CRISIS INTERVENTION

A Practical Guide

Sara Miller McCune founded SAGE Publishing in 1965 to support the dissemination of usable knowledge and educate a global community. SAGE publishes more than 1000 journals and over 800 new books each year, spanning a wide range of subject areas. Our growing selection of library products includes archives, data, case studies and video. SAGE remains majority owned by our founder and after her lifetime will become owned by a charitable trust that secures the company's continued independence.

Los Angeles | London | New Delhi | Singapore | Washington DC | Melbourne

CRISIS INTERVENTION
A Practical Guide

Alan A. Cavaiola
Monmouth University, New Jersey

Joseph E. Colford
Georgian Court University, New Jersey

Los Angeles | London | New Delhi
Singapore | Washington DC | Melbourne

FOR INFORMATION:

SAGE Publications, Inc.
2455 Teller Road
Thousand Oaks, California 91320
E-mail: order@sagepub.com

SAGE Publications Ltd.
1 Oliver's Yard
55 City Road
London, EC1Y 1SP
United Kingdom

SAGE Publications India Pvt. Ltd.
B 1/I 1 Mohan Cooperative Industrial Area
Mathura Road, New Delhi 110 044
India

SAGE Publications Asia-Pacific Pte. Ltd.
3 Church Street
#10-04 Samsung Hub
Singapore 049483

Copyright © 2018 by SAGE Publications, Inc.

Printed in the United States of America.

Library of Congress Cataloging-in-Publication Data

Names: Cavaiola, Alan A., author. | Colford, Joseph E., author.

Title: Crisis intervention : a practical guide / Alan A. Cavaiola, Monmouth University, Joseph E. Colford, Georgian Court College, New Jersey.

Description: Los Angeles : SAGE, [2018] | Includes bibliographical references and index.

Identifiers: LCCN 2017029908 | ISBN 9781506322384 (pbk. : alk. paper)

Subjects: LCSH: Crisis intervention (Mental health services) | Counseling.

Classification: LCC RC480.6 .C378 2018 | DDC 362.2/04251—dc23 LC record available at https://lccn.loc.gov/2017029908

This book is printed on acid-free paper.

Acquisitions Editor: Abbie Rickard
Editorial Assistant: Jennifer Cline
Production Editor: Andrew Olson
Copy Editor: Janet Ford
Typesetter: Hurix Systems Pvt. Ltd.
Proofreader: Laura Webb
Indexer: Maria Sosnowski
Cover Designer: Karine Hovsepian
Marketing Manager: Jenna Retinal

SUSTAINABLE FORESTRY INITIATIVE
Certified Chain of Custody
Promoting Sustainable Forestry
www.sfiprogram.org
SFI-01268
SFI label applies to text stock

17 18 19 20 21 10 9 8 7 6 5 4 3 2 1

Contents

4 Child Maltreatment

7   Alcohol and Drug Crises   143

8   The Crisis of Sexual Assault   177

9   Intimate Partner Violence & Domestic Violence   197

10 Crises Involving Bereavement, Grief, and Loss   231

11   Crises Involving Suicide, Homicide, and Lethality   265

15 Disaster Response   385

Acknowledgments

I am very appreciative of the work my graduate assistants, Erin Brennan and Christine Hennigan did in reviewing and editing the initial drafts of my chapters. I also want to thank Dr. Stephanie Hall for her insightful review and comments of the Bereavement chapter. In addition, I'd also like to thank those colleagues who reviewed my chapters and provided insightful comments and recommendations for revisions, most notably: Dr. Amanda Faulk, Richmond Community College; Dr. Mark Fox, Hawaii Pacific University; Dr. Rejoice Addae, Arkansas State University; Dr. Michelle L. Williams, Paradise Valley Community College; Dr. Wendy Killam, Stephan F. Austin State University; David B. Saltman, Florida International University; LaShauna M. Dean, William Paterson University; Mikal Crawford, Husson University; Nancy Sherman, Bradley University; Robert G. Parr, University of Alaska Fairbanks-Community and Technical College; and Susan Wycoff, California State University, Sacramento. I am grateful for my family's support throughout this entire project. (AAC)

I want to thank Moshe Deutsch, one of my graduate students, for his research assistance and for his help in updating the statistics pertinent to my crisis chapters. A special thank you also goes to my wife Jeanne for helping me with the typing and for giving me the space to complete this book in the midst of a challenging and burdensome year in academia. (Joe C)

We also wish to extend our heartfelt thanks to our SAGE Editors, Abbie Rickard and Nathan Davidson for their incredible patience, encouragement, and tenacity in bringing this book to fruition. We are very grateful for all the work that Alissa Nance had done in making certain that all copyright permissions were obtained. It was such a pleasure to work with her. We also wish to thank Janet Ford for her meticulous editing and to Andrew Olson for his help in the final production of this book. We are also grateful to Barry Fetterolf, our literary agent and friend who also worked diligently to bring this and previous works to print.

Finally, we'd like to dedicate this book to all those who have endured crisis and trauma in their lives and who have managed to persevere in the face of tragedy and heartbreak. Especially our those closest to us, our family, our friends, our students, and our patients who have shared their stories of hope, strength, and resilience.

About the Authors

Alan A. Cavaiola, PhD, LPC, LCADC is a full Professor in the Department of Professional Counseling at Monmouth University where he is currently serving as the Director of the Addiction Studies program. Prior to teaching at Monmouth, he was an assistant professor in the psychology department at Rowan University. Dr. Cavaiola is the former clinical director of the addiction treatment programs at Monmouth Medical Center, which included a 49-bed adolescent substance use disorder residential program. He has coauthored six books and has authored several journal articles. Dr. Cavaiola is currently an associate editor of the journal *Substance Abuse* and serves on the board of the International Coalition for Addiction Studies Education (INCASE) and the National Association of Substance Abuse Educators (NASAC). Dr. Cavaiola is a licensed psychologist, a licensed professional counselor (LPC), a licensed clinical alcohol and drug counselor (LCADC) in New Jersey.

Joseph E. Colford holds a PhD in child clinical psychology from Seton Hall University; he is a licensed psychologist and a certified school psychologist in New Jersey. Dr. Colford worked in the public schools, primarily at the middle and high school levels, for almost 27 years before leaving the public sector for higher education. He now is in his 13th year at Georgian Court University in Lakewood, New Jersey, as a professor of psychology and the director of the graduate program in school psychology. A former president of the New Jersey Association of School Psychologists (2012-13), he also is the coauthor with Dr. Cavaiola of two previous books: *A Practical Guide to Crisis Intervention* and *Crisis Intervention Case Book*. On a personal note, he and Jeanne, his wife of 40 years, recently became grandparents for the first time to Eleanor Rose, the daughter of son Matthew and daughter-in-law Nyla; their other son, Michael, will wed his fiancée Jayne several months before this book is released.

C H A P T E R   1

Understanding Crisis

Boston Marathon Bombing: April 15, 2013: Two bombs went off near the finish line of the Boston Marathon, killing three spectators and wounding more than 260 other people, many of them with catastrophic injuries. Coverage of the disaster saturated all forms of media for weeks, bringing into everyone's living room images of destruction. The search for the two terrorist brothers also shut down the entire city of Boston.

Superstorm Sandy: October-November, 2012: Hurricane Sandy, dubbed a superstorm because of its ferocity, was the deadliest and most destructive hurricane of the 2012 Atlantic hurricane season as well as the second costliest in U.S. history. It resulted in the deaths of 233 people in eight different countries before it hit the east coast of the United States. The states of New Jersey and New York were particularly hard hit. Flooding and high winds resulted in property damage, loss of power, and relocation of families to temporary shelters throughout the area. School buildings also were destroyed, keeping children and families in a recurring nightmare as relief efforts faltered.

9–11 and the Twin Towers; President Vows Exact Punishment for "Evil:" (New York Times September 12, 2001, New York City): Hijackers rammed jetliners into each of New York's World Trade Center towers yesterday, toppling both in a hellish storm of ash, smoke, glass and leaping victims; third plane crashes into Pentagon in Virginia and a fourth plunges to the ground near Pittsburgh; military is put on highest alert; National Guard units called at Washington and New York, two aircraft carriers are called to New York harbor.

Tales of crisis and of people in the throes of crisis appear in all forms of media on any given day, in any city or town in the United States. Whether the article is about a terrorist attack, a domestic violence incident, a kidnapping, a school shooting, a rape, an earthquake, or any other natural disaster, it can resonate across communities and whole nations. Suddenly, unexpectedly, and without forewarning, individuals are left to their own devices in the immediate aftermath of such events. Most individuals do find some means of coping after a crisis, relying on assistance from their own social support networks consisting of extended family members, friends, or trusted individuals like clergy or other members of the community. However, there are those who feel overwhelmed and immobilized, or who find that they are unable to cope, even with the assistance of well-meaning friends or family members. Some also find that the ways they might have used to cope in the past are not working for them in dealing with the present crisis.

Often when one hears the term, "crisis intervention," one may immediately think of those services which would ordinarily be provided by mental health professionals in a mental health clinic, a private practitioner's office, or a hospital emergency room. While psychiatrists, psychologists, psychiatric social workers, and professional counselors often do provide these services, one must also consider the array of other individuals who are either at the scene of the crisis event or who arrive shortly after. Police officers, teachers, school counselors, college counselors, firefighters, rescue workers, community volunteers, first aid squads, nurses, physicians, clergy, funeral directors, attorneys, employee assistance counselors, human resource managers, neighbors, friends, roommates, family, and other relatives may find themselves performing crisis intervention services, sometimes without realizing it.

It might appear that there are more crisis situations and traumatic events that take place in today's society, but this perception is due, in part, to the media coverage of such events. What is clearly different today is that there are many more types of crisis delivery services than there were forty or fifty years ago: hotlines; mobile emergency teams trained in crisis intervention; school intervention personnel, such as school psychologists and student assistance counselors; workplace intervention specialists, such as employee assistance counselors; and emergency room services, which include crisis services for both psychiatric emergencies and substance abuse.

This chapter provides an overview of crisis intervention, definitions of and types of crises, and diagnostic considerations that are part of the crisis experience. Multicultural issues related to crisis considerations also is discussed. Finally, the chapter includes a brief historical overview of the field of crisis intervention and some examples of the assessment and intervention models that have evolved.

DEFINING CRISIS

As suggested by Graf (personal communication, August 19, 2002), a broad definition of crisis is *a predictable or unpredictable life event which is perceived by an individual as stressful to the extent that normal coping mechanisms are insufficient.* Gerald Caplan, one of the early pioneers in the crisis intervention field, was the first to articulate what he referred to as crisis theory. In order to understand his crisis theory, it is helpful to look at how he defined *crisis.* For Caplan (1964), a crisis is a temporary state of upset and disorganization, characterized chiefly by an individual's inability to cope with a particular situation using customary methods of problem solving, and by the potential for a radically positive or negative outcome. There are many assumptions made by Caplan which are implicit in his definition.

First, *a crisis begins with a precipitating event.* These precipitants can be specific predictable life events, such as getting married, graduating from school, moving to a new town, a planned pregnancy, and retirement; or they can be unpredictable, such as natural disasters, accidents, an untimely death of a loved one, or other traumatic events, such as being a victim of rape. The second assumption made is that a crisis state, by its very definition is "*time-limited.*" Caplan claimed that the immediate impact of a crisis usually lasts from six to eight weeks, depending on the nature and intensity of the crisis. This is not to say that there are not long-lasting effects to many of the crises that are experienced. The third assumption is that *crises create a state of disequilibrium and disorganization* for the individual. Therefore, individuals who tend to be organized and operate with a certain degree of predictability, now are faced with days filled with chaos as the crisis event sometimes controls or dominates their every waking moment.

Another assumption of Caplan's is that once the crisis event takes place, there is a *cognitive interpretation* or appraisal of the event, which accounts for the notion that not everyone reacts to a crisis in the same way. For example, being fired from a job may seem like the end of the world to one person, while for another, it can be a chance to take a few months off, do some traveling, and relax between jobs. The Greek philosopher, Epictetus, once said, "It's not the events of life that make men mad, but rather the view we take of them." It's the "view we take of them" that suggests this cognitive interpretation of crisis events.

Finally, *crisis events will cause a breakdown in one's ability to cope.* The goal of crisis intervention, therefore, is to help clients mobilize their own coping resources in an effort to restore balance or equilibrium. In developing his crisis theory, Caplan was interested not only in identifying the crisis itself, but also in assessing the individual's ego functioning in the aftermath of the crisis situation as they attempt to cope with it. According to Caplan, adequate ego functioning was the basis of one's mental health.

DANGER VS. OPPORTUNITY

According to Slaikeu (1990), the word *crisis* itself is very rich in psychological meaning. In Chinese, the word for *crisis* is made up of two symbols, "danger" and "opportunity" (Wilhelm, 1967). The word, therefore, connotes not only a time of danger, which may be physical (as with assault, natural disaster, medical illness) or psychological (losing one's job or going through a divorce), but also the opportunity for personal growth that results from having experienced a crisis and having come to the realization of one's inner strength. This would be the case with rape victims who come to the realization that they have survived and can use their strength to help other rape victims, or the person who experiences a job layoff and obtains training to get a better or more satisfying job. Of course, while a person is going through a crisis, the notion of "opportunity" probably doesn't make much sense. It sometimes isn't until months or years after the crisis has passed that one realizes the personal growth and self-efficacy that has been achieved. Perhaps the old English proverb sums this up best, "A smooth sea never made a skilled mariner."

The English derivative of the word *crisis* is taken from the Greek word, *krinein* that means "to decide" (Lidell & Scott, 1968), emphasizing that a crisis is a time for decision making, a turning point or moment of reckoning. In some instances, these decisions will help to improve one's life. Slaikeu (1990, p. 15) notes the potential for a "radically positive or negative outcome" in the aftermath of a crisis. In a fundamental way, the direction that the outcome takes depends on the decisions made by the affected individuals as part of the crisis resolution process. Often the decision reached because of a crisis enables that individual to thrive. In other instances, however, these decisions may lead to a life that is negatively impacted and/or diminished in some way. To acknowledge this potential for positive or negative outcomes and the role of the individual's decisions in determining the outcome is not as simple as implying that all the person in crisis needs to do is to "think positively." To suggest this would be to deny the unique complexity of crisis events and the often-insurmountable difficulties that they pose to affected individuals.

TYPES OF CRISES

Based on these definitions, one could argue that just about any stressor could bring about a crisis situation. In order to further delineate this term, it is helpful to conceptualize crises as being grouped into three areas: normal *developmental* crises, *traumatic event* crises, and *existential* crises (Brammer, 1985). A fourth area, *psychiatric crises,* also can be included, since there are many instances where a psychiatric condition can serve as the catalyst to the crisis state (e.g., a person who suffers from bipolar disorder may begin to experience a manic episode which results in a gambling spree). Conversely, a crisis can exacerbate an already existing psychiatric condition (e.g., stops taking her medication after being evicted from the boarding home where she had been living).

Developmental Crises

What is unique to developmental crises is that the precipitating event of the crisis or the stimulus event is embedded in normal maturational processes (Slaikeu, 1990). Throughout the lifespan, human beings are constantly changing; yet the normal growth process is characterized by continuity, as one passes from one stage to the next, through a series of life transitions.

Erikson (1963) was one of the first developmental theorists to point out that development continues through the lifespan. What was also unique to his approach was his assertion that at each stage of development, there is a major task or conflict to be resolved by the individual in order to move onto the next stage. The table below summarizes Erikson's developmental stages, outlining both the transitional theme and the developmental tasks associated with each stage. It also identifies conflicts or events that could potentially precipitate a developmental crisis for an individual at each identifiable stage. What Erikson referred to as a potential crisis imbedded in each of his eight stages might also be considered a "challenge" instead; that is, a test of the individual to master the needs of each stage before moving onto the next one. The Latin derivation of the word "impediment" comes from the word "impedimenta," meaning "heavy baggage," and it is just this excess baggage that individuals drag with them to the next developmental stage. It is as if their unfinished business at one stage will impede their ability to master the challenges of subsequent ones.

Erikson (1963) considered a major task of adolescence to be identity formation. He believed that by the end of the teen years, healthy individuals must develop some sense of identity, including who and what kind of persons they are in relationships, what their strengths and weaknesses are, and what they see as future life goals and/or directions. The teenager who is unable to "find" their identity may wander aimlessly from job-to-job, or from college-to-college feeling depressed and lonely. "Stuck" in a developmental crisis that Erikson refers to as "role confusion;" these individuals may be unable to proceed with the

Table 1.1 Erickson's Developmental Stages

Stage	Transitional Theme	Developmental Tasks	Potential Conflicts
Infancy (Birth–1 yr.)	Trust vs mistrust	Development of a trusting relationship with a caregiver who will tend to his/her needs	Lack of trust that needs will be met by others; attachment issues may linger
Toddlerhood (1-2 yrs.)	Autonomy vs shame and doubt	Development of independence	Independence thwarted by overprotective or neglectful caregivers
Early childhood (2-6 yrs.)	Initiative vs guilt	Continued development of independence; child given freedom to explore, practice newfound motor skills; toilet training	Feelings of self-blame and guilt as caregivers discourage child's need to explore
Middle Childhood (6-12 yrs.)	Industry vs inferiority	Development of academic mastery; consolidation of social network; comparison of self with others	A sense that the child doesn't "measure up" to others in academic, social areas
Adolescence (12-18 yrs.)	Identity vs role confusion	Adjusting to puberty; defining one's identity; acknowledging one's strengths, weaknesses	Self-consciousness re: body image, sexuality; indecisiveness about life goals
Young adulthood (18-34 yrs.)	Intimacy vs isolation	Development of intimate relationship with significant other; settling down with career choice established	Rejection by others; difficulty with intimacy in relationships
Middle adulthood (35-retirement)	Generativity vs stagnation	Adjusting to middle age, parenting; dealing with aging parents; developing sense of productivity, advancement in the workplace	Workplace issues challenging and unrewarding; parenting concerns with growing children
Older adulthood (after retirement)	Ego integrity vs despair	Adjusting to retirement, to aging; evaluating level of success in one's career, in one's personal/family life; dealing with health issues and physical decline	Despair over perceived lack of productivity; sense of loss as health declines, friends begin to die

later developmental tasks of young adulthood, including establishing intimate, committed relationships, and achieving occupational stability.

Male midlife crisis is another example of a developmental crisis (Mayer, 1978; Levinson, 1978). This crisis may occur as men begin to experience various emotions of anxiety or sadness or fear of death as they contemplate and take stock of the accomplishments in their lives. These emotions may be exacerbated as they take on the developmental tasks of adjusting to aging and preparing to retire. Women may experience a similar type of midlife crises with the onset of menopause or as grown children leave home, resulting in "the empty nest syndrome." Certainly, not every man or woman experiences a crisis as they navigate these life transitions, but for some individuals the normal developmental passages do indeed precipitate crisis responses.

It should be emphasized that when individuals are experiencing what may be a developmental crisis, it is not always certain that they will seek professional help, nor will they identify their problem as "developmental" in nature. Instead, they may experience frustration, anxiety, loneliness, depression or may express other complaints. It should also be noted that developmental crises can sometimes occur simultaneously, as would be the case with a 50-year-old man or woman who is going through a divorce and having to make decisions regarding the care of his or her elderly parents.

Traumatic Event Crises

Traumatic event crises are what most people imagine a crisis to be, and each of the events reported at the beginning of this chapter were, in fact, traumatic event crises. The most distinguishing characteristic of traumatic event crises is that there is a clear external precipitating event. The traumatic event is usually an uncommon or extraordinary incident, which one cannot predict, nor control. Unlike the developmental crises described above, traumatic event crises can occur at any time in one's development, commonly have a sudden onset, are unpredictable, have an emergent quality, and can impact more than one person (e.g., an entire state, county, or community). Examples of traumatic event crises include community-wide disasters (e.g., fires, floods, tornados, devastating nor'easters, man-made disasters, train/airline crashes, nuclear and toxic waste accidents, terrorist attacks, school shootings, homicides, suicides, car accidents, industrial accidents, sudden medical illnesses, domestic violence, and crimes, including assaults, robberies, murders, rapes, child sexual abuse, and child abuse.

The ruthless destruction of human life caused by terrorist bombings at the Boston marathon site, by hijacked planes used as bombs at the World Trade Center and Pentagon, or the bombing of the Federal Building in Oklahoma City, are examples of unpredictable traumatic emergencies that create untold suffering, leaving the survivors, and surviving family members with tremendous grief as they try to rebuild their lives. The "time-limited" nature of such crises cannot take into account how these events will permanently scar those who are affected.

Existential Crises

An existential crisis takes place when one begins to question the meaning of life or the meaninglessness of one's existence, the lack of connectedness with other people, or the futility of one's work or profession. This type of crisis is often experienced in the wake of some particular crisis event. For example, in the aftermath of a high school student's suicide, many of her friends began to question the importance and meaning of their own day-to-day existence. Having made certain choices in life or perhaps by not being given choices, the realization that one's life has been inexorably altered in profound ways can induce a personal crisis in many individuals. This was best illustrated in the film, *It's a Wonderful Life,* when George Bailey experiences an existential crisis, which brings him to the brink of suicide on the realization that his lot in life cannot be changed.

Existential crises are probably the most difficult to identify because, as with developmental crises, the person experiencing this type of crisis, may present with other complaints or with other symptoms. It is only once the crisis intervention counselor begins to scratch the surface of the presenting complaints that they begin to find that the individual's issues go much deeper than an upset over day-to-day hassles or annoyances.

Psychiatric Crises

As with developmental and existential crises, the triggering psychiatric crisis event may not be readily discernible. For example, a person with bipolar disorder who stops taking medication will often begin to re-experience the extreme mood fluctuations that represent the "highs" of the manic state or the "lows" of the depression that usually follows. This information may not be reliably conveyed to the crisis worker. Or a person with a substance use history may unintentionally overdose on painkillers, yet when that person is brought to the emergency room, he may appear to be sedated and unable to provide an accurate account of what pills he had taken. When psychiatric crises take hold of some persons, they sometimes may come on without rhyme or reason, yet they can be so debilitating and send the person into an intense state of crisis. It is important to note, however, that not everyone with a psychiatric condition necessarily experiences crisis as part of their illness. However, when those who suffer from psychiatric conditions experience crisis situations or traumatic events, it can often add to the feelings of devastation.

It should be noted that it is quite possible for people to be experiencing more than one crisis at the same time. It would be helpful if crises only came along one at a time or at intervals that allowed people to resolve one crisis before having to tackle another. However, this is often not the case. Instead, it is common for people to experience multiple and rather complex crises simultaneously. Such would be the case with a woman whose husband was killed in the World Trade Center, who is now faced with major decisions about whether to move; whose 8- and 10-year-old daughters are going through major grief reactions and are now failing in school; as a result, whose in-laws are pressuring her to sue the U.S. government rather than accept her portion of the victim compensation funds; and who herself is naturally going through major grief reactions over the loss of her husband. Crises have no timetable, nor do they wait for people to prepare for them.

CRISES REACTIONS: A CONTINUUM OF RESPONSE

People who experience any of the aforementioned crises often vary in the way they respond to that particular crisis event. As stated earlier in the various definitions of *crisis,* the person in crisis usually does experience extreme upset and disorganization in functioning. One result of this disorganization is increased vulnerability, and the normal defenses that may have helped the person to cope in the past are no longer effective. Acute crisis reactions are debilitating and can result in extreme levels of perceived psychological distress. However, until such time that some sense of equilibrium has been restored and the crisis has been constructively resolved, these individuals may feel that they are "going crazy."

Many individuals in crisis will experience a "fight, flight, or freeze" response in the face of the immediate crisis event. The fight or flight response is that programmed, biological response that allows human beings to react in the face of imminent danger by either fighting off the danger (fight) or by fleeing (flight). This adrenalin surge and redirection of blood flow to the large muscles of the legs and arms allows the fight or flight response to occur. However, it is also natural for people to "freeze" in the face of imminent danger. People who have experienced car accidents will often describe a feeling of being "suspended in time" or in "slow motion" as they watch the other car collide with theirs. The "freeze" response is also common in rape and sexual assault victims who fear for their lives, but are unable to scream, run, or fight. There are also some individuals who will not experience psychological distress in the aftermath of a crisis event. These individuals seem to have the capacity to repress the event and, therefore, will go about their daily business as if nothing had happened. The ego defense mechanism of repression, first described by both Sigmund Freud and elaborated on by his daughter, Anna, allows the mind to repress the traumatic event or push it out of conscious awareness.

Some individuals will experience various symptoms in response to the crisis they have experienced. The American Psychiatric Association's *Diagnostic and Statistical Manual of Mental Disorders*, Fifth Edition (*DSM-5*, 2013), presents various diagnoses which may occur in the aftermath of some of the aforementioned crisis events. Many crises will reach some resolution within the six to eight-week period, and those individuals will attain some degree of equilibrium; however, there may also be more enduring reactions or responses to crisis events. Although the goal of crisis intervention is not to label individuals or to pathologize their reactions to trauma or crisis, the rendering of a diagnosis does serve the purpose of conveying to other professionals that the person who is victimized by a trauma or crisis event is experiencing a particular set of symptoms or sequelae, the identification of which may become important in effectively treating that individual.

For example, it is common for victims of sexual assault, such as a rape or molestation to blame themselves for the incident: "I shouldn't have gone out to the store that night," or "I should have dressed differently." These are common statements of self-blame. In the treatment of sexual abuse victims, it is important to help the sexual abuse survivor relinquish these self-blaming perceptions. Hence, it is important that the diagnosis convey to other professionals some similar features they have experienced among people suffering from the same crisis or trauma.

The three most common diagnoses given to individuals who experience trauma or crisis events are posttraumatic stress disorder (PTSD), acute stress disorder, and adjustment disorder.

PTSD is a rather complex diagnostic entity which encompasses thoughts, feelings, interactions with others, changes in self-concept, and in overall daily functioning. Trauma can have a tremendous impact on the individual, whether they are a combat veteran, a rape victim, a domestic violence victim, a car accident victim, or a person who witnesses violence like a shooting. A diagnosis of PTSD also lends itself more readily to traumatic event crises as described above. One of the criteria for PTSD specifies that the individual must have experienced or witnessed a traumatic event in order to qualify for this diagnosis.

Those who *witnessed* the horrifying scene of hijacked planes crashing into the World Trade Center, for example, also experienced PTSD reactions, just as those people who were in the Towers at the time and experienced the impact of the crash, but managed to escape.

The *DSM-5* also includes the following indicators of PTSD:

- Exposure to a traumatic event via directly experiencing it, witnessing it, or learning that it happened to a close family member or friend

- Recurrent distressing memories or dreams of the event

- Flashbacks in which the individual feels as if the event were recurring

- Distress caused by any internal or external cue that serves as a reminder of the event

- Persistent avoidance of stimuli associated with the event

- Persistent negative cognitions and moods in the aftermath of the event

Related, but slightly different indicators of PTSD for children six years of age or younger also can be found in *DSM-5*. Individuals with acute stress disorder experience the same severity and type of symptoms as the person with PTSD; however, what is unique to this diagnosis is the time frame. Acute stress disorder reactions are reserved for those who experience symptoms within the first month after exposure to the traumatic event; unlike PTSD, these symptoms last from three days to one month. Those who continue to experience symptoms after this time period would be diagnosed with PTSD. This is why the symptoms listed for both posttraumatic stress disorder and acute stress disorder are similar.

It is rare that a person going through a developmental or existential crisis would meet the *DSM-5* criteria for PTSD. For those individuals, a diagnosis of adjustment disorder would most likely characterize their symptoms. The adjustment disorder diagnosis indicates that a "stressor" is the catalyst to the symptomatology. These stressors might include a breakup in a relationship, a separation, a divorce, a layoff from one's job, or could emanate from various developmental events, such as going away to school, leaving home, getting married, becoming a parent, failing to attain occupational goals, or retiring. The subtypes also allow for the clinician to determine what is the predominant response to the stressor: for example, is it depression, anxiety, acting out behavior (disturbance of conduct), or a mixed emotional or behavioral state? Again, it is important to note that individuals react quite differently to stressors.

DSM-5 lists the diagnostic criteria for adjustment disorder:

- Emotional or behavioral symptoms occurring within three months of the onset of a stressor

- Distress is out of proportion to the severity or intensity of the stressor

- Significant impairment in social, occupational, or other areas of functioning

- Subtypes of the disorder include those which present with: depressed mood, anxiety, mixed anxiety and depressed mood, disturbance of conduct, mixed disturbance of emotions and conduct, or unspecified

The issue of diagnosis pertaining to crisis intervention is quite controversial. This is true especially among individuals who are victims of domestic violence or rape. Many professionals who work with domestic violence and rape survivors feel that to diagnose these women is to pathologize otherwise normal reactions to horrific situations. The women's movement has made significant inroads in this area by educating both mental health and medical professionals about the psychological/emotional impact of victimization. While domestic violence survivors and rape survivors like Vietnam veterans may share similar symptomatology, this should not be interpreted to mean that these individuals are "sick," "crazy," or "weak of character." The question then becomes, "why diagnose at all?" As indicated earlier, a diagnosis allows professionals to communicate information about an individual without needing to come up with an endless list of symptoms. A diagnosis may also help the survivor to understand that what they are experiencing is to be expected, given the trauma. For example, a rape survivor who is experiencing emotional numbing or who is unable to recall specific events of the rape may understand that this is a normal PTSD reaction to rape trauma. This, in turn, may also help significant others in her life to understand that the numbing reaction is part of the PTSD reaction and not indicative of indifference to the traumatic event. On a practical level, a diagnosis also allows survivors of trauma to use their medical insurance benefits, should they decide to seek professional counseling.

MULTICULTURAL AWARENESS AND CRISIS INTERVENTION

Whether you are a professional crisis counselor or the first police officer to arrive at the scene of a crisis event, it is of utmost importance to take cultural, ethnic, and religious backgrounds into consideration in order to fully appreciate an individual's response to a crisis. For example, consider a person who states in a crisis interview that she is "possessed by evil spirits." At first glance, and without any prior knowledge of this individual's cultural background, the crisis counselor may begin to think that this person is suffering from some type of profound psychiatric disorder. However, what if this individual is of Native American ancestry, a culture that is rich with tales of spirit influence? Or what if this person is of Hispanic or Latino ancestry, a culture which has many beliefs about white magic as well as evil or black magic? Or what if this person is of Italian ancestry, a culture that believes that bad people can cast "the evil eye" on others? Arthur Kleinman (1991) has done extensive research into multicultural aspects of psychiatric disorders. He points to the example of a Native American from one of the Plains nations who may hear the voice of a deceased relative from the afterworld, and how that experience would be considered normal from that cultural perspective. Yet, if a non-Native American were to hear such "voices," he or she might be considered psychotic.

It is also important to consider that there is often a great deal of diversity within a particular racial group, culture, or ethnicity. For example, Spanish-speaking individuals may prefer to be called Mexican Americans, Spanish Americans, Cuban Americans, Puerto Rican Americans, Hispanics, or Latinos depending on their country of origin.

Native Americans represent a very diverse population composed of 554 federally recognized tribes or nations and Alaskan native villages each with its own social organization, rituals, customs, and language.

Similarly, there are some who prefer the term Black, as opposed to African American, because these individuals do not identify Africa as their country of origin or with pre-slavery connotations. It is important for counselors to be aware of these differences and to be careful not to make assumptions that because one is of a particular racial, ethnic, or religious group that they necessarily identify with a particular cultural heritage.

Religious beliefs and culture may also influence how a particular crisis is defined or how it evolves. Examples of this are found within suicide rate statistics. In Catholic and Muslim countries, suicide rates are lower, presumably because those religions view suicide as sinful. In Western industrialized countries, suicide rates are higher. In Japan, suicide may be viewed as an "honorable" solution to one having dishonored one's family. Or in the instance of kamikaze pilots during World War II, it was considered an honor to die for one's country. The following excerpt helps to illustrate cultural influences: A young Japanese woman living in Los Angeles was distraught over discovering that her husband was having an affair. She had no work skills, spoke no English, and felt worthless and helpless. She became increasingly depressed and dysfunctional. One spring day, she took her infant and four-year-old to the beach, bought lunch, and then walked into the ocean with the children to commit family suicide. Bystanders witnessed the act and were able to summon help. The woman survived, but both children drowned. Although she was jailed and accused of murder, the Japanese American community, sympathetic to her effort to resolve her dilemma through the suicide that included her children, rallied to her support. They argued that in traditional Japanese communities, the family is the unit, not the individual, and they called it Japanese suicide, not American murder (Group for the Advancement of Psychiatry, 1989).

Multicultural considerations must be taken into account, especially when providing crisis intervention services. For example, Dr. Marilyn Aguirre-Molina (Aguirre-Molina & Molina, 1994) describes how a counselor not familiar with Hispanic culture can offend the head of the family (often the father) by not asking their permission to see the identified patient (for example, the son or daughter). By demonstrating *respeto* (respect) to elders and persons of authority, one is being culturally sensitive to an important Hispanic value, the importance of showing deference and obedience to elders and those in authority (Marin & Marin, 1991). Similarly, a crisis counselor working with an African American family must be aware of the important role of spirituality. Strong spiritual belief is thought to have sustained African Americans through the horrors of slavery and racism (Robinson, Perry, & Carey, 1995). For the counselor working with an Asian American individual or family, awareness of the importance of the family as the unit of social and cultural activities is important (Dana, 1993). The counselor should also be aware that in many of the diverse Asian cultures, it is considered a sign of disrespect to look someone directly in the eye. Instead it is considered deferential to look away, so as to not appear to be "staring the person down." For the crisis counselor unaware of this custom, they may misinterpret this behavior as being disrespectful, instead of as a sign of respect.

It is important therefore, that all counselors develop a sense of *cultural competence.* According to Castro, Proescholdbell, Abeita, and Rodriquez (1999) cultural competence refers to "the capacity of a service provider or an organization to understand and work effectively with the cultural beliefs and practices of persons from a given ethnic/racial group" (p. 504). They conclude that cultural competence is of utmost importance in the delivery of effective mental health and human services to diverse special populations. When counselors or agencies fail to acknowledge and appreciate the important differences in values, beliefs, and rituals then individuals from these diverse populations may feel skeptical, misunderstood, and untrusting that these counselors or agencies will be able to meet their needs (Castro et al., 1999).

Box 1.1: Intervening in Crisis: The L-A-P-C Model

Name: _____   Age: _____

       Listen   Assess   Plan   Commit

L   I   S   T   E   N

I   What are they saying about the crisis?

S   What happened?   When did it happen?

T   What type of crisis was it? (Traumatic Event, Developmental, Psychiatric, Existential)

E   Did they mention anything that indicates danger?

N   Other relevant information about the crisis

A   S   S   E   S   S

S   Feeling: Is their predominant emotional state one of:

S   anger   sadness   hopelessness

E   anxiety   panic   numbness
        suicidal? If yes, complete lethality assessment/suicide.
        homicidal? If yes, complete lethality assessment/violence.

S   Acting: Is their behavior
        active/restless   consistent with mood
        passive/withdrawn   good eye contact

S   Thinking: Are they
        logical/making sense   coherent/expressing self well
        insightful   focused on topic
        evasive/changing subject

    Other: Any medical problems?   Physical limitations?
        Hospitalizations?   Need for hospitalization?

P   L   A   N

L   What needs to be done now?

A   What alternative plans have been discussed?

N   Are these plans reasonable? Able to be carried out?

C   O   M   M   I   T

O   Which plan of action have they chosen?

          Do they have the resources/support to implement the plan?

M   Are they motivated to implement the plan?

          What other resources/support may be needed?
M   friend   family member
              neighbor   mental health provider
              public agency (law enforcement, child protective
I   services, social services)
              medical (hospitalization, medication)

T

Several authors have conceptualized the ability to work with members of diverse popu-lations as existing along a continuum (Castro et al., 1999; Cross, Bazron, Dennis & Isaacs, 1989; Kim, McLeod, & Shantzis, 1992). At the far end of this continuum is *cultural destruc-tiveness,* which can be defined as counselors or agencies manifesting negative attitudes toward diverse populations or considering them to be inferior to the mainstream, domi-nant culture. The next step along the continuum is one of *cultural blindness,* a philosophy which advocates that all people are alike and therefore should be treated equally. However, the problem with this service delivery approach is that it fails to consider the many cultural differences *necessary* to acknowledge in order to help someone effectively resolve their crisis. The next step along the continuum is *cultural sensitivity,* which is where the coun-selor or agency is open to acknowledging and working with issues of multicultural diver-sity. The next stage is *cultural competence* that was defined earlier, followed by *cultural proficiency,* the highest level of cultural capacity, here defined as the counselor's ability to understand the nuances of cultural diversity in greater depth and to implement new and more effective service delivery approaches based on the appreciation and understanding of these differences.

For the crisis counselor, the first step toward cultural competence and hopefully toward cultural proficiency, is not to assume that everyone views things from your own values or beliefs systems. When one does this, it reflects *ethnocentrism,* which is the cultural equivalent of egocentrism, only here, the belief is that all cultures function in the same way that one's own culture does. Therefore, when in doubt about particular customs, rituals, values, or belief systems it is better to ask rather than to assume.

The L-A-P-C model of crisis intervention found in Box 1.1 (see pages 12–13) is the model proposed by the current authors. It will appear throughout the book.

RESOURCES FOR CHAPTER ENRICHMENT

Suggested Readings

Caplan, G. (1961). *An approach to community mental health.* New York, NY: Grune & Stratton.
Caplan, G. (1964). *Principles of preventative psychiatry.* New York, NY: Basic Books.
Dana, R. H. (1993). *Multicultural assessment perspectives for professional psychology.* Boston, MA: Allyn & Bacon.
Erikson, E. (1963). *Childhood and society* (2nd ed.). New York, NY: Norton Press.

Suggested Websites

Crisis: The Journal of Crisis Intervention & Suicide Prevention (www.hhpub.com/journals/crisis) This is a journal devoted exclusively to crisis intervention and provides an excellent example of how crisis intervention has become accepted as a specialized field within the human services professions.

Trauma Response (http://www.aaets.org) This is the journal of the American Academy of Experts in Traumatic Stress. Both the journal and the AAETS provide excellent, up-to-date information within the field of crisis intervention and traumatic stress response. The AAETS also provides specialized certifications for qualified professionals.

Journal of Traumatic Stress (http://www.wkap.nl/journalhome.htm/) This is the official journal of the International Society for Traumatic Stress Studies. The journal contains excellent, up-to-date information on various empirical studies dealing with trauma resulting from domestic violence, rape, sexual assault, combat, work-related trauma, and natural disasters.

Crisis Intervention Models: An Exploration of Historical and Contemporary Models

Since the inception of crisis intervention as an area of specialization, many models have been developed that were designed to serve as guidelines for counselors performing crisis intervention services. The crisis models that evolved can be broken down into two types: Crisis assessment models and crisis intervention models. Although most models fit into one of these two categories, there are several hybrid models that combine aspects of both. The first part of this chapter explores various crisis assessment models while the second part of the paper is devoted to an exploration of crisis intervention models. Finally, we'll explore the historical development of crisis intervention models and how crisis services have evolved in the 21st century.

CRISIS ASSESSMENT MODELS

The ability to accurately assess an individual who is in crisis is an important prelude to providing effective crisis intervention services. Crisis assessment must be quick, accurate, and relevant to be effective. For example, in crisis situations it is important to focus on the "here and now" rather than conducting an extensive, in-depth assessment of past history other than that which is pertinent to the crisis. Crisis counselors often must be familiar with how to assess a variety of crisis situations, such as domestic violence, suicide, homicide, child abuse, and substance abuse emergencies in order to intervene effectively. Client safety in each of these situations is of paramount importance, therefore, counselors must be able to focus on essential information and not get sidetracked by irrelevant details. In order to accomplish this, various assessment models have been proposed that are designed to help crisis counselors in rendering an accurate evaluation of a client. In summarizing the most important aspects of a crisis assessment model, Myer (2001), indicates an assessment model should be parsimonious and user friendly . . . the model should be adaptable for use with many types of crisis situations . . . the model needs to be holistic, considering all aspects of clients in their experience of the crisis situation . . . the model must be appropriate for the time-limited nature of the crisis situation and guide the intervention process . . . the assessment model must recognize that people from different cultures react differently to crisis events . . . an assessment model for crisis intervention should be fluid and continually usable during the intervention process. (p. 23)

One such model is the BASIC assessment model of Karl Slaikeu (1990). Using the acronym B-A-S-I-C, Slaikeu provides counselors with an assessment model that is both parsimonious, as well as user friendly and can be applied to many different types of crisis situations. Emphasis is placed on assessing the client's thoughts, feelings, behavior, and the social impact of the crisis. In the acronym, *B* represents observable ***behaviors*** like changes in the client's day-to-day functioning behavioral responses, such as suicidal and homicidal behavior, and agitation or slowing of behavioral response. *A* represents ***affect*** or emotional response. What is the client feeling, and how has the crisis impacted on him or her emotionally? *S* represents ***somatic*** complaints and somatic issues, such as clients who report headaches, muscle aches or muscle tension, stomach aches, and any other physical problem they may be experiencing. In many instances, crises will exacerbate an existing medical or physical problem. *I* represents ***interpersonal*** or social functioning. Here, the counselor assesses how the crisis event has changed the client's relationships with friends, family, coworkers, and others in the community. Some people will isolate in the face of crisis, while some find it helpful to reach out to others. *C* represents ***cognitions*** or thoughts relevant to the crisis. For example, a person who is going through the crisis of a marital separation may blame himself or herself for the break up, by saying, "I'm a failure at everything, I can't even keep my marriage together." Cognitions would include self-statements or thoughts expressed to others. In performing a BASIC assessment, Slaikeu suggests that the counselor not limit themselves to just talking with the client, but also with the client's family or referral sources where appropriate.

The Hendricks and McKean assessment model is considered a "frontline model" (Hendricks & McKean, 1995) in that it was developed specifically for crisis intervention counselors working with clients "on the streets" or on the immediate scene of the crisis, such as a crime scene, a disaster location, or the scene of an accident. The assessment process involves two phases. The first phase involves the crisis worker's assessment of the scene itself. For example, is the crisis scene secure? Are there weapons present or other potential hazards? As the crisis counselor tries to gather relevant information, an assessment is also made regarding the "who, what, where, and how" of the crisis situation. The second phase of the assessment is geared toward evaluating the individual(s) in crisis. Here, the crisis counselor attempts to discern their current level of functioning as well as their pre-crisis functioning abilities, their medical and psychiatric history, the person's mood, and intensity of emotional expression. This model is unique in that it focuses primarily on the crisis situation or scene. The Hendricks and McKean model appears to be most useful for police, firefighters, or EMT's who may be working with individuals in crisis; however, it appears to be limited when applied to psychiatric, substance abuse, or other types of crisis intervention.

The triage assessment model (Myer, Williams, Ottens, & Schmidt, 1991), provides one of the most parsimonious, user-friendly models of assessment. Indeed, Myer (2001) criticizes the two aforementioned models for being too cumbersome and not providing a sufficient guide to the development of intervention services. In the triage assessment model, the counselor assesses the individual's crisis responses in three domains: *affective* (emotional), *cognitive* (thinking) and *behavioral* (actions) (Myer, 2001). The model also helps counselors to identify the complex interactions between these domain areas. Each domain area is divided into three possible crisis responses or reactions. So, for the affective area, counselors are asked to rate whether the client is experiencing *anger/hostility, anxiety/fear, or sadness/melancholy* as their primary emotional response to the current crisis. For the cognitive domain, counselors assess whether the client perceives the crisis event as a *transgression, threat, or loss.* A transgression would pertain to the client's perception of a present violation. Client's experiencing a threat would experience the crisis as having the potential to harm in the future, whereas a loss would be experienced as something irretrievable and would carry the notion that there is no way to recover the lost object or person in the future. Myer, William, Ottens, and Schmidt (1991) have developed a form to be used for triage assessment which appears in Myer's (2001) *Assessment for Crisis Intervention: A Triage Assessment Model* (pp. 147–149). Myer's recommends that since client reactions will vary throughout the crisis period, that counselors adjust their interventions/treatment to meet the client's needs at that moment. In this way, the triage assessment model helps to guide the counselor's interventions with the client. For example, if a client had experienced a traumatic event crisis in which they were physically assaulted in a robbery, the crisis counselor would assess the primary affective response (e.g., anger/hostility), the primary cognitive response (e.g., a sense of loss brought on by the violation of one's physical safety and loss of property), and the primary behavioral response (e.g., immobility as evidenced by the client's not having called the police yet or having taken steps to be medically checked out in the emergency room). Having done this assessment, the counselor would assist the client in expressing their anger over the losses they are experiencing and in doing so, to then mobilize them to report the assault to the police and then to seek medical attention.

In some of their early pioneering work in the crisis intervention field, both Parad and Caplan (1965) were especially interested in examining the impact of particular types of crises on families, and ways to help restore equilibrium. In assessing families, both Parad and Caplan felt it was important to examine the family's "lifestyle," which included their value system

> the family's ". . . system of ideas, attitudes and beliefs which consciously and unconsciously bind together the members of the family in a common culture";

> the family's pattern of roles (defining "what is to be done, in a family, [obviously influenced by the system of values], who is to do it, and who is to decide on allocation of tasks (leadership)."

Finally, communication is the third dimension by which families are assessed. Here, communication refers to the ". . . carrying of messages and transmitting information, feelings, ideas, among the various family members of the nuclear family [internal communication] as well as between the family and the outside community" [external community]. (Parad & Caplan, 1965, p. 58)

Parad and Caplan also felt it was important to look at what immediate mechanisms were being used for problem solving and adapting to the emotional difficulties associated with various crisis situations. These "immediate mechanisms" refer to the family's own unique style of trying to restore equilibrium at the time the crisis impacts on the family.

In looking at the impact of crisis, Parad and Caplan, outlined five aspects which they felt were central to how the family responded to the crisis situation:

1. *The stressful event poses a problem, which is, by definition, insoluble in the immediate future.* The stress of tuberculosis and hospitalization is obviously beyond the control of the family as a group. The family has no knowledge of the probable duration and outcome . . . of the illness.

2. *The problem overtaxes the psychological resources of the family, since it is beyond their traditional problem-solving methods.* Here Parad and Caplan are referring to the fact that the crisis at hand is so "massive" that it often overtaxes the traditional problem-solving approaches or methods that may have worked in the past.

3. *The situation is perceived as a threat or danger to the life goals of the family members.* Here the notion that the crisis interferes with the overall goals or functioning of the family is of importance.

4. *The crisis period is characterized by tension, which builds to a peak, then falls.*

5. This is similar to Caplan's notion that crises in and of themselves are time-limited in nature.

6. *Perhaps of greatest importance, the crisis situation awakens unresolved key problems from both the near and distant past.* This aspect of the crisis suggests that a present crisis may resurface unresolved feelings or tensions from prior crises or trauma (Parad & Caplan, 1965).

Each of the aforementioned assessment models focuses on a particular aspect of the crisis. For example, Slaikeu's BASIC model and Myer's triage assessment model both focus assessing the individual in crisis. The Hendricks/McKean model focuses on assessing the crisis situation, while the Parad/Caplan model focuses on an assessment of the family in crisis.

One of the more recent crisis assessment models is the Developmental-Ecological Model developed by Collins and Collins (2005). Using an A-B-C-D-E acronym, the A-B-C refers to affective, behavior, and cognition which is defined similarly to Myers's model. However, the "D" refers to developmental considerations. Here, it is recommended that the crisis counselor take into consideration the client's developmental stage, given that people in differing developmental stages will often react to crisis differently. For example, a 6-year-old child's concept of the death of their parent will differ in intensity and expression from that of a 25-year-old who experiences the loss of a parent. The "E" refers to "ecological" considerations, here referring to the need to take one's immediate environment factors (i.e., support systems, financial, and other resources) into consideration. By adding these two dimensions (developmental and ecological), to the crisis assessment, the counselor develops a more complete picture of the individual in crisis.

Before concluding this section on crisis assessment models, it is important to point out that there may be crisis situations that call for a specific type of assessment. Such would be the case with lethality assessments. Here, a crisis counselor may be called up to assess the danger of suicidal risk, homicidal risk, or intimate partner violence. Fortunately, there are some excellent tools for assessing these various types of risk. For example, for assessing suicidal risk, Linehan (1999, p. 158) has compiled a series of indicators and risk factors for assessing imminent suicidal danger. With regards to homicidal risk, Cavaiola and Colford (2006, p. 147) provide a lethality assessment checklist for assessing homicidal risk and risk of violent behavior. Similarly, Edelson and Tolman (1992, p. 28) have compiled a list of assessment issues and a checklist for violence risk to be used with male batterers.

CRISIS INTERVENTION MODELS

Just as there are various factors that are important in judging crisis assessment models, so too there are various elements that are necessary in judging a crisis intervention model. Many of the same proscriptions that Myer (2001) outlines for assessing crisis assessment models are also applicable to crisis intervention models. For example, he indicates that

> models should be parsimonious and user friendly . . . the model should be adaptable for use with many types of crisis situations . . . the model needs to be holistic, considering all aspects of clients in their experience of the crisis situation . . . the model must be appropriate for the time-limited nature of the crisis situation and guide the intervention process . . . and must recognize that people from different cultures react differently to crisis events . . . . (p. 23)

In order to appreciate the current crisis intervention models, it is important to first explore some of their historical influences. It is difficult to pinpoint the exact inception of crisis intervention although it is likely that people were performing crisis intervention services long before it was labeled as such. For example, during World War I and World War II, the devastating and often long-term effects of combat trauma resulted in some rather unusual interventions. In an attempt to treat conditions known as "shell shock" and "battle fatigue" (Shephard, 2001) many techniques (ranging from the barbaric to the therapeutic) were employed to help military personnel overcome these effects with the primary goal of returning the soldier to combat. Barbaric approaches included the administration of faradic electric shock to the vocal cords of mute soldiers. However, some early interventions resulted in humane and innovative therapeutic approaches for helping soldiers experiencing combat trauma. For example, Freudian psychoanalysis, referred to as the "talking cure" was just one of the therapeutic techniques used during World War I for treating "shell shock." Group therapy was also first employed in British veteran's homes during World War II with better success than many of the individual approaches developed (Shephard, 2001). It was also the British who came up with the first "crisis model" for dealing with combat trauma where the acronym P-I-E was coined. The acronym stood for "proximity," referring to the notion that soldiers were to be treated as close to the frontlines as possible, "immediacy," referring to the recommendation that treatment be provided as soon as possible following the traumatic event, and "expectancy," referring to the goal or expectancy that the soldier would be returning to combat quickly. Those who could not return to combat however were often evacuated to long term respite care provided in homeland veterans hospitals (Shepard, 2001).

On November 28, 1942, a tragic event took place, which proved to set the stage for modern crisis intervention theory. The event was the Cocoanut Grove fire in Boston, Massachusetts. Cocoanut Grove was a large nightclub where 493 people perished when flames swept through the nightclub. Many of the victims died of smoke inhalation or were trampled to death trying to find poorly marked exits. Dr. Eric Lindemann was working at Massachusetts General Hospital at the time and noted that the symptoms of the grieving survivors were very similar. Many of these survivors kept returning to Mass General "to talk" about the loved ones whom they had lost in the fire or to relive their own harrowing experiences in trying to escape the smoke and fire. Lindemann (1944) also saw how important the role of community caregivers and clergy was in helping the Boston community to grieve. In fact, out of this early work, Lindemann developed his later work on grief theory. Another discovery was that this group of survivors had actually benefited from short-term intervention, which ran counter to the prevailing psychoanalytic thinking of the day, which advocated for long-term analysis as the only proper way to achieve therapeutic results. The Cocoanut Grove disaster was considered by most to mark the beginning of modern crisis intervention; although Gerald Caplan (1961) who had worked with Lindemann in the aftermath of the Cocoanut Grove Nightclub fire, was said to have been the one to articulate the notion of crisis theory. Caplan (1964) emphasized the need for early intervention and is considered "the master architect of preventative crisis intervention" (Parad & Parad, 1990, p. 13) as the founder of the Harvard Family Guidance Center. The Guidance Center directed their preventative crisis efforts to study the impact of four major stressors: premature birth, birth of a child with congenital abnormalities, birth of twins, and tuberculosis. Howard Parad was the social worker assigned by Caplan to the mental health and public health teams who began to explore and elaborate on methods and techniques for crisis intervention.

In 1958, Leopold Bellak started the first 24-hour walk-in psychiatric clinic (called The Trouble-Shooting Clinic) in Elmhurst City, New York. This clinic became the framework for Bellak and Siegel's (1983) work on "brief emergency psychotherapy" which was based on psychodynamic theory. In 1962, Gerald Jacobson, a psychiatrist, began a similar clinic (based on Caplan's theories) called the Benjamin Rush Center for Problems of Living in Los Angeles (Jacobson, Strickler, & Morley, 1968). The Center was essentially a walk-in clinic which offered six sessions to individuals and families who were experiencing various life crises. The following year, 1963, the Community Mental Health Centers Act was passed which required 24-hour crisis intervention services as one of the five mandated program features in CMHCs (Community Mental Health Centers). Although Community Mental Health Centers did not proliferate as planned (Sharfstein, 2000), the dire need for such services was validated at that time with the ever-growing number of psychiatric patients who were literally "dumped" into the community with the advent of "deinstitutionalization" and the closing of many state psychiatric hospitals.

It is important to note that all this early work in crisis intervention gave way to some of the following contemporary crisis intervention models.

MASLOW'S HIERARCHY OF NEEDS AND CRISIS INTERVENTION

Although Abraham Maslow is not usually associated with crisis intervention, much of his writings on the hierarchy of needs do have a bearing on crisis intervention work (Maslow, 1958). Most often, the hierarchy of needs would be included in introductory psychology texts under chapters examining motivation or drive. Yet Maslow's work also does a good job in explaining how crisis counselors may work effectively with people in crisis. Also keep in mind the common recommendation for anyone doing human service counseling . . . *Start where the client is*. Below is an example of the hierarchy of needs:

Figure 2.1   Maslow's Hierarchy of Needs

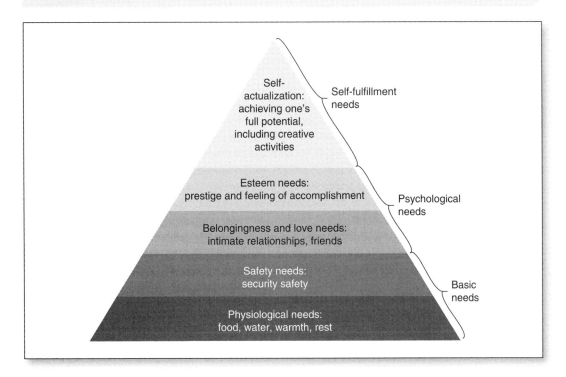

Say you're helping a person who just lost their home and belongings in Hurricane Katrina or Superstorm Sandy. In order to "begin where your client is" you would need to focus on making certain that the individual has adequate food, water, shelter, clothing, or those basic *physiological needs* described at the very lowest rung of the hierarchy. Similarly, in counseling a person who has been physically or sexually assaulted, you would be most likely dealing with physical *health and safety needs*, therefore you would want to help ensure that this person feels that they are in a safe place in the aftermath of the traumatic assault. If you were working with someone who has just separated from their spouse, fiancé, or partner, you would be helping them with *belongingness and love needs*. Those experiencing a developmental crisis (e.g., midlife crisis) may be examining *esteem needs* according to Maslow, while those experiencing an existential crisis (e.g., where he or she may be examining the meaning of life) may be dealing with *self-actualization needs* according to the hierarchy. Put in another way, wouldn't it be ludicrous for a crisis counselor helping someone who has just gone through a traumatic event like a horrible car accident to say to them, "Okay I understand that you've been in a horrible accident, but I think we need to talk about your self-esteem issues."

SLAIKEU'S COMPREHENSIVE MODEL FOR CRISIS INTERVENTION

Karl Slaikeu, PhD began formulating his comprehensive model for crisis intervention while working at the Eric County (Buffalo, NY) Suicide Prevention and Crisis Service and continued this endeavor while at the University of South Carolina and the University of Texas. What is unique to Slaikeu's model is that he was one of the first crisis interventionists to make a distinction between what he terms, "psychological first aid" or first order intervention, and crisis therapy or second order intervention. The length of treatment, the specific crisis service delivered, and the goals and training of the counselor/therapist distinguish the two approaches. First order intervention or psychological first aid refers to the immediate assistance offered to an individual in crisis and "usually takes only one session" (Slaikeu, 1990, p. 102). The goals of first order intervention are to reestablish immediate coping by providing support, reducing lethality, and helping link the person to other intervention resources. It is implied that individuals with various levels of training can offer first order intervention. For example, a police officer called to the scene of a domestic dispute, a teacher working with an angry student, a clergy member providing words of solace to a grieving family, or a medical doctor or nurse who is treating a distraught accident victim all are providing psychological first aid. Crisis therapy refers to the therapeutic process that goes beyond the immediate "first aid" and attempts to bring about some resolution to the crisis. In some respects, crisis therapy is like other types of counseling, however the main difference is that the major focus is on the crisis.

Slaikeu (1990) conceptualizes psychological first aid as consisting of five stages:

1. *Making Psychological Contact:* Here the counselor is empathically listening to the client as they describe the crisis and is trying to establish connection with him or her.

2. *Exploring Dimensions of the Problem:* In this stage, the counselor is concerned with exploring the events leading up to the crisis as well as the crisis itself. The counselor inquires about the "who, what, when, where, and how" of the crisis. However, Slaikeu points out that this is not done as a strict step-by-step interrogation, since people in crisis will offer this information spontaneously.

3. *Examining Possible Solutions:* This stage is devoted to discovering and identifying a wide range of possible alternative solutions. It is suggested that the crisis counselor ask the client about what they already tried to do to remedy the situation, and then to ask them to generate alternatives, at which point, the counselor can then offer other solutions.

4. *Taking Concrete Action:* At this point, the person is encouraged to take some concrete action to deal with the crisis at hand. This action step can be as simple as planning to meet the next day to discuss how the person is coping, or it can be rather complex, as would be the case if someone needed to be evaluated for admission to a psychiatric unit because of suicidal intentions. Slaikeu points out that at this stage, the helper/counselor takes either a "facilitative or directive stance in helping the client deal with the crisis" (p. 115). If the client can make sound judgments and there is no indication of danger to self or others, then the counselor can take a facilitative role. However, if the client is incapacitated in some way (e.g. under the influence of alcohol or drugs) or they pose a danger to themselves or others, or are too emotionally distraught to make sound decisions, then the counselor needs to take a more directive stance.

5. *Follow Up:* This last stage involves agreeing on a follow-up procedure to check on the individual's progress and/or his or her status. Follow up may entail a face-to-face meeting, a phone call, or a visit to a clinic or hospital. The objective of follow up is to ascertain that the goals of psychological first aid have been achieved.

FLANNERY & EVERLY'S CRISIS INTERVENTION MODEL

Raymond Flannery, Jr., PhD, and George S. Everly, Jr., PhD are usually names that are associated with *critical incident stress management (CISM)* and *critical incident stress debriefing* that will be presented later in the text. Flannery and Everly (2000) conclude that traumatic events, or what they refer to as critical incidents, often result in "disruptions in reasonable mastery of the environment, in caring attachments to others and in sustaining a purposeful meaning in life" (p. 119). As a result, individuals who are exposed to critical incidents or traumatic life events will often experience many reactions like those common to posttraumatic stress disorder (e.g. hypervigilance, sleep difficulties, intrusive recollections of the event, and a tendency to withdraw from involvement in everyday activities). Therefore, the goal of emergency mental health (EMH) clinicians is to restore the individual back to equilibrium, restore "independent functioning," and to lessen the impact of the trauma and PTSD-like symptoms (Flannery & Everly, 2000, p. 120). In order to accomplish this, emergency mental health practitioners are encouraged to use the following guidelines:

1. **Intervene immediately:** Here Flannery and Everly (2000) emphasize the importance of responding as quickly as possible in the aftermath of the traumatic event or critical incident.

2. **Stabilize:** The immediate goal is to stabilize the person who has been impacted by the traumatic event by finding out who their support systems are and mobilizing them to help. This will allow the traumatized person to begin to function independently.

3. **Facilitate Understanding:** Here the counselor is assisting the person impacted by the trauma to gain some understanding as to what has happened. It is important therefore to gather facts about the critical incident as the traumatized person recounts the chain of events leading up to the traumatic event.

4. **Focus on Problem Solving:** The goal at this stage is to help the victim of the traumatic event to use their support network and available resources in order to assist him or her with problem solving. It is important to do this within the context of the victim's emotional reactions to the traumatic event.

5. **Encourage Self-Reliance:** The emphasis here is on empowering the client by having them accomplish those tasks that they are capable of performing. Although victims should be helped in assessing the current problem and the options that they have available to them, the goal is to restore self-reliance.

These guidelines were developed based on the works of Butcher, 1980; Everly & Mitchell, 1999; Flannery, 1998; Raphael, 1986; Robinson & Mitchell, 1995; Sandoval, 1985; Wollman, 1993.

AGUILERA'S MODEL OF CRISIS INTERVENTION

Donna C. Aguilera, PhD is a renowned expert in the field of crisis intervention. Her text, *Crisis Intervention: Theory and Methodology* (Aguilera, 1998), is considered one of the most influential works within the field. In terms of her theoretical approach, Aguilera's work is greatly influenced by Caplan's crisis theory. Crises are perceived as events that upset one's equilibrium, therefore the goal of crisis intervention is to help restore equilibrium by mobilizing the individual's coping resources and support systems. Aguilera's crisis model provides recommended steps to follow, however each of the steps do not always take place in a clearly defined, discrete pattern, even though typical interventions usually follow a similar sequence:

Assessment: Aguilera recommends that an accurate assessment of the presenting problem be performed, not an in-depth or thorough diagnostic assessment of the individual. The focus, therefore, is on the precipitating crisis that caused the person to seek professional help. The assessment also includes a lethality assessment.

Planning Therapeutic Intervention: Once an accurate assessment is made, the counselor then plans appropriate interventions. Given the short-term nature of crisis intervention, these interventions are obviously not designed to bring about changes in personality structure, but instead are geared toward restoring the individual to pre-crisis equilibrium. Accordingly, it is important for the crisis counselor to know how much the crisis event has disrupted the individual's life and how this disruption has impacted significant others in his or her environment. It is also important to be aware of how the individual has handled prior crises and what types of supports he or she have used in the past. Although the types of intervention techniques will depend on the nature of the crisis, and the skills and creativity of the therapist, the following intervention techniques are suggested (Morley, Messick, & Aguilera, 1967):

1. *Helping the individual to gain an intellectual understanding of his crisis.* If the client is unable to see a connection between the crisis event and the degree of discomfort and disequilibrium they are experiencing then the role of the counselor to explain the role of the crisis in creating this discomfort.

2. *Helping the individual become aware of his or her present feelings.* Similarly, individuals experiencing crisis events may have difficulty in accurately labeling the feelings they are experiencing. It is also possible that this person may be suppressing or blocking feelings in an effort to cope with the crisis. According to Aguilera, an immediate goal of intervention is to provide some relief from tensions, by providing the individual with a means of recognizing their emotional states, bringing these feelings into the open and validating them. In some instances, counselors may need to bring about emotional catharsis, by giving the individual permission to cry, or express their anger, guilt, or other feelings.

3. *Exploring coping mechanisms.* Here, the counselor is assisting the individual in exploring past coping styles as a means of finding ways to cope with the present crisis.

4. *Reopening the social world.* Since many crises usually involve loss, for example in the death of a loved one or divorce, the possibility of using significant others from one's social milieu to help fill this loss becomes a highly effective means of providing coping resources; as in the case of a widow or widower who joins a bereavement support group.

Resolution of the Crisis and Anticipatory Planning: In this last phase, the therapist is trying to consolidate those gains made during the crisis intervention period and to reinforce those adaptive mechanisms that the individual has used effectively to reduce tension and anxiety. The counselor may also address ways in which the present crisis may help in dealing with future crises.

Aguilera's crisis model can be considered a hybrid model given that it is both an assessment model and a "problem-solving" model designed to assist individuals in the restoration of equilibrium. Throughout her text, *Crisis Intervention: Theory and Methodology,* there are numerous diagrams that describe how and why some individuals may regain equilibrium, while others may not. This depends in part on the individual's perception of the crisis event and whether they have adequate social supports and coping resources. As indicated above, the crisis counselor helps the individual to gain a more accurate intellectual and emotional understanding of the crisis event. Other aspects of crisis counseling involve assisting the client to mobilize social supports or summon their own coping resources. The overall goal is to assist the client in developing coping strategies that they can use in the future.

ROBERTS'S SEVEN-STAGE CRISIS INTERVENTION MODEL

Albert R. Roberts, a professor of social work, and criminal justice at Rutgers University, advocates that crisis counselors be active and directive; however not to the extent that they take ownership of the crisis or its solutions away from the individual. Roberts's writings (1990, 1996, 2000) credit Caplan (1964), Golan (1978), and Parad (1965) with having influenced his model of crisis intervention. Roberts also advocates that crisis counselors convey acceptance and optimism so that individuals are aware that their situation is not hopeless and therefore they can successfully survive the crisis.

Roberts's model is a stage model in that the crisis counselor helps the client by addressing specific points within each stage of the model. Roberts's seven-stage model is as follows:

1. *Plan and conduct a Crisis Assessment (including lethality measures).* In this initial stage, the crisis counselor determines if the person in crisis is in imminent danger. For example, do they require medical attention or is this person suicidal? Is this person a victim of domestic violence or are this person's children in danger? Is there a threat or history of violence? Or is there a history of psychiatric difficulties or a history of chemical dependency? If so, is this person under the influence of alcohol or drugs at present or are they able to accurately interpret reality?

2. *Make psychological contact, establish rapport, and readily establish a relationship.* Here the crisis clinician's goal is to establish a connection or rapport with the person in crisis. To accomplish this, Roberts recommends that the clinician convey a respectful, nonjudgmental attitude toward the client.

3. *Identify major problems and examine the dimensions of the problem in order to define it.* Roberts recommends that the clinician try to find out a) the 'last straw' or precipitating event that led the client to seek help; b) previous coping methods; and c) danger or lethality (Roberts, 2000).

4. *Encourage an exploration of feelings and emotions.* Roberts feels that this stage is most closely related to the previous stage. He feels that crisis counselors often overlook this step, because they may be too focused on conducting an accurate, assessment or in gathering factual information about the crisis. Roberts indicates that it is important to allow the client to express their feelings in a nonjudgmental, supportive

environment. To accomplish this task, crisis counselors are advised to employ active, empathic listening techniques.

5. *Generate and explore alternatives and assess past coping attempts.* The focus here is on uncovering past coping tools that were successful. It is assumed that the present, precipitating crisis is overwhelming to the individual or that the crisis impacts on the individual beyond their normal coping abilities. Roberts feels it is important for the crisis counselor to bring into conscious awareness those coping responses that may exist just beneath the surface, at a preconscious level. Also, the crisis counselor is trying to get the client to modify maladaptive coping responses. Roberts believes that solution-focused approaches are especially helpful at this stage. For example, a person experiencing a crisis over the death of a parent might be asked, "If your deceased parents are in heaven looking down on you, what could you do to make them proud?" (Roberts, 2000, p. 19).

6. *Develop and formulate an action plan.* Roberts stresses the importance of addressing cognitive factors as a means of moving the client and crisis clinician toward the eventual goal of developing an action plan. For this to occur, three conditions must be met. First, the client needs to have a realistic understanding of what factors led up to the crisis and why it occurred. Second, it is important that the client have an understanding of how the crisis event interferes with his or her expectations, life goals, and belief systems. Here, the crisis clinician must be aware of any cognitive distortions, overgeneralizations, or irrational beliefs (e.g., "If she does not come back to me, I simply can't go on living"). Third, the crisis counselor begins to help the client get rid of these faulty, maladaptive cognitive misperceptions or distortions as they begin to adopt healthier, adaptive rational beliefs and new cognitions. The action plan that evolves from these steps will often include having the client generate some alternatives (e.g., in the case of an abused partner, helping them to find temporary shelter where they will be safe).

7. *Establish a follow-up plan and agreement.* Follow-up plans may involve referrals for ongoing counseling, referral to self-help support groups or an agreement may be made between the crisis counselor and the client that a follow-up phone contact will take place at a specific time and date to make certain the client continues to regain equilibrium and balance in their lives. Obviously, the nature of the follow up would depend on the type of crisis.

Roberts's seven-stage model can be applied to a variety of crisis events and crisis situations ranging from addictions, incest, child abuse, school violence, hospital emergency room cases, HIV clients, telephone crisis calls, walk-in crisis centers, and mobile crisis units. This is clearly a definite strength of Roberts's model. Students of crisis intervention will often find this type of stage model very helpful in guiding both crisis sessions and intake sessions, as it provides them with a clearly defined, systematic guide that they can use. With time and experience, they may find that they are using these steps somewhat automatically.

JAMES AND GILLILAND'S SIX-STEP CRISIS INTERVENTION MODEL

Richard James and Burl Gilliland are both professors of psychology at the University of Memphis and like Roberts's model, they developed a six step model of crisis intervention. The James and Gilliland model (2002) is also very pragmatic and can be used in a variety of situations. The first three steps of the model are defined as "listening" steps, where the crisis counselor is primarily listening, observing, gathering information, responding with genuineness, and using active listening skills to establish rapport and provide the client with support. The latter three steps are referred to as the "acting" steps. The six step model of crisis intervention follows these steps:

1. *Defining the problem*

2. *Ensuring client safety*

3. *Providing support*

4. *Examining alternatives*

5. *Making plans*

6. *Obtaining commitment*

In Step 1, *defining the problem,* the crisis counselor discerns the precipitating crisis event that resulted in the client's seeking assistance. This is where the "who, what, where, when, and how" of the crisis event is discussed. Background gathering is usually limited to the crisis event itself and not so much to the past history of the client, other than how it relates to the event itself. For example, if a man or woman were to seek help because of a crisis pertaining to a present breakup in a love relationship, it may be helpful to explore other past events surrounding loss. This would be done to determine if the pain of the present loss is being exacerbated by prior similar losses. In Step 2, *ensuring safety,* the crisis counselor ascertains whether there are imminent danger aspects to the crisis, such as suicidal or homicidal ideation or intent, intimate partner violence, or any potential threat of future violence. In Step 3, *providing support* the counselor is offering supportive encouragement to the client to help reassure them that they will get through the crisis at hand. In Step 4, *examining alternatives,* it is important that the counselor find out what steps the client has tried already and considered taking to remedy their situation.

In Step 5, *making a plan,* it is suggested that the client and the counselor work together toward a collaborative plan. The client is more likely to follow through with a plan in which they feel some sense of ownership.

In Step 6, *obtaining commitment,* the client consents to implement and follow the plan that has been agreed on. This sometimes is accomplished through a written contract or perhaps a tacit verbal agreement.

There is a quite a bit of overlap between the Roberts's model and the James and Gilliland model even in the terminology they use. They both start off with an assessment of the crisis situation, and both are concerned with making contact with the person in crisis. Both models then explore various alternatives to dealing with the crisis and then develop a plan of intervention based on those alternatives. Finally, there is a commitment made to implementing a plan of action. Both the Roberts and the James and Gilliland models provide crisis counselors with a pragmatic format for assessing and managing clients who present in crisis. The other advantage to these models is that they can be adapted to a variety of crisis situations (Gilliland & James, 1997).

GREENSTONE AND LEVITON'S CRISIS INTERVENTION MODEL

The Greenstone and Leviton model (2002) also presents a six-step model for counselors to follow:

   I. Immediacy

  II. Control

  III. Assessment

  IV. Disposition

  V. Referral

  VI. Follow up

Immediacy: Act immediately to stop emotional bleeding. Here, Greenstone and Leviton suggest that the counselor do their utmost to make certain that the client does not harm himself or herself or others, relieve anxiety, and prevent disorientation. The goal of this stage is to provide immediate assistance to clients to help them cope with their immediate responses to the crisis.

Take Control: Greenstone and Leviton recommend that the crisis counselor take control of the session by letting the client know that you are there to assist them. In doing so, the counselor is attempting to bring some structure and direction to the session in order to prevent chaotic feelings from escalating. In this stage, the goal is not for the counselor to control the client, but to add structure and definition to the crisis and reduce feelings of apprehension and anxiety.

Assess the Situation: Here, Greenstone and Leviton recommend the assessment focus on both the crisis situation (i.e., the who, what, where, why of the crisis) as well as trying to ascertain how the crisis can best be managed in the present and what variables may interfere with managing the crisis. They caution that this is not the time to do a lengthy assessment or to explore a life history. Instead they recommend that counselors focus on assessing the present crisis and the events leading up to the crisis. It is also suggested that the counselor not overwhelm the client with too many questions, which might only increase their confusion. Instead, direct clarifying questions are suggested.

Decide How to Handle the Situation After You Have Assessed It: In this stage, the crisis counselor will explore options with the person in crisis and will creatively explore possible solutions to the crisis situation. It is at this point, that the crisis counselor will also help the individual to identify what resources they have at their disposal and help mobilize both personal and social resources.

Follow Up If Possible or as Agreed. Refer as Needed: Here, the crisis counselor will refer the individual to any appropriate resource that may help them in resolving the crisis. Greenstone and Leviton feel it is imperative that crisis counselors have a good working knowledge of community agencies, social service resources, medical treatment providers, state, county and national referral hotlines, clergy, and legal resources. It is also suggested that counselors have knowledge of any fees that may be charged for services and whether these resources will accept individuals with limited financial resources. There is nothing more frustrating to individuals in crisis than to have doors slammed in their face because of an inability to pay for services or a lack of healthcare insurance coverage. So, it is imperative that crisis counselors make successful, appropriate referrals and that they follow up to make sure the client was seen.

The Greenstone and Leviton model is unique in including suggestions regarding the types of skills that crisis counselors may use in ameliorating crises, for example attending skills; questioning (using both open-ended and close-ended questions); clarifying (using paraphrasing and verifying statements); reflecting (reviewing positive, painful, ambivalent feelings); and summarizing (tying together important facts, feelings, subjective distress with the precipitating event). This model is also somewhat unique in that Greenstone and Leviton are strong advocates for effective referral and follow up.

KANEL'S A-B-C MODEL OF CRISIS INTERVENTION

Dr. Kristi Kanel (1999) is a licensed marriage and family counselor who received her doctorate in counseling psychology. She derives her model from her work with victims of domestic violence and from her private practice work with couples and families. The A-B-C model was developed specifically so that it could be used in both nonprofit, social service type agencies, as well as in private practice settings. The A-B-C model follows these steps:

A—Developing and Maintaining Contact: In this stage, Kanel stresses the importance of establishing rapport with the client. She defines rapport as "a state of understanding and comfort" (Kanel, 1999, p. 55) and feels that before the counselor can really delve into the client's personal world, that rapport must be established. Kanel suggests various counselor skills that are essential for establishing rapport. These include attending skills (such as maintaining eye contact, body posture, vocal style); questioning (using both open-ended and close-ended questions); clarifying (using paraphrasing and verifying statements); reflecting (reviewing positive, painful, ambivalent feelings); and summarizing (tying together important facts, feelings, subjective distress with the precipitating event).

B—Identifying the Problem: This stage involves both an exploration of the crisis and an assessment of the client's response to that crisis. Here the precipitating event is explored in more detail, as well as how that crisis event is creating impairment in the person's life behaviorally, socially, academically, and/or occupationally. Kanel also suggests that the client's pre-crisis level of functioning should be assessed to determine how much the current crisis accounts for functional impairment. Also at this stage, a suicidal assessment should take place, as well as an assessment of the client's use of mood-altering substances. In addition, this stage lays the groundwork for therapeutic interaction. Here, the counselor might provide educational information, provide statements of empowerment, make supportive statements, or reframe the crisis.

C—Coping: This step is similar to James and Gilliland's or Greenstone and Leviton's stages that investigate alternatives and options. First, Kanel suggests that the counselor survey how the client has attempted to cope to date and then explore some alternatives, as a means of helping the client to develop some new coping behaviors.

CAVAIOLA AND COLFORD'S L-A-P-C MODEL OF CRISIS INTERVENTION

After the above review of a variety of different models, we would like to present a model that is simple and effective to use with most crisis clients. The L-A-P-C model involves four steps:

L—Listen

A—Assess

P—Plan

C—Commit

In the *listening* step, the crisis counselor is listening to the client's explanation of the crisis. When it took place, where, who was there, the events leading up to the crisis, and what happened in the immediate aftermath. This is an active listening step, because the counselor is asking the client questions, and is encouraging him or her to talk about whatever details come to mind. The counselor also is supportive of any attempts to cope with the crisis. This step is like listening to a friend or family member who is relating a crisis or incident they have just experienced. You would not sit there indifferent to what they were saying nor would you criticize them or act outraged. Instead, you would listen, hear them out, ask them clarifying questions and offer support.

In the *assessment* step, the counselor is trying to get a read on how the client is responding to the crisis. What is their behavior (e.g., are they agitated, pacing around the room, or are they sluggish and slow in their movements)? What is their emotional state (e.g., are they angry, sad, crying, anxious, or feeling overwhelmed)? What is their interpretation of the event (e.g., is it the worst thing that has ever happened to them, are they feeling guilt or remorse, are they blaming themselves)? In this step, the counselor may also assess the client's own personal strengths and possible social supports that may have helped them to deal with crises in the past.

In the *planning* step, the counselor is either trying to help the client generate some various options that they can support and process or the counselor is being directive in planning what steps need to be taken. For example, the planning done with a person who has experienced a job loss is different from the necessary planning involved with a suicidal client or a rape victim.

In the final *commit* step, from the plans discussed above, one is agreed on and implemented.

This model is unique in that it provides counselors with a quick checklist form which can easily be used to guide counselors through the process of providing crisis intervention counseling with clients.

CRISIS INTERVENTION SERVICES IN THE 21ST CENTURY

Crisis intervention services have evolved quite a bit since their inception with the first crisis hotlines in New York City in 1906. As an example, just about every major hospital offers full-time, face-to-face psychiatric screeners for individuals who present with mental health and/or substance use disorder crises. In addition, many county social service departments (and many medical centers) offer mobile psychiatric screening for children, adolescents, and adults where the crisis counselor travels to the individual rather than having that person transported to an emergency room. Now there are also a proliferation of crisis hotlines and self-help groups for various types of crises (similar to the crises that are covered in this textbook), such as national clearinghouses (e.g., https://healthfinder.gov), and statewide hotlines and self-help groups (e.g., in New Jersey there is a Self-Help Group Clearinghouse which lists self-help groups and hotlines by county at www.njgroups.org; and in Missouri there's a comparable clearinghouse at www.mha-em.org/self-help-groups). Additionally, first responders receive more extensive training in managing mental health, substance use disorder, and bereavement crises. For example, police, firefighters, and EMTs have been trained to administer Narcan for opioid overdoses. In most towns and cities, police have the most difficult of task of doing "next of kin notification" whenever a loved one has died in an accident, shooting, or under other atypical circumstances. Imagine being the police officer who must tell a parent that their child was struck and killed by a car while crossing the street? All next of kin notifications are usually done face-to-face with the victim's family. Also, police and EMTs are often called on to respond to various types of mental health and psychiatric crises. In some states and counties, mobile crisis response teams are dispatched from medical centers to assist individuals who are experiencing mental health or substance use disorder crises often accompanied by police officers or EMTs.

Another development in crisis intervention service delivery is the emphasis on disaster crisis counseling. Many states offer courses that lead to certification in disaster crisis counseling. These counselors are then deployed at times of state or national emergencies, such as when tornadoes struck Joplin, Missouri, or Superstorm Sandy in New Jersey, or the recent flooding in Louisiana.

Concurrently, the number or undergraduate and graduate courses that focus on crisis intervention reflects the increased crisis intervention service delivery programs. Since 2009, the Council for the Accreditation of Counseling and Related Educational Programs (CACREP) (2009) has mandated that crisis intervention be included as part of the curriculum for CACREP accredited graduate programs. Some graduate clinical and community psychology programs also offer specializations in crisis counseling.

SUMMARY

In reviewing the aforementioned models of crisis intervention, a few important points need to be clarified. The first point is that there is a definite historical evolution to crisis intervention theory, which began with the early work of Lindemann and Caplan. This early theoretical work then gave way to the work of Parad, Aguilera, and Slaikeu, and more recently to the models proposed by Roberts, James and Gilliland, and Greenstone and Leviton. The second major point is that there is certainly more similarity to these models than there are differences. Although some models incorporate assessment strategies into their step-by-step approach, others stress the importance of connecting with the person in crisis. However, all models follow a similar sequential procedural format. For example, James and Gilliland stress the importance of exploring alternatives and then making a specific plan based on an exploration of these alternatives, which bears similarity to Roberts, Greenstone, and Leviton, and Kanel's approach.

Again, in exploring similarities it is important to point out that these models all focus on providing psychological first aid, making certain that the client feels heard and supported. The counselor then assesses the crisis situation and explores alternatives or optional ways to deal with the crisis. An agreement is made as to what options will be enacted and appropriate referrals are made. Some type of follow up then takes place, to make certain that the client has adhered to the selected options or alternatives and that some beginning steps have been taken to resolve the crisis. The strength of all these models is that they help provide the beginning counselor with some very rudimentary, systematic procedures that can be followed to assist clients in a variety of crisis situations. Each theorist has attempted to devise a model that can be used whether the crisis is situational, developmental, environmental, or existential. The down side of these models is that the success of resolving the crisis will depend in part on the experience of the crisis counselor in comfortably applying the model to a variety of situations, and also to their knowledge of resources. In exploring options and alternatives, the counselor's own creativity and resourcefulness comes into play by proposing some acceptable alternatives for dealing with the problem at hand. Naturally, most models recommend that the counselor actively engage the client in this exploration of alternatives. The other downside with these models is that they assume the client is a cooperative, active participant in the crisis counseling process who will explore alternatives and follow through with the recommendations. Unfortunately, from experience counselors know all too well that this is not always the case. By their very nature, crises can be immobilizing and it is not unusual for clients to repeat past methods of coping, even though they are ineffective. Take for example, a crisis involving intimate partner violence. A crisis counselor may spend hours making certain that they have secured a bed at a local domestic violence shelter, only to find out that the victim has returned to their abuser. Unfortunately, it is common for battered individuals to not follow through with an agreed-on referral from the crisis counseling session. Or take for example, a person with a substance use disorder who against medical advice leaves a detox program after one day, after you spent hours getting him or her admitted to that program. It is clear that no single model has all the answers, but each does contribute to a more complete understanding of how to provide effective crisis intervention services.

RESOURCES FOR CHAPTER ENRICHMENT

Suggested Readings

Aguilera, D. C. (1998). *Crisis intervention: Theory and methodology.* St. Louis, MO: Mosby-Year Book.

Bellak, L., & Siegel, H. (1983). *Handbook of intensive brief and emergency psychotherapy.* Larchmont, NY: C.P.S.

Caplan, G. (1964). *Principles of preventative psychiatry.* New York, NY: Basic Books.

Council for the Accreditation of Counseling and Related Educational Programs. (2009). *Accreditation Standards.* Retrieved from http://www.cacrep.org

Flannery, R. B., Jr. (1994). *Post-traumatic stress disorder: The victim's guide to healing and recovery.* New York, NY: Crossroads Press.

James, R. K., & Gilliland, B. E. (2002). *Crisis intervention strategies* (4th ed.) Pacific Grove, CA: Brooks/Cole.

Kanel, K. (1999). *A guide to crisis intervention.* Pacific Grove, CA: Brooks/Cole.

McGee, R. K. (1974). *Crisis intervention in the community.* Baltimore, MD: University Park Press.

Puryear, D. A. (1979). *Helping people in crisis.* San Francisco, CA: Jossey-Bass.

Roberts, A. R. (2000). An overview of crisis theory and crisis intervention. In A. R. Roberts (Ed.), *Crisis intervention handbook: Assessment, treatment, and research.* New York, NY: Oxford University Press.

Slaikeu, K. A. (1990). *Crisis intervention: A handbook for practice and research* (2nd ed.). Boston, MA: Allyn & Bacon.

Shephard, B. (2001). *A war of nerves: Soldiers and psychiatrists in the twentieth century.* Boston, MA: Harvard University Press.

Wainrib, B. R., & Bloch, E. L. (1998). *Crisis intervention and trauma response: Theory and practice.* New York, NY: Springer

Recommended YouTube Viewing

https://www.youtube.com/watch?v = VCiBBFe6xE4

This is a brief documentary by Dr. Eric Lindemann of the infamous Cocoanut Grove disaster, which was described earlier in this chapter. By viewing the video, students will get a clearer sense as to why this disaster was so tragic and how it gave birth to the field of crisis intervention.

CHAPTER 3

Essential Crisis Intervention Skills

David was a 35-year-old probation officer who was attending graduate school in the evening for a degree in counseling. He prided himself on setting and achieving goals, particularly in the area of education, as he was the first member of his family to be able to attend college. A regular visitor to the local gym and an avid runner, he was accosted one night while on an evening boardwalk jog by two armed men who ordered him off the boardwalk and demanded his watch and any cash he might have. They held the gun to his head and told him not to leave the beach until after they were long gone. David remained there for almost six hours—when he finally returned to his apartment where he remained for the next week. A coworker only learned of the attack when he called David to check with him on the reason for his very uncharacteristic fifth consecutive missed workday.

Ancient Greek and Roman tragedians managed crises with little effort. In order to avert the demise of a protagonist in the throes of crisis, they often lowered onto the stage, via a primitive mechanical crane, a device intended to whisk the actor away to safety. This technique, known as the *deus ex machina* ("god from the machine"), typically represented divine intervention in resolving the crisis. Hollywood also was not immune to such a technique: the cavalry arrives just in time to rescue the film hero, and a favorite television character survives the crisis of the season-ending cliffhanger to return the next year for another go at it.

However, without the benefits of a stage prop or a screenwriter's pen, it is up to crisis workers to bring order out of the chaos of real life crises using only their training, ingenuity, and clearheadedness. In crises of all types, counselors must attempt to have crisis survivors return to some semblance of the lives they enjoyed prior to the crisis event. Crisis counseling requires a different set of skills than those learned in an introductory counseling class. In non-crisis counseling, clients tend to seek out treatment to resolve self-defeating patterns of behavior, to understand what lurks in the dark corners of the mind, or to comply with the urgings of a spouse, supervisor, teacher, or attorney.

Crises, however, are random and unpredictable. Recovery requires more inner resources than the survivors can sufficiently muster at the time, pushing them to seek comfort and support from those willing and able to help. The purpose of this chapter is to outline the techniques that are critical to the assessment of victims in crisis and to the intervention required to bring them to a sense of equilibrium. The chapter addresses these issues in four parts: physical, emotional, and cognitive responses to crisis; characteristics of effective crisis intervention; characteristics of effective crisis counselors; and effective intervention techniques. The L-A-P-C model of crisis intervention (listen, assess, plan, commit) also is discussed.

RESPONSES TO CRISIS

Since, by nature, crisis is a time limited phenomenon, some victims will recover from the crisis state without the aid of outside intervention. Caplan (1964) considered the duration of a typical crisis state to be four to six weeks, although there has been some confusion regarding this timeline (Roberts, 2000). Other studies suggested that acute symptoms of stress in the majority of people exposed to severe trauma tend to subside within three months, and only 25% of victims eventually develop stress disorders (Goode, 2001). Crisis victims are most willing to accept help during this approximate month to three-month period (Golan, 1978), and the appropriate intervention will help them emerge from it functioning at higher adaptive levels (Kanel, 1999).

Myriad factors influence crisis recovery, including the pre-crisis level of function, the type and intensity of the crisis encountered, and the availability of a support system. For example, the individual with a preexisting anxiety disorder who never managed transition or change well will be at far greater risk after a crisis event than the resilient individual who has always accepted change. Similarly, the ascetic loner without a family or social group will have to cope with the crisis alone, while the victim who is surrounded by a large extended family will have access to much needed support. Understanding the reactions of the victims of crisis enables counselors to provide appropriate interventions to meet the needs of individual victims.

Biological systems theory proposed that the rules of complementarity apply to the functioning of the living organism. That is, maintaining a steady state of functioning, a balance known as homeostasis is one of the functions of the central nervous system; the individual is aroused to action when such action is called for and then returns to a state of equilibrium when the arousal period passes. The driver who has to activate her own emergency response system in order to swerve suddenly to avoid hitting a deer in the road will calm down before her trip is over. Tourists who must remain on alert to negotiate unknown city streets will return to a steady state once they complete their tours.

Individuals also contribute to the maintenance of their own reassuring states of equilibrium. They develop routines, cultivate templates through which they view themselves and the world; establish specific rules of order for cause-and-effect, justice, and fairness; draw on resources from their support systems to help sustain them. Changing any one of these elements would be a source of stress for most people. However, when a sudden, random event (crisis) occurs, its victims experience a complete disruption of these established requisites of equilibrium. Crisis dislodges people from their comfort zones and makes it difficult for them to restore their balance. Senseless events throw individuals into the maelstrom, leaving them to tread water until exhaustion sets in and, it is hoped, help arrives.

According to Roberts (2000), there is a general consensus among many mental health professionals regarding the characteristics of a person in crisis. The person in crisis

- perceives an event as being meaningful and threatening;

- appears unable to modify or lessen the impact of a stressful event with traditional coping methods;

- experiences increased fear, tensions, and/or confusion;

- exhibits a high level of subjective discomfort; and

- proceeds rapidly to an active state of crisis—a state of disequilibrium.

THE PHYSICAL RESPONSE

The physical response to crisis is one which has significant survival value for the individual. It is the same response experienced by the earliest members of humankind who had to spring to action to either run from or ward off potential predators and other impending disasters. This fight or flight reaction is the mobilization of the individual's defenses in times of threat; the body's internal device that enables it to survive another day.

When a crisis occurs, this reaction enables individuals to ready themselves for a response. Crisis victims go on alert status: pupils dilate, heart rate and blood pressure increase, digestion is inhibited, and adrenalin is secreted. The "call to arms" that the stressor sounds for the individual enables the utilization of familiar coping strategies to address the source of the stress. However, the more common stressors that lead to the mobilization of the body's defense system tend to pale in comparison to the types of crises discussed in this book. Crisis presumes a traumatic event alien to the victim, one that is beyond the range of typical experiences. Thus, the lack of familiarity with the crisis event prevents the individual from successfully employing the usual coping strategies.

THE EMOTIONAL RESPONSE

Despite the state of physical arousal, victims of crisis often experience a state of frozen fright (Young, 2001), a state of shock, disorientation, and numbness. Victims are left with only the sensation that something is terribly wrong and without an understanding of the event itself or of its impact.

They may suffer a psychological paralysis, an inability to react at all; for example, a parent who returns to sleep after a 3:00 a.m. phone call informing him of the death of his teenage son in a car accident. Roberts (2000) described the crisis victim as being anxious, confused, and helpless, as well as appearing to be disorganized, withdrawn, and apathetic. Finally, since the level of physical arousal cannot be sustained indefinitely, the individual eventually will collapse with exhaustion. Whether this exhaustion is manifested as sleep or unconsciousness, the response will serve as a break from the traumatic event (Young, 2001). The crisis victim also will experience profound sadness and grief, depending on the level of involvement with the crisis, and will vacillate between irritability and anger, between self-blame and blaming others.

THE COGNITIVE RESPONSE

Whereas crisis counselors can observe the physical and emotional aftermath of a crisis event, a victim's belief systems that are also shattered are hidden from the naked eye. The standard rules of order have been violated, and the victim's understanding of how they fit into society may be forever altered (Berglas, 1985). Particularly for crime victims, crisis contradicts their views about themselves and their safety in the world. Additionally, in order to reinforce their belief in a just world where bad things only happen to bad people, they change their belief systems regarding their roles in the crisis events.

For example, if David (see the introduction case) attributed the cause of his mugging to an isolated mistake of jogging alone late at night, he might emerge from the event with some resolve, believing that he could avoid future muggings by jogging earlier in the day or in better-lit surroundings. However, if he assigned the cause of the event to a more generalized sense of personal failure or to outside events that could not be controlled, he would recover slowly from the experience, unable to regain an expectation of safety or to trust in his own competence to provide for his safety.

Similarly, a woman's appraisal of a physical assault by her husband will, among other factors, affect how she recovers from it. Consider the following case of Gail:

> Gail was a 32-year-old woman who had been married for three years to Steve. Both were successful business people, earning six-figure salaries each. Gail's career was on the rise due to the good fortune of her company, which she joined in its infancy, while Steve's career had stalled. In fact, it seemed that he would be a casualty of the impending downsizing of his company. Although nothing was definite in this regard, Steve assumed that the end was near. Gail, concerned about her brooding preoccupied husband did her best to cheer him up. One night as they were getting ready to attend a dinner party with some friends, Gail suggested that Steve wear a different color shirt than the one he had chosen. At this point, Steve stormed toward her, striking her across the face and knocking her to the floor. He stood over her and warned her not to tell him what to do again.

Will Gail blame herself for being too "bossy" by telling Steve what to wear and, therefore, blame herself and assume responsibility for the abuse? Will she consider Steve's quick temper to be indicative of his despair and resulting poor judgement in managing his own frustrations, thereby freeing herself from recriminations over the incident? The crisis counselor eventually must be able to find the answers to these types of questions to effectively intervene.

CHARACTERISTICS OF EFFECTIVE CRISIS INTERVENTION

When Medea was rescued from the hands of a fast-approaching, vengeful Jason by a serpent-driven flying chariot (the *deus ex machina*), her crisis was avoided, and she lived to go onto other adventures. Although a neat and tidy ending, this resolution of crisis is as far removed from contemporary crisis intervention as the Greek theater is from the contemporary Broadway stage.

Crisis intervention is not about "rescue." More often than not, rescuing benefits the rescuer more than the victim; rescuers make the mistake of maintaining control over the victim when control should be placed in the hands of the individual in crisis. Crisis intervention is about the foundation of the Chinese symbol for crisis: danger and opportunity.

Understanding the notion of opportunity in crisis is critical to effective crisis intervention. The crisis event drives the individual to seek help, just as hunger drives the search for food, thirst for water, and loneliness for greater connectedness with others. The search for help presents an opportunity to acquire more effective problem-solving skills, greater self-awareness and fulfillment, and more positive feelings of competence and self-efficacy. Effective crisis intervention should empower the individual to rise from the devastation and to resume control of daily life with a regained sense of hopefulness. In order to be effective, therefore, crisis intervention must be both empowerment-focused and flexible.

EMPOWERMENT-FOCUSED CRISIS INTERVENTION

Young (2001) suggested that the primary goal of crisis intervention is to help victims restore control in their lives. Crisis intervention literature also presents the goal of crisis intervention as the restoration of functioning of the individual to the level enjoyed prior to the crisis event itself. However, Frazier (1990) suggested that a counselor intervening in a crisis should assist the victim in striving for something more, and he maintained that crisis should be an opportunity to help people grow beyond their previous levels of functioning to higher, more competent levels.

To accomplish this latter goal, it is important for those involved in effective crisis intervention to approach a crisis event in two ways: viewing victims as resilient individuals and as resourceful individuals. Walsh (1998) refers to resilience as a person's ability not only to cope with and to survive traumatic experience, but also to continue to move toward greater psychological growth. Resilient people are able to draw on their internal and external resources and to recover from adversity, perhaps stronger than before. They are not easily defeated, and they are able to integrate their crisis experiences into their belief system, and learn from them. Seligman's (1990) version of resilience is based on his notion of "learned optimism." In his model, optimistic/resilient people can bounce back from adversity quickly and do not hesitate to undertake other challenging novel tasks or experiences. Consider the case of Jessie:

> *Jessie, a 13-year-old seventh grader in middle school had become lethargic in class and her performance in school had declined. One of her classroom teachers became concerned, as Jessie was generally an outgoing cheerful young adolescent with a wide circle of friends. The social worker who was asked to intervene with Jessie was able to uncover her secret. Although the school was aware of the car accident in which Jessie's parents had been involved a few months before, the staff did not comprehend the full impact of this event. Jessie's mother had lost a limb in the accident and suffered*

considerable facial scarring. Upon discharge from the hospital, she took to her bed, refusing to show herself outside the home, lest people see her disfigurement. Jessie, as a result, assumed a domestic role and undertook all household tasks: shopping, cooking, cleaning, and seeing to the general welfare of her younger brothers. She reported having no time for after-school tutorial assistance, nor for socializing with her friends. Her father became less and less available to her, as her mother believed she had lost all physical appeal and repeatedly told him to go and meet somebody else. He began to spend more and more time outside the home.

Effective crisis intervention would include viewing Jessie as a resilient individual, as she was assisting her family by assuming a new role in the family system after the car accident. Although the new role was a self-defeating one for her, it also indicated that she was able to adapt to changing circumstances; for this reason, an empowerment–focused crisis counselor would see Jessie as resilient, even prior to the intervention. This same counselor would also view David and Gail as resilient, and she would initiate intervention with the expectation that these people would emerge from their respective crises and acquire greater feelings of competence in the process.

Resourceful individuals have a variety of tools for extricating themselves from difficult situations. In effective crisis intervention, belief in the resourcefulness of the victim is essential to good practice. Counselors who entertain the rescue fantasy cannot provide effective intervention because they believe the source of the solution lies in their hands rather than in the hands of crisis victims. For example, the assumption that Gail will forever be stymied by her assaultive husband and that she needs a solution handed to her prevents effective crisis intervention and makes only the rescue possible. Additionally, telling Jessie and David how to exit their crises achieves little more than a short-term reprieve.

FLEXIBLE CRISIS INTERVENTION

Although in the field of geometry it may be true that the shortest distance between two points is a straight line, such a simplistic linear view has no place in the exploration of the complexities of human behavior. A direct cause and effect analysis of the aforementioned cases might indicate that the car accident that disfigured her mother caused Jessie's depression; that the mugging incident caused David's absences from work; and that Gail's request that her husband change his attire caused the assault. Although each of these triggers had some bearing on the outcome of the crises, they were only a part of the much larger picture. Assuming a direct cause-and-effect relationship might lead a counselor to draw the conclusion that all individuals who experienced similar events would respond in similar, if not identical, ways. However, in effective crisis intervention, flexibility is essential, requiring the counselor to make a quick evaluation of the multiplicity of factors that may have influenced the reaction of the victim.

Flexibility in crisis intervention requires that counselors ask questions like these:

- "What was it about Jessie and her total milieu, including all factors both internal and external to her, that resulted in her reaction to the crash?"

- "Why did David react to the mugging in the way that he did?"

- "What was it about a simple request for a clothing change that caused Steve to assault Gail?"

Cognitive Factors

Cognitive behavior-oriented clinicians have long appreciated the role that one's cognitions play in one's emotional experiences. Between any event and the individual's emotional reaction to that event comes a cognitive mediation of the event. That is, people experience and evaluate a situation or event before assigning it meaning. Thus, as people appraise the same event in different ways, their emotional and behavioral reactions to these identical events may be drastically different. For example, given similar circumstances to Jessie's, a 10-year-old may have reacted to the crash by running away. A victim of a similar mugging to David's may have gone to work the next day to be around familiar friends and surroundings. A husband other than Steve may have reacted to Gail's request in a very benign way.

Ecological Factors

Flexible crisis intervention, however, requires more than just an appreciation of the different ways in which people cognitively mediate crisis events. Crises play havoc, not only with internal affected individuals (i.e., family, friends, coworkers, etc.), but also with the larger ecological systems (i.e., community, school, place of worship, etc.) (James & Gilliland, 2001) Conversely, the surrounding interdependent system where one lives, works, and plays impacts the individual as well. For example, consider the following case of a family affected by a nationwide economic downturn that resulted in the layoffs of thousands of employees:

> Bill Bland received his pink slip after 22 years with the company. He still asserted, however, that as long as there were children in the home, his wife of 20 years would never have to work; they still had two teenage sons at home. After three months of dwindling financial resources and a mortgage to pay with no employment possibilities, Bill started drinking heavily. His wife took a job at a local business, as much to get away from Bill's increasingly abusive behavior as to earn an income. Meanwhile, his 16-year-old son took part-time employment as well, but the night hours eventually affected his schoolwork. His relationship with his parents became quite contentious, as they fought over his failing grades. The situation reached crisis proportions when Bill, drunk again by midday struck and killed an elderly woman while driving to his son's high school for a conference with the vice principal. His wife called the local crisis center when she received the call from the police.

This case illustrates the interplay between an individual and the circumstances in which he lives. The individual factors exert reciprocal influences on each other: a poor economy leads to unemployment, which leads to family dysfunction, which leads to the additional crisis of a woman's death. This is a system of complex interacting parts, each of which affects the others.

Bronfenbrenner (1979) articulated the complexity of the systems that are relevant to the coping behavior of individuals:

- *Microsystem*—consists of family members and the individual's immediate social group (i.e., Bill's wife, sons, and friends)

- *Exosystem*—contains the community at large, including neighborhood social networks, work-related structures, and governmental agencies (i.e., Bill's workplace, his son's school, etc.)

- *Macrosystem*—represents the largest environment that influences and, in turn, is influenced by the individual; this level includes the individual's culture and belief system that impacts the person, his/her family, and the community as well (i.e., the economic conditions that affect Bill's income, the belief that wives should stay home and be supported by the husband, etc.)

Counselors must practice flexible crisis intervention by following the precept that no crisis takes place in a vacuum. Crisis responses cannot be understood without appreciating a victims' family and social milieus, community resources, and cultural backdrops (Slaikeu, 1990) as well as the manner in which individuals, these various systems, and the environment interact with each other. To be cognizant of these multiple influences is to create a template that will guide the crisis counselor's view of the individual's response to crisis in a meaningful way.

CHARACTERISTICS OF EFFECTIVE CRISIS COUNSELORS

Perhaps the following metaphor can best describe the role of the effective crisis counselor and the nature of crisis work:

Maritime Jack, the owner and captain of a 30-foot schooner, the Random Sea, awakened below deck one night to the heaving and thrashing of his ship by an unanticipated squall. Stumbling to the deck in the hopes of determining what had happened, all that was clear to Jack was that his ship had been blown far from the course he had set for his original destination; everything else was shrouded in the darkness of the night and the turbulence of the sea.

Once on deck, Jack scurried about tending sails, checking gauges and compasses, and assessing damage to the ship's instruments in an attempt to minimize further damage and to right his course. After a seemingly unending struggle to steady the ship, Jack finally was able to do so, leaving him to ponder other more salient issues.

He wondered to himself where his next port of call should be, where he must steer the ship for repairs and supplies. "Surely," he thought, "It may be not be possible to return to the port that I left some time ago, and I may not have the necessary supplies to continue to my intended destination." It was at that time that Jack noticed in the horizon a sole beacon of light, beaming as if reassuring him that there was a harbor in which he could set anchor. Being mindful of this light throughout the rest of the storm enabled Jack to set his course accordingly. Jack then was able to put in at this port, one neither too distant from where he had originally embarked, nor quite the same. A safe place, nevertheless, for Jack to anchor the Random Sea for a brief repair before he set sail again.

This metaphor epitomizes the nature of crisis and crisis work: an unanticipated event disrupts the intended course of events, leaving the victim in rough waters. Throughout the course of the intervention, the victim remains captain of the ship. The role of the crisis worker is to provide the beacon of light that guides the ship to calmer waters. Were it not for the storm, Jack would not have learned to chart his course as he did, and were it not for the light, his destination would have remained unclear. Even though the beacon was not able to lead Jack back to his home port, it did beckon him to a safe place where he could drop anchor and take on those supplies that would enable him to set sail again. Those personal characteristics and professional abilities that make for an effective counselor in a more typical therapeutic setting also are essential for the crisis counselor. However, given the intensity level of crisis events, other traits are necessary as well.

Tolerance for Ambiguity

When chaos reigns, crisis counselors must be able to enter poorly defined, high stress environments and wade through the morass of high emotions to conduct their work. Without a complete understanding of an event and the victim's involvement in it, the counselor must wait to hear from the victim about the experience. The counselor also must avoid the projection of a personal belief system onto the victim's experience. The crisis worker's ability to distinguish personal thoughts or feelings about the event from the actual feelings or thoughts of the victim is a critical component to crisis work. The meaning assigned to such an ambiguous event should be established by the victim rather than the counselor.

A Calm Neutral Demeanor

The crisis counselor must be able to maintain a calm, reassuring demeanor throughout the initial crisis session. Without this ability, the counselor would be swept away by the waves of emotion. The counselor's calm reserve in the face of the client's strong emotions communicate to the client that it is safe to express strong emotions without overpowering or frightening the counselor. Additionally, the counselor can serve as a model of strength and serenity for the client to emulate in the face of the crisis.

Tenacity

Crisis sufferers may rebuff the best intentions of even a well-trained counselor, as recovery may be far more difficult for some than others. It may be only determination and tenacity that enable a counselor to withstand a client's intransigence, to hang in there, and to persist through the crisis until a resolution is reached.

Optimism

For effective crisis intervention, the counselor must believe that people are resilient and resourceful creatures, capable of recovering from horrific events and perhaps emerging stronger than before. Otherwise, without any optimism or confidence in success, the counselor would have difficulty developing an action plan for the client.

Adventuresomeness

Crisis work is not for the fainthearted, but rather for the adventurous spirit. The unpredictable nature of crisis, the sense of never knowing what to expect, and the frenetic pace all necessitate this adventurous quality in a crisis counselor. If one's preferences are for a quiet sail around the local pond, then it might be a good idea to avoid rafting trips down the Colorado River during the Spring thaw. Similarly, if one is not prepared for dealing with raw emotion and uncertainty, then crisis intervention work may be something to avoid.

Capacity for Empathy

In addition to employing techniques learned in undergraduate or graduate schools for demonstrating empathy to a client, the crisis counselor should exhibit a capacity for openness to others, the ability to experience the world from another's point of view. Training may provide the counselor with the techniques, but only the ability and willingness to be open separates effective crisis workers from the ineffective.

Flexibility

As client needs and crisis demands shift and change over time, counselors must adapt to these changes and be flexible enough to adjust the course of the intervention.

Confidence

For crisis counselors, knowledge of oneself and the strong belief in one's ability and efficacy are critical ingredients for success. Being strong and steady in the chaos of crisis helps the counselor weather the vagaries of crisis events. Similarly, knowing oneself and understanding one's relationship to the client helps the counselor maintain realistic expectations for the intervention and maintain the client's confidence in the intervention.

Little Need to Rescue

Counselors who entertain a rescue fantasy invite troubles of over involvement with clients and tend to assume ownership of clients' problems. Rescuers also tend to become involved in crisis work more for their own self-aggrandizement than for the benefit of crisis sufferers. The absence of this fantasy makes for greater clarity and objectivity in crisis work.

Capacity For Listening

The crisis counselor must be able to demonstrate effective listening skills. The counselor with a capacity for listening knows

- when to be passive and let the client lead the way;

- when to be active, gathering information and moving toward resolutions; and

- when to seek information without being intrusive and interfering with the process.

Awareness of Trauma Indicators

The counselor must be prepared to make decisions based on observations of the client's response to crisis. Are there critical safety issues that should be addressed? Medical concerns? The counselor should be prepared to make a judgment regarding the client's response to the event by observing as well as listening.

Openness to Individual Crisis Reactions

Individuals react differently to the same crisis event. They each bring to the experience a legacy of family relationships, learning histories, unmet and satisfied needs, and unique modes of perceiving and responding to the world. The effective crisis counselor will not approach the intervention with any preconceived notions about how the client should react to crisis. Rather, the counselor will come to understand individual clients by listening to their expressions and reactions to the crisis experience.

Capacity for Information Management

When counselors receive a flood of information, they must be able to sort through it and develop analyses pertinent to action plans. Information will appear contradictory at times, but the role of the counselor is to organize and process it.

EMPATHY, GENUINENESS, AND ACCEPTANCE AND POSITIVE REGARD

The work of other theorists, primarily Carkhuff (1969), Carkhuff and Berenson (1977), and Rogers (1951) actually sets the framework for the following section. Their research, and the research of others has focused on the importance of the core conditions of empathy, respect, genuineness, and positive regard in establishing beneficial relationships and in attaining positive counseling outcomes. Individual approaches to counseling, notwithstanding, these researchers demonstrated that the presence of an empathic, involved, and genuine counselor is critical to a successful counseling relationship.

Empathy

Empathy is the message that counselors relay to crisis victims, indicating that they not only understand what happened, but also how victims feel about it (Slaikeu, 1984, 1990). Empathy involves sharing of the victims' pain and letting them know that the counselor truly understands what it feels like to be in their situation. Counselors must be able to "walk a mile in their shoes" and to communicate this ability to victims. To understand the essential feelings and beliefs that clients express, and to be able to communicate that understanding, is the core of empathy (Carkhuff, 1969; Gladding, 1999). There is a caveat regarding the development of empathy in crisis work, however; counselors must maintain a delicate balance between empathy and over involvement with victims (Myer, 2001). That is, the counselor must strike a compromise in the almost dichotomous relationship between involvement and detachment in crisis work: To feel as the victim rather than to be the victim, to have a subjective understanding of the victim's feeling state without the objective experience of it. Over involvement breeds dependence on the counselor and, conversely, clouds the judgement and problem-solving abilities of the counselor, who may become lost in the victims' pain.

Genuineness

The essence of genuineness is honesty (James & Guilliland, 2001): honesty with oneself, honesty with others. This quality is essential in any intimate interpersonal encounter, but is a particular prerequisite for the crisis counseling relationship. The genuine, honest crisis counselor is comfortable with a range of client emotions and is not threatened by them, is confident in the role of helper without having to hawk professional degrees as proof of expertise, and is not averse to self-disclosing personal information when appropriate. The client sees honesty, consistency, and reliability in the genuine counselor. Although in an earlier section of this chapter this quality was discussed as a characteristic of an effective crisis counselor, the purpose of the section to follow is to provide specific strategies for communicating genuineness to the crisis victim.

Acceptance and Positive Regard

When the crisis counselor feels and communicates an unconditional positive regard for the client, the client will feel accepted and will move toward resolution of the crisis event. The counselor accepts all clients, regardless of differences in race, ethnicity, class, gender, size, or shape. The counselor sees only someone needful of help, someone requiring a lifeline out of the chaos and pain of crisis. This positive regard is offered without an expectation of its reciprocity; regardless of the client's expressed feelings toward the counselor, the counselor remains steadfast in caring for the client.

CRISIS INTERVENTION TECHNIQUES: THE L-A-P-C MODEL

The purpose of this section is to provide an overview of intervention strategies and techniques designed to guide the crisis counselor through the foggy haze that usually surrounds the chaos of crisis. Despite the best intentions of people purporting to be effective counselors, crisis intervention can be all for naught unless it is guided by techniques that allow victims not only to regain some semblance of control in their lives, but also to forge ahead with renewed hope and resolve. In addition to these techniques, the counselor also should be guided by a master plan, a frame of reference for crisis intervention that serves as a template through which the counselor's skills and techniques are applied.

Several key components of crisis intervention emerge from the common underpinnings of a number of models. Slaikeu's (1990) five-stage psychological first aid model, and Roberts's (2002) seven–stage model share many common features. Central to each of these models are steps involving making contact and listening, exploring dimensions of the crisis event, securing agreement to an action plan, and providing follow up. The goals of each of these models also are similar: providing safety, reestablishing coping mechanisms for clients, and facilitating linkages for them with other resources.

Myer (2001) stated that crisis intervention models should be simple and user-friendly, adaptable for use with many types of crises, and able to encompass all aspects of a client's experiences. Crisis counselors should be able to use a straightforward model and apply it in an effective intervention to a variety of crisis situations, such as those involving domestic violence (see Chapter 8), suicide and homicide (see Chapter 10), sexual assault (see Chapter 6), child abuse (see Chapter 12), and substance abuse (see Chapter 5). Whether a police officer called to the scene of a domestic dispute, a school counselor consoling a terrorized student after a school shooting, or a clergy member providing solace and support to a grieving family, crisis counselors require their own action plans to assist them in their work.

The following model provides a simple, straightforward plan for crisis counselors. This four-step approach incorporates the critical features of previously developed models and addresses the need for a flexible model, or template, that the practitioner can apply to multiple crisis settings. Known as the L-A-P-C model, its steps are as follows:

Listen: What is the victim saying? What is he or she NOT saying?

Assess: What is the victim feeling? How is he or she acting? What is he or she thinking?

Plan: What plans can the victim make now? Are the plans reasonable? Can they be carried out?

Commit: Has the victim agreed to follow the plan? What other resources will be needed to see the plan through?

The remainder of this chapter focuses on these four stages, and particularly on those listening skills that are critical to any helping relationship. They compose an important first step to the L-A-P-C model; listening begets an assessment capability that leads to a viable plan based on the client's needs, and eventually to the client's commitment to implement such a plan. Finally, family community or other resources are enlisted as needed to assist with this plan.

Step 1: Listen

The first step of the L-A-P-C model accomplishes one of the goals of effective crisis intervention by communicating three important messages to victims of crisis: that they are safe, they are heard, and they are in control.

Communicate Safety

In the immediate aftermath of a crisis, a well-intentioned counselor can be either an intrusive or a positive presence. The numbers of people performing various functions at the crisis location can be overwhelming, leaving the victim needful of reassurances. Some simple strategies can help reassure victims.

Introduce Yourself

Regardless of an identifying name, the victim simply needs the counselor to be there, to be attentive, and to be a constant in the chaos. Nevertheless, a simple uncomplicated introduction is essential:

Hello. My name is John, and I am from the Brookside Counseling Center. I am here to listen and learn from you what I can do to help.

Announcing one's name role, and intentions will go a long way toward providing much needed structure and support for the victim. It is essential to communicate to the individual, by a calm demeanor the notion that perhaps order can be restored. The emphasis, however, during this introductory phase should be simplicity: the counselor should keep it simple and neither ask too many probing questions nor make any promises until he or she has engaged the individual in a helping and caring relationship. Delving into the crisis details prematurely also should be avoided. The relationship has not been developed yet.

Act Immediately and Take Control

- The assertive crisis counselor will take care of some of the details, including some of the small and inconsequential details, that can loom large for the victim in structuring and reordering the crisis. For example, the following type of details:

- Keep representatives from the media away from the victim.

- Move the victim from the crisis situation to as neutral a location as can be arranged.

- State simply, "You are safe now." That is, if the assailant was indeed apprehended, if the fire was brought under control, or if the motor vehicle accident site has been secured by the police. False promises, however, should never be made regarding the individual's safety.

- Take care of other tangential distracters that weigh heavily on the individual's mind: for example, if there are children at home who may be unattended, arrange with the victim's cooperation and input, to call a family member, friend, or other individual to provide child care. Additionally, if the victim worries that the accident will make her late for an appointment, with her permission arrange to call to cancel or reschedule. Securing permission for even these details serves as a way of restoring some control and authority to the individual.

- Guarantee that you will indeed be there to listen and to help, but do not promise things that you cannot control. After all, everything may NOT turn out all right; for example, even law enforcement officers cannot control the length of incarceration of an assailant.

Begin Handing Over Some Control to the Victim

In order to restore control to the victim eventually, it is important to begin to do so at the beginning of the process, albeit in small, relatively benign steps. The victim can make decisions and exert some influence over even those minor issues that are part and parcel of the intervention relationship, particularly immediately following the crisis event itself. Asking questions like the ones listed below can introduce some decision making on the victim's part.

- Where would you like me to sit/stand?

- What name would you like me to call you?

- Would you like me to get you something before we talk?

- Would you prefer if we stay/stood over there instead?

- Is there anyone you would like me to call at this time?

In addition to the need to feel safe, crisis victims, particularly victims of physical or sexual abuse, also have a need to control their own boundaries. That is, once their sense of safety and security has been breached and their physical space violated, they require some control over these very issues in their relationships with crisis counselors. They need to know that their preferences are important and that they do not have to respond to any way other than how they wish (Schmookler, 1996). In cases of physical or sexual assault, victims have to feel that they will be able to control who may touch them, if anyone at all, during the course of the crisis work. Victims also must know that they are entitled to give permission to the crisis worker to do almost anything: discuss the crisis details, talk at all, or ask any questions.

Finally, the calm demeanor of the crisis counselor communicates to the victim a sense of detachment, of neutrality, of a proverbial "blank slate" onto which the victim may place any thought or emotion experienced as a result of the crisis. Doing so lets the victim know that without being judged, it is all right to express their thoughts and emotions, regardless of their intensity level or their content. The counselor, despite the strong feelings that the victim's own story creates, must remain a staid, nonjudgmental individual who allows the victim to control the amount and the content of the feelings expressed.

Communicate the Message that the Victim is Heard

Once safety has been assured as much as possible in the wake of a crisis, the primary goal of the crisis counselor is to listen. The pitfalls that often get in the way of the simple process of listening, however, are varied. Myer (2001) discussed several of the more common mis-steps of overzealous crisis counselors who interfere with the recovery process of victims by intervening with well-intentioned, albeit counterproductive attempts at helping.

He decried those crisis counselors who offer premature suggestions before listening fully to victims' stories. For example, 15-year-old Angela, in the aftermath of a failed suicide attempt, rebuffed the counselor's repeated suggestion that she confide in her parents about her secret pregnancy as a way of resolving this hidden dilemma. However, if he were a more attentive listener, he may have learned eventually that Angela feared that her stepfather was the father of her child after several years of sexual abuse in the home; thus, her inability to disclose her secret to them. Angela undoubtedly heard similar advice from her friends; now she just needs to tell her story to someone more adept at listening to her.

A second pitfall that results in ineffective crisis intervention is the tendency to ask for too many details (Myer, 2001). Detective Joe Friday, an earnest, clue-obsessed investigator from the old Dragnet television series, would doggedly pursue the crime scene witnesses, wanting only to uncover "the facts, ma'am, just the facts" about the crime. However, crisis intervention is not a crime scene interrogation designed to gather facts in the manner of a Joe Friday. Rather, it is the beginning of a helping relationship that requires a good listener who allows the victim to lead the way and control the direction that the intervention takes.

The crisis counselor as information-gatherer would leave Angela bereft of support. This same counselor also would stymie Jessie in her aimless search for hopefulness in the midst of her family crisis. Questions related to the time and location of the car accident, the nature and extent of her mother's injuries, and her recent failing report card grades would miss the mark and would result in the continuation of Jessie's emotional malaise. An interrogation would communicate to her that the counselor was more interested in minutia, in facts that were of concern to others, but not to Jessie, and that her feelings of despair were only of secondary importance.

Although there will be a time when the crisis counselor will require specific information about the crisis event, there are ways it can be gathered. Suggestions for collecting information that clients may choose to minimize or to leave out altogether are included later in this chapter. However, the following section discusses those strategies and techniques designed to help the crisis counselor create a supportive emotional climate conducive to a helping relationship and to the growth of the individual in crisis.

PUTTING EMPATHY, GENUINENESS, AND ACCEPTANCE INTO PRACTICE

Attending, listening, and questioning skills are the cornerstone techniques for the counselor in communicating to crisis victims that they are truly the focus of the intervention and that they indeed have been heard.

Attending

Attending to another's words and actions is a nonverbal technique. It requires presenting oneself as attentive by looking and acting the part. Body posture, facial expression, and proximity to the client are only a few elements that communicate attention. Words can only suggest the condition of attentiveness, but they cannot produce it. Nonverbal behaviors often betray the meaning of words, so it is crucial that one practice attending behaviors rather than attending statements or phrases. For example, the crisis counselor who professes unyielding attention to the client yet sits in profile to the client belies the words. Similarly, the counselor who utters all the reassuring key phrases to the client, yet furtively glances at the clock on the wall or at other activities around them presents as less than sincere in the verbalized claims of attentiveness. The crisis counselor demonstrates attention by engaging in the following nonverbal behaviors (Greenstone & Leviton, 1993; James & Gilliland, 2001; Kanel, 1999):

- Establishing and maintaining eye contact with the client;

- Nodding one's head in acceptance of key elements of the client's verbalizations;

- Maintaining close physical proximity to the client, as long as the counselor does not invade the client's space (the counselor should also remember to get the client's permission regarding how close to sit or stand without being threatening);

- Leaning forward in the direction of the client and facing him or her;

- Maintaining an open stance (no crossed legs, folded arms across the chest, or closed fists);

- Unbuttoning one's coat or if possible, avoiding formal attire better suited to a wedding reception than to a crisis counseling interaction; and

- Demonstrating an appropriate range of facial expressions; for example, a smile to reassure and to relax the client, a serious expression to show commitment.

Crisis counselors can display attentiveness to clients by being mindful of the above nonverbal behaviors. Even though it takes practice and some self-reflection to master the skill of attending, overlearning the above skills may be just as contraindicated as avoiding them altogether. The rigid application of eye contact, for example, may present as a stare, invoking a feeling of discomfort in clients rather than comfort, while the open stance practiced to the extreme may give the counselor a slovenly appearance. An overlearned nod may be more reminiscent of one of those perpetually nodding bobblehead dolls than an attentive counselor.

In addition to practicing these skills prior to applying them, it is essential that counselors also monitor the reactions of clients during interactions and are attentive to their impact. Does the client lean back as the counselor leans forward? Does the client avert his or her eyes at the counselor's steady gaze? Does the client's rather formal predilections cause unease with a counselor determined to be very casual? If so, then it is imperative for the counselor to modify his or her nonverbal behaviors to keep the client engaged.

More importantly, are there cultural considerations that would account for the clients' unexpected responses to the attending behaviors listed above? That is, should the counselor interpret reactions to those nonverbal indicators of attention (i.e., eye contact) differently for non-European-Americans? Is physical closeness unsettling for some cultures? Questions like these require the attention of the counselor. Just as individuals respond differently to crisis events, different cultural and ethnic groups also respond in their own unique ways. Although it is beyond the scope of the present discussion, it is incumbent on the crisis counselor to develop an awareness and an understanding of cultural values as they pertain to the business of this textbook.

Listening

The primary technique for identifying and clarifying a client's feeling and emotions is active listening (Roberts, 2000). Slaikeu (1984, 1990) presents the following definition of active listening:

In active listening, the therapist attends carefully, both physically and psychologically, to the messages transmitted by the client. The therapist communicates understanding and empathy by reformulating and summarizing the client's explicit statement, by attending to and commenting on the client's nonverbal or para-verbal signals, and by guiding the client toward an expansion of the issues addressed. It is important to allow the client to direct the flow of the conversation and to avoid critical or judgmental statements (Slaiku, 1990, p. 295).

The specific techniques that compose active listening are varied, and they encompass many of those nonverbal strategies already discussed in the previous section. In fact, to separate verbal from nonverbal active listening behaviors is to create an almost artificial dichotomy between these two intricately entwined sets of skills. They do not stand alone, since the true empathic listener demonstrates congruence in words and actions when interacting with a crisis victim. For example, the look of disinterest on the counselor's face belies all those well-chosen empathic words and actions that are key to active listening, just as a fleeting eye contact betrays the professed interest in the client.

Listening is an active process that combines a repertoire of not only the aforementioned nonverbal techniques, but also the following verbal ones. The purpose of these verbal techniques is to communicate understanding to clients and encourage communication.

Clarifying

Eliciting more information about previous statements is the purpose of clarification. This technique is essential in dealing with the rush of emotions and the resulting cascade of verbalizations regarding the crisis experience. It enables the counselor to place into better perspective the meaning that the event had for the victim and to clear up any confusion or ambiguity in the victim's statements. The actual experience of the death of a sibling in a car accident, for example, may conjure up common images of loss, but the more personal symbolic meaning (i.e., feelings of guilt over not being able to protect the younger sibling) may elude the crisis worker who doesn't clarify the victim's description of the crisis aftermath. If the crisis worker and the client are essentially talking about two different experiences of the crisis, then little will be achieved with this intervention. Clarifying also supports a problem-solving approach to crisis intervention. The problem-solving approach is discussed later in the chapter.

The two most common clarification techniques, particularly in the early stages of crisis intervention, are paraphrasing and verifying. Counselors use paraphrasing to highlight the factual content of what they are hearing rather than the emotional content, which may be premature immediately after the crisis. When paraphrasing, counselors use the clients' own words and phrases to summarize what they said; new or equivalent words are to be avoided at this point, as in the following example:

Client: *I keep hearing my wife scream as the fire raced through her office building. I wasn't even there, but I just keep imaging it over and over again. I can't concentrate at work, and I can't sleep.*

Crisis worker: *In other words, ever since your wife died in the fire, you keep hearing her screams and can't seem to concentrate or to sleep.*

Client: *I just can't imagine what life is going to be like without her. I am just so lonely and my days all seem so long.*

Crisis Worker: *Without her, you are so lonely that your days seem to be very long.*

Frederick Lanceley (1999) suggested that paraphrasing in the client's own words keeps the client from being on the defensive and demonstrates that the listener has heard and has understood the client's story. Other benefits of paraphrasing include creating empathy and rapport, clarifying content, and highlighting issues for the client.

Unlike paraphrasing, which is a simple restatement of what was heard, verifying involves actually questioning what the client said in order to ensure that the statement is understood. The following exchange is an example of verifying:

Client: *I'm 48 years old and I just read that people my age have a real hard time finding employment, once they are downsized out of a job.*

Crisis worker: *Are you saying that you are worried about not being able to find another job?*

Client: *This is the second time in 7 years that my home has been destroyed by a tornado. My family wants me to move, but I've lived my whole life here. All my friends and family are here.*

Crisis worker: *Are you thinking that your family wants you to leave your hometown and relocate someplace else?*

When using this clarification technique, the counselor should avoid making an inferential leap regarding what the client said. It is important to remember that the purpose of this step is simply to communicate an understanding of what was said, not to interpret the content of the message.

Reflecting/Mirroring

Using this technique, the counselor uses the client's own words and phrases to direct the session to their emotional responses to the crisis situation. Reflecting is essentially a statement rephrasing the emotional content of the session, and is a powerful tool in creating an empathic environment (Kanel, 1999). The crisis counselor does not interpret, but rather points out the affective state seen or heard in the client's own statements. The counselor can maintain a sense of congruence by using the client's own words. Although assigning an affective label to the client's verbalizations may also be essential. The counselor, however, must exercise caution in doing so; assigning a label to the client's emotional state that does not reflect the reality can make the client defensive or simply frustrated. Following are some examples:

Client: *This is so typical for me! Five years of nothing but rotten luck, and now this!*
Crisis worker: *Sounds like you've had quite a run of bad luck, even before today's accident.*
Client: *I can't face her any more. I mean, I love her, but I am at a loss as to how to avoid the constant fights we have.*
Crisis worker: *You seem confused when you try to figure how to love each other without fighting.*

Summarizing

Another important indicator that a crisis counselor is truly hearing what the victim has to say is the ability to summarize–to encapsulate in a simple, verifiable statement—all that the victim has said during the crisis interview. The essence of summarizing is distilling into one or two meaningful and accurate sentences all that has been said.

To accomplish this technique, the counselor must combine in summary fashion the facts of the crisis (as perceived by the victim) with the feeling state expressed by the victim. Successful summarization of the material should lead to the development of a working definition of the problem attendant to the crisis situation and, ultimately to an intervention plan for the victim. Here are some examples of summarizing statements:

In other words, you are feeling not only tremendous grief over your husband's death, but also a lot of guilt, since you had a fight just before he left and said some unkind things to him. If you knew he was going to be killed in a car accident on the way to work, you wouldn't have said those things.

So, your home has just been lost to the twister, and being new to the area yourself, your entire family is still back east. You are frightened and are feeling all alone with this situation.

You thought that if you kept what your father has been doing to you a secret, he would leave your younger sister alone. Now that you've found out that he has started doing it to her, you are feeling very angry, and you want to do something to stop him.

If the counselor's summarizing statements truly depict the victim's experience of the crisis, then the counselor will be able to move the victim to the next level of crisis intervention: defining the problem and developing an intervention plan. However, if the statements do not accurately summarize, the victim may feel little validation of his or her crisis experience, and may be unable to move forward toward some sense of resolution. The crisis counselor must understand that summarization of the crisis should be from the victim's vantage point, not the counselor's.

Using "I" Messages

Messages that communicate to the client the impact that he or she is having on the crisis counselor are called "I" messages. The "I" in the message is the counselor, and the message is what "I" think/feel/wish regarding the explanation of the crisis experience by the client. Additionally, referring to "I" allows the counselor to exercise some referent power with the client; the use of "I" messages allows the counselor to communicate to the client that they may share a common experience, thus enabling treatment to continue unimpeded.

"I" messages are better alternatives to "you" messages, which tend to be more threatening and can put the victim "on the hot seat" to account for feeling or reactions to the crisis. "I" messages, according to James and Gilliland (2001) "are probably more important in crisis intervention than in other kinds of therapy because of the directive stance the crisis worker often has to take with clients who are immobile and in disequilibrium" (p. 49). Nevertheless, such statements still should be used sparingly, since their overuse would make the counselor rather than the client, the focus of treatment.
Appropriate "I" messages are as follows:

I agree that it is very confusing to try to understand all that has happened.

I know how difficult it is to talk about all of these things, and I applaud you for taking such a big step.

I need you to agree to take the steps that we talked about today.

Managing Silence

A skill that eludes many counselors is the ability to manage silence. Silence makes many people uncomfortable, since it represents the absence of communication. They then respond to this absence with some attempt to fill the void; they find words, whether well-chosen or not, to generate some discussion of the event with the client, to give advice, or simply to comment on the content of the client's crisis description.

However, it is critical for the crisis worker to view silence as just another form of communication, not the absence, similar to other forms of nonverbal communication. Counselors generally should be silent themselves, although always observing the behavior (silent and otherwise) in clients, with a particular emphasis on what clients do NOT say.

Questioning

The quality of the questions put to a crisis victim can make the difference between communication and obstructing communication. The purpose of questioning during a crisis interview is twofold: to elicit information and to provide a forum for the client to speak openly and freely with the counselor. Knowing how to question and the types of questions to use in an interview are important skills for the crisis counselor.

One of the cardinal rules for counselors is to avoid the use of "why" questions. Such questions take on an accusatory tone and imply blame or responsibility where none exists. "Why" questions only reinforce and encourage self-blame, particularly in the case of a crisis victim who harbors some sense of guilt over an imagined role played in the crisis situation. For example, the father of a young child killed in a car accident on the way to school blames himself for the death, since he decided against keeping her home from school that day despite a slight head cold. Asking "why" he sent his daughter to school can only immerse the grieving father in tremendous guilt and can suggest that the counselor may also view him as blameworthy. Communication under these circumstances is thwarted, leaving an individual in pain without the support of a counselor now perceived as accusatory. Crisis sufferers do not want to defend their actions related to the crisis.

There are at least two distinct types of appropriate questions, and each has a place in a crisis interview: closed questions and open questions. Closed questions enable the counselor to collect factual information related to the crisis victim and to the crisis itself. They ask for specific data that the counselor then will organize and use to formulate the best possible plan for assisting the client. However, care must be taken so that these questions are not perceived as an interrogation rather than a crisis interview. Gathering factual information is important in any such encounter, but too much data collection can easily put a client on the defensive at a time when the counselor really wants the client to be at ease. In short, a search for too many details will miss the overall emotional picture the client wants to paint, leaving the client frustrated and convinced that the counselor has little interest in helping. Similarly, the counselor should also consider the pacing of these questions: rapid-fire questioning allows little time for reflection before responding and will shut down communication, and increase rather than decrease the client's level of agitation.

Overuse of closed questions also creates another pitfall: the tendency to forestall the development of a true helping relationship by allowing the client to respond "yes" or "no" only. The information gathered by these types of questions prevents a more thorough exploration of the feelings and thoughts related to the crisis. However, there is a place for closed questions that require communication of specific information, provided that they are used sparingly. Examples of appropriate closed questions include:

- *How many years had you been married at the time of his death?*

- *Was it before or after your job relocation that you were assaulted?*

- *Who first told you that your son was missing?*

Examples of closed questions to be avoided include:

- *Are you worried that your son is still missing?*

- *Did you try to tell him that you didn't want to have sex that night?*

- *Have you ever tried to talk to your mother about these feelings?*

Whereas closed questions result in specific responses, open-ended questions do not limit the client to a carefully circumscribed response set; they are not counselor imposed dichotomies to frame the client's responses. Rather, these types of questions are designed to elicit feeling, thought, and perceptions of those events that brought the client to the counselor in the first place. Equipped with the right questions, the counselor is less an interviewer than a facilitator. The client, unencumbered by the counselor's restrictions, responds with a genuine disclosure of the crisis experience. Examples of appropriate open-ended questions include:

- *Could you tell me more about what happened after he entered your apartment with you?*

- *What were you thinking about just before you picked up the knife to cut your wrists?*

- *How did you feel when your teacher told you about the man with the gun in school?*

Step 2: Assess

The second step of the L-A-P-C model involves an assessment by the crisis counselor of all the verbal and nonverbal communication received from the client during the listening state. Body language speaks volumes, but it can be far more difficult to interpret than the words actually spoken by the client. If the counselor reads the body language as being out of synch with the expressed verbal message describing the client's feeling state, then the counselor must question the verbal message further. Using the listening techniques described above, being open, accessible to the client, and committed fully to hearing the client's words, enables the counselor to make an informed assessment of the client, which leads to the third and fourth step in the L-A-P-C model.

Although assessment is an ongoing and dynamic process that changes throughout the course of an intervention, the crisis counselor must assess the client across several dimensions in order to understand the impact of the crisis event on the client.

Emotions—Is the client inconsolable? sad? hopeless? anxious? angry?

Behavior—Is the client agitated? pacing the room? sluggish or slow? wanting to leave? wanting to linger?

Thoughts—How does the client interpret the crisis? What is its meaning for the client? Is the client hopeful or hopeless about the outcome? How devastating is it for the client? The client's future? How does the client judge his or her ability to cope?

Support system—How large a family or friendship network does the client have? Is the client alone and solitary, or social with many friends? Who can be called on to assist the client at this time?

Answers to the above questions will guide the counselor in determining the direction to be taken in the next two steps of L-A-P-C.

Step 3: Plan

The ultimate goal in crisis intervention is actually twofold: first, assist the client in recovering from the emotional impact in the immediate aftermath of the crisis; then impart to the client a sense of hope and empowerment via a plan. This two-part approach includes a return to some state of equilibrium and a plan to help maintain this balance long after the crisis has passed. Of course, this plan requires a skilled crisis counselor who is able to strike a balance between several competing counselor and client needs.

These needs include:

Counselor		Client
Need to be active	*vs*	*Need for autonomy*
Need to model hopefulness	*vs*	*Need to grieve first*
Need to help with problem	*vs*	*Need to retain ownership of problem*
Need to express universality	*vs*	*Need to communicate individuality of crisis experience*
Need for short-term treatments	*vs*	*Possible need for long-term work*

Balancing these two sets of needs can be accomplished within the context of crisis intervention. Most individuals possess a reservoir of problem-solving inner resources that will aid their recovery. Crisis victims tend to be more resilient and resourceful than they originally thought they were, and it is the work of crisis counselors to enable them to tap these inner resources to move forward. People solve problems on their own every day, and although these problems rarely reach crisis proportions, the strategies that are used to solve them can also be applied to larger, seemingly insurmountable problems. In effect, the crisis counselor's job is to help the client apply innate problem-solving skills to more crisis-specific dilemmas.

Communicating the Message that the Client is in Control

The assumption that the individual is resourceful enough to generate multiple solutions is one of the cornerstones of effective crisis intervention. The function of the counselor is not to change people, but rather to serve as a catalyst for victims to discover and to use their own resources. There is an expectation that people haven't yet identified those skills that they already possess and that they have all they need to help solve their problems (Roberts, 2000). Even though familiar coping methods may fail the person in crisis, an expectation of victim resourcefulness would lead the crisis counselor to elicit from the individual other, perhaps less familiar, solutions to the crisis situation. Following is the case of Nicole, which illustrates this key element of crisis intervention.

Nicole was a recent widow as a result of the September 11 attacks on the World Trade Center. Several weeks after the death of her husband, she acknowledged to a crisis counselor's queries that she experienced all the signs of depression: sleep and appetite disturbances, a sense of helplessness and hopelessness, frequent crying episodes, and an inability to mobilize her own inner resources to return to work and, even more significant, to leave the house altogether. She explained to the counselor during the initial interview that she had experienced a similar episode as an adolescent when, in the aftermath of a car accident in which she was wounded psychologically rather than physically, she remained housebound for two whole years. The initial crisis interview concludes with the following exchange:

Counselor:	*What was it that enabled you, after two whole years, to leave the house?*
Nicole:	*It was the church; I went back to church for the first time in a while.*
Counselor:	*Tell me what it was that drew you to the church for help.*
Nicole:	*It was because I remembered that, as a girl, I always felt safe in church. I remembered that whenever I was in church there was nothing to fear.*

Once Nicole suggested that her support in times of great distress, as evidenced by her past history, was the church, a key component of the counselor's intervention plan involved her return to church. Plans were made to initiate contact with a priest from a neighboring parish and to seek him out for support. It was Nicole, with the assistance of the counselor, who devised this plan; she had known this priest in the past and had always considered him to be a soothing and spiritual man. Thus, her plan was set in motion, and she eventually contacted this priest.

The plan chosen for Nicole certainly would not necessarily be the plan chosen for other crisis victims. It was specific to Nicole, and to her needs. More importantly, it used Nicole's own resources, her own ideas. She enlisted her reconnection of what helped her emerge from trauma in the past and applied it to the present. In doing so, she began to shed the cloak of grief and to don that of empowerment; this outcome exhibits the essence of crisis intervention that capitalizes on the client's strengths and inner resources to put her back into control.

Step 4: Commit

In this final step in L-A-P-C, the client, either through the facilitative or directive stance of the counselor, agrees to commit to a plan of action to help alleviate the strains of the crisis and to regain some level of equilibrium. Even though several different plans may be discussed along with the advantages and disadvantages of each, a specific plan that is appealing to the client and that he or she believes can be enacted is chosen. Additionally, follow up becomes a component of this commitment. Once the client agrees to enact the plan, the client also commits to ongoing follow up with the counselor or with some other member of the support system.

The content and protocol for this follow up, of course, depends on the needs of the crisis client. For some, follow up may be with a medical professional (for medication, possible hospitalization, etc.), or a mental health professional (for ongoing counseling, etc.), while for others, follow up may be a somewhat less formal arrangement for the client returning to work (maintaining telephone contact only with the crisis counselor, etc.). As described above, Nicole for example, committed to accessing her local priest, while her involvement with a sizable group of friends and community members also contributed greatly to her recovery.

It is important to note that there is a problem-solving component to the planning stage. One action plan is chosen by the client for implementation. However, the counselor and the client also may discuss several others before deciding on the most viable one. One of the advantages of the fourth L-A-P-C step is that it also affords the client the ability to follow up with the counselor or with another member of the support system to choose another plan, should the initial one not result in a successful outcome. Commitment to the plan as well as to the follow up are equally important in Step 4.

CHAPTER 4

Child Maltreatment

In a story that stunned the nation for days and weeks after its discovery, Penn State University assistant football coach, Jerry Sandusky, was indicted on 52 counts of child molestation (Ganim, 2011). Although four charges were dropped, he was found guilty of 45 of the remaining 48 counts and sentenced to 30 to 60 years in prison. Most of his victims were underprivileged, at-risk youth who participated in "The Second Mile," a nonprofit organization he founded to help just such a population. Some of the evidence presented in his trial suggested that college officials missed opportunities to report the suspected abuse to Child Protective Services (Moulton, 2014). His case persuaded state and national lawmakers, child welfare workers, and the community at large to reexamine and enforce mandated reporting laws (Krase & DeLong-Hamilton, 2015).

DISCUSSION QUESTIONS

What are some common disciplinary practices used by parents these days? Which practices are promoted by the popular press or by visiting child psychologists on your local talk shows?

Did you ever suspect that someone you were friends with or attended school with was being maltreated by his or her parents? Or by someone else (clergy, teacher, coach)? What was your response?

What do you consider to be some of the typical stresses and strains in family life today that might influence the manner in which parents discipline their children?

INTRODUCTION

Child maltreatment is a tragedy of human error and human consequences, a serious and prevalent public health problem, responsible for substantial morbidity and mortality (Fang, Brown, Florence, & Mercy, 2012). At its most basic level, child maltreatment denotes parenting failure—a failure to protect the child from harm, and the failure to provide the positive aspects of a parent-child relationship that can foster development. The responsibility for this failure is shared not only by the individual parents for not adequately providing for their child, but also by society, for not adequately providing the parents with supports and safety nets (Wekerle & Wolfe, 2003).

Child maltreatment, the term used to include physical abuse, sexual abuse, psychological abuse, and neglect is a significant problem, not only for America's youth, but also for society in general.

Individual reactions to child maltreatment vary widely and are affected by a combination of factors. The Child Welfare Information Gateway (2014) suggests that the following factors play a role in the child's ability to survive abuse:

- The child's age and developmental status when the abuse occurred (i.e., the egocentric young child who blames herself as being deserving of the maltreatment versus an older child who faults the perpetrator, not herself, for the abuse)

- The type of maltreatment (i.e., physical abuse, sexual abuse, or neglect)

- Its frequency, duration, and severity (i.e., episodic, chronic, and over many years)

- The relationship between the child and the perpetrator (i.e., parent? stranger? coach? other relative?)

Another significant factor which determines the outcome of maltreatment for some children is their level of resilience, an inherent trait that results from a mixture of both risk and protective factors that result in either a child's positive or negative reaction to adverse experiences (Shaffer, 2012). There are those children who possess a sense of resiliency which protects them from these lifelong problems. A relatively new term in the psychological lexicon, "resilience" refers to the tendency for some children to develop psychological and behavioral competence, even in the face of other multiple risk factors (Weis, 2008). Those protective factors that make up resilience occur spontaneously and are rarely planned. Shaffer (2012), and Mash and Dosois (2003) list several:

- "Easy" temperament, which makes the child good-natured and easy to deal with

- High intelligence and scholastic competence

- Effective problem-solving skills

- Positive self-esteem

- Will to be or do something

- Positive attachment early in life with a caregiver

- Ability to regulate one's emotions

- Sense of humor

- Independence

Weis (2008) also describes the protective value of a child who has a supportive relationship with a significant adult outside the family (e.g., a teacher, coach, or neighbor who values them and serves as a positive role model); the importance of adequate educational opportunities; or the possession of a special skill which is valued by others (i.e., sports, music, art). These factors as well as others serve as buffers between some children and the possible toxic aftereffects of a legacy of maltreatment. However, for those children who do not have a high level of resilience, they may pay a much higher cost for the abuse to them over the course of their lifetimes.

CONSEQUENCES OF CHILD ABUSE AND NEGLECT

Here is a list of just some of the broad range of physical, psychological, behavioral, cognitive, and social effects caused by this social ill:

Physical

Child maltreatment can have a multitude of long-term effects on physical health. The National Survey of Child and Adolescent Well-Being (U.S. Department of Health and Human Services, 2013) found that at some point during the three years following a maltreatment investigation, 28% of children had a chronic health condition. Although victims of physical abuse often suffer broken bones, bruising, burns, and a host of other perpetrator-inflicted wounds, abusive head trauma caused by shaking and blunt impact is the most common cause of traumatic death for infants. These injuries also may not be immediately noticeable, and, since significant brain development takes place during infancy, this process can be seriously compromised in maltreated children. Approximately 25% to 30% of infants who are victims of Shaken Baby Syndrome (SBS), the violent shaking of an infant back and forth, die from their injuries. The Center for Disease Control and Prevention (2013) found that one in every four victims of SBS dies, while all of its victims experience serious health consequences, often suffering varying degrees of visual, motor, and cognitive impairments (National Center on Shaken Baby Syndrome, 2009).

Other nonfatal results of abusive head trauma result in long-term consequences vis-à-vis cognitive, language, mental health, and academic functioning, leading to special education supports throughout the school years (Tarullo, 2012). Other studies have demonstrated a relationship between maltreatment and poor physical health (Felliti & Anda, 2009; Widom, Czaja, Bentley, & Johnson, 2012). Among these problems were

- cardiovascular disease
- lung and liver disease
- hypertension
- diabetes
- asthma
- obesity
- malnutrition

Psychological

Children who suffer maltreatment experience an elevated risk of developing not only adverse health conditions, but also many other mental health and behavioral issues. The NSCAW suggested that more than half the youth reported for maltreatment were at risk for such problems. For example, the immediate emotional effects of abuse and neglect (isolation, fear, and an inability to trust) can result in lifelong consequences related to depression, low self-esteem, and future relationship difficulties. Felitti and Anda (2009) found that approximately 54% of cases of depression and 58% of suicide attempts in women were related to adverse childhood experiences; problems with emotional regulation which usually persists into adolescence and adulthood also were found to be another aftereffect of maltreatment (Messman-Moore, Walsh, & DiLillo, 2010).

Behavioral

Also found as a result of maltreatment were increased rates of smoking, alcoholism, substance abuse, eating disorders, depression, suicide, and sexual promiscuity (Runyan, Wattam, Ikeda, Hassan, & Ramiro, 2002; Messman-Moore et al., 2010).

Maltreated children also are more likely than non-abused peers to develop anxiety disorders, particularly posttraumatic stress disorder (PTSD), a condition whose symptoms can last years beyond the abuse itself (Weis, 2008).

Other conditions which often result from child maltreatment include a number of disruptive behavior disorders; one such condition is oppositional defiant disorder (ODD), a condition characterized by argumentativeness toward caregivers and teachers, poor self-control, and an open defiance of established rules. Older children and adolescents also may develop conduct disorder (CD), a condition which involves serious antisocial behaviors, such as stealing, cheating, animal cruelty, and physical assault (Weis, 2008). The correlation between child abuse and future juvenile delinquency has been documented with the high likelihood (nine times) that abused children would be involved in criminal activities (Gold, Sullivan, & Lewis, 2011).

Cognitive

Maltreated children also show more cognitive delays and lower IQ test scores than their non-abused peers. These problems include difficulties with executive functioning (planning, organizing, and problem solving), working memory (the ability to hold information temporarily in memory while performing some operation with it), and language (Eigsti & Cicchetti, 2004). Cognitive problems like these are long-lasting and have a significant impact on a child's performance, both outside school and within it. Academic achievement of abused children also suffers significantly across all areas of functioning, resulting in higher rates of learning disabilities, special education placement, grade retention, and school dropouts. The combination of the aforementioned behavioral difficulties associated with maltreatment as well as the cognitive sequalae of abuse contributes to the academic woes of abused children (Kolko, 2002).

Social

A history of troubled relationships with others, even into adulthood, often characterizes the life of the maltreated child. These children may experience a lifelong pattern of absent or troubled relationships as they find it difficult to trust others and participate in interpersonal relationships (Prevent Child Abuse America, 2006). Infants and young children who suffer severe neglect also are at risk for a specific psychological condition known as reactive attachment disorder (RAD) in which children do not initiate or respond physically or emotionally to others, even to caregivers, when physical comfort is offered; they are difficult to soothe, since they avoid close contact with caregivers. On the other hand, disinhibited social engagement disorder is marked by the child's indiscriminate sociability; that is, these children seek comfort and attention from anyone, including strangers, and are often described as "needy" and as requiring constant reassurance from others (*DSM-5*).

Abused children also were found to be more likely than non-abused children to be abusive parents themselves. Xiangming & Corso (2007) found that male victims of child sexual abuse were 1% to 17% more likely to commit interpersonal/domestic violence and girl victims were 3% to 12% more likely to do so.

The costs to society of child maltreatment are incalculable in so many ways, but some research (Fang et al., 2012) has estimated that the total lifetime economic cost resulting from new cases of fatal and nonfatal child maltreatment in the United States was $124 billion in 2012. The researchers considered long- and short-term health care costs, lifetime productivity losses, child welfare costs, costs of involvement with the criminal justice system, and special education costs in their calculations.

Maltreatment that occurs at an early age also can damage children in ways which extend well beyond the present day. Abuse and neglect contribute to a legacy of chronic problems for children which last well into adolescence and adulthood, including poor school performance, an increased need for special education services, juvenile delinquency, relationship difficulties, and adult criminality.

Prevent Child Abuse America's Annual Report (2006) documented the following long-term effects of maltreatment.

- 90% of imprisoned male felons were abused as children;

- 70% of teenage drug abusers reported abuse in childhood;

- More than 50% of female criminals were sexually or physically abused as children;

- 95% of teenage prostitutes have child abuse histories; and

- Abused children often become adults who repeat these violent abusive acts.

DEFINITIONAL ISSUES IN MALTREATMENT

The key piece of federal legislation which addressed child abuse and neglect was the Child Abuse Prevention and Treatment Act (CAPTA), originally enacted in 1974 and amended and reauthorized in 2010. In addition to providing federal funding to the states in support of prevention, assessment, and treatment of child abuse and neglect, CAPTA also set forth a minimum definition of abuse and neglect and identified the federal government's role in supporting research, technical assistance, and data collection activities. It also established the Office on Child Abuse and Neglect and mandated Child Welfare Information Gateway, a service which provides access to print and electronic resources for all individuals concerned for the welfare of children and families in many areas, including child abuse and neglect.

Within CAPTA's minimum definitional standards, each state must provide its own definitions of child abuse and neglect. CAPTA's definition of child abuse and neglect refers to "Any recent act or failure to act on the part of a parent or caretaker which results in death, serious physical or emotional harm, sexual abuse, or exploitation; or an act or failure to act which presents an imminent risk of serious harm."

Most states recognize four major types of child maltreatment:

- Physical abuse
- Neglect
- Sexual abuse
- Emotional abuse

Physical Abuse

Generally defined as any non-accidental physical injury to the child, the definition can include striking with a hand, stick, strap, or other object, kicking, burning, shaking, throwing, stabbing, choking, or otherwise harming a child at the hands of a parent, caregiver, or other person who has responsibility for the child. The definitions in approximately 36 states also include acts or circumstances that threaten the child with harm or create a substantial risk of harm to the child's health or welfare.

Neglect

Frequently defined in terms of deprivation to the child of adequate food, clothing, shelter, medical care, or supervision, neglect also may include the failure to provide for educational needs (failure to educate or to attend to special education needs), and emotional needs (failure to provide psychological care or permitting a child to use drugs or alcohol). Approximately 21 states actually include failure to educate in their definitions of neglect, and seven states define as medical neglect the withholding of medical or mental health care needed by the child.

Sexual Abuse

All states include sexual abuse in their definitions of child abuse. States vary in how it is defined; however, some states refer to it in general terms, whereas others specify various acts as sexual abuse. This form of abuse typically includes activities by a parent or caretaker, such as fondling a child's genitals, penetration, incest, rape, sodomy, indecent exposure, and exploitation of children through prostitution or the production of pornographic materials.

Emotional Abuse

All states except two include emotional maltreatment as part of their definitions of child abuse and neglect. Approximately 22 states provide specific definitions of emotional abuse or mental injury to the child. Although difficult to define, the language usually used in these definitions include "injury to the psychological capacity or emotional stability of the child as evidenced by an observable or substantial change in behavior, emotional response, or cognition" or by "anxiety, depression, withdrawal, or aggressive behavior." It is generally agreed, however, that the definition of emotional abuse involves those behaviors which impair a child's emotional development or sense of self-worth, such as constant criticism, threats, or rejection, as well as withholding love, support, or guidance.

The problem with this type of abuse lies in the fact that it is difficult to prove, thereby preventing the local Child Protective Services (CPS) personnel from intervening; without evidence of harm to the child, CPS help is not likely. However, emotional abuse is considered to be almost always present when other forms of abuse are identified and documented.

PREVALENCE OF CHILD ABUSE AND NEGLECT

Among the many amendments to CAPTA was the mandate for the Department of Health and Human Services (DHHS) to establish a national data and analysis program for child abuse and neglect reporting information. Because of this mandate, the DHHS created the National Child Abuse and Neglect Data System (NCANDS) as a voluntary national reporting system. The National Data Archive on Child Abuse and Neglect (NDACAN) promotes secondary analysis of child abuse and neglect data by providing researchers with high quality datasets, documentation, and technical support, and encourages collaboration within the scientific community. NCANDS 2014 data included in its report statistics on types of maltreatment, victim characteristics, and perpetrator characteristics.

In NCANDS's *Child Maltreatment 2014,* 6.6 million children were referred to Child Protective Services (CPS) for investigations of child maltreatment. Of these referrals, approximately 3.9 million children were deemed appropriate for CPS response. An estimated 1,580 children died from documented abuse and neglect, 70% of whom were children younger than three years of age. According to this report, however, these data reflect only a small part of the problem, since many cases of abuse and neglect are never reported to the police or to social service agencies. The report also included the following data:

Types of Maltreatment

- 75% of the confirmed child victims experienced neglect
- 17% were physically abused

- 8.3% were sexually abused

- 6% were psychologically maltreated

- 2.2% were medically neglected

- 6.8% experienced other maltreatment like threatened abuse of parents' substance abuse

Victim Characteristics

- 51% of the victims were girls; 47% of victims were boys

- the youngest children were the most victimized of all age groups, with the highest rate of victimization (27%) occurring among infants and children from birth through three years of age; shaken baby syndrome alone, the violent shaking of an infant or child, affects 1,200 to 1,600 children each year (National Center on Shaken Baby Syndrome, 2009).

- the rate of victimization was inversely related to the age of the child, with ages 4 through 7 listed as the second most victimized group, followed by ages 8 through 11, ages 12 through 15, and ages 16 through 17

- about one-half of all victims were white, one-quarter were African American, and 17% were Hispanic; highest rates of victimization by race were found among African American children followed by American Indian/Alaska Native children and Pacific Islander children; white children and Hispanic children had similar rates of victimization

- although living arrangements of victims were not reported by many states, more than 20% of victims were living with a single parent

- children with a disability requiring more care and attention than is typically required of children without a disability accounted for nearly 8% of the victims of abuse and neglect

Perpetrator Characteristics

- most abusers (79% of victims) were parents acting alone or with another person

- 28% of victims were maltreated by their mothers acting alone; 15% by fathers acting alone, and 21.8% by both parents

- women abusers typically were younger than men (31 years versus 34 years, respectively); almost half of these women (45%) were younger than 30 years

- 55% of abusers were white, 21% African American, and 18% Hispanic

- most abusers (61%) neglected children, whereas 11% physically abused them and approximately 8% sexually abused them

- non-parents (kin and child care workers) accounted for 15.7% of child fatalities

Although there is no single profile of the child abuser, multiple risk factors that contribute to child maltreatment include mental health problems and substance abuse in the parent or caregiver, ineffective and coercive discipline practices used, domestic violence, and single parenthood which often means high stress, low income, and poverty.

POSSIBLE INDICATORS OF CHILD ABUSE AND NEGLECT

There is no single indicator of child maltreatment, nor is there a "profile" of a maltreated child. Physical signs or behavioral problems alone are unreliable indicators of abuse. A child's direct verbal report is far more reliable (McConaughy, 2005). Nevertheless, those who work with children should be aware of some of the more common signs of child maltreatment. The Child Welfare Information Gateway and the National Children's Advocacy Center provide information on these signs and symptoms:

The following four cases are varied; the first two involve the events surrounding the reporting of child abuse by responsible adults, and the second two concern intervention directly with an abused child.

Case Presentation: Physical Neglect and the Neighbor

Billy was a seven-year-old boy who frequently played an assortment of games and activities with his neighbor's five-year-old son, David, in a neighborhood which was short of school-age children and long on older, mature families. As a result of this demographic, the two boys were locked into a friendship due to mutual need rather than to a true friendship bond. Billy had Fetal Alcohol Syndrome (FAS), a condition caused by his mother's excessive use of alcohol during her pregnancy with him. He was undersized for his age, very thin and frail, and his facial features were distinctive and were characteristic of others with FAS. Billy's mother had not been employed in some time, and she had recently been widowed, leaving her as the sole caregiver for Billy. After repeated suspicions among the neighbors that Billy had been unsupervised for extended periods of time, these suspicions became acute when Billy was invited to have dinner with his friend's family. The way he ate ravenously, as if he hadn't eaten in a while, prompted his friend's father to inquire about his eating habits at home.

Table 4.1   Indicators of Abuse

Type of Abuse		
Physical Abuse	**Child Indicators** • unexplained bruises in various stages of healing • unexplained burns, especially cigarette burns or immersion burns • unexplained fractures, lacerations, or abrasions • swollen areas • evidence of delayed or inappropriate treatment for injuries	**Child Indicators** • self-destructive • behavioral extremes: withdrawn and/or aggressive • arrives at school early or stays late as if afraid to be at home • seems frightened of the parents and protests or cries when it is time to go home • shrinks at the approach of adults • reports injury by a parent or another adult caregiver • chronic runaway (adolescents) • complains of soreness or moves uncomfortably • wears clothing inappropriate to the weather in order to cover body • bizarre explanation of injuries **Parent Indicators** • offers conflicting, unconvincing, or no explanation for the child's injury • describes the child as "evil" or in some other very negative way • uses harsh physical punishment with the child • has a history of abuse as a child
Physical Neglect	**Child Indicators** • abandonment • unattended medical, dental needs, immunizations, or eyeglasses • consistent lack of supervision • consistent hunger, inappropriate dress, poor hygiene • lice, distended stomach, emaciated • inadequate nutrition	**Child Indicators** • states that there is no one at home to provide care • frequent absences from school; tardy often • begs or steals food or money • regularly displays fatigue or listlessness, falls asleep in class • self-destructive • school dropout (adolescents) • extreme loneliness and need for affection **Parent Indicators** • appears to be indifferent to the child • seems apathetic or depressed • behaves irrationally or in a bizarre manner • is abusing drugs or alcohol
Sexual Abuse	**Child Indicators** • torn, stained, or bloody underclothing	**Child Indicators** • suddenly refuses to change for gym or to participate in physical activities

	• pain, swelling, or itching in genital area • difficulty walking or sitting • bruising or bleeding in genital area • contracts venereal disease or becomes pregnant, particularly if under age 14 • frequent urinary or yeast infections • massive weight change	• reports nightmares or bedwetting • sudden change in appetite • demonstrates bizarre, sophisticated, or unusual sexual knowledge or behavior • runs away • reports sexual abuse by a parent or other adult caregiver • excessive seductiveness • role reversal, overly concerned for siblings • suicide attempts (especially adolescents) • threatened by physical contact, closeness **Parent Indicators** • is unduly protective of the child • severely limits the child's contact with other children, especially those of the opposite sex • is secretive and isolated • is jealous or controlling with family members
Emotional Abuse	**Child Indicators** • delayed physical or emotional development • substance abuse • ulcers, asthma, severe allergies	**Child Indicators** • habit disorder (sucking, rocking, biting) • antisocial, destructive • neurotic traits (sleep disorders, inhibition of play) • delinquent behavior (especially adolescents) • shows extremes in behavior, such as overly compliant or demanding behavior, extreme passivity, or aggression • is either inappropriately adult (parenting other children) or inappropriately infantile (frequently rocking or head banging, for example) • has attempted suicide • reports a lack of attachment to the parent **Parent Indicators** • constantly blames, belittles, or berates the child • appears unconcerned about the child • refuses to consider offers of help for the child's problems • overtly rejects the child

Intervention

Father: Billy, you seemed very hungry tonight.
Billy: I was!
F: Did you have any lunch today?
B: No, my mom was asleep.
F: Does she sleep a lot?
B: She usually sleeps in the daytime, and I sleep in the nighttime.

F: Who feeds you during the daytime?

B: I usually get food myself.

F: What did you have for dinner last night?

B: I made myself some cereal (naming his two favorite breakfast cereals).

F: Do you have cereal for dinner a lot?

B: Yeah.

F: Do you get hungry sometimes for other kinds of food?

B: Yeah, but sometimes my mom tells me that she can't go to the store to buy stuff, and sometimes she just tells me to have cereal.

F: What are some of your favorite foods?

B: Well, when my daddy was here, he used to take us to the diner where I used to get different things. I don't know what it was called, but it was good. My mom says that she doesn't have enough money now to take me there anymore.

F: It sounds like you would like to have other kinds of food for dinner besides cereal. I know that there are ways that I can help you and your mom have enough other kinds of food to eat. I know that there are people I can call whose job it is to help families who need help with things like food and money.

B: Really?

F: Yes. First, let's go over to see your mom so that I can tell her about my plan to call these people. They are social workers who will come to visit you and your mom.

B: O.K.

Case Conceptualization/Crisis Resolution

When David's father escorted Billy home later that evening, there was no answer to a knock on the door. Left unlocked, Billy and David's father entered the house to find his mother, Helen, slumped across the kitchen table, oblivious to their presence until Billy nudged her to awaken her. Sensing that it was clear that she was unable to provide for Billy's needs that night, David's father walked Billy back to his own home in order to spend the night with David. Meanwhile, David's father called the local CPS office to report his concerns over the apparent physical neglect of Billy and then returned to Billy's home to make sure that his mother was not in any danger herself. When he told her that he had called CPS to report his observations, she was neither angry nor upset; rather, she told him that she already had a caseworker, having been reported to CPS once before when pulled over by the local police for driving under the influence of alcohol with Billy in the car with her.

David's father took care to express his concerns to Helen that his call to CPS was not a vindictive one, but rather one borne out of his concerns for Billy's safety as well as for her need for assistance from other agencies, given her single-parent status and other life stresses. Helen nodded in agreement with this assessment and awaited the next phone call and home visit from the CPS worker assigned to the family.

In applying Cavaiola and Colford's L-A-P-C model of crisis intervention, it is important to review this case with the four steps in mind:

Listen

Be attentive to Billy's description of his dietary habits at home. Questions posed to children, particularly someone like Billy, a seven-year-old developmentally challenged boy, must be short and simple and geared toward the understanding of the child. It is important not to be judgmental nor reactive to the content of his answers, lest one runs the risk of having him "shut down" as a result of one's reactions to him. One also must listen not only to the verbal responses to the questions asked, but also to those nonverbal messages that accompany the verbal (i.e., avoidance of eye contact, squirming in discomfort due to the questions, possible withholding of information out of shame, embarrassment, etc.)

Assess

What does all this information mean? The lingering suspicions of neglect, Billy's overall appearance, and his ravenous approach to the meal offered to him all suggested that the course of action chosen by the father was the appropriate one. Although seemingly not forlorn or depressed, his physical health continued to be compromised due to lack of proper nutrition and to a mother struggling with a probable alcohol addiction. The father's assessment of all these factors which he observed and heard from Billy guided him in deciding to call the local Child Protective Services (CPS) office.

Plan

Of primary concern, based on his assessment, was for the physical well-being of Billy and his mother, thus the immediate plan to keep Billy for the night for a "sleepover" with David and to establish the safety of his mother as well. The plan for a longer-term intervention was for the father to contact CPS so that Billy's health and safety would be assured via the agency's monitoring of the family by providing it with appropriate financial and other resources.

Commit

In this step of the process, it is important to get the client to commit to following the plan as outlined in the previous step. In the case of Billy, however, it was preferable, but not required, that Billy and his mother make a commitment to the plan to call CPS. That is, whether they agreed to it or not, the father was still legally obligated to contact CPS, even if Billy's mother asked him not to do so; his strong suspicion of neglect bound him to be proactive to make sure that Billy's health and safety was monitored by CPS. Billy's mother's consent to the plan to call CPS was fortunate in this case, but not essential.

Case Presentation: Physical Abuse and the Third Grader

Ms. Spatzer, a third-grade teacher in one of the neighborhood public schools, came to see the school psychologist one day to ask his opinion about her concerns about one of her students. She reported that she had just observed for the second time in as many weeks suspicious bruising on the upper arms of her student, Lloyd. Thinking nothing of it at first, attributing it to a "boys will be boys" bit of horseplay with one of his friends, she asked him about the bruises several days later when she happened to have a quiet and private time with him. According to her, Lloyd's behaviors, both verbal and nonverbal, raised some suspicions in her when she questioned him about the source of the bruises. She said that he became noticeably agitated when questioned, averted eye contact when Ms. Spatzer raised the issue with him, and began to pull down on his sleeves as if to cover the bruising. His hesitation in presenting an explanation about the cause of the bruises, as if he were struggling to create a fictional account of their cause, also alarmed her.

Lloyd's reticence in this encounter also convinced Ms. Spatzer that some of her previous observations of Lloyd may indeed have been significant after all. She always thought that he tended to be more withdrawn and passive immediately after a weekend break from school, and there were times when he wore clothing which was not particularly seasonal, particularly long-sleeved shirts on hot, humid days. She also learned from conversation in the teachers' room that his parents had separated recently and that he stayed with his father on weekends. After consideration of these observations, Ms. Spatzer decided to seek out the school psychologist for a consultation.

Intervention

Teacher: I have a strong suspicion that one of my students, Lloyd, may be being abused by one of his parents, probably his father.

Psychologist: Tell me about your suspicions.

T: Well, it's just that I have noticed a second set of bruises in the last couple of weeks, and when I tried to talk with him about it, he became very secretive and uncomfortable and couldn't tell me clearly any reason that might account for the bruises. I also recall sometimes when he wore oversized clothing which was not in keeping with the weather conditions. Could this also be a sign that he was hiding some other signs of physical abuse?

P: All of what you have just told me could be the result of several things, but one of them is possible child abuse. Since you have these suspicions, you are required to report it to the local Child Protective Services (CPS) agency. It is up to them to investigate suspicions like yours and to make sure that Lloyd is safe. Have you ever made a call like this before?

T: No, I haven't. I've only been teaching for three years, and I have never had this experience before. One of my college professors warned us, though, that one day we would experience an abused child in our classes. I don't even know what to do; couldn't you make the call for me with all that I told you? And what if I am wrong? Can I get in trouble? I mean, what if his bruises really are the result of his playing around with his friends? I just am not sure what to do.

P: I certainly can assist you with the call, but the CPS intake worker will have some specific questions about what you saw and what Lloyd told you, all things that only you can answer accurately. I will sit with you and make the call with you, but you are the best one to speak directly to the CPS worker. Just remember that you also can make the call anonymously and that anyone who makes a report of suspected abuse "in good faith" cannot be held liable, even if the suspected abuse was not corroborated by the investigation. Your observations seem to me to be sufficient reason for contacting CPS.

T:	Is there anything else I need to do after I make this call?
P:	That will be up to the CPS worker assigned to Lloyd. There is a good chance that they will come to school to interview him today; they also may want to see you as well. Afterward, they will visit Lloyd's parents and ascertain the ongoing danger to his health and safety and then decide on the best placement for him. Just be assured that your call will go a long way toward guaranteeing his protection from further abuse.
T:	O.K., I'm new at this, fortunately, but let's go make the call. Can we use your office?
P:	Of course.

Case Conceptualization/Crisis Resolution

Within minutes Ms. Spatzer and the psychologist were in his office making the call to CPS. Although he initiated the contact with the intake worker, Ms. Spatzer handled the telephone interview and answered all the intake worker's questions related to her observations of Lloyd's suspected abuse. A subsequent CPS investigation of her suspicions corroborated them as factual, leading to several interventions for Lloyd and his family.

Even though the largest percentage of calls to CPS offices regarding suspected child maltreatment come from educators, making such a call is nevertheless unnerving for most professionals. Fears of being wrong in their suspicions, worries over lawsuits from angry parents, and general uneasiness with being the one to call, all contribute to this sense of dread. All school districts are required to have in place an Emergency Response and Crisis Management Plan (see Chapter 12), which is designed to address all potential crises that might arise within the school or the community. Among the issues addressed are the school's organized responses to many potential crisis events, including school shootings, natural and man-made disasters, and teacher or student reported suspicions of suicidal talk or child abuse.

Ms. Spatzer followed the protocol for a reporting of child maltreatment as outlined in her district's crisis plan: contact the psychologist first with your suspicions and be prepared to be the one to contact CPS. Although Lloyd was the individual who was most in crisis and needful of CPS intervention, Ms. Spatzer herself required some reassurances for her actions. According to the L-A-P-C model:

Listen

The psychologist heard what Ms. Spatzer said about this crisis: Lloyd definitely showed signs of possible abuse that seemed to peak after visits with his father. The case required a call to CPS on behalf of Lloyd, but despite the appropriateness of this response, the teacher also was at a high state of agitation over this course of action. Her reaction became quite clear to the psychologist after listening to her description of Lloyd's physical condition and observing her nonverbal messages of hand-wringing, voice shaking, and general level of anxiety over being in this situation.

Assess

The psychologist had to make a dual assessment in this case: whether or not CPS was to be contacted and determine the emotional state of the reporting teacher. He decided that it was clearly a case for CPS to make sure that Lloyd would be safe from further harm; he also concluded that Ms. Spatzer required a lot of support herself in making the CPS call.

Plan

After assuring her that her suspicions warranted CPS involvement and that her call was to be made "in good faith," thus precluding any legal actions against her, the psychologist spelled out for her the plan of how the call would be made and what the outcome would be.

Commit

Ms. Spatzer agreed with this plan and made the phone call along with the psychologist.

Case Presentation: Self-Disclosure of Abuse

Brian visited the nurse's office in his middle school one morning several times. He was a frequent visitor, she reported, so his multiple visits this one particular morning did not raise any suspicions in her mind. It was during his fourth trip that morning, however, when he announced to her that his father had beaten him with a belt the night before.

Brian's family had a contentious relationship with the school district for a variety of reasons, so this self-disclosure of abuse was a delicate one indeed. The school nurse reported Brian's statements to the school principal who was unclear as to how to proceed, considering the sensitive nature of the issue that was superimposed on a difficult home-school relationship. Fears of a lawsuit and of other repercussions from the family clouded her thinking for the moment.

The first person she consulted with was the school counselor who had experienced most of the contact with the family ever since Brian's arrival in the school one year earlier. She asked the counselor to speak with Brian and to proceed with the appropriate CPS referral.

The school counselor asked Brian's classroom teacher to send him to the counselor's office after his lunch period had ended. In sensitive matters like this, the counselor always tried to be as unobtrusive as possible in singling out students for a visit to her office, lest other classmates suspect that something dire was up with their friend. Confidentiality and privacy issues are paramount, particularly in cases of child maltreatment. Brian himself was considered somewhat of an oddity by his peers, since he lacked those social skills typical for his age group. Although not disliked by them, they viewed him as just a bit "different," and they were not inclined to invite him to many of those weekend birthday and holiday parties that included so many of his other classmates.

When Brian entered the counselor's office, he looked perplexed as to the purpose of his visit. He had been in the counselor's office many times before, but he usually was the one who initiated the visit, dropping in from time to time to talk about nothing of great consequence. This visit was different, he suspected.

Intervention

School counselor:	Hello, Brian. Please take a seat.
Brian:	Sure. Why did you want to see me? Am I in trouble?
SC:	No, of course not, Brian. I just wanted to talk with you about something, that's all.
B:	Should I close the door (looking nervously at the entrance to the office)?
SC:	Yes, Brian. I would like to talk with you about what you told the school nurse this morning.
B:	What do you mean?
SC:	She told me that you said that your father beat you with a belt last night.
B:	Oh, that! No, I was only kidding! Nothing like that really happened. My father's a great guy; he would never do that to me! I was just kidding! (Brian averted eye contact with the counselor and started to stare at the floor while uttering his protest. He was noticeably agitated.)
SC:	Brian, one of my jobs here as counselor is to do what I can to make sure that all children in this school are safe and that no one hurts them.
B:	You mean, like, other kids, bullies, people like that?
SC:	Yes, certainly, but I also mean parents; they also don't have the right to hurt their children, even though they love them and want them to behave.
B:	So, a father, I mean, a parent can hit their kids and still love them, right?
SC:	Yes. It's just that are better ways for a parent to deal with their children's behavior without hitting or hurting them.
B:	Oh.
SC:	I'm wondering if that might not be true for your father; you know, loving you and hitting you sometime?
B:	(Sitting silently with his eyes welling up with tears.)
SC:	(Allowing for a period of silence first) Is it, Brian?
B:	(Starting to cry) I just don't want to get him in trouble, and I don't want to be taken out of my home! I'll just tell everyone that I made it up before! Can't we just keep this a secret?
SC:	Remember what I told you once before, Brian? There are many things that a counselor can keep secret or confidential, but when a counselor learns that children are thinking of hurting themselves or someone else, or if they themselves are being hurt, then the counselor must break confidentiality and tell other people in order to make sure that those children are safe. Do you understand?
B:	Yes, but it's not his fault! He has used the belt before, but last night I talked back to him and made him mad, so he hit me more than he usually does. I just don't want to get him in trouble for something that I did.

SC: Brian, when a child is hurt by a parent, it's never his fault. Parents are adults and have to learn ways of disciplining their children without hurting them or humiliating them. It sounds like your father has to learn other ways to deal with you when you talk back or do other things that children do.

B: Now what are you going to do?

SC: Brian, the law says that I or anyone else who works in a school has to contact a group of people called Child Protective Services if they suspect that a child has been hurt. I will make the phone call now and tell them all that you have told me and the school nurse. They then will either come to the school to meet with you first or make direct contact with your father. The way they proceed will be their decision. Their job is to help families by having them change the ways they deal with their children.

B: But, I won't be in trouble, will I?

SC: No, Brian. The caseworker who visits you or your family will try to make sure that you don't get in trouble for telling us what happened. In fact, what you did was a very hard thing to do; it took a lot of courage to come forward to tell us what happened. I also will be here when the caseworker comes and sit with you, if that's OK with you.

B: Sure.

Case Conceptualization/Crisis Resolution

The counselor then made the phone call to the agency. Although inclined to make a visit to Brian's home within 24 hours, the agency instead dispatched a caseworker to see Brian in school before the end of the school day, since he let it be known that he was afraid to return home that afternoon.

Generally, the messages that should be communicated clearly to the child throughout this process include (Cavaiola & Colford, 2006, 2011):

- Children are entitled to be safe and not hurt

- Children shouldn't have to be afraid to go home

- Adults, even parents, are not permitted to hurt children

- Abuse is not the child's fault

- A child will not get into trouble for telling someone about abuse

- Hitting is not the right way for parents to punish bad behavior

- There are ways that counselors and other people can help parents so that they will stop doing hurtful things

- The goal of the involvement of Child Protective Services is to help the family

The familiarity that Brian had with the school counselor made the counselor's role less problematic than it could have been, had they not known each other. There was undoubtedly a level of trust which facilitated the counselor's L-A-P-C intervention.

Listen

The counselor listened to Brian's initial denial of the abuse admission, then heard him minimize it by accepting the blame for it. One of the protective factors for children experiencing physical abuse is whether or not they blame themselves for the abuse (Grych, Jouriles, Swank, McDonald, & Norwood, 2000). That is, children who blame the abusers rather than themselves for the abuse tend to have a better outcome than those who think that they were the ones who deserved the abuse. The counselor heard statements of self-blame from Brian, his wish to protect his father and to keep the family intact, and his eventual relief that something was going to be done about it.

Assess

The counselor's assessment was that abuse had taken place at the father's hands and that Brian continued to be at risk for future harm. Of great concern to the counselor was Brian's acceptance of blame for the abuse. It was clear that a call to CPS was essential at this point.

Plan

The counselor described his plan to Brian to let him know what the next step in the process was. Ideally, he hoped that Brian also agreed to the plan, even though he was obligated to make the call, with or without Brian's agreement.

Commit

With the counselor's support, Brian committed to the counselor's plan.

Case Presentation: Self-Blame and Abuse

Cindy, an eight-year-old second grader in the local public school, presented as a very frail, undernourished young girl. Although the teachers who knew her never really suspected anything in the way of abuse at home, they always encouraged her to eat more. She was very affectionate, appearing at times to be very "clingy" with her teachers. She interacted well with her fellow classmates, although she tended to be quite passive and to take orders from others in her class. Her appearance, including the dark circles under her eyes, escaped her teachers' scrutiny to assess whether there were any more dire goings-on in the home. A neighbor of Cindy's, however, had many more opportunities to observe her home life. He decided to make a call to CPS, citing multiple instances of abuse and neglect which he observed around the neighborhood. He had witnessed her father and her mother strike her several times, and he voiced other concerns about the time she was left alone to take care of her younger brother,

Jake. The social worker from CPS received the neighbor's phone call and went to see her in school that same day. The principal summoned Cindy from class when the social worker arrived.

Intervention

Social worker:	Hello, Cindy, my name is Jane.
Cindy:	Hello. (Looking very confused and uncertain of why she was sitting with a stranger in the principal's office.)
SW:	I just wanted to ask you a few questions, if I might. You are not in trouble in any way. I am what they call a social worker. My job is to talk to parents, children, and families just to make sure that everything is going well. Do you mind if I ask you some questions?
C:	O.K.
SW:	First, how old are you?
C:	I am eight.
SW:	And you are in the second grade, right?
C:	Yes, I am in Ms. Fielder's class.
SW:	Tell me what your favorite thing to do in school is.
C:	(Smiling, as if comfortable with this initial neutral line of questioning.) My favorite part of school is the specials; I like Art, because we get to do lots of different things. We draw, play with clay, and look at pretty pictures that the teacher shows us.
SW:	What other specials do you like?
C:	Gym, because we get to run around a lot and play different games. I get a little tired, though.
SW:	Yes, I remember how I also liked to play gym when I was in school. Do you mind if I ask you some more questions?
C:	O.K.
SW:	Tell me, Cindy, who else lives at home with you?
C:	My mom, my stepdad, and my brother, Jake.
SW:	How old is Jake?
C:	Five, I think. Yeah, he's five, that's right. He's funny, but sometimes he bothers me, like he takes my stuff and cries a lot.
SW:	And who takes care of Jake?
C:	Mostly I do, because my stepdad works, and my mom works sometimes and sleeps sometimes.
SW:	What kinds of things do you do for Jake?
C:	Well, I wake him up and give him his breakfast, get his clothes out for him to wear—he goes to kindergarten here—and then I get dressed. Oh yeah, and then I wake my mom for her to drive us to school.
SW:	And what do you do after school?
C:	Well, I wait for Jake and we sometimes walk home together, because sometimes my mom forgets to pick us up.
SW:	Is your mom or stepdad home when you eat dinner?
C:	Sometimes, but if she isn't, she leaves us something to eat ourselves.

SW:	You and Jake?
C:	Yes.
SW:	Do you get punished sometimes, like if you didn't do your chores or something?
C:	(Looking more and more apprehensive.) Yes.
SW:	Tell me what your punishment is.
C:	Sometimes I have to kneel in the corner on the floor in my kitchen until my mom tells me I don't have to any more.
SW:	Have your mom or stepdad used other kinds of punishment?
C:	(Clearly uncomfortable at this point and silent.)
SW:	Cindy, I know that these questions are hard questions to answer, but I really appreciate how you have been able to talk with me here today. I know that it is hard for lots of children your age to talk about these things. I really would like you to tell me the other kinds of punishment that is used at home.
C:	(Starting to cry.) Sometimes, if I'm really bad, I get hit and I cry.
SW:	Who hits you?
C:	Mostly my stepdad, but he hits my mom too, sometimes, and sometimes my mom hits me, too, like if I forget to clean up or if I have a fight with Jake. But, I'm older, I should know better.
SW:	You should know better?
C:	Yeah, I am older and I should know better. I should be more responsible. I should be better, too. Jake looks up to me, he needs me to be better.
SW:	Cindy, you are such a good, caring big sister, but maybe being an eight-year-old is too young to have to do so much at home. I don't think that you have to be better at all. One of the things that I do is to talk to parents about ways to help their children without hurting them or hitting them. Sometimes parents make mistakes and hurt their children, but nobody should hurt other people, especially children. I also want to make sure that your mom is safe and that your stepdad doesn't hurt her any more. What I want to do is to go to see your mom and stepdad and talk to them about other ways of helping you and Jake. I can talk to them about lots of other things that they can do instead of hitting you and hurting you. There also are other people that they can see who can help. I also will tell them that I talked with you today.
C:	But, I don't want to get into more trouble.
SW:	I will tell your mom that you were very brave in answering some very hard questions and that you shouldn't get in trouble for it. I also will give her some help so that she also is safe.
C:	O.K.

Case Conceptualization/Crisis Resolution

As with the case of Brian (above), Cindy blamed herself for the maltreatment; if she were only "more responsible" it wouldn't have happened. In other words, she deserved it. The social worker who responded to the neighbor's call was aware of this belief of Cindy's and tried to reassure her that that was not the case. The social worker used the L-A-P-C approach in her interview of Cindy.

Listen

She sensed Cindy's initial discomfort with the interview, talked first about more neutral school-related issues, and then gradually introduced the more emotionally laden topic of her home life. She also heard the blame for the abuse that Cindy heaped on herself.

Assess

The assessment was clear to the social worker that Cindy was the victim of maltreatment within the confines of a home where there also was domestic violence. The blame she accepted for it made her numb to what was happening and undoubtedly required additional community and mental health services for Cindy and her family.

Plan

Making a visit to the home was critical in this case to assess the level of safety for the children and for mom.

Commit

As with the previous cases in this chapter, even a child's refusal to commit to the plan cannot be heeded, given the ethical and legal obligations to report abuse and to allow CPS to intervene on behalf of children. Nevertheless, Cindy did seem to be agreeable to the plan after the social worker's explanation of what she intended to do.

GENERAL GUIDELINES FOR REPORTING SUSPECTED CHILD ABUSE AND NEGLECT

Estimating the actual number of cases of child maltreatment is difficult, considering that as many as half of all suspicions go unreported (Krase & DeLong-Hamilton, 2015). States vary in their reporting laws concerning child maltreatment. Eighteen states have enacted Universal Mandated Reporting laws which require that all adults, regardless of their position in the community, report suspicions of child maltreatment to CPS personnel. The remaining 32 states delegate mandated reporting to professionals generally involved with children, such as school personnel, social workers, mental health professionals, child care providers, medical examiners, and law enforcement.

Once an individual observes signs of maltreatment in a child (see above indicators), he or she must contact the local CPS office with these suspicions. Although the standards used to determine when a mandatory report should be made vary from state to state, a report must be made when the reporter suspects that a child has been abused or neglected. Reporters may make these reports anonymously, although states find it help-ful to know the identity of the reporter. Most states have provisions to maintain the con-fidentiality of the reporters and to protect the disclosure of their identity to the alleged abuser. Failure to report suspected child maltreatment or filing a false report against someone in most states results in penalties ranging from fines to imprisonment. However, professionals are protected from civil and criminal liability in all states if reports are made in good faith, even if later the reports are deemed unfounded by the investigation.

The most recent NCANDS report claimed that 24% of reports of physical abuse were made by teachers, 23% by police officers or lawyers, and almost 12% by medical staff. Overall, professionals accounted for 75% of reports of physical abuse and non-professionals provided the other 25%. However, reports of neglect and sexual abuse were made primarily by police officers and lawyers.

Considering the high rate of reports made by teachers, it is incumbent on them to famil-iarize themselves with the laws of the state in which they teach regarding the reporting of abuse and neglect as well as of the school district's policy identifying procedures for reporting and for those designated as reporters. Investigating reported allegations of mal-treatment, however, is not within the purview of teachers, but rather the responsibility of the CPS staff or of other professionals who have received special training in interviewing children, particularly in the investigation of abuse claims. Nevertheless, school-based pro-fessionals often are the first ones to know if a child has been abused; children spend almost 40 hours per week in the schools, raising the likelihood that a teacher may observe evi-dence of possible abuse, that a child may self-disclose abuse at home, or that a friend will report on the abuse of a peer.

When disclosure of possible maltreatment of a child is made, the local CPS office will be contacted. Prior to this contact, however, the initial interviewer often will be another professional, perhaps a school teacher, counselor, psychologist, or social worker. McConaughy (2005) provided general guidelines for responding to all children who report maltreatment. These guidelines are not investigative in nature, since it is not the job of the interviewer to gather evidence or to establish guilt; rather they are designed to provide a framework for reassurance and support for a maltreated child after a disclosure has been made. These guidelines suggest that the professional:

- Conduct the interview in a private place

- Maintain an atmosphere of informality and trust

- Believe the child (or at least take the child's report at face value)

- Reassure the child that he or she has done nothing wrong and will continue to have your support

- Does not display negative reactions, such as horror, shock, or disapproval of the child or parents

- Be sensitive to the child's nonverbal cues

- Ask for clarification if what the child says is ambiguous

- Use language that the child understands

- Use the child's terms for body parts and sexual behaviors, but also obtain the child's definition of such terms

- Does not suggest answers to the child and avoid probing and pressing for answers

- Give the child a clear and understandable reason why reporting to the local CPS agency is necessary

- Does not suggest that the child conceal the interview from the parents

- Keep clear notes of the interview and the child's disclosure statements, as well as of any subsequent actions regarding reporting

Fears of retribution by the abuser, concerns about the break-up of the family after the disclosure has been made, and guilt over reporting an abuser, particularly if he or she is a parent, are only some of the reasons why children are reluctant to self-disclose or to participate in an interview with a professional after being reported by a peer. Therefore, in age-appropriate terms and language, the interviewer must validate these fears for children, recognize their courage in coming forward, and provide other reassurances that the outcome of the process will result in keeping them safe. Discussing the limits of confidentiality with the child also is critical (the need to report whenever someone has been hurt or is intending to hurt themselves or someone else). CPS investigators of the report also should be portrayed to the child as being in a position to protect the child so that further abuse does not happen. The initial interviewer, however, should not make personal promises to protect the child.

All professionals who work with children should learn how to contact their local CPS or law enforcement agencies. Many states have toll-free numbers to call to report suspected child abuse or neglect. Additionally, the National Child Abuse Hotline is staffed 24 hours per day, seven days per week, by trained crisis counselors who have access to a database of over 50,000 emergency, social service, and support resources and all calls are anonymous.

The phone number is: 1–800–4-A-CHILD.

RESOURCES FOR CHAPTER ENRICHMENT

Recommended Films

This Boy's Life: Leonardo DiCaprio portrays the stepson of a brutal and controlling stepfather played by Robert DeNiro. The emotional and physical abuse handed down by the stepfather culminates in a final confrontation between the two men. Even before the actual abuse begins, the film suggests a cold, detached emotional climate in the household.

Radio Flyer: Two young brothers are the chronic victims of their violent, drunken stepfather's physical abuse. Resorting to fantasy to escape the abuse, they imagine that their Radio Flyer wagon can take them away and allow them to escape the torment they must endure.

Dolores Claiborne: The title character in the film is a middle-age woman who is a suspect in the mysterious death of the elderly woman for whom she had provided help for several years. There also were strong suspicions that she had a hand in her husband's death 15 years before. When her estranged daughter, a newspaper reporter, visits her to inquire about the case, the family secret of sexual abuse rises to the surface.

Suggested Activities

Contact the local Child Protective Services agency and interview one of the caseworkers there about their caseloads, the kinds of cases they have investigated, and some of their most difficult cases.

Research how your particular state defines different forms of child maltreatment, mandatory versus permissive reporters, and the consequences of failing to report suspicions of abuse and neglect, or of filing a knowingly false report.

Research the issue of corporal punishment and the roles that culture, ethnicity, and religion play in its acceptability as a parenting practice. What are your thoughts on the use of spanking as an appropriate discipline strategy?

Student Activity: What Would You Do?

You are a college student who befriends another student during the first semester of freshman year. You both begin a cordial relationship with each other, taking classes together when possible, and socializing on weekends. You enjoy each other's company, and little by little, you begin to share personal stories. Your friend, Sasha, tells you laughingly one Monday morning about how drunk her stepfather was over the weekend. Although a commuter to campus, Sasha holds down a part-time job on the weekends, so she was out of the house and not around much to witness firsthand the entire drunken episode. Much of what she reports to you came from the personal account of her 11-year-old stepbrother, Ian.

Ian apparently told Sasha that his father "took the paddle to him" and gave him a good "whooping." Corporal punishment like this type was not new to Ian or to Sasha, according to her. Sasha explained that it was just that her stepfather was more abusive than usual when he was drunk and that no one knew this more than Ian. When you questioned Sasha further about all this, she laughed and said that she was just waiting to be able to afford an apartment so that she could get away from her stepfather entirely. When questioned about Ian, she told you that she didn't have time to worry about him and that "he would just have to deal with it like she did all those years."

Answer the following questions as if you were the friend to whom Sasha disclosed this information:

1. How would you respond to Sasha's stories of abuse, particularly the ongoing stories about Ian's abuse?

2. Would you take any proactive steps to get it to stop?

3. How would you respond to Sasha if she told you not to tell anyone about her story, lest it lead to additional repercussions at the hands of her stepfather?

4. Does her threat of her loss of friendship with you deter you from doing what you might have planned to do about this issue?

CHAPTER 5

Adolescent Crises

DISCUSSION QUESTIONS

Talk to your parents or a few other adults who are the same age as your parents. Ask them about the major issues they faced as adolescents. Then talk to your own peers about the issues that adolescents face today; how would you compare the stresses and strains faced by your parents or their peers with those faced by the adolescents of today?

Watch a little television. Look for those stations that broadcast the popular shows from the 1960s to 1970s and watch them with an eye toward their depiction of the typical American family and the major obstacles they faced on a week-to-week basis. Compare those issues with the ones portrayed in a contemporary situation comedy today. What impact on the adolescents of today have the attacks of 9/11 had on their development? Similarly, how have technological advances like the internet, multipurpose cell phones, and access to personal web pages like *My Space* affected the lives of adolescents today?

INTRODUCTION

What exactly is adolescence? Who determines what it is? Is it synonymous with the teenage years? Is it a life stage determined by age alone, or by mastery of certain developmental tasks? Finally, is there really a discernable beginning and an end to this period?

The word itself, adolescence, is from the Latin word, *adolescere,* a word meaning *to grow* or *to grow into maturity* (Rice & Dolgin, 2008). Although perhaps not a sufficient enough definition of the term to satisfy some of the questions raised above, it nevertheless suggests a period of transition, a bridge of sorts between an earlier time of childhood and the eventual stage of adulthood. The World Health Organization takes a more simplified approach, defining it as the ages of 10 to 19, and the American Academy of Pediatrics defines it as the interval between child and adult status, acknowledging also that the exact period of adolescence varies in length, according to differences in certain historical periods, cultures, and societies.

In fact, deciding on when adolescence begins and ends may be more a matter of opinion rather than of actual fact (Steinberg, 2005). Does one consider the physically precocious fourth grader, all of nine years of age, to be an adolescent or a child? Is the 23-year-old graduate school student who still lives at home and is dependent on parents for support considered an adolescent or an adult?

Using puberty as an indicator of adolescence always is misleading. From the Latin word, *pubescere,* meaning *to grow hairy or mossy,* the appearance of body hair varies considerably from person to person and from one racial or ethnic group to the next, thereby precluding it as a reliable and universal marker of adolescence. The signs of puberty also come years before a child becomes fertile, so the physical signs that accompany puberty are not, in themselves, sufficient to reveal the onset of adolescence.

What is clear, however, is that the period of adolescence has lengthened considerably in recent years. Over the last century, physical maturation for young people has started earlier and earlier due to advances in medical treatment and in nutrition, whereas individuals at the other end of this age range delay entering the world of work due to longer stays in undergraduate and graduate education programs. They also put off marriage for longer and longer periods. The median ages for marriages in 1970 were 23.2 for men and 20.8 for women; in 2004, these ages increased to 27 for men and 26 for women (Popenoe & Whitehead, 2005). These data suggest that the parameters which previously had defined adolescence have been expanded significantly in recent decades. For these reasons, it may make more sense to think of adolescence as beginning around age 10 and ending in the early 20s (Steinberg, 2005).

HISTORICAL PERSPECTIVES IN ADOLESCENCE

Adolescence has been the focus of much debate among the psychological establishment over the years. G. Stanley Hall was the first psychologist to use scientific methods to study adolescence. He described this life stage as a period of *sturm und drang* ("storm and stress"), a reflection of his views of adolescence as a time of great turbulence and unrest.

Sigmund Freud did not focus much of his time or attention on adolescence, other than to discuss it in terms of his stages of psychosexual development. His own daughter, Anna, assigned much greater importance to adolescence than her father. She saw it as playing an important role in character development and characterized it as a time of great inner conflict and erratic, unpredictable, and contradictory behavior: submissive and rebellious; selfish and idealistic; enthusiastic and apathetic.

These theorists and others have long viewed adolescence as a stressful developmental time, complete with pitfalls that are unavoidable to the typical adolescent. The media also tends to portray adolescents as being only a failed romantic relationship away from a mass killing or a suicide attempt. Still other portrayals suggest that adolescents, as a group, are shiftless and aimless, caught in an existential void of meaninglessness and pessimism. And then there are those who view them as highly emotional and as much more random and unpredictable in their behavior than when they were children or become adults. Anecdotal records of individual adolescent's mental health problems and behavioral shortcomings tend to be generalized to all members of this developmental stage.

More contemporary thinking (Rice & Dolgin, 2008), however, suggests that certain problems, such as conflicts with parents, mood swings, and risk-taking behaviors are more common in adolescence than in childhood or adulthood, but that their presence does not mean that these issues are universal throughout this stage. Rather, the majority of adolescents do not get into serious trouble, and if they do, these troubles are very intermittent and of short duration.

Steinberg (2005) claimed that adolescents were one of the most stereotyped groups in contemporary society:

> *If they are not cast as juvenile delinquents—the usual role in which they are cast—adolescents are depicted as sex-crazed idiots (if they are male), giggling school girls (if they are female), or tormented lost souls, searching for their place in a strange, cruel world (if they aren't delinquent, sex-crazed, or giggling). It's not only fictionalized portrayals of teenagers that are stereotyped—studies of local television newscasts find that the majority of stories on youth are about violence.* (p. 18)

None of the theorists mentioned above had any scientific evidence that the period of adolescence was any more turbulent than that of other life stages, but the stereotype to which they contributed persists. The Carnegie Foundation of New York (1995), in its book *Great Transitions: Preparing Adolescents for a New Century,* concluded

> *Most American adolescents navigate the critical transition years from ten to eighteen with relative success. With good schools, supportive families, and caring community institutions, they grow up to meet the requirements of family life, friendship, the workplace, and citizenship in a technically advanced, democratic society. Even under difficult conditions, most young people grow into responsible, ethical, problem-solving adults.*

A more balanced view on the influences on the adolescent journey appears to consider that an interactive effect between the social and cultural influences of contemporary society and the inner biological/cognitive influences promulgated by many of the earlier researchers in the field provide a clearer picture of today's adolescent.

WHAT THE DATA SAY

Data on the behavior of American adolescents and their involvement with drugs and with other risky pursuits often considered typical for this age group are equivocal. That is, they are encouraging on the one hand, yet not altogether promising on the other hand. The data below provide a look at three areas of concern in the study of the adolescent of today: drug and alcohol use, high-risk behaviors, and sexuality practices.

Alcohol and Drug Use

In its comprehensive survey of approximately 45,000 high school adolescents, the University of Michigan as investigators in conjunction with the Department of Health and Human Services published *Monitoring the Future* (DHHS, 2015), a long-term study of adolescents, college students, and adults through age 45. Their survey found the following among eighth, tenth, and twelfth graders:

- A significant decline in the use of any illicit drug between 2015 and 2016;

- A sharp drop of 9.4% in the use of marijuana among 8th graders too; among 10th graders the drop was 24%, while use among 12th graders remained somewhat steady over the years at 36%;

- A substantial decline in heroin use since its peak in the late 1990s; only .3% of 8th graders reported using it in the prior 12 months, the same percentage reported by 12th graders;

- Although more prevalent than marijuana, alcohol use also is continuing its downward trend; the three grade levels surveyed (8, 10, 12) reported historic lows of alcohol consumption in the 12 months prior to the survey; and

- Tobacco use also has seen a steady decline among the three groups.

High-Risk Behaviors

These behaviors also appear to be part of the adolescent experience. Perhaps due to Elkind's (1967) idea of the *personal fable,* the typical adolescent believes that "nothing can happen to me, despite the risks presented by my behavior," thus putting them at risk of death or injury. It's as if adolescents usually perceive themselves as invulnerable and immune to the laws that apply to others. Yet again, contemporary neuroscience research suggests that the rational, organized, problem-solving part of the brain, the frontal lobe, is not yet fully developed until later in adolescence, thus the behavior of many adolescents is not governed by rational thought.

In its Youth Risk Behavior Surveillance Survey (YRBSS), (CDC, 2015), the Centers for Disease Control and Prevention reported on the findings of its survey of those health-risk behaviors that contribute to the leading causes of morbidity and mortality among youth and adults. The reporting period of the survey was September 2014 to December 2015; students were asked if they had participated in such behaviors in the 30 days prior to the survey.

The YBRSS found an overall decrease in the prevalence of most health risk-taking behaviors among high school students, but it found the following among those participating in the survey:

- 71% of all deaths among persons 10 to 24 years of age result from four causes: motor vehicle crashes, other unintentional injuries, homicide, and suicide

- 41.5% of high school students nationwide who drive a car or other vehicle admitted that they drove while texting or emailing

- 32.8% had used alcohol; 21.7% used marijuana

- 20.2% had been bullied on school property in the previous 12 months

- 15.5% had been bullied electronically

- 8.6% had attempted suicide during the 12 months before the survey

- 30.1% reported being sexually active, with 11.5% reporting sexual intercourse with four or more persons

- 56.9% had used a condom during their last sexual intercourse

- 10.8% had smoked cigarettes in the 30 days before the survey

- 41.7% reported having played video or computer games unrelated to school work for an average of three or more hours per school day

- 13.9% admitted to obesity, and 16% reported being overweight

- During the 30 days preceding the survey, many high school students increased their risk of death by engaging in any one of four behaviors: driving a car while under the influence of alcohol (9.9%); carrying a weapon (18.5%); drinking alcohol (43.3%); and using marijuana (20.2%)

- 37.2% of sexually active high school students had not used a condom during their last sexual intercourse, thus exposing themselves to pregnancy and to a sexually transmitted disease (STD).

- 8.6% had attempted suicide in the previous 12-month period

- 67% did not attend daily physical education classes

- 10.2% of students had rarely or never worn a seat belt when riding in a car driven by someone else

- 28.5% had ridden in a car or other vehicle driven by someone else who had been drinking alcohol

Sexuality Practices

The YBRSS also surveyed the sexual practices of adolescents, and the Kaiser Family Foundation (KFF), a nonprofit organization which researches health care issues, completed a survey of the *Sexual Health of Adolescents and Young Adults in the United States* (2014). Below are some of the findings from both surveys:

YBRSS

- 9.2% of students had been hit, slapped, or physically hurt by their boyfriend or girlfriend in the year preceding the survey.

- 6.7% of high school females were forced to have sexual intercourse

- 41.2% of students have had sexual intercourse

- 11.5% reported having had sexual intercourse with four or more partners

KFF

- Nearly half (47%) of high school students reported having had sexual intercourse in 2013

- 17% of male teens and 13% of female teens reported sex with more than four sexual partners

- 34% of high school students are sexually active

- 10% of high school students reported having experienced dating violence

- 7% of students have been forced to have sexual intercourse (11% female, 4% male)

- One in four sexually active young people contract a STD every year

- Young people feel a great pressure to have sex

- 75% of sexually active adolescents engage in oral sex

- 13% admitted to "sexting," the practice of having shared a naked photo or video of themselves via digital communication

- 22% of sexually active teens reported having unprotected sex after drinking or taking drugs

Although surveys such as the ones discussed above are far from perfect in the information they gather, their data suggest that many of today's adolescents place themselves at risk of a number of physical, psychological, and sexual dilemmas. The data provided do not necessarily imply that the individuals surveyed possess chronic and persistent problems in these areas, but they do portray a trend in the behaviors of many adolescents of today. Even if many of these behaviors do not reach crisis proportions for most adolescents, they reveal patterns of behavioral choices for some members of this age group which reflect the uncertainties of this developmental period, and the adolescent's search for identity, for independence from parents, and for acceptance by peer group members.

ADOLESCENT CRISES

This next section addresses those crises in adolescence which are more chronic and aberrant than typical for the average adolescent. Adolescents who experience a crisis that requires mental health treatment do not constitute the norm; rather, they are in the minority. A discussion of all the potential problems of non-clinical significance which might befall a typical adolescent is beyond the scope of this chapter; issues related to school underachievement, family conflict, and other challenges to the mastery of adolescent developmental tasks are left to chapters on adolescent development rather than to those devoted to adolescent crises. Instead, the following narrative and case examples focus on three crises which often are associated with the adolescent stage: eating disorders, suicide, and non-suicidal self-injury (NSSI; aka: cutting). Another case regarding identity development is included here as well, not because it is a crisis in the magnitude of the aforementioned three, but because it represents a challenge common to many adolescents.

Eating Disorders

An eating disorder is a psychological disorder which is characterized by an excessive desire to be thin as well as an intense fear of gaining weight. Individuals with the disorder limit their food intake to health-threatening small amounts, or use other techniques (excessive exercising, laxatives, diuretics, and vomiting) as weight control strategies. Eating disorders tend to be placed into three categories: anorexia nervosa, bulimia nervosa, and binge-eating disorder. A summary of the diagnostic criteria for each disorder contained in the American Psychiatric Association's *Diagnostic and Statistical Manual of Mental Disorders*, Fifth Edition (*DSM-5*) follows:

Anorexia Nervosa

- Intense fear of gaining weight or becoming fat

- Significantly low weight that is less than minimally expected for adolescents

- Disturbance in view of body weight/body image

- Persistent lack of recognition of the seriousness of the low body weight

DSM-5 considers two types on anorexia. In the restricting type, the individual focuses on weight loss primarily through dieting, fasting, or excessive exercise. However, the binge-eating/purging type of individual maintains the weight loss through recurrent episodes of binge-eating, then purging, either by self-induced vomiting, or overusing laxatives, diuretics, or enemas. Despite their obsession with weight gain, those with this disorder do experience hunger pains.

Bulimia Nervosa

- Recurrent episodes of binge eating

- Recurrent compensatory behaviors to prevent weight gain through self-induced vomiting; overuse of laxatives, diuretics, or other medications; fasting; or excessive exercise

- These behaviors occur, on average, once a week for three months

- Body shape and weight has undue influence on self-image

According to the *DSM-5*, to meet the criteria for bulimia, the binge eating must be done within a specific period of time (i.e., two hours) and must include an amount of food that is much more than what most individuals would eat during that same time period. Additionally, the individual must have a sense of lack of control over the eating during that period; that is, a sense that one cannot stop eating or control the amount of food being eaten.

Binge-Eating Disorder

- Recurrent episodes of binge eating characterized by the bulimia nervosa criteria described above

- Episodes are associated with at least three of the following: eating much more rapidly than usual, eating although feeling uncomfortably full, eating large amounts without being hungry, eating alone to avoid embarrassment, feeling depressed, disgusted, or guilty after episodes

- Distress experienced during binge eating episodes

- Binge eating occurs at least once per week for three months

Research suggests that 15% of young adult females and 6% of young males are affected by eating disorders. Those with the restricting type of anorexia limit their intake of food to the point where they experience starvation, whereas the binge-eating and purging types use various inappropriate compensatory behaviors like self-induced vomiting after they eat. The emaciated appearance of individuals with anorexia is an external indicator of the disorder. Bulimia is diagnosed twice as often as anorexia, and bulimia sufferers are more likely to seek out treatment.

There are more estimates of the prevalence of eating disorders than there are actual statistics, particularly among adolescents, since most individuals who suffer with eating disorders keep them secret and fail to acknowledge their symptoms. Therefore, survey data may reveal only a minimal estimate of the disorder, considering the large number of unreported cases. Another confounding problem in determining the prevalence of eating disorders is the number of adolescents, primarily female, who do not exhibit all the diagnostic indicators of the disorders as determined by the *DSM-5*, yet who exhibit disordered eating habits and other excessive dieting regimens.

Estimates of the number of those adolescents actually diagnosed with an eating disorder are approximately 1% for anorexia, 4% for bulimia among college-age women, and 1% for binge eating (Anorexia Nervosa and Related Eating Disorders [ANRED], 2004). Earlier estimates (Polivy & Herman, 2002), however, placed the number at between 3 to 10% of women between the ages of 15 to 29.

Documenting this larger number was the YRBSS survey that, in tracking all health-risk behaviors of adolescents, also surveyed the dieting practices of this age group. Some of its findings among adolescent females and their attempts to lose weight are listed below:

- 31.5% described themselves as overweight (higher among females at 38.2% than males at 25.3%)

- 13.9% reported obesity

- 45.6% reported that they were trying to lose weight (higher among females at 60.6% vs males at 31.4%)

- 60% had exercised to lose weight

- 17% had gone for 24 hours or more without eating

- 8.1% had taken diet pills, powders, or liquids without a doctor's advice within 30 days of the survey

- 6.2% had vomited or taken laxatives in the last 30 days

The health risks involved with eating disorders are significant: irregular heartbeat, liver and kidney damage, loss of tooth enamel and damage to the esophagus due to excessive vomiting, loss of muscle mass and of the menstrual cycle, a weakened immune system, and anemia and malnutrition. Additional psychological effects include depression, anxiety, guilt and shame, a sense of hopelessness and helplessness, and suicidality.

Case Presentation: Danielle, A Story of Anorexia

For Danielle, it all started as a 12-year-old seventh grader who had just entered the middle school in her local district. A sensitive girl conscious of her appearance and of her body shape, she began what was to be years of food restricting in an attempt to get to and maintain a weight that seemed to her to be reasonable; one that was more comparable to the tall, thin young girls with whom she danced. However, to her friends and to her teachers, there was nothing reasonable about her weight status; they brought it to her attention and explained to her this thing called anorexia nervosa, but Danielle didn't think that that problem applied to her at all. Changes in her life over the years of her disorder were stressful for her and made it difficult for her to maintain a normal weight: her family's move in the eighth grade to a different town, the death of a close grandfather, and finally the death of her own mother after a long struggle with cancer.

When she entered the tenth grade, her thin frame didn't escape the notice of her friend's mother who promptly called Danielle's mother to express her concerns. Her first appointment with a psychologist who specialized in the treatment of eating disorders followed after her mother confronted her about her food restriction. Danielle saw the psychologist only once, preferring not to return to him after he attributed her eating disorder to anger at her parents for the forced middle school relocation, a conceptualization with which she strongly disagreed. However, she did see another therapist on a regular basis along with a nutritionist who developed a meal plan for her and supervised her adherence to it.

Although she continued in therapy, she got better at lying about her dietary habits, even to her therapist. She even went so far as to put things in her pockets so that she would be heavier at her regular weigh-ins. Her charade was over, however, when, as a 15-year-old tenth grader, she passed out on the way to her first period class. Helped up by her friends and escorted to the class, Danielle recalled not remembering much for the next few minutes until the school nurse arrived with a wheelchair and took her to her office. A call to Danielle's parents summoned them to school where they took her to the first of many hospitals she was to visit in the next few years.

Visits to inpatient units, outpatient units, day treatment programs, and partial hospitaliza-tion programs became part of her routine through her high school years and beyond. At the end of her 11th grade when her mother was diagnosed with brain cancer, she completely fell apart, eating no solid food for 18 straight days; all that sustained her was water and coffee with a little milk.

Case Conceptualization/Crisis Resolution

Now several years into recovery, Danielle can reflect on her journey through her anorexia. She can speak of it publicly and has, in fact, become a leader of a support group at a local eating disorder treatment center. She also is nearing completion of a graduate program in social work with further plans to obtain her license as a clinical social worker so that she can become a therapist for others with eating disorders. "I want to raise aware-ness; it helps keep me in recovery."

In the following interview, she provides some insight and some advice for those who treat eating disorders and for other adolescents themselves. Unlike other cases in this book, the following exchange between Danielle and her counselor provides a retrospective rather than an interventionist look, on the early stages of her anorexia.

Counselor: We all know what the research says about the personality type of the individ-ual who develops an eating disorder. Tell me what you were like as a young person.

Danielle: I was just a typical kid. I was teased by the proverbial school bullies just like everyone else my age, but I took it more personally than the others. It always bothered me more.

C: Tell me when things started to change for you.

D: In grade seven when I was 12-years-old, things were important; looks became important, clothes were important, all those shallow things. I didn't want to wear glasses, and my shoes and everything had to be a brand name.

C: Middle school can be a significant transition for young adolescents. Was that transition a smooth one for you or a difficult one?

D: It was around that time that things started to change for me. I started gaining weight, but not growing taller; I was a little pudgy, maybe at most, 10 pounds overweight.

C: Was that a problem for you?

D: It wasn't only that. I had been a dancer from ages three through 15 or 16, and I started to compare my body to other dancers' bodies, those tall, lean bodies. My stomach was a sore issue, then my thighs. I could never have a flat enough stomach.

C: What did you do about these thoughts and feelings?

D: Well, I decided that perhaps a diet was in order, so I cut back drastically on my food intake. I stopped eating breakfast and lunch completely. I was unable to avoid having dinner with my family, so I had to eat at that time in order to keep from arousing suspicion in my parents.

C: Was there a change in your eating habits after you moved with your family to a new town? I know that you were angry over having to leave your friends behind, and you were now an eighth grader.

D: I just added new tricks to my dieting. I still refused to eat any breakfast or lunch, and I avoided dinners whenever possible, telling my parents that I ate dinner at a friend's house or that I had something to eat on the way home from school. I would make food, and then either throw it out in the outside garbage so my family wouldn't notice or feed it to the dogs. Sometimes I would put the food in my mouth and then spit it into a napkin, but I tried not to do this too often, because I was afraid of absorbing any of the calories.

C: Weren't your parents suspicious?

D: They said nothing to me at the time, but they told me years later that they had their suspicions of my problem.

C: How did the rest of your eighth grade go?

D: I had a growth spurt in the eighth grade that added a few more inches in height, which accentuated my thinness even more. However, I was into my "grunge-look phase"; all that large, oversized, and ill-fitting clothing let me be fashionable while using it to conceal my shrinking frame from my parents. The only one to notice was my health teacher who took me aside one day and told me about eating disorders, but I was convinced that the problem didn't apply to me.

C: So, things began to peak in the eighth grade. What was your high school experience like?

D: In high school, I met another girl my age who also thought that she was overweight, so we began to compare notes with each other about our food restricting, and we learned tricks to not eat. I would leave dirty knives and forks around the kitchen to suggest that I had eaten, and I'd pack a picnic lunch at home, only to throw it all in the dumpster, once away from my parents. Eventually two high school teachers approached me and talked to me about not eating lunch in the school cafeteria. I dreaded the cafeteria with the conflict between the smell of good food, and the desire not to eat anything. I only put food in my mouth if somebody was watching me, otherwise I just pushed the food around the plate.

C: When did you make your first visit to the hospital?

D: I was 15 years old and in the tenth grade. I passed out in school; I hadn't eaten in days. The hospital didn't admit me, though. I know now that it was because of some insurance issue, but I was convinced at that time that the hospital was telling me that I was not sick, that I didn't have an eating disorder. But I was still too weak to attend school, so I stayed home from school for two weeks.

C: Any other hospital visits?

D: Many more!! I had many more hospital visits and all sorts of other treatment program stays. I was in and out of them for the next few years.

C: And now, how are you?

D: My last stay in an eating disorders treatment program was when I was 23 years old. I knew that it was my last resort. I am in recovery now, but I will always struggle. For me, it was always an issue of control. I couldn't control my family's moving; I couldn't control my mother's dying; but I could control eating or not eating. I will never be happy with my body, but it doesn't control me anymore.

GUIDELINES FOR INTERVENING WITH EATING DISORDERS

One of Havighurst's (1972) developmental tasks of adolescence had to do with *accepting one's physique,* and it is precisely this task that many adolescents, particularly females, are hard pressed to do. The causes of eating disorders are varied, and it is the interplay among multiple factors than determines the course the disorder follows in individuals who suffer with it. Both internal and external factors share responsibility in the occurrence of the disorder.

One of the internal factors at play is the personality trait of perfectionism, which is central to eating disorders. Individuals with the disorder also tend to be over achievers, popular, and academically successful (Weis, 2008). Rigidity and need for control also mark individuals with eating disorders; they are eager to please and are overly concerned with their appearance and the way they present themselves to others. Low self-esteem also haunts them (Tozzi, Thornton, Klump, Fichter, Halmi, & Kaplan, 2005).

Other external/environmental factors that play a causative role in the disorder are the media-driven ideal of the perfect body, and the glorification of a standard of beauty that is more the ideal than the real. In particular, the demands on young girls to lose weight and to be attractive are powerful. Seligman (1998) referred to *the pursuit of thinness* in describing these contemporary pressures on young women, a notion echoed by other researchers. Smolak (2005) addresses the *idealization of thinness* that contributes to body dissatisfaction and, as a result, various dietary restrictions to get to the ideal body size and shape. Other researchers also point to the influence on the development of eating disorders as being perceived by one's parents as overweight in middle childhood (Allen, Byrne, Oddy, Schmidt, & Crosby, 2014).

Individuals with anorexia in particular are convinced that they must lose weight. Their sense of body distortion leads them to overestimate their weight and the size of their bodies. Denial about the disorder keeps them from addressing this health-threatening condition. What causes them psychological and emotional distress is not the emaciated appearance of their bodies, but rather the chronic fear that they will continue to remain overweight.

Danielle's case illustrates much of what is true for others with the disorder: denial that her extreme weight loss was a problem, an inability to view one's frame as far too thin, and a sense of perfectionism and a need for control. She illustrated these issues in her description of one of her six-week hospitalizations. She spent most of this time being fed through a feeding tube, a practice which accounted for a four-pound weight gain in the first week. Her only thought, however, was that the staff was trying to make her fat.

ADOLESCENT SUICIDE

Even though deaths by suicide are relatively rare, suicidal thoughts and other related behaviors are much more common (Lieberman, Poland, & Cassel, 2008). The Center for Disease Control (CDC, 2016) claimed that suicide was the second leading cause of death among 10- to 24-year-olds. Despite the best guess at the prevalence of suicide, it is important to note that the number of reported suicides may be an underestimate of the actual number (Berman, Jobes, & Silverman, 2006). The American Foundation for Suicide Prevention (2016) claimed that, for every successful suicide, there are approximately 25 suicide attempts. Clouding the issue are those single-victim deaths in automobile accidents and in other tragic events in which the cause of death could indeed be either accidental or purposeful, yet which lack compelling enough evidence to classify them as suicides.

The CDC reported that there are 100 to 200 suicide attempts for every completed suicide among young adults ages 15 to 24. According to the CDC, 32,000 people kill themselves each year, the equivalent of 89 per day or one every 16 minutes, and another 425,000 people are treated in hospital emergency rooms for self-inflicted injuries each year. Males between the ages of 15 to 19 take their own lives at more than four times the rate of females, yet the latter group attempt suicide more frequently than males (Berman et al, 2006).

In its survey of American high school youth, the YRBSS (CDC, 2015) reported some staggering statistics regarding the prevalence of those feelings and suicidal behaviors which often are precursors to a completed suicide. In the 12 months preceding the survey, adolescents reported the following:

- 29.9% felt sad or hopeless almost every day for two weeks or more that they stopped doing some usual activities (39.8% of females made this report vs 20.3% of males)

- 17.7% had seriously considered attempting suicide (23.4% of females, 12.2% of males)

- 14.6% made a plan about how they would attempt suicide (19.4% of females, 9.8% of males)

- 8.6% actually attempted suicide one or more times (11.6% of females, 5.5% of males)

- 2.8% made a suicide attempt resulting in an injury, poisoning, or overdose that had to be treated by a doctor or nurse (3.7% of females, 1.9% of males)

Common risk factors for suicide include symptoms of depression, such as feelings of sadness, helplessness, and hopelessness (Brock, Sandoval, & Hart, 2006). The CDC also included among its list of risk factors:

- previous suicide attempts
- history of mental illness
- alcohol or drug abuse
- family history of suicide or violence
- physical illness
- feeling alone, depressed
- feelings of helplessness and hopelessness

Although situational factors, such as physical abuse, legal troubles, the breakup with a boyfriend or girlfriend, academic failure, bullying or victimization, the death of someone significant, and knowing someone who died by suicide may serve as precipitants to suicidal behavior, they only lead to suicide among those individuals who also satisfy a host of other risk factors as well.

Case Presentation: Georgia, A Threatened Suicide

Georgia was a 17-year-old high school junior. Although not an outgoing, gregarious individual, she maintained a small group of friends who tended to look out for each other. She was an average student who spoke of attending college, even though she hadn't made any overtures regarding readying applications or visiting campuses of preferred colleges. Her friends talked of going away to school and spoke in generalities about what they could see themselves doing as a career, but Georgia was always non-committal. Her group tended to spend weekends together, seeing movies or attending parties hosted by other high school friends. No one knew much about Georgia's family, just that her mother had passed away a year earlier after a bout with stomach cancer. She and her mother had been very close.

One day two of her friends dropped in to see the school counselor at the high school, asking to see her right away because of an "emergency." The counselor sat down with the two who both expressed concern over Georgia. They told her that Georgia had been acting "standoffish" lately, preferring not to accompany the rest of the group on their weekend activities. According to them, she also started to look sloppier than usual in her attire, something out of character for someone who always took great care with her appearance. Her friends went on to describe a phone call they each had received the night before from Georgia in which she told them that she wanted them to have several of her CDs of her favorite rock group. She also told them that she might not be around much longer, thus her wish for them to have the CDs. Putting all these signs together and having recently had a suicide awareness program in their health class, they rushed to see the counselor for assistance.

Intervention

Friends: Before you do anything with what we told you, please don't tell anybody else. Georgia would get real mad at us. We just wanted to find out from you what we should do.

Counselor: First of all, I am ethically bound to maintain confidentiality in my interactions with my clients. However, I also am ethically bound to break that confidence in the event that I am told that someone intends to hurt themselves or somebody else, or if someone is hurting them. Then I am obligated to tell those who are in a position to provide help and protection in order to ensure the safety of the individual. That is the case here with your friend, Georgia. You have done the right thing to come to me with your concerns. I agree with you that these concerns are real ones.

F: But you're not going to tell her that we were the ones who told you, are you? She really will be mad at us!

C: No, I won't tell her who alerted me to this situation, but my experience tells me that when I speak with her, she will know who gave me her name. But wouldn't you rather have a friend who is alive to yell at you rather than one whose obituary you read about in tomorrow's newspaper?

F: O.K. You're right.

As soon as the students left her office, the counselor went to Georgia's classroom and asked her to accompany her to her office.

C: Hello, Georgia. I haven't seen you in a while since the semester began. I saw that you were working in groups in class just now. What was it you were working on?

G: (Looking down at the floor as she spoke in a low monotone.) It was social studies class, and we were working on analyzing the major causes of the civil war.

C: It sounds like you weren't really into it.

G: It was boring and stupid. The other three people in the group talked too much. I just didn't want to be there. It's just stupid; the civil war is over, anyway, so why go over it again?

C: I'm concerned that you seem pretty down right now. In fact, that's the reason I wanted to see you today. Some of your friends came to see me earlier today to tell me that they were very worried about you.

G: (Interrupting angrily) I know, it was (names both students)! I told them not to tell anybody! I know that I shouldn't have come to school today!

C: I know that you are angry with them; they were afraid that you might be angry with them for coming to me, but what they did was out of a great concern for you. They like you and value your friendship. They did the right thing by coming to me. That's why I wanted to see you, because what they told me concerned me a great deal. You are certainly not in any trouble, but you do seem down.

G: (No acknowledgement, only silence and staring at the floor.)

C: Tell me Georgia, have you thought about killing yourself?

G: (Mumbling) Yeah.

C: About how many times have you thought about it?

G: I don't know, a bunch, maybe 10 to 12 times.

C: O.K., so you really have been feeling pretty down for a while now, am I right? Tell me the last time you thought about it.

G: I guess I've been thinking about it this week.

C: Has anything been going on in your life recently that might have something to do with your thoughts of suicide?

G: I don't know, since my mother died, I've been kinda lonely. And all this talk of going away to college (her voice trails off).

C: And going away to college is not something that appeals to you at this time?

G: Not now. I just wish that everybody else would just let everyone do what they want to do.

C: Let's go back again to what you told me before, that you were thinking about killing yourself. You said that you have been thinking about it as recently as this past week. How did you plan to do it?

G: Well, there are lots of pills and things in my bathroom medicine cabinet. My dad is on antidepressants, and there are different kinds of pills left over from the time when my mother got cancer. My father doesn't do much to throw the old pills away, so I figured that I could take a whole bunch of them and do the job.

C: Why have you decided not to take these pills up until now? I mean, you knew how to get them, right?

G: Of course, I know where to get them.

C: I am glad that you did nothing about those pills and that you told your friends instead. What stopped you from taking them?

G: Well, I did try taking a bunch of the pills a few weeks ago, but all it did was put me to sleep; I woke up real groggy and dizzy, but everyone thought that it was because I was hung over from the night before. No one knew that I took them to try to kill myself. I thought about it again, but then I thought that my dad would be so upset, first with my mom dying, and then me! I couldn't bear to see him that upset again.

C: So, it sounds as if you have some mixed feelings here, wanting to die, yet not wanting to because of what it would do to your father, right?

G: I guess so.

C: Have you thought about taking these pills again? Or doing something else to kill yourself?

G: I don't know any more, but maybe.

C: Georgia, I am still concerned about you. Since I want to make sure that you are safe, even after you leave here, I have to call your father. I am concerned that, once you are home, you may have those thoughts again. I want your father to take you to see some other counselors who will decide if you need to talk to someone else about these feelings of yours.

G: Whatever.

Case Conceptualization/Crisis Resolution

The counselor considered Georgia to be at a high risk for another suicide attempt. She had already made a previous attempt, she had access to the methods she needed to kill herself, and she sent out clear indicators that she had intentions to complete the act. That is, she essentially said "good-bye" to her friends and had sent out other signals (giving away her favorite CDs) that she would not see them much longer. Her friends also were able to describe changes in her behavior, and her admitted sense of loneliness on the death of her mother also was alarming to the counselor. Another major life transition, the possibility of going away to college or of her friends all leaving her for college, was a frightening prospect for her. Georgia also did not convince the counselor that she would not make another attempt on her life, making it clear that she could do so at any time.

Whether a high risk or not, the counselor explained to Georgia that she was obligated to call her father in order to notify him of the danger and to have him take her to the local emergency psychiatric screening unit. Although Georgia was not pleased when the counselor told her that she was going to call her father, she did not resist the notion, as if relieved. She requested to be allowed to go back to her next class while awaiting the arrival of her father at school, but the need for close supervision made the counselor deny this request. Instead, Georgia remained in the counselor's office, and the counselor also accompanied her on a visit to the women's room an hour later.

Although her father seemed somewhat resistant to leaving work early to come to school and pick up his daughter for a trip to the local crisis unit, he eventually agreed to do so when the counselor told him that, in his absence, she would be obligated to contact the local Child Protective Services unit to take her instead. When her father appeared in the high school, the counselor explained in detail her concerns and made sure that he understood the importance of making his home "suicide proof" by removing all medications in the medicine chest or in other places where Georgia might have access. He agreed to do so, and he signed an agreement with the counselor that he would bring Georgia to the unit and would follow up on its recommendations for additional help or treatment. The counselor promised to keep track of Georgia's progress and to develop a plan for her to return to school with the appropriate services.

It was important for the counselor to make a carefully considered intervention, once Georgia's friends brought their concerns to her attention. She was able to follow the **L-A-P-C** model and to *listen,* both to what her friends said and to what Georgia had to say, both verbally and nonverbally, to her questions. She remained nonjudgmental, used active listening, and was able to *assess* the fact that she was at a high risk for another suicide attempt. The *plan* was to contact the father, have her screened by the local crisis unit, and to create a follow-up system when Georgia returned to school. Although Georgia appeared quite depressed and lethargic and not willing to *commit* to the plan, her father did so. Georgia's sense of relief that her suicidal thoughts were finally addressed was palpable.

GUIDELINES FOR DEALING WITH A SUICIDAL ADOLESCENT

Many of these warning signs were present in Georgia's case: a previous attempt, making final arrangements, having access to the means of suicide, the loss of a parent, the specter of a major life transition (college), and depression. Those who were in a position to observe these signs, including her loss of interest in her previous social activities, were able to report their concerns to the appropriate person, Georgia's school counselor.

Whenever in doubt about whether or not a seemingly depressed adolescent poses a suicide risk, the best thing to do is to ask them directly if they have thoughts of hurting or killing themselves. Of course, if they answer in the affirmative, the adult who posed the question must be able to make the appropriate intervention or provide the right referral for help. Once identified, they must also be monitored closely until the proper help is provided. Not all depressed adolescents are suicidal, but if they satisfy many of the risk factors described above, the potential for suicidal behavior increases considerably.

Perhaps the best way to make sure that suicidal adolescents are identified and treated is to be proactive and preventive in nature. Providing education for those who come in contact regularly with adolescents regarding the warning signs of suicidal thoughts or behaviors is an important step. Teachers, parents, coaches, mentors, community groups, and even other adolescents can all benefit from some form of training in recognizing the warning signs of a depressed and potentially suicidal adolescent. Educating these individuals and groups about what to do and whom to tell about their concerns is of equal importance in this training.

One such program, which is school-based is *Signs of Suicide,* designed for middle and high school students. It involves training in the warning signs of suicide in addition to a depression screening for the individuals involved. Parents, school staff, and students themselves go through this training program and are able to contribute to the prevention of adolescent suicide by learning the warning signs and the appropriate means of intervention (Lieberman, Poland, & Cassel, 2008).

ADOLESCENTS AND NON-SUICIDAL SELF-INJURY (NSSI): AN OVERVIEW

It is difficult to address the issue of adolescent suicidal behavior without also addressing one of the least understood behaviors of adolescence that appears to be increasing at an alarming rate and which is eliciting increased attention and concern around the world: non-suicidal self-injurious behaviors (NSSI) (Muehlenkamp, Claes, Havertape, & Plener, 2012). It is defined as: "the deliberate, self-inflicted destruction of body tissue without suicidal intent and for purposes not socially sanctioned, includes behaviors such as cutting, burning, biting, and scratching skin" (p. 2).

It is especially prevalent during adolescence, with estimates of NSSI occurrence as high as 18% among the general population (Muehlenkamp et al., 2012), with an increase to 40% in a clinical population (Swannell, Martin, Page, Hasking, & St. John, 2014). Those who engage in this behavior also are known as "cutters," those individuals who engage in direct, intentional, repetitive behavior which results in mild to moderate physical injury (McVey-Noble, Khemlani-Patel, & Neziroglu, 2006).

Non-suicidal self-injurious behaviors (NSSI) need further study (Zetterqvist, 2015), so the *DSM-5* has only included it among its "Conditions for Further Study." Its proposed criteria include:

- five or more days within the last year of intentional self-inflicted damage to the surface of one's body likely to induce bleeding, bruising, or pain by cutting, burning, stabbing, hitting, or excessive rubbing; the expectation is that the injury will lead to only minor or moderate physical harm (i.e., there is no suicidal intent);

- the expectations of the injury are to obtain relief from a negative feeling or emotional state, to resolve an interpersonal difficulty, or to induce a positive feeling state; and

- the intent of the self-injury is associated with interpersonal difficulties or other negative feeling states (depression, anxiety, etc.) prior to the act, a preoccupation with the self-injury which is difficult to control, or thinking about self-injury frequently, even when it is not acted on.

People who engage in NSSI use knives, razors, the metal scraper from the plastic pencil sharpener, thumb tacks, or any other sharp instruments to make slices in their skin, usually in some little noticed body part, like the inner thighs, the abdomen, or the inside of their upper arms (Zila & Kiselica, 2001), all the areas that can be concealed easily from others. However, their attempts at keeping these marks secret don't always escape the watchful eye of gym teachers, parents, or sports coaches. They tend to engage in these cutting behaviors secretively; they may also do so in the school bathrooms, locker rooms, or other isolated and secluded areas. Although cutting is the most common form of self-injury, other self-injurious behaviors are scratching, burning oneself, hitting oneself (head against the wall), picking at old wounds, and hair pulling (trichotillomania) (Winkler, 2003).

Of the approximately 150,000 to 360,000 adolescents around the country, more than 70% of whom are female, the estimates are that for every 100,000 adolescents, approximately 750 to 1,800 of them will engage in self-injurious behaviors (Suyemoto & Kountz, 2000). Almost all of those who engage in self injurious behaviors (90%) begin in adolescence (Bowman & Randall, 2004). Other researchers also think that 13% of adolescents engage in these practices (Ross & Heath, 2002), although it is difficult to determine the actual number due to the secrecy attached to these behaviors.

There is a common misconception that adolescents who engage in self-injurious behavior like cutting are doing so in a conscious attempt to commit suicide. In fact, there appears to be no conscious suicidal intent on the part of the cutter; it is as if they are cutting themselves so that they do not kill themselves. Even the wounds they inflict on themselves are relatively superficial and not life-threatening, for example like slitting the wrists in a true suicide attempt. It is primarily the skin that is damaged, and not the veins, arteries, or ligaments, so the long-term harm is limited to scarring (Levenkron, 1998).

They may be engaging in self-injurious behavior like cutting, since self-mutilation may actually create a sense of relief, calm, and satisfaction due to the release of the brain's natural antidepressants, the endorphins. For this reason, it is considered an impulse disorder not unlike eating disorders, shoplifting, and substance abuse. The behavior is controlling them; they are not controlling the behavior.

Although not a sign of a suicidal attempt, adolescents who self-injure are troubled and are crying out for help, and their actions are not to be taken lightly. It is as if they are putting into practice what they cannot put into words; they convert their emotional pain that they cannot express into physical pain, a form of self-punishment in order to help them gain greater control over their own emotions (Lieberman, 2004). Other functions of self-injury (Kress, Gibson, & Reynolds, 2004) include:

- Feeling concrete pain when psychic pain is too overwhelming

- Reducing numbness and promoting a sense of being real

- Keeping traumatic memories from intruding

- Modulating affect

- Receiving support and caring from others

- Discharging anger, anxiety, despair, or disappointment

- Self-punishing

- Gaining a sense of control

Another phenomenon regarding self-injury is the issue of contagion, the imitation of the behavior of others in the environment. That is, having a friend or relative who self-injures raises the likelihood of the same imitative behavior in another adolescent. Such behaviors often spread through peer groups, grade levels, and campus clubs, serving as a "rite of togetherness" to consolidate certain friendships and romances (Froeschle & Moyer, 2004). Nevertheless, many students who self-injure will invariably be assessed at low risk for suicide and will not demonstrate any overt emotional disturbance.

Case Presentation: A Case of Self-Injury/Cutting

Jessica was a cheerleader for her local high school basketball team. She was active in the squad as well as in other school activities. Several of her teachers thought that she ran with the wrong crowd, but she was well liked by the staff, nevertheless. She was not a very talkative individual, although her grades were acceptable. She tended to keep to herself except for the cheerleading activity which she appeared to enjoy along with her friends who also were on the squad with her. They were a cohesive group of adolescents, both on and off the court.

One day the cheerleader coach called Jessica aside to tell her of her concerns. During several of the practices, she had noticed numerous cuts along Jessica's stomach as she jumped high in a routine with a short waist-length jersey that easily leaped up, exposing her abdomen. Since the faculty had recently had an in-service workshop on the issue of cutting, the coach was immediately suspicious, thus her explanation to Jessica for pulling her aside. Even though Jessica told her that it was "nothing," that all the girls were doing it, the coach nevertheless brought her concerns to the school psychologist and to Jessica's parents. Her parents were vaguely familiar with the phenomenon of cutting and decided to seek out a therapist in the community.

Intervention

Counselor: Jessica, how are you feeling? You know that you are here because your parents had concerns about you.

Jessica: I know, I know, but this is stupid! My coach told them that I had cut myself, but it's not a big deal. She should mind her own business, anyway; it's none of her business what I do with my body.

C: Jessica, you are not in trouble here. I know other young women like you who started cutting themselves. I know that many of them were hurting and came here for help.

J: What do you mean, help?

C: Well, they were hurting for different kinds of reasons. They came for help. I am wondering if you are hurting or upset about something also. If I can't help, I can find someone else for you to talk to.

J: I just feel so weird being here for this, talking to you about some cuts on my stomach. I mean, it's embarrassing!

C: There is nothing to be ashamed of here. Sometimes hurting yourself is the best way to deal with your feelings. And sometimes hurting oneself is a sign of other things. Tell me, have you ever had thoughts of suicide?

J: (Immediately) No! That's got nothing to do with my cutting.

C: So, you haven't had those thoughts?

J: No! I definitely don't want to die. I just get so stressed out sometimes, with all the practices and the school work, and all the stuff going on at home, that I just need a relief, so I started slicing my stomach one night when I was shaving my legs. In a weird way, it actually felt good. I don't know what it is, but it took a lot of my stress away.

C: Others have also said that cutting helps them deal with their stress, but there also are other ways of dealing with those things without having to hurt yourself.

J: What kinds of ways?

Crisis Conceptualization/Crisis Resolution

Like many individuals who self-injure, Jessica did not appear to be at risk for any suicidal intent. What she did highlight, however, was her shame and embarrassment over being "caught" for what she had done. What also was important, though, was that the counselor did not react in a directive judgmental way, but rather reassured her that there was nothing to be ashamed of and that she knew of many other adolescents who engaged in the same behavior.

In this very early stage of the counseling relationship, the counselor used active listening in an attempt to engage her in a therapeutic relationship. She used these techniques to *listen* to her thoughts and feelings about the cutting; she used these observations to *assess* her feeling state and her level of potential suicidality; and her *plan* was to either refer Jessica to another helping professional or to present to her other ways of coping with her life stresses. Finally, the counselor's last step would be to get Jessica to *commit* to working on this very plan.

GUIDELINES FOR TREATING AN ADOLESCENT FOR SELF-INJURY

Despite what, to most people, is the unsettling practice of purposefully cutting oneself, it is important to avoid alienating the adolescent by reacting with shock, disgust, or disbelief. Rather, building trust is critical, since the cutter is someone in pain and in need of a nonjudgmental professional.

As can be seen in the case above, once a cutter has been identified and referred to the appropriate professional, an assessment should be made regarding whether or not they are safe. Many of those who self-injure are not suicidal, but it should be ruled out by a trained professional. This assessment would determine whether or not the individual was safe or in need of additional emergency services. Whether suicidal or not, those who self-injure are looking for a way to cope with their psychic pain. For Jessica, this pain was related to the many stressors in her life for which cutting provided considerable relief. Acknowledging not only these feelings, but also the use of cutting as a means of coping with them is reassuring and soothing for them. Providing her with more appropriate means of stress reduction and with better problem-solving and coping skills is the direction that therapeutic intervention would take.

AN IDENTITY CRISIS IN ADOLESCENCE

Erik Erikson was a developmental psychologist and psychoanalyst known for his theory on psychosocial development of human beings. He may be most famous for coining the phrase "identity crisis." He modified many of Freud's views on development of the individual, particularly those on adolescence. He de-emphasized Freud's notion of the strength of sexual and biological drives as primary forces in personality development. What he proposed instead was a *psychosocial* rather than a *psychosexual* theory of development, placing greater emphasis on social and cultural influences on development.

Stage five of his eight-stage theory, *identity versus role confusion,* is the most germane to a discussion of adolescent development. He believed that acquiring a strong identity was dependent on the consistent and positive recognition of the child's achievements throughout the earlier stages. As the individual develops, interactions with peers, with other significant adults outside the family, and with the community in general help to shape the adolescent's identity.

The adolescent "tries on" different identities, just as one might try on a suit of clothes to see how it fits before deciding to purchase the right one. The feedback received from these other sources influences the adoption of the one true identity that just seems to "fit." Thus, Erikson explained, the adolescent life stage is filled with experimentation and exploration as a means toward the development of a firm identity. To master the challenge posed by the question, "Who am I?" is the goal of this developmental stage.

Case Presentation: David, A Case of Identity

David, a 17-year-old high school junior, always appeared to be wandering through his adolescence searching for an identity that fit him just right. Like any other adolescent who was trying on different identities in an attempt to find the most comfortable one, David had a hard time finding the right "fit."

From all accounts, his middle school years, the early stage of his adolescence, was marked by a delayed onset of puberty, and his slightly overweight body type was characterized by some of his peers as "girly," a reference to his soft, chubby appearance and breasts considered oversized for boys of his age group. His teachers reported at the time that he never seemed to have settled into a regular group of friends, preferring instead to wander from group to group, as if looking for one which would accept him. He also spent many an afternoon after the school day had ended hanging around with any one of several teachers whom he professed to like. Whereas other students his age were at home socializing with friends, David chose instead to spend this time with trusted adults.

Although David was a bright young man, his grades always hovered around the "C" range. A self-described avoider of homework and of out-of-classroom assignments, he was content with just getting by with his grades. By the time he entered high school, his teachers, almost to a person, began their descriptions of him with the statement, "He's so bright, but __." The latter part of this statement typically ended with observations of his lack of effort, his failure to complete important assignments, or some other achievement-related shortcoming. But never did teachers ever complain about his classroom behavior; David remained respectful of teachers and compliant with school rules, despite the fact that he completed little, if any, work. Although he cut classes from time to time and reported smoking marijuana with some regularity, his discipline record was unremarkable. Despite grades which kept him on the brink of academic failure and with the threat of being a five- or six-year high school student, he presented the outward demeanor of a satisfied, happy-go-lucky individual, always greeting passersby in the school corridors with a big smile.

A number of things happened for the better for David when he entered high school, the most important of which was his discovery of, and acceptance by, a new group of friends. This group of approximately ten students in all was just like David: disenfranchised from the typical school experience, particularly its emphasis on academic achievement and largely ignored by other more "mainstream" social groups. Nevertheless, David felt very much at home with this newfound group of friends, regardless of the identity it provided for him. His membership in this "fringe" group helped him define himself by giving him an identity that, for him, seemed to "fit." Researchers may refer to such a group as part of a resistance culture (Woolfolk, 2007), but David would describe it as being home among friends.

David's identifiable "trademark" was a full-length, trench coat-like black leather duster that he wore consistently every day, regardless of the weather; days of low temperatures and days of high humidity did not dissuade David from this attire. The trench coat became his "calling card;" the one thing that set him apart from others, even the other members of his own social group. Whereas some adolescents sport purple hair and others, multiple facial piercings to make a statement of their identity, David chose this coat as his statement.

The trench coat, however, also served another purpose for David. Still a slightly overweight chubby individual, there was an air of body-consciousness to David, an explanation of his cutting of his gym class more often than other classes and of his refusal to change for gym on those days when he did attend. Exposing his body to others in the locker room was something he preferred not to do at all costs. Therefore, his trench coat allowed him to cover his body and to keep it from the judgmental eyes of fellow students.

Then, on April 20, 1999, two students, Eric Harris and Dylan Klebold, entered the halls of Columbine High School in Colorado armed with several guns, killed 12 fellow students and a teacher, wounded 24 others, and then committed suicide. The shooters had been members of a fringe group not unlike David's group, a counterculture, resistance culture group which had been labeled informally as the Trenchcoat Mafia because of the black leather dusters worn by the shooters. Like David's group, the Columbine group had banded together for much the same reason: to form a haven for those not accepted by the mainstream students. The Trenchcoat Mafia had been in existence long before the shooters had joined it, and none of the other members were implicated in the shootings.

In a knee-jerk reaction to the media-saturated images of Harris and Klebold dressed in their trench coats before the killings, many school districts, including David's, banned the wearing of trench coats in school, fearing that those who wore them could easily conceal firearms and bring them into school. And so it was with David: within days of the news of the Columbine killings, the school principal called David into his office, the lone wearer of a trench coat in his school, and told him to remove it. David reluctantly complied and then found his way to the school psychologist's office; as well as he knew David, the psychologist also had never seen him without him wearing his trademark trench coat.

Intervention

David:	(Pushing open the door to the office with such force that the psychologist had never before seen in him) I can't believe it, I'm gonna kill him!
Psychologist:	I've never seen you angry like this before. Let's sit down together so that you can tell me about it.
D:	It's Clement (the principal)! He says I can't wear my coat!
P:	You can't wear your coat?
D:	Yeah, he says that it's a new rule because of what happened in Columbine. What does he think, that I'm going to go out there and shoot somebody? I haven't hurt anybody in my entire life!
P:	It sounds as if that coat is very important to you.
D:	Yeah, I've been wearing it since middle school, and nobody told me I couldn't wear it until now!
P:	Is there anyone else in the high school, a friend of yours maybe, who also has been wearing a similar coat?
D:	None of my friends do, and I don't know of anyone else who might. But that doesn't really matter to me, anyway. I just want to wear my coat. I just feel too weird without it. Like I said, I've been wearing it since the seventh grade.
P:	Was there anything special about seventh grade that made you decide to start wearing it then?
D:	No, but that's when I started to feel funny, like not really fitting in. Lots of kids in the middle school had families with lots of money, and we didn't have that much. You could tell from the clothes that they wore. I just didn't fit in with that crowd.
P:	It sounds like middle school was a tough time for you.
D:	Well, it wasn't fun, that's for sure, all those smart kids and rich kids looking so cool and all. I was a pretty good student in sixth grade, though, getting mostly As and Bs. But when seventh grade started, I figured that I just didn't want to get into a competition for grades with all those other kids. They were all growing, and I was staying short, so I figured that there was no point in trying to be like them. I didn't want to cause any trouble or anything, I just wanted to do my own thing.
P:	Is that when you came up with the idea for the trench coat?
D:	Yeah, but really I saw it once in a store, and it reminded me of one of those Clint Eastwood movies, I don't know which one, but where he wore a coat like that. So, I thought it would be a cool thing to wear, and nobody else was wearing one like it. But then those two Columbine clowns had to wear one and ruin it for me!
P:	So, the coat has become your own unique trademark, is that right?
D:	Yeah, I guess you could say that. But I never caused any trouble at all in school. Ask my teachers, they're all cool. I know that I don't do a lot or work or anything, but I never cause trouble.
P:	It sounds like you're not doing work, even though you know you can, is as much a trademark for you as your coat is, is that right?
D:	(Smiling) I never thought of it like that.

P: O.K., so let's see. Why don't we figure out how you can present your case to the principal to get permission to wear your coat again. We can practice here how to talk to him about it in a non-confrontational way. You also may need some sort of a backup plan in the event that he refuses to grant you permission.

D: Like what? Like wearing something else instead?

P: Sounds reasonable to me.

D: I'll think about that when the time comes, but I don't want to deal with the whole thing until next week.

Case Conceptualization/Crisis Resolution

Unlike the other crisis case vignettes in this chapter, David's case does not suggest a danger to life or limb. Many adolescents struggle with issues of identity, and its importance as a normal developmental struggle for many individuals made it a fitting topic to address here.

David was quite agitated without his cherished trench coat. He vacillated between anger and tears; it wasn't necessarily the loss of his trench coat which bothered him, but rather all that it represented. To him, it was as if he were asked to stroll naked throughout the school building. His coat was his protection as well as his signature attire, which set him apart from others and contributed to his identity and to his sense of self-esteem. Without it, he was bereft of any comfortable sense of who he was.

David didn't attend school for the next couple of days, despite his professed willingness to talk to the school principal. When he returned, however, he sported another long, baggy jacket of some type which served the same purpose as his original trench coat. After some time had gone by after the Columbine news and after the psychologist had intervened for David with the school principal, the trench coat ban was lifted, and David was permitted to wear it again in school. Despite his struggle with his grades, he did manage to earn his diploma. However, most people lost track of David after he graduated. Did he continue to struggle in his search for an identity that fit? Or did his experiences to date provide him with more information about who he was and where he was going?

Like other adolescents who grapple with a version of Erikson's *identity crisis,* David found solace, however temporary, in the identity he had assumed and in the social group he found that accepted him. However, David still had a long way to go before he accomplished so many of the other developmental tasks enumerated by Havighurst. What can often be expected in this age group is a sense of exploration as adolescents try on one identity at a time before settling on one that feels right for them. Significant adults in their lives have to be accepting of those identities, provided that they are not self-destructive, and allow them to "test the waters" and to experiment with different possibilities.

The psychologist followed the L-A-P-C approach with David. He *listened* to the verbal and nonverbal material he offered in his reaction to the trench coat ban, *assessed* his emotional state and David's need for support and assistance in coping with this issue, came up with a *plan* to help him address it with the principal, and asked David to *commit* to the plan.

GUIDELINES FOR ADDRESSING ISSUES OF IDENTITY DEVELOPMENT

As Erikson (see above) suggested, the major crisis for the adolescent is the development of an identity, answering the question, "Who am I?" Toward this end, experimentation with different looks, different attitudes and beliefs, and different lifestyles is not only typical for the adolescent, but healthy as well. Without having this range of other experiences to choose from in order to establish one's own identity, adolescents would be hard pressed to come up with one of their own. Difficulties arise, of course, in the reactions of teachers and caregivers to these individual "experiments." Do they try to thwart the adolescent's attempts at trying on new roles and identities and make them "tow the mark," or do they allow them some "space" in their search for that identity that seems just right for them? A social context which allows and encourages this experimentation is necessary for the adolescent.

Having the time and opportunity to experiment with these different roles is actually a prelude to the development of an identity. Erikson's version of the *identity crisis* comes during the period which he referred to as the *psychosocial moratorium,* a time when the adolescent actually delays or takes a "time out" from other excessive responsibilities before making a commitment to a particular social or occupational role (i.e., identity). It is during this time that the aforementioned experimentation takes place. However, those who are unable to take this "time out" usually miss the opportunity to undertake the requisite steps to the formation of their own identity. The 16 year old who drops out of school after his father, the sole wage earner in the family, dies in order to go to work at the local factory is not afforded the luxury of a moratorium period, nor is the young adolescent girl who finds herself pregnant and the primary caregiver of a young baby.

In addition to the moratorium stage, Erikson and others (Marcia, 1994) discussed several other *identity statuses,* or outcomes, in the search for an identity:

Identity foreclosure—a very undesirable outcome, foreclosure is commitment to an identity without any exploration. Instead of considering a range of possibilities, this adolescent commits prematurely to a role usually determined by parents or other authority figures. For example, the adolescent who was predestined from childhood to follow in the family tradition and become a dentist just like his father and grandfather before him.

Identity diffusion—an incoherent sense of self without any firm direction; diffusion varies in intensity from adolescent to adolescent. A sense of self-consciousness and low self-esteem makes some adolescents unable to make a decision about their lives, whereas others may become openly rebellious and simply follow whatever crowd accepts them (Kroger, 2000). Is David in this stage?

Identity achievement—a healthy identity status; achievement means that a commitment is made after many options have been explored. However, since the moratorium stage is often lengthened for many adolescents by virtue of their remaining in school for undergraduate and graduate degrees, identity achievement may not be attained until several years after adolescence is over.

Negative identity—an indication that there are problems in identity development. After failing to receive positive recognition and support from significant adults in their lives, adolescents assume an identity that is completely contrary to their family values and unwritten codes of conduct. In other words, being known as a "rebel" is more desirable than being known as a "nobody." The son of the local police chief breaks the law repeatedly and is known to all local law enforcement officers, and the daughter of accomplished concert pianists drops out of school to pursue a career as a rock singer against the mandates of her parents. Is David in this stage?

Identity formation is a process which takes time to unfold. The number of times that college students change their major courses of study speaks to the changing nature of the process, and it suggests that identity formation may indeed begin in adolescence, but not end until after the college years are over.

RESOURCES FOR CHAPTER ENRICHMENT

Recommended Films

Thirteen: (2003) (stars Evan Rachel Wood, Holly Hunter, & Nikki Reed). Tracy is at the precipice of adolescence. A straight A student, she eventually befriends Evie, the most popular and beautiful girl in school, who leads her down the path of sex, drugs, and small-time crime. Tracy transforms herself and adopts a new identity, putting her at odds with all who knew her, especially her mother, her teachers, and her old friends.

The Breakfast Club: (1985) (stars Emilio Estevez, Judd Nelson, Molly Ringwald, & Ally Sheedy). Trapped in a day-long Saturday detention in their high school library, a group of five adolescents, strangers to each other at the start of the day, bond together in response to the villainous school principal. Each of the five students represents a social group within the school's "caste" system: the princess, the jock, the criminal, the brain, and the basket case. Commonalities among them emerge throughout the course of the day, however, as they discuss issues about their lives, their relationships, and their views of the adults in their lives.

The Virgin Suicides: (1999) (stars Kirsten Dunst, John Hartnett, & James Woods). The Lisbon family seemed ordinary enough. The father was a math teacher at the local high school, and the mother was a woman of great religious faith. Their five daughters ranged from 13 to 17 years of age. Their lives all changed, however, when the youngest daughter, Cecelia, falls into a deep depression and makes a suicide attempt. Family adjustments to the event and the advice of a psychiatrist are to no avail, as Cecelia eventually makes good on her decision to kill herself. The film depicts how family is changed in dramatic ways.

Dead Poets Society: (1989) (stars Robin Williams & Ethan Hawke). Depicts the suicide death of a young teenager who feels trapped by his father's expectations of him.

Suggested Activities

1. Seek out a mental health counselor in your local middle or high school; they might be a school psychologist, social worker, school counselor, or substance abuse counselor. Interview them about the prevalence of suicide attempts or completions they have experienced in their careers. Discuss what is involved in a suicide assessment. Inquire also about the themes involved in these cases (precipitating events, risk factors present, etc.).

2. Contact a school administrator with many years of experience in either a middle school or high school. Discuss with him or her their perceptions of how the adolescent has changed throughout the course of their careers. That is, in what ways have adolescents changed over the years? Are contemporary issues for them different from the issues of 10 years ago? 20 years ago?

3. Look up the 10 most popular movies among adolescents from each of the last few decades (1970s, 1980s, 1990s, 2000s). Compare and contrast them according to themes and main characters. Are there discernable differences among these different eras in the way adolescents, families, or school personnel are portrayed?

The School's Response to Crisis

DISCUSSION QUESTIONS

In your own experiences in school, what would you consider the most disruptive crisis-type event you remember? How did the school staff and administration cope with it? What was your own reaction to it?

Think back to those individuals with whom you attended school. Were there any whom you "profiled" in your own mind who might be the type who would instigate some level of violence within the school? What contributed to your impression of that individual?

Who were those groups in your school who were the likely ones to engage in bullying of others? Who were the likely ones to be the victims of bullies?

INTRODUCTION

This chapter provides a model of crisis intervention designed to address a variety of crises which can, and will continue to, have an impact on school communities. The focus is on elementary, middle, and high school students.

School crises come in many forms. They can be from internal or external sources, from the hands of individuals or from nature itself. Internal crisis types are varied: the student who brings firearms to school for the purpose of settling a score with a teacher, administrator, or other student; the random, unplanned shooting of rival gang members in the school corridors; the suicide of a popular student or staff member; or the untimely death of any member of the school community. External crisis types are equally as varied: motor vehicle accidents which claim the lives of students and staff, armed school intruders, industrial accidents, and natural weather disasters which devastate communities.

Nothing resonates more with the American public, however, than yet another evening news story of violence within its schools. School shootings, as rare as they are horrific, lead the list of such events which have shaken forever the image of schools as safe and secure environments in which students learn and flourish. Televised images of traumatized children being comforted by rescue workers and parents in the aftermath of such tragedies are encoded forever in the consciousness of the television-viewing public.

School shootings tend to lead to knee-jerk reactions by communities as they cry out for more enforceable security measures: zero tolerance policies (i.e.,: "just say no to bad behavior"); armed guards in schools; metal detectors; bullet-resistant doors, backpacks, and lunch boxes; and suggestions that teachers be permitted to carry weapons. However, despite the media coverage, which keeps graphic details of these events front and center for days and weeks at a time, they are far less frequent than one would ever guess. But first, it is necessary to examine the most unthinkable of these tragedies to understand how these stories could shake anyone's belief in the safety and security of school buildings.

No images have cast a greater pall on the American public than those of the events of December 14, 2012, when 20-year-old Adam Lanza, the morning after killing his own mother as she slept, shot his way into Sandy Hook Elementary School in Newtown, Connecticut, and systematically worked his way through a first-grade classroom, killing 20 six- and seven-year-old children in addition to six members of the school staff, including the principal and school psychologist. He then took his own life shortly before law enforcement arrived.

In addition to days of speculation in the press about the cause of Lanza's action (due to autism? Asperger's? personality disorder?), there also were widely publicized photos of the murdered children for all to see. And the debate about increasing school security measures had a new life.

The killing at Newtown overshadowed yet another school shooting of April 20, 1999, in Littleton, Colorado, when Eric Harris and Dylan Klebold, students at Columbine High School, entered the school with an arsenal of weapons and killed 12 students and one teacher before turning the guns on themselves. They also wounded another 23 of their fellow students in the rampage, making this event the nation's deadliest school shooting at that time.

However, despite the coverage of such high-profile events, schools have been considered one of the safest places for children (Poland & Gorin, 2002). Only a few of the approximately 60 million school children in this country who attend the nation's 119,000 schools will ever fall prey to a serious instance of violence in the schools they attend. It can be argued that the extensive media coverage of such incidents of school violence has significantly exacerbated fears over school violence, suggesting a probability of harm that is out of proportion to the reality of harm for the typical student (Reddy, Borum, Berglund, Vossekuil, Fein, & Modzeleski, 2001).

Stephen Brock (2015), president of the National Association of School Psychologists (NASP), also reported that such high-profile coverage has "led many of us to believe that schools are horribly flawed, fatally violent institutions, and that the chances of a young person being killed in school are great." "In fact," he added, "schools are objectively the least likely place for young people ages 5 to 18 years to be killed" (p. 1). Drawing on data from the National Center for Education Statistics and the U.S. Department of Education, Brock concluded that the odds of a 5- to 18-year-old being killed at his or her school were 1 in 4.5 million, whereas the odds of a same-age child or adolescent being killed in a motor vehicle accident were only 1 in 20,000.

Others (Brooks, Schiraldi, & Ziedenberg, 2000) also reported that youth were over 50 times more likely to be murdered away from school and almost 150 times more likely to commit suicide when they were away from school than at school. Even immediately after the Columbine shooting, it was argued that the odds that a child would die in school from homicide or suicide were close to one in 2.5 million. Students simply are safer at school than they are away from school (DeVoe, Peter, Noonan, Snyder, & Baum, 2005).

ACTIVE SHOOTER INCIDENTS: RESULTS FROM THE FBI AND THE SECRET SERVICE

The FBI's "A Study of Active Shooter Incidents in the United States between 2000 and 2013" (Blair & Schweit, 2014) examined 160 shooting incidents that occurred in the United States. However, the locations of these shootings were varied, from commerce settings to open spaces, and even houses of worship. The data discussed in this chapter includes just those findings of shootings in pre-K to grade 12 school settings, and refers to 27 of the 160 incidents, or 16.9% of the total.

A striking statistic is that exactly 50% of the 52 individuals killed in a school setting during the period of this study were from the Newtown shooting alone; 59 individuals were wounded as well in those 27 incidents. Other schools with multiple fatalities included Santana High School (CA); Ricori High School (MN); Red Lake (MN); West Nickel Mine (PA); and Chardon High School (OH). Most of these incidents took place in a high school (14), followed by middle school (6), elementary (4), and pre-K to grade 12 school (1).

Here are the FBI findings:

- There was no significant increase in incidents between the time periods 2000 to 2006 (13) and 2007 to 2013 (12), unlike other environments where there was a dramatic increase in incidents;

- In most middle school and high school incidents, the shooter was a student at the school: 12 of the 14 high school shooters and 5 of the 6 middle school shooters (Note: the Newtown shooting technically cannot be categorized as a school shooting, since Lanza was an intruder, and not a student in the school.);

- At the elementary level, incidents increased from one to three across those same time periods; those shooters were all adult males, ages 26, 48, and 20; that type of violence perpetrated by adults is virtually impossible to anticipate or prevent;

- In 64% of the school incidents, either citizens or law enforcement resolved the incident; citizens included unarmed teachers, administrators, other students, counselors, coaches, or other school employees; and

- The percentage of youth homicides occurring at school is less than 1% of the total number of youth homicides.

In 2002, the United States Secret Service and the United States Department of Education issued the results of a joint study, the Safe School Initiative (SSI), a look at school shootings and other school-based attacks which took place between 1974 and 2000. The study focused on what the agencies defined as "targeted school violence," those incidents of violence where an attacker selected a particular target (i.e., fellow student(s), teacher, administrator, etc.) prior to the violent attack; in fact, in over half the incidents, the shooter had targeted at least one school administrator, faculty member, or staff member. Those other random, unplanned, and impulsive shooting episodes in the schools were not included in the SSI. Although there have been over 20 school shootings since the period included in the SSI, the report examined a total of 37 incidents of targeted violence involving 41 student attackers. The purpose of the study was to identify those aspects of school shooters and shootings which might be identifiable before other shootings occur, thereby preventing additional ones.

In addition to an exhaustive review of records from multiple sources, the SSI investigators also interviewed 10 of these school shooters. The study arrived at 10 key findings:

- *Incidents at school are rarely sudden, impulsive acts.* More than half of the shooters developed the idea to harm the victim(s) at least two weeks prior to the attack; more than half planned the actual attacks at least two days before they struck. Most shooters had revenge as a motive, and many communicated their grievances to others prior to the attack. (Note: the great exception to this finding was the Columbine attack which the shooters had planned for over a year.)

- *Prior to most incidents, other people knew about the shooter's intent and/or actual plan.* In almost all of the cases studied in the SSI, the shooters told a peer (friend, schoolmate, or sibling) about the plan; they told more than one person in over half the incidents.

- One attacker told two friends about what he had planned and had arranged for several others to be in a safe place at the time of the shooting. When the fateful morning arrived, the word had spread to a total of 24 students, all of whom had assembled on the mezzanine over-looking the school lobby (the site announced beforehand by the shooter). One of the students who knew of the attack in advance even brought a camera to take pictures of the event.

- *Most attackers did not threaten their targets directly before the attacks.* Instead, worrisome behaviors or communications from the shooter were not heeded by others and did not prompt a response from the schools before the attacks.

- *There is no accurate "profile" of students who engage in targeted school violence.* Ages ranged from 11 to 21. They came from a variety of racial and ethnic backgrounds, from a variety of family situations, and from a wide range of academic performance (from excellent to failing). Some shooters were popular socially, some were social isolates; some had no documented behavioral problems, whereas some had a history of such. In short, there was no school-shooter "type" which the SSI uncovered. The only common thread throughout all shooters was simple: they were all male.

- *Most shooters engaged in some behavior prior to the incidents that caused others concern, usually adults.* These behaviors included expressed wishes to obtain a gun and themes of homicide or suicide in conversations or in classroom writing assignments.

- *Most attackers had problems coping with personal loss or failure.* Many (nearly three-fourths) also had threatened or attempted suicide.

- *Many attackers felt bullied, persecuted, or injured by others.* A number of them experienced bullying and harassment which was chronic and severe.

- *Most attackers had access to and had used handguns.* In almost two-thirds of the cases, the shooter got the gun used in the attack from his own home or that of a relative. The gun also had been a gift from the shooter's parents in some cases.

- *Other students were involved in the attack in some capacity.* Although most shooters acted alone, in almost half the cases others encouraged them to complete the act. One shooter was convinced by his friends that the only way for him to get other students to stop harassing him was to actually shoot kids at school in order to appear tough.

- *Despite the response of law enforcement to the attacks, most attacks were brief and were stopped by people other than law enforcement.* In over half the attacks, faculty or fellow students stopped the attack, or the attacker killed himself. Although the Columbine High School attack lasted over three hours, half of these incidents were over in 20 minutes or less, long before law enforcement arrived.

IMPLICATIONS FOR SCHOOLS

The school's response to threats to school safety require as much prevention as it does intervention. Schools must be clear that shutting the barn door after the proverbial horse gets out is too late; prevention first, then intervention to follow. The implications for school practice are discussed in accordance with the U.S. Department of Education's four phases of crisis management: prevention/mitigation, preparedness, response, and recovery.

Prevention/Mitigation

Establish physical and psychological safety procedures for schools. Physical safety issues include, but are not limited to:

- Insure building access only to those individuals who have an expressed/scheduled reason for being there: intercom voice message to be retrieved by school personnel who then allow the approved visitor to enter the building

- Designate only one entrance to the building, despite the availability of multiple doors throughout the building

- Plant shrubs, bushes far from the school building itself to prevent a possible assailant from hiding there

- Require personnel ID of all employees

- Understand and enforce school conduct code, a code which focuses on reinforcing and rewarding positive, prosocial behavior rather than relying primarily on punishing negative behaviors

- Develop and strengthen the school's anti-bullying policies

- Have staff available, visible, and able to supervise and monitor

- Allow data to inform additional measures as individual districts' needs dictate

Psychological safety issues include, but are not limited to:

- Collect data; reengineer whole school communities to promote positive and lasting behavior change

- Promote student resiliency (internal & external)

- Foster school bondedness/connectedness

- Enhance positive school climate

- Provide adequate school mental health services (psychologists, counselors, social workers)

- Reach out proactively to needy students and families in need of support

- Endorse evidence-based reading, academic instruction

- Support evidence-based humane discipline policies that promote prosocial behavior rather than just eliminating antisocial behavior

- Screen at-risk children; the earlier, the better

- Train all staff and students in suicide awareness education

The findings from the FBI and the SSI suggested strongly that some school attacks may be preventable; many people, particularly students themselves, are often the first ones to detect such threats, and play a critical role in prevention efforts. Additional preventive efforts that school districts can implement include:

- **Convincing students of their roles in the prevention of school violence.** It is silent "bystanders" who learn of threats, either directly or indirectly, yet alert no one in a position to investigate and to stop such events before they happen who are complicit in these attacks. Schools must be proactive in convincing students of the importance of their roles in violence prevention by bringing any suspicions or any other information gathered by their observations to staff members who can intervene. Perhaps redefining what is meant by "friendship" is also a goal, freeing students from the unwritten code of not "ratting out" a classmate to school authorities regarding suspicions of future violent behavior. Some of these attacks may indeed be preventable, provided that students take an active role in reporting their suspicions to the proper school authorities.

- **Eliminating barriers to effective student-staff communication.** Students are inclined to avail themselves of the opportunity to seek out a school staff member to report suspicious behavior on the part of a fellow schoolmate if a number of factors are in place, including:

o disseminating information to school children regarding policies and procedures for reporting such suspicions; this information should include:

o an emphasis on the importance of student vigilance in violence prevention

o the types of observed and unsettling behavioral and communication messages that should serve as "warning signs" worthy of reporting to a school official

o the manner in which this information should be reported, emphasizing ease of access to the proper authority

o the school resources available to all students outside the classroom, including school counselors, school psychologists, social workers, substance awareness counselors, and general school-based administration

o Instilling a sense of belongingness with school in order for all students to feel connected to a system which values their welfare; this sense of belonging benefits both bystanders and potential perpetrators of violence alike. Students with a sense of school bondedness will be inclined to report their suspicions, since they would anticipate a positive outcome for their efforts and would expect school personnel to be willing and able to assist a fellow student in pain. The troubled students in question also would view themselves as being part of a larger system which was concerned for their welfare.

• **Reaching out in a proactive way to students in distress or in some need for assistance.** Since most of the shooters in the SSI study exhibited some troubling behaviors prior to the attacks, it is incumbent on school districts to reach out to such individuals beforehand and provide help in the form of counseling or referrals to local mental health or social service agencies outside the school district. A student observed coping with a major loss or any other perceived failure warrants attention. Caution should be exercised, however, in not alienating or stigmatizing the student in question.

o Disaffected, disconnected students with no sense of bond with the school not only are more inclined to drop out, but also are more likely to engage in antisocial behavior. If these students were asked the question, "If you no longer returned to school, who besides your friends would notice that you were gone and miss you?" Their answers would reveal how connected to the school they felt. It is this type of student who requires some kind of outreach by school personnel.

• **Discussing with the school community, particularly with parent groups, the importance of gun safety and storage.** Since most attackers obtained the firearms they used in the attacks from their own homes or those of relatives, it is imperative that all community members understand the importance of making their weapons accessible only to those individuals who have the right to use them.

- **Establishing strong anti-bullying policies and programs in the schools.** Although bullying was not a factor in every case examined by the SSI, in a number of cases the shooters described their experiences of being bullied to the extent that it approached torment. Therefore, it is incumbent on schools to adopt a formal anti-bullying policy and accompanying procedures to ensure that no student is bullied in the schools and to empower other students, the bystanders to such events, to notify other staff members of any instances of bullying.

- **Create a warm, nurturing school climate.** A school district is truly proactive in its attempt to prevent school violence if it promotes positive behavior and communicates it clearly to all school community members; practices positive disciplinary approaches; and provides mental health services for students in distress. Also, critical to student success and to building a student's feeling of connectedness to the school is a strong bond between the school and home; working together, a good home-school connection can address the needs of the whole child. Finally, training staff in crisis procedures and in the identification of potential sources of violent acts is critical for true violence prevention.

Echoing these recommendations was the American Psychological Association's (APA) Zero Tolerance Task Force (2008) which investigated the effectiveness of zero tolerance policies in the schools as an approach to discipline enforcement. These policies, originally developed as a means of drug enforcement, are those that require a predetermined consequence applied to a behavior, regardless of its severity, mitigating circumstances, or situational context. The kindergarten boy who pointed a "finger gun" at a fellow kindergartner during recess and said, "Bang, bang, I shot you," for example, was suspended from school pending a psychiatric evaluation attesting to the fact that he was not a danger to anyone. Eight days later he was able to return to school.

In concluding that these zero tolerance (tolerance is the word) policies were ineffective and, in fact, did more harm than good, the APA Task Force echoed the importance of many of the prevention issues discussed above. It suggested that schools improve school climate, reconnect alienated youth to the school community, and evaluate threats of violence in the context of situational, developmental, and other factors.

Another suggestion from the joint SSI study was for school districts to develop a threat assessment protocol to be able to evaluate the risk of violence posed by someone who has communicated an intent to harm someone. Threat assessment considers the context and circumstances surrounding a threat in order to uncover any evidence that indicates the threat is likely to be carried out. It also includes interventions designed to manage and reduce the risk of violence. Unlike zero tolerance, threat assessment considers the context and meaning of a student's behavior, not just the behavior itself, and it is designed to determine the seriousness or danger of a student's behavior, prompting an appropriate response. Such a practice permits flexibility in how schools respond to threats, and it does not require the same severe consequence for all infractions. The understanding is that there is a difference between posing a threat and making a threat (posers may not threaten, and those who threaten may pose no harm).

Preparedness

Every school district should have a crisis policy developed by school and community representatives and an actual crisis plan that describes clearly the roles and responsibilities of each member of the plan's crisis team. The federal law No Child Left Behind required that

Each local board of education shall establish *plans, procedures, and mechanisms for responding to emergencies and crises.* The plan should consider defining *roles of district and building staff,* establishing parameters for *memorials,* coordinating with communications media, community agency networking, *crisis response teams,* training and development, guidelines for working with communications media, and establishing guidelines for *parent outreach.*

Part of a crisis policy really begins with evaluating those factors unique to the district, so a thorough needs and risk assessment should drive the contents of the policy. For example, a coastal community would have to address potential weather hazards, such as flooding and devastating nor'easters, unlike areas of the heartlands where tornados pose the likely threat instead. Urban districts would have to address issues related to gangs, a high unemployment and school dropout rate; still other areas affected by the downturn in the economy will have greater needs than more affluent areas. Once needs are established, the policy yields a plan with the school's stated intentions as to how a crisis of any kind will be addressed.

The U.S. Department of Homeland Security (DHS) developed the National Incident Management System (NIMS), which it required all federal agencies to adopt; part of the NIMS was the Incident Command System (ICS), basically a structure used across agencies to manage emergencies (DHS, 2004). In a school setting, the ICS is known as the school crisis team. The ICS Division of Labor includes the following functions, each with a team leader:

Incident command: the managers, typically the school principal or superintendent of schools who organizes and coordinates the crisis response

Planning and intelligence: the thinkers, those who coordinate the team and review status of the crisis response

Operations: the "doers," those who provide immediate services to those affected by a crisis, typically district psychologists, counselors, nurses, and social workers, although practitioners in the community may be called on if the needs of the school overwhelm the district resources

Logistics: the "getters," those who take care of communication and supplies

Finance: the "payers," those who track costs and finance requirements

The National Association of School Psychologists (NASP) has developed a school crisis prevention and intervention protocol known as PREPaRE (Prevent and Prepare, Reaffirm, Evaluate, Provide, and Respond, Examine) (Brock, Nickerson, Reeves, Jimerson, Lieberman, & Feinberg, 2009). It incorporates the crisis response model promoted by the Department of Homeland Security's NIMS, which provides an organizational structure and a common set of concepts and principles pertaining to crisis. Designed for school-based mental health

Table 6.1 Characteristics of Effective Crisis Team Members

Tolerance for ambiguity	Ability to remain focused
Calm, neutral demeanor	Tolerance of confusion and chaos
Tenacity	Ability to monitor their own stress
Optimism	Sensitivity to and familiarity with
Capacity for empathy	diverse cultures and people
Flexibility	Ability to function without seeing
Confidence	immediate results
Little need to rescue	Ability to "think on their feet"
Capacity for listening	Ability to view crisis-related problems
Awareness of trauma indicators	as challenges rather than as
Openness to individual crisis reactions	burdens

professionals, PREPaRE also follows the Department of Education's four phases of Emergency Response and Crisis Management (ERCM): prevention/mitigation, preparedness, response (crisis intervention), and recovery.

A school crisis team functions along ICS lines. Those who serve on school crisis teams typically are volunteers who, ideally, possess the following illustrated characteristics.

Once the ERCM team is established, training is provided, roles are distributed among team members, and all are now prepared to respond to a call regarding a crisis. Other preparedness issues have to do with enabling the crisis team and all school personnel and students alike to "practice" the school's response to particular crisis events. Some practice crisis drills include:

Lockdowns (intruder in school; the practice of holding children in class, locking the door, moving students out of sight, and having them remain quiet)

Evacuations (fire, bomb threat)

Reverse evacuations (the practice of having students outside the building return inside if intruder on school grounds, severe weather)

Duck-cover-hold positions (earthquakes, tornados)

Shelter-in-place (chemical/biological weapons, severe weather)

Other drills as the data and as school needs dictate

Even though the practice of lockdowns during a potential crisis has been the standard approach for almost two decades (NASP & NASRO, 2014), the U.S. Department of Education (2013) has relaxed the lockdown only procedure and allows for more decision-making among school staff. A new approach to threatening situations, acronym A.L.I.C.E. (Alert, Lockdown, Inform, Counter, Evacuate), considers lockdowns to be inadequate as a primary response to the crisis of a school intruder, insofar as it encourages individuals to be passive in the face of potential danger. A.L.I.C.E. trains school staff and others to consider lockdown as an opportunity for the group to consider its options, one of which is to counter (attack) an intruder, or to evacuate the building if they have been informed that the intruder is not in the immediate vicinity of their classroom.

Response

Once news of a tragic event becomes known, the crisis team leader (principal or superintendent) alerts the crisis team of the news and summons the members together to determine the level of response needed and the responsibilities of each member. However, it is important to remember:

- Individuals do not react the same way to the same violent event, whether distant or proximate (i.e., one size does not fit all);

- Most individuals exposed to a violent event recover on their own without help;

- Providing crisis intervention for children who don't need it does more harm than good; therefore, make sure you provide it only for those who need it.

In order to determine the extent of the problem, one of the first responsibilities of the crisis team is to conduct psychological triage, which the National Institute of Mental Health (NIMH) described as "The process of evaluating and sorting victims by immediacy of treatment needed and directing them to immediate or delayed treatment. The goal of triage is to do the greatest good for the greatest number of victims" (p. 27).

There are four factors in evaluating risk as part of triage:
Crisis exposure

- Physical proximity; Who were those individuals who were closest to the crisis event? Who was witness to it? Who only heard about it through a third person?

- The closer the individual was to the crisis event, the more traumatic the experience.

- Emotional proximity; Who were those students who had a close relationship to victims of the crisis, which increases the likelihood that they, too, would be traumatized? Family members? Best friends? Neighbors? Teammates? Classmates?

1. One of the first tasks of the crisis team is to make a determination about how many children were in close physical or emotional proximity to the impacted child. Networking with individual school staff members more familiar with such students is a good place to start to collect this information.

   Geselle, 16-year-old high school junior with an undiagnosed heart condition dropped dead in class one day during chorus rehearsal. However, a combination of factors kept the need for a large crisis response to a minimum. First, the chorus room was in a distant part of her large high school, far removed from the academic areas where most students were engaged, so physical proximity was not great, keeping her death far from their awareness. Second, she did not enjoy a very high social standing among her peers, so there was little emotional proximity with anyone beyond her very small circle of friends. As a result, the crisis team provided some outreach to just those friends and to several students who were with her in chorus when she passed away. Conversely, had she been a high profile, popular, and well-liked individual, more services would have been required.

In yet another situation, Sam, a six-year-old first grader new to his school at mid-year, was the victim of an accidental shooting at the hands of a young neighbor. The principal called together the crisis team to provide a response the next day. During triage, the school psychologist met with the teaching staff to determine who was most in need of some outreach services. However, as with the case of Geselle, Sam was new to the school, and neither well known nor well-liked by his peers, so his teacher was hard-pressed to come up with the names of any of his classmates who might be impacted by his death. The principal's observation that he was considered a friend by the students of varying grade levels who rode the same school bus with him each day resulted in the bus group becoming the primary target for intervention.

2. Understanding Individuals' Vulnerability Factors

The crisis team also must be able to identify those students whose ability to cope with tragedy, whether within their personal sphere or not, is seriously compromised by personal factors, such as the ones listed in the Table below.

3. Understanding threat perceptions

Subjective impressions can be more important than the actual crisis exposure, consequently triage also requires the crisis team to understand

- o What the crisis means to individual students

- o How students may identify with the event or with the victim

- o How adult reactions to crises are important influences on students' threat perceptions

Table 6.2   Factors Affecting Response to Tragedy

Internal Factors	External Factors
Avoidant coping style	Not living with nuclear family
Preexisting mental illness	Ineffective/uncaring parenting
Poor regulation of emotion	Family dysfunction
History of trauma	Poverty/financial stress
Poor self-efficacy	Social isolation/few friends
External locus of control	Lack of social support
Low self-esteem	Recent loss
Lower IQ	Caregivers not coping well

Larissa was an eight-year-old third grader who died suddenly one night at home due to a serious asthma attack. The principal summoned the school psychologist to arrange a crisis response the following day. Some of the outreach provided by the crisis team went to her classmates and to the fifth grade where her older brother had been enrolled. However, during triage, the school nurse sought out the crisis team to report that Joey, a second grader in the school, had been making repeated visits to her office with very vague somatic complaints. As the psychologist found out when he reached out to Joey, he, too, had asthma and was quite concerned that he also might meet the same fate as Larissa. Although he didn't know her personally, he identified with her condition and with her fate.

4. Understanding crisis reactions

   Most children have their own reservoir of resiliency to rely on to survive a crisis experience. Most lean on their own social support network of family, friends, and community, but the following list of more severe reactions (i.e., posttraumatic stress disorder effects), suggest the need for additional help beyond what the school-based personnel can offer:

   o Dissociation

   o Hyperarousal

   o Persistent re-experiencing of the event

   o Persistent avoidance of reminders

   o Significant depression

   o Psychotic symptoms

   o Suicidal/homicidal talk; abuse of self or others

Once the crisis team completes its triage work, its members are able to determine which children require services immediately, which ones can wait a few hours or days, and which ones might not require any outreach at all by the psychologists, counselors, and social workers from the team.

The following cases illustrate how crisis teams work. Teams consist of individuals who have been delegated certain carefully circumscribed tasks in an attempt to organize as much as possible the multitude of tasks which are necessary during and after a crisis. Although school shootings are exceptionally rare events that impact a small percentage of students, because of their horrific nature and high profile it seems an appropriate type of crisis to discuss first. Most crisis teams are more likely to encounter the crises situations that follow this example: the suicide of a student at school and the deaths of students in a motor vehicle accident.

Case Presentation: A Case Involving a School Shooting

Students at the local junior high overheard fourteen-year-old Victor complain bitterly about the perceived maltreatment he received at the hands of the school vice-principal, an out-of-school suspension for an assortment of transgressions. "Wait 'til they see what I can do!" he claimed aloud as he left the vice principal's office; a number of students heard him, according to later reports. Later that same day, Victor was overheard by a teacher decrying his science teacher and swearing to "get even" for writing him up for a discipline infraction that ultimately lead to his suspension.

Three days later, one day before his suspension was up, Victor arrived at school in the middle of the day, anticipating that the vice principal and his science teacher both would be in the school cafeteria providing supervision for approximately 100 students or so. He walked through the school corridors, much to the surprise of teachers and students alike since he was back in school one day prior to the end of his suspension. The heavy jacket he was wearing, considering the unseasonably warm day, also contributed to the suspiciousness of his appearance. Victor stormed into the cafeteria, pulled a handgun from his jacket pocket, and opened fire about 50 feet from the vice principal, sending students and other staff members screaming and scrambling for cover. When he finished firing, the vice principal lay dead and three students were wounded. When the gun emptied, staff members disarmed him and restrained him until the police arrived.

A postmortem analysis of the event yielded the information that the day before the shooting Victor told a small group of students that he knew where he could get "a real gun with bullets." Some of his friends reinforced his disdain for the vice principal.

Case Conceptualization/Crisis Resolution

The above case is a composite of several actual school shooting incidents. Many of the components of school attacks are contained in this incident: a chronic history of school problems, a triggering event, verbalized threats overheard by several peers, and access to a firearm. When such an event takes place, safety of all members of the school community is paramount; collaboration with local law enforcement is critical toward accomplishing this goal. Discussion of the case will include suggestions about what to do during the event, as well as the role of the school crisis team, both immediately after, and in the longer-term postvention period.

Once the shooting was over, approximately five minutes after it began, there were numerous tasks which had to be accomplished. The crisis coordinator, the school principal, was involved with coordinating law enforcement efforts at the crime scene, so another administrative designee was assigned as the crisis team coordinator. She called a formal meeting of the crisis response team which made a quick assessment regarding the collective emotional state of both students and staff. The functions of the team members were reviewed and assigned.

The team made a list of all the wounded students' classes and assigned members of the team to make special visits to each class to address the tragedy with them and to ascertain those students in need of more individual attention. Additionally, the team summoned other crisis teams from its own district schools and alerted another team from a neighboring school district to stand by to assist with these special needs. These team members maintained high visibility throughout the school building, providing many opportunities for students and staff to express their own thoughts, feelings, and fears about what happened.

Cavaiola and Colford (2006, 2011) reviewed other important tasks which must be addressed after a crisis like this, and which are part of the crisis plan:

Completion of a Crisis Fact Sheet: A factual account of the day's events was summarized in an announcement that was distributed to all classes, most of whom were not aware of the cafeteria shooting.

Planning for the afternoon faculty meeting: In order to provide an update of the event and to allow the staff to process it, the meeting was held to better prepare the staff to offer comfort for the students on their return to school.

Planning the schedule for the first day back after the shooting: Since the return to routine is helpful after a crisis, the team decided to follow a regular class schedule when students returned.

Planning for the evening parent meeting: An important component for any crisis response is the parent/community meeting. Among other things, parents were given information about children's reactions to traumatic events and suggestions for dealing with them at home.

Planning follow-up for the next day: The crisis team decided that the counseling liaison would devote much of the day after the shooting to providing outreach to those thought to be most needy.

Scheduling of regular crisis team meetings: In order for the team to continue to function as efficiently as possible, regular meetings were deemed essential to keep pace with the changing demands in the days and weeks following the crisis.

Other responsibilities for crisis team members included the medical liaison, the school nurse, who kept in contact with medical personnel and with families for ongoing updates on the health of the wounded. The media liaison proved to have one of the most difficult tasks of the crisis team; her primary responsibility was to make sure that members of the media, when they arrived at the school, remained in an assigned location, preferably some distance from the school building itself, where they would receive updates on the event from a designated school staff member. Wandering media personnel looking for distraught middle school students to speak with on camera can be overwhelming and intrusive at times like this, thus the need for separation of media and schools after a crisis. The media liaison was advised to use local law enforcement personnel to enforce the "no media allowed in school" policy, if needed.

The parent/family liaison greeted parents who arrived at school to address their concerns and advised them on how to talk with their children about the shooting. The security liaison for the team maintained regular contact with the local police and with other law enforcement agencies; he also began the process of evaluating the district's own safety and security systems.

After several days had passed, a sense of equilibrium returned to the school. Many students attended the funeral along with their parents. The wounded students returned to school, and teachers returned to academics as their primary function after days of crisis debriefing. Nevertheless, the crisis team remained available on an as-needed basis.

Case Presentation: Suicide and the School's Response

As students and staff arrived at their high school for another day of class, they were turned away by police who were standing guard by the front gate while stretching yellow tape across the entrance to the school. Early in the morning, Frankie, one of the members of the senior class of this 700-student high school had leaped to his death from the roof of the building. His family had reported him missing when he didn't show up at home the night before, and the first teacher to arrive at the school discovered the body. Rumors began to spread among the students and staff members arriving shortly after, both students and staff alike, regarding the presence of the police and of the diversion to different entrances to the school building. Left behind by the victim were writings consistent with suicide. He also had sent numerous e-mails and text messages to his friends telling them that he loved them and saying, in essence, "good-bye." Until those messages were discovered, none of his friends or classmates noted any disturbing signs in his comments or in his behaviors that might have alerted them that something was amiss. In fact, he was active in several clubs in the high school, was a straight A student, and was known as personable, hard-working, and very bright. His acceptance into an Ivy League college, which he planned to attend and a new relationship with a girl at school seemed to indicate, if anything, that all was well with him.

Case Conceptualization/Crisis Resolution

Time was of the essence in responding to this crisis. So many things had to spring into action before the remainder of the student body and staff arrived at school that morning. Diverting the incoming individuals from their typical front gate entrance to the school to any one of several side entrances was important to keep potential onlookers from the site of the deceased. This unusual diversion, however, raised many suspicions as to what had occurred, especially with the presence of the police yellow tape stretched across the better part of the entranceway. Rumors were rampant as the students and staff entered the building. The school crisis team members, notified of the suicide only an hour before the school day was to begin, gathered together to decide on the distribution of responsibilities for the crisis intervention that day.

So many things had to happen very quickly. Routine had to be established in the school, beginning with the typical morning homeroom; a factual account of what had happened also had to be communicated to the students and staff. Counseling had to be provided and access to this service also communicated to both these groups. Specific outreach services also were to be offered to those closest, both physically and emotionally, to the deceased. These individuals included the teacher who discovered the body, the teachers and friends of the deceased, especially those who received his farewell text messages beforehand and hadn't responded to his pleas, his girlfriend, and all other classmates who had been his friend for many years. Others who were at risk for many other reasons (see below) also were included in this outreach effort.

Counselors from the school decided to follow Frankie's schedule, sharing the class time with his teachers and allowing discussion of his death. However, the discussion included the notion that suicide was an unfortunate decision, one designed as a permanent solution to a temporary problem. The emphasis during these discussions was on using better problem-solving and coping strategies than suicide as a solution. Other interventions included providing after-school and evening counseling and feedback sessions for students, parents, and other members of the school community regarding the meaning of the death and ways of coping with it.

GUIDELINES FOR DEALING WITH A SCHOOL-RELATED SUICIDE

According to the Centers for Disease Control (2016), *suicide* ranked as the second leading cause of death among those 10 to 24 years of age, with a steady increase in incidents since 2007 among adolescents between the ages of 15 to 19. Young people were more likely to use firearms, suffocation, and poisoning as the preferred methods of death, with firearms the more common choice among adolescents and suffocation among children. There may be as many as 25 suicide attempts for every completed suicide.

The challenge for any school crisis team is to act very quickly after being notified of a student suicide, regardless of whether it occurred on school grounds or somewhere in the community after school hours. The fear of suicide contagion (Brock, 2002), imitative suicidal behavior, particularly among other adolescents, places others at risk of a "copycat" suicidal attempt as well, thus the need for swift action. The following steps should be taken immediately.

Engaging the School Crisis Team

The first thing that should be done, typically by the crisis coordinator, is to summon together the school crisis team. If the school is a particularly large facility with a large student body, then additional mental health resources may be requested from other local crisis teams. The coordinator also should verify the facts of the case, making sure that a suicide has been pronounced by medical authorities; speculation should never replace fact-finding. If suicide has not been confirmed by these authorities, then the cause of death should be considered "unknown" at this time. Only verifiable facts should be shared with the crisis team and with others.

Contacting the Victim's Family

The team's parent/family liaison should reach out to the family to provide comfort and support and to determine the family's wishes regarding student expressions of grief and outreach efforts to other students.

Calling Together the School Staff

Whenever possible, the school staff should assemble prior to the return of students to the school building in order for them to receive the information about the suicide and to be apprised of the school crisis team's plan for the reentry of the students. This meeting also is an opportunity for the crisis team to assess any faculty members who might have difficulty addressing this issue with their students.

Informing Students of the News

Students should be informed in small intimate settings like individual classrooms rather than in large, open venues, such as auditorium assemblies or via large-scale intercom announcements through the school. One of the reasons for the preference for small settings is to allow the teacher to be able to conduct a discussion of the facts of the case and to monitor students' reactions to the news. Should they find that some students have an inordinate amount of difficulty handling the news, they can then summon additional counseling resources for these students.

Any information must be truthful. A death by suicide must be described in those exact terms in any notification to the general student body. It also should include some mention of suicide being a poor decision by the victim in his/her attempt to solve a problem. The crisis coordinator, in collaboration with the crisis team, should compose an announcement distributed to the staff and read by teachers to their classes. The announcement should be relatively brief, as the following sample indicates

> John Doe, a senior in our high school, committed suicide early yesterday morning. As a faculty and school community we extend our sympathies to John's family and friends. We encourage all students to consider the tragic nature of this death and to realize that death is final. John's death is a reminder to us all that the act of taking one's life is not an appropriate solution to any of life's problems, nor is it an act of courage. There will be counselors available in school today and for the next few days in (specify locations in the building where counselors will be found) for any student wishing to talk to someone about John's death.

> Funeral services will be held in _____. Expressions of sympathy may be sent to _____.

Brock, Sandoval, and Lewis (2001) provided a sample of an announcement designed for students' parents:

> It is with a heavy heart that I write this letter to you today. I have some very bad news to share. I have just learned that the death of a member of our school family has been ruled a suicide by the coroner's office. John Doe, a senior in our school, killed himself yesterday. Our school staff has made the choice not to speculate on what it was that may have led to the suicide. Rather, our focus will be on what we can do to prevent other such losses.

> Part of what makes this death especially tragic is that it did not have to happen. Clearly, this was a permanent solution to problems which could have been dealt with in other ways. Perhaps some good can come from this loss if it generates a greater awareness of the signs of possible suicidal thinking and of school and community resources available to help people cope with their problems. To this end I would like to share with you some of the signals or warning signs suggesting the need for counseling support. These warning signs include the following:

The letter then would close with information regarding warning signs as well as available counseling services during the day for any student wishing to seek them out, including information about where in the school building the counselors were located. The list also would include a list of local mental health agencies and their phone numbers and information regarding the funeral arrangements. In the event of a suicide, student attendance at the funeral during the school day should be allowed on an individual basis with parental permission only; the school district should not provide any *en masse* bus trips to the funeral, nor should it cancel classes during the time of the funeral.

Identifying At-Risk Students

A variety of emotional reactions are noted in individuals affected by the death by suicide of a close friend or family member. However, there are some individuals who might be more inclined than others to imitate the suicidal act. Imitative suicidal behaviors account for approximately 1% to 3% of all adolescent suicides (Moscicki, 1995). Factors to consider when assessing the risk for imitative suicidal behavior, according to Brock (2006), include those who

- facilitated the suicide;
- failed to recognize the suicidal intent;
- believed they may have caused the suicide;
- had a relationship with the victim;
- identified with the victim;
- have a history of suicidal behavior;
- have a history of psychopathology;
- have suffered significant losses; and
- lack social support resources.

Crisis team members themselves may not be aware of all such at-risk students, but they should be able to reach out to staff members, including teachers, the school nurse, drug and alcohol counselors, and school staff responsible for discipline; each one of these individuals would undoubtedly know of students who fit into one of these risk categories. Once known, the counseling liaison should facilitate an outreach program for these students, calling them from class to ascertain their level of distress and to make the appropriate referrals, if needed, to other mental health resources.

Reinforcing Prevention and Coping Among All Survivors

- Providing ongoing information to students regarding a host of proactive practices
- Knowing where to turn for help: for self or others (provide contact information for school and community mental health services)
- Recognizing warning signs among friends and knowing when to make referrals for assistance
- Understanding that problems can be solved without resorting to suicide

Arranging for Appropriate Memorials for the Deceased

Postvention services and activities, those provided for people affected by a completed suicide, have the potential of doing more harm than good by increasing the risk of contagion (Brock, 2003). It is essential that the victim's death not be sensationalized and that the victim not be glorified or vilified in any way, thus giving the victim more notoriety in death than they ever had in life. Too much attention to the victim and too many details of the death just encourage identification with the victim, thereby increasing the risk of contagion.

Postvention activities that are contraindicated and potentially harmful include permanent memorials like planting trees, installing plaques, dedicating yearbooks, flying the flag at half mast, or having assemblies to honor the deceased. Rather, appropriate activities should be proactive and preventive in nature: contributing money to a local hot line, developing student assistance programs, or contributing in some way to suicide prevention programs in the school or community.

CASE PRESENTATION: ACCIDENTAL DEATH OF A STUDENT

Two of the five high school students in the car were just five days away from their graduation in this large, sprawling urban school district where the size of the high school alone approached 5,000 students. Three other friends, all juniors in the same high school, had cut class to join their older friends right after their graduation practice for one last trip to a local fast food restaurant just a couple of miles from the high school. Only one rider was wearing his seat belt.

After picking up their fast-food fare, they decided to visit a large shopping mall about 10 miles away. Their 80 mile-per-hour trip down a heavily traveled highway proved fatal to the driver and to one additional passenger. Another car entering the highway from a small strip mall caused the students' car to spin, hit a tree, and flip over several times. Two students were pronounced dead a short time later at the local hospital; one of them was due to graduate four days later. The three other passengers suffered only nonlethal injuries; one of them planned to attend his graduation ceremonies later that week.

Responding to Accidental Death: The School's Response

Sudden and unexpected deaths like these are especially difficult, since the survivors have no time to prepare for the loss of the lives of friends and acquaintances (Jimerson & Huff, 2002). Complicating the school's response to this tragedy were several factors. The major ones included

- **The immediacy of the event**: There was practically no time to prepare; news spread of the accident while school was still in session.

- **The size of the high school:** Student enrollment in this exceptionally large school exceeded 5,000 students.

- **Cultural differences among the deceased and the survivor family members:** One of the fatalities was foreign born. His parents spoke little English, and additional family members were on route from their homeland to attend the funeral services. The other victim was Hispanic. Sensitivity to cultural norms and practices at times like these was critical.

- **Loss of contact between the school and the student body:** It would only be four days before all students would be gone for the summer break, making outreach by the counseling staff an immediate need, particularly for those vulnerable students (see above) who would soon be removed from the reassuring and predictable routine of the school day and from those counseling services offered by the school district.

The Immediacy of the Event

This tragic accident took place during the school day, and the cell phone and text message capabilities of today's youth allow news, both good and bad, to circulate quickly. Before the school day was over, a large number of students within the school building had heard of the crash and of the fatalities. The crisis coordinator had to act quickly to obtain the facts of the event and communicate them to staff and students alike. This step in the district's crisis response was accomplished by distributing an announcement to each individual classroom which was to be read by the teachers to the class. The announcement (see above section) included a brief description of the accident, the names of the deceased, and the counseling services available to any student wishing to use them. Although a hand-delivered announcement is the most frequent recommendation for distributing this type of tragic news (National Association of School Psychologists, 1998), the public address system also may be used in the event of a death while school is in session. However, the administrators or their designees must plan this announcement carefully and rehearse what they will say. The delivery style, including choice of words used and the tone of voice, can indeed set the tone for the school's management of the tragedy. An emotionally charged announcement can exacerbate students' own emotional reactions to the news; yet a calm, dispassionate delivery can be reassuring to the student body. A school-wide announcement, however, is contraindicated if the death is due to a suicide.

Teachers were summoned to an after-school faculty meeting to address the tragedy as well as the district's crisis intervention plans. The decision also was made to have counselors available after the school day had ended and into the evening.

The Size of the High School

Another daunting factor was the size of the student body; school size alone can present a significant obstacle to effective crisis intervention. However, the development of an effective crisis plan would have taken this factor into consideration. In the case of this high school, the student body was separated into five separate, but connected sections, thereby reducing in size the number of students who may have been personally connected to the victims. Each section also had its own crisis team, all of whom assembled when notified of the tragedy; among the items discussed in this meeting was the likely section of the school attended by the deceased, therefore said area would be most affected by the tragedy. Counseling "drop in" centers were prepared for those sections, and notification of these services was communicated via individual classroom announcements (see above section). A list of vulnerable students, particularly close friends of the deceased, was assembled, and outreach was planned for them by the team's counseling liaison and other mental health personnel. A list of any siblings of the deceased who attended any of the other district schools also was prepared, and the crisis teams in those schools were alerted to the need to respond to them as well.

Cultural Differences Among the Deceased and the Survivor Family Members

Another consideration that had to be made in this tragedy involved the cultural and linguistic differences among the deceased: one foreign-born Polish young man and one Hispanic. Any crisis plan developed by a school district also should include participation by community groups, particularly representatives of the different cultural and ethnic groups which make up the district's surrounding community. Among those issues addressed in the crisis plan: determining what languages are spoken in the community; its prevailing religious beliefs and cultural practices, especially as they pertain to the meaning of tragedy to the families involved; and the way these families grieve and bury their dead (Athey & Moody-Williams, 2003; Sandoval & Lewis, 2002).

Prior to reaching out to the victims' families, the district first communicated with community groups for assistance; this assistance included securing the services of an interpreter for any families requiring language assistance and consulting with them regarding the appropriate form of communication for the school district to use in its family outreach efforts.

Loss of Contact Between the School and the Student Body

Plans also were made to provide counseling in the high school for several days after the graduation ceremonies, even though the school year had officially ended. Concerns over students' reactions after the graduation ceremony and after the funeral services themselves prompted the extension of this counseling service. The school district summoned the assistance of personnel from the local mental health community to assist in this endeavor.

MEMORIALS

It is a common sight for motorists to find along the highways throughout the country makeshift memorials marking the actual locations of a motor vehicle-related death, which consist of flowers, posters and letters with emotional testimony, and an assortment of other memorabilia designed to honor the dead. Although it is unclear what value these commemorative practices serve in recovery from tragedy, society in general has established certain rituals and ceremonies for tragic events (Pagliocca, Nickerson, & Williams, 2002).

Young (2002) suggested that school crisis plans in cases like these approach memorialization in two parts: memorial services immediately after an event, typically within a week, and permanent memorials. What must be emphasized, however, is that memorials of any kind should not be provided in the case of a death by suicide. Another suggestion (Young, 2002) is that permanent memorials also not be encouraged if the death is due to the victims' own misconduct, including, among other causes, reckless driving. Determining the conditions surrounding the deaths of any young people might be germane to a district's decision regarding a permanent memorial in their honor.

In the case of these accidental deaths, the district administrator composed a tribute to the victims on the district website. He also provided symbolic empty seats for the two seniors at the graduation ceremony just a few days after the tragedy. Representatives from each family also ascended the stage and received diplomas for them.

The decision regarding a permanent memorial should include student participation, but should be guided by school administrators and other staff. However, allowing for the passage of time and some emotional distance from the actual event before planning the memorial is advisable for emotions to have an opportunity to subside and for reason to replace emotion in establishing a commemoration that is appropriate to the event (Cavaiola & Colford, 2006, 2011). Otherwise, permanent memorials that are too obtrusive only serve as daily reminders of tragedy, long after the event took place. Rather, they should be in a location where students may choose to look at it and where it would not confront students every time they enter the school grounds (Paine, 1998). Some of the more common memorials are plaques, tree plantings, and annual events in honor of the deceased. Poland and McCormick (1999) suggest "consumable" gestures instead, such as the establishment of a scholarship in the names of the victims, whereas schools and communities, in the aftermath of a tragedy, look for activities and projects designed to make a difference and to prevent similar tragedies in the future. Activities and curriculum projects that address tolerance and bullying, for example, are appropriate "memorials" after a violent event in the schools.

Case Presentation: Middle School and 9/11

When the twin towers were attacked that fateful day, resulting in the deaths of almost 3,000 people, schools in many parts of the country had just opened their doors for the beginning of another school day. A suburban middle school within just an hour commuting distance from New York City was in the early part of the first academic period. Only a handful of teachers were aware of the jet airliner collisions with the towers, since they were without an assigned teaching period at that time and were watching the news unfold on a television set in the teacher's room. Gradually, however, other teachers gained access to the television and spread the grim news to their colleagues and students. The crisis team's concern was that rumor would replace fact and that students and staff alike would experience considerable anxiety.

Case Conceptualization/Crisis Resolution

After some time had passed, the specific impact the event had on this middle school became clear: a student had a father who worked in the towers, and a secretary had a son in the same location. Two popular teachers in the school also had husbands employed there. Superimposed on the grand scale of nationwide horror were these personal stories of anxiety and fear over the unknown fate of these family members. The tasks facing the school's crisis team were significant.

Among the difficulties encountered by the middle school staff were

- hordes of parents arriving at the school to pick up their children and take them home, despite the school psychologist's explanation to them that school was the best place for them to be at the time. Remaining in school among friends and in a familiar routine was a better alternative to going home and watching the televised horror over and over again. Parental prerogative superseded professional advice, however, and many children left school with their parents before the day was over.

- the school district's inability to summon additional district resources (counselors, psychologists, or social workers) to assist with the middle school staff, since all schools in the district were in the same crisis mode in their respective school buildings. Although each school should have its own contained crisis team, those schools with low enrollment and limited staff often enlist the services of crisis team members from neighboring school districts or from other schools within the district. However, the magnitude of the crisis on this day precluded any assistance from other sources.

- the sudden nature of the crisis which prevented the crisis coordinator, the school principal, from summoning the crisis team together to sort out roles and responsibilities. In most cases involving crisis, there is a time interval between an event and the return of children to school (i.e., a popular student dies in a motor vehicle accident over the weekend, allowing time for the crisis team to assemble before school resumes on Monday morning). In this case, however, the school was already midway through the first period when the attacks occurred.

Nevertheless, those crisis team members who were present in the middle school decided to get to work. First, the crisis coordinator composed a brief, informative note for the teachers to read in their classrooms; the note presented only the facts as known at the time which had not yet included confirmation about a terrorism connection. Notes distributed during times of crisis must be dispassionate and objective in presenting facts about the crisis as well as reassuring for students that the familiar routine of the school day was going to continue. The principal had his secretarial staff distribute the notes to each of the classrooms with instructions that they be read aloud in each class.

Throughout the entire day, the crisis team's counseling liaison, the school psychologist, the school counselors, and the school social worker made themselves available by their visibility in the school building, monitoring students' and staff members' reactions, and intervening with those individuals who exhibited particularly strong reactions to the news. Besides attending to the needs of all members of the school community, however, the crisis team also had to reach out to those groups of people who were particularly vulnerable to the current crisis. The groups included any student or staff member who had a parent, other relative, friend, or loved one working in the Twin Towers. Although deaths were not confirmed until later in the day, the team sought out these individuals, both students and staff alike.

One teacher whose husband worked in the towers, overcome and inconsolable at the news, asked to leave school to be with her family; she was escorted home once it was clear that there would be some other relatives waiting for her there. Yet another teacher with a spouse employed in the towers was asked to leave her class to meet with the school psychologist and principal in order for them to offer support and reassurance. She stated emphatically that she felt strongly that her husband was indeed safe, and she then asked to return to her class to continue teaching. The team continued to monitor her during the remainder of the school day. The team, after consulting with many staff members, determined that one student only had a parent working in the towers. His mother decided to pick him up from school and take him home. A school secretary also had a son working there; she, too, left school to be with her family. Both the student and the secretary had the deaths of their father and son confirmed the next day.

In the days following the attacks, the school crisis team continued to monitor the emotional health of students and staff. Teachers who requested assistance from one of the school mental health specialists were able to secure their assistance in the days that followed to help them address the attack-related issues in class discussions. Crisis team members also were able to determine who those students were who had some special personal connections to the deceased; and follow-up consultations with them were accomplished by the team members. It would be days before everything would settle down for most members of the school community.

CRISIS BY PROXY

In a culture where instances of terrorism, death, and destruction are widely circulated by all forms of media, school-age children are exposed to crises. Even though distant events for the typical child, these images are displayed repeatedly on their televisions, making the events more near than far. The Newtown shootings, the Boston Marathon bombing, images of the Towers coming down on 9/11, the Oklahoma City bombings, and the pictures of all the young children and adults slain that day are incessant, including repeated broadcasts of acts of terrorist bombings.

Psychological triage may have to be applied to those children who tremble with these images, and fear that they, too, could be a victim. Keeping track of those children may be as important as attending to the children who have been personally involved with some tragedy. Some suggestions for adults and caregivers in helping children cope with these constant images (NASP, 2017)

1. Maintain calm and control (remember that children take their cues from adults)

2. Reassure children that they are safe (even if it means showing them that all school doors are locked and that strangers can't get in)

3. Remind them that people are in charge who will take care of them

4. Let them know that it's O.K. to be upset

5. Tell them the truth (no graphic details, but the facts that are known)

6. Don't stereotype groups of people who do bad things

7. Keep explanations developmentally appropriate

8. Stay with a typical routine and schedule as planned

9. Monitor and restrict exposure to scenes of violent events as much as possible

10. Continue to monitor their emotional state

11. Encourage helping, acts of kindness

RESOURCES FOR CHAPTER ENRICHMENT

Recommended Films

The Killer at Thurston High : (2000). This documentary film chronicles the life of Kip Kinkel, a teenager who entered his high school cafeteria in September 1998 with a semi-automatic rifle, firing 50 shots into the crowd, killing two students and wounding 25 others. He also killed both his parents at home the night before. The film includes family videotape footage and interviews with those who knew him.

Untold Stories of Columbine : (2000). The two teenage gunmen entered Columbine High School armed with numerous weapons and roamed throughout the building firing at students and staff members who tried to run away and hide from the terror. Before turning the guns on themselves, they left 13 dead and 23 wounded. This documentary focuses on the death and life of one of the murdered students, Rachel Joy Scott; it features interviews with her father and excerpts from her diary. The issue of her Christian faith provides a focus as well.

Suggested Activities: What Would You Do?

School had just ended for the day for this suburban high school. It was the beginning of the fall season, and the freshman and sophomores headed for the school buses to take them home. Meanwhile, the upper class students, those juniors and seniors with permission to park on campus, hurriedly raced through the parking lot to get to their cars for a quick trip home. One of the school security officers took to the parking lot and directed student traffic out of the lot and into the local street in an orderly fashion.

Sandra, a popular senior and member of the student council, was one of those who exited the lot. She was only several blocks from the school when she reportedly failed to stop for a stop sign and went through an intersection; a car driven by another high school senior, an acquaintance of Sandra's, hit her broadside, killing her instantly, according to the coroner's report. An analysis of the accident by the local police revealed that Sandra had been changing a CD in her CD player and probably never noticed the stop sign. The school day had only ended 20 minutes prior to her death.

Answer the following questions as if you were a member of Sandra's school district's crisis team:

1. What should the crisis coordinator do right away?

2. What issues should be addressed with Sandra's friends? With the driver of the other car?

3. What should the counseling liaison's primary responsibilities be in the immediate aftermath of the crash?

4. From what other agencies might the crisis team request assistance?

5. With school not in session at the time other students hear of this tragedy, what are your biggest concerns about making sure that all students are provided counseling or other supports?

6. What kinds of memorials, both immediate and permanent, might be appropriate?

7. What school-based prevention practices might come out of this event?

Alcohol and Drug Crises

DISCUSSION QUESTIONS

Have you ever experienced a situation where you had to take care of a friend who was intoxicated or under the influence of drugs? What was the experience like? At any point did you have any concerns for his or her safety?

Did you ever have a friend who was injured or arrested because of being under the influence of alcohol or drugs? How did you react when you first heard about his or her injury or arrest?

James is 21-years-old and is in his senior year at a state university. He was driving home from a party on Saturday night when he was involved in a car accident. Because he had to be taken to an emergency room with a possible head injury, and because the police suspected he was under the influence at the time of the crash, a blood test was taken which revealed a high blood alcohol level (.26) and an opioid in his system. When being interviewed by the psychiatric screener in the emergency room, James admitted to having taken a prescription opiate medication (Roxicet) which had been given to him by a friend at the party. Because James lives off-campus and commutes by car to classes, James is worried that if he's charged with a DUI (Driving Under the Influence), his parents will be angry and this may impact his ability to graduate on time.

Substance use disorders can affect anyone, whether young or old, rich or poor, regardless of educational achievements, abilities, race, ethnicity, or religion. Alcohol and drug-related problems are pervasive in American society and, so too, are a variety of crises related to these disorders. Although we discuss general information pertaining to substance use disorders (e.g., information pertaining to diagnosis and models of addiction), the goal of this chapter is to provide the reader with an understanding of how alcohol and drug use can develop into a variety of crises. For example, many people who manifest substance use disorders experience life crises given the unpredictable nature of one's behavior while under the influence of mood-altering substances. In the case example described above, most likely, when James set out for an evening of fun and partying, he didn't plan to end up in an emergency room. Because alcohol and drug use is so widespread in American culture, it is common for individuals who abuse alcohol or drugs to present in crisis in a variety of settings, such as hospitals, schools, mental health clinics, or the courts. Naturally, not everyone who uses or misuses alcohol or drugs experiences a crisis, therefore the goal of this chapter is to focus on those crises that arise as a direct result of substance abuse.

Alcohol and drug crises parallel the three major diagnostic categories found in the *DSM-5* (American Psychiatric Association, 2013). These include substance intoxication, substance withdrawal, and substance use disorders. Examples of crises related to *substance intoxication* include a college student like James who ingests large amounts of alcohol along with other substances; or a young woman in a state of intoxication from ecstasy who becomes dehydrated and loses consciousness. *Substance withdrawal* crises occur when someone who has been physically dependent on a substance begins to experience withdrawal symptoms after a period of time without the substance. This includes an alcoholic who begins to experience tremors and may have a seizure, or a person addicted to pain medication like Vicodin or Oxycontin who begins to experience muscle cramping and extreme agitation when the drug is leaving his or her system. A *substance use disorder* crisis includes problems directly as a result of repeated alcohol or drug use, such as a person fired from a job, or failing classes. For anyone who has not had prior legal involvement like James, a DUI becomes a crisis event, as he must now deal with a court appearance, financial loss due to court fees and fines, and worries over how to get to and from classes. Generally, people with substance use disorders experience a variety of problems because of alcohol or drug use, and their lives become increasingly more unmanageable. Crisis counselors (along with other mental health counselors, nurses, social workers, and psychologists) can help people with alcohol and drug problems safely manage these crises provided that proper assessment occurs that allows for effective intervention. This chapter focuses on what to do and what not to do to help individuals with substance use disorders manage these crises.

THE SCOPE OF DRUG AND ALCOHOL PROBLEMS

What is unique to substance use disorders is not only how ubiquitous these disorders are, but also how dangerous they can be. For example, according to the Center for Disease Control (2015), it is estimated that from 2006 to 2010, approximately 434,000 people died each year from complications related to smoking cigarettes. There were approximately 88,000 deaths annually attributed to excessive alcohol use. In fact, excessive alcohol use is the third leading lifestyle-related cause of death for people in the United States each year, while approximately 60,000 individuals die each year from drug use and overdoses (Center for Disease Control, 2013b). According to the World Health Organization alcohol alone is the third leading risk factor for disability and disease (WHO, 2010).

Within the United States, drug use trends often tend to regionalize. For example, the Midwestern and Southwestern states have been experiencing an epidemic of crystal methamphetamine (such as that depicted in the A&E television series *Breaking Bad).* The designer drug *Mollie,* which some claim to be a much purer powder form of Ecstasy or MDMA originated in the Syracuse, New York area (Steinhardt, Moore, & Casella, 2014; Ohlheiser, 2015), while a new, very potent, synthetic form of cannabis called "spike" has become widespread in the Syracuse and Buffalo, New York area. What is most worrisome about "spike" is that it causes users to become paranoid and physically violent (Featherstone, 2015). Nationally, the United States has been in the grips of a prescription opioid and heroin epidemic, with the Northeastern, Mid-Atlantic, and "rust belt" states like Ohio states especially impacted. According to a recent study by the Kaiser Family Foundation (2015), 16% of Americans know someone who has died from a prescription opioid painkiller overdose with 9% having seen a family member or close friend die of an overdose. According to the Center for Disease Control (2015), there were 47,055 lethal overdoses in 2014, with opioids accounting for a large portion of these overdoses (18,893 overdose deaths related to prescription pain relievers and 10,574 deaths related to heroin). In exploring the mortality rates from the opioid epidemic, the death rates appear to be rising consistently, especially for White European Americans ages 25 to 34, while the death rates have either flattened or fallen for Hispanic Americans and African Americans. These astounding statistics were validated in a recently published study by Princeton economists, Anne Deaton and Angus Case, who found an increase in mortality rates among White, European American men of lower education most often due to either drug overdose or suicide (Case & Deaton, 2015). For the past three decades, it has been estimated that approximately half of all highway fatalities were linked to driving under the influence of alcohol or drugs (National Highway Traffic Safety Administration, NHTSA, 2012). It is also estimated that 56% of domestic violence cases involve alcohol. Alcohol and drugs also figure heavily into both violent crimes like homicides and in property crimes, such as assaults and burglary. Of the 10.1 million persons who were ages 12 to 20 who indicated that they drink, nearly 6.8 million or 19% were binge drinkers and 2.1 million or 6% were heavy drinkers (Substance Abuse and Mental Health Services Administration, SAMHSA, 2011). For prescription opioids alone (e.g., Percoset, OxyContin, Vicodan), workplace costs (driven by lost earnings from premature death and reduced compensation due to lost employment) are estimated to be around $25.6 billion annually, while healthcare costs (driven by excess medical/prescription costs) are estimated to be about $25 billion annually, and criminal justice costs (driven by correctional facility and police costs) are estimated to be approximately $9 billion annually (Birnbaum, White, Schiller, Waldman, Cleveland & Roland, 2011).

Substance use disorders (SUD) also overlap or coexist with other mental health disorders. For example, it is estimated that approximately one-third of psychiatric patients admitted to inpatient units have an active drug or alcohol problem at the time of admission. It is also estimated that approximately 60% of those seeking assistance at community mental health clinics have a primary or co-occurring substance use disorder. Among the 20.7 million adults with a past year substance use disorder, 40.7% (8.4 million adults) had co-occurring mental illness in 2012. In comparison, among adults without a substance use disorder, 16.5% had mental illness. In 2014, among the 20.2 million adults with a past year SUD, 7.9 million (39.1%) had another mental illness (AMI) in the past year. In contrast, among adults without a past year SUD, 16.2% (35.6 million adults) had AMI in the past year. Among adults with a past year SUD, the percentage of adults with co-occurring AMI in 2014 was similar to the percentages of adults with AMI in most years from 2008 to 2013. The 7.9 million adults with AMI who met the criteria for an SUD in the past year represent 18.2% of the 43.6 million adults with AMI. In contrast, 6.3% of adults who did not have past year AMI (12.3 million adults) met the criteria for an SUD. Among adults who had AMI in the past year, the percentage of adults with a co-occurring SUD in 2014 was similar to the percentages of adults with a co-occurring SUD in most years from 2008 to 2013 (Center for Behavioral Health

Statistics & Quality, 2015). Substance use disorders also account for many medical crises requiring immediate medical attention in emergency departments. Emergency room statistics are tracked throughout the United States by the Drug Abuse Warning Network (DAWN). In 2011, over 125 million visits were made to emergency departments, and DAWN estimates that over 5 million of these visits were related to drugs, a 100% increase since 2004. Broken down by substance, about 1.25 million emergency department (ED) visits, or 51%, involved illicit drugs; approximately 1.24 million, or 51%, involved nonmedical use of pharmaceuticals; and 0.61 million, or 25%, involved drugs combined with alcohol (SAMHSA, 2014).

Although substance use disorders are referred to as an "equal opportunity" disease, in that they can affect anyone, there are some variations that deserve mention. For example, there are high rates of multiple substance abuse among young people. In some instances, this pattern may result in higher rates of psychological dependence rather than physiological dependence. Young people are also more likely to abuse inhalants and hallucinogens than adults. Furthermore, African American youth tend to have lower rates of substance use when compared to European American or Latino Americans (Delva, Wallace, O'Malley, Bachman, Johnston, & Schulenberg et al., 2005; Galea, Nandi, & Vlahov, 2004). It also appears that low parental education may be more of a risk factor for "White students than for Hispanic or African American students." (Bachman, O'Malley, Johnston, Schulenberg, & Wallace, 2011, p. 281). Among the elderly, prescription drug abuse is a major problem. Regarding gender differences, men tend to manifest alcohol and drug problems in their late teens and early twenties while women in their 30s are at higher risk for developing alcohol and drug problems. Native Americans and those of Irish and English ancestry also tend to have higher rates of alcohol use disorders (Rouse, 1995).

What is clear in the aforementioned statistics, is that regardless of what human service occupation one pursues (whether as a teacher, police officer, emergency room psychiatric screener, family counselor, nurse, attorney, social worker, or psychologist), it is likely that you will be dealing with the direct or indirect impact of alcoholism or drug addiction. Therefore, it is important to know the facts about substance use disorders in order to deal with these types of crises effectively. In no other area is so much harm done by human services workers with good intentions than in dealing with alcohol or drug problems. The police officer who drives the DWI (driving while intoxicated) offender home rather than making an arrest; the teacher who ignores signs of drug abuse in one of his or her students, or the doctor who continues to write prescriptions for painkillers or tranquilizers to an addicted patient year-after-year, may all unwittingly become "enablers;" that is rather than becoming part of the solution, they become part of the problem. Indeed, it is estimated that among physicians, the diagnosis of alcoholism or other drug dependency is missed in approximately 60% to 70% of the cases they treat (Doweiko, 2014).

DEFINING SUBSTANCE USE DISORDERS: DIAGNOSTIC CONCERNS

What is alcoholism and drug addiction? What distinguishes those who drink "socially" from those whom we consider alcoholics? What separates the alcoholic or addicted drug user from the recreational or social user? To answer these questions, it is important to explore the definitions of substance use disorders.

The most widely used and accepted classification system for diagnosing substance use disorders is the *Diagnostic and Statistical Manual of Mental Disorder*, 5th Edition (*DSM-5*) (American Psychiatric Association, 2013). As stated earlier, there are three main categories of substance disorders, which includes **substance use disorders**, **substance intoxication**, and **substance withdrawal**. In other words, when assessing a client who presents in an alcohol or drug-related crisis, the counselor would try to determine if that individual is currently under the influence of drugs or alcohol (intoxication), or in withdrawal from drugs or alcohol, as would be the case with someone who is experiencing heroin withdrawal or delirium tremens (DTs) from alcohol withdrawal. Both of these categories relate to the person's condition at the time they are being evaluated.

Substance Use Disorders

The diagnosis of a substance use disorder (SUD) is given when an individual's alcohol or drug use has impacted on his or her ability to function over time; one would not diagnose a substance disorder based on a single incident where alcohol or drugs impaired one's judgment or decision-making abilities (e.g. someone who drinks too much at a wedding reception and gets arrested for a DUI on his or her way home). So, with a substance use disorder we're basically looking for whether alcohol or drugs *interferes* with the individual's ability to function on a daily basis. According to the *DSM-5*, the 11 diagnostic criteria for substance use disorders can be grouped into four major categories: *impaired control* (Criteria 1–4), *social impairment* (Criteria 5–7), *risky use* (Criteria 8–9), and *physiological impact* (Criteria 10–11). In the first major category *impaired control,* these criteria include Criterion 1 where the individual may use substances in larger amounts or over longer periods of time than he or she intended. Such is the case with someone who stops off at the bar to have one or two beers after work, but ends up getting drunk; or the person who vows to only do one or two lines of cocaine, but ends up going on a three-day binge. Criterion 2 includes the individual's persistent desires to cut down or quit substance use and repeated unsuccessful attempts to stop using. Criterion 3 addresses the symptom that many individuals with substance use disorders spend a great deal of time getting the substance, using it, or recovering from its effects. Such is the case with a person using heroin who spends a better part of the day finding the substance and a place to use it. Criterion 3 also addresses the impact of alcohol or drug hangovers. Criterion 4 deals with craving, here defined as an intense desire or urge for the substance especially when triggered by environmental cues likely to occur in places where the individual previously used the substance. Criteria 5 through 7 describe *social impact;* for example, Criteria 5 describes how repeated use often results in failures to fulfill major obligations at work, home, or school. Criteria 6 describes how the person continues with substance use despite knowing the impact on their social and interpersonal life caused by their substance use. For example, an individual who has lost friends or love relationships because of how belligerent he or she becomes when they drink, or continues to use substances despite knowing it was their substance use that caused their relationship problems. Often individuals give up important social, occupational, or recreational activities because of their substance use, which is addressed in Criteria 7. Here people begin to withdraw socially because of their alcohol or other substance use. *Risky use* is addressed in Criteria 8 and 9. With Criterion 8, the person continues to use in situations where it is physically hazardous (e.g., a person arrested for a DUI after drinking at a wedding). People who drink and drive on a regular basis or those who continue to drive following a DUI arrest reflect Criterion 8. Criterion 9 is somewhat similar in wording to Criterion 6, however, here the individual continues to drink or use substances despite knowing that physical or psychological problems are caused by or exacerbated by substance use. For example, the person who continues to drink despite knowing it's causing liver disease, or the person who continues to use cocaine despite knowing that it exacerbates his or her depression. Finally, the ***physiological impact*** discussed in Criteria 10 and 11 basically addresses physiological substance dependence as evidenced by tolerance (Criterion 10 whereby the person requires increasingly more of the substance to obtain the desired effect), and withdrawal (Criterion 11), whereby cessation of alcohol or substance use results in withdrawal symptoms specific to that substance type. It should also be pointed out that many individuals who misuse or abuse substances often use more than one substance at a time, therefore, it is not uncommon to assess someone who is abusing both alcohol and prescription medication, as was the case with James, described at the beginning of this chapter. It is also very important to keep in mind that an individual need not be physiologically dependent on a substance to be diagnosed with a SUD. For example, a person who uses cannabis on a regular basis may experience that he or she craves getting high when at work or school (Criterion 4) AND has given up former friends and recreational activities (Criterion 7) because of smoking cannabis, thereby meeting the criteria for a cannabis use disorder.

In order to meet the criteria for substance use disorders a person must meet the benchmarks of **at least two of the eleven criteria within a 12-month period.** Also, it is important to keep in mind that the term substance use disorder is a generic term and that when actually diagnosing someone, the professional rendering the diagnosis would specify the use substance (e.g., alcohol use disorder; cannabis use disorder; cocaine use disorder; inhalant use disorder; opioid use disorder; sedative, hypnotic or anxiolytic disorder; tobacco use disorder). Table 7.1 (see p. 151) provides a list of risk factors that place individuals at risk for developing substance use disorders along with a list of protective factors that may help to prevent these disorders from occurring.

Substance Intoxication and Substance Withdrawal

There are three commonalities with substance intoxication and substance withdrawal. First, they are both state-dependent, meaning these diagnoses refer to the individual's state or status at the time he or she is being assessed. Second, both substance intoxication and substance withdrawal are substance-specific. Very simply, the "high" or intoxication effect from smoking crystal methamphetamine is specifically different from the "high" or intoxication effect of injecting heroin. The same applies to substance withdrawal whereby the withdrawal from alcohol or benzodiazepine (e.g. Xanax or Librium) may be more severe and potentially fatal than the withdrawal from cannabis. Continuing with the example of assessing someone in crisis, after determining if the client is under the influence of drugs or alcohol (intoxication) or is in withdrawal, the counselor then tries to determine whether the client manifests *physiological dependence*. The reason for this is that a client can be diagnosed with an SUD even though they are *not* physically addicted to the substance. This may sound confusing, however, think about a "periodic alcoholic;" that is someone who drinks once or twice a year, however, when they do, they drink to excess, experience blackouts, miss days from work, get into accidents and so on. This person would not necessarily be physically dependent on alcohol, yet he or she experiences a loss of control and might spend a great deal of time using the substance and recovering from its effects, or they end up neglecting important occupational activities. It is also possible for a person using cannabis several times per week, to not experience any symptoms of physical dependence. Yet according to the *DSM-5*, a person can suffer from Cannabis Withdrawal, which suggests that regular marijuana users do experience a substance-specific withdrawal from cannabis, characterized by symptoms, such as irritability, sleep disturbance, nervousness, or anxiety, decreased appetite or weight loss, restlessness, depressed mood, and physical symptoms, such as sweating, chills, or headaches. Since cannabis has been legalized in Washington State, Colorado, and Oregon, there have been reported instances of individuals seeking emergency room assistance because of adverse reactions to Cannabis Intoxication especially from more THC-potent strains of cannabis, or because of ingesting too many "edibles." A recent study done at the University of Colorado Medical Center found that emergency room visits doubled from 2013 to 2014 (85 per 10,000 in 2013 to 168 per 10,000 in 2014) for Colorado tourists (McGhee & Munio, 2016).

Finally, the third commonality between substance intoxication and substance withdrawal is that they are both reversible. For example, a person who is intoxicated on alcohol, cannabis, opioids, or hallucinogens will eventually metabolize these substances after a period of hours or perhaps days, depending on how much of the substance was ingested and will return to a normal or non-intoxicated state. The same holds true of substance withdrawal. With the passage of time, the person who has been ingesting substances on a daily basis for weeks or months will eventually begin the withdrawal process which may also take days, weeks, or months to successfully complete. This process may require that the individual is treated in an inpatient detoxification facility (e.g., a hospital setting or detox program) and may require medication to safely detoxify from the substance. Such is the case with alcohol detoxification where a person can experience withdrawal symptoms ranging from headaches and tremors to alcohol hallucinosis, grand-mal type seizures, and delirium tremens (delirium tremens is a substance-induced psychotic-like state characterized by extreme agitation and dangerous increases in heart rate). The following are some examples of various types of substance–specific intoxication and substance withdrawal.

Alcohol Intoxication: After ingesting alcohol (e.g., beer, wine, hard liquor) individuals may experience problematic behavioral or psychological changes (e.g., inappropriate sexual or aggressive behavior, mood lability, impaired judgment) that develop during, or shortly after, alcohol ingestion.

Alcohol intoxication is also characterized by one or more of the following: Slurred speech, incoordination, unsteady gait, nystagmus, impairment in attention or memory, and after ingesting a great deal of alcohol, stupor or coma may result at very high blood alcohol levels (e.g., .25 to .40).

The aforementioned symptoms are not the result of another medical condition or mental health disorder or due to ingesting another substance.

Alcohol Withdrawal: Within several hours or a few days after the cessation of or reduction in the amount of alcohol intake which usually has been heavy and prolonged, individuals may experience two or more of the following symptoms: autonomic hyperactivity (e.g., sweating or pulse rate greater than 100 bpm), increased hand tremor, insomnia, nausea or vomiting, transient visual, tactile, or auditory hallucinations or illusions (i.e., hallucinosis), psychomotor agitation, anxiety, and generalized tonic-clonic seizures.

Cannabis Intoxication: Because of cannabis use, the individual may experience problematic behavioral or psychological changes (e.g., impaired motor coordination, euphoria, anxiety, sensation of slowed time, impaired judgment, social withdrawal) that develops during, or shortly after, cannabis use. Two or more of the following symptoms may be observed: Conjunctival injection, increased appetite, dry mouth, tachycardia. These symptoms are not caused by another medical condition or mental disorder and are not caused by intoxication with another substance.

Cannabis Withdrawal: Following the cessation of heavy or prolonged cannabis use, individuals may experience the following: irritability, anger or aggression, nervousness or anxiety, sleep difficulty (e.g., insomnia, disturbing dreams), decreased appetite or weight loss, restlessness, depressed mood, and at least one of the following physical symptoms: abdominal pain, shakiness/tremors, sweating, fever, chills, or headache. These symptoms are not caused by another medical condition, another mental health disorder, or intoxication or withdrawal from another substance.

Opioid Intoxication: Because of opioid use the individual experiences problematic behavioral or psychological changes (e.g., initial euphoria followed by apathy, dysphoria, psychomotor agitation or retardation, impaired judgment) that develop during, or shortly after, opioid use. Pupillary constriction (or pupillary dilation due to anoxia from severe overdose) and one (or more) of the following: drowsiness or coma, slurred speech, impairment in attention or memory. These symptoms are not caused by a medical disorder, a mental health disorder, or intoxication with another substance.

Opioid Withdrawal: Following the cessation or reduction in use of opioids (e.g., heroin or prescription opioid), after prolonged or heavy use, the individual experiences the following: dysphoric mood, nausea or vomiting, muscle aches, lacrimation or rhinorrhea, pupillary dilation, piloerection, or sweating, diarrhea, yawning, fever, or insomnia. These symptoms are not caused by another medical condition, mental health condition, or another substance.

Stimulant Intoxication: Following the use of a stimulant medication, cocaine, or methamphetamine, some individuals may experience problematic behavioral or psychological changes (e.g., euphoria or affective blunting; changes in sociability; hypervigilance; interpersonal sensibility; anxiety, tension, or anger; stereotyped behaviors; impaired judgment) that develop during, or shortly after, use of a stimulant. Along with symptoms, such as tachycardia or bradycardia, pupillary dilation, elevated or lowered blood pressure, perspiration or chills, nausea or vomiting, weight loss, psychomotor agitation or retardation, muscular weakness, respiratory depression, chest pain, or cardiac arrhythmias, confusion, seizures, dyskinesias, dystonias, or coma. These aforementioned symptoms are not caused by another medical condition, another mental health disorder, or other substance use.

Stimulant Withdrawal: Following the cessation of (or reduction in) heavy or prolonged amphetamine-type substance, cocaine, or other stimulant use the individuals may experience the following within a few hours or within several days: fatigue, vivid, unpleasant

Box 7.1: An Alternative to Treating Opioid Addiction

The New York Times reports that Vancouver, British Columbia, Canada is attempting a rather unique approach to treating individuals who are addicted to heroin (Levin, 2016). Like the United States, Canada is also experiencing a heroin epidemic and in response, a new program called Crosstown is offering a treatment that is referred to as "heroin maintenance." Having found that opioid replacement medications like methadone or suboxone were ineffective for some heroin-addicted individuals, Crosstown provides diacetylmorphine to their clients. Diacetylmorphine is the active chemical ingredient in heroin. To be eligible for the heroin maintenance program, potential clients must be able to prove a five-year history of injecting opioids and have at least two failed attempts at some other replacement therapy (e.g. methadone or buprenorphine, or suboxone). Clients report to the clinic anywhere from one to three times a day and are monitored by nurses who provide the clients with clean needles and an average dose of 200 mg of diacetylmorphine. The process takes a few minutes. Clients are assured of the purity of the opioid they are injecting unlike street heroin which varies in purity and adulterants (e.g., fentanyl which is reported to account for many of the fatal overdoses in the United States and Canada).

Thus far, research studies on this approach have been positive. The first research trial, known as the North American Opiate Maintenance Initiative, studied clients from 2005 to 2008 and found that "prescribed diacetylmorphine saved an average of $40,000 in lifetime societal costs per person compared to methadone." The clients who were interviewed indicated that unlike methadone or buprenorphine, diacetylmorphine allowed them to function on a daily basis. Most importantly, to date, the Crosstown program reports that there has been no fatal overdose.

Source: Levin, Dan (2016, April 21). Vancouver finds success in treating drug addicts: Prescription program gains new attention. *The New York Times,* pp. A4, A9.

dreams, insomnia or hypersomnia, increased appetite, psychomotor retardation, or agitation. These symptoms are not caused by another medical condition, mental health disorder, or withdrawal from another substance.

As alluded to in the criteria, substances can either differ greatly or be similar in the intoxication they produce. For example, alcohol, benzodiazepines (such as Valium, Librium, Xanax, and Tranxene), barbiturates (such as Seconal and pentobarbitol), and opioids (such as heroin, codeine, Oxycontin, Percoset and Methadone) are all Central Nervous System depressants, and therefore produce a somewhat similar intoxicating effect; that is speech and movement are slowed down, gait may be unstable, reaction time is slowed, cognitive processing or thought processes are slowed down and the person may appear to be drowsy or may fight to stay awake. Alcohol is mistakenly thought to have an initial stimulating effect; however, some intoxicated people report that this excitation is often the result of inhibitions being anesthetized by the impact of alcohol on GABA neurotransmitters. Stimulant drugs produce similar effects. Therefore, substances like cocaine, amphetamines like "crystal meth," or methylphenidate (Ritalin)• produce excitation, rapid speech, agitation, increased speech, and movement as well as a decreased need for sleep. In Substance Withdrawal, the adage, "What goes up, must come down" can be applied. In other words, usually substances that produce a stimulation effect or an "upper" effect (such as cocaine, crack, or amphetamines) often produce a withdrawal effect that is opposite to the effect of the substance. In the instance of stimulants, the withdrawal effects are usually characterized by depressive states with accompanying irritability.

Nicotine, which is a stimulant, produces a depressant withdrawal effect characterized by lethargy, irritability, and craving. With the CNS (central nervous system) depressant drugs, such as alcohol, benzodiazepines, barbiturates and opioids, the withdrawal effect is usually one of stimulation or agitation. Of the various CNS depressants, alcohol can produce the most potentially fatal withdrawal and is certainly a more dangerous withdrawal than that produced by heroin. Alcohol withdrawal effects can range from mild agitation, to tremors, to hallucinosis, and the most severe form, delirium tremens (DTs). DTs are likened to an extreme form of withdrawal agitation and many alcoholics die from DTs because cardiac or respiratory arrest comes about due to extreme exhaustion. At one time, it was estimated that 5 % to 25 % of those who experienced DTs would die (Lehman, Pilich, & Andrews, 1994; Schuckit, 1995); however, with improved medical care the mortality rate from DTs has decreased to approximately 1 % to 5 % (Milzman & Soderstrom, 1994; Yost, 1996).

Interestingly, while many of the hallucinogen drugs produce rather dangerous "intoxication effects" (phencyclidine or PCP, is a prime example), this class of substances often produces very little withdrawal effects. For example, there are no documented instances of someone experiencing LSD withdrawal. An LSD flashback may produce an unexpected feeling of "tripping" with accompanying visual hallucinations, such as seeing colors or "trails" (colorful afterimages); however, a flashback is not a withdrawal phenomenon, as evidenced by the fact that not all LSD users experience flashbacks.

The intoxicating effects of many substances can often lead to several types of crises, such as fights, arrests, domestic violence incidents, suicide attempts, and other forms of violent or extreme behavior. For example, phencyclidine (PCP) abusers are often known to become agitated and sometimes violent when under the influence of the drug. They can become easily overwhelmed by any visual or auditory stimulation and, as a result, they can become unpredictably violent. This is quite different from the person who is under the influence of CNS depressants, such as Percoset or Darvon and is usually quite placid and nonreactive. Contrast that to the cocaine abuser who may be experiencing "coke paranoia," a cocaine-induced psychotic-like reaction that is estimated to affect 53 % to 65 % of regular cocaine users (Beebe & Walley, 1991; Decker & Ries, 1993).

When assessing individuals who are experiencing crises related to alcohol or other substances, it is important to consider that there is often an overlap between SUD and other mental health disorders. In 2014, among the 20.2 million adults with a past year SUD, 7.9 million (39.1 %) had a mental illness in the past year. In contrast, among adults without a past year SUD, 16.2 % (35.6 million adults) had another mental disorder (AMD) in the past year. Among adults with a past year SUD, the percentage of adults with a co-occurring mental health disorder in 2014 was similar to the percentages of adults with co-occurring mental health disorders in most years from 2008 to 2013.

The 7.9 million adults with another mental disorder who met the criteria for an SUD in the past year represent 18.2% of the 43.6 million adults with AMD. In contrast, 6.3% of adults who did not have past year AMD (12.3 million adults) met the criteria for an SUD. Among adults who had AMD in the past year, the percentage of adults with a co-occurring SUD in 2014 was similar to the percentages of adults with a co-occurring SUD in most years from 2008 to 2013 (Center for Behavioral Health Statistics and Quality, 2015).

CRISIS INTERVENTION AND CASE MANAGEMENT

By virtue of the information presented thus far in this chapter, hopefully you have an appreciation of the fact that not all crisis situations pertaining to alcohol or drugs are the same. For example, a person may present in crisis because they are under the influence (*substance intoxication*), or they may be in a state of alcohol or drug withdrawal (*substance withdrawal*). It is also possible that an individual may present in crisis because they are unable to stop using or every time they use, they end up getting into trouble (*substance use disorder*). This is why it is of utmost importance to make an accurate assessment of the individual who presents with an alcohol or drug crisis. What complicates this assessment, however, is that the counselor may not be able to rely on the patient's self-report of how much he or she may have used of a particular substance and over what time period. In addition, given the lack of "quality control" among drug producers/dealers, it is often impossible to tell the potency of a particular drug, such as heroin, marijuana, or cocaine. It is also not unusual for individuals with substance use disorders to blame their problems on anything other than their substance use or to outright deny that they have been using substances at all. Nevertheless, this should not discourage counselors since minimization, rationalization, and denial are often an integral part of substance use disorders. How counselors help individuals with SUD in crisis very much depends on the extent of the person's use at the time when crisis intervention takes place. For example, it is impossible to conduct a thorough crisis interview with someone who is totally intoxicated or incoherent due to the influence of drugs. The following case presentations illustrate ways in which crisis counselors can help manage substance abuse crises.

Case Presentation: A Crisis Involving Substance Intoxication

Let's return to the case of James that we presented at the very beginning of this chapter. James's crisis starts off as both a *legal crisis* (because of the DUI charge), and a *medical crisis* given that he has both an extreme blood alcohol level (.26) and that he has an opioid pain reliever (Roxicet) in his system. The combination of the two central nervous system depressant substances could have been lethal if James had not been brought to the emergency room following the accident. Therefore, most instances of **substance intoxication**, especially when a person is intoxicated to the point of being either unconscious, unable to wake up, or incoherent (i.e., disoriented, not making sense), should be handled as a medical crisis, and the person should be brought to an emergency room or to an immediate health care center, where he or she can be observed and properly treated. The worst thing

Table 7.1 Risk Factors and Protective Factors for Alcoholism & Substance Dependence

Risk Factors	Protective Factors
Family history of alcohol or drug problems	Absence of any family history of alcohol or drug problems
Family history of psychiatric problems	Absence of any family history of psychiatric problems (e.g., bipolar disorder, depression) or (antisocial personality) or (neurochemical model)
History of diabetes	Absence of family history of diabetes
Prior history of trauma (e.g. childhood sexual or physical abuse)	Absence of any trauma
Friends drink and/or use drugs	Friends do not drink or do drugs and are supportive of abstinence
Family members drink and/or use drugs, encourage use or are afraid to confront use	Family does not drink or use drugs and are supportive of abstinence

to do is to leave the person alone, assuming that he or she will just "sleep it off." Also, don't assume that because you have rolled the person on their side, that they can't aspirate (regurgitate) food and asphyxiate (suffocate).

Intervention

In James's situation, once his medical crisis was stabilized, he was evaluated the following day. The crisis counselor approached the situation as follows:

Counselor: Hi James, my name is Dave Roberts, I'm a counselor here at the university medical center. The doctor who treated you last night asked that I come in and check on you to see how you're feeling today. I understand you were in a car accident. Do you recall being brought to the ER?

James: I remember most of it, I remember my car sideswiping a parked car. And then the cops showed up. That was pretty scary. They called an ambulance because they thought I might have a head injury.

C: Yes, I see in your chart that they gave you a CT scan, but the results are not back yet. How is your head feeling?

J: My head is killing me. Do my parents know I'm here?

C: No, I don't think they've been called yet. I'll check with the ER doctor. Do you want them to be notified that you're here?

J: No! Please don't call them. If they find out I was taken to the ER they'll probably make me come home to live and I'll have to attend a community college or go to work. I can't believe I sideswiped that car. Am I going to be charged with a DUI? I can't believe this is happening again.

C: Has something like this happened before?

J: Well, it wasn't quite this bad, but it was when I was in high school. I went to one of the school dances and really got wiped out on some Jack Daniels that a friend and I stole from my parent's liquor cabinet. We thought that no one would be able to tell we were wasted until my friend, Kylee started puking all over the gym floor. It didn't take them long to figure out that we were drinking together. I remember they sent us both to see the school drug counselor; boy was that a waste of time, we ended up lying our way out of it. My parents threatened me, that if I ever got into trouble like that again for drinking they wouldn't let me go away to college. They are going to kill me, are you sure my parents were not called? Could you check now?

C: Sure, I'll check at the nurses' station and then we'll talk some more. I'd like to get more information about what happened.

J: Okay, who did you say you are? Do you work here at the hospital?

C: Yes, my name is Dave Roberts and I work as a crisis counselor here at the hospital. Dr. Chung asked that I speak with you. I know she is really worried about you.

J: I'm going to be okay, as long as my parents don't find out about this.

At this point, the counselor checks to see if James's parents have been contacted. Many universities and hospitals have policies that allow for parental contact in the event of their son or daughter being treated in an emergency room. Although James is legally an adult, universities will request that students sign FERPA release forms that allow for contact with parents in cases of emergencies. When the counselor returns he informs James that his parents have been notified. James asks if he can call them to let them know he is okay.

C: James, besides this incident, have you been having other problems at the university? Any relationship or academic problems?

J: No, not that I can think of. Oh wait, yeah, I did have something happen a couple of years ago during the spring of my freshman year. My roommate and I threw a party in our dorm and I was caught bringing beer and hard liquor on campus. They put me on some kind of disciplinary probation. I was told that if I didn't have another incident, they would clear my record, whatever that means. Will this get back to the University? I didn't hurt anyone.

C: Not from what I was told, but it sounds like you don't have much recollection of what happened last night? Has that happened to you before?

J: Not every time I drink, but it has happened a bunch of times I guess.

C: Can you tell me what you recall from last night? Did you intend to drink as much as you did?

J: No, I really figured that I would just have a couple of beers and then I was supposed to meet my roommate over at the dining hall and go get something to eat.

C: What do you make of the fact that your evening turned out a lot different from how you planned it?

J: I know there are times when I can control my drinking and other times when I can't, I guess.

C: James, it says on your chart that your blood alcohol level was .26, which is really extreme. The lab also found opioids in your bloodstream. You're really lucky you didn't go into a coma especially with having a head injury. What type of opioid had you taken?

J: I was prescribed Percoset for back pain. I was injured playing lacrosse last year, but when I run out, I have a friend who gives me Roxies (Roxicet).

C: James, it's important that you answer this question very truthfully, were you deliberately trying to harm yourself by drinking and taking drugs? People can overdose by combining alcohol and drugs.

J: You mean like was I suicidal? No, I know that things are pretty screwed up for me right now, but I'd never do something like end it all. I would never do something like that. I just had more to drink than I thought I would, that's all. You don't think I'm a druggie or some kind of psycho case, do you?

C: No, it's just important for me to make sure that you weren't trying to harm yourself intentionally because you did take a potentially lethal combination of drugs. Would you tell me more about your use of Percoset and Roxies?

J: No, I'd never do anything stupid to hurt myself. I'm upset because of the accident and the possibility of getting a DUI. I like began using Percosets when I had a lot of back pain, then I began using them in order to relax.

C: Is there any history of drinking or drug problems in your family?

J: My mom and dad almost broke up a few years ago because of my father's drinking. He then started to go to AA and counseling. I don't think he drinks anymore. Not that I know of.

C: Did you feel that your father had a drinking problem?

J: I guess. He would come home just about every night either drunk and stumbling or buzzed and slurring his words. A couple of times he stayed out all night and my Mom was worried he was in a car accident or thought he might have been involved in an affair or something. I was glad when he quit. He was a nasty drunk.

C: James, did you know that alcohol and drug problems run in families? Some researchers feel there is pretty convincing evidence that it's a genetic illness.

J: Yes, I've heard that, but just because I party every once in a while, it doesn't mean that I'm like my father or that I have a problem. I'm young and this is what we do to blow off steam.

C: Sure, I see what you mean. I was thinking, though, that when you set out last night to have a good time, you didn't think you would end up in an emergency room, right?

J: Right, but this happens to my dorm mates all the time, they get wasted and end up being brought to the ER. That alone doesn't mean I have a problem, does it?

C: You have had a lot of problems related to your drinking and drug use. I appreciate your being honest with me. Is there anything you might have left out that would be important for me to know?

J: No, not that I can think of. I'll do anything in order not to be kicked out of school. I don't want to go back home to live.

C: Since you've already tried the counseling center, why don't we set up an appointment with an intensive outpatient program here at the medical center. I can't guarantee that you won't be expelled from school, but going to an intensive outpatient program would be a good step for many reasons.

J: Like I said, I'll do anything. Would you talk with my parents when they get here? I'm afraid of facing them alone.

C: Sure, I'd be happy to meet with them. That sounds like a good idea. Let's see if they will agree with the plan we've discussed.

Case Conceptualization/Crisis Resolution

The crisis session described above, attempts to do two things. First, the crisis counselor is trying to get needed background information from James pertaining to his alcohol and drug use in order to determine the nature of the present crisis. Another goal pertaining to the alcohol and drug use is whether this represents an isolated instance of excessive drinking and/or drug use or whether it may represent a pattern of substance use and consequential problematic behavior that may suggest a diagnosis of substance use disorder. Also, the counselor attempts to determine if the incident may have represented a possible suicide attempt. There are many instances where people will overdose accidentally or will use alcohol and drugs with suicidal intentions.

How does one approach the alcoholic or addict in order to work effectively with them and to assist them in resolving the crisis in a professional, competent manner? As in any counseling situation, it is important to first establish rapport. The person in crisis needs to know that you are there to help them, not to criticize them, nor to judge them. Individuals with SUDs are often very attuned to judgmental attitudes. In James's case, it was also important for the counselor to *listen* to his concerns and account of what he was able to recall. The next step is to *assess* the extent and nature of his alcohol and drug use. Some say, "Why bother, most alcoholics or addicts lie anyway." Others suggest that whatever the alcoholic or addict tells you they are using, simply double that amount and you probably have a more accurate picture of their substance use pattern. That is why, whenever possible, it is helpful to get information from significant others, such as roommates, friends, family, and coworkers. However, we must caution you that except for a life-threatening medical emergency, federal confidentiality laws pertaining to alcohol and drug patients dictate that you must obtain a signed written release from the patient, before you can contact anyone. James probably would not have allowed the crisis counselor to speak with his parents or friends unless absolutely necessary. It was also noteworthy that James disclosed that his father had a problem with alcohol, which suggests a genetic risk factor to James's alcohol and drug problems (Legrand, Iacono, & McGue, 2005).

Prior to James's release from the hospital, it is of utmost importance that some definite *Plan* be set up for continued assessment and counseling. The tendency of most individuals in similar situations is to deny the need for counseling once the crisis has passed. That is why it is important that definite appointment times be established before he is medically cleared to leave, and that in the meeting with his parents, James *Commits* to following through with that plan.

Case Presentation: A Crisis Involving Substance Withdrawal

Ophelia is a 28-year-old single retail manager who has been living with her boyfriend Ray for the past three years. They met while in college and began dating in their senior year. They've had many "ups and downs" in their relationship; they separated for 10 months, at which point they decided to give things one more try. Most of their problems have revolved around Ophelia's drinking and drug use. Ophelia explains that she began drinking in high school with friends on weekends. During the summer, she would rent a house at the beach with these friends and there would be continuous, wild parties. Ophelia had a DUI last year, but she chalked it up to "being in the wrong place at the wrong time." Ray was really upset with her. Although he drinks, he feels that he never lets his drinking get out of hand. He feels that Ophelia becomes like Dr. Jekyll and Mr. Hyde after a few drinks. One evening at a dinner party, after Ophelia consumed several margaritas, Ray caught her in a sexually compromising situation with one of his best friends. Ophelia sought crisis counseling because Ray moved out. Ophelia was out drinking with her friends last night and did not come home until 4:00 in the morning only to find that Ray had left her. Ophelia is upset, is crying, and doesn't know how she can live without Ray. She did not want to ruin their relationship. She feels that her life is out of control. As the crisis counselor begins to gather more information, Ophelia reveals that in addition to drinking almost a pint of hard liquor per day, she supplements that with a "few glasses of wine" in the evening, and then takes a Valium to "calm" her nerves in the morning. About 30 minutes into the session, Ophelia's hands are noticeably trembling.

Ophelia sought crisis counseling with the presenting complaint that her boyfriend, Ray, left her (It is not unusual for alcoholics or addicts to present for help for many other problems other than their drug or alcohol abuse.). However, as the session progresses and more information is gathered, it is obvious that Ophelia has a drinking and drug problem. What is significant, although not unique about her pattern of use, is that she is a functional alcoholic who is also dependent on Valium (another depressant drug). It is likely that her use of Valium became a means of preventing the withdrawal symptoms (such as hand tremors and shakiness), which she experienced in the morning because of her drinking. Very similar to the crisis of substance intoxication, **substance withdrawal** is also a medical emergency. The worst thing a crisis counselor can do is to let this patient leave an outpatient office unattended, or without being escorted to an emergency room for a medical evaluation. Also, very similar to the case of James described earlier, the crisis counselor's approach is to establish rapport with Ophelia, and to gather as much information as possible about her recent use of alcohol and drugs, in order to relay this information to the physician who will be assessing her in the emergency room. It is also important to gather this information in a sensitive, nonjudgmental manner, which is why it is very important to establish rapport and connection first. With Ophelia, for example, it is important to hear out her distress about Ray and to offer support. Supportive statements might include, "I can see how upset you are about Ray's leaving," or "This separation must be really difficult for you right now." It is best to steer clear of statements like, "Don't worry, you'll get him back," or "I know how you feel, it's tough to go through a breakup." In making statements like these, the counselor may be promising something that may not happen ("you'll get him back"), or presuming how Ophelia feels ("I know how you feel").

The most difficult scenario that comes up with a case involving substance withdrawal is when the person refuses medical attention. Some states have laws that make it permissible to hold an intoxicated person in an emergency room for 48 to 72 hours for observation. The supposition of these laws is that a person who is intoxicated or in a state of substance withdrawal may not be coherent and reasonable enough to make an informed decision regarding his or her treatment. However, others would argue that keeping a person in an emergency room against his or her will is a violation of their civil liberties. Naturally, there are horror stories of intoxicated people leaving the emergency room against medical advice and getting killed as they tried to cross the street. There are no simple solutions. Also, an important point of clarification: the diagnoses of substance intoxication and substance withdrawal refer to the patient's current status at the time he or she is being seen for crisis intervention. However, once that crisis passes, for example the person is no longer under the influence of the drug or he or she has been detoxified from the substance, then the patient still needs to be evaluated to determine if he or she meets the criteria for a substance use disorder. It is important to remember that a person need not be physically addicted in order to be diagnosed with a substance use disorder. Think, for example, of a binge alcoholic who can often go weeks or months in between binges without drinking; however, once he or she does pick up a drink, their binge can last for days, weeks, or months. If you were to evaluate the person during one of their periods of abstinence, he or she could still meet the criteria for substance dependence and still require some type of intensive treatment.

For the crisis counselor, the task becomes trying to talk the person into seeking medical attention or staying in the emergency room. The following dialogue is an example of how a crisis counselor might try to convince Ophelia that she needs medical attention.

Intervention

Counselor: Ophelia, from everything you've told me so far, I am really worried about your plan to stop drinking without medical intervention.

Ophelia: Oh, I've done this before, no big deal. One time, Ray was angry with me after I got drunk at his father's birthday party, and I was completely sober for a few days.

C: I recall your mentioning that, but Ophelia, you mentioned earlier that you were not drinking as much then, plus now you are taking Valium. Taking these two together is a really dangerous combination, that's why I'm really worried what would happen if you try to stop on your own.

O: I see what you're saying, but I need to get Ray back; I need to talk with him right away. Hell, I don't even know where he is or even if he would talk to me anyway.

C: Right, Ophelia, besides you really need to take care of yourself right now. It's really important that you let the doctor take a look at you. Would you at least agree to having Dr. Ruiz check you over to make sure you are okay?

O: I guess so. I am really shaking, and I don't know if I have enough Valium to get me through the night.

C: Sounds like we have an agreement. Let's have Dr. Ruiz take a look at you and see what she recommends.

O: I'm okay with that, but what if she wants me to stay in the hospital overnight? I'm afraid I won't be able to talk with Ray.

C: Let's see what Dr. Ruiz recommends, and if you'd like, we can try to call Ray. Would you like to use the phone while we're waiting? Would you like me to talk with Ray?

O: No, but I would like to try to call him again. If he doesn't believe that I'm here, could you talk with him then?

C: Sure, I'd be happy to talk with him.

Case Conceptualization/Crisis Resolution

In the illustration above, the crisis counselor tries to appeal to Ophelia's sense of reason in a nonthreatening way. The counselor also reinforces the idea that for right now, it is okay for Ophelia to take care of herself and not focus so much on Ray or trying to regain the relationship. Naturally, if these strategies are not working, the counselor may need to use more persuasive tactics, such as bringing up some of the dangers of trying to detox on her own. Again, while scare tactics are usually to be avoided, some of the realities of withdrawal complications (such as tremor, seizures, hallucinosis) can be brought up in such a way as to try to make a more persuasive argument for treatment. In some instances, there may be a family member or friend present who can also help persuade the patient to stay and get the proper medical attention. It is important that the crisis counselor not lose his or her patience or attempt to force the person into making a decision too hastily, as this usually produces resistance or treatment refusal. It is better that the crisis counselor tries to help diminish the client's fears of the detoxification process, and stress that you and the other staff will help see them through this difficult period with as little distress or pain as possible. A detoxification in a medical setting may take about three to seven days on average, depending on the drug of choice. Detoxifications involving opiate drugs (such as heroin, morphine, codeine, and oxycontin) usually take longer, but can be done on an outpatient basis.

Case Presentation: A Crisis Resulting from a Substance Use Disorder

Federico is a 45-year-old attorney who has a thriving law practice. Last night he was arrested after getting into an argument with his wife. The argument got very heated and Federico ended up shoving his wife, Claire, down on the floor, which resulted in her hitting her head. She called the police and Federico was arrested for domestic violence. When asked what they were arguing about, Federico admitted to the counselor that he had been using cocaine that night. He stated that he began using cocaine "socially" about six years ago. He described his use as occasional at first, usually with some of his golfing friends; however, over the past two years, he was using consistently. Federico said he was also prescribed Vicodin for back pain, which he also takes on a daily basis. He described that on some weekends he would rent a hotel room and would continue to snort lines of cocaine until Monday morning. He states that he would often get paranoid and would be afraid to come out of the hotel room. He would then take Vicodin just to calm down enough to go into his office or court on Monday. Federico explained that Claire doesn't do drugs and never had any interest in them whatsoever. She resented Federico's use because of the time and money it had taken away from her and their son. Federico felt that Claire was overreacting and was being very prudish. He stated that if Claire would just get off his back, he could work this problem out on his own. He was referred for crisis counseling by the court because of the domestic violence complaint. Federico presently feels he can cut down on using cocaine, especially if he goes back to intranasal (snorting) use and refrains from freebasing, as he has been doing the past two years. However, he does not feel that he can stop using all together, nor does he feel that is necessary. At the time of the crisis session, Federico reports feeling depressed, lethargic, and apathetic, which he attributes to his arrest.

This case raises some interesting questions. For example, does Federico have a primary drug problem, or is the primary problem with his wife Claire, given her domestic violence complaint? Also, because Federico feels, "depressed, lethargic, and apathetic" is this primarily a psychiatric problem? Is Federico really depressed? In this case, Federico's crisis is illustrative of **substance use disorder**. In his bravado (many cocaine dependent individuals often exhibit a sense of invulnerability), Federico declares, "I can cut down," yet later admits that he probably will not "stop using altogether." Federico clearly has a cocaine use disorder. As was pointed out earlier, although one does not have to use on a daily basis, nor experience tolerance or withdrawal in order to be diagnosed with a substance use disorder, it appears, however, that Federico does exhibit many symptoms of substance dependence. For example, he does report a progression to his cocaine use, having started with occasional use then progressing to daily use punctuated with many weekend cocaine binges. His report of feeling "depressed, lethargic, and apathetic" are probably due to cocaine withdrawal. One could also make the argument that Federico is experiencing guilt and is feeling depressed over the domestic violence arrest, yet he plans to continue using despite his knowledge that his cocaine use is causing major disruption in his marriage. Additionally, it appears that in order to fend off his guilt, Federico blames Claire as the source of his problems and will not admit that his cocaine use is the root cause of his difficulties. This is a common defense among many individuals with substance use disorders.

In terms of providing crisis intervention counseling to Federico, it is necessary to establish rapport or connection with him by hearing him out, listening to his explanations of what happened and the events leading up to the arrest. Then, the counselor needs to help to assist Federico to realistically define the current crisis. For example, even though he wants to view Claire as "the problem," it is necessary to provide feedback to Federico regarding the events he describes.

Intervention

Counselor: So, it sounds as if it weren't for Claire, you wouldn't be having all these problems, right? Had you been considering a divorce?

Federico: No, of course not, I could never divorce Claire. Besides, divorce is frowned on in my religion.

C: But, isn't Claire the source of your problems, the reason why the domestic violence arrest took place? You said before she was "overreacting."

F: No, she's not the source of the problem. I just wish she would be okay with my doing a few lines (of cocaine) every once in a while, after all, what's the harm in that? It's the only way I get to relax or have any fun, like a mini-vacation.

C: Federico, you said before that you couldn't use a few lines once in a while. Your use is beyond that, right?

F: Yeah, I guess. But, I still think I can cut back.

C: Federico, you've spent thousands of dollars on cocaine, how much did you tell me your last weekend binge cost you? Also, you now have a domestic violence charge pending. It sounds like things have gone beyond the point where cutting down a little will really work. Besides, do you really think Claire would accept you back under the condition that you've "cut back"?

F: No, you're right. No way would she take me back if I was still using.

C: So, I guess the question becomes, "how are you going to stop getting high?"

F: Got any ideas?

C: Yes, let me present some different treatment options to you and then we can discuss which ones that may interest you. One treatment you may consider would be a residential program (rehab). Is that something you would consider?

F: I really don't think I need it, but if you think it would help me get my wife back, and it would keep the court from disbarring me, I'd consider it.

Case Conceptualization/Crisis Resolution

Naturally, not all crisis sessions go this smoothly. In an actual session, it would probably take some time to get Federico to focus on his cocaine use, since he would most likely be too invested in blaming Claire. The main goal of a crisis session with someone who is substance dependent is to get them to question their own faulty addictive logic and accept treatment. As Vernon Johnson (1991) states, the approach used in interventions is to "present reality in a receivable way." The reality of Federico's situation is that his cocaine use is out of control and is causing major problems in functioning. The task of the counselor is to present this "reality in a receivable way," with the hope that the alcoholic or addict will commit to treatment, usually in a residential or inpatient setting as a beginning. Other modalities and sequences of treatment are discussed in the last section of this chapter.

Families in Crisis

Before concluding this section on intervention techniques, it is important to say a few words about family crises. In many crisis intervention settings, it is not unusual for the family to present in crisis, requesting help rather than the substance abuser. Family members often live with an active alcoholic or addict for years, feeling powerless and frustrated in not being able to change their loved one's drinking or drug use (Johnson, 1991). Most families begin to live their lives "around" their loved one with a substance use disorder. This may work temporarily, because sooner or later, a crisis will eventually occur (e.g. an arrest, an overdose, being fired from a job, etc.) In these instances, it is important to encourage the family to "strike while the iron is hot"; in other words, to take advantage of the crisis as an opportunity to intervene with their loved one and encourage him or her to go for treatment. The other rule of thumb in working with families in crisis is to look for denial in various family members. The dynamics of the families where substance use disorders are present is often unique not just in the various roles of family members, but also in terms of various instances of *triangulation* and *collusion* that may occur. (These terms are used by family therapists to describe family dynamics). In triangulation, for example, an unstable couple, say the husband and wife, will often drag a third party, usually a son or daughter into their conflicts as a means of creating a dysfunctional balance. In collusion, you may have a parent who will collude or confide in a son or daughter who then takes sides with them against the other parent). Therefore, in helping families impacted by a SUD crisis it is often common to find some family members who will perceive the crisis to be caused or related to some other mental health problem or some other stressor (e.g., like job stress), while other family members will be keenly aware of the crisis being related to or caused by alcohol or drug use.

GENERAL GUIDELINES FOR WORKING WITH INDIVIDUALS WITH SUBSTANCE USE DISORDERS

First determine if the person is in a state of intoxication or withdrawal. This is not always as easy as it sounds. Some alcoholics and addicts have built up such an extreme tolerance to alcohol or drugs that they may be capable of functioning somewhat "normally," but with relatively high levels of chemicals in their bloodstream. If the person is under the influence or in a state of intoxication or withdrawal, you may be dealing with a medical crisis where it might be best to have him or her seen in an emergency room. Here, a toxicology screen can be performed that will determine what substance he or she may have taken and in some instances how much. Also try to find out if this individual identifies as a person in recovery who may have recently relapsed. First, is the person in a state of medical emergency (as noted above) due to substance intoxication or withdrawal? Second, the counselor must then determine if there is a pattern of substance use resulting in serious life problems, in which case a diagnosis of substance abuse or substance dependence may be rendered. Obviously, if a person is in a state of substance withdrawal, it's easier to diagnose a substance use disorder. The intoxication and withdrawal diagnosis is important for immediate crisis planning while the diagnosis of a substance use disorder is important for longer range planning beyond the medical crisis.

Next determine if there is an ongoing alcohol or drug problem. Crisis counselors who assess individuals with alcohol and/or drug crises are really making two major determinations.

It is common for individuals with substance use disorders (SUD) to minimize, rationalize, or outright deny the seriousness of their chemical use. Don't be put off by this or take it personally as this is common among individuals with SUDs.

Avoid being judgmental or blaming the person with a SUD for their seemingly irrational behavior. This only adds to their resistance to treatment. It is always best to take a nonjudgmental, concerned approach.

Treatment planning may be driven by medical insurance coverage. Individuals with insurance coverage usually have a wider range of treatment options open to them, while those without insurance are usually limited to state-funded programs with often lengthy waiting lists. Similarly, not all insurance plans are alike; those who are covered by health maintenance organizations (HMOs) are often limited to attend certain programs. Also, the length of treatment stay is also determined by the HMO. Most counselors will tell you that prior to HMOs, the challenge was trying to convince the person with the substance use issue to enter treatment. Today, the challenge is trying to convince the HMO administrator to let the addict or alcoholic into treatment!

Box 7.2: Screening, Brief Intervention, and Referral to Treatment (SBIRT) approaches

With the vast number of individuals who manifest substance use disorders in the United States, there has been a national effort to attempt to use various points of contact, such as hospitals, schools, doctors' offices, mental health clinics and university health centers, to try to encourage individuals to seek treatment when there are signs or symptoms of a substance use disorder. According to the Office of National Drug Control Policy, healthcare practitioners have the important responsibility of looking after their patients' general health and welfare. In this role, they must be vigilant in identifying a host of potential health problems, including problems related to substance use. It is critical, therefore, to focus resources and efforts on expanding the continuum of care health practitioners provide for their patients. With SBIRT, substance abuse screening is incorporated into mainstream healthcare settings, such as college health clinics, hospitals, trauma centers, and dental clinics, as well as into tribal and military healthcare settings. Practitioners screen patients to assess substance use; then, based on the screening results provide the appropriate intervention and recommendations for treatment if necessary. SBIRT is a four-part process: Universal screening assesses substance use and identifies people with substance use problems. Brief intervention is provided when a screening indicates moderate risk. Brief intervention uses motivational interviewing techniques focused on raising patients' awareness of substance use and its consequences and motivating them toward positive behavioral change. Brief therapy continues motivational discussions for persons needing more than a brief intervention. Brief therapy is more comprehensive and includes further assessment, education, problem solving, coping mechanisms, and building a supportive social environment. Referral to treatment provides a referral to specialty care for persons deemed to be at high risk. A key aspect of SBIRT is the integration and coordination of screening, early intervention, and treatment components into a system of care. This system links community health care and social service programs with specialty treatment programs. In each of the SBIRT grantee programs, healthcare professionals and clinical support staff conduct universal screening that targets risky to harmful use, thereby helping to reduce the number of people who move from substance use to addiction.

Office of National Drug Control Policy (ONDCP). (2012, July). Substance Abuse and Mental Health Services Administration (SAMHSA) *FACT SHEET: Step 1, Steps 2 and 3, and Step 4.*

Source: Retrieved from http://www.integration.samhsa.gov/clinical-practice/SBIRT

Individuals with substance use disorders are often ambivalent about change and therefore may try to avoid "Committing" to treatment. It is often better to offer a menu of treatment choices. However, in instances where detoxification is needed or there are severe medical complications, then crisis counselors may need to strongly suggest what constitutes a safe treatment option. Some states provide a civil commitment option for those individuals who need treatment, but refuse (Cavaiola & Dolan, 2016).

Whenever possible involve family members or significant others in the assessment and crisis planning process. Here it is important to always include family members and/or significant others in the assessment and treatment planning process. Family members may be an invaluable source of information (e.g. regarding past treatment attempts) regarding what resources may be available to their loved one. For example, if a family member indicates that their loved one has tried outpatient several times and not done well, then it may be time to consider a more intensive form of treatment. Or a family member may be able to provide background information; for example, the history of bipolar disorder in other family members that can impact on the crisis counselor's current assessment and treatment planning decisions.

Don't get frustrated by "revolving door" clients. Substance use disorders are often said to be "chronic relapsing diseases," therefore it is not unusual to see the same client in crisis over and over again. You never know when this crisis intervention may be the one that helps motivate that individual into long-term recovery.

Find out what has worked in the past. If an individual with a SUD has put together any appreciable amount of sober/clean time in the past, try to find out what factors helped him or her accomplish that sobriety. Also, what "strengths" does this person have that helped them put together this clean time.

Don't get roped into the "treatment may work for others, but not for me" approach. Just because this individual has been in detox or rehab before, doesn't mean that it won't work for him or her this time around (Washton & Zweben, 2006).

Don't leave an intoxicated person unattended or let them get out of your sight. A medical center and a crisis screener were both sued when an intoxicated patient wandered out of the emergency room and was hit and killed by a car.

TREATMENT OPTIONS

There are many different treatment modalities that are available to treat those with substance use disorders. It may be helpful to think of these modalities as existing on a continuum from most intensive to least intensive. Regarding individuals who manifest substance use disorders, it is important to think of these treatments as being sequential rather than as discrete entities (See Table 7.2).

For example, in the case of Ophelia, described above, once the initial substance withdrawal is managed effectively in a medical setting, ideally, she would then be immediately transferred to an inpatient substance treatment facility for further management. Detox was the first step in the process, however, it is important that inpatient treatment extend beyond the initial detox phase which may only last a few days to a few weeks at most.

Table 7.2 Alcohol and Drug Crisis Management

Assessment			
• gather alcohol & drug history • obtain information on recent use • determine prior treatment history • assess for medical complications			
Intoxication	**Withdrawal**	**Substance Use Disorders**	
Medical Evaluation	Medical Evaluation	Medical Evaluation	Outpatient
Hospitalization or Medical Supervision	Hospitalization Outpatient Detox	Admission to Rehab or Intensive Outpatient	Education
Chemical Dependency Assessment	Referral to Rehab	Family Counseling	Family Counseling

Once Ophelia completed the inpatient phase of treatment, she might be transferred to a halfway house, where she might go to work or school during the day, while participating in group counseling and Alcoholics Anonymous/Narcotics Anonymous (AA/NA) meetings in the evening at the halfway house. Or she may return home and then would immediately begin an intensive outpatient program. In an intensive outpatient program (or IOP), she would attend groups three to four nights a week, while going to Alcoholics Anonymous meetings on the weekends, as a means of reinforcing her sobriety/recovery. Usually an IOP lasts three or four weeks, at which point, Ophelia would most likely begin an outpatient group on a weekly basis or she may be seen for individual counseling about once a week, while she actively attends AA meetings in between those sessions. Although many recovering people (the correct term is "recovering," not "recovered" alcoholic or addict, because addictions are considered to be chronic, lifelong diseases, therefore, a person is never fully "cured," hence the term "recovering" is acceptable), often continue to attend counseling for years into their sobriety, this is not always necessary although it is highly recommended that the person continue to actively participate in either AA or NA (Narcotics Anonymous) or some other 12-Step program (12-Step programs are the mainstay of most substance disorder treatment modalities). So, while a person may be in an inpatient program, they will be introduced to the 12-Step philosophy on how to stay clean and sober.

For individuals without medical insurance coverage or for those with managed care insurance plans, they may not be as fortunate as Ophelia to have such a comprehensive array of treatment options at their disposal. For these individuals, their options may be limited to often over-crowded federally funded or state-funded programs. However, these programs often have lengthy waiting lists which adds to the difficulty in treating individuals effectively. From the case vignettes provided, one can see how crucial the timing is when encouraging an individual with a SUD to agree to treatment. Usually, this search for treatment occurs in the wake of a major crisis. Unfortunately, to finally have someone agree to go into treatment and then to have him or her placed on a lengthy waiting list is inhumane.

Sober living facilities are another option for individuals who may have been living in homes or areas where alcohol or drug use was rampant or they are sometimes referred to as *Oxford Houses*. These are basically homes or large apartments that are shared by individuals who have been clean and sober for several weeks or months and whose prior living arrangements are not conducive or supportive of his or her recovery. For example, a person who lives in a crime-ridden, drug-ridden neighborhood where his or her drug dealer stands on their corner everyday would have more support by living in a different neighborhood with "like-minded" individuals who are also clean and sober and who are also working actively on their recovery by attending outpatient treatment and/or 12-Step meetings. Similarly, for an individual who may have siblings or other family members who are active drug/alcohol users, returning to that environment may present too many relapse triggers, and therefore a sober living facility may be a better choice for that individual rather than returning home.

Many of the aforementioned treatment programs usually include some type of family counseling. Family counseling programs usually vary in terms of their length and intensity. For example, some inpatient programs offer an intensive residential family program which usually lasts for about a week. While in the program, family members often participate in both educational and counseling groups, sometimes with their addicted family member, other times without them. The purpose of these family programs is to assist family members in identifying how their loved one's addiction has impacted on them and the role they may have played in perpetuating the addiction, for example as an enabler, or as the equivocator. Naturally, the goal of such programs is to assist family members in breaking free of pathological family roles. Just as the alcoholic or addict is introduced to AA or NA philosophy during the inpatient treatment process, so too, the family members are being introduced to Al-Anon and Nar-Anon. (For a complete listing of 12-Step Programs, see Table 7.3).

Similar to the alcoholic or addict, treatment does not end once they step foot out of the rehab and the same applies to the family. Family members should ideally continue to participate in their own counseling beyond the inpatient program stay, and continue to attend Al-Anon and Nar-Anon meetings regularly. A question arises in terms of when is the best time to begin couples counseling or family counseling with the alcoholic or addict present. This is not always a black-or-white issue. Obviously, the alcoholic or addict must be stable enough in their recovery to be capable of hearing the sometimes not-too-flattering feedback from their family. Sometimes, family members see the initial counseling sessions as a safe means to vent all their anger and resentment toward the alcoholic or addict for the disruption their addiction has caused them. In some instances, if this is handled in the same manner as an intervention, it can certainly help to break down any remnants of denial. However, the caveat is that the alcoholic or addict must be stabilized enough to withstand some of the anger that may get thrown his or her way. This is why some addiction treatment providers prefer to hold off on any heavy-duty family or couples counseling until the alcoholic or addict is well into their recovery (perhaps at least six to

Table 7.3   12-Step Programs

To learn more about specific 12-Step programs for various types of addictions or programs for family members, contact the phone numbers listed or visit their websites for information about meetings and services. There may also be local listings for these 12-Step groups listed in the white pages of your phone book. Remember, 12-Step programs are FREE!!! and are very effective in helping many addicts, alcoholics, and their families.

A.A. (Alcoholics Anonymous)
World Services
Box 459
Grand Central Station
New York, NY 10163
(212) 870-3400
www.aa.org

Adult Children of Alcoholics
World Service Organization
PO Box 3216
Torrance, CA 90510
(310) 534-1815
www.adultchildren.org

Al-Anon & Alateen
For adult and teenage family members of an alcoholic and other friends or relatives
Al-Anon Family Group Headquarters
1600 Corporate Landing Parkway
Virginia Beach, VA 23454-5617
(888) 4AL-ANON
www.al-anon.org

Co-Dependents Anonymous
For people whose lives are impacted by alcoholics or addicted individuals and who cannot seem to break free from problematic roles in which they may enable the addict or alcoholic to continue drinking
PO Box 33577
Phoenix, AZ 85067-3577
(602) 277-7991
www.codependents.org

Debtors Anonymous
General Services Office
PO Box 920888
Needham, MA 02492-0009
(781) 453-2743
fax (781) 453-2745
www.debtorsanonymous.org

Gam-Anon
For family, friends and significant others of someone with a gambling addiction
International Service Office
PO Box 157
Whitestone, NY 11357
(718) 352-1671
fax (718) 746-2571
www.gam-anon.org

Gamblers Anonymous
International Service Office
PO Box 17173
Los Angeles, CA 90017
(213) 386-8789
fax (213) 386-0030
www.gamblersanonymous.org

Narcotics Anonymous
World Service Office
PO Box 9999
Van Nuys, CA 91409
(818) 773-9999
fax (818) 700-0700
www.na.org

Overeaters Anonymous
World Service Office
PO Box 44020
Rio Rancho, NM 87174-4020
(505) 891-4320
fax (505) 891-4320
www.overeatersanonymous.org

Sexaholics Anonymous (S.A.)
PO Box 111910
Nashville, TN 37222
(615) 331-6230
fax (615) 331-6901
www.sa.org

Sex Addicts Anonymous (S.A.A.)
International Service Office
PO Box 70949
Houston, TX 77270
1-800-477-8191
www.saa-recovery.org

(Continued)

Table 7.3   (Continued)

Sexual Compulsives Anonymous (S.C.A.) International Service Office PO Box 1585 Old Chelsea Station New York, NY 10011 1-800-977-HEAL www.sca-recovery.org
Sex and Love Addicts Anonymous (S.L.A.A.) The Augustine Fellowship PO Box 338 Norwood, MA 02062-0338 (781) 255-8825 www.slaafws.org
S-Anon International Family Groups For family members and significant others of sex addicts PO Box 111242 Nashville, TN 37222-1242 (615) 833-3152 www.sanon.org
Solvency Ideas and support for those in debt, compulsive spenders, plus listings for Debtors Anonymous meetings. www.solvency.org
Sober Space Information on AA meetings across the United States by state. Also, there are the phone numbers for local AA Intergroups and e-mail addresses state-by-state. www.soberspace.com
Original Group Download a copy of the AA Big Book in Windows 95 Format www.originalgroup.com/on-the-net/bb_index.html

12-months sober). The problem with this approach is that many more couples break up in recovery than they do during active addiction, so the question remains whether it is truly better to hold off on couples/family counseling. Research studies seem to suggest, however, that there is a better prognosis for those families who do participate in treatment when compared to those families that don't.

The American Society of Addiction Medicine (ASAM) offers a rubric for determining the level of care of individuals with substance use disorders. In the ASAM-3 patient placement criteria (Mee-Lee, 2013), there are ten levels of treatment ranging from the least intense, early intervention level that focuses on psychoeducational approaches in an outpatient setting (Level .05), to medical managed intensive inpatient services for individuals requiring 24-hour medical and nursing care due to severe and potentially life-threatening medical complications and/or withdrawal (Level 4). The ASAM-3 criteria provide a useful way to determine what treatment options best meet the patient's needs.

SUMMARY

Alcohol and drug use is pervasive in American culture and therefore, it's not surprising to see so many people who are impacted by substance use disorders and substance use crises. And it is estimated that for every person with a substance use disorder, six other people in that person's life are affected. This may account for the vast numbers of individuals who enter treatment programs each year. It is also well-known among mental health professionals that many individuals who seek mental health treatment are seeking help because of their own substance use issues or those of a friend or family member. Therefore, it is very important that crisis counselors are aware of the three subtypes of substance-related diagnoses (i.e. substance intoxication, substance withdrawal, and substance use disorders) and are aware and knowledgeable about how to effectively intervene in these situations.

RESOURCES FOR CHAPTER ENRICHMENT

Suggested Readings

Goodwin, D. W. (1984). Studies of familial alcoholism: A review. *Archives of General Psychiatry, 45,* 14–17.

Hari, J. (2015). *Chasing the scream: The first and last days of the war on drugs. NY: Bloomsbury Press.*

Johnson, V. (1990). *I'll quit tomorrow: A practical guide to alcoholism treatment.* (Rev. ed.). San Francisco, CA: HarperCollins.

McCrady, B. S., & Epstein, E. E. (Eds.). (2014). *Addictions: A comprehensive guidebook* (2nd ed.). Oxford, UK: Oxford University Press.

Stanton, M. D., & Todd, T. C. (1982). *The family therapy of drug abuse and addiction.* New York, NY: Guilford.

Vaillant, G. E. (1995). *The natural history of alcoholism revisited.* Cambridge, MA: Harvard University Press.

Quinones, S. (2015). Dreamland: The true tale of America's opiate epidemic. NY: Bloomsbury Press.

Washton, A. M., & Zweben, J. E. (2006). *Treating alcohol and drug problems in psychotherapy practice.* New York, NY: Guilford.

Suggested Websites

National Institute of Alcohol Abuse & Alcoholism (NIAAA)
This the website for the National Institute of Alcohol Abuse & Alcoholism in Washington, D.C. It contains a plethora of useful information, including incidence and prevalence statistics, factual information about alcohol, alcohol abuse and alcoholism, mortality statistics, treatment resources, and a section of "Frequently Asked Questions." This is an excellent website to gain some good basic knowledge about alcohol and alcoholism: www.niaaa.nih.gov

National Institute of Drug Abuse (NIDA)
This is the website for the National Institute of Drug Abuse in Washington, D.C. This website is like the NIAAA website cited above, only it deals specifically with drugs of abuse. It also contains a great deal of factual information about incidence and prevalence rates, up-to-date information about a variety of drugs, treatment resources, and other worthwhile statistics: www.nida.nih.gov

Substance Abuse & Mental Health Services
This is the website for SAMHSA, which is the Substance Abuse & Mental Health Services Administration, an agency of the U.S. Department of Health & Human Services. This site contains up-to-date information on incidence and prevalence rates, treatment resources, and information on drugs and alcohol: www.samhsa.gov

National Clearinghouse of Alcohol and Drug Information
This is the website for the National Clearinghouse of Alcohol and Drug Information, which is a service of SAMHSA, which is the Substance Abuse & Mental Health Services Administration which is a branch of the U.S. Department of Health & Human Services. This site also provides excellent up-to-date information on topics pertaining to drugs and alcohol. Each drug of choice has its own page that contains vital information about the effects of the drug as well as the dangers and consequences associated with that particular drug. There is also information about treatment resources. This page is quite useful for those providing education and/or prevention services to a variety of individuals from different backgrounds, as the site contains specific pages for various groups; for example, teens, elderly, gay and lesbians, as well as a variety of racial and ethnic minorities: http://ncadi.samhsa.gov

National Council on Alcoholism and Drug Dependence
This is the website for the National Council on Alcoholism and Drug Dependence. This site also contains useful, up-to-date information on alcohol and drugs as well as treatment services: www.ncadd.org

Alcohol & Drug Abuse Commission
This is the website for the Alcohol & Drug Abuse Commission. It also contains a lot of information pertaining to drugs and alcohol, negative effects, and treatment options: www.aadac.com

The Web of Addictions
This is an excellent website that provides a great deal of information for those with addictive illnesses. The page contains links to many other resources and mailing lists: www.webofaddictions.com. Recognized as a noted person in the addictions field, Dr. Grohol's webpage offers a review of this website at http://www.grohol.com/reviews.htm

Recommended Films

Clean and Sober: **(1988)** (stars Michael Keaton & Morgan Freeman). This film portrays the life of a young stockbroker who is addicted to cocaine and alcohol and whose life spirals out of control as a result of the progression of his addictions. Morgan Freeman plays the role of the counselor. The portrayals of the rehab, the groups, and especially the denial of those in the throes of active addictions is chilling and accurate.

28 Days: **(2000)** (stars Sandra Bullock, Dominic West, & Viggo Mortensen). This film portrays the life of an active alcoholic and addict whose life goes into crisis when she gets drunk at her sister's wedding, embarrasses herself and her sister in front of guests, then proceeds to steal the bridal limo, which she ends up running through the front porch of someone's home. The remainder of the film takes place in a Hazelden-model, 28-day rehab center (The Hazelden model is the term used to describe the traditional 28-day inpatient/residential treatment programs for treating alcohol use disorders. These programs were traditionally designed to coincide with AA principles). The depiction of this type of rehab is realistic and portrays the many types of individuals who struggle with addictions. The film also does a fairly good job in depicting the denial and anger that other family members of the addict and alcoholic experience.

When a Man Loves a Woman: (1994) (stars Meg Ryan & Andy Garcia). This film depicts an alcoholic marriage, only this time, it is the wife who is the alcoholic. One unique and important aspect of this film is that it dispels the common stereotype that only husbands or boyfriends become alcoholics. This film is a good portrayal of the impact that alcoholism has on a marriage and family. It also does not give a sanitized version that once the woman enters recovery, everything is wonderful. Far from it, as this couple struggles now with reorganizing itself in recovery. It helps bring to light why more couples break up or divorce in recovery than they do in active addiction.

Traffic: (2000) (stars Michael Douglas, Benicio Del Toro, & Catherine Zeta-Jones). This film is multilayered in that one theme depicts the life of a drug trafficker, while the other theme depicts the life of a politically appointed presidential drug czar, whose teenage daughter's life is spiraling out of control because of her progressive cocaine addiction. The film is poignantly frightening in its depiction of the drug addiction and the dark side of the drug world.

Requiem for a Dream: (2000) (stars Ellen Burstyn, Jennifer Connolly, & Jared Leto). This film provides a gritty depiction of the impact of drug addiction on three individuals. It provides an interesting contrast of legal prescription addiction with illegal drug addiction; however, in all cases the results are the same. The film also depicts the progression of addiction and how it robs these individuals not only of their life goals, their dreams, but also of their dignity, their values, and their self-worth.

Trainspotting (1996): (stars Ewan MacGregor & Ewen Bremner). This film is set in Edinburgh, Scotland, and depicts the impact of heroin addiction on a group of young men who are enslaved to their addiction. The depiction of drug-seeking behavior and heroin withdrawal are surrealistic, but powerful in its portrayal of the progressive nature of addiction.

T2: Trainspotting (2017): this film reunites the main characters of the 1996 film (described above).

Sherrybaby: (2006) (stars Maggie Gyllenhall, Ryan Simpkins, & Sam Bottoms). This film portrays the life of a young woman who has just been released from prison after serving a sentence for drug possession. As Sherry tries to start her life over again after prison, there are several problems and stressors she encounters. This film also portrays the impact of child sexual abuse that is a common form of trauma among many individuals with substance use disorders.

Flight: (2012) (stars Denzel Washington, Nadine Velazquez, & Don Cheadle). This film depicts the life of an airline pilot who has both a cocaine and alcohol use disorder who has been able to keep his use hidden for many years until an accident occurs in which several passengers and crew are killed.

Bill Moyers PBS Series on Addictions: **(2008).** This is probably one of the best documentaries made on alcohol and drug addiction. The series is divided into several 30- to 45-minute segments each of which deal with a different aspect of addiction. Some of the segments include several chemically dependent individuals who describe how the progression of drug and alcohol use took over their lives; another segment, called "The Hijacked Brain" deals with the neurochemistry of drug use and the similarity that all drugs of abuse have in hijacking the dopamine producing system within the brain. Another segment deals with the societal impact of drugs and alcohol and the government's "War on Drugs."

HBO Series on Addictions: **(2007)** This is one of the most up-to-date documentaries on the market. The videos (which can be obtained for a nominal fee through www.hbo.com) contain a 60-minute segment with basic information about various facets of drug and alcohol addiction and its impact on adolescents, families, and adults, as well as cutting-edge treatments for a number of addictions. This lengthy segment is then followed by a number of shorter segments dealing with specific issues (e.g. the impact of drug addiction on a parent, new medications to combat drug and alcohol addiction, the impact of drug courts, etc.).

Heroin: Cape Cod: **(2015)** This HBO documentary explores the heroin epidemic in the Northeast with interviews with several young adults in small towns throughout Cape Cod who had become addicted to heroin.

Dope *Sick Love:* **(2005)** This HBO documentary looks at the lives of two heroin addicted couples as they try to live out a bare-bones existence on the streets of New York City.

Suggested Activities

1. Attend an open AA (Alcoholics Anonymous) or NA (Narcotics Anonymous) meeting. You can find information about when and where meetings take place by calling the number listed in the white pages of the phone book under "Alcoholics Anonymous" or "Narcotics Anonymous" (not under their abbreviations AA or NA). It is best to attend on Open Speakers meeting, as these meetings are open to anyone and as a student you will be more comfortable with the format. In an open speakers meeting, two speakers tell their stories of their addictions and how they came to recover in AA and/or NA. Sit and listen, do not take notes. No one will ask you to speak, just sit and listen. Also remember that the program is anonymous so you cannot reveal to anyone people you see there that you may know. After the meeting, take note of what stands out the most about what you heard and observed. Does it match with your impressions of what AA and NA are about? Were the people at the meetings similar or different from what you expected? If so, in what respect?

2. Watch one of the films mentioned above, for example, "Clean and Sober," "Requiem for a Dream," "28 Days" or "Traffic." What are the crisis points in these movies? How did the main characters use denial to convince themselves (and others) that they didn't have an alcohol or drug problem?

3. If you had a friend or relative who needed alcohol or drug detoxification followed by an inpatient treatment program, where would you send them? Look for alcohol and drug treatment resources in your area. Go online and see what alcohol and drug treatment programs are available within a 50-mile radius of where you live. How are these programs similar, how do they differ? Does the program require that the person being admitted have health insurance or can they accommodate people who cannot afford to pay?

4. What if you had a family member or friend who was just arrested for drug possession? He or she is frantic and reaches out to you for help with their crisis. What would you do to help them with their crisis?

5. Interview someone who is in recovery from drug or alcohol dependence. In your interview see if you can find out, what brought that individual into recovery. What crises did they experience while they were actively addicted. When did they realize that they had a problem with drugs and alcohol? Before they reached that realization, how did denial manifest itself to convince them (or others) that they didn't have a problem?

6. Interview someone from law enforcement (a police officer, a state trooper, someone from the courts or prosecutor's office or public defender's office) and ask them how alcohol and/or drugs impact their community or state. What types of alcohol or drug problems have they seen? What types of alcohol or drug crises have they been called on to help manage?

Recommended YouTube Viewing

Substance Withdrawal

https://www.youtube.com/watch?v = CrTlI6seM0A This video presents information on alcohol withdrawal and alcohol use disorders.

https://www.youtube.com/watch?v = rU2B-HfnaNc Excellent clinical lecture on alcohol withdrawal and how to treat alcohol withdrawal symptoms.

https://www.youtube.com/watch?v = PBGaJnsVx7w This video provides a good clinical description about benzodiazepine withdrawal (i.e., withdrawal from antianxiety drugs, such as Xanax, Ativan, Valium, Klonopin). When you go onto YouTube and type in benzo withdrawal, you'll also see many first-person accounts of how difficult it is to withdraw from benzodiazepines.

https://www.youtube.com/watch?v = LjpD41mMG8o This is another informative video on benzodiazepines and how addictive they are.

https://www.youtube.com/watch?v = UsjhqdE7–6A This is a brief video by Dr. Heather Ashton who is a world-renowned expert on benzodiazepines. Dr. Ashton is from the University of Newcastle in the United Kingdom and her website (http://www.benzo.org.uk/profash.htm) provides valuable information on benzodiazepine intoxication, benzodiazepine use disorder, and benzodiazepine withdrawal.

https://www.youtube.com/watch?v = 3vKLU5_Hgco This video explains the neurobiology behind opiate tolerance and withdrawal. Please note that YouTube also contains many first-person accounts for people experiencing opioid withdrawal some of which are very informative.

Substance Use Disorders

https://www.youtube.com/watch?v = lqdmWRExOkQ This documentary video addresses prescription opioid disorders and was produced by the FBI and NIDA. Very informative.

https://www.youtube.com/watch?v = qEQ6O4PZRWA This short video also addresses opiate addiction and withdrawal.

https://www.youtube.com/watch?v = zIGaGkBVfK8 This documentary also addresses opiate use disorders. Very good information.

https://www.youtube.com/watch?v = nRuxZyGCzaI This documentary was produced by CNN's Sanjay Gupta, MD and contains some up-to-date information on cannabis and cannabis use disorders.

https://www.youtube.com/watch?v = -mo3pA2KpLQ Informative documentary on cannabis.

https://www.youtube.com/watch?v = PY9DcIMGxMs Interesting TED talk on substance use disorders which addresses etiology or what causes addiction.

CHAPTER 8

The Crisis of Sexual Assault

DISCUSSION QUESTIONS

Take this simple True-False quiz to test your knowledge of sexual assault. Discuss your answers with your classmates before checking them against the correct answers found at the end of the chapter. This 2008 quiz is courtesy of *Men Against Sexual Assault,* University of Rochester:

1. She was asking for it because of the way she was dressed.

2. Use of drugs and alcohol lead to more occurrences of rape.

3. Persons who commit rape are usually psychopaths or stalkers who jump out of the bushes at night.

4. A person can be raped even if they have had sex before.

5. If the victim has had sex with their attacker before, it is not rape.

6. When men are sexually aroused, they have to have sex.

7. If the victim does not actually fight the attacker, then it is not rape.

8. Rape is a crime of aggression and violence, motivated by anger and the desire for power and control.

9. A woman can be raped even if she willingly goes to a man's room.

10. Women rarely lie about being raped.

INTRODUCTION

The word "rape" is from the Latin word, "rapere," which means "to seize quickly." Exact definitions of "rape," "sexual abuse," "sexual assault," and other related terms differ by state. Some of the general guidelines from the U.S. Department of Justice, however, describe "rape" as an act of forced sexual intercourse, including vaginal, oral, or anal penetration by a body part or an object, and "sexual assault" as unwanted sexual contact that stops short of rape and which may include sexual touching and fondling.

The National Women's Health Information Center (NWHIC) and the U.S. Department of Justice (2016) report from the Office on Violence Against Women define sexual assault more broadly, however, as any type of sexual activity that an individual does not consent to, including the following:

- Vaginal, anal, or oral penetration
- Inappropriate touching
- Sexual intercourse that a person says "no" to
- Rape (a common form of sexual assault)
- Attempted rape
- Child molestation
- Anything verbal or visual that forces a person to join in unwanted sexual contact or attention, such as voyeurism, exhibitionism, incest, and sexual harassment

In addition to the above forms of sexual assault, the U.S. Department of Justice's Office on Violence Against Women (2016) also defined sexual assault as any type of sexual contact *without the explicit consent of the recipient of the unwanted sexual activity* and added several other definitions:

- Forcing an individual to perform or receive oral sex
- Forcing an individual to masturbate or to masturbate someone else
- Forcing an individual to look at sexually explicit material or forcing an individual to pose for sexually explicit pictures

In general, state law also assumes that individuals cannot give consent to sexual activity if they are forced, threatened, unconscious, drugged, a minor, developmentally disabled, chronically mentally ill, or believe that they are undergoing a medical procedure.

The Federal Bureau of Investigation revised its own definition of rape in 2012 and removed the word "forcible" from it: "the penetration, no matter how slight, of the vagina or anus with any body part or object, or oral penetration by a sex organ of another person, without the consent of the victim."

STATISTICS

The Federal Bureau of Investigation's Uniform Crime Report issued by the U.S. Department of Justice estimated that 90,185 rapes were reported to law enforcement in 2015, an increase of 6.3% from the year before. The Rape, Abuse & Incest National Network (RAINN) (2016) calculated that there is one sexual assault every 98 seconds.

Considering the fact that a staggering number of rapes and sexual assaults go unreported, any estimation of their occurrence must be viewed as minimal. RAINN puts the number of rapes and sexual assaults reported to the police as only 310 out of every 1,000 assaults. In its report on Estimating the Incidence of Rape and Sexual Assault (2013), **the** National Research Council stated that the "crimes of rape and sexual assault are substantially undercounted through police reports" (p. 36). The report documented an 84% non-reporting of assaults as far back as 1992 and a similar percent (81%) in 2006. Truman, Langton, and the Bureau of Justice Statistics (2014) put the number of unreported cases at 66%, whereas the University of Kentucky's Center for Research on Violence Against Women placed the percent of unreported cases even higher, from 66 to 72%.

The reasons for non-reporting of these crimes are varied. RAINN has found several reasons:

- To prevent retaliation by the perpetrator (20%)

- The belief that law enforcement could not or would not be able to do anything to help (13%); the National Research Council (2013) saw an increase in this percent to 20%

- The belief that the assault was a personal matter only (13%)

- It just wasn't important enough (8%)

- Others: fear of being blamed for the rape; fear of the social cost if the information becomes public

Some cases go unreported, however, due, in part, to the relationship of the assailant to the victim. The National Violence Against Women Survey (NVAWS) (U.S. Department of Justice, 2011) found that many more rapes/sexual assaults committed by strangers were reported to the police (41%) than those committed by intimates (i.e., boyfriend, spouse: 24%). In fact, almost 75% of all rapes and sexual assaults are committed by someone known to the victim (acquaintances, current or former spouses, boyfriends, or girlfriends), thus the wish to keep the attack private and unreported (Dobie, 2016; RAINN, 2016). The two most likely locations where a date rape occurs are in the victim's own residence, followed by the perpetrator's (Gannon, Collie, Ward, & Thakker, 2008).

REACTIONS OF VICTIMS TO SEXUAL ASSAULT

There are a multitude of factors which have a direct impact on the reactions of victims after a sexual assault. The victim's age and developmental level, the relationship to the assailant, the presence of a support system for the victim, the reactions to the assault by family, friends, the police, and medical personnel, and the severity and duration of the attack all contribute significantly to the victim's response to it. The National Center for Victims of Crime (2007) listed the following typical responses to a sexual assault which might apply to many, but not all, victims:

Table 8.1 Rape Trauma Syndrome Phases

Physical Effects	Emotional/Psychological Effects
• Pain • Injuries • Nausea • Vomiting • Headaches	• Shock/denial • Irritability/anger • Depression • Social withdrawal • Numbing/apathy (detachment, loss of caring) • Restricted affect (reduced ability to express emotions) • Nightmares/flashbacks • Difficulty concentrating • Diminished interest in activities or sex • Loss of self-esteem • Loss of security/loss of trust in others • Guilt/shame/embarrassment • Impaired memory • Loss of appetite • Suicidal ideation • Substance abuse • Psychological disorders
Physiological Effects	
• Hypervigilance (always being "on your guard") • Insomnia • Exaggerated startle response (jumpiness) • Panic attacks • Eating problems/disorders • Self-mutilation (cutting, burning, or otherwise hurting oneself) • Sexual dysfunction (not being able to perform sexual acts) • Hyperarousal (exaggerated feelings/responses to stimuli)	

A combination of any of these signs could also be part of a larger problem known as rape trauma syndrome (RTS), which includes several posttraumatic stress disorder (PTSD) symptoms specific to the experience of rape or sexual assault. RAINN (2016) describes three phases to RTS:

1. **Acute phase**: occurs immediately after the assault and usually lasts a few days to several weeks. Reactions in this phase typically fall into three categories:

   • Expressed—victims are openly emotional, appearing agitated or hysterical, and suffering from crying spells or anxiety attacks;

   • Controlled—victims appear to be without emotion and act as if nothing happened; this calm may be a state of shock; and

- Shocked disbelief—victims are disoriented, suffering from difficulties in concentrating, making decisions, or doing everyday tasks; poor recall of the assault also may result.

2. **Outward adjustment phase**: victims resume what appears to be their normal lives while suffering from considerable inner turmoil. Many of the emotional and physiological symptoms listed above appear during this phase. Victims tend to use any of five coping techniques:

- Minimization—pretending that "everything is fine" or that "it could have been worse"

- Dramatization—inability to stop talking about the assault; it dominates their lives

- Suppression—refusal to discuss it, acting as if it never happened

- Explanation—overly analyzing what happened

- Flight—attempts to avoid the pain (moving, changing jobs, relationships, or appearance)

3. **Resolution phase**: the assault is no longer the central focus of the victims' lives. The rape is accepted as part of their lives, yet they move on and the pain lessens over time.

Courtney, a rape survivor herself (see below), summarized those similarities among the reactions of rape victims whom she currently helps to counsel:

- Feeling terribly alone

- Not being sure of who you are any more

- Being terrified, experiencing nightmares

- Having flashbacks brought on by colors, smells, or other reminders of the assault

- Feeling angry—those who can't express their anger go into deep depression

- Feeling unable to relate to other people

WHO ARE THE PERPETRATORS OF RAPE AND SEXUAL ASSAULT?

Those who rape do so for a variety of reasons, but most motives involve anger, power, eroticized cruelty, and opportunistic mating (Miller, 2014). Rape is committed largely by young males: 46% of them are under the age of 25 (Gannon et. al., 2008). RAINN (2016) also places 15% of rapists at 17 years of age and younger.

Miller (2014) reviewed some typologies of rapists:

- Anger/retaliatory rapists—those who wish to use force to degrade and humiliate women as their way of expressing contempt for them

- Power/assertive rapist—those who wish to dominate women; control is the primary objective

- Sadistic/hedonistic rapist—those who enjoy hurting women; these acts may involve bondage and torture

Neuropsychological theories about rape point to brain dysfunction in the perpetrators in areas associated with verbal skills, attentional control, and behavioral inhibition. Some psychological theories, more psychodynamic than others, suggest that deviant sexual behavior has its roots in unresolved infantile sexual urges and feelings of sexual and personal inadequacies. More behaviorally oriented theories make the connection between sexual arousal and aggression cues or between such behavior and pleasure as reinforcement. Still others view rape as an instrument of male dominance and superiority, fueled by demeaning media portrayals of women.

WHAT TO DO WHEN SEXUAL ASSAULT IS REPORTED

Although a victim is not required to report a sexual assault, the local prosecutor's office may decide to pursue prosecution with or without the victim's participation in the process. However, it also is unlikely that they would proceed with the case without the victim's cooperation. Reasons for reporting range from the importance of prosecuting sexual offenders and "keeping them off the streets" to helping the victims regain a sense of control, an important component in their recovery.

Making a report requires a call to 911 by the victim herself or by a friend or family member whom she may have called first. However, if ever there is a question of any kind regarding the process of reporting a sexual assault, victims themselves or their friends and family members can call the National Sexual Assault Hotline for free, confidential advice about anything related to the process. The 24 hour a day, seven days a week hotline number is:

1-800-656-HOPE

Most prosecutors' offices have an established Sexual Assault Response Team (SART), which is activated whenever a sexual assault is reported. The SART is a multidisciplinary team composed of professionals involved in the immediate response to a report. Although SART components vary by community, members typically include:

- Rape care advocates: they will be involved in initial contact with the victim via hotlines or in face-to-face meetings. Called as soon as the report is made, they may accompany the victim to the local police station or to the hospital for treatment and for the collection of evidence, or simply provide any other supportive assistance requested by the victim. In most communities, the local women's shelter or rape crisis center provides these advocates.

- Forensic medical providers: a Sexual Assault Nurse Examiner (SANE) is a medical professional trained in the treatment of victims and in the collection of key physical evidence, such as hairs, fluids, and fibers from the victim after the assault. They typically coordinate with rape care advocates to ensure that victims receive crisis intervention and support during and after the examination process. Other health care personnel may also include emergency medical technicians, gynecologists, surgeons, or other private physicians. The purpose of this forensic examination is to provide any evidence necessary to establish that a crime occurred and to help identify the assailant.

- Law enforcement representatives: police officers or detectives assigned to investigate the report, interview the victims, and coordinate the collection of evidence to assist with the prosecution of the case. The officers assigned typically have specialized training and experience in sexual assault investigations. They also perform other tasks like providing transportation to the local medical facility.

- Prosecutors: their role is to decide whether there is sufficient evidence to prosecute the case. Some communities involve them more actively, but the Office of Violence Against Women (OVAW) in the Department of Justice suggests their full participation in SART.

The OVAW in the U.S. Department of Justice developed *A National Protocol for Sexual Assault Medical Forensic Examinations* (2004) and emphasized the importance of a timely, appropriate, sensitive, and respectful response to the disclosure of a sexual assault. The protocol calls for all involved to put the needs of the victim first throughout the exam process and afterward, particularly being mindful of the victims' needs for privacy, for advocacy, and for information regarding each step of the examination and of subsequent legal steps in the possible prosecution of the case.

The purpose of SART is to help the victim make informed choices and decisions about how to proceed. The SANE leads the interview with the victims and explains the services available to them as well as the various options they have in accepting them as offered. That is, they can choose whether or not they want to proceed with the forensic medical examination, the services of a rape care advocate, and law enforcement (i.e., filing a report and agreeing to an interview with a police officer). Providing victims with these choices throughout the process is intended to empower victims to do what's in their own best interests at the moment. Thus, they have the right to accept or reject any one or all of the services offered to them.

Caution: The following four cases provide accounts of sexual assault which are relatively graphic and descriptive. Please be advised.

Case Presentation: Anita, A Case of Sexual Assault

Anita was an 18-year-old high school senior in a school of approximately 1,200 students in a suburban setting in one of the southern states. She was an average student who had plans to attend the local community college the following year, with the intention of eventually completing a four-year program for a bachelor's degree. Her longer-term professional plans, she told her school counselor, were unclear; all she knew, she claimed, was that she wanted to work with children in some capacity. Anita's academic record was without any significant blemish; aside from one or two "Cs" on her high school transcript in some of her college prep classes, she did well. Her discipline record also was unremarkable. Except for leaving school with a host of other students on the annual "cut day" for which she received the penalty of a detention, there were no other offenses worthy of note.

It was just after the semester break that the vice-principal assigned to the senior class noticed a slight change in her performance, however. Anita started a pattern of lateness to school in the morning, causing her to miss close to 20 minutes of her first period English class. A failure in this class since it was a requirement for graduation, would result in her inability to graduate unless she took the class in the district's summer school program. The vice-principal grew concerned about this possibility and spoke with Anita several times about this pattern, only to have her reassure him that she would desist with her lateness and do her best to be timelier in her arrival to school. The reasons she gave for being late were varied: over-sleeping, car trouble, and having to babysit her younger stepbrother whenever her mother worked overtime at her night shift job.

Always alert to the goings-on among the seniors for whom he was responsible, the vice-principal regularly consulted with the school psychologist about those students who concerned him, particularly his seniors who hoped to graduate in June of that year. If he saw something in their academic or behavioral record that concerned him, he sought out the psychologist for some problem-solving feedback. So, because Anita's lateness pattern began to mount, the vice-principal asked the psychologist if there was anything in the presentation of her case which might suggest the need for psychological intervention. The psychologist, seeing nothing in her record to indicate any long-term pattern of difficulties that would threaten graduation, except for this recent tardiness, suggested that the vice-principal speak with Anita again about the risks that this pattern posed to graduation. Because the vice-principal had a well-earned reputation as a fair, even-tempered school administrator whose sage advice many students valued, the psychologist was comfortable in knowing that he would address this problem with Anita in a professional and benevolent manner. The psychologist was a virtual stranger to her, whereas the vice-principal had known Anita for several years, making him the logical person to speak with her.

It was later in the week after this last conversation when the vice-principal left an urgent message for the psychologist to see him right away. He told the psychologist that only a few minutes earlier Anita had disclosed to him the reason for her lateness; the explanation was nothing that either of these school professionals anticipated. According to Anita, her stepfather who had moved into her home after marrying her mother about a year ago, had begun fondling her, rubbing her breasts, and placing his hands on her buttocks, usually when her mother was not around. He would laugh when she recoiled and pushed him away, claiming that she was making a "big deal" over nothing. Rather than tell her mother about what was happening, she kept quiet about it, lest she upset her mother who seemed to be in love with her husband after having been on her own as a single parent for several years. Anita felt that she would be able to survive as long as she avoided being alone in the house with him; she also planned to be out of the house and on her own after graduation just a few months later.

Anita went on to explain to the vice-principal that her stepfather's job change several months ago also resulted in a change in his work hours. Instead of having to leave the house to make the 6:20 a.m. train, he now could sleep later and catch the 7:15 train, keeping him in the home while Anita went through her morning ritual of preparing herself for the start of her school day at 7:40. Part of this ritual was her morning shower. What she realized at one point was that her stepfather had unlocked the locked bathroom door and stared at her in the shower. Although she suspected that it may have been happening for several weeks, she doubted her suspicions, lacking any real evidence to confirm this awful truth. Finally, she saw him one morning looking at her through a small opening in the door; when she screamed, he offered the excuse that he was unaware that she was in the bathroom and only wanted to retrieve his razor from the medicine chest.

So, Anita told the vice-principal, her lateness coincided with the realization of her stepfather's voyeurism. She had to wait until he left the house for work each day until she dared undress for the shower, thus her late arrival at school each day.

Intervention

The response of the psychologist and the vice-principal was to call the local Child Protective Services (CPS) office to report the abuse, but Anita's age (18 years) placed her beyond the reach of CPS. The psychologist explained to her, therefore, that she had the right to contact the police, since what her stepfather had done to her constituted sexual assault.

Psychologist: If you would like, Anita, you can call the police and report to them what your stepfather did to you.

Anita: But, why would I do that? I mean, what can they do? It's not like I have any proof or anything. What if it's just my word against his?

P: You're not convinced that the police will believe you?

A: That's right. My stepfather has lived in this town all his life. I just moved here with my mother when they got married last year. They'll probably just believe him. I just know that he'll deny doing anything.

P: Have you considered talking to your mother about it?

A: No way! She's really stuck on him; she thinks he's the greatest! Besides, my mother caught me making out with my boyfriend a few weeks ago, and she went crazy, calling me all kinds of names and things. I wouldn't be surprised if she even blamed me for what happened.

P: It seems that there are so many things that you are thinking about. Would you like to talk to someone who works with young women like you who have had similar experiences? This person may have some advice for you that you might find helpful.

A: Who are you talking about?

P: There is an agency nearby that provides not only shelter for victims of domestic violence and sexual assault, but also counseling and advice and other support services. There is a hotline number you can call if you wish to talk to someone there. The advantage in calling them is for you to ask them any questions at all about this problem.

A: Do they keep a record of the call?

P: You can call anonymously if you want; they don't need to have your name to be able to talk to you.

A: O.K., then, I'll call them.

Case Conceptualization/Crisis Resolution

Anita spent a considerable amount of time with the advocate exploring the options available to her. However, she eventually decided not to pursue the matter with the police. Although she clearly had not decided how to address the issue with her mother, Anita told the psychologist that she planned to call the advocate again to discuss with her how to talk to her mother about it.

Case Presentation: Nicole, A Case of Date Rape

Nicole, a 16-year-old high school sophomore, had it all figured out. Assuming that her parents would never let her attend the end-of-season football party at the home of the team captain due to the preponderance of seniors who would be in attendance, she concocted a plan along with her friend, Cherise, to make it all happen. Nicole told her parents that she planned to attend a "sleepover" at Cherise's home with a few other classmates; Cherise's parents, she assured them, would be home to supervise the gathering.

Instead, both girls went to the party. Not only were the captain's parents not at home at the time, but in attendance among the dozens of familiar faces were many other outsiders, including older-looking "young" people who seemed to be the ones who provided the underage partygoers with a large supply of alcohol. Nicole had one beer, then another, and as her inhibitions loosened, she began to take her turn atop the dining room table and dance to the loud rock music resounding through the room. After several minutes of entertaining the crowd, she stepped down from the table, woozy and unsteady on her feet, and went upstairs to use the only available bathroom.

Following her upstairs, however, was one of the partygoers, Kevin, a 17-year-old senior who also was in Nicole's biology class. As she exited the bathroom, Kevin greeted her in the hallway, pulled her into the bedroom, and fell with her onto the bed covered with the coats of the party attendees. Some kissing and "making out" followed. When he told her that he wanted to "do it," she pushed him away, telling him that what they had just done was "enough" and that she wanted him to leave her alone so that she could get back to the party. Kevin, however, was able to overpower her easily, and he restrained her and penetrated her. It was at the time when he rolled over in exhaustion that someone opened the door to the room looking for a coat that allowed Nicole to leave the room and rejoin Cherise downstairs.

Nicole said nothing of the assault until the next morning when she told Cherise. The response she received was not what she expected. Cherise pleaded with her not to do anything about it, because the report to the authorities might get both of them into trouble for lying to their parents about their whereabouts the night before. Nicole agreed at that time, but a lingering dread about the incident lead her to tell her aunt later the next day; her aunt convinced her of the importance of reporting the assault to the police.

Nicole's next step was to tell her parents who then accompanied her to the hospital for a forensic examination. The Sexual Assault Nurse Examiner (SANE) collected the forensic evidence, and a rape care advocate interviewed Nicole, telling her also of the options available to her. One of these options, the choice not to proceed with law enforcement, was the one which Nicole chose out of her concerns over publicity for herself and for her family.

She also expressed some fear that the prosecution of the case would have an adverse impact on her social standing in the high school; Kevin was a popular student, Nicole thought, and pursuing charges against him legally might result in her social ostracism. Discussion with her family over this course of action confirmed her decision not to proceed with the case.

Case Conceptualization/Crisis Resolution

A SANE sees Nicole's case as not uncommon. "Most of the cases I've seen are victims between the ages of 15 and 25 and are date or acquaintance rapes," she explained. "Many are alcohol-related and involve house parties where there is a lot of drinking" (personal communication, 2010). Since the purpose of the collaborative efforts of SART members is to empower the victims of sexual assault to make informed decisions in the aftermath of the attack, individuals have the right to stop the process at any time.

A trained SANE staff member averages between 120 to 140 hospital visits each year to conduct forensic examinations; however, only 100 to120 exams are completed. Those calls to the hospital which do not result in exams, she explained, are due either to the fact that the victims "are too drunk and can't give accurate information" or that they "just opt out." And she also learned that the primary reasons for victims opting out of the process fall into the following categories:

- Fear of the medical process
- Fear of involvement with law enforcement
- Fear of social repercussions, especially for teens
- Encouragement by parents to pursue the process, despite the victim's reluctance to do so. In these cases, the victim eventually opts out.

A registered nurse and coordinator of a rape care program in an agency devoted to providing services and advocacy for women, men, and children affected by domestic violence and sexual assault, described the same reasons why young women decide to forego the exam process (personal communication, 2009). She added that, as was true in Nicole's case, "Sometimes they're doing something they're not supposed to be doing, like drinking, so they fail to report to avoid trouble at home." Still others, she claimed, don't see themselves as victims, particularly if the assailant was a former or current boyfriend.

Any one of the agency's 62 trained rape care advocates are available at all hours, seven days a week, to respond to a reported sexual assault. Their role, and the role of the entire SART team, is to explain to the victim what to expect throughout the process of making the report, consenting to the forensic medical examination, and following up with law enforcement. However, she explained, "Our role is to empower them to be able to say 'no' at any step in the process." The victim, whether a minor child or adult, has the right to consent to these steps, to refuse them altogether, or to withdraw initial consent later in the process. The advocate's role involves obtaining the victim's consent, regardless of age, even if it is contrary to the wishes of a parent.

Case Presentation: A Case of Date Rape and Date Rape Drugs

She was 20 years old at the time, attractive, energetic, and popular, and still reeling from the breakup with a long-term boyfriend. Despite numerous offers from other potential suitors, Courtney stayed far from the dating scene, expecting instead that she and her former boyfriend would one day be reunited. Finally, however, she took the advice of family and friends to return to an active social life and accepted the offer of a date from Tom.

Tom was more than just an average guy. "A golden boy," Courtney called him, a young man from a high-profile local family enjoying a successful professional career, personable, handsome, and charming. Courtney's later retrospective analysis of some of the events of that night suggested that there may have been some warning signs present early in the evening to which she attributed little meaning until it was too late. For example, he requested that the night before the date she allow him to spend an hour with her parents when he came to pick her up that night; he asked her specifically not to "rush him out the door." Although an odd request, Courtney thought, for a whole hour to get acquainted, she nevertheless dismissed it as due to his typical friendliness and affability. When he arrived that night, he kissed Courtney's mother on the cheek, shook her father's hand, and sat down at the kitchen table with them. Tom's questions of the father concerned his occupation, his long morning commute, and the hours he arose in the morning and returned home in the evening. All the time, however, Courtney thought that Tom was not really her type and that this date would be a one-time-only encounter.

After close to an hour had passed, Courtney left with Tom. He said that he would take her to a local bar/restaurant, even though Courtney was not of drinking age, a fact she repeatedly reminded him that evening. Despite several refusals to accept a drink from the bartender, however, she eventually relented and agreed to take one. The bartender, a personal friend of Tom's, didn't ask to see any form of identification from Courtney to verify her drinking age, probably as a favor to Tom, Courtney assumed.

Within minutes of just a few sips of the drink, Courtney recalled, she felt sick and light-headed. She fell off her barstool as she attempted to make her way to the restroom, but she managed to get there. She knew that she felt very uncomfortable, both physically and emotionally, so she decided that she would ask Tom to take her home. Another large frosted drink greeted her at the bar on her return, however, and Tom lingered at the bar ignoring her request to drive her back home. Courtney just knew that there was something in that first drink.

Tom finally paid the bar bill, and as they walked to his car, his cell phone rang. "I'm with her now," he told the caller, "Oh yeah, we'll stop by." Her protests against this side trip, however, were silenced, and she assumed that she passed out once she entered the car. "It's the strangest thing I have ever had happen," she said, "I opened my eyes and I was in an entirely different place." The now disoriented and confused Courtney awoke to realize that Tom had taken her to a go-go bar with exotic dancers to meet up with his friends.

After a few introductions, she overheard Tom say to his friends, "Give me five minutes and I'll get her into bed." Now an irate Courtney demanded that he take her home immediately. First, he insisted, she had to look at the dancers, so he put his hands on her shoulders and turned her in the direction of the bar area. Then, he took her to the car. Courtney once again passed out in the car which, she assumed, was en route to her home. Instead, she recalled something hitting her on the head, only to realize that it was the storm door which she banged into as Tom carried her up the steps to his house. The only other person present was a room-mate of Tom's who was inside the house watching television. Courtney immediately went to the bathroom and threw up.

When she exited the bathroom, the roommate was no longer there, and the only light on in the house was in a first floor bedroom, which was empty. She entered the room, fell facedown on the bed, and promptly passed out again. When she awoke, still disoriented and confused, Courtney realized that the sensation of paralysis in her right arm was her arm stretched behind her and handcuffed to the bed post; the heaviness on her chest which made it difficult to breathe was Tom lying on top of her, struggling to remove her pants and underwear. Her one-armed struggle was unsuccessful in stopping him from raping her; within minutes, he was inside her. "I remember crying, screaming so that the roommate would hear me," Courtney reported, but no one came. She also recalled blacking out several times.

When he was finished, he just rolled over and slept. In the morning he woke up, threw Courtney's clothes at her ("like I was yesterday's trash"), and told her that he would drive her home. He told her at one point that he wanted to keep her there locked to the bed so that "he could do that every day after work." The ride home was bizarre, she thought. Tom apologized for what he did, claiming that he got "carried away." He also maintained that he wanted to have her as his girlfriend and to take her shopping that weekend.

It was early in the morning, just 15 minutes before her father woke up, when Tom dropped her off at home. Courtney quickly went upstairs, took off her clothes, and hopped into bed. Was the reason that Tom expressed such an interest the night before in her father's working and commuting hours to help him ascertain the best time to have her home without having to run into the father? Courtney asked herself this question and others in trying to make sense of the experience.

Case Conceptualization/Crisis Resolution

Courtney didn't plan to tell her mother about the rape, despite their closeness and open-ness with each other. She did plan, however, to contact the local women's shelter to speak with a counselor. When her mother arrived home later that day after Courtney awoke, she sensed that something was wrong. Courtney's repeated denials that something was amiss did not stop her mother from probing: *Did something happen last night? What did he do to you?* Finally, Courtney broke down and told her of the ordeal. Unsure of how to proceed, Courtney's mother consulted with her own mother about the best course of action. Court-ney ultimately decided not to report the rape to the police, preferring instead to seek out therapy at the women's center.

What changed her mind eventually about pursuing the matter with law enforcement, however, was her discovery that Tom had raped another young woman in the same man-ner a little more than a week after her assault. This second victim, on learning Courtney's identity, contacted her and asked her to corroborate her story with the county prosecutor. "Out of pure guilt," Courtney claimed, she visited the prosecutor and told her story, but she remained ambivalent about pressing charges as the prosecutor suggested until several days later. Finally, she relented and went to trial. A third victim who suffered a similar fate at Tom's hands eventually came forward as well.

The trial was an ordeal for Courtney and for the second victim, but Tom was acquitted of the charges. However, Courtney and the other two victims took their case to an administrative law hearing which, after one unsuccessful try, resulted in Tom's loss of his public service job. Courtney reported that she and the other two women "felt empowered" by exercising their right to pursue the hearing after the courts found him not guilty.

What Courtney did next illustrated one of the core concepts of the meaning of crisis: "danger" and "opportunity" (see Chapter 1). She used her experience as an opportunity to emerge from it stronger than before. Courtney now serves as a speaker during training sessions for rape care advocates sponsored by her local women's crisis center; she speaks to these groups about her rape experience as a survivor, not as a victim, as well as of the opportunities it afforded her in the aftermath. "It was almost a blessing," she claimed, "because I got angry enough to help other people. I'm a better person for it; I'm one of the lucky ones."

Courtney remains in group therapy with other rape survivors at the same center she called immediately after the rape. In her experience, she claimed, most rape victims don't report it to law enforcement nor follow through with all the steps in the process described above, but they do go to therapy. "I acquired a different mind frame and moved from the victim to the survivor stage. It changed my life for the better."

Case Presentation: Kristin, A Case of Rape

Note: Similar to Courtney's story, Kristin tells of her ordeal and of her decision not to file a police report after her rape. And just like Courtney, she talks of her response to the assault in a manner which illustrates the "opportunity" offered in the aftermath of her crisis (see Chapter 1).

Currently a medical school student with an intended specialization in oncology, Kristin was a college senior attending a large, prestigious university somewhere in the heartland of America at the time of her rape. Bright, popular, and active in a campus sorority, Kristin lived off-campus in an apartment with several of her sorority sisters. It was the friend of one of these sisters who visited one weekend and met Kristin. Steve was a senior at another university not far from Kristin's, one which enjoyed a fierce competitive sports rivalry with her school.

Kristin and Steve got to know each other that Saturday night, spending a few hours at a local bar with other friends before parting company. Kristin returned to her apartment; Steve departed to parts unknown. A short while later, however, her phone rang; it was Steve who asked her if it was all right for him to come over to her place to see her again. Although second-guessing her decision to allow him to visit now, Kristin recalled, she agreed to it then.

Steve came to the apartment, which was far from empty; it contained several other friends and sorority sisters, some of them sleeping in the living room. Nevertheless, before long Steve had Kristin in her bedroom and had overpowered her and raped her.

"I told him to stop, but he told me to 'just hold on,'" she remembered. She thought about screaming to awaken her sleeping friends, but in a decision that she considered not to be a conscious one, she thought better of doing so. Perhaps out of embarrassment, she thought, or perhaps for some other reasons she kept quiet; a sense of powerlessness and dread compromised her reasoning during this most personal of assaults. Instead, she maintained her silence and tried to survive the attack by dissociating herself from it, claiming, "I closed my eyes and pretended to be somewhere else."

Soon after the assault, Steve left the apartment. Kristin remained in her bed while several of the other overnight guests packed up their sleeping bags and left. Unclear as to what to do in the aftermath of her rape, Kristin finally left her room and decided to confide in one of her roommates about her ordeal. Hoping for some solace and support from her friend, Kristin received none. "She told me to try not to make not a big deal out of it," Kristin recalled her friend telling her. "Watch the 'Gilmore Girls' and it'll be fine," her roommate told her. Despite feeling rebuffed and minimized by this reaction, Kristin reached out one more time, this time to someone she described as her best friend, Tom, another fellow senior at the university. However, the same sense of rejection she experienced at the reaction of her roommate she experienced yet again with Tom. "No offense, Kristin, but you put yourself in that position," he told her. "He made me feel that it was my fault, so I decided not to tell anyone else," Kristin recalled regretfully.

She decided to go about her business and kept quiet about the rape. About two months later as she became increasingly more aware of the possibility of having contracted a sexually transmitted disease (STD) from Steve's attack, she visited the university health center to be tested and treated, should she test positive for the disease. As part of the STD assessment protocol, the attending physician asked Kristin why she was concerned about the disease at that time. Thinking that this question was "another chance for me to tell somebody," Kristin seized the opportunity and said, "Because I was raped." The physician's response, however, was not what Kristin had hoped to find; instead of being supportive, she maintained, the physician appeared to be taken aback and simply asked Kristin, "Are you taking care of that?" Feeling "shut down again," Kristin vowed to keep her secret to herself.

When asked about her decision not to report her rape to the police, she replied, "Emotionally, I couldn't press charges. The first two people I told as well as the physician at the health center completely shut me down. Besides, stopping the perpetrator by reporting it is not the victim's responsibility."

Case Conceptualization/Crisis Resolution

As the next few months passed and graduation approached, Kristin began experiencing multiple indicators of Rape Trauma Syndrome (see above). "I had nightmares, cold sweats, and even if I smelled the same cologne he wore on someone else, it triggered flashbacks. Sometimes while sitting in class, I would just start crying," Kristin remembered.

Finally, the turning point came for Kristin. A university sponsored *Take Back the Night* rally was planned on campus. The purpose of these rallies is to empower men and women both to stand up to violence, particularly sexual violence and rape, and to assert the rights of all people to be free from violence. These rallies typically are followed by speak-out sessions where survivors of violence are offered the opportunity to speak publicly to the rally attendees about their experiences with violence.

Kristin attended the rally and seized the opportunity to ascend to the podium during the follow-up speak-out session to tell the story of her rape. She recalled thinking that "telling my story felt good"; a visit to the campus women's center for a social gathering immediately after the speak-out session that night also convinced her that she was on the road from victim to survivor. "I was able to spread the word to a lot more people; I wanted to get involved," she stated.

When she returned home after graduation, Kristin contacted the local women's shelter and eventually completed a training program to become a rape care advocate, a role she continues to this day whenever her medical school studies permit. She not only serves on the local SART, but also speaks to numerous groups of professionals about her experiences and what it takes to become a survivor rather than a victim. She participates in the training of other rape care advocates as well. "Being an advocate has been my calling; I couldn't imagine my life without it now, it has become an important part of me. I'm in a great position to try to help people," this survivor asserted. As for suggestions she has for other victims of sexual assault, Kristin offered the following: "Get a support system, but you might not find it when you expect to find it; some people just don't know how to respond. Don't be discouraged by people's reactions, just find someone who believes you and supports you."

GUIDELINES FOR TREATING VICTIMS OF SEXUAL ASSAULT

The National Center for Victims of Crime also lists additional suggestions for those who respond to a sexual assault victim once the disclosure is made, whether to a friend or family member first, or to a member of the law enforcement community:

- **Listen without judging**. Sexual assault is a crime which can have staggering consequences for the victim. Coming forward and disclosing the attack to a friend or to a professional is an important, yet difficult step, making it incumbent on the listener to provide a safe and accepting environment for this disclosure to occur. Communicating a belief that the attack really did happen is one of the most important things to be communicated to the victim. Unconditional acceptance of the victim's story by using reflective listening techniques is critical.

- **Let them know that they did what was necessary to prevent further harm.** If the victim blames herself for not fighting back enough to avoid or to stop the assault, reassurances should be provided for her that such behavior may indeed have resulted in greater harm to her; fear of the kind which engulfed her during the attack often immobilizes people out of a need for survival. Guilt over not doing enough to stop it may linger, so constant reassurances to the contrary are important.

- **Encourage them to seek medical attention.** If the victim has not received medical attention or if she has not yet reported it to the authorities, she should be encouraged to do so. Calling 911 or a local or national hotline phone number (see above, **1-800-656-HOPE**) is the easiest way to do so.

- **Let them know that they do not have to manage the crisis alone.** Social support is a powerful mediator of symptoms suffered after a sexual assault. The fact that the victim has already disclosed the attack to someone should start the process of engaging others in a helping capacity. Communicating to the victim the network of helping people available to her is important in the recovery process.

QUIZ ANSWERS

1. She was asking for it because of the way she was dressed.

    Answer: False. This belief is little more than one of those "rape myths," those stereotypical beliefs about rape "that serve to deny, trivialize, or justify sexual violence exerted by men against women" (Bohner, 1998, p. 14). Acceptance of this and other rape myths places women in a disempowered position and is associated with greater rape proclivity in men (Malamuth & Check, 1983).

    Rape myths place responsibility for sexual assault on women by attributing to them certain indecent behaviors or other instances of lapses in moral judgment that actually cause the rape to occur. Walking in a certain manner deemed seductive by the assailant, wearing provocative attire, or considering eye contact as inviting are just some of those behaviors which assailants consider causally related to the act of sexual assault. Individuals who ascribe to rape myths truly do believe, "She asked for it by the way she was dressed and the way she looked at me." Other rape myths (Scully, 1990) are generated by beliefs that women could indeed avoid rape *if they really fought hard enough;* that victims *ask for and secretly enjoy rape*; and that they *only conjure up reports of rape to punish men for some perceived wrongdoing.*

2. Use of drugs and alcohol lead to more occurrences of rape.

    Answer: True. Alcohol and sexual assault often occur together. Approximately one-third of all sexual assaults happen when the assailant is under the influence of alcohol (30%) or drugs (4%). The victim also is intoxicated in some cases. However, one must be careful not to attribute the assault to intoxication only; being inebriated does not cause the assault, but rather it allows the assailant to ignore sexual boundaries. A drunken victim also finds it more difficult to defend themselves against an attack.

    In relatively recent years, the appearance on the nightclub and dating scene of what are commonly known as "date rape" drugs also has placed individuals at risk for sexual assault. The concern over the proliferation of these drugs resulted in the passage in 1996 of the Drug Induced Rape Prevention and Punishment Act making it a felony to give a controlled substance to anyone with the intent of committing sexual assault or any other crime on them.

    These drugs cause the individual to pass out, making them unable to resist an assault and unable to recall the next day whatever happened the night before. Many victims of these drug-induced assaults fail to report them to the authorities, blaming themselves for being too drunk to remember any details; a state of confusion caused by the drugs that may last for several days, and also may result in the destruction of necessary evidence to charge the assailant with the crime. The most commonly used "date rape" drugs are rohypnol, gamma-hydroxybutyerate (GHB), and ketamine.

3. Persons who commit rape are usually psychopaths or stalkers who jump out of the bushes at night.

Answer: False. According to the National Crime Victimization Survey (U.S. Department of Justice, 2005), the typical assailant is neither a psychopath nor anyone else with a major psychiatric disorder. They do not hide in dark alleys or behind bushes waiting for their next victim to arrive. Rather, non-strangers, individuals known to the victims as family members, acquaintances, or intimate partners accounted for almost two-thirds (73%) of all sexual assaults; 38% of the perpetrators were a friend or acquaintance of the victim, 28% were intimates of the victim, and 7% were other relatives. Only the remaining 27% of assailants were strangers, unknown to the victim.

The Rape, Abuse & Incest National Network (RAINN), the nation's largest anti-sexual assault organization, reported that four out of ten sexual assaults take place at the victim's own home, with another two in ten occurring in the home of a friend, neighbor, or relative.

4. A person can be raped even if they have had sex before.

Answer: True. A victim's sexual history has nothing at all to do with a case of rape. One doesn't have to be a virgin to be a victim of a sexual assault. A victim even could have had sexual relations with the assailant at an earlier time and can still be raped by them. The major issue pertains to consent (see next section), and if the victims do not give consent, regardless of their sexual history with the assailants beforehand, a rape can still take place.

5. If the victim has had sex with the attacker before, it is not rape.
Answer: False. See answer to # 4 above.

6. When men are sexually aroused, they have to have sex.

Answer: False. A state of sexual arousal (i.e., an erection) is not causally connected to sexual assault. There are no adverse physical consequences to a man if he does not have sexual relations when sexually aroused.

7. If the victim does not actually fight the attacker, then it is not a rape.

Answer: False. There are too many reasons why a victim might not fight back during a sexual assault. Verbal threats of harm to herself or to her friends and family members, the presence of a weapon used to intimidate her, or a state of complete terror are just some of the reasons why victims sometimes are silent during an attack.

8. Rape is a crime of aggression and violence, motivated by anger and the desire for power and control.

Answer: True. Although there are too many different kinds of rape for a single explanation to satisfy each of them (Cavaiola & Colford, 2006), contemporary research suggests that no more than approximately 10% of all rapes are committed for purposes of sexual pleasure (Kendall & Hammen, 1998). Other social-cultural explanations view sexual assault as an act of men's control over women in a culture that is more patriarchal in nature and which socializes males to associate power with masculinity and passivity with femininity (Odem & Clay-Warner, 1998).

9. A woman can be raped even if she goes to a man's room.

Answer: True. If a woman does not give consent for a sexual encounter, whether she is in a public place or a private place, such as a car, home, or college dormitory room, then the sexual encounter is rape. In cases of date rape (a.k.a., acquaintance rape), agreeing to be with a person in a dating relationship, for example, does not imply consent for sex; and sexual contact without consent is still rape. Another far less common type of rape is spousal rape, which occurs in dysfunctional marital relationships where there is sexual assault against a spouse. Even if committed in the couple's own home and in the context of marriage, sex without consent is still rape.

10. Women rarely lie about being raped.

Answer: True. One of the reasons why so many rapes go unreported is the victim's belief that people will not believe him or her. However, false reports are very rare; only 8% of reported rapes are false.

RESOURCES FOR CHAPTER ENRICHMENT

Recommended Films

The Accused: (1988) (stars Jody Foster [as Tobias] & Kelly McGillis). Based on a true-life incident, the movie tells the story of Sarah Tobias, a working girl who likes to party with her friends and flirt with the guys. One night after several hours of drinking and flirting, she is brutally gang raped atop a pinball machine in the bar while onlookers cheered on the proceedings. The film challenges viewers to re-assess their own beliefs in those rape myths which abound regarding a woman's responsibility in her own rape.

Dead Man Walking: (1995) (stars Sean Penn & Susan Sarandon). This film presents the viewer with difficult choices about capital punishment as an effective or humane punishment for the crime of rape and murder. Sean Penn plays the sexual assailant and murderer on death row.

Casualties of War: (1989) (stars Michael J. Fox, Sean Penn, & Don Harvey) Set in the jungles of Vietnam during the Vietnam War, the film chronicles the lives of soldiers in combat and their gang rape of a young, innocent Vietnamese girl. Michael J. Fox plays the troop's conscience as he attempts to reason with the assailants about their intended action.

Suggested Activities

1. Contact the SART in your own counties of residence. Interview a member of the team about the process it follows in responding to reports of sexual assault. Find out information regarding the numbers of calls it receives annually, the types of calls it gets, and the choices made by victims in the services they accept or reject.

2. Interview a rape care advocate in your area. Inquire about what they perceive as the most important skills and/or traits required of an advocate for sexual assault victims. What have their experiences been like in their work? What have been their most distressing or frustrating cases?

3. Download a copy of the 2004 *National Protocol for Sexual Assault Medical Forensic Examinations (Adolescents/Adults)* from the U.S. Department of Justice's Office on Violence against Women and review it for more detail regarding the process of sexual assault response.

CHAPTER 9

Intimate Partner Violence & Domestic Violence

Gerry and Laura have been married for the past thirteen years. Almost from the beginning of their relationship, Gerry was very critical of Laura. If she made an error in the check-book, he called her "stupid" or "retarded." He constantly criticized her appearance. If she tried to look nice for Gerry, he accused her of being a "slut." When she put on weight after having their first child, Gerry referred to her as "the mother cow," or said she looked like "a Mack truck." At first, the name-calling was confined to the home when no one else was in hearing distance; however, Gerry soon began to call Laura names in public or around friends and family members. He got very jealous if she spent time on the phone with her mother or sister and went into a rage if she spent any time talking with her girlfriend. Gerry also threatened to take Laura's cell phone and to take her checkbook and credit cards away from her. Laura said she began to feel "like a prisoner in my own home" and felt beaten down by Gerry; nothing she ever did was right or good enough for him.

Vinnie and Sophia have been living together for the past three years. They dated for about six months before moving in together, over Sophia's mother's vehement objections. She didn't feel that Vinnie was a good match for her daughter and although at first, he made a good impression, there was something about him that Sophia's mother didn't like. But, Sophia brushed aside her mother's protests stating that no matter who she went out with, he would never be good enough, in her mother's eyes. After only a few months of dating, Vinnie and Sophia started to get into heated arguments. Vinnie was very critical about how much money she spent and Sophia was often angry with Vinnie because of the amount of time he spent with his friends down at the local sports bar. Sophia also complained that Vinnie was drinking too much and spending too much money on sports gambling. Yet, whenever she confronted Vinnie, he went into a tirade and would storm around the house sometimes smashing things. One night, in one of these heated arguments, Vinnie punched Sophia giving her a black eye. He then stormed out of the house to "cool off." Then he would come back after a few hours with flowers for Sophia, and tell her he was sorry and that it "would never happen again." Unfortunately, four weeks later, Vinnie's sports teams lost and he lost a lot of money. When he came home late, Sophia was angry with him as they were invited to go over to her mother's house for dinner. She told Vinnie to pack his things. Instead, he started turning over furniture and then beat Sophia so badly that she ended up having to go to the emergency room with a broken jaw and fractured ribs.

DISCUSSION QUESTIONS

1. Usually when people hear the term "domestic violence," they think of physical abuse that occurs when a husband beats his wife, but this is just one variation of intimate partner violence. What are some other types of abusive intimate relationships?

2. It is common when you hear of someone who is involved in an abusive relationship to question, "why don't they just leave?" Why is this often "easier said than done"?

3. What causes people to become batterers? What do you think motivates this type of physically abusive behavior?

4. There's been quite a bit of controversy regarding mandatory reporting of intimate partner violence. Some states have laws that mandate that police make an arrest whenever they are called to intervene in a domestic violence incident. Some states have laws similar to child abuse reporting laws that mandate that medical and human service staff report any instance where they suspect intimate partner abuse. What do you think are some of the advantages and disadvantages of these laws?

Both cases described above, represent a different aspect of intimate partner violence. Vinnie and Sophia represent what most consider to be a more typical case of intimate partner violence. However, Gerry and Laura's relationship is also illustrative of the devastating impact of verbal and emotional abuse, which can often be just as damaging to the relationship as physical abuse. The terms "intimate partner violence" and "domestic violence" are often used interchangeably. Although domestic violence had been the preferred term, it was limiting in that it was often associated with physical abuse among married couples. Intimate partner violence is more inclusive because it takes into account, non-marital partner violence; for example, in dating relationships, couples that are living together, violence between siblings, violence between parents and adult sons or daughters, and violence in LGBT (lesbian, gay, bisexual, and transgender) intimate relationships.

In this chapter, various terms associated with intimate partner violence/domestic violence are defined along with the scope of the intimate partner violence in the United States. We also present some of the theories as to why intimate partner violence occurs in relationships as well as psychological characteristics that are common to batterers. Finally, various types of interventions for both batterers and their victims are discussed.

SCOPE OF THE PROBLEM

Intimate partner violence whether discussing spousal or partner violence or abuse is a major societal problem in the United States. The National Coalition Against Domestic Violence approximates that over ten million Americans are victims of domestic violence each year (NCADV, 2015). Estimates of the American Medical Association (1991) suggest that domestic violence injures more women than car accidents, muggings, and rapes combined. Recent trends in intimate partner violence indicate that there was a decline in the number of reported incidents from 1993 to 2010 (Bureau of Justice, 2012) for women of all marital statuses. Separated females experienced the highest rate of intimate partner violence from 1994 to 2010; however, the rate declined from 151.4 victimizations per 1,000 females age 12 or older in 1994 to 59.6 per 1,000 in 2010. On average, nonfatal intimate partner violence accounts for 22% of violent victimization of girls and women 12 years and older (Bureau of Justice, 2014). For homicide, intimate partner violence accounts for 30% of women and 5% of men. One must keep in mind however, that intimate partner violence often goes underreported. Nonfatal serious violence comprised more than a third of intimate partner violence against females and males from 2002 to 2011 (Bureau of Justice, 2012). Of the 3,032 homicide incidents involving women in 2010, 39% were committed by an intimate partner, while 37% were committed by a non-intimate individual who was known to the female victim, and 24% by an unknown offender. During the same year, of the 10,878 homicide incidents involving males, 3% were committed by an intimate, partner, 48% by a non-intimate, and 50% by an offender with an unknown relationship to the victim (Bureau of Justice, 2012). According to the National Coalition Against Domestic Violence, a woman is fatally shot by a spouse, ex-spouse, or dating partner every 14 minutes in the United States (NCADV, 2015).

Racial and ethnic factors must also be considered when looking at the statistics pertaining to intimate partner violence. Between 2004 and 2005 it appears that rates of intimate partner violence remained stable for European American women and African American women, but rates were generally higher for Native American and Alaskan Native women. From 1993 to 2005 the rates of intimate partner violence fell by two-thirds for women of Hispanic origin (Bureau of Justice, 2009).

The problem of intimate violence is one of immense proportions with far-reaching implications that have been well documented in the literature (Dutton, 1995, 1996, 1998; Hilton, Harris, & Rice, 2007; Jacobson & Gottman, 2007; Walker, 1994, 2000). Not only is there often lasting psychological damage to the victim (Herman, 1997; Miller, 1994; van der Kolk, McFarlane, & Weisaeth, 1996), but rates of recidivism suggest ongoing unresolved problems for both batterers and their victims (Hilton, Harris & Rice, 2007; Lachkar,1998; Simpson & Rholes, 1998; Stosny, 1995;). Furthermore, intimate partner violence can have serious effects on children, both in terms of immediate concurrent emotional problems, and "sleeper effects" in terms of replicating modeled violence in future relationships. (Dutton, 1995; Smith & Williams 1992). The societal costs are therefore tremendous, when one includes the medical costs, judicial costs, time costs spent by police officers in providing initial intervention, facility costs (e.g., the need for battered women's shelters), and the costs of counseling programs and the like.

It's important to keep in mind that intimate partner violence can impact couples from all socioeconomic strata, from all educational levels, and from all racial and ethnic groups as discussed above. In addition, LGBT couples also experience intimate partner violence as evidenced by a recent meta-analysis by Badenes-Ribera, Bonilla-Campos, Frias-Navarro, & Pons-Salvador (2016) of 687 studies of intimate partner violence in self-identified lesbians in same-sex couple relationships. All of the studies that were selected were carried out in the United States. The findings revealed that most of the participants were European American, of higher educational level, and although all forms of partner violence were represented, the most prevalent form was emotional/psychological violence.

DEFINITIONS AND TERMINOLOGY

Often the terms battering, abuse, and assault are misused interchangeably. Battering is most frequently used to denote forms of physical violence like actual injuries, but also can include the coercive control that so often entraps the victim of battering in the relationship. Young and Long (1998) define *battering* as

> . . . a pattern of behavior in which one person establishes power and control over another person through fear and intimidation, often including the threat or use of violence. Battering occurs when batterers believe they are entitled to control their partners. Battering includes emotional abuse, economic abuse, sexual abuse, manipulation of children, exercise of male privilege, intimidation, isolation, and a variety of other behaviors designed to maintain fear, intimidation, and power. (p. 188)

More recently, definitions of partner violence have been developed by several researchers. For example:

> . . . intentional use of physical force with the potential for causing death, disability, injury or harm. Physical violence includes but is not limited to: scratching, pushing, shoving, throwing, grabbing, biting, choking, shaking, hair-pulling, slapping, punching, hitting, burning, use of a weapon (gun, knife, or other object), and the use of restraints or one's body size, or strength against another person. Physical violence also includes coercing other people to commit any of the above acts. (Brieding et al., 2015, p. 11)

and

> . . . an act carried out with the intention of or perceived intention of causing physical pain or injury to another person. (Strauss, Gelles, & Steinmetz, 2006, p. 17)

and

Partner violence is when one partner knowingly behaves in a way that may hurt the other partner, without the other partner's explicit (informed and free-will) consent. (Winstok, 2016, p. 97)

According to the definitions cited above, abusive relationships are defined by the *intentional* harm of one's partner by the other partner that may include physically violent behaviors, such as hitting, punching, kicking, slapping, and often includes both emotional and verbal abuse. In contrast, assault is a legal term and may include both simple assault and aggravated assault subtypes. Assault is defined as the intentional inflicting of injury on another person (U.S. Department of Justice, 2000). As indicated earlier, even though assault is the most common form of intimate partner violence, other forms of partner violence can include rape, sexual assault, robbery, and verbal threats to inflict harm on the other person; all of which are criminal offenses. It is especially noteworthy that only about half of the incidents of intimate partner violence get reported to the police.

In instances where physical battering has taken place, the abused partner may seek a temporary restraining order (TRO) or Order of Protection against the batterer. Most states have laws that allow for temporary restraining orders. Once a judge issues a TRO it means that the batterer must leave the premises where the victim resides and cannot have any face-to-face, written, or phone contact with them. Many abuse victims worry that by requesting a TRO it will lead to retaliation by the batterer; unfortunately, retaliatory violence is common. Research suggests that women are most in danger of assault or murder around the time a TRO is issued by the court. In most states, however, if a police officer witnesses signs of physical abuse (such as a black eye, bruises, etc.) then the police officer can make an arrest and a TRO would then be issued by the municipal court judge. There was a great deal of controversy over whether police should be granted the authority to make an arrest, even if the battered partner does not wish to make a formal complaint. However, once a TRO is issued, it then necessitates that the battered partner appears before a judge, at which point, the restraining order is made permanent, or the complainant may decide to drop or vacate the restraining order. Prior research suggests that there are few demographic differences between those victims who decline to process a restraining order versus those who keep them (Klein, 1996), with the exception that a history of requesting a restraining order in the past, is a predictor of those who elect to make a restraining order permanent. Once a permanent restraining order is granted by the court, the batterer is then usually referred to a treatment program for batterers (either inpatient or outpatient). Stark (1996) notes that when an offender arrest is combined with treatment, batterers were 10 times less likely to be recidivists. However, more recent research (Briody, Albright, & Denman, 2016) found that there were no substantive differences in subsequent incidents of partner violence when batterers: 1) were arrested, 2) had a civil protection order (restraining order), or 3) both arrest and civil protection orders were put in place. Recent research has found that older batterers with more distorted thoughts of violence and who had been child abuse victims were at significantly greater risk for treatment failure and re-offending

(Fernandez-Montalvo, Echauti, Martinez, Azcarte, & Lopez-Goni, 2015). While Rock, Sellbom, Ben-Porath, and Salekin (2013) found batters with higher levels of psychopathic traits and impulsive antisociality were significantly more likely to drop out of treatment and to re-offend. This suggests that treatment for batterers, when combined with a legal mandate, can be effective in preventing future instances of intimate partner violence. However, this is not the case for all batterers. While legal sanctions like restraining orders are necessary, they do not provide the batterer with strategies to change their behavior, nor are they a guarantee that they won't become abusive in the future (Harrell & Smith, 1996).

Emotional, psychological, and verbal abuse is an important aspect of intimate partner violence, which often gets overlooked. Prior research has shown that emotional abuse is always part of the physical abuse cycle, whether as part of the escalation stage (Jacobson & Gottman, 2007) or as a replacement for physical abuse when the abuser wants to avoid re-arrest (usually following the realization that arrests are not made on the basis of their being verbally abusive). Verbal and emotional abuse are often powerful domination tactics because they carry the threat of physical violence (Jacobson & Gottman, 2007). It has been hypothesized that many offenders initiate control over their spouse or partner first by verbal or emotional means (psychological abuse), which can take many forms. Examples include such behaviors as intimidation (e.g., screaming at or insulting the intimate partner); degradation (e.g., shaming in public); terrorization (e.g., harassment at work); control of freedoms (e.g., preventing going to work, stopping ability to use the car, or a telephone) (Evans, 2010).

BATTERED WOMEN

The research literature indicates that there are some characteristics common to women who are victimized by verbal, emotional, or physical abuse. It is important to discuss these characteristics because in crisis intervention situations, intimate partner abuse is not always readily identified and many battered women are too afraid to discuss the battering with the crisis counselor. We are sensitive to the fact however, that in discussing common characteristics it is important not to stereotype women who have been battered. The danger in creating stereotypes is that crisis intervention professionals may miss the battering incident that created the crisis. For example, if one thinks of the battering as occurring more frequently in undereducated, lower socioeconomic status relationships, then counselors can miss identifying abusiveness in professional and higher socioeconomic status partner relationships where battering is just as likely to occur.

One of the most common characteristics found in battered women was that they had grown up in homes where they were abused physically or sexually by their parents or significant others (Walker, 2000). In keeping with learning theory, Walker hypothesizes that these women "learned" that when someone loves you they have the right to physically abuse you. In Walker's sample, 67% had been physically abused, while 48% had been victims of childhood sexual abuse.

Rosewater (1982, 1985a, 1985b) concludes that it could be quite easy to misdiagnose a battered woman as having a mental health disorder thereby missing the fact that the symptoms she is presenting are brought about by trying to cope with the trauma of abuse. What was surprising in Walker's (2000) study of battered women using various psychological measures, is that they did not demonstrate consistent patterns of low self-esteem, depression, or an external locus of control (i.e., one who feels they are not in control of their own destiny). Walker (2000) concludes ". . . our sample of battered women was not consistent in demonstrating the negative cognition and moods we would have expected" (p. 112). She points out that the impact of trauma can often be affected by the time of the trauma; by one's own coping resources and resilience; the person's level of stress response; and whether one receives any support from friends, family, and the community. A more recent study however, found depressive symptoms to be the most common reaction to intimate partner violence (IPV), especially among low income women (Kastello, Jacobsen, Gaffney, Kodadek, Sharps, & Bullock, 2016). Also, PTSD symptoms were common reactions among women who were victims of intimate partner stalking (Dardis, Amoroso, & Iverson, 2016). More recent research found that although women who are survivors of intimate partner violence are encouraged to become economically independent as a means of having options to free themselves from their abusers; in reality, IPV survivors often experience several obstacles to their becoming financially independent: for example, damage to the survivor's health due to the impact of long term abuse, low socioeconomic status, affiliation with a marginalized ethnic or racial group, and continued violence by the perpetrator (Peled & Krigel, 2016). In a recent literature review of employment and IPV by Showalter (2016) it was determined that having a steady job was an important factor in being able to live an abuse-free life; however, even those women who reported steady employment, also reported losing paid work time, job loss, and periods of unemployment resulting from IPV incidents. Yet, women who were survivors of IPV benefitted from neighborhood community resources that often included protection against re-victimization.

Walker (2000, 2009) identifies three components to the battered woman's syndrome. The first component is comprised of 1) posttraumatic stress disorder symptoms (PTSD). Because violence is traumatic and outside of the range of normal human experience, the victim begins to develop several symptoms of PTSD. The trauma of intimate partner abuse may be re-experienced in nightmares, in the numbing of feelings, avoidance of situations, or any conflict which may be associated with victimization trauma, or he or she may feel detached, experience a loss of interest, have increased anxiety, and have difficulty falling asleep. The second component, is 2) learned helplessness. This develops as a result of attempts to escape the abuse without success. Here, the abused partner learns to survive rather than try to escape the battering. The third component is the 3) self-destructive coping response to violence. Here, the abused partner, after perceiving that there are no alternatives or that their only choice is to stay, may begin to actively self-destruct by abusing drugs or alcohol, or attempting suicide.

For someone who has not worked with battered partners or has not experienced physical, emotional, verbal, or psychological abuse, the question often arises, "Why do they remain in the relationship? Why don't they just leave?" To an outside observer, leaving may seem like a simple, rational, and reasonable thing to do. However, for the victim who is caught in the web of intimate partner violence, leaving may be anything but simple, rational, or reasonable. For example, anyone who is experiencing the impact of PTSD symptoms—or who is experiencing learned helplessness, feels immobilized, depressed, numb, hopeless, and helpless—is not in any emotional condition to leave the relationship. Another important factor is that batterers are often quite adept at convincing their partners that they are worthless, that no one else would want them, essentially stripping them of their dignity, their sense of self-worth and self-esteem. Intimate partner violence is essentially brainwashing. In order to brainwash a captive individual, one must constantly exert total control over their lives, threatening to kill them one minute, while treating them sympathetically or benevolently the next. The captive person never knows what to expect and they never know how their captor will act toward them. Prisoners of war often break under the strain of unpredictability in addition to physical torture. So, too, the abused partner experiences the same unpredictability from their batterer. It is also noted in the research literature that when subjected to physical and psychological IPV, victims were likely to romanticize the controlling behaviors of their partners (e.g., believing that jealousy was an expression of romance or commitment from their partners). (Papp, Liss, Erchull, Godfrey, & Waaland-Kreutzer, 2016).

Box 9.1: Keeping Abuse Victims Safe . . .

A *New York Times* article (Sontag, 2002) raises many important controversial issues pertaining to domestic violence and how counselors handle these cases. From a rational perspective, most counselors want to ensure the safety of the abused victim and to end the cycle of violence by encouraging them never to return to the batterer. However, this is not always the goal of the battered woman, whose life may be inextricably intertwined with their abuser. As Sontag points out:

> Well-meaning professionals often find themselves in an uncomfortable and sometimes adversarial relationship with victims. Prosecutors especially, become frustrated by the many women who balk at testifying against their boyfriends or husbands . . . As Ruth Schulder, a social worker in the Bronx, says: "Nobody has the right to say to a woman, 'You can't be with this guy.' So, we have to deal with the reality."

As indicated in the Discussion Questions, it is often easy to recommend that someone leave an abusive relationship and to provide referrals to women's or men's shelters, however, the reality of taking this step is extremely difficult and involves many factors. Crisis counselors must be able to offer options to battered victims even with the realization that they may chose not to exercise these options at this particular point in time. Therefore, as mentioned earlier, it is of utmost importance that the crisis counselor is nonjudgmental in discussing these alternatives.

Source: Sontag, D. (2002, November 17) Fierce Entanglements. *The New York Times.*

There are often many other reasons why the abused stays. For example, Kanel (1999) provides a list of possible reasons: 1) religious beliefs forbid him or her from leaving the marriage ('til death do us part); 2) the children need a father or mother; 3) the fear of retaliation or that he or she will kill the children, pets, or other family members; 4) the lack of financial resources (no transportation, no money, no place to live); 5) the hope that the batterer will change; 6) the insecurity and the fear of not being able to take care of themselves; 7) the fear of being alone; and 8) the influences of pro-family societal messages (keep the family together at all costs). Denial can certainly be added to this list, as many abused partners will stay, while rationalizing that the abuse is "not that bad," or may believe "he or she will change eventually."

CHARACTERISTICS COMMON TO BATTERERS

Prior research regarding the psychological profile of men who are abusers suggested that these perpetrators tend to be a rather heterogeneous group; however, the research literature suggests that there appears to be particular subtypes of batterers, as well as common characteristics that describe the majority of batterers.

In some of the initial attempts to determine whether subtypes of male batterers existed, Hamberger and Hastings (1986) labeled three subtypes. The first is "schizoid/borderline," which describes the batterer as moody and sensitive to any interpersonal criticism; having a "Jekyll and Hyde" type of personality (e.g., cool and calm one minute, angry and full of rage the next). These descriptions are similar to the *DSM-5* diagnosis of borderline personality disorder. The second type is the "narcissistic/antisocial," who is described as very self-centered, out for themselves, and cold and calculating in their violence toward their partners. The violence they inflict is explained as more "instrumental" in nature, meaning that they use intimidation, threats, and violence in a cold, calculated way, not impulsively or on the spur of the moment (as is true of some of their counterparts). The third type, the "passive-dependent/compulsive" is described as passive, but also rigid and tense. This type tends to want things their way, and everything has to be exactly the way they want.

From an extensive research project with severely violent couples, Jacobson and Gottman (2007) discovered that not only are personality disorders critical to understanding differences in batterers, but that these correlate with physiological differences among batterers as well. Jacobson and Gottman (2007) labeled these two abusive styles the "cobra" and "pitbull." Cobras show evidence of antisocial, criminal traits, which are more generalized to other settings and relationships, and are not only manifested in the intimate relationship. Furthermore, cobras tend to act out in a more sadistic way. Physiologically they become calmer as their violence escalates, like a cobra snake that focuses with clear attention on its victim before striking. This appears to relate to their cold, remorseless, and independent style. The movie *Sleeping with the Enemy*, where the husband played a cold, calculating type of batterer is an excellent portrayal of this type of abuser.

Figure 9.1 Issues to Address in the Assessment of a Male Batterer

Nature of Abuse:
  frequency
  chronicity
  severity
  type (e.g., physical, psychological, sexual)
  injury inflicted
  other targets of abuse (family members, outside the family)
  violence in family of origin (observed, victim)
  type of denial
  agreement of corroborating sources
Individual Characteristics:
  behavioral deficits
  depression
  hostility
  alcohol and drugs
  sex roles and attitudes
  psychopathology
  reading level/intelligence
  language skills
Environmental Factors:
  current living situation (e.g., separated, living together)
  social network (e.g., supportive of abusive behavior)
  external stressors
Likelihood of Follow-Through:
  level of remorse
  desire to reunite with partner
  involvement with criminal justice system
  effectiveness and saliency of external motivators
  match of program with client ability
  cultural sensitivity of program
Current Risk of Violence:
  increased frequency or severity of violence
  implicit or explicit threats
  client concern about ability to control himself
  use of alcohol or drugs
  availability of a weapon
  past history of abuse
  level of denial
  violence normalized in employment setting
  pronounced psychological disturbance
  recent separation
  custody decisions

Reprinted with permission from J. L. Edleson & R. M. Tolman (1992). *Intervention for Men Who Batter: An Ecological Approach* (p. 28). Newbury Park, CA: SAGE.

The pitbull, on the other hand, may exhibit less severe violence, which tends to be manifested only in the intimate partner relationship. Physiologically, their biological markers like blood pressure escalate with their violence. Psychologically they tend to be more insecure and dependent, fearing abandonment when they become calm and will express remorse. The name "pitbull" is derived from the idea that this type of abuser may always be "in your face," barking, yelling, screaming, and making threatening gestures; however, they may not always act out viscously. As with the animal, the pitbull may attack only when they feel most threatened, insecure, or when they feel cornered (Jacobson & Gottman, 2007).

Another critical focus of study and treatment (Kassinove,1995) is research focused on anger styles among batterers. Much of the research literature suggests that abusive patterns in batterers relate to deficits in how anger is perceived and controlled (Eckhardt, Barbour, & Davison, 1998); similarly, anger style in the victim is central to systemic treatment models. Interestingly, PTSD has also been determined to be important in the background of batterers. (Dutton, 1998; Stosney, 1995; van der Kolk et al, 1996). There have also been links between intimate partner violence (both emotional abuse and physical abuse) and substance use disorders (SUD). Although not all individuals with SUD experience IPV, research suggests that substance use is prevalent among both batterers and victims (Kraanent, Vedel, Scholing & Emmelkamp, 2014; Schuerger & Reigle, 1988). Fitch and Papantonio (1983) also found that family of origin violence, as well as SUD and economic stress were highly correlated with spousal abuse. In a more recent study, Thomas, Bennett, and Stoops (2012) compared a group of batterers who manifest concurrent alcohol and drug problems (AOD) with a group who did not manifest alcohol or drug problems; they found that batterers with AOD were more likely to perpetrate more severe violence toward their partners. The AOD batterers also reported more anger and past trauma and had a greater proclivity toward Borderline Personality traits. Generally, when compared to most

Box 9.2: Baltimore Ravens Running Back Star Ray Rice Suspended by the NFL Following Domestic Violence Incident

In March 2014, Rice was arrested and subsequently indicted for third-degree aggravated assault relating to an incident in which he punched his then-fiancée (now wife) Janay Rice in the face. The blow knocked her unconscious. The incident became a prominent controversy after celebrity news website TMZ released a video of the encounter, which led to an NFL policy change regarding how it handles domestic violence cases. Rice's contract was terminated by the Ravens in September 2014, following the release of an additional video of the incident. He was subsequently suspended indefinitely by the league, but was later reinstated after he successfully appealed the decision in federal court. Rice has currently returned to the Baltimore Ravens in the role of educator, as he talks with rookies about life management skills and life skills. He has not returned to play for the Ravens since the March 2014 incident, which continues to be a scandal for the NFL.

Source: http://www.breakingnews.com/topic/ray-rice-domestic-violence-incident/

substances, alcohol use is most often linked to violent behavior (Foran & O'Leary, 2008; Langenderfer, 2013; McKinney, Caetano, Rodriguez, & Okoro, 2010). However, in a recent meta-analytic review of IPV and SUD, in which data from 285 studies were examined, the findings indicated significant correlations between SUD and IPV victimization and perpetration. Surprisingly, drug use yielded significantly stronger correlations with IPV than alcohol use. Yet, there was no significant differences in the use of different drug types and no significant differences between the impact of stimulant versus nonstimulant drug use on IPV perpetration (Cafferky, Mendez, Anderson, & Stith, 2016). The research within this area points to the fact that men who drink or abuse drugs are certainly at higher risk to act out violently and abusively to their intimate partners.

THE CYCLE OF VIOLENCE

Much of the literature pertaining to partner violence, points to a pattern of abuse that tends to be cyclical. The Walker cycle theory of violence (Walker, 1980, 1989) indicates that there are usually three phases in the partner violence sequence: 1) the tension building phase, 2) the acute battering phase, and 3) the loving contrition phase.

In the tension building phase, there is a gradual escalation of tense emotions, as the batterer often uses critical or demeaning remarks, verbal abuse, name calling and other intentionally intimidating remarks to keep his or her partner in their place. During this phase, the woman or man may try to placate their partner, agree with them, do things that will please them, do things that will calm them down or diffuse their anger. Eventually, both out of sheer exhaustion and learned helplessness (i.e. "no matter what I try to do, I can't control the anger"), the victim begins to withdraw from their partner. As they withdraw, the controller begins to pursue more vehemently, at which point, the tension is unbearable. Usually, it does not take much for a battering incident to occur; this begins the second phase, The acute battering phase. Here, "the batterer typically unleashes a barrage of verbal and physical aggression, that can leave the woman severely shaken and injured" (Walker, 2000, pp. 126–127). It is obvious that this is the phase where physical injuries take place and sometimes the police may be called. This is the pinnacle of the crisis. This phase ends when the battering incident has stopped. The batterer often experiences a reduction in tension and anger, a feeling of calm or relief, which unfortunately only reinforces the violent behavior. In the loving contrition phase, the batterer apologizes for his or her behavior, promises they will never do this type of thing again and expresses regret or guilt. In some instances, according to Walker, this phase is accompanied by a reduction in tension; however, this can also be the phase at which lethality is at its greatest, especially in the absence of any contrition or remorse. This phase more often occurs with "cobra" type batterers, who are incapable of experiencing true remorse. Cobras are also least affected by the cries or pleas of their abused partners.

Recent research has examined the concept of what's referred to as "bidirectional violence" in couples that experience IPV. This is a rather controversial topic in that it examines the propensity of both partners toward violence and violent behaviors. While counselors and other professionals are always mindful of not "blaming the victim," this research examines the role of bidirectional violence within a couple's relationship. (See Bates, 2016; Langhinrichsen-Rohling, Misra, Selwyn, & Rohling, 2012).

MULTICULTURAL CONSIDERATIONS

Intimate partner violence does not occur in a vacuum. There are many other factors to take into consideration when assessing a case of domestic violence. For example, it is important to look at the cultural milieu of the couple. A recent meta-analysis of cross-cultural factors (Mallory et al., 2016) examined the impact of whether the couple had come from a collectivist or individualistic society.

Unfortunately, many cultures support male dominance as opposed to gender equality. Although in the United States there have been major strides toward gender equality, in many ways the United States is still considered a patriarchal culture as evidenced by the larger proportion of men who are elected to public office, or who rise to administrative posts in major corporations. In many households, men make the majority of decisions. However, a patriarchal culture alone does not necessarily constitute a precursor to domestic violence. It appears that cultural attitudes where women are viewed as subservient or inferior to men, or where women are viewed as sexual objects or objects to be possessed, can be significant contributing factors to a result of increased intimate partner violence.

Although intimate partner violence cuts across all socioeconomic, racial, and religious boundaries, it appears that there are some subcultures and societal attitudes that may inadvertently contribute to domestic violence. A crisis worker or police officer who is called to intervene in a domestic violence dispute with some couples may be running headlong into these cultural differences. For example, in one such case, the police were called by neighbors to a home where yelling and screaming were heard. The neighbors feared the wife was being beaten. When the police arrived at the scene, the outraged husband was at the door to confront them. He told the police that in his country of origin, women were considered "property," and that the police had neither rights nor jurisdiction to intervene. He demanded that the police leave his property immediately. The officers begged to differ with him, given that he had admitted to physically abusing his wife. In the state where this incident took place, this admission of physical abuse allowed the officers to make an arrest.

Religious factors can also play a role. In religions where divorce is considered "sinful," there may be instances where an abused spouse will stay in an abusive relationship in order to try to work things out "for the sake of the children," or to avoid committing a sin. Although more contemporary clergy would have no hesitancy in recommending a marital separation and divorce for couples experiencing intimate partner violence, there are instances where some pastoral counselors, despite the abuse, might advocate that couples try to work on saving the marriage.

SURVIVOR THERAPY WITH BATTERED WOMEN

Walker (1994) outlines five states of treatment with battered women that she calls "Survivor Therapy." It should be noted that Stages I and II are often the focus of crisis intervention with battered women, whereas Stages III, IV, and V cover ongoing treatment, usually over the course of several weeks, or months. The stages are as follows:

Stage I: Assessment and Labeling of the Abuse

Stage II: Helping the Woman Get Safe

Stage III: Dealing with the Trauma Effects

Stage IV: Dealing with Other Psychological Effects of the Abuse and Underlying Issues

Stage V: Preparation for Termination

In Stage I: Assessment and Labeling of the Abuse, a complete assessment of the battered woman takes place. This assessment combines both traditional methods of evaluation and data gathering, as well as educational histories, job and medical histories, and other relevant information. Open-ended questions are suggested as a means of helping to spontaneously elicit information. Walker advocates using "the four incident technique" for gathering an abuse history. Here, the battered partner is asked to recall four specific incidents: the first abusive incident she can recall, the most recent incident, the worst incident or one of the worst abuse incidents, and a typical incident.

Other areas to focus on while gathering information are childhood history, adult relationship history, support networks (family and friends), medical history, and alcohol and drug history. Psychological testing may provide additional sources of information as well. When reviewing childhood history, for example, it is important to focus on anything in the abused partner's history that may help to reveal whether the victim or perpetrator had experienced or witnessed abuse in their homes during childhood or adolescence. Walker feels it is important that the abuse is labeled as such in order to present the reality of the situation to the battered partner. While labeling the abuse is important, Dr. Walker refrains from criticizing or verbally denigrating the batterer. To do so, usually elicits defense reactions from the battered partner. Walker often asks the battered partner to describe some positive characteristics about the batterer to lessen the likelihood that the battered partner defends their batterer.

In Stage II, a safety plan is discussed. Here the battered partner is asked to consider what they would do and where would they go should they see their mate begin to escalate their anger or resentments. The battered partner is asked to come up with a plan of how to get out, where they would go, and what to take. Some partners keep a packed suitcase in the hall closet that they can grab if they need to make a quick getaway. Stage III initiates the therapeutic work of coping with the emotions surrounding the abusive incidents. Battered partners often blame themselves for the abusive incidents and feel inferior for not being better lovers, partners, or spouses. The goal in this stage is to help the battered partner to begin to see how emotionally they have been impacted by the abusive incidents.

Here it is important for the counselor to ask the battered partner about their feelings in different situations. Feelings of guilt, low self-esteem, self-deprecation, and feelings of responsibility are all quite common. Counseling in this stage focuses on helping the battered partner to begin to understand their feelings as a means of facilitating the healing process.

Stage IV addresses the psychological effects of abuse and other related issues. For example, at this juncture, there can be a more in-depth exploration of family of origin issues, childhood trauma, exploration of the emotions associated with having experienced or witnessed trauma, and coping responses to these various issues. It is very important to listen for previous methods of coping, as these may provide helpful clues to assist in empowering the battered partner. Naturally, a woman who experiences a sense of learned helplessness has more therapeutic work to do before she can begin to feel a sense of empowerment. In Stage V, the counselor and client begin the process of preparing for termination. Included here is a summation of the work that has taken place and an exploration of future directions. It is important to remember that the majority of battered partners do not become re-involved with batterers, as was originally assumed. If anything, according to Walker, these women are often sensitized to behaviors that are suggestive of battering, such as difficulty in controlling temper, alcohol or drug abuse, sexual jealousy, and a prior history of stormy or conflictual relationships.

PROGRAMS FOR BATTERERS

During an intimate partner violence crisis, the batterer is more than likely to focus attention on issues of finance, food, and shelter and often will place blame on the partner for his or her arrest. The crisis counselor who works with batterers regularly deals with their outrage over the arrest or for having been put out of the house. They often blame their partner for their "losing control" of their temper, or accuse them of "pushing my buttons." The goal of the crisis intervention worker is to address the batterer's outrage and to assess whether further abuse is possible (e.g., does the batterer verbalize a plan to see retaliation against their partner? If so, the crisis worker may need to report these threats to the police and to the potential victim). Once the batterer is in a counseling program, the goal of treatment programs for batterers is to shift this focus back onto the batterer and to the behaviors that resulted in the arrest. Programs for batterers are offered in prisons, jails, or as part of outpatient court-mandated programs. Many of these programs, as well as an experiential group process, are designed to work with batterers in phases or stages. For example, the first stage usually focuses on defining and labeling the abuse as a precursor to encouraging the batterer to begin to take responsibility for their actions, verbal, emotional, and physical abuse. Here, batterers are encouraged to identify and relate to the information they are receiving. The next stage is to focus on breaking through or confronting areas of denial, where the batterer may blame their partner for the abuse, or blame external factors. In order for change to take place, the batterer must admit that they have a problem and take responsibility for their actions. The third stage focuses on assisting the batterer to develop new tools and strategies for managing their anger in order to develop alternatives to verbal, physical, or emotional abuse (Stordeur & Stille, 1989).

Many programs for batterers offer both stress management and anger management. It is interesting to note, however, that studies have not made a strong connection between external stress and battering (Hotaling & Sugarman, 1986). In anger management training, the goal is to help the batterer to modulate angry feelings, and in doing so, refrain from acting these feelings out. The assumption is that anger management and assertiveness training help batterers better control their emotions, making them less likely to abuse their partners. Many batterers (and unfortunately, therapists and lay people) operate on the myth that it is better to vent their anger rather than to bottle it up. Unfortunately, venting often leads to an escalation of angry feelings, in which case, venting anger may not be the best alternative. On the other hand, bottling up anger is also not a very good alternative, because eventually the feelings may reach explosive proportions, very much like a cork in a soda bottle that is constantly being shaken.

The viable alternative is assertiveness training. Here, batterers may be taught to make "I" statements rather than "You" statements like "You did...." or "You should have." In both of these instances, blaming or accusing only results in an escalation of anger and resentments. This is where the tension building stage described earlier begins to escalate. The caveat to this approach with batterers is whether the work done in the session will generalize to their intimate partner relationships. There are several factors that need to be considered however, in making this prediction; for example, does the batterer engage in regular drug or alcohol use; do they have an extensive history of violence toward their partners and toward non-familial individuals? is there an absence of guilt or remorse for the battering incidents? do they have any other criminal history? and do they exhibit sexual jealousy? If the answer to these questions is "yes," then the likelihood of successful generalization is not very favorable. Most programs advocate that it is better to stay with a separate approach in treating the abused partner and the batterer, rather than to attempt some type of couple's therapy. Why do you think this is a common treatment recommendation? The answer to this question is addressed later in this chapter.

There have been several studies that examined the effectiveness of treatment programs for male batterers, and the factors that impact on treatment efficacy. For example, Waller (2016) found high dropout rates in programs for African American male batterers when comparing the Duluth model and cognitive behavior therapy models. While these models are effective with most populations, they may not be suitable for use with African American males due to other societal factors (e.g., systemic racism). Waller makes the point that fixing the treatment system for batterers is essential given that African American women are murdered at a parallel rate to the percentage of African American males who drop out of treatment. In another study, Cuevas and Bui (2016) found that batterers who witnessed childhood abuse; who witnessed sibling and parental violence; who had distant relationships with their fathers; and whose parents divorced, these were all significant factors in predicting treatment completion. Boira, del Castillo, Carbajosa, and Marcuello (2013) examined the role of the therapeutic alliance in treatment programs for male batterers and found a significant relationship between therapeutic alliance and treatment effectiveness. In a study of male batterers mandated to treatment in Spain, there was an approximate 85% improvement rate; however, older males, along with those who had distorted thoughts about violence and who had been victims of childhood abuse were more likely to drop out of treatment (Fernandez-Montalvo et al., 2015).

As alluded to earlier, couples therapy is usually contraindicated in the early stages of treatment, especially when the counselor suspects that physical violence is still taking place. However, couples counseling may be used in instances where verbal or emotional abuse takes place, provided that the safety of the battered victim is ensured. Couples therapy is also predicated on the supposition that the abusive partner has sufficient control of their anger that they will not act out violently. According to Geffner, Mantooth, and Franks (1989), and Geffner and Pagelow (1990), couples therapy would only be undertaken in situations that meet the following preconditions: 1) both the perpetrator and the abused partner desire this type of treatment; 2) the abused partner has a safety plan and understands the potential dangers; 3) there are no custody issues if the couple is divorcing; 4) a lethality evaluation suggests a low presence of danger; 5) the therapist or counselor treating the couple is trained in both family systems and domestic violence counseling; 6) neither partner is abusing alcohol or drugs; 7) if there has been substance abuse in the past, then there is appropriate treatment for this issue; and 8) neither partner exhibits psychotic behavior.

INTIMATE PARTNER STALKING

Of all the forms of intimate partner violence, intimate partner stalking is one form of partner violence/intimidation that often gets overlooked. Intimate partner stalking has been defined as "a pattern of repeated, unwanted attention and contact that causes fear or concern for one's own safety, or the safety of someone else (e.g., family member, close friend)" (Brieding, Basile, Smith, Black & Mahendara, 2015, p. 14). Research by Black and colleagues (2011) suggests that approximately one in six women experienced lifetime intimate partner stalking. Intimate partner stalking has been found to correlate with both physical and sexual IPV (Basile, Arias, I., Desai, & Thompson, 2004). Intimate partner stalking is also associated with posttraumatic stress disorder symptoms, in both a national sample of women (Basile et al., 2004) as well as among women veterans (Dardis et al., 2016). According to the National Coalition Against Domestic Violence (NCADV, 2015), approximately 19.3 million women and 5.1 million men in the United States report having been stalked.

Case Presentation: Physical & Verbal Abuse in a Dating Relationship

Verbally and physically abusive relationships are quite common among dating relationships with both teenage and college-age populations. One national epidemiological data suggest that approximately 12% of adolescents reported physical violence while 29% reported psychological victimization in the past 18 months (Halpern, Oslak, & Young, 2001). However, a more recent survey found that 20% of adolescents reported physical violence, while 44% reported psychological victimization, and 11% had experienced and reported sexual victimization, including date rape (Ybarra, Espelage, Langhinrichsen-Rohling, & Korchmaros, 2016). Korchmaros and colleagues (2013) examined the use of computer-mediated communication (e.g., text messaging, social media) as a means of perpetrating psychological victimization. The following is a case involving violence in a dating relationship.

> *Nicole and Dan are college sophomores who have been dating for the past year. They met in their freshman year at an off-campus party and have been seeing each other exclusively ever since. After coming back to school from winter break, Nicole decided that she wanted to take a break from the relationship so that she could begin to see other guys. She felt that Dan was monopolizing too much of her time and was becoming too possessive. Dan did not take the news very well. He planned on spending spring break with Nicole and had already made arrangements for them to go to Florida. Nicole felt bad about backing out of their spring break plans, but she felt it would not be fair to Dan to go with him, given her change of heart. Dan tried to convince Nicole to reconsider, resume the relationship and go to Florida with him, but she was firm in her decision. Dan began to stalk Nicole and was constantly calling her and leaving angry and threatening messages on her cell phone. One Thursday evening, Nicole went to a party with some of her friends. Dan found her there and began to yell and scream at her, then hit her, giving her a black eye. Nicole left the party crying and returned to her dorm feeling depressed and blaming herself for going to a party where she might see Dan. Her Residential Assistant (RA) convinced her to see the counselor in the college counseling center.*

In exploring the safety aspects of this case, it is important that the counselor has a clear understanding of what took place and the history of Nicole's relationship with Dan. It is also important that the counselor take every possible step to ensure Nicole's safety given the physical incident that occurred. To accomplish this task, the counselor explores whether Nicole is willing to file a restraining order against Dan.

Intervention

Nicole was referred by the Residential Assistant from her dormitory to see a therapist at the college counseling center. Nicole's black-eye was obvious to the counselor who proceeded to make sure that Nicole had gone to the Student Health Center to be checked out medically. Nicole then described the incident that occurred at the party where Dan had become violent and punched Nicole. The counselor reassures Nicole that she did the right thing by coming to the university counseling center. She then asks Nicole whether she feels safe going back to the dorm. Nicole indicates that Dan had been aggressive before, but never quite as bad as he did in the most recent incident. She is aware of her option to file a restraining order because a girlfriend of hers had to file a restraining order against her ex-boyfriend. Nicole is uncertain what to do, but she does know that she wants to continue attending classes and socializing with her friends. However, she doesn't feel that Dan is going to allow her to have her personal space and freedom.

Case Conceptualization/Crisis Resolution

It is common for crisis counseling to take place over the course of several meetings following the initial session that Nicole has with the counselor. Nicole decides to file a restraining order that prevents Dan from having any contact with her. In subsequent sessions, Nicole is encouraged to express and process her feelings surrounding the abusive incidents in the relationship. As was discussed earlier, it is common for many abused partners to minimize these incidents or to downplay their significance, thereby creating a more favorable image of the relationship. It is important for the counselor to question Nicole about how she felt about these incidents. Here, the "four incident technique" described by Walker (1994) may be particularly useful. The counselor would also focus on *behavioral adjustments* that Nicole could make. For example, Nicole might be encouraged to spend time with her friends or to resist the urge to respond to Dan's attempts to contact her. She may also be encouraged to develop a safety plan whereby, she would be able to stay with a friend if she felt threatened. This phase of counseling would also focus on *cognitive mastery*. As was mentioned in the vignette, Nicole initially blamed herself for Dan's violent reaction. Nicole would be encouraged to refrain from taking responsibility for Dan's behavior and to realize that she did not cause him to be abusive. Only he can make that decision and only he can be responsible for whether or not he becomes abusive. In order to provide Nicole with some immediate skills she may be encouraged to do some reading on abusive relationships. The counselor would also work with Nicole on developing coping strategies such as those provided by Rizo (2016).

Case Presentation: A Case of Physical & Verbal Abuse

Let's return to the case example Sophia and Vinnie presented at the beginning of this chapter. In addition to representing a rather common illustration of physical and verbal battering, Vinnie also represents an insecure batterer or a pitbull (Jacobson & Gottman, 2007) who constantly uses verbal and physical intimidation to "keep Sophia in her place." It is unlikely that individuals like Vinnie will present in treatment on their own and usually will only do so when mandated into treatment by the courts. It is also common for batterers to project blame for their explosive anger on their spouses or partners. Sophia finds herself constantly "walking on eggshells" in fear that something she will say or do will incite Vinnie's rage.

Sophia and Vinnie have been living together for the past three years. They had dated for about six months before moving in together, which Sophia's mother had very much objected to. She felt that Vinnie was "no good" and that there was something about him that she just didn't like. Sophia felt that no matter who she went out with, he wouldn't be good enough for her, in her mother's eyes. Sophia and Vinnie often got into heated arguments usually about his spending time with friends down at the local sports bar. She felt he was drinking too much and spending too much money on sports gambling. Whenever she confronted Vinnie, he would go into a tirade and he would storm around the house sometimes breaking things. In one of these arguments, Vinnie hit Sophia and then stormed out of the house to "cool off." He came back a few hours later with flowers for Sophia and told her he was sorry and that it "would never happen again." Unfortunately, four weeks later, one of Vinnie's favorite teams lost a playoff game and he lost a lot of money. When he came home Sophia was angry with him, as they had planned to go over to her mother's house for dinner. She told Vinnie to pack his things. Instead, he started turning over furniture and then hitting her, telling her, "No one is going to tell me what to do."

Most beginning counselors make the mistake of assuming that reasoning and rational explanation is all that is needed is to convince Sophia to leave Vinnie. Usually, women in Sophia's situation will keep the abuse a secret from their friends and family because they don't want to hear those dreaded words, "Why don't you just leave him?" This would especially be true if Sophia were to tell her mother about the abuse. Sophia may feel invested in making the relationship work, or to try to prove to her mother that Vinnie is "not such a bad guy." As indicated earlier however, there are many reasons why battered women stay in the relationship, so it is best that counselors listen for these various reasons in a nonjudgmental manner. Again, it is best to ask open-ended questions and to stifle the impulse to criticize Vinnie and his abusive behavior. In conceptualizing abuse cases like this from the viewpoint of modern crisis intervention models such as those developed by Roberts (1998), the most important step is that of assessing lethality or ensuring safety. As the Nicole Brown Simpson case suggests, verbal and physical battering, sexual jealousy and lethality often go hand-in-hand.

In the following case transcription, excerpts from an initial session with Sophia will be presented. As this case unfolds, see if you can pick out how some of this ties in with suggested "four incident technique" questions used in the survivor therapy approach (Walker, 2000).

Intervention

Counselor: Sophia, I understand that your sister referred you here. Why did she suggest that you come to the Women's Center?

Sophia: Oh, she has it in her head that my boyfriend, Vinnie, is abusive or something. I agreed to come, mostly to get her off my back. No offense to you, I just don't see why my sister gets so upset.

C: Had something happened that caused her to be concerned?

Although the counselor notices some bruising, she refrains from asking about this too early in the session. Her goal, at this point, is to help Sophia feel comfortable with having come to the Center. This is usually a big step, although it is not uncommon for the battered spouse to deny the importance of having taken this step. Often, they may feel that others are beaten or abused more severely than they are, therefore, they do not deserve to access counseling services. Sophia goes on to explain the incident described in the vignette at the beginning of the chapter.

C: The incident you described sounds really frightening. How did you feel?

S: Yeah, I guess I was afraid, but I can usually get Vinnie to calm down, or if he goes for a walk or goes down to the bar, he usually calms himself down.

C: What was Vinnie like when he came home?

S: Well, he was checking for phone messages and was snooping around to see if I had been talking to anyone or if I had anyone over. He does get kind of crazy, thinking that I'm fooling around.

Remember, it is not unusual for male batterers to display a great deal of sexual jealousy, some of which may border on paranoid-like suspicions.

C: How did you feel at that point?

S: I was really, really afraid. Usually, when he gets crazy like that, it usually means he is going to blow up. I just try to lay low and not argue with him, but that only lasts for so long.

Sophia is describing the "tension building" phase, which often precedes explosive physical violence. It is not unusual for many abused women to try to placate their abuser in order to try to reduce the tension. The counselor's goal at this point in the session is to try to get Sophia to explain as much of what she can remember as possible and to elicit her feelings and reactions.

C: What happened then?

S: Well, I told Vinnie I wanted him to leave and that's when he really blew up. He started throwing furniture, and then he started hitting me. He finally left and I called my girlfriend, Jennifer. I think she was the one who told my sister what happened.

C: Why do you think Jennifer did that?

S: Well, I guess she thought she was helping me or something. I was really angry with her at first, but then I thought about it and realized she was trying to help.

C: And what was your sister's reaction?

S: She was really angry. She and Vinnie never got along, but I thought it was because our mother never really liked Vinnie from the get-go.

C: How did you feel about your sister's reaction?

S: Well, I guess I could see her point; I think she's overreacting though by wanting me to come here to a women's crisis center. It's not like I'm an abused woman or something.

C: Sophia, could you tell me about the first time that Vinnie lost his temper with you?

At this point, the counselor begins to get some history using Walker's four incident technique (the first abuse incident, the most recent, the worst incident, and a typical incident). Sophia relates other incidents like this one, at which point, the counselor says:

C: Sophia, everything you've told me so far, is very similar to the stories of women who seek help here at the Women's Center. Is it possible that you are an abused woman?

S: I guess, as I was listening to myself, recalling all those incidents with Vinnie I began thinking that maybe I am, or that you're thinking that I'm some kind of nut case for staying with him.

C: Not at all, you are not a "nut case," there are many reasons why women stay with guys who are abusive. Plus, it sounds like you've tried many different things to try to survive a very difficult situation. I'd like to talk about what you would like at this point, what are your goals?

At this point in the session, the counselor provides Sophia with feedback about her situation. It is not uncommon for woman to vehemently deny that they are abused or some compare themselves to other battered women they know or know of and rationalize that their situation is not nearly as bad. This minimization sometimes is used as the rationale for why they haven't sought help ("their situation is so much worse than mine"). Here it is important to reinforce that any woman who is verbally, emotionally, or physically abused should have access to counseling no matter what type of abuse or how severe the abuse may be. It is important that the counselor gather information about Sophia and her relationship with Vinnie in a nonjudgmental manner. It is also important to keep the focus on the here and now. This is not a time for exploration of prior relationships or family history. The emphasis is purely on the abusive relationship and how to ensure that Sophia is safe moving forward.

Case Conceptualization/Crisis Resolution

Although the aforementioned case focuses on Sophia and her reactions to the abuse incidents that resulted in her sister bringing her in for crisis counseling, it is important to keep in mind that batterers also need to be referred for ongoing treatment. In working with Vinnie (and batterers in general), there are usually four main goals that are the focus of this treatment: 1) to ensure the safety of the victimized partner, 2) to alter the batterer's attitudes toward relationship violence, 3) to increase the batterer's sense of personal responsibility rather than to project blame on the victimized partner, and 4) to learn nonviolent alternatives to dealing with conflict in order to change past behavior (Edleson & Tolman, 1992). Generally, couples counseling is contraindicated because it may place the victim at greater risk for battering. For example, if the battered partner were to bring something up in counseling that angers the batterer, this could then lead to a battering incident once they leave the office. What is considered "best practice" is to treat the couple separately and to continue to do so until the battered partner either safely leaves the relationship, or until such time as all parties agree the batterer has demonstrated sufficient progress in their own treatment that they no longer pose a risk for becoming either emotionally or physically abusive.

Case Presentation: A Verbally and Emotionally Abusive Relationship

In the case of Dashawn and Cherie, a verbally abusive relationship is presented. Dashawn displays many of the characteristics of verbally abusive men.

Dashawn and Cherie have lived together for the past three years and dated for about year prior to living together. Cherie recalls that Dashawn began to be critical of her from the time they moved in together. Often, he would criticize how she dressed. So, if she tried to look nice for Dashawn, he would accuse her of being a "slut." He would even criticize her for squeezing the toothpaste from what he considered to be the "wrong end." At first, Dashawn was only critical of Cherie at home, but eventually he became very critical of her in public and when they went to social events. Dashawn would also get very jealous of Cherie if she was on the phone with her mother or sister. Dashawn began to accuse Cherie of having affairs with other men and would sometimes follow her to work or would take her cell phone away from her to see who she was talking to. Cherie began to feel trapped. No matter what she did, she couldn't convince Dashawn that she was faithful. She began to feel increasingly isolated from her friends and family.

Intervention

Dashawn is threatening, controlling, critical, and intimidating toward Cherie. Although abusive patterns like this often go on for years, it is also likely that they can erupt into physical violence. Assuming that there have been no instances of physical violence and also assuming that Dashawn would not come in for counseling either with Cherie or individually, it is likely that Cherie would seek counseling individually. It is common however, that Cherie might be too fearful to initiate counseling herself, so let's assume that Cherie was referred for counseling by her physician who noted possible symptoms of depression (e.g., Cherie reported that she wasn't sleeping well). In the crisis session with Cherie she eventually admits that she is having problems in her relationship with her boyfriend, Dashawn. She goes on to describe instances of his verbally denigrating her, calling her names, and threatened violence over his suspicions that she is in communication with an ex-boyfriend. Cherie admits that Dashawn has never hit her, but she is afraid he might get to that point, as he becomes so angry sometimes that he "loses control" and once threw a lamp against the wall.

Given what Cherie has shared, it is important for the counselor to cautiously explore some of the types of verbal abuse that might be involved, such as those put forth in a book called, *The Verbally Abusive Relationship* (Evans, 2010). Additionally, to explore some of the items listed by Tolman (1989) in his assessment scale called *The Psychological Maltreatment of Women Scale (PMWS)*. It is also important that the counselor not attack or criticize Dashawn, as this will only alienate Cherie or add to her feelings of guilt or responsibility. Cherie feels that it's her responsibility to calm Dashawn down and she often goes into lengthy justifications to explain that she has not had contact with her ex-boyfriend. As is often the case, these attempts to calm Dashawn work momentarily until he finds some excuse to launch into another tirade.

Case Conceptualization/Crisis Resolution

This case provides so many examples of a verbally abusive relationship. From Cherie's description, Dashawn tries to control just about every aspect of her life. Cherie plays the dutiful codependent, as she tries to placate Dashawn, fearing that his anger will escalate out of control. However, no matter what Cherie does, Dashawn continues to use his temper outbursts as a means to control and manipulate Cherie. This is a common characteristic of verbally abusive relationships. Victims of verbal abuse often become brainwashed into believing that nothing they do is right and develop a sense of learned helplessness (e.g., "no matter what I do, it won't make a difference"). This is one of the reasons why victims so often present with depressive symptoms as Cherie did when she sought help from her family doctor.

Box 9.3: LAPC Form: Laura

Name: _____Laura_____   Age: __42__

Listen   **A**ssess   **P**lan   **C**ommit

L   I   S   T   E   N

I   What are they saying about the crisis?
Laura states that she feels depressed because of financial stress at home.

S   What happened? *No particular triggering event*

T   What type of crisis was it? (Traumatic Event, Developmental, Psychiatric, Existential)

E   *Developmental because of problems in the marital relationship*

N   Did they mention anything that indicates danger? *No, Laura denies physical abuse in the relationship, although this should be explored further in subsequent sessions.*

Other relevant information about the crisis: *Laura is referred by her primary care physician and is willing to allow communication*

A   S   S   E   S   S

S   **F**eeling: Is their predominant emotional state one of:
anger	sadness *X*	hopelessness *X*

S   anxiety   panic   numbness

          suicidal? If yes, complete lethality assessment/suicide. *No*

E   homicidal? If yes, complete lethality assessment/violence. *No*

S   **A**cting: Is their behavior
          active/restless   consistent with mood *Yes*
          passive/withdrawn *Yes*   good eye contact

S   **T**hinking: Are they
          logical/making sense *Yes*   coherent/expressing self well *Yes*
          insightful *No*   focused on topic *Yes*
          evasive/changing subject *No*

          Other: Any medical problems? *No*   Physical limitations? *No*
                 Hospitalizations? *No*   Need for hospitalization? *No*

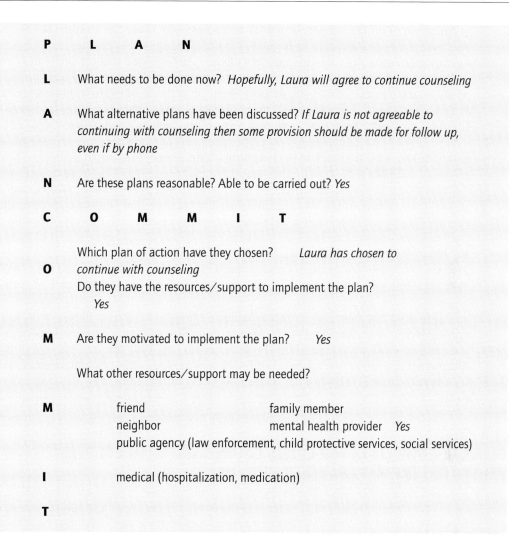

P   L   A   N

L   What needs to be done now? *Hopefully, Laura will agree to continue counseling*

A   What alternative plans have been discussed? *If Laura is not agreeable to continuing with counseling then some provision should be made for follow up, even if by phone*

N   Are these plans reasonable? Able to be carried out? *Yes*

C   O   M   M   I   T

O   Which plan of action have they chosen?   *Laura has chosen to continue with counseling*
        Do they have the resources/support to implement the plan?
          Yes

M   Are they motivated to implement the plan?   *Yes*

        What other resources/support may be needed?

M   friend   family member
            neighbor   mental health provider   *Yes*
            public agency (law enforcement, child protective services, social services)

I   medical (hospitalization, medication)

T

Evans (2010) makes several recommendations for individuals who find themselves in verbally abusive relationships. She suggests that it is first important for partners to know when they are being put down, ordered around, or yelled at. They also need to develop awareness that they are dealing with an abusive partner who is trying to dominate or control them, but that there is nothing that they have done to cause the abuse. Finally, she suggests that partners take a firm, authoritative tone in dealing with verbal abuse, to convey that this type of verbal behavior will not be tolerated. Hopefully, Cherie continues in counseling beyond this crisis phase and is open to exploring the issues that Evan's recommends.

Since we're on the subject of verbal and emotional abuse, let's return to the case example of Gerry and Laura presented at the beginning of this chapter, as it portrays an important aspect of intimate partner violence. As discussed earlier, Gerry and Laura illustrate a case where verbal and emotional abuse are key factors. Gerry displays many of the characteristics of verbally abusive men. He is threatening, intimidating, critical of Laura and controlling. Assuming that Laura might come for counseling on her own, the crisis counselor begins by exploring some of the factors leading up to Laura's decision to come in for counseling. The crisis counselor begins to explore the nature and extent of Laura's difficulties in the **listening** phase. Suspecting verbal abuse, the counselor can then begin to explore the types of verbal abuse, such as those described by Tolman (1989) in his assessment scale (e.g., "My partner prevented me from using the phone," "My partner threatened to have me committed to a mental institution," or "My partner threatened to leave me."). In the **assessment** phase, the counselor concludes from Laura's description, that Gerry tries to control just about every aspect of her life; however, there is no evidence that his temper outbursts escalate into physical violence. In response to Gerry's outbursts and accusations, Laura has tried to appease and placate him; however, this strategy provides only momentary de-escalation of Gerry's anger.

Working with someone in Laura's situation is a long-term process, although the initial crisis intervention counseling is designed to hopefully get Laura to agree to continued counseling, which becomes part of the **plan,** which hopefully she will then **commit** to. Although it is obvious that Laura is not financially irresponsible, she believes that she is to blame for Gerry's wrath. This is the L-A-P-C form filled out after the session with Laura.

GENERAL GUIDELINES FOR CRISIS COUNSELING WITH COUPLES EXHIBITING INTIMATE PARTNER VIOLENCE

Battered women may present for crisis counseling in a variety of settings. They may be first seen in criminal justice settings by judges or court personnel who may be involved with the legal aspect of the battering situation, such as when the police make an arrest or when the battered spouse applies for a restraining order for protection. The battered partner may seek assistance at a shelter for battered women and their children. The battered spouse may appear in an emergency room with broken bones, a broken nose, bruises, or similar physical trauma. They may also seek help in a mental health clinic for PTSD symptoms, for treatment of some other anxiety disorder, depression or alcohol or drug abuse. It is also possible that the battered spouse may seek help from a clergy member with hopes of obtaining marital counseling to help preserve the marriage or with hopes that the priest, minister, or rabbi will admonish the batterer for their abusive behavior and in so doing, somehow get them to stop. The battered spouse may reach out to other family members or friends for help. They may be seeking financial help, a place to stay, or just emotional support. Whatever the point of entry into the crisis intervention delivery system, there are certain "givens" that effective crisis counselors must take into consideration in any of these cases.

1. It is common that the battered partner will not identify their crisis as being one of domestic violence or intimate partner violence. Perhaps, the only two exceptions to this may be in instances where the battered partner seeks a restraining order from the courts or specifically seeks assistance at a battered women's shelter. In those instances, the woman must have been victim to an unusually violent threat or suffered intense physical harm in order to access those services. Although there may still be evidence of denial as to the nature and extent of the intimate partner abuse (e.g., the woman may still blame herself for her injuries), there is usually less likelihood that the abuse will be denied altogether. In the other points of entry, the battered partner may deny that their injuries are the result of their partner's abusive, violent behavior. This is not unusual, because the abused partner may be fearful of being discovered. They may fear retaliation, they may also fear they will have no place to go, or financial means to support and protect their children.

2. It is important that crisis counselors take into account that they may be working with an abused partner who may be in denial that they are actually in an abusive relationship, or they may present with other symptoms that can lead the crisis counselor down the wrong path of assessing the crisis as being something other than a domestic violence situation.

3. If abuse is suspected, do not interview the partners together. This is suggested for two reasons. First, it is unlikely that the abused partner will give up much information, while under the watchful, threatening eye of their abusive partner. In many instances, abuse victims have been coached by their abusers in terms of what and what not to say. Therefore, if the abusive partner is present it is better to conduct a separate interview. The second reason is the same: in outpatient counseling centers, if the counselor suspects abuse then they refrain from doing any couples or marital counseling. Even in couples counseling, once abuse is discovered in the relationship, it is a basic tenet **NOT** to treat the couple together, but rather to work with the couple separately. The prevailing theory is that by working with the couple together, it puts the battered partner in too much danger. For example, if that partner were to say or do "the wrong thing" within the session, the likelihood of abuse once the session is over is greatly increased.

4. It is of utmost importance to ensure the safety of the battered partner. Regardless of the setting where this individual presents, it is imperative that the crisis worker explores every possible alternative for making certain that the battered partner cannot be re-victimized. This usually means that legal charges are pressed against the batterer and that the abused partner has a safe place to go, preferably a location unknown to the batterer or one that he or she cannot access. Just as locks are only effective with honest people, restraining orders also have their limitations if not effectively enforced. The police cannot be in all places at all times. It is common

for batterers to defy restraining orders by trying to establish phone contact with their partner in order to pressure them into dropping the restraining order. Although restraining orders make provisions that there is to be no phone or written contact as well as face-to-face contact, this part of the court order cannot be enforced if the abused partner falls unwittingly into the trap of the abuser (e.g., "see you broke the law by taking my call, you're as guilty as I am"). Some treatment providers and those working in shelters for battered women, feel that a restraining order can sometimes represent a challenge to the masculinity of the batterer, and therefore some batterers purposely defy the court order, or escalate their level of violence. Lethality increases when a restraining order is initially filed. It is important to take collaborative steps in order to help ensure the battered partner's safety. Although it is difficult to predict the next act of violence, in order to assess the immediate danger to the battered partner, it is important to take into account as much as possible the history of the batterer: the frequency and severity of violence, the frequency of intoxication and drug use, the threats to kill or threats to harm the children, their access to weapons, current stressors in his or her life, attitudes toward violence, any reports of psychiatric impairment, forced sexual acts, and the battered partner's suicide threats or prior attempts at suicide (Sonkin & Durphy, 1997; Walker, 1994). It is important for crisis counselors to provide the battered partner with phone numbers of domestic violence shelters as well as other emergency numbers.

5. In working with intimate partner violence victims, it is important that the counselor not judge, preach, or blame, nor should they force the victim into choosing a course of action that they cannot follow or are not willing to follow. It is important that the crisis counselor convey acceptance. Since most abused partners often understate their case, it is also important that the counselor believes what they have to say pertaining to the abuse, and not convey disbelief about the abuse incident or a lack of understanding. The battered partner must trust the counselor and also believe that this trust will not be betrayed.

Klingbeil and Boyd (1984) developed a protocol that can be used in hospital emergency rooms and involves the triage nurse, the physician, and the crisis counselor. Each has a specific role to play. The triage nurse plays a key and vital role in determining whether the woman presenting for treatment may be an abuse victim. Medical records of prior emergency room treatment or hospitalizations are useful in determining if a cycle of violence may exist based on the type of injuries the victim has sustained. The crisis counselor is then called and their initial role is to help calm the battered partner and support her decision to seek help. Once this is accomplished, a history of the events leading up to the crisis is taken. Although the focus is on the immediate crisis, it is important to also explore recent abuse incidents. The physician provides medical attention and also fully explains any medical procedures performed and the potential dangers of the medical injuries. The crisis counselor reiterates these dangers in an attempt to head off any denial or minimizing of the abuse that may begin to take place at this point. Permission to take photographs needs to be obtained by either the triage nurse, the physician, or the crisis counselor. Also, if the victim is willing to press charges then the police are called to take a statement. The next item of business involves ensuring the safety of the battered spouse. Here, it is determined if there is a safe house of a friend or family member where she can stay, or preferably, if she willing to enter a battered women's shelter. Interestingly, there were only seven emergency shelters for battered women in 1974 (Roberts, 1981); however, by 2015 it is estimated that there are over 1,500 shelters and crisis intervention services for women and their children across the country (Battered Women's Shelters, 2015).

ELDER ABUSE AND OTHER TYPES OF DOMESTIC VIOLENCE

Another form of domestic abuse that is also underreported occurs when an adolescent or adult son or daughter is verbally and/or physically abusive to a parent. By using threats of violence, physically abusive behavior, constant demeaning comments, and other forms of intimidation, a teenage or adult son or daughter can make a parent's life a living hell. In many of these instances, the son or daughter emotionally batters their parent not only to have the upper hand or control, but also to intimidate that parent into giving them money, or doing favors for them. In these situations, parents become apprehensive of reaching out to others for help in fear that their son or daughter will retaliate in some way. Just as the battered intimate partner becomes helpless from having been constantly worn down by physical and mental abuse, so too, does the parent become helpless and hopeless over time. In some instances, social services or the police become involved if a neighbor or a relative becomes aware of the abuse taking place; however, the conspiracy of silence that is common in these situations results in this type of domestic abuse occurring for years.

Elder abuse is a variation on the domestic violence theme. Similar to other forms of intimate partner violence, elder abuse can take many forms, including physical and sexual abuse, neglect, financial exploitation, emotional abuse, and abandonment (U.S. Department of Health and Human Services, 2013). In the case of elder abuse all 50 states have enacted mandatory elder abuse laws that are similar to child abuse reporting laws; however, there is a great deal of variability in the content of these mandatory reporting laws and, in general, most cases of elder abuse, neglect, or exploitation go unreported and undetected. Most of the recent studies on the incidence of elder abuse estimates that approximately 7.6% to 10% of study participants experienced abuse in the prior year. (Acierno et al., 2010; Lifespan of Greater Rochester, 2011) This same study also found that an estimated 1 in 10 adults who were experiencing abuse, were not experiencing financial abuse. It also appears that data gathered from adult protective services agencies shows an increase in cases of reported elder abuse. Yet, one study estimated that only 1 in 14 cases of elder abuse are reported; while the New York State Elder Abuse Prevalence Study found that only 1 in 24 cases get reported. Interestingly, financial exploitation cases were more often self-reported at a rate of approximately 41 per 1,000 surveyed (Lifespan of Greater Rochester, 2011).

Case Presentation: A Case of Elder Abuse

Throughout his adult and married life, Carl was always proud of his independence. Even now at age 84, he is proud of the fact that he is living in his own apartment and able to bathe and dress himself and walk to the local park to talk with neighbors and friends. However, Carl's daughter Denise must cook meals for him, as Carl often leaves the stove on, or forgets to put food away in the refrigerator. Denise resents having no help from her siblings as they claimed their work schedules and family responsibilities did not allow time to take care of their father. Denise's resentments towards her siblings surfaced one time after her father burned a dish that Denise brought over to him, so she pushed him and punched him. The visiting nurse noticed several new bruises on his arm.

As in this case, elder abuse poses several problems, as the abusers can sometimes be other family members, or abuses can occur at the hands of caregivers in nursing homes, or other senior care facilities. With the aging of the baby boomer generation, elder care facilities and senior daycare programs have increased dramatically. Given that these facilities and programs are licensed under state licensure standards, it is imperative that these licensing entities are diligent in making sure that elders are never abused by family or staff.

SUMMARY

Intimate partner violence continues to be a source of crisis in American society. Although initially, intimate partner violence was thought to occur only in marital relationships (hence the terminology, domestic violence), it is well-known that abuse can take place in just about any intimate partner relationship, including violence in dating relationships, violence in LGBT relationships, and abuse of elders. Crisis counselors need to become familiar with the signs of IPV, as it is common that abuse victims will not divulge their abuse for fear of further retaliation and further mistreatment. Elder abuse, violence in other types of family relationships, and partner stalking are other forms of relationship violence explored in this chapter.

RESOURCES FOR CHAPTER ENRICHMENT

Suggested Readings

Dutton, D. (1996). *The domestic assault of women.* Vancouver, Canada: UBC Press.
Dutton, D. (1998). *The abusive personality.* New York, NY: Guilford Press.
Edleson, J. L. & Tolman, R. M. (1992). *Intervention for men who batter.* Newbury Park, CA: SAGE.
Evans, P. (2010) *The verbally abusive relationship.* 3rd ed. Avon, MA: Adams Media Corporation
Jacobson, N., & Gottman, J. (2007). *When men batter: New insights into ending abusive relationship.* New York, NY: Simon and Schuster.

Jones, A. R. (1993). *When love goes wrong: What to do when you can't do anything right.* New York, NY: Harper Trade.

Pizzey, E. (1974). *Scream quietly or the neighbors will hear.* London, England: Penguin Books.

Roberts, A. R. (1991). *Sheltering battered women.* New York, NY: Springer.

Shupe, A., Stacey, W. A., & Hazlewood, L. R. (1987). *Violent men, violent couples.* Lexington, MA: Lexington Books.

Walker, L. (2000). *The battered woman syndrome* (2nd ed.). New York, NY: Springer.

Suggested Websites

Family Violence & Prevention Services
Leading medical experts explore new methods to improve health care response to domestic violence.
https://www.acf.hhs.gov/fysb/programs/family-violence-prevention-services

Partnership Against Domestic Violence
http://padv.org/campaign/

National Coalition against Domestic Violence
Information and referral center for public media, battered woman, agencies, and organizations.
http://www.ncadv.org

National Network to End Domestic Violence
Site provides news and information for advocates about domestic violence. Get national perspective on legislation and public policy, advocates in the news, training, conference, and employment opportunities.
http://www.nnedv.org

National Domestic Violence Hotline
In 1996, President Clinton established a toll-free domestic violence hotline (1–800–799-SAFE). This hotline receives about 11,000 calls a month. There is also a number for those who are hearing impaired. That number is: TDD 1–800–787–3224.

Recommended Films

Bed of Lies: (1992) Based on the true story, *Bed of Lies* tells the story of Vicky Moore (Susan Dey), a low-born Texas waitress who marries Marion Price Daniel, Jr., the son of Texas governor Price Daniel, thinking she is going to live happily ever after. She realizes that her husband is an alcoholic, drug addict, and abusive husband, which eventually leads to her husband's shooting death. She is accused of murder and fights for custody of her children.

Black and Blue: (1999) The story centers around Frances Benedetto (Mary Stuart Masterson), a victim of domestic violence. The movie follows Frances's relationship to her increasingly abusive NYPD officer husband (played by Anthony LaPaglia), who has the police force on his side, and her eventual escape to Florida with her son (played by Will Rothaar). Eventually her husband finds them and attacks her. Her son's sports coach comes to the house when she does not pick her son up from practice on time and finds her beaten and bruised in the hallway. Meanwhile, her husband kidnaps their son. Five years later, she has married the coach and has a daughter, although she has never found her son.

Her son meets up with his aunt by chance on the street, and Frances (her name now changed to Beth) receives a phone call from him.

The Burning Bed: (1984) This classic film is based on the true story of Francine Hughes who is imprisoned within her marriage by a husband who beats her viciously while in uncontrollable fits of rage. Eventually, no longer able to withstand the constant battering, Francine sets fire to her house, killing her ex-husband. This film portrays an accurate depiction of battered women's syndrome and the devastating impact of abuse on victims and families. It also provides an accurate depiction of the "pitbull" type of batterer as described by Jacobson and Gottman (2007).

Domestic Violence: Faces of Fear: (1996) This documentary (although dated) provides excellent background information into the issues surrounding intimate partner violence (e.g., impact on families, children, jobs, legal considerations). Narrated by investigative news reporter, Diane Sawyer, this film provides interviews with battered women, attorneys, doctors, employers, and counselors who work with intimate partner survivors. One problem with the documentary is that the batterers depicted are exclusively men and disproportionately, men of racial and ethnic minorities.

Duma: (Dolls in Arabic) (2011) is a ground-breaking and controversial documentary about the abuse of women in Arab and Palestinian society. Made by Palestinian female director Abeer Zeibak Haddad, it sheds light on sexual abuse of women in Arab society. "Duma is an extremely powerful documentary. Brutally realistic; revealingly provocative, and exceedingly enthralling" wrote Dr. Eylem Atakav on October 5, 2012, in a blog for the Huffington Post.

Enough: (2002) After running away fails, a terrified woman (Jennifer Lopez) empowers herself in order to battle her abusive husband.

*Escape from Terror: The Teresa Stamper Story: (*1995) Teresa Walden-Stamper is happily married to her husband Paul Stamper and together they have one daughter Katie Stamper. The marriage seems happy until Paul starts abusing Teresa and becomes obsessed with her. Teresa divorces Paul and gets a restraining order against him, but this doesn't stop Paul and he kidnaps Teresa and shoots her boyfriend Chris Butler. Paul is later caught by the police and is taken to jail, but escapes from jail and Teresa knows that now she must protect herself and her daughter and that they're in real danger. Based on a story from Unsolved Mysteries.

If Someone Had Known: (1995) Katie marries her boyfriend and at first, they are very happy together. But when their first son arrives, her husband becomes nasty and jealous about the boy, beating her, and hanging around with friends all day leaving all the work to her. When their second child is on its way things get even worse, so that Katie decides to leave the house, but when she packs her suitcase the conflict climaxes and he gets shot.

Men Don't Tell: (1993) This movie shows another side to spousal abuse that not too many people thought is possible—the husband as the victim and the wife as the abuser.

Private Violence: (2014) The film focuses on the issue of domestic violence, as told through two survivors. Ultimately, the film centers on dispelling the logic of the commonly asked question: "Why didn't she just leave?

Sleeping with the Enemy: (1991) This film portrays intimate partner violence in a married couple where the husband (played by actor Patrick Bergen), portrays a controlling, compulsive, and violent husband. This film depicts an excellent example of a "cobra" type of abuser, as described by Jacobson and Gottman (2007).

Reviving Ophelia: (2012) Lifetime original movie that documents the life of a teenage girl suffering from an abusive romantic relationship.

What's Love Got to Do with It: (1993) This film depicts the life of rhythm & blues (R&B) icon, Tina Turner, and the physical, emotional, and sexual abuse she suffered by her then husband, Ike Turner. This film provides chilling and brutal depictions of intimate partner violence.

Suggested Activities

1. Every county court hears cases pertaining to intimate partner violence, some on a daily basis, others establish one day of the week to hear these cases. These cases are heard in open court; therefore, anyone can attend. Although it is inadvisable for a large group of students to attend a court session, it may be possible for a few students to attend. In many instances, judges welcome students to their court because they want future counselors, social workers, and psychologists to be aware of the devastation of intimate partner violence. Students can report back to the class what they heard and their reactions to attending the court session, with strict instructions not to disclose the identity of any of the people who appear before the court.

2. Students can watch one of the suggested films and then discuss how the film matches with their perceptions of intimate partner violence.

3. Students can explore what resources exist for victims of intimate partner violence in their county. They can explore what kinds of hotlines exist, outpatient programs, and the availability of battered women's shelters in their area.

4. Unfortunately, intimate partner violence is common among college-age students. If asked to create an awareness and prevention program on their campus, what would they include? What types of marketing might help to get the word out about intimate partner violence and to make potential victims aware of resources on or off campus?

5. Law enforcement personnel deal with intimate partner violence on a daily basis. Some statistics indicate that police officers are more at risk for injury in domestic violence disputes than in any other type of police work. Arrange to have a state, county, or local police officer come to class to talk about their experiences with intimate partner violence or arrange to interview a law enforcement officer regarding his or her experiences with intimate partner calls they have responded to. How do they manage situations and mandatory arrest laws when a couple is accusing one another to arrest or not to arrest? Is it true that police are often called to intervene with the same couple or family repeatedly and if so, do they approach those cases differently?

Recommended YouTube Viewing

https://www.youtube.com/watch?v = 9cG3gT9gU40; this is a short film which portrays intimate partner violence.

https://www.youtube.com/watch?v = Kv2ldkoJtYE; this is another short film depicting intimate partner violence.

https://www.youtube.com/watch?v = V1yW5IsnSjo; this is a very informative TED talk on the secrets of domestic violence. Excellent!

https://www.youtube.com/watch?v = A5Adq-jVQ1s; this is a TED talk on intimate partner violence. Provides first person account of intimate partner violence. Excellent!

https://www.youtube.com/watch?v = NDWk-rKRTCs; this is a very informative TED talk on intimate partner violence.

Crises Involving Bereavement, Grief, and Loss

Robert is 55 years old and has been married to Betty for the past 28 years. They have two daughters, ages 24 and 22. About eight months ago, Robert began to experience stomach pains and also began losing weight. His primary care physician did several blood tests and suspected cancer. It was later confirmed by an oncologist that Robert had an advanced case of pancreatic cancer. Within four months of the diagnosis, Robert died at home with the aid of hospice care. All of Robert's family was devastated by his death, especially his wife, Betty. Betty was referred for crisis counseling by an emergency room physician who examined her for chest pains and difficulty in catching her breath.

DISCUSSION QUESTIONS

1. Usually when people think of bereavement, they tend to think of losing a loved one who has died. What other kinds of losses can people experience that may produce similar grief reaction?

2. Many cultures, racial, and ethnic groups have their own special ways of grieving the loss of a loved one. We often see this in funeral rituals. Can you think of some ways in which your culture, race, or ethnicity influences grieving rituals? Give examples.

3. Is it possible for a person to grieve the loss of a pet more intensely, than for a friend or family member? Can you think of situations where this might occur?

This chapter examines the types of crises that come about as a result of loss. Whether these losses come about suddenly and unexpectedly or whether the losses occur after a long, chronic illness, the reactions to the loss are often no less intense or less difficult to process. However, not all losses result in a person experiencing a bereavement crisis. For example, a wife whose husband has died after a long battle with lung cancer most certainly experiences grief reactions, yet there may also be a sense of relief that he is no longer suffering. It is also possible that the time period from when the initial diagnosis was made to the time of death, may have allowed the wife to prepare for this loss emotionally. If there was a crisis period, it was more likely to occur at the time of the initial diagnosis. Yet, even with time to prepare, surviving family members and significant others are thrown into crisis. This chapter also provides recommendations for crisis counselors to help people manage their loss.

DEFINING GRIEF AND CRISES OF BEREAVEMENT

In her seminal work on grief, Rando (1984) makes important distinctions between terms used throughout this chapter. Rando defines *grief* as

> the process of psychological, social, and somatic reactions to the perception of loss. This implies that grief is (a) manifested in each of the psychological, social, and somatic realms; (b) a continuing development involving many changes; (c) a natural, expectable reaction (in fact, the absence of it is abnormal in most cases); (d) the reaction to the experience of many kinds of loss, not necessarily death alone; and (e) based on the unique, individualistic perception of loss by the griever, that is, it is not necessary to have the loss recognized or validated by others for the person to experience grief . . . (p. 15)

Rando defines *mourning* as having two historical meanings. The first involves a wide range of intrapsychic processes, both conscious and unconscious, brought on by the experience of loss, and the second involves the cultural response to grief. Implied here is that there is no one acceptable style of mourning. *Bereavement* is defined as "The state of having suffered a loss" (p. 16). Losses can take many forms, including the death of a pet, moving, the death of a spouse or partner, graduation, the end of an addiction, major health changes, financial changes brought about by retirement, the aftermath of holidays, legal problems, and an empty nest as all are examples of the types of loss that one can experience; yet, with the aforementioned list, not all of these losses are necessarily associated with grieving. Rando (1984) suggests that losses can be either physical or tangible (such as losing a desired possession, or the death of friend); or they can be symbolic (such as in the case of a divorce or losing job status because of a demotion).

More recently, further distinctions have been made which include *traumatic bereavement* that specifically includes the loss of a loved one through traumatic circumstances, for example deaths involving violence, damage to the loved one's body, if harm was caused to a loved one by a perpetrator, and if the death was perceived as being preventable, unfair, or unjust (Barlé, Wortman, & Latack, 2015).

Grief is normal in the face of loss. However, there are many mediators (Worden, 2008) that influence how one experiences feelings of grief. Despite many of the similarities found in the bereavement process, there are many variations in how each individual grieves. This is evident within families where siblings may grieve the loss of a parent very differently and in parents who grieve the loss of a child in their own unique way. One study, for example found that parents who lost a younger child were more likely to have suicidal ideation than parents who lost an older child (Zetumer et al., 2015). Traumatic bereavement can also occur in instances where a loved one has died as a result of a tragic accident, e.g. a car or plane crash, or death by drowning. What is important however is for counselors to refrain from making judgments about what constitutes the "right or proper" way to grieve. The reasoning behind this becomes clear as you read through this chapter.

Grief can be experienced on several levels and in several different ways, which accounts for why there are multiple variations in how people grieve. For example, on an **affective** or emotional level, feelings of sadness, despair, guilt, loneliness, anxiety, helplessness, hopelessness, numbness, disinterest, or apathy regarding work or school, or feelings of emancipation and relief are all common reactions. On a **cognitive** or thinking level, shock, disbelief, preoccupation, or self-deprecation are all possible experiences, which may be expressed in the form of "would've, could've, or should've," (e.g., "I should have told my son how much I loved him while he was still alive"). On a **behavioral and somatic** level, a grieving person may experience disturbed sleep, a loss of appetite, crying, fatigue, or a loss of desire to interact with others. Some may also experience physical symptoms, such as panic attacks, a feeling of emptiness, heart palpitations, loss of sexual desire or increased sexual drive, hollowness or aching in the stomach, headaches, muscle pain or muscle weakness and other physical manifestations of their grief. It is not unusual that grief may be expressed more as physical problems than emotionally or cognitively (Worden, 2008). This is the example in the first case vignette describing Betty.

A question that often arises is, "When does normal grief cross over into problematic or pathological grief?" Similarly, "How does bereavement differ from depression?" While the *DSM-5* (American Psychiatric Association, 2013) is considering a new diagnosis called ***persistent complex bereavement disorder*** under its section on "Conditions for Further Study;" the International Classification of Diseases (ICD) is including a diagnosis called ***prolonged grief disorder*** in the 11th edition of the ICD (Rosner, 2015). Although it is common that most crisis intervention and grief counselors refrain from diagnosing or pathologizing situations that are considered to be part of the normal grief process, there are some instances where grief can cross over into a mental health condition. The following case example illustrates such a situation:

Sara is a 20-year-old college student who had been dating Jason, for the past two years. They talked about the possibility of getting married after college, depending on whether or not Jason got into law school. However, their plans ended when Jason was killed in a fire in the apartment complex he lived in off campus. Sara presented at the student counseling center on campus distraught and crying. She felt she just could not go on living without Jason and explained that she had not only thought about suicide, but also had a means of carrying out her plan by taking pills she had accumulated.

This case example demonstrates not only an extreme and persistent reaction to grief, but also illustrates how intense a sudden unexpected grief can be. Sara was serious about suicide as evidenced not only by suicidal ideation, but also by her having a plan and a means to carry out that plan. Some studies conclude that approximately 12% to 15% of bereaved individuals will experience intense and prolonged reactions (Clayton, Desmarais & Winokur, 1968; Parkes & Weiss, 1983; Schaal, 2015; Zisook, Shuchter, & Lyons, 1987).

The symptoms of normal grieving and depression may overlap in several areas, although qualitatively they may differ. Worden (2008) suggests that there are distinctions between normal, difficult, and pathological grief. Determinants of normal grief reactions are discussed in the next section. Schaal (2015) feels that while there are overlaps between prolonged grief disorder and depression, the symptom clusters of both have yet to be resolved. Difficult reactions are often determined when the conditions of the person's death are exceptionally arduous; for example, in the case of the death of a young child in an accidental shooting, or the death of an infant or a new spouse, or deaths that occur as the result of tragedy, as in the September 11th deaths. Pathological grief reactions are often characterized by major psychiatric symptoms (such as severe depression, suicidal ideation, extreme agitation, restlessness). Although there is no time frame to resolve grief feelings, pathological reactions are often described as equally intense several years after the loved one has died as they were at the time of death. Another way to think about pathological grief reactions is that when a person suffers a loss and they experience a crisis because of that loss, it is natural that they will be immobilized for a period of time by the loss. Even once the person does resume everyday activities, they often report as if they are going "through the motions." In a pathological grief reaction, the mourner continues to remain immobilized even after many months or years have passed. The person may be unable to work, to attend religious services, or may refrain from any social contact. A recent study of bereaved who lost family members in the 2004 Southeast Asian tsunami (Kristiansen, Weisaeth, Hussain & Heir, 2015) found that symptoms of depression and posttraumatic stress disorder were prevalent among family members within the two to six years following the tsunami, while 36% of the bereaved still suffered from psychiatric disorders even after six years, most notably prolonged grief disorder, generalized anxiety disorder, and agoraphobia.

Finally, another distinction can be made regarding the more immediate crisis intervention counseling and ongoing bereavement counseling. Naturally, not everyone who experiences a loss will access or need formal counseling. In some instances, people adapt to the loss and we think of those individuals as resilient because they were able to adapt and cope with loss (Bonanno, 2004; Sandler, Wolchik, & Ayers, 2008). A great deal of grief work is done informally with the help of family, friends, clergy, and sometimes coworkers. For those who do access formal counseling, crisis bereavement counseling usually constitutes the initial contact the bereaved person makes to seek formal counseling. This might be in the immediate aftermath of the loss or tragedy. However, in the case vignette interventions presented later in the chapter, you can see, that many individuals often access formal counseling when they are in a state of crisis, which can sometimes be several months (or possibly even years) after their loss. Why is this? Just as trauma reactions can have a delayed onset, so too can grief reactions. Much of how a person reacts to loss is determined by several factors, which are presented in the next section.

DETERMINANTS OF GRIEF REACTIONS

Grief can take so many forms and be so individualized, in part, because of the many factors that can influence the grief reaction. For example, in the list of affective reactions listed above, feelings of sadness or loneliness are obvious grief reactions. However, what about feelings of relief or emancipation? A death that comes about after a lengthy, chronic, and painful illness may bring about feelings of relief, which often leads to feelings of guilt, as well as sadness. In a highly conflictual relationship with an abusive, possessive, alcoholic spouse, their death may bring about feelings of emancipation among the surviving spouse and children. The loss of a part of one's body (such as a limb, a breast) can also bring about grief reactions; so too can a loss of mobility due to paralysis. Rando (1984) provides a list of many psychological factors that can influence the grief reaction. Here are some of them:

The Unique Nature and Meaning of the Loss Sustained or the Relationship Severed: This refers to the idiosyncratic meaning of the loss to the individual. As Rando points out, there are some who may grieve more intensely to the death of a pet, than they would to the death of a sibling. This suggests that the impact of the loss is very much determined by nature and meaning of the relationship to that individual and how attached the mourner was to the deceased.

The Roles that the Deceased Occupied in the Family or Social System of the Griever: Here again, the nature and quality of the relationship determine the intensity of the grief reaction. When one loses a spouse, it can represent the loss of a companion, a friend, a lover, an income provider, an accountant, a gardener, a babysitter, a chauffeur (Parkes, 1970). Therefore, when a loved one dies, it often forces new roles on the surviving family and it takes time for the family to regain its sense of balance. In providing effective crisis intervention, it is important that the crisis counselor take into account the role of the deceased in the survivor's life.

Grief is Determined by the Individual's Coping Behaviors, Personality, Mental Health, their Level of Maturity, and Intelligence: Coping with grief is determined in part, by how the person coped with crisis in the past. Has this individual coped with other crises in their lives in a positive way? According to Rando,

> . . . most will cope with grief using the responses they have become familiar with. The mourner will tend to grieve (and the dying patient will tend to die) in much the same manner in which the rest of her life has been conducted. (p. 45)

The behaviors of the individual mourner also determine individual grief reactions; for example: avoidance of painful stimuli; distraction; abuse of drugs, alcohol, or food; obsessive rumination; impulsive behavior; reliance on prayer; rationalization or intellectualization; and socialization, whether one engages in contact with others. The mourner's level of emotional maturity also plays an important role. For example, an overindulged 38-year-old daughter incessantly made a hysterical scene every time she stepped onto the oncology ward where her dying father was being treated. Just as individuals grieve based on their prior ability to cope with loss, families also cope in a similar manner to how they managed crisis in the past. From clinical observation, it is no surprise that grief brings out the best or worst in families. Families with a strong identity that value trust and honesty, or that value the opinions and feelings of each family member often support each other in their grief. Conversely, families with strained interactions tend to become even more dysfunctional in the face of a bereavement crisis; for instance, families that spend years contesting the deceased's will and communicate with one another only through their attorneys.

Grief Reactions are Influenced by the Individual's Past Experience with Loss and Death: Current or present reactions to loss are very much influenced by one's past experiences with grief, such as a person who as a young child perceived the death of his grandparent as horrific because it caused his father to have a major falling out with his aunt and uncle over the grandfather's estate. This person rightfully perceives grieving as a dangerous enterprise that can result in even more loss. On the other hand, a person who perceives grieving as a process that helps to bond family and community members together and, in doing so, allows them to work through their feelings and to make meaning of their loss, naturally has different expectations of the grieving process. Although crisis intervention focuses more on the here and now, it is important that crisis counselors understand the client's past experiences with loss and death, in order to effectively intervene in the present.

Grief Reactions are Influenced by the Individual's Social, Cultural, Ethnic, and Religious/Philosophical Background: As has been emphasized throughout this text, it is of utmost importance in any counseling endeavor to take culture, race, ethnicity, and social milieu into account; this is especially true in crisis counseling with the bereaved. Look at how much multicultural influences affect the expression and the process of working through grief. For example, grief reactions in individuals from highly expressive cultures, races, or religions are naturally much different than the reactions of individuals from less expressive cultures. A New Orleans African American funeral procession complete with a seven-piece jazz band differs greatly from a New England Protestant funeral of sixth generation New Englanders. In order to understand these rituals, one must understand the cultural context. In the New Orleans African American and Creole community, death is often viewed as similar to a graduation or emancipation from the struggles of life and a promise of paradise in the life hereafter. In the Anglo-Saxon Protestant tradition, extreme forms of emotional expression are often frowned on. Instead, rationality and a stoic "stiff upper lip" attitude is expected. Also, death which occurs by suicide also has a particularly strong impact on survivors from religious backgrounds where suicide is viewed as sinful behavior. For crisis counselors, it is important that they take these cultural factors into context and not be fooled into thinking that because someone does not express their grief outwardly, that it is not as heartfelt as for those who do. In taking a multicultural perspective toward grief and mourning rituals, it is important that counselors are open to exploring how their client's racial, cultural, or ethnic origins influences views toward death, dying, and funeral rituals. For example, Kristiansen (2016) describes a Muslim woman's bereavement as she experiences the death of her husband to lung cancer while they were living as refugees in Denmark. The widow's bereavement narrative describes how her religious beliefs help to shape her ability to cope with his loss. Derived from Christian tradition, there is a concept that the "milestones" of grief follow the old adage of "two weeks, two months, and two years." This suggests that the first two weeks after the death of a loved one are the most difficult as significant others are caught up in making funeral arrangements, seeing friends and family who come to pay their last respects (e.g., at the wake or by making home visits). Mourners may also experience shock or emotional numbing during these first two weeks, as if they are on "automatic pilot" (i.e., going through the motions of trying to hold things together emotionally). Two months are said to represent the difficulty of making it through the first two months of trying to readjust to life without the deceased, of getting back to work or household routines. The significance of two years is to represent getting past the first year where anniversaries weigh heavily, or the first

Christmas, or New Year's, or Thanksgiving. By the second year, these anniversaries and holidays take on a different feel and may be approached with less trepidation. However, in the Jewish tradition, these milestones are somewhat different. Instead of "two weeks, two months, and two years," it is "one week, one month, and one year." For example, in Jewish tradition a Shiva Minion is held during the first week after the loved one's death. Also, Jewish tradition states that the burial should take place by sundown of the day of the loved one's death unless there are special circumstances that prevent the burial from taking place so quickly (e.g., when an autopsy has been ordered). The significance of "one month" refers to the time frame during which the bereaved tries to get back to work or resume other household routines. The significance of one year represents the unveiling of the headstone at the cemetery. This is an important religious milestone as it marks the one-year anniversary of the loved one's death. Worden (2008) found that anniversary reactions are often common for up to ten years following the death of a loved one.

Grief Reactions are Influenced by Age: Children, adolescents, and adults all grieve differently. Even among adults there are tremendous variations in grieving that are not only influenced by some of the aforementioned factors (e.g., relationship with the deceased, maturity, or multicultural considerations), but also by whether one is a young adult, middle-age, or elderly. For example, in the elderly, because many have experienced the death of their peers, it may seem as if they are outwardly impervious to the death of yet another friend or loved one. Death is perceived as inevitable, whereas at the death of a young adult, expressions, such as "They were cut down in the prime of their life" or "They had their whole lives ahead of them, what a pity to be taken at so young an age" can often be heard.

Yet, age may not be such an important a factor in determining grief. Take the case of an 80-year-old man who loses his 78-year-old wife. As Rando (1984) points out, "Age is irrelevant to him—he lost his life's companion" (p. 49). Children and adolescents also tend to express their grief differently. This outward expression, or lack thereof, should not be construed to mean that the child or teenager is experiencing any less emotional distress. In the aftermath of a parent's death, a child may regress by becoming more dependent on their surviving parent, or he or she may regress to thumb-sucking, bedwetting, or to "baby talk." When one parent dies, the child often feels the pain of losing both parents, because the surviving parent is also experiencing grief. In addition, the surviving parent must now take on new roles, deal with financial problems, and take on the tasks of becoming a single parent. Adolescents (and some children) may be more prone to "acting out" behaviors, such as getting into fights, or trouble in school. Teenagers may resort to drug or alcohol use to avoid the pain of the loss. Others may throw themselves into a whirlwind of activity, thereby avoiding the pain of their loss.

Grief is Influenced by the Characteristics of the Deceased: Not only the age of the person, but the personality type of the deceased also influences grief reactions. A well-known, well-loved high school student who died at the hands of a drunk driver had mourners lined up around the block of the funeral home. As Rando (1984) points out there is a ". . . tendency for our society to approve of grief for those who are good and worthwhile, but not for those who are bad. The death of a criminal in the midst of a robbery does not arouse much social concern . . ." (pp. 49–50)

Grief is Influenced by the Individual's Perception of the Deceased Fulfillment in Life: Here, the more the grieving individuals perceive the deceased as having lived a full life, the more readily their death can be accepted and the more likely grief work can take place. When a child or a young person dies, there is always a sense that they were robbed or cheated out of having a full life with many types of experiences. When a young graduate student died in a car accident, the pain of his death was magnified by the fact that this was an individual with so much promise and a true commitment to helping others.

Grief is Influenced by Whether the Death is Sudden or Expected: It is generally agreed that when death is expected, as is the case when someone is diagnosed with a terminal illness, it allows time for anticipatory grieving to take place; for example, unfinished business can be taken care of, and one can prepare for the loss and say farewell to the dying person. A client commented that by the time her father died after a long bout with cancer, she was struck by the fact that she did not cry or mourn as she thought she might. In exploring this unexpected reaction, it was clear that this daughter had been mourning her father's loss throughout all the months of his illness and felt relief when he died. With a sudden death, however, this is not the case. The shock of a sudden, unexpected loss can often be immobilizing. Such was the case with those who lost loved ones in the September 11th attacks as they expected to see their loved ones again. Unexpected losses and deaths resulting from violence often overwhelm a person's coping abilities (Murphy, Johnson & Cain, 1998; Parkes & Weiss, 1983).

Grief Can Also be Influenced by Concurrent Stresses or Crises: A person who is experiencing ongoing stressors (e.g., a physical illness, job loss, financial problems, or other interpersonal stressors), may have difficulty with grieving. For example, a couple who were considering divorce after the wife had been discovered having an affair, were two months into marital counseling when the husband was stricken by a hit and run driver and instantly killed. The wife's grief was naturally further compounded by her guilt over having the affair. In the instance of families who lost loved ones in the World Trade Center attack, these loved ones reported several concurrent crises, such as being badgered by the media, or being called by the New York City Medical Examiner to identify remains of their loved ones, which was accompanied by fears over the long-term impact of the loss on their children.

THE GRIEVING PROCESS

As previously discussed, crisis intervention has its roots in Erich Lindemann's clinical work following the Cocoanut Grove fire. Specifically, Lindemann found that acute grief reactions are a normal response to tragedy, and that grief has five characteristics:

- Somatic distress
- Preoccupation with the image of the deceased
- Guilt
- Hostile reactions
- Loss of patterns of conduct (daily life disruptions)

Bowlby (1969), most famous for his work on attachment theory and separation/loss as viewed from a psychodynamic perspective, also described phases of mourning. Initially,

Bowlby described three phases: 1) the urge to recover the lost object (person); 2) disorganization and despair; and 3) reorganization. Bowlby (1980) later modified these phases when Parkes (1970) discovered another initial phase that Bowlby had omitted. The revised phases were as follows:

Phase of Numbing: Here shock and disbelief prevail, often including varying degrees of denial.

Phase of Yearning and Searching: The bereaved individual often demonstrates strong urges to find, recover, or reunite with the loved one they lost. Feelings of anger, restlessness, and irritability are most evident in this stage. Strong preoccupations with visual memories of the deceased are also present.

Phase of Disorganization and Despair: This phase is marked by the bereaved giving up the search for the deceased. Feelings of depression are most prevalent in this phase, along with an inability to look to the future or see purpose in life.

Phase of Reorganization: Here the bereaved breaks their attachment to the deceased and begins to establish ties to others. There is a gradual return to former interests and appetites.

Perhaps the most well-known work on the grieving process was done by Elizabeth Kubler-Ross (1969), a Swiss psychiatrist who was working with terminally ill children and adults when she developed her stage theory. What is noteworthy is that when Kubler-Ross first wrote about death and dying, she discovered that these stages applied to the dying individual. However, it was later concluded that these same stages applied to the mourning family members as well. More recently, Kubler-Ross's stages have been applied to describe the process by which individual's come to accept any medical illness (including mental illness and substance use disorders). These stages are as follows:

Denial and Isolation: Denial is a natural initial reaction to the dying process. Denial can also be a healthy reaction in that it may help the individual continue on with daily functioning. It may also help to cushion the patient from the initial shock or despair.

Anger: Once the reality of the illness begins to set in, denial begins to decrease and anger takes center stage. Patients may question, "Why me?" and their anger may be directed to doctors, health professionals, family members, or God. They may experience rage, bitterness, and envy.

Bargaining: The bargaining stage can take different forms, but usually is characterized by a secret pact made with God, in which the dying patient agrees to change or do something in return for more time or a return of health. For example, one woman diagnosed with uterine cancer secretly prayed that God spare her life until she could see her daughter graduate from high school.

Depression: This stage occurs when the inevitability of death is prominent and overwhelming. As with clinical depression, feelings of hopelessness, helplessness, and despair are paramount.

Acceptance: Not all individuals reach this stage. Perhaps the best way to characterize this stage is one of being at peace. The person is no longer wrestling emotionally with the inevitability of their death or for the loss of their loved one or family member, they have reached a point of acceptance when they can reflect back on their loved one's life with fond memories now devoid of the sharp pain that grief often brings. The dying patient may appear to be void of feeling. They begin to disengage from life or disengage from battling their illness.

There are several noteworthy points in Kubler-Ross's stages. First, not everyone experiences these stages in sequence, even though these stages are said to be sequential. From clinical observation, we find that people often bounce between stages at various points during the course of their illness. So, it is not unusual, for example, for a person to be feeling depressed one week only to find they have gone back into anger the next, or denial and isolation the next. This does not negate the importance of this stage model. Instead, it is important for counselors to roll with these changes and to be able to work with the person, no matter where they are in their grief process at any particular moment in time. Please keep in mind, that prior to Kubler-Ross's work, no one really took the time to talk with dying patients, or to listen to their feelings, and their needs. Her work not only pioneered the field of grief counseling, but also made course work in grief counseling and communication with dying patients and their families, mandatory in many medical schools. Second, in doing crisis intervention in bereavement situations, it is possible for individuals to present in any of these stages (except for acceptance, because with acceptance there is usually no crisis). So, patients in crisis may present with anger, bargaining, or depressive feelings.

THE TASKS OF MOURNING

Related to the notion of stages of mourning are the tasks or goals in the bereavement process. This is somewhat analogous to developmental tasks. In other words, in the developmental stage of adolescence, there is a time frame that demarcates this stage, usually somewhere between the ages of 13 and 19. However as Erik Erikson (1968) suggests, in order to "complete" this stage, teenagers must complete particular tasks relevant to this stage before they go on to become young adults. Tasks, such as forming a sense of who they are (identity); career decisions; defining interpersonal relationships; and separation from one's family of origin are all important tasks in this process. In the mourning process, Worden (2008) described four *tasks* of mourning:

1. *To accept the reality of the loss:* As noted in Kubler-Ross's stages, denial is often encountered when dealing with a dying patient or a family member who has lost a loved one. One grieving spouse continued to set a place at the dinner table for her husband for several months after he died. She demonstrated that she had reached some acceptance of his death when she stopped doing this, and also when she gave his clothes away to a local homeless shelter. This task involves coming to the point of facing the "reality that the person is gone and will not return" (Worden, 2008, p. 39).

2. *To process the pain of grief:* One of the most difficult tasks in grief work is experiencing the feeling associated with grief, whether they are feelings of sadness, rage, guilt, depression, or other feelings. Anthropologists explain that feelings of anger toward loved ones who have died is normal, and may have engendered important funeral rituals, such as placing tombstones on graves as a means of "holding down" the spirit of the deceased individual who might come back to haunt us. The supposed origin of the 21-gun salute was from primitive tribes who would throw rocks and spears into the air with the intent of driving away the deceased's spirit, lest they come back and retaliate. These traditions originated because of our anger at the deceased for leaving us. Individuals experience the intensity of the pain of grief in different ways. Some may try to avoid the pain, however as Bowlby (1980) stated, "Sooner or later, some of those who avoid all conscious grieving, break down—usually with some form of depression" (p. 158). As Worden (2008) points out, the role of bereavement counseling is essentially to help people process the pain of grieving.

3. *To adjust to a world without the deceased:* Coping with the loss of a loved one is difficult enough, however, coping in the world without the loved one is even more of a challenge. Worden (2008) indicates that there are three areas of adjustment that need to be addressed when a loved one dies: 1) External adjustments, such as a widow learning where to have her car repaired; a widower learning to cook for himself; or a child learning to pick out clothes in the morning all represent an attempt to come to terms with living without the deceased. These external adjustments often involve learning new skills. 2) Internal adjustments that often involve developing a new sense of self or a new identity. For a widow or widower, this might include no longer seeing themselves as half of a couple, but rather as an individual. Bereavement impacts not only one's identity, but also a person's sense of self-esteem and self-efficacy. It often takes time for bereaved people to gain a new sense of who they are and what they are capable of doing. 3) Spiritual adjustments refer to those changes that occur in how the person perceives the world and to reexamine their prior assumptions; for example, the world is fair and just, the world makes sense, or the belief in a benevolent God. The death of a loved one often challenges one's core beliefs or assumptions. Worden (2008, p. 49) provides an example of a mother whose child is killed in a drive-by shooting who questions how God could allow something that tragic to happen.

4. *To find an enduring connection with the deceased in the middle of embarking on a new life.* The very thought of withdrawing emotional energy away from the deceased may be viewed as being disloyal or may be accompanied by a sense of betrayal or guilt. Even for parents who experience the death of a child, they often report that they find themselves pulling away from their surviving child or children. It may take years before the person is able to trust and love again, to reinvest their emotions in another person. This process takes time and there is often concern when a person throws himself or herself into another love relationship too quickly. In one such instance, a widower quickly became involved with another woman, about three months after his wife died, rationalizing that he "just wasn't meant to live alone."

After a quick marriage, he soon realized that he and his new bride were very different and although he thought she possessed many of the same character traits of his deceased wife, he now found he had deluded himself into searching out these similarities. This couple grew more and more disillusioned and miserable with each passing month as the tension and fights between them took over their day-to-day interactions. It was of no surprise when they announced their divorce.

CRISIS INTERVENTION IN SITUATIONS INVOLVING BEREAVEMENT AND LOSS

Rynearson (1987) contends that a crisis intervention approach is "generic" to all bereavement or grief counseling as the counseling focus often overlaps. For example, the need to emphasize strengthening self-esteem, ameliorating anxiety, expressing emotion, enhancing human supports, and strengthening of resources are all common to both approaches.

Worden (2008) offers guidelines for crisis bereavement counseling. They include the following:

1. *Help the survivor to actualize the loss.* Here it is important for crisis counselors to allow the grieving individual to talk about the loss, including the details of what happened and how the death occurred as a means of helping to make the loss a reality. Often survivors of loss feel a sense of unreality, as if the death really didn't occur.

2. *Help the survivor to identify and express feelings.* Don't assume that the client is able to readily identify their feelings. They may be burdened with guilt, anxiety, or anger, but may be unaware of these feelings. Crisis counselors can help the grieving individual identify or clarify their anger or guilt. Therefore, it is important that the counselor listen for affect as the client tells their story of their loved one's death. Body language and facial expression can also provide cues to affective state. If the person is having difficulty with guilty feelings the counselor could approach this by asking, "If there was something you could have changed when your loved one was alive, what would it be?"

3. *Assist the survivor to live without the deceased.* Here basic crisis counseling skills of helping the client to explore alternative approaches to problem solving is useful. It is important to remind clients that they often do not need to make major decisions right away and to allow themselves time to make decisions.

4. *Help find meaning in the loss.* Counselors can help clients find meaning in the death of their loved one. This may be difficult in instances where the loved one's death was sudden and tragic. Meaning may be found by survivors becoming involved in philanthropic, political, or caretaking activities that may help the surviving loved ones make sense of an unnecessary or senseless death(s). An example is the political pressure for gun reform which became the cause of the parents and other survivors in the aftermath of the Sandy Hook Elementary School shootings.

5. *Facilitate emotional relocation of the deceased.* Here counselors are helping survivors to find a new place for the deceased in their lives. The loved one is never forgotten and it is important for grieving loved ones to keep a special place for him or her in their hearts. The goal here is to find a special place that allows the grieving loved ones to move on and establish new identities and connections with others. It is important that grieving loved ones not interpret "moving on" as jumping into another relationship or marriage, as this often interferes with the grieving process.

6. *Provide time to grieve.* Grieving has no time table and requires time to heal the wounds of loss. Also, the process of grieving is gradual and can't be rushed. Sometimes, we've seen instances where families try "too hard" to establish normal routines, thereby not allowing other family members to experience their sadness or grief. One 19-year-old client recalls his ex-Marine Corps uncle telling him to "be strong" for his parents in the aftermath of the murder of his sister by an ex-boyfriend. The 19-year-old brother brought this recollection up when he was being treated for an opioid addiction.

7. *Interpret "normal" behavior.* As alluded to earlier, clients often question whether their reactions are normal or not. One widow questioned whether it was normal to cry whenever she was in church, several months after her husband had died. While he was alive, she and her husband had been actively involved in the church and his funeral service was in this same church. Naturally, each time she was in church, the painful memories of the funeral service came flooding back.

8. *Allow for individual differences.* Grief reactions tend to be unique. Some people grieve openly and intensely, others grieve quietly and privately. Some cry every day for weeks or months, others not at all. It is important for counselors to be sensitive to individual differences in grieving styles.

9. *Examine defenses and coping styles.* This step does not take place during the bereavement crisis counseling, but once a rapport has been established with a client. Clients are encouraged to develop healthy coping skills, such as involvement in bereavement groups or regular social activities with friends. Blaming, social withdrawal, denial, alcohol or drug abuse, self-harm are examples of coping attempts that interfere with the grief process. The timing and manner to discuss unhealthy or unproductive coping defenses with the client is of utmost importance as the goal is to present this interpretation in a way that the client will hear it.

10. *Identify pathology and refer.* Counselors have to be aware if clients need more than traditional bereavement counseling. Here, crisis counselors may have to serve in a "gatekeeper" role to help determine if a professional referral (e.g., a referral to a psychologist or psychiatrist) may be needed; such as when clients exhibit signs of major depression or suicidal thoughts.

Case Presentation: George, A Husband Grieves the Loss of his Wife

George is a 56-year-old sales manager and the father of two daughters, ages 24 and 22. Three months ago, his wife Joan died of pancreatic cancer. Approximately eight months ago, she complained of nausea, upper stomach pain, and was losing weight even though she was not dieting. Her physician suspected cancer and sent Joan to see an oncologist who made the diagnosis. After going through two months of radiation and chemotherapy, Joan died approximately six months after the initial diagnosis was made. The loss devastated George. He and Joan were very proud of their two daughters; one is married and living in Paris where both she and her husband work for a large investment firm. The youngest daughter is currently in her junior year of college. George feels a lot of loneliness, especially when he's not occupied with work. The minister of the church George attends noticed that George was inconsolable at all church meetings and during church services, so he referred George for bereavement counseling.

George is dealing with the recent loss of his wife and "empty nest" grief resulting from his adult daughters living away from home. The goal of the initial counseling session was to **listen** to George's grief and to get a sense as to what feelings he is grappling with most at this point. Initially, it is helpful to determine if he is experiencing one of the stages of grief, such as the stages described by Elizabeth Kubler-Ross, specifically, denial and isolation, anger, bargaining, depression, or acceptance.

Intervention

Counselor: Hello George, my name is Susan Reilly, I'm from the counseling center here at Southern Regional Medical Center. I understand that your minister suggested that you come in today. Do you mind if we talk for a while?

George: No, I don't mind. Reverend Paul is a great guy. He could see I was having a tough time.

C: What have you been struggling with?

G: Well, my wife Joan died a few weeks ago. In fact, she was receiving chemo treatments here at Southern. We spent a lot of time in this place. I guess we were hoping for a miracle cure, but everything I read on pancreatic cancer was not good. It advances and spreads so quickly. Joan put up a brave fight though (George starts to weep).

C: You must miss her a great deal?

G: Sometimes I can't believe she's really gone. There are times when I'll come home from work and I'll see her car in the driveway and I'll think to myself, "oh look, Joan's home from work," and then it'll hit me that she's gone. It's weird how you always think about how you'll grow old together, somehow you never expect that things will turn out like this.

C: This must have come as quite a shock to you?

G: She was fine and then one day she began complaining of some pains up around her stomach area and it seemed like the next thing we knew she was diagnosed with cancer and then the treatment started. That was the worst part.

C: How so?

G: The "chemo" really knocked her for a loop. She couldn't keep any food down. It seemed that she had already lost a lot of weight, but the chemo made her look emaciated, like a concentration camp victim. She hated wearing that wig too. She said it made her look like one of those Barbie dolls the girls used to play with when they were kids. It was really horrible.

C: Sounds like you have very painful memories of these past months. How are your daughters taking the loss of their mother?

G: They're both taking it hard. They were both very close to their mother and she was such a good mother. She was always there for them. My one daughter who lives in Paris with her husband was able to take a few weeks off, but she hated going back. My younger daughter, Jamie, is in college. She'll be home for winter break soon. She's having a tough time also.

C: George, how have you been managing your days since your wife passed away?

G: I'm okay when I'm at work, I keep pretty busy, but once I get home I get really depressed. Sometimes I feel like I'm numb or like I'm on automatic pilot or something. Just going through the motions. Weekends are really tough (George starts to tear up).

C: In what way?

G: Well I just lay around the house. It takes me hours just to get going to do simple chores or errands like going to the bank or post office.

C: Did you and Joan do things on the weekends?

G: That's what makes weekends so tough. Joan and I used to do everything together. We had a lot of friends that we used to get together with, you know like to go out to dinner or the movies.
      Now I feel like the third wheel. They ask me to go out with them, but it's not the same.

C: Have any weekends been less difficult for you?

G: Actually, I did have one decent weekend. My sister and brother-in-law invited me to go to a movie and out to dinner. It really helped to take my mind off of things for a while. They really understand how much her loss means to me and I'm not embarrassed if I tear up over nothing.

C: It sounds like most days are a struggle though, which is normal. It's good to hear that you had a pretty good weekend when you saw your sister and brother-in-law. It also sounds like a lot of what you're experiencing is part of the painful grief process that people go through when they lose someone they loved very much. Do you know of anyone who had gone through something similar to what you're experiencing?

G: I do have one friend that I used to work with. His wife died of a brain tumor. It was really awful. I remember Joan and I saying to each other, how horrible it was and we didn't know how our friend Victor got through it.

C: Are you still close to Victor?

G: Yes, he did come to the funeral. It was so nice to see him. He told me to call him if I wanted to talk or go out for dinner some time. I guess I should take him up on it, huh?

C: Do you feel ready to?

G: It actually does feel good to talk with somebody, like talking with you today.

C: Then let's set up another time to meet. When you are ready, I also know of some small group sessions for people who are going through similar grief. And, if you're ready, call Victor, he may be a good support.

Case Conceptualization/Crisis Resolution

George's case presents an interesting illustration of how other losses often compound grieving (e.g., the empty nest of the daughters living away from home, and the loss of friends and social contacts). George describes the loss of his wife, Joan, and how she managed to just keep going through all of it, yet his life is now in crisis. It is important that the counselor not label George's reactions as unusual. He uses the word "depressed" for example, not the counselor. Since grief reactions vary from person to person, it is inadvisable to label grief as pathological unless the person's functioning is severely impaired for lengthy periods. The goal of the session then becomes to establish a plan for ongoing support for George that will help him to reestablish some equilibrium in his life. It sounds like his job is helping him keep busy, but non-work hours are most difficult for him. It is important to note that the counselor does not "push" George toward any one crisis plan, but rather presents him with some alternatives that he can then chose. A collaborative crisis plan is always preferable to a plan that's imposed by the counselor.

Case Presentation: James and Barbara, A Couple Grieves the Tragic Loss of their Son

James and Barbara sought counseling following the death of their son in a car accident. The accident took place two months ago when their son, Dave, was driving home from work late at night. According to the police report, Dave either fell asleep at the wheel or was picking up a CD or cell phone from the floor of his car when he veered off the road and hit a tree. Both James and Barbara are devastated by losing their 19-year-old son. They have another child, a 21-year-old daughter who is away at college. Since the accident, both James and Barbara have been unable to function. Just getting through the first two weeks with planning the funeral was an ordeal. Now most of the family and friends that supported them through this most difficult time have gone home and on with their lives, and James and Barbara find themselves feeling lost, isolated, and angry.

Accidents like this are among the three leading causes of death in individuals aged 15 to 24 (suicides and homicides are the other two causes). James and Barbara find that they are unable to function and unable to communicate their grief to one another. The following dialogue recounts the crisis session which took place approximately two months after their son's death. As indicated earlier in this chapter, there are unspoken "milestones" during the grieving process. It is said that these milestones occur temporally, and are reached at "two weeks, two months, and two years." In the first two weeks, a loved one comes to grips with the reality of the death; however, there is usually a lot of support, family, and friends around to help buffer the grief. The next milestone, "two months," occurs when the reality of the loss sets in. James and Barbara are currently at the "two month" milestone and are experiencing difficulty in talking about their son's tragic death.

Intervention

Counselor: Hello Barbara and James, my name is Bob Kane. I understand from your phone call that you're here because of having lost your son recently. I'm so sorry for your loss. When did this happen?

James: This has been the worst thing we have ever been through. No parent ever expects to be burying their son or daughter (James starts to cry).

Barbara: It seems like the past two months have been a blur. Like we were both on automatic pilot, just going through the motions. At least that's how I felt.

C: What was the worst part of these past two months?

J: I just keep going back to the night we got the phone call from the police. At first, I thought it was one of Dave's friends playing a joke or something and then it sank in that it was for real. We still don't really know what happened. How the accident happened. We just know that there was no other driver involved, no alcohol or drugs in his system, and they say it was unintentional.

C: But, that doesn't tell you what did happen, only what didn't happen. Barbara what was the worst part for you?

B: Like Jim said, getting the call, but then going to the Medical Examiners to identify David. I'll never get that image out of my mind. Jim didn't want me to go in, but how could I not see my baby for the last time?

C: This is such a tragic loss. You both miss David so much.

Here the counselor is joining with Barbara and James by hearing their story of their son's death, what they remember, and what was the worst part. These are tough memories to relive, but necessary to the grief process and to help actualize the loss. The main goal of the counselor is to create an environment where Barbara and James feel comfortable in expressing any feelings.

Case Conceptualization/Crisis Resolution

It's important that the counselor stay with Jim and Barbara, and convey to them that their feelings are being heard. If they express guilt, it's important not to put a Band-Aid on the guilt, rather to let Jim and Barbara know that their feelings are being heard. Often the impact of grief is determined in part by how the death occurs. It is obvious that it is difficult to come to grips with a horrible tragedy like a car accident. It is also important that Jim and Barbara are aware that it is normal for couples to grieve in different ways and not to judge each other harshly because of these differences.

Case Presentation: Ryan, A Child Grieves the Loss of his Mother

Ryan is 8 years old and is in the 3rd grade at the Middlebrook Elementary School. Last month, his mother died in a car accident. Ryan's parents were divorced when he was 4 years old and his father was transferred to a new office in another city out of state last year. Ryan's teacher noticed that since returning to school, he was getting into fights with other students and his grades had gone down. The teacher also noticed that Ryan was avoiding playing with his friends and would not join in any activities, so the teacher referred him to the school counselor who provided the initial crisis session with Ryan. This session was subsequent to the school's threat of expulsion after getting into another fight with a classmate.

Ryan's case offers an important perspective on the differences in childhood bereavement. As discussed earlier, children and adolescents have distinct grieving patterns as compared to adult grieving patterns. Much of how a child copes with grief is determined by how much preparation they may have received prior to the death, and how the mourning is addressed after the death (Furman, 1974). Generally, it is thought that the older the child, the better their chances of understanding the permanence of death, therefore, the better their overall adjustment. This naturally depends on how independent and emotionally stable the child is prior to the parent's death. Children between the ages of four and five have particular difficulty with accepting the concept of the permanence of death. Coping is also determined by how the child's questions and curiosities about the death are handled. For example, if a child's questions are met with harshness or anxiety, this only increases the child's confusion. Yet, on the other hand, too much or too little information can also be detrimental to overall adjustment. For example, Furman (1974) points out that children often express concerns about losing the surviving parent by asking, "Will you die too, Daddy?" Although concerns about misleading or deceiving the child by replying, "No, daddy will not die" are valid, giving too much information about the unpredictability of life or our shared ultimate fate, only serves to increase the child's anxiety. Similarly, even with younger children, where the parent dies from a terminal illness, it is best to properly label the disease, for example, "Daddy is dying because of cancer," as opposed to saying, "Daddy is sick." By not giving proper information, one runs the risk that the next time anyone in the child's life gets sick (including the child), that he or she fears that they too will die and leave them, in the same way that Daddy did. In the sudden unexpected death of a parent, the surviving parent or guardian can broach this by saying, "I have something very sad to tell you." Sometimes, all the details are not known; however, children seem to feel better when the parent promises them that details will be shared with them just as soon as they know (Furman, 1974). Children naturally cannot deal with a flood of frightening details, but they can cope with the surviving parent or being upset or crying. The child also benefits from reassurance that they will be well taken care of; therefore, explaining the arrangements is very important. There are often questions about whether a child should attend the wake or funeral service. With very young children it is usually advised that they not attend the wake. However, older children can attend even an open-casket viewing if they can sit at a comfortable distance and an adult is with them to support and comfort them, as well as to respond to their questions and concerns. It is often advised that it is best to explain to the child what a funeral is and that it is his or her choice whether to attend the funeral. It is also important to recognize that the child's longing to be with their deceased parent is also part of the normal grief process as are the accompanying feelings of sadness and/or anger. Part of successful grieving in children (and adults for that matter), is their ability to withstand these feelings of longing or yearning to be with the deceased.

Case Conceptualization/Crisis Resolution

Ryan's fights with his classmates are a good example of how a child's grief can be displaced behaviorally. It is easy to see how through his fighting, Ryan's anger at his mother's death is being displaced onto his classmates. The role of the school counselor is to help validate Ryan's anger and frustration and hopefully to get him to accept counseling. Although the school counselor can help Ryan, especially regarding his school behavior and academic performance, it might still be more helpful for Ryan to see a bereavement counselor to work with the entire family to process their feelings as they move through the grief. The role of the school counselor is to help Ryan with his adjustment at school and to deal with the immediate crisis surrounding his mother's death.

Case Presentation: Tara and Bill, Parents Grieving The Loss of their Newborn Daughter

Tara and Bill have been married for two years. Tara is 24 years old and Bill is 26. They were both looking forward to having a baby and becoming parents. After having two miscarriages, Tara finally gave birth to a baby girl. They were both ecstatic; however, the neonatologist then told them that their baby had been born with "respiratory complications" and was having difficulty breathing. A pulmonary neonatologist was called in on a consultation and told Tara and Bill that the baby had major heart and lung abnormalities and "was not expected to live." Having never left the hospital, their baby died approximately two weeks after she was born.

The death of a child is probably the singular most traumatic event that a parent can face. It is universally assumed that a child will outlive their parents. As Rando (1984) points out, when an adult loses a parent they lose their past, but when they lose a child, they lose their future. It was once assumed that the divorce rate for bereaved parents who do not receive grief counseling could be as high as 92% (Kanel, 2003). However, a 1999 survey concluded the divorce rate remains low among bereaved parents when it found that only 12% of those marriages had ended in divorce (Kanel, 2003). A 2006 survey commissioned by Compassionate Friends found the divorce rate was slightly higher at 16%, however this rate was still lower than the divorce rate in the general population (Fox, 2009). In the aftermath of losing a child, it is common for couples to feel that they are no longer the same. Also, it is not unusual for parents to grieve differently, and these differences may elicit feelings that their partner is being callous. For example, if the husband (or male partner) views the death as something the couple can get over by trying to have another child, then their spouse may perceive this response as cold and discounting her feelings. Likewise, if the wife is experiencing tremendous grief, then the husband may feel that he is not doing enough for her, or in contrast he may want his wife to move on with their lives as a couple. In addition, it is also very important to acknowledge that a woman's identity is often linked to her ability to have children (Rando, 1986). Finally, since both husband and wife are experiencing grief, they often are unable to support one another through this process. They begin to feel isolated and disconnected from each other. According to a systematic review conducted by Albuquerque, Pereira, and Narciso (2016), the death of a child can both divide and join a grieving couple. Variables, such as the couple's pre-death relationship characteristics, communication, and family factors (e.g., having surviving children, or the family's history of grief and trauma) can impact their functioning as a couple, and in turn, their adjustment as individuals (Albuquerque et al., 2016).

In the case example described above, it is Tara who seeks counseling approximately four days after their baby died. Her grief is further compounded by her two miscarriages prior to the birth of their daughter. A miscarriage can be as devastating emotionally as any other tragic loss and may compound her current feelings. Unfortunately, there have been only a few medical centers and crisis intervention providers who were attuned to the need for some more formal ways to grieve the termination of a pregnancy by miscarriage or abortion. Some medical centers now provide grief counseling for those who have experienced a pregnancy loss. Some even provide a grieving ritual like planting a tree to memorialize these losses.

Intervention

In counseling Tara and Bill it is important that the counselor first **listen** to what they have just gone through over these past two weeks since their daughter was born; to hear out their individual experiences in terms of moments of hope just following the birth to feelings of hopelessness and despair on learning their baby would most likely not survive given the medical complications. It is also important to **assess** where both Tara and Bill are in their grief as it is possible they are experiencing shock or denial and the reality of their daughter's death is not impacting them in the same way now. There may also be gender differences in how couples grieve the loss of a child as men tend to be less expressive of their pain and/or sometimes more "task-oriented" in terms of suggesting that they keep trying to have a child. Tara may also be experiencing dramatic hormonal changes that contribute to and exacerbate her postpartum grief. In **planning** with Bill and Tara there are two issues that are important. Depending on how soon counseling initiates for Bill and Tara following the death of their daughter, the practical issues of funeral arrangements might need to be discussed. It is important that Bill and Tara agree about the type of funeral service they wish to have. In some instances, family members (such as Bill and Tara's parents) may be helpful in planning the funeral service and making necessary, but extremely difficult calls to extended family and friends. The other important issue of planning involves discussion of ongoing counseling for both Bill and Tara. Here it is important to help support the couple as they are experiencing various stages of grief and as they address the tasks of mourning that we discussed earlier in this chapter. Finally, getting Tara and Bill to **commit** to a plan is the final phase of this crisis session.

Case Conceptualization/Crisis Resolution

It is important that both Tara and Bill commit to ongoing bereavement counseling as this is a positive sign that they are willing to support one another through the grieving process. The days and weeks ahead are the most difficult. Also, it is important for the crisis counselor to point out that couples often grieve differently and that this is normal, and to further emphasize the importance of communication between the couple. It is also important to mention to Tara and Bill that there are support groups specifically for parents who have lost newborns and infants. Of all the counseling treatments available, support groups are one of the most beneficial modes of therapy, because it allows for honest sharing with couples who have experienced the same loss and can better understand the pain that Tara and Bill are going through.

Case Presentation: Tanya, A Case of Traumatic Bereavement

Tanya was very proud of her 24-year-old son, Tyrone, when he decided to become a corrections officer. After graduating high school, Tyrone served in the army for four years with the military police, both here in the United States, as well as having served two tours in Afghanistan. Once Tyrone was discharged he figured it would be easy for him to find work either as a state trooper, or in a county or municipal police department. However, at the time that Tyrone was honorably discharged, many police departments were forced to make cutbacks because of the economic recession. Tyrone was frustrated that he couldn't find work as a police officer so he began to look around for other job opportunities and eventually decided to go into corrections work. After going through extensive training, Tyrone was assigned to work at a state prison. This particular prison was noted for being particularly volatile because there were several rival gangs that were housed in that facility. Tanya often worried about Tyrone's safety, similar to when he was serving in Afghanistan. She had a strong religious and spiritual faith and believed with God's care that Tyrone could take care of himself. Tanya was watching TV one evening when the local news announced there was a prison riot at the facility where Tyrone was working. The news reports said that several guards were taken hostage and that two correction officers had been reported killed. Tanya tried to call Tyrone on his cell phone, but did not get any response. At first, she thought that Tyrone had not had to work that day. She prayed that was the case and that her son was safe. She tried calling some of Tyrone's friends and even the prison warden's office to determine if Tyrone was safe. Later that evening, there was a knock on the door and it was the head of the corrections officer's union and Tyrone's supervisor informing Tanya that her son was killed in the riot. Tanya asked if her son's body had been recovered and she was told by the supervisor (who became very anxious at that point) that they were in the process of recovering Tyrone's body. Tanya later heard on the news that the prison rioters had tortured the guards and burned their bodies in the prison courtyard.

This sad case has all the characteristics of traumatic bereavement as described earlier in this chapter. This is a sudden, untimely traumatic loss that involves harm to the loved one (Tyrone) by a perpetrator(s) who intended to harm him and there are certainly feelings that Tyrone's death was unfair or unjust. Tanya is now facing, not only the loss of her son, but also the traumatic circumstances that surrounded his death. As we discuss in Chapter 14 dealing with work crises, corrections officers are among those groups who are most likely to be killed or injured on the job. We can expect that Tanya is experiencing high levels of grief, depression, and posttraumatic stress disorder symptoms. Also, it is important to note that becoming fixated on anger and obtaining justice may delay the grief process. Traumatic grief also takes much longer to process (Rando, 2003). Often the bereaved comes to regard their continued emotional and psychological distress as a sign of their inability to cope or some personal inadequacy (Lehman, Wortman, & Williams, 1987).

According to Barlé et al. (2015) with those experiencing traumatic bereavement, there are particular "core issues" that need to be considered in their bereavement counseling. First, a traumatic death shatters one's basic life assumptions. Here, for example, Tanya always believed that her son would be safe and that God was watching over him. Her spiritual faith helped her to see the world as operating on principles of fairness and justice or that the world was safe. However, these beliefs are now shattered. Tanya may question how her son could survive being in combat only to be murdered here at home. This raises another core issue as Tanya tries to make sense of or find meaning in her son's death. As imagined, these attempts to find meaning tend to complicate the bereavement process given that her son's death was both tragic and meaningless. Survivors of traumatic loss often experience feelings of guilt and ruminate over the loss. Here, Tanya may obsess over what her son's last minutes or hours were like being held hostage and whether he might have struggled with his killers. In the following crisis intervention session, the minister of her church convinces Tanya to see a bereavement counselor at a local mental health clinic.

Intervention

Tanya: Thank you for coming over to see me. I can't believe Tyrone is gone.

Counselor: I am so sorry to hear of your son's death. Could you tell me what happened?

Here Tanya describes the details of her son's death and how she came to learn he was murdered in the prison riot.

T: I can't help being angry . . . with God for taking him. Why did he survive all that time in Afghanistan, only to be killed by vicious thugs right here at home? None of this makes sense. Why did God allow this to happen?

C: It doesn't make sense.

T: I can't get the thoughts about how Tyrone died out of my head. I can't sleep because I'm afraid I'll have nightmares, but even during the day I can't turn these thoughts off. They are constant.

C: It must be so hard for you to have these thoughts every waking moment, and at night as well.

T: It is so hard; I keep expecting that Tyrone is going to call me or stop over unexpectedly the way he used to just to check in on me.

Here Tanya expresses difficulty accepting that Tyrone is gone and difficulty in coping with the ruminations about how he died. Earlier in the conversation she expresses her struggle to find meaning in his death. The counselor is careful to validate Tanya's feelings while avoiding any judgment or dictates about what she "should do." For example, if the counselor were to tell Tanya to accept that Tyrone is gone, that statement is in effect telling her how she should feel, which is not the role of crisis counseling.

C: It is very difficult to think of Tyrone no longer being here with you.

T: It is the most difficult thing I've ever had to do. I don't know what to do, what not to do. I just know that I hurt and the pain is overwhelming.

C: The pain must be overwhelming. It is so important that you agreed to come here and to talk with me today. Are there other people you feel you are comfortable talking with?

T: The minister at my church has been very helpful. He brought me here today. I also have a lot of friends at the church who have been calling me and dropping off food. They have been so kind.

C: Sounds like you have a lot of friends and support.

T: Yes, these are good people and they all knew Tyrone and were so proud of all the things he did both while in the army and as a corrections officer. I also have a brother, Tyrone's uncle, who is coming up from Virginia to spend time with me and to help me with the funeral arrangements. My brother is a tremendous source of support for me. I was so relieved when he said he would be coming up to help with the funeral.

C: It is helpful that he will be here for you through these difficult days ahead. Would you be willing to come back so we can talk again?

T: Yes, I appreciate that very much.

Case Conceptualization/Crisis Resolution

Tanya took an important step first by reaching out to her minister during her time of grief and pain rather than isolating from others and her community, and also by agreeing to see a bereavement crisis counselor. In this excerpt, the counselor **listens** as Tanya describes her struggles with ruminations and trying to make sense of her son's tragic murder. Often there are no "magic words" that can soothe Tanya's feelings of trauma and grief, but what is important is that the counselor is willing to be with Tanya in her grief and to listen to her emotional pain, worries, and fears. Tanya is experiencing both PTSD symptoms along with her overwhelming feelings of grief, which is evident in the intrusive thoughts and nightmares of her son's death. Ongoing bereavement counseling can assist Tanya in managing these most difficult symptoms. This is known as "trauma-informed counseling" (SAMHSA, 2015). According to the Substance Abuse and Mental Health Services Administration (SAMHSA), trauma-informed counseling realizes the widespread impact of trauma and understands potential paths for recovery; recognizes the signs and symptoms of trauma in clients, families, staff, and others involved with the system; responds by fully integrating knowledge about trauma into policies, procedures, and practices; and seeks to actively resist re-traumatization of the individual.

Case Presentation: John, The Grief of Divorce

John is a 46-year-old married father of two daughters ages 20 and 18, both away at college. He and his wife, Mary, met at work and were engaged for about a year; they have now been married for the past 21 years. John thought that they were both happy and content in their relationship, however, one day Mary confronted John and told him that she no longer loved him and that she had fallen in love with a guy she met in one of her yoga classes. John was devastated. He tried to get Mary to go for counseling with him, but she refused. She felt that all through their marriage she was always low on John's priority list. She saw no reason to rehash those issues that had been sources of conflict throughout their marriage. John did get Mary to agree to go to one marriage counseling session; however, he soon realized that she no longer loved him, there was no hope of salvaging the marriage, and the separation was final. John sought crisis counseling at the urging of his brother, after he told him that he saw no reason to go on living and that he was so depressed, he had not even been to work in three weeks.

In the case of John, a different type of loss is presented, that of separation and divorce. However, there are many who feel that the emotional pain associated with a divorce is tantamount to losing someone through death. In addition, just as there are also hidden losses that one experiences when a loved one has died, it is also true that divorced individuals experience many other losses: loss of time with children, loss of income, loss of a home, loss of friends, loss of contact with in-laws, or loss of companionship. Even in the most amicable divorces, the sense of loss is tremendous and overwhelming; however, in the case of a contentious divorce there may also be accompanying feelings of anger, rage, guilt, envy, and jealousy. When children are involved, the pain of loss often becomes greater. Such is the case when the noncustodial parent is now faced with limited time with their sons or daughters, as was so vividly depicted in the movie, *Kramer vs. Kramer*.

Crises involving divorce are quite common, mostly because the United States has the highest rates of divorce (6.8 per 1,000), compared to other countries (United Kingdom 2.97 per 1,000; Sweden 2.40 per 1,000; and Germany 2.07 per 1,000) (Center for Disease Control & Prevention, 2014; United Nations Secretariat, 1996). It is estimated that approximately 40 to 50% of marriages in the United States will end in divorce. However, there are several factors that should be considered when examining these comparatively extreme U.S. divorce rates. First, there is a greater acceptance of divorce in the United States with marriage not viewed as having the same permanence that it once had. Second, the roles of women have shifted. With more and more women in the workforce, women are no longer as financially dependent on men and therefore, are less willing to stay in unfulfilling marriages. Third, the sanctity of marriage as a religiously bound union does not have the same strong level of acceptance as was the case several years ago. Fourth, culturally there is a greater emphasis on seeking satisfaction of personal goals and higher expectations for marital happiness (Weitzman, 1985). Fifth, people now live longer, therefore, it is not unusual for couples to divorce after their adult children have gone off to college or have married and moved away from home. It is also important to take into consideration that many marriages end in divorce because of problems related to infidelity and substance use disorders (Granvold, 2000).

Overall, even in amicable separations, divorces tend to have a deleterious effect on one's mental and often physical health. Indeed, divorce is associated with higher rates of *depression* (Anthony & Petronis, 1991; Gallo, Royall, & Anthony, 1993; Weissman, Bruce, Leaf, Florio, & Holzer, 1991); *suicide* (Cantor & Slater, 1995; Trovato, 1986) and *substance abuse* (Beck, Wright, Newman, & Liese, 1993). A more recent study (Symoens, Van de Velde, Colman, & Bracke, 2014) found that both men and women divorcees experienced higher levels of depression and lower levels of self-esteem and competence. In a study of military couples, comparing couples who had divorced with those who remained married, divorcees were significantly more likely to screen positive for "new-onset" posttraumatic stress disorder, depression, smoking initiation, binge-drinking, alcohol-related problems, and experience moderate weight gain. However, those military men and women divorcees scored in the 15th percentile on physical fitness measures (Wang, Seelig, Wadsworth, McMaster, & Crum-Cianflone, 2015). Granvold (2000) recommends a thorough risk assessment when divorced individuals present for crisis intervention services because of these aforementioned mental health and substance use risk factors. Yet, Symoens, Colman, and Bracke (2014) also found that when divorcees went on to live together with a new partner (either in marriage or in cohabitation) there were beneficial effects on mental health, even in cases of high conflict with an ex-spouse.

As discussed earlier in this chapter, just as bereavement reactions are often determined by the factors surrounding the death, such as cause of death, the survivor's relationship with the deceased loved one, age, and ethnicity; so too, in cases of divorce, the events and factors surrounding the divorce also play a role. For example, marital infidelity, physical violence, verbal and/or emotional abuse, alcoholism and substance abuse, physical and/or sexual abuse of the children, gambling, gross financial irresponsibility, and episodic violation of trust (e.g. lying, deceit) to name just a few (Granvold, 2000).

Intervention

John was brought to the counseling center by his brother, Barry, who had just become aware of John's veiled suicidal threats and absence from work. Here it was important for the counselor to **listen** to John's story of the loss of his wife and how her announcement that she had fallen in love with someone else had such a devastating impact on him. There are no "magic words" or platitudes that can ease John's emotional pain at this crisis point, so it's often better for the counselor to validate John's pain and to convey a willingness to understand what he's going through. In **assessing** John, it is important to distinguish John's bereavement from depression as it appears that John has stopped going to work and has also expressed suicidal ideas and possible intent. It is helpful therefore to do a suicide lethality assessment like the one described later in this chapter.

Case Conceptualization/Crisis Resolution

At this point, John appears willing to accept these referrals as alternatives to staying "stuck" with his depression and anger, which appear to be part of his grief reactions. It is fortunate that his brother Barry is attending the session with him because Barry can help monitor whether John makes these contacts. A few follow-up sessions can be set up to make certain that John is safe and beginning to make progress. If necessary, a referral for psychotropic medication may also be needed to help move John out of the immobilizing aspects of the grief. In some instances, an antidepressant may be helpful on a short-term basis to get John functioning again.

SUICIDE BEREAVEMENT

Although not any less painful than some of the other types of grief and losses discussed in this chapter, the bereavement following the death of a loved one by suicide differs in how it impacts family members and significant others, such as partners, friends, and coworkers. This is evident in the stages of grief following a suicide death (Lifeline, 2016). The first stage is **shock**, which is often described as a state of emotional numbness which takes over when one first learns of the suicide death of a loved one. The feeling of shock and numbness sometimes allows loved ones to detach emotionally in order to get through the initial hours after learning of the loved one's death. **Denial** also serves the purpose of limiting the amount of pain that the surviving family member or loved one can handle. In one example of denial, after they got home from the hospital after identifying their son's body and then calling the funeral home, a parent recalled making their son's favorite meal waiting for him to come home. Denial is common when one learns or hears of the death of a loved one, however, when the death occurs because of suicide, denial becomes an important protective defense mechanism because the thought of someone killing themselves is so disturbing and incomprehensible. **Shame** encompasses all of the feelings that somehow the survivor has failed as a parent, a partner, a wife/husband, a friend in being able to recognize the emotional pain of their loved one. There are also questions about what to tell others and how much information to give, which also reflects the survivor's feelings of shame. The next stage, **guilt,** tends to be more about those things the survivors feel they "would have," "could have," or "should have" done while their loved one was alive that maybe would have prevented their suicide. In actuality, thoughts and decisions about suicide are usually the result of a number of factors and usually not just determined by one isolated occurrence; however, in the survivor's perceptions, he or she may question whether spending more time with their loved one or being there for them would have prevented their death. **Anger** is a very common reaction in grieving, however it becomes even more complex when the death occurs because of suicide. Anger sometimes can be directed at the loved one for taking his or her own life or can be directed at others whom the survivors feel should have been more careful or responsible for their loved one, which could have prevented them from committing suicide. What many survivors report is that they often feel a lack of **trust** in the aftermath of losing a loved one by suicide. The trust that was taken for granted with others often disappears. There may even be suspiciousness or doubt about the intentions of others who try to console the survivors in their grief.

The next stage, **loneliness** is tied with feelings of pain regarding a future that the deceased loved one is no longer part of. Because suicide is so sudden and unexpected, the sense of having that person in your life one minute and having them gone the next, brings such incredible pain to survivors. **Depression**, which is accompanied by feelings of despair, lethargy, feeling that life is pointless with no reason to go on, are all part of this next stage. Fortunately, as the grief progresses these feelings of depression begin to lift; however, survivors often find it very difficult to accept help from their supports during this period of depression. Finally, with the help of friends, family, counselors, and support groups, survivors begin to find some **resolution and integration**, which in some ways can represent an acceptance of the loss and the beginnings of being able to see a life ahead (Lifeline, 2016). As we've talked about with other stages of grief, these are not a smooth, linear path, but rather a road with a lot of twists and turns, as one may feel anger one day, feel lonely and depressed the next, or bounce back into denial the next. That is why it's important for crisis counselors and bereavement counselors to work with individuals in whatever stage he or she presents.

GRIEVING THE LOSS OF A PET

Only recently has pet loss been recognized as a loss that often necessitates grief counseling. Today there are many support groups that solely address pet loss and there are even condolence cards specifically for those who have experienced the loss of a pet. Also, pet loss can often be just as difficult for children as it can be for adults. A pet can become an important part of the family and is perceived as being there through thick and thin providing unconditional love to all family members. For adults living alone, a pet is there to greet him or her when they come home, and provides comfort and companionship. Many pet owners talk about how their cat or dog is very much attuned to their moods and responds accordingly. It is no coincidence that horses have been used in equine-assisted therapy with returning Iraq and Afghanistan veterans because horses are so attuned to the emotions of humans. For anyone who has had to "put down" or euthanize a pet, it is one of the more emotionally painful experiences that they have gone through. That brings us to the case of Bertha described briefly below. Bertha's loss not only demonstrates the grief over the loss of her dog, Jackie, but also how her grief taps into the grief she felt at the time her husband, Carl died, several years prior.

Bertha is a 70-year-old widow who lives alone. Her husband, Carl, died about eight years ago after a sudden heart attack. Bertha has three grown children who live near Atlanta and, because of their work schedules, she sees them and her grandchildren during the summer and around the Christmas holidays. Bertha sought crisis counseling at the urging of some of her friends in the senior citizen complex where she lives. Bertha explains in the session that a few days ago, she had to put her little terrier, Jackie, to sleep because she had developed kidney disease. Bertha explained how she and her husband Carl had adopted Jackie from the local animal shelter around the time her husband retired. Jackie and Carl were inseparable and when Carl died, Jackie became Bertha's devoted companion. In some ways, Bertha felt that Jackie provided her with a connection to Carl because of their similar bond with Jackie. Bertha reports that she's been crying all the time and has not been able to eat or sleep since her dog's death.

Case Conceptualization/Crisis Resolution

Bertha found it comforting to talk with the crisis counselor, even though, at first, she didn't think she would ever need to talk with someone about grief issues. The counselor was careful to **listen** to Bertha's explanations of what it was like to lose her husband, Carl, and the dreams and plans they had for when he retired. The counselor also validated how painful it is to lose a pet and how pets often are part of our family and our lives, just as Jackie had become part of Bertha and Carl's family. In **assessing** Bertha's grief, the counselor noted that she is not eating or sleeping, but felt that this might be part of Bertha's immediate reaction to having to put Jackie to sleep, and makes a note to monitor Bertha's appetite and sleep patterns as time progresses. In **planning**, Bertha agreed to come back to talk with the counselor again. The counselor felt it was too early to introduce the recommendation of a pet bereavement group, but in the future, it might be something that Bertha may want to try out. At which point, the counselor will provide Bertha with as much information about the group as possible and perhaps even set up a meeting with the group facilitator prior to Bertha's joining the group. At the moment, it is important that Bertha is **committed** to returning for another meeting with the counselor. There are several books written on pet loss, some of which offer very practical recommendations about making decisions on euthanasia, and pet burial (Dolan-Delvecchio & Saxton-Lopez, 2013; Kowalski, 2012).

GENERAL GUIDELINES FOR COUNSELORS IN MANAGING CRISES OF LOSS AND BEREAVEMENT

Although there are no "hard and fast" rules when it comes to crisis intervention in bereavement situations, there are some guidelines that might be useful for counselors to keep in mind as they are working with people in the throes of these types of crises.

1. Join the bereaved individual at whatever stage they present in. (For example, if the person is angry, it is important to hear out their anger and let them vent.)

2. Don't try to force the person to the next stage, gently guide, but don't force them. (The aforementioned stages of grief are meant as a guide, not as a directive. Counselors can sometimes "preview" what the next stage in their grief may feel like or sound like, but again this is not meant to be a dictate.)

3. While it's important to be a good empathic listener, you don't want to become overwhelmed in the person's grief to the point where you also become immobilized by their story of grief. In other words, don't become like the "deer caught in the headlights." It is most important that you as the counselor, convey the confidence and knowledge to see the person through this grief process, no matter how overwhelming it may seem initially.

4. It is important for bereavement and crisis counselors to be cognizant of the tendency of loved ones to idealize the deceased, almost to the point of elevating the deceased loved ones to sainthood. This is easy when the person was indeed a good, kind-hearted type of person; however, this can also occur even when the person was quite the opposite. Even a miserable, vitriolic, abusive spouse can be deified in death. This is a common reaction and it is helpful for crisis counselors to be aware of this and not feel that they need to confront these "misperceptions." Those types of issues may be addressed in long-term bereavement counseling.

5. Crisis counselors should also avoid giving directives and being critical of the bereaved (Dershimer, 1990). Here it is important to avoid making any statements that might result in exacerbating the client's feelings of guilt, shame, or self-doubt. As Dershimer points out, bereaved individuals often have their "radar" set for anything that might suggest that their grief is abnormal, so statements that might be misconstrued as being judgmental or critical are to be avoided. For example, a well-meaning crisis counselor might suggest to a bereaved widower that eventually they will be able to move on and their grief will not be as intense. This type of statement could be misinterpreted by the grieving husband as a criticism of their present feelings.

6. Don't become impatient if the client seems "stuck" in their grief (Dershimer, 1990). It is important to remember that grief has no timetable. Grief counselors estimate that grief sometimes takes five to seven years to resolve. Also, people tend to grieve in their own way and at their own pace. Those in mourning may appear to be coping well at one moment, only to fall apart emotionally the next. This is common.

7. Be careful not to brush aside, offer platitudes, or judge the client's deep-seated fears or doubts (Dershimer, 1990). Bereaved individuals most likely have received enough platitudes or sometimes well-meant advice from their friends or family members, so it is best that they not feel their fears or doubts are dismissed by the counselor. Accordingly, they obviously don't need to hear platitudes, such as "you'll meet someone new," "you'll be able to have another child," or "you'll get over it" or "this was God's will." Also in working with those who have experienced traumatic bereavement, Barlé and colleagues (2015) recommend that counselors prepare loved ones for often unexpected hurtful or uncaring remarks that may be made by

relatives, friends, or acquaintances. For example, can you imagine someone coming up to Tanya a few weeks after her son was killed and saying, "How is Tyrone doing at his new job?" By preparing the bereaved for these types of remarks, how to respond emotionally, and what to say, it can help loved ones from being blindsided or caught off guard at vulnerable moments.

8. No matter how many times you hear the same story about the deceased, treat it as if it is the first time you are hearing the story, instead of responding verbally or non-verbally with the statement "you already told me that." One of the differences between formal crisis counseling and grief counseling is that counselors continue to listen when all the bereaved's friends and family have gone away, or may be telling them, "it's time to move on," "I don't want to hear the same stories about the deceased anymore" (which may be said overtly or covertly). As with post-trauma counseling, each time the person relives a story of the deceased, it usually helps to bring them closer to resolving their feelings of loss.

9. Listen for prior instances of resolved or unresolved grief. Unresolved grief issues surely exacerbate the current bereavement crisis (Klingspon, Holland, Neimeyer, & Lichtenthal, 2015), while prior grief issues that resulted in a positive resolution can help to illustrate prior coping styles that were effective.

10. Generally, it is best to refrain from physically touching the client, unless they reach out for you. Putting your hand on someone's shoulder, or placing your hand over their clasped hands can be comforting; however, it is most important to honor the client's physical boundaries. Empathy and compassion can be respectfully conveyed and demonstrated verbally.

11. Assist the person in determining those individuals within their social support system they can rely on. Here, it is important for the crisis counselor to begin to address the issue of who is in the client's social support system. The old saying, "you really know who your friends are when the chips are down" is very applicable here. Some friends or family members may "head for the hills" and avoid dealing with the person in mourning. Often, this arises out of their own discomfort in dealing with death and mortality or other unresolved grief issues. On the other hand, sometimes unexpected friends or family members may surface as empathic supports. Often, these are individuals who may have gone through some type of grieving process themselves and are willing to listen and help.

12. Be mindful of anniversary reactions. It's common for mourners to experience intense emotions on specific anniversary dates, such as the deceased's birthday, wedding anniversary, and naturally the anniversary of the death. Anniversary reactions may occur, sometimes up to ten years after the death of a loved one.

SUMMARY

Crises involving grief stemming from a loss are a challenge for most professionals who find themselves in the role of helping someone who has lost a loved one. Whether it is a police officer executing a next-of-kin notification of a death of a loved one, a nurse who informs a wife that her husband did not survive the car accident, or counselors or social workers who are providing bereavement counseling for children or adults who lost loved ones; these are all very difficult situations that call for empathy and genuineness. We must also be mindful that in grief crisis counseling there are no "magic words" that can take the pain away from those we console; however, our ability to be with that person in the moment and to listen to his or her pain becomes our most important role.

RESOURCES FOR CHAPTER ENRICHMENT

Suggested Readings

Boss, P. (1999). *Ambiguous loss: Learning to live with unresolved grief*. Cambridge, MA: Harvard University Press.

Bowlby, J. (1980). *Attachment and loss: Loss, sadness, and depression* (Vol. III.). New York, NY: Basic Books.

Cobain, B., & Larch, J. (2006). *Dying to be free: A healing guide for families after suicide*. Center City, MN: Hazelden.

Dolan-Delvecchio, K., & Saxton-Lopez, N. (2013). *The pet loss companion: Healing advice from family therapists who have led pet loss groups*. North Charleston, SC: Create Space.

Donnelly, K. F. (2001). *Recovering from the loss of a child*. New York, NY: Dodd, Mead.

Edelman, H. (1994). *Motherless daughters*. New York, NY: Delta Press.

Fine, C. (1997). *No time to say goodbye: Surviving the suicide of a loved one*. New York, NY: Broadway Books/Random House.

Gates, P. (1990). *Suddenly alone: A woman's guide to widowhood*. New York, NY: Harper Perennial.

Huntley, T. (1991). *Helping children grieve*. Minneapolis, MN: Augsburg.

James, J. W., & Friedman, R. (2001). *When children grieve*. New York, NY: Harper Collins.

Kowalski, G. (2012). *Goodbye, friend: Healing wisdom for anyone who has ever lost a pet*. Novato, CA: New World Library.

Kubler-Ross, E. (1969). *On death and dying*. New York, NY: Macmillan.

Kushner, H. S. (1981). *When bad things happen to good people*. New York, NY: Avon Press.

Lukas, C., & Seiden, H. M. (2007). *Silent grief: Living in the wake of suicide*. London, UK: Jessica Kingsley.

McDowell, A. R. (2015). *Making peace with suicide: A book of hope, understanding and comfort*. Riverside, CT: White Flowers Press.

Parks, C. M., & Weiss, R. S. (1983). *Recovery from bereavement*. New York, NY: Basic Books.

Rando, T. (1984). *Grief, dying and death: Clinical interventions for caregivers*. Champaign, IL: Research Press.

Rando, T. (1986) *Parental loss of a child*. Champaign, IL: Research Press.

Secunda, V. (2000). *Losing your parents, finding yourself*. New York, NY: Hyperion.

Worden, J. W. (1982). *Grief counseling and grief therapy: A handbook for the mental health practitioner*. New York, NY: Springer.

Wrobelski, A. (1991). *Suicide survivors: A guide for those left behind*. Sutherlin, Afterwords Publishing.

Suggested Websites

Crisis, Grief, & Healing

The PsychCentral website is devoted to a variety of topics, including grief and loss issues and provides information designed to help people to better understand the grief process. http://psychcentral.com/lib/category/grief-and-loss/

Hospice Information

These websites provide basic information on hospice care along with resources for those seeking hospice. https://www.medicare.gov/what-medicare-covers/part-a/how-hospice-works.html; http://www.webmd.com/balance/tc/hospice-care-topic-overview#1

Maternal Grief

This scholarly article is devoted to women who have experienced pregnancy loss through miscarriage, stillbirth, neonatal death, sudden infant death, and infertility. http://scholarworks.gvsu.edu/cgi/viewcontent.cgi?article = 1431&context = theses

Bereavement Information

This website provides definitions of bereavement and information on the bereavement process. https://www.psychologytoday.com/conditions/bereavement

GriefNet

This website also provides a list of varied resources for those experiencing grief. http://www.griefnet.org/

Suicide Bereavement

Lifeline provides crisis support and information for those who have lost a loved one to suicide. In addition, this website provides many information downloads, including Fact Sheets, a Survivors of Suicide Booklet, and information on how to facilitate a Bereavement Support Group. https://www.lifeline.org.au/Get-Help/Facts—-Information/Suicide-Bereavement/Suicide-Bereavement

Common Ground is a self-help organization composed of those who have lost loved ones to suicide. They provide information on support groups, resources, and hotlines. http://commongroundhelps.org/wp-content/uploads/2015/02/Survivors-of-Suicide-Loss-Packet.pdf

Recommended Films

Ordinary People: **(1980) (**stars Mary Tyler Moore, Donald Sutherland, & Timothy Hutton). This film provides an accurate and emotionally powerful portrayal of a family who is unable to grieve the loss of the oldest son, Buck. Donald Sutherland and Mary Tyler Moore play the role of the parents, while Timothy Hutton plays the role of Conrad, Buck's younger brother, who survives the sailing accident in which Buck drowns. Conrad becomes the "symptom bearer" of the family and at the beginning of the film has just come from a psychiatric hospitalization after a failed suicide attempt. The film sensitively portrays the family dynamic that takes place following the death of Buck, the family hero.

In the Bedroom: (2001) (stars Sissy Spacek, Tom Wilkinson, Marisa Tomei, and Nick Stahl). This film portrays a very realistic depiction of the grief experienced by parents after the murder of their son. What is unique about this film is that unlike many films which merely allude to parental grief, this film delves into the parent's grief over the course of several weeks following their son's death and perfectly illustrates how differently both parents grieve and how those differences lead to conflict and tension.

Monster's Ball: (2001) (stars Halle Berry and Billy Bob Thornton). This film is replete with death and grief issues. Halle Berry plays the role of a single mother, whose son is killed in a hit-and-run incident that she witnesses and is powerless to help save her son's life. Billy Bob Thornton plays the role of a corrections officer whose son commits suicide by shooting himself as he tells his father that he had always loved him. Issues pertaining to capital punishment and its impact on family members are also addressed. This film is a powerful portrayal of grief and exhibits how mourning becomes complicated when the causes of death are so tragic.

Men Don't Leave: (1990) (stars Jessica Lange). This is the story of a young woman, mother of two, whose husband is killed suddenly in a construction accident. The film traces the life of this young widow as she tries to reestablish a life for herself and her children as a single, working mother, while at the same time, trying to cope with her own grief and that of her children.

Stepmom: (1998) (stars Susan Sarandon, Julia Roberts, and Ed Harris). This film portrays the grieving of a divorced mother of two whose husband is dating a younger woman. The film provides a realistic portrayal of the transitions the family experiences as the mother is dying of cancer.

Kramer vs. Kramer: (1979) (stars Dustin Hoffman and Meryl Streep). The film depicts a couple's divorce and the impact of the divorce on their son. It accurately portrays the grieving process that the husband faces and the feelings of hopelessness and rage that often accompany this grieving process as the father tries to cope with the grief of the lost marriage and then losing custody of his son.

A Single Man: (2009) (stars Colin Firth and Julianne Moore). It's November 30, 1962. Native Brit George Falconer, an English professor at a Los Angeles area college, is finding it difficult to cope with life. Jim, his personal partner of sixteen years, died in a car accident eight months earlier when he was visiting with family. Jim's family were not going to tell George of the death or accident, let alone allow him to attend the funeral. This day, George has decided to get his affairs in order before he commits suicide that evening. As he routinely and fastidiously prepares for the suicide and post-suicide, George reminisces about his life with Jim.

Rabbit Hole: (2011) (stars Nicole Kidman and Aaron Eckhart). Grief in the family—what happens after the unthinkable happens? *Rabbit Hole*, based on the Tony-winning play by David Lindsay-Abaire and deftly directed by John Cameron. Mitchell slowly reveals the answer: something else unthinkable. *Rabbit Hole* is a moving, dark character study of what happens to a happily married couple, Becca and Howie, who suddenly lose the love of their lives, their 4-year-old son. As in real life, the grief portrayed in *Rabbit Hole* takes peculiar twists and turns, and the deep sorrow and tragedy of the story is leavened by dark humor– much of it coming from Kidman.

Lorenzo's Oil: (1993) (stars Nick Nolte and Susan Surandon). A true story about a battle for the life of Lorenzo who suffers from ALD rare disease which destroys all basic functions like speech and movement and in the end, takes the life of the person. In this movie, the parents fight the clock by doing their own research and investigation.

Three Colors: Blue: (1993) (stars Juliette Binoche and Zbigniew Zamachowski). The first part of Kieslowski's trilogy on France's national motto: Liberty, Equality, and Fraternity. *Blue* is the story of Julie who loses her husband, an acclaimed composer, and her young daughter in a car accident. The film's theme of liberty is manifested in Julie's attempt to start life anew, free of personal commitments, belongings, grief, or love. She intends to numb herself by withdrawing from the world and living completely independently, anonymously, and in solitude in the Parisian metropolis.

The Son's Room: (2001) (stars Nanni Monette and Laura Morante). Giovanni is a successful psychoanalyst who has to put up with the seemingly endless string of trivial details his patients ramble on about. Yet his family provides a loving and steadfast foundation for his life that can even survive the problem of their son, Andrea, who is accused of stealing a rare fossil in school. That foundation is profoundly rocked when Andrea dies in a scuba diving accident. Although the usual arrangements run smoothly, the emotional harm is profound. Giovanni begins to obsessively dwell on the missed chances he had with his son that might have saved his life, even blaming his patients. In addition, his wife is inconsolable and his daughter is becoming antisocial in their loss.

My Dog Skip: (2000) (stars Frankie Muniz, Kevin Bacon and Diane Lane). This is a story of a shy boy, Willie, who grows up in 1940's Mississippi with the help of his dog, Skip, who becomes his companion through his childhood and up until the time he leaves for college. This film deals with pet loss and the type of important emotional bonds we form with pets. The film is based on the best-selling, Mississippi memoir by the late Willie Morris.

Suggested Activities

1. Watch the film "In the Bedroom" or select one of the other films listed above. As you're watching the film, try to determine how the family depicted in the film deals with crisis of loss. What differences did you see in how various family members grieve? Do they reach a point of acceptance?

2. Find out how certain burial customs or rituals in our society came about. Discuss the purpose or function of these customs: wakes, sitting Shiva, different cultures funeral and burial customs.

3. It is said that when people grieve they go through various stages. Elizabeth Kubler-Ross described some of the most widely known stages of grief: denial/ isolation, bargaining, anger, depression, and acceptance. From your experiences with grieving various types of losses, do these stages ring true? Do they match with your experience of grieving a loss? Write about what you personally experienced regarding a significant loss.

Recommended YouTube Viewing

https://www.youtube.com/watch?v = Jjh1W_TbUNY Families who have lost loved ones by suicide speak out. Very informative brief video.

https://www.youtube.com/watch?v = nmtzEFRwYXU This video provides some good basic information on bereavement counseling and an example of a session with a client experiencing grief issues.

https://www.youtube.com/watch?v = jTxOiq3V7Bw A full-length documentary with renowned grief expert, Dr. Elizabeth Kubler-Ross.

https://www.youtube.com/watch?v = juET61B1P98 Very informative TED talk on living after loss and grieving losses.

https://www.youtube.com/watch?v = T4oTIJ-4mlE TED talk that provides interesting insights on the grief and mourning process.

https://www.youtube.com/watch?v = 2mTV5UgE9rA This video provides portrayal of a bereavement counseling session using role play.

https://www.youtube.com/watch?v = T7BvnzRPuPk This brief video provides interviews with individuals who have suffered losses and examples of counseling sessions.

https://www.youtube.com/watch?v = W7suv8xWOfk This video addresses grief support groups and how to make effective referrals to support groups.

https://www.youtube.com/watch?v = NIwQn4nmzYY Discusses grief counseling from the perspective of those doing hospice work.

CHAPTER 11

Crises Involving Suicide, Homicide, and Lethality

*B*eth is a 24-year-old separated mother of a 10-month-old daughter. She called the hot-line of the local mental health clinic today because she felt so depressed that she could not get out of bed. Beth explained to the hotline crisis worker that she has felt this way for the past six months. Beth described feeling "lifeless and hopeless" that she has no energy to do anything. She also said that nothing is really enjoyable to her anymore, and as a result, she has become increasingly reclusive and prefers to be left alone. Since Beth's husband left her to run off with one of her best friends, Beth feels that she doesn't "have anything to live for." When questioned directly about suicidal intent, she denied feeling like killing herself, but then admitted that she tried to cut her wrists a few days ago when she received a copy of the divorce papers, but "lost the nerve" and could not go through with it. "Besides," she said, "I could not leave my baby all alone, with no one to look out for her."

DISCUSSION QUESTIONS

1. If you were the crisis hotline worker who spoke with Beth, what would you say to her? What recommendations would you make?

2. What would you do if a friend or family member is threatening to hurt themselves or threatens to hurt someone? Would you know what to do or who to contact?

3. On April 16, 2007, Virginia Tech experienced one of the deadliest shooting rampages in U.S. history when a student, Sueng-Hui Cho murdered 32 students and faculty. The perpetrator of this tragedy was ordered to receive mental health treatment by a judge in December 2005. He was also known to express bizarre thoughts to those who interacted with him on campus. Could this tragedy have been prevented? If so, how?

INTRODUCTION

Of all the types of crises that are presented in this text, crises involving suicidal risk, violence, and homicidal risk are probably the most difficult and most frightening to manage. Unlike other crises where intervention plans are often collaboratively agreed on between the counselor and the client, suicide and threats of violence may result in a safety plan enacted without the client's cooperation or consent. Such would be the case where a suicidal or homicidal client refuses to be admitted to an inpatient unit for evaluation and a civil commitment order must be issued by the courts. The overriding goal of crises involving suicide or homicide is to preserve life. Therefore, if someone threatens to harm themselves or someone else, it is unethical, negligent, and potentially dangerous for a crisis counselor to send this person home with instructions to return to see them the following day. Therefore, enacting a crisis plan with those individuals who are either suicidal or homicidal requires decisive clearheaded action. This is not the time for passive therapeutic reflection as you can see in the cases presented in this chapter.

SCOPE AND DEFINITION OF THE PROBLEM

The statistics regarding suicide are rather alarming. Not only in the United States, but in many industrialized countries, suicide ranks among the leading causes of death. According to the National Alliance on Mental Illness, suicide is the 10th leading cause of death in the United States; and the 2nd leading cause of death for people ages 15 to 24 (Centers for Disease Control, 2014). In addition, more than 90% of children who die by suicide have a mental health condition (Centers for Disease Control, 2015), and each day an estimated 18 to 22 veterans die by suicide (Hudenko, Homafar & Wortzel, 2016). There were 41,149 suicides in 2013 in the United States—a rate of 12.6 per 100 is equal to 113 suicides each day or one every 13 minutes (Centers for Disease Control & Prevention, 2014) and the use of firearms accounted for 50.5% of these deaths. The fact that firearms account for such a high percentage of suicide deaths can largely be attributed to the high likelihood that self-inflicted gunshot wounds will result in death, with reported lethality rates between 82.5% and 92%. States with stricter gun control laws have lower overall and firearm-related suicide rates (Briggs & Tabarrok, 2014; Yang & Lester, 2009). In Washington, D.C., the suicide rate abruptly decreased by 23% after individuals were required to obtain a license to buy a firearm (Anestis et al., 2015, p. 2059). Prior studies found that handguns were used in 43% to 72% of firearms related suicides in Iowa, Washington, and Tennessee between 1987 and 1991. Furthermore, data from the National Violent Death Reporting System indicate that in 2011, handguns accounted for 65.4% of all firearm suicides across the 17 states involved within that reporting system (Anestis et al., 2015; Briggs & Tabarrok, 2014). In a study of firearm deaths, Neill and Leigh (2009) found that in Australia, a 20% reduction in guns as a result of a firearms buy-back program resulted in an 80% reduction in gun suicide deaths.

Interestingly, the state of Montana had the highest rate of suicide per capita with Wyoming and Alaska ranking 2nd and 3rd (CDC, 2014). Overall, suicide was ranked the

10th leading cause of death in the United States in 2013; however, suicide is the third leading cause of death among persons ages 10 to 14; the 2nd leading cause of death among persons ages 15 to 34 years; the 4th among persons age 35 to 44 years; the 5th among persons age 45 to 54 years; the 8th among persons 50 to 64 years; and the 17th among persons 65 years and older (Centers for Disease Control & Prevention, 2014). Approximately 90% of people who commit suicide have a diagnosable mental illness (National Institute of Mental Health, 2002), most often depressive disorders, bipolar disorder, substance use disorders, and schizophrenia. Suicides outnumbered homicides 3 to 1 and were twice as common as deaths related to HIV and AIDS (Briggs & Tabarrok, 2014; National Institute of Mental Health, 2002). Young people between the ages of 15 and 24 years old are considered to be a high-risk group, because suicide ranks among the top leading causes of death in this age group (along with homicide and car accidents). In fact, between 1950 and 1996 suicide rates within this age group tripled (National Center for Health Statistics, 2001). Suicide is the 4th leading cause of death for the 25- to 44-year-old age group. Firearms caused most of the suicide deaths in the 15- to 24-year-old age group; however, it should be noted that firearms constituted the leading cause of death for both adult men and women (National Center for Health Statistics, 1998). According to Maris (1992), therefore, the issues of suicide prevention and gun control are very much intertwined.

Adolescents and young adults are not the only group considered to be at higher risk for suicidal behavior. Males 45 years and older constitute another high-risk group. The research literature suggests that the risk of suicide in men increases with age; however, in recent years, rates of suicide are also increasing in middle-age women (see Box 11.1 on p. 272). The risk of suicide in older adults is often exacerbated by chronic medical conditions, especially those involving chronic pain. With regard to race and ethnicity, there have been indications that suicide rates have increasing among young African American men (Centers for Disease Control and Prevention, 1998; Shaffer, Gould, & Hicks, 1994). Also in a recent study by Case and Deaton (2015), increases in suicide rates were found in middle-age, underemployed, white males. Risk can also be compounded by several other factors, including particular psychiatric illnesses, alcohol and drug abuse, and social isolation. Lifetime data indicates that men outnumber women, 4.6 to 1 in their suicide completion rates (Centers for Disease Control & Prevention, 2013; Kochanek, Murphy, Anderson, & Scott, 2004); however, adolescent and adult women outnumber men in nonfatal suicide attempts and in overall rates of depressive disorders (Andrews & Lewinsohn, 1992; Garrison, McKeown, & Valois, 1993). Recent national studies indicate that suicide rates have been dramatically changing over the past ten years (see Box 11.1 on p. 272). Veterans comprise 22.2% of all suicides. As the wars in Iraq and Afghanistan were winding down and troops were coming home, a rather frightening statistic began to emerge—an alarming increase in suicide deaths among returning veterans (Hudenko et al., 2016). These were often servicemen who had seen combat and witnessed the deaths of their comrades. A similar trend was found in returning Vietnam veterans. There are estimates that there were as many suicide deaths in the years following the end of the Vietnam War as there were deaths in combat; however, this has not been substantiated (Hendin & Haas, 1991). There are many hypotheses regarding the extreme number of veterans who take their own life. Some contend it is because of PTSD (posttraumatic stress disorder), others contend it is due to post-combat depressive disorders (Hudenko et al., 2016).

Of the psychiatric disorders most often associated with suicide, schizophrenia, depression (both major depression and bipolar depression) and substance use disorders (alcohol and drug dependencies) are often correlated with suicide. Research indicates that approximately 10% of schizophrenics end up committing suicide. Risk factors for suicidality in this population include being male, younger than 30 years old, unemployed, with a high level of education, a chronic relapsing course, prior depression in the last episode of active schizophrenic symptoms, and a recent hospital discharge. Schizophrenics who commit suicide are often painfully aware of their condition and as a result often feel inadequate and hopeless. In the majority of instances, schizophrenic individuals rarely communicate their suicide intent to others. In addition, alcohol and drug abuse exacerbate suicidal risk in this population (McGirr et al., 2006; Siris, 2001). In general, alcohol and drug abuse tends to increase suicidal risk in any of the aforementioned "at risk" populations. Intuitively, alcohol or substance intoxication often intensifies an already existing depression, which then adds to feelings of hopelessness and helplessness. Alcohol and drug intoxication often have a disinhibiting effect thereby making the likelihood of suicidal action much greater. Mood-altering chemicals can also increase the chances of "indirect" suicidality, as is the case when someone "accidentally" overdoses or "accidentally" is killed in a single car motor vehicle fatality (Weiss & Hufford, 1999). Suicide also increases in instances where people have endured severe psychological trauma. According to Chu (1999), individuals who were subjected to severe childhood physical or sexual abuse often manifest two traits that place them at substantial risk for suicide, that is, profound mistrust and self-hate.

Naturally, these are just a partial list of discrete risk factors. Often, several predictors must be taken into account when assessing someone suspected of being suicidal. Here is a partial list of predictors: suicidal risk is considered to be much greater when the individual is male; 45 years old or older; separated, widowed, or divorced; lives alone; is unemployed or retired; is in poor physical health; has a mental disorder; drinks heavily; had medical care within the past six months; has a suicidal plan involving the use of firearms, hanging, jumping, or drowning; has made a prior attempt in the spring or summer months; made the prior attempt at home and was discovered immediately; and finally does not report his suicidal intention to others (Drapeau & McIntosh, 2015). The other difficulty is that a person may manifest three or four of these risk factors and might actually be at a lower risk for suicide, while another person may have only one of these risk factors and be at a high risk for suicide (e.g., a depressed teenager with undefined suicidal ideas might be at a lower suicidal risk than a teenager with a prior history of suicide attempts who voices a suicide plan and began giving away prized possessions). Assessment of risk is therefore best accomplished on a case-by-case basis. The dilemma of what weight to give to risk factors is perhaps best summarized by Schneidman (1999), one of the leading authorities on suicide.

My central belief is that in the distillation of each suicidal event, its essential element is a psychological one; that is, each suicidal drama occurs in the mind of a unique individual. Suicide is purposeful. Its purpose is to respond to or redress certain psychological needs. There are many pointless deaths, but there is never a needless suicide. Suicide is a concatenated, multidimensional, conscious and unconscious "choice" of the best possible practical solution to a perceived problem, dilemma, impulse, crisis or desperation. (p. 85)

Table 11.1   Risk Factors Associated with Suicide

Risk Factors Pertaining to Adolescents and Young Adults
• A family history of suicide
• Male
• Having access to firearms (when other risk factors are present)
• History of prior attempts and covert attempts (not identified as suicide attempts)
• Being Native American or African American
• Presence of mental health disorders (e.g. mood disorders or substance use disorders)
• Mini-epidemic in community (e.g. copycat suicides)
• History of delinquent or semi-delinquent behavior
General Risk Factors
• A past history of suicide gestures or attempts (it is a myth that those who talk about suicide rarely act on those threats; all suicide threats, statements or comments should be taken seriously
• A family history of suicide or mood disorders (e.g. bipolar or major depression)
• Active alcohol/drug use (may have disinhibiting effects resulting in the person being more likely to act on suicidal feelings
• A history of mental health disorders: the following disorders have the highest rates of suicide: schizophrenia, bipolar disorder, major depression and substance use disorders
• A history of severe trauma, such as sexual molestation or assault, incest, physical abuse
• Isolation from others: those who live alone or who are recently widowed, separated or divorced
• Radical shifts in mood or behavior, such as giving away prized possessions, saying "goodbye" to loved ones, or taking care of unfinished business, putting one's affairs in order. Also abrupt changes in sleep or eating habits, work or school behaviors.
• Expressions of a profound sense of hopelessness or helplessness e.g. "no matter what I do or say, nothing will ever change" or "I can't go on living without him/her".
• Chronic medical conditions, especially those which cause chronic pain.
• Expressing suicidal ideas and plan along with a concrete plan for carrying out suicide
• Gender: male (women make more attempts but males complete suicide at higher rates)

When a person is assessed for suicidal risk in a crisis situation, usually their entire history and family history is taken into account, as well as their current mental status. A mental status exam usually includes an assessment of the person's present physical appearance, behavior, speech, emotional expression, thought processes, perceptions, attention and concentration abilities, memory, judgment, intellectual functioning, and ability to form insight (Kilgus, Maxmen, & Ward, 2016). There are also a number of suicide rating scales which can be used for the purpose of assessing suicide risk as described in Table 11.3 below.

One of the difficulties inherent in assessing suicidal risk is the issue of when does suicidal ideation transition to suicidal behavior (i.e., a suicide attempt)? In their meta-analysis study, May and Klonsky (2016) found that much of the research they examined was unable to answer this most important question. They concluded that a clinician's traditional approach of exploring risk factors with clients may not actually

Table 11.2 Suicide Lethality Checklist

I. CURRENT STATUS	LOW	MODERATE	HIGH
1. Chronic pain condition, chronic illness	___None at present	___Intermittent pain, able to function on daily basis	___Chronic debilitating pain, terminal illness
2. Socially isolated	___Infrequently	___Frequently	___Currently alone
3. Daily functioning	___Fairly good	___Moderately good	___Not good
4. Support systems (friends, family, etc.)	___Several available	___Few available	___Only one or none
5. Willingness to receive mental health treatment	___Very willing and positive attitude	___Willing but ambivalent	___Unwilling and negative attitude toward treatment
II. MOOD	**LOW**	**MODERATE**	**HIGH**
1. Depression, dysthymia, anhedonia	___Mild	___Moderate	___Severely depressed unable to function
2. Anxiety or agitated depression	___Mild	___Moderate	___High (cannot sleep, agitated throughout day
3. Isolation from others	___None, willing to be around others	___Isolates intermittently	___Refuses to socialize or be around others
4. Disorientation with time, place, person, and disorganized thinking	___None	___Some	___Marked
5. Helplessness/ hopelessness	___Sees hope for future, feels some ability to affect change	___Sees some hope for future, some ability to bring about change	___Feels no hope for future or ability to change
6. Anger and hostility	___Calm	___Angry and Argumentative	___Total Rage
III. BEHAVIORAL SYMPTOMS	**LOW**	**MODERATE**	**HIGH**
1. Suicide plan When Where Method	___In the future ___Unplanned ___Unclear ___Will have to obtain	___Within 24 hrs ___Clear plan ___Has plans ___Means is close by	___Immediately ___Is at location ___Well planned ___Able to carry out
2. Drugs, alcohol consumption	___ Abstinent	___Intermittent use or intermittent binge use	___Currently using and using daily
3. Previous attempts & prior hospitalizations	___None for both	___Attempt within past 6 mos. or hospitalized	___Many prior attempts or one within the last 30 days

Table 11.3 Suicide Risk Scales

Name of Scale	Description	Author
Columbia-Suicide Severity Rating Scale (C-SSRS)	6-item scale translated into over 100 languages can be used in various settings, adult/child	Posner, Brown, Stanley, et al. (2011)
Harkavy-Asnis Suicide Survey (HASS)	self-report survey designed to assess suicidal behavior in clients & families	Harkavy Friedman, Asnis (1989)
InterSePT Scale for Suicidal Thinking (ISST-Plus)	12-item measure for assessing current suicidal ideation in pts with schizophrenia & schizoaffective disorder	Lindenmeyer, Czobar, Alphs et al. (2003)
Suicide Behaviors Questionnaire Revised	4-item questionnaire that assesses suicidality	Osman, Bagge, Gutierrez, et al. (2001)
Beck Scale for Suicide Ideation	5 screening items, 21 items total, Spanish/English	Beck, Kovacs, & Weissman (1979)
Sheehan-Suicidality Tracking Scale (S-STS)	16-item, Likert scale simple, specific	Sheehan, Giddens, Sheehan (2014)
Cultural Assessment of Risk for Suicide (CARS)	52 items assess 4 cultural risk categories	Chu, Floyd, Diep, Pardo, et al. (2013)
Geriatric Suicide Ideation Scale (GSIS)	31-item, Likert scale Suicide Ideation composite scale which is composed of three subscales: Death Ideation, Loss of Personal & Social Worth, and Perceived Meaning in Life	Heisel & Flett (2006, 2016)

be examining risk factors for suicidal behavior at all, but might be limited to assessing suicidal ideation. Bryan and Rudd (2016) propose that rather than looking at suicidal risk derived from a list of static "risk factors," the key to determining suicide ideation are time factors and what Rudd (2006) refers to as "fluid vulnerability theory," where some risk factors often vary in intensity from day-to-day. Take for example the intensity of depressive affect for a particular individual. In the pits of depression, some individuals may lack the energy to follow through with suicidal behavior even though their suicidal ideation might be extreme during those periods. This may account for why suicidal action or behavior might be more likely during periods when a person's mood is improving and his or her energy level returns. Take for example the risk factor previously discussed, substance use. Ostensibly, a person who is under the influence may be more likely to act on suicidal ideation during an alcohol or drug binge or in the aftermath of a binge when he or she is feeling hungover. The aforementioned examples are temporal or time factors that Bryan and Rudd (2016) refer to as possible "tipping points" that may account for the transition from suicidal thought to suicidal action or behavior.

The following case examples provide illustrations of ways that crisis counselors can intervene when individuals are experiencing a crisis involving suicidal intent.

Box 11.1: U.S. Suicide Rates Reach a 30 Year High

In a recent article by Sabrina Tavernise (2016), suicide rates were reported to have surged to a 30 year high according to federal data (National Center for Health Statistics, 2016). What is most troubling about these statistics is that almost every age group experienced increases in suicide rates, with the EXCEPTION of older adults, who have traditionally been considered one of the "at-risk" age groups for suicide. The overall suicide rate increased by 24% from previous years. Since 2006, the suicide rate has increased by 2% every year. The increase in suicide deaths was particularly steep for women and for middle-age Americans (groups who had previously experienced stable or falling rates of suicide since the 1950s). In addition, the suicide rate for middle-age women ages 45 to 64 increased by 63% while the rate for men of that same age group increased by 43%. A total number of 42,773 Americans died from suicide (21,175 as a result of firearms) in 2014 compared to 29,199 in 1999.

Source: Adapted from Tavernise, Sabrina. "U.S. Suicide Rate Surges to a 30-Year High," *The New York Times*. Apr. 22, 2016.

Case Presentation: Beth, A Case Involving a Vague Threat of Suicide

Let's go back to discuss crisis management with Beth, whom we presented at the beginning of this chapter. What makes this case especially difficult is that Beth has called a crisis hotline. Therefore, it is more difficult to ensure her safety. Additional case detail is provided below.

With Beth, we see an individual who is considered to be at high risk for suicide. Even though she claims that she tried to cut her wrists a few days ago and was unable to go through with it, there is still a real danger of a future potentially fatal suicide attempt. Beth is young and she and her baby live alone without much immediate family or social support. She has experienced the trauma of both a marital separation and learning of an extramarital affair in which her husband left her for her best friend. Beth's recent suicide attempt occurred when she was served with divorce papers. What makes this case difficult to assess is that the initial contact occurred when Beth called a mental health crisis hotline. If she had presented at a clinic or emergency room, this assessment could have been conducted face-to-face, which affords many advantages. However, crisis counselors are usually quite limited in how much information they can obtain over the phone. Obviously, the crisis counselor working with Beth first needs to establish rapport or try to connect with her. Asking Beth about her baby or some other aspect of her life that would be less threatening might help accomplish this. Also, the crisis counselor needs to convey a willingness to listen to Beth's problems nonjudgmentally and convey to Beth that he or she is there to help her work out some solutions to these problems. The counselor needs to be very definite in convincing Beth that treatment works, that he or she can help Beth explore effective alternatives and solutions to her problems, and that he or she will she see Beth through her current emotional crisis. It is of utmost importance to provide hope (Bohen, 2002). This is sometimes difficult, as many suicidal individuals often feel that there are no solutions, therefore suicide is perceived as the only viable alternative to end emotional pain. However, Beth did call the crisis hotline, which can be viewed as a positive step in that it represents a cry for help. The crisis counselor basically needs to ally with that part of Beth that wants to live; that part of her personality that wants to continue to be a good parent to her daughter; or that part of her personality that gave her the courage to call the hotline.

Beth goes on to explain to the crisis counselor that she previously sought counseling after her mother died and it really helped. She also had contacted her aunt to stay with her baby. These factors can be seen as positive signs. At this point, the counselor is able to persuade Beth to come down to the mental health clinic, where the counselor can speak with her in person. Beth agrees because she feels some trust in the crisis counselor and is willing to get help. Beth makes an agreement with the counselor that she will come to the center and she will bring her aunt with her. They set up a specific meeting time. Beth allows the counselor to speak to her aunt over the phone, in order to make certain that Beth makes the appointment. If the crisis counselor had assessed Beth as being in danger at that particular moment and she was alone, then it would have been necessary for the counselor to have the call traced by the police, who would then dispatch a police officer and/or a mobile mental health crisis outreach team to Beth's home. In that case, Beth would then have been brought to the local emergency room or mental health clinic for assessment and probably would be admitted to a hospital for observation and treatment.

Once Beth is assessed at the mental health clinic, it is determined that she is not actively suicidal and can be treated on an outpatient basis with a combination of counseling and antidepressant medication. With the support of her therapist and her aunt, Beth agrees to daily contact with her counselor in between her appointments. In some instances, a "No-Suicide Contract" may be used. According to Motto (1999), contracts may be a useful therapeutic tool; however, this depends on whether there is a strong, mutually trusting relationship with the therapist. Contracts can be formal written documents that the therapist, the patient, and a significant other sign (in this instance, Susan's aunt is involved in the contract), or they can be simple verbal agreements (e.g., "Would you agree to call me or come in for a session if you're feeling overwhelmed or feeling like you might hurt yourself?"). Contracts are still a subject of research study and debate and are certainly not a panacea or a substitute for inpatient treatment when it appears that they may be the only way to ensure client safety (Davidson, Wagner & Range, 1995; Egan, 1997; Miller, 1999). More recently, there is an emphasis on "safety plans" rather than "contracts" as an alternative means to preventing suicide. A safety plan is also a collaborative written document that provides suicidal individuals with steps they can take if their suicide risk increases.

Case Presentation: Maria, a Case Involving a Threatened Suicide

Maria is a 19-year-old college student in her sophomore year. She told her roommate that she has been feeling depressed over problems she was having with her boyfriend. Recently, Maria found out that her boyfriend was cheating on her with a mutual friend. When she confronted her boyfriend, he denied the accusations and told Maria she was "just being paranoid and crazy," but seized the moment to break up with her. This made Maria feel more angry and depressed. Maria now feels taken and used. She can't get out of bed and has been missing classes. She did well in her freshman year, but is receiving a scholarship and is afraid that if her grades drop she'll lose the scholarship which means that she'll have to return home and attend a local community college. Maria reports that she feels overwhelmed. She feels that nothing she does will make things any better. She tried calling the hotline of the local mental health clinic today because she felt so "upset" that she was considering taking her roommate's prescription medication and washing it down with vodka. Maria explained to the hotline crisis worker that she had been in counseling while she was in high school after her parents separated. Maria describes feeling "lifeless and hopeless," having no energy to do anything. She also reports that nothing is really enjoyable to her anymore and that as a result, she has become increasingly reclusive, preferring to be alone. Maria also states that she has not been eating or sleeping very well. Although she initially told the crisis worker that she was not feeling suicidal, she states that since the problems with her boyfriend began she feels she doesn't have anything to live for.

Maria's history and presenting complaint reveals someone who is considered at risk for suicide. She feels isolated, angry, hopeless, and helpless. Maria is experiencing the loss of the relationship with her boyfriend and is in danger of losing her educational opportunity. In addition, she has thought about a plan of how she would kill herself. What makes this case difficult to assess is that the initial contact occurs by Maria calling a psychiatric hotline. If she had been seen in a clinic or emergency room, the many advantages to conducting an assessment face-to-face could prevail, however, the crisis counselor is usually quite limited in how much information they are able to obtain over the phone. The crisis counselor first needs to establish rapport and try to connect with Maria. Also, the crisis counselor needs to convey a willingness to listen to Maria's problems nonjudgmentally, and that she is willing to help her work out some solutions to the problems she is encountering. The counselor needs to be very definite in convincing Maria that treatment works, and that she can help her get through the present crisis. It is of utmost importance to provide hope (Bohen, 2002). This is sometimes difficult, as many suicidal individuals often feel that there are no solutions; therefore, suicide is perceived as their only viable alternative and solution. However, Maria did call the crisis hotline, which is a positive step and a cry for help.

Intervention

The crisis counselor basically needs to ally with that part of Maria that wants to live and that part of her personality that gave her the courage to call the hotline. Once Maria reveals that she was experiencing suicidal feelings and has thought of a plan, the counselor then needs to assess Maria's current feelings regarding suicidal intent:

Counselor: Maria, I was wondering, given what you've told me so far, if you're feeling like harming yourself or wanting to end your life?

Maria: Well, what if I do? Does that mean you're going to lock me up? Then I know I'd be thrown out of school.

C: No, Maria, I want to help you find some answers to the problems you've been having, which is why you called isn't it? From what you've told me, you've really been going through a tough time.

M: I have. It's really been horrible. I can't sleep, I can't eat. When I do sleep, I wake up at like 3:00 am and begin thinking about Jimmy having sex with one of my best friends. I can't stand it.

C: How long have you been feeling like this?

M: It's been a few weeks I guess. I can't keep track of time. I've also been missing all of my classes and now I know I'll fail everything.

Maria has avoided answering the counselor's original question about feeling suicidal, so the counselor redirects Maria back to the question.

C: With all that you've been going through, have you had any suicidal thoughts?

M: I have been thinking that I would just be better off dead. At least it would be a way of ending all this pain.

C: Maria, are you feeling suicidal right now? Is that why you called today?

M: No, I think I just needed to talk to someone. I was feeling really alone and lonely, so I heard about this crisis hotline and thought it might be helpful to talk. Besides, I don't think I really want to die. I just want the hurt to stop.

C: I'm glad you decided to call. From what you've told me, I can hear how much pain you've been in. It must be really tough to be trying to deal with all this on your own. Let's talk about some things that might help you begin to feel better.

M: I'd like that. I really don't want to flunk out and have to go back home.

C: I know that your college has a counseling center. If you were to go and speak with one of the counselors there, they can often help with talking to your professors to let them know that you're trying to get back to your studies.

M: Will the counselor have to tell them the details of why I've missed classes?

C: No, they won't give details just that you've had to miss classes.

M: That sounds like it would be helpful.

C: The counseling center can also arrange for ongoing counseling at no cost because you're a student there. Usually they refer students over here at the medical center if they think that medication may be helpful. Have you ever been in counseling before or taken any medication?

M: I saw someone for counseling when I was in high school and my parents were separating. They had me on medication for about four months, then my parents got back together and I began to feel better.

C: Was the counseling helpful?

M: It was helpful to talk about how I was feeling. My parents were fighting a lot and I began to develop IBS (irritable bowel syndrome). I guess because of the stress.

Case Conceptualization/Crisis Resolution

Maria goes on to explain to the crisis counselor more about her parents' separation. The counselor was able to use this information to illustrate to Maria how she was able to make it through previous crises in her life, therefore she will make it through the present crisis. They also go on to talk about Maria's relationship with Jimmy and some of the problems they had. Maria had been feeling that Jimmy was taking her for granted and was verbally and emotionally abusive to her. Maria felt that she couldn't break free of the relationship, but she wasn't really happy either. At this point, the counselor obtained a commitment from Maria to see someone in the college counseling center (Malley, Kush, & Bogo, 1994), and Maria allowed the counselor to call so that she could be seen that day. Maria also agreed that she would come to the medical center and speak with someone if she felt suicidal again. If the counselor had determined that Maria was in danger of harming herself at that particular moment, it would have been necessary for the counselor to trace the call through the telephone operator and to send the police or a mobile mental health outreach team to Maria's apartment. If that had occurred, Maria would then be brought to the local emergency room or mental health clinic for assessment and likely be admitted to a hospital for observation.

Whereas, if it was determined that she was not actively suicidal, then she might be treated on an outpatient basis with a combination of counseling and antidepressant medication.

The crisis hotline intervention with Maria raises three issues that are central to working with suicidal patients. First, is that suicidal individuals often view their death as a solution to their problem or as a means to end the psychological, emotional, or physical pain they are experiencing. Second, suicidal individuals often feel that their lives are out of control or often feel overwhelmed by their problems and that the only way to take control of their situation is through taking their own lives. Third, some suicides are motivated by revenge. There's an old saying, that "behind every suicide, there is a homicide." This notion is derived primarily from psychoanalytic theory that indicates that suicide occurs in instances where anger is "turned inward" or against the self. This is true with many adolescents and young adults who view suicide as a means of getting back at a boyfriend or girlfriend who has rejected them or getting revenge against an overbearing parent.

In providing crisis intervention to a person in the throes of a suicidal crisis, the L-A-P-C model can be used as a format to help manage the crisis. In the **listening** phase, the crisis counselor first establishes rapport with Maria by talking about nonthreatening topics. The counselor then begins to gather information about the crisis by asking about the particulars regarding Maria's reasons for seeking help and the difficulties she is experiencing. It is also important to determine when Maria first began to feel suicidal, if she has any previous history of suicidal ideation, intent, or attempts. If so, what happened as a result of these feelings or actions. Suicidal risk factors can also be determined at this point.

In the **assess** phase, the counselor notes Maria's predominant emotional reactions. Maria expresses feelings of hopelessness and also states that she feels overwhelmed and is not able to function. It is also noted that although Maria has every right to feel angry and betrayed by Jimmy, she instead feels defeated and helpless. Given the presence of past depression and current suicidal ideation, the counselor gathers information for a lethality assessment. A lethality assessment involves a thorough exploration of the suicide risk factors that Maria is manifesting. A lethality assessment also includes questions pertaining to whether Maria has a suicidal plan and a means to carry out that plan. Usually, plans that are more concrete, specific, and feasible are considered more dangerous than the lack of a plan, or a plan that is vague and unlikely. One of the ultimate questions of the lethality assessment pertains to whether Maria falls into high risk factor status. It is noted that Maria manifests several risk factors: she has a previous history of depression when her parents separated; she currently manifests many symptoms of depression; she is isolated and is feeling the loss of her relationship with her boyfriend; and she is experiencing the psychological turmoil over Jimmy's affair with her best friend. Maria's thinking appears to be impacted by the depression and suicidal thoughts otherwise she is able to reason logically and express herself coherently. Her attention span is adequate and there are no indications of any current medical problems.

In the **planning** phase, the counselor attempts to determine if there is anyone who Maria can reach out to for help. Maria's safety is the main priority and here the counselor is making certain that Maria has support, in this instance through the college counseling center. The **plan** agreed on is that Maria will see a counselor at the counseling center who will also help Maria get back into her classes without being penalized. Regarding the **commitment** stage, it appears that Maria does have the resources to carry through with the plan to begin counseling and appears to be motivated, at this time, to follow through with the agreed on plan.

The major concern in providing crisis counseling to a person who is suicidal is that they are SAFE. But, what if the person refuses help? Most states provide some procedure for an involuntary hospitalization or commitment of persons who present as a danger to themselves or others. According to Frierson, Melikian, and Wadman (2002) there are essentially three categories of potentially suicidal individuals: 1) patients with suicidal ideation, plan, and intent; 2) patients with ideation and plan, but without intent; and 3) patients with ideation, but no plan or intent. Patients that fall within the first group (especially when they have accompanying psychosocial stressors and access to a lethal means of suicide), should be psychiatrically hospitalized (either voluntarily or involuntarily if necessary). Patients that fall within the second group (suicidal ideation and plan, but without intent), may be treated on an outpatient basis provided they have a good social support network and no access to lethal means of suicide. Some patients within this group, however, may require hospitalization if the environment cannot be assured as being safe, or if they are not adequately supervised. For patients in the third group, outpatient treatment is recommended, however, again only if the environment is safe (e.g., all weapons are removed from the dwelling) and there is adequate social support and supervision. For patients in the second and third groups, their willingness and motivation to seek treatment and follow through with therapy naturally plays a significant role in determining their suitability for outpatient treatment.

What happens if the son or daughter is not a child or adolescent, but a young adult (e.g., a college student)? Confidentiality regulations and professional ethical guidelines are clear in that they specify that patient-doctor privilege allows for information discussed in counseling to remain strictly confidential, *except* in instances involving danger to self or others. Many counselors, psychologists, and treatment agencies use an Informed Consent

---

Box 11.2: The Urge to End It All

According to Scott Anderson's (2008) *New York Times* article, the National Institute of Mental Health (NIMH) statistics show that 90% of all those who commit suicide have some form of a diagnosable mental disorder. Yet, despite advances in mental health treatment, psychotropic medications, the proliferation of hotlines, and crisis centers and psychiatric screeners in nearly every emergency room throughout the United States, the overall suicide rate in the United States in 2008 is the same as it was in 1965. The numbers of those who commit suicide are often nearly twice the rate of those who die via homicide. In Scott Anderson's (2008) *New York Times* article, he raises some other astounding facts regarding suicide. Anderson points to the fact that much of suicide research focused on the question "why" rather than "how," especially when trying to figure out how to reduce the number of suicides. Yet, the means by which people take their own life becomes an important factor, as Anderson found out. Take for example what happened in Great Britain prior to 1960 when coal gas heated most homes. Although coal was cheap and plentiful, when burned it released high levels of deadly carbon monoxide. This meant that by literally sticking one's head in the oven, one could easily commit suicide, as was the case with the famous American poet, Sylvia Plath. According to Anderson, in the late 1950s carbon monoxide poisoning accounted for nearly half of England's suicide deaths. Fast forward to 1970 when Britain converted to natural gas that contained zero levels of carbon monoxide, and the suicide rate dropped by nearly one third. Fast forward again to the 1980s and the Ellington Bridge in northwestern Washington, D.C., which had become known as the "suicide bridge." In 1985, a suicide barrier was erected. Those who opposed the barrier said that people intent on killing themselves would merely go to another bridge a few blocks away; except those opponents were wrong.

A study of 515 people who attempted suicide by jumping from the Golden Gate Bridge in San Francisco, but who were either pulled off the bridge or who survived the jump revealed that only 6% had gone on to commit suicide by other means. Also, Anderson points out that guns account for approximately 54% of all completed suicides. A 2007 survey of gun ownership across 21 states found that the fifteen states with the highest gun ownership had suicide rates that were three times higher than those states with the lowest gun ownership.

So, what does this tell us about suicide and suicide plans?

Source: Adapted from Anderson, Scott. "The Urge to End It All," *The New York Times.* July 6, 2008

to Treatment form (signed by patients at the onset of treatment), which specifies that confidentiality can be broken in instances of suicidal or homicidal threat or suspected child abuse. In a lawsuit filed against the Massachusetts Institute of Technology, it is alleged that MIT administrators had not acted responsibly in preventing the death of an MIT student who purposely set herself on fire in her dorm room (Sontag, 2002). The suit alleges that the MIT staff did not inform the parents of their daughter's suicidal threats.

GUIDELINES FOR MANAGING CRISES INVOLVING SUICIDE

1. *Don't ignore the warning signs:* references to suicidal thought, "my family would be better off without me," or "life's too much of a struggle."

2. *When in doubt, don't be afraid to ask about suicidal feelings, or intentions:* For example, if someone expresses feelings of hopelessness about the present or future, ask "Have you had thoughts of taking your life? When did you have these thoughts, and do you have a plan for ending your life?" "Have these thoughts ever gotten to the point where you attempted to end your life?" Suicide risk scales like the Columbia Suicide Severity Rating Scale (Posner, Brown, Stanley et al., are described in Table 11.3 and provide a structured series of questions that can be used to assess someone who may be suicidal.

3. *Validate the client's emotional pain:* Suicide is often viewed as a means of ending emotional (and sometimes chronic physical) pain (Maltsberger, 1992).

4. *Be patient:* Working through suicidal feelings takes time, there are no magic pills to immediately take away suicidal pain.

5. *Stay calm and listen:* Don't overreact to expressions of suicidal thoughts or intentions.

6. *Understand what suicide means to your client:* Suicide often has many motivations; for example, revenge, to end emotional pain, to end physical pain, or to end despair. How did your client come to view suicide as a solution?

7. *Understand that suicidal individuals are ambivalent:* Therefore, you provide a sense of constancy in that you want to help preserve life.

8. *Remind the client that suicide is a permanent solution to a temporary situation.*

9. *It is important to be proactive, have a plan, take action.*

10. *Help figure out ways to treat the underlying mental health disorder.*

11. *Document your treatment plan, assessment, actions, consultations, contacts, and so forth.*

CRISES INVOLVING HOMICIDE, LETHALITY, AND THREATS OF VIOLENCE

Scope of the Problem

In 2013, homicide was the 16th leading cause of death in the United States with a total of 16,291 deaths. Milwaukee was at the top of the list of violent cities, with a 76% increase in homicides. The Centers for Disease Control and Prevention (CDC) (2010) reported that 14 to 34 school age children (ages 5–18) were victims of homicide at school (including travel to and from school) each year from 1992 to 2010 (Roberts, Knox & Tesh, 2013).

In contrast, a far larger number of school age children were murdered outside of school. For example, the CDC identified 19 school-associated homicides during the 2009 to 2010 school year and 1,377 homicides outside of school (CDC, 2010; Nekvasil, Cornell, & Huang, 2015). School-based homicides represent only one to two percent of homicides of school age children. Homicides are among the top three leading causes of death among teenagers and young adults ages 15 to 24 (accidents and suicides are the other two leading causes of death). What is astounding is that most of these homicides are committed by same-age perpetrators. Homicides are more likely to occur in cities than in rural areas according to the FBI's Uniform Crime Reporting statistics (2015), in 2015 for example, there were 2,424 homicides in urban areas compared to only 861 in rural areas. However, there were 3,822 homicides in suburban areas, which includes small cities with populations of fewer than 50,000 residents. Milwaukee experienced the largest increase in homicide deaths from 2014 to 2015; however, Baltimore had the largest number of homicide deaths in 2015 (215 deaths), which represented a 56% increase (See Table 11.4 below).

Assessing Violence/Lethality Risk

Just as suicide risk is best assessed on a case-by-case basis, the same also applies to assessing the potential risk for violence and homicidal behavior. Risk assessment ideally considers factors, such as a prior history of violent behavior, age, social stressors, substance abuse, personality traits, and psychopathology. It is well accepted in the mental health field that "the best predictor of future violence is a past history of violence." In terms of personality traits and psychopathology, there are particular personality characteristics that are often associated with violent, acting-out individuals. These traits include: low frustration tolerance, impulsivity, immaturity, poor problem solving, and individuals who see violence as glamorous or a viable solution to life's problems. Three types of psychiatric disorders are often associated with violence and homicidal behavior. They include: Intermittent explosive disorder, paranoid schizophrenia, and antisocial personality disorder. While not all individuals with antisocial personality disorders are violent, many resort to violence to achieve personal goals, as is the case with psychopaths who use violent assault in a robbery or rape, or the example of a spouse abuser who uses violence as a means of control and intimidation. Some of this violent behavior is impulsive and therefore,

Table 11.4 Homicide Rates in United States Cities 2014-2015

City	2014 Homicides	2015 Homicides	% Change
Milwaukee	59	104	76%
St. Louis	85	136	60%
Baltimore	138	215	56%
New York	190	208	9%
Philadelphia	165	171	4%

Table 11.5 Homicide/Violence Lethality Checklist

1. Is there a past history of any of the following?	Yes	No
Violent behavior		
Property destruction		
Attempted homicide		
Other criminal behaviors		
Intimate partner violence		
Other family violence		
Bullying of others		
Child abuse (client)		
Incarceration		
Job loss due to threats		
School expulsion		
Animal cruelty		
Psychiatric treatment		
Alcohol/drug abuse		
If yes, specify which substance		
2. **Present threats of violence?**		
3. **Violent or homicidal plan?**		
4. **Recent homicidal plan or behavior?**		
5. **Violent ideation or obsessions?**		
6. **Means or methods to carry out plan?**		
7. **Recent disruptions in interpersonal relationships (e.g., separation)?**		

spontaneous, while other psychopaths are very calculating in their violent behavior (Hare, 1993). Table 11.5 provides a list of risk factors for violence/lethality.

Given that one of the *best predictors of violent behavior is a past history of such behavior* (Litwack, Kirschner & Wack, 1993; McNeil & Binder, 1991, 1994; Meloy, 1987; Monahan, 1995; Mulvey & Lidz, 1995; Slovic & Monahan, 1995; Truscott, Evens, & Mansell, 1995), *it is vital to thoroughly explore past history and to gather prior legal and treatment records as quickly as possible.* Individuals with criminal histories, which include assault and battery offenses, arson, sexual assault, weapons possession, aggravated felonies, domestic violence, drunk and disorderly, property damage, reckless and/or drunk driving, a history of assaultive behavior while hospitalized, and naturally prior homicidal threats are considered to be at high risk for violent behavior (Blumenreich & Lewis, 1993; Klassen & O'Connor, 1988). This risk is further increased when the individual is male and has a history of prior victimization (Cavaiola & Schiff, 1988). Although women can also become violent and assaultive, it should be noted that the majority of women imprisoned for murder have usually committed these acts as "crimes of passion" (i.e., referring to the murder of a spouse, boyfriend, or lover in the heat of a jealous rage or as self-defense against a physically abusive partner).

Violent behavior can also occur situationally. Such as in the case of "road rage" where a person acts out violently, or in instances where a person becomes outraged by a boss or coworker. Violent behavior also can be exacerbated when individuals are under the influence of alcohol or drugs. Because alcohol intake can have a disinhibiting effect, it is not unexpected that there are correlations between criminally violent behavior and alcohol use (Bradford, Greenberg, & Motayne, 1992). Other mood-altering chemicals also associated with a propensity toward violence include stimulant drugs, such as amphetamines and cocaine. It is noted that violent behaviors (e.g., accidents, suicide, and homicide) are the leading causes of death among stimulant users and accounts for the vast majority of emergency room visits, especially among young people (Whiteside, Bonar, Blow, Ehrlich, & Walton, 2015). Violent behavior is also associated to certain types of hallucinogens, particularly PCP (phencyclidine); however, some research suggests that PCP does not induce violence in individuals unless they are prone to violence (Brecher, Wang, Wong, & Morgan, 1988). Steroids have also been known to increase violent behavior, as in the well-known "roid rages" (Pope & Katz, 1990, 1994). Similarly, some types of inhalant abuse are also linked to violent behavior and delinquency in adolescents (Reed & May, 1984) and in adults who inhale solvents (Dinwiddie, 1994).

The ability to effectively manage individuals who become aggressive or violent is an essential skill for any crisis counselor, police officer, teacher, nurse, or anyone who is involved in human service work, including customer service representatives, consumer complaint representatives, human resource personnel, and flight attendants. All of the aforementioned individuals can be faced with people who may become aggressive or violent. At one time, it was thought that the ability to manage violent or aggressive behavior was needed only for corrections and police officers working with violent criminal types, or for psychiatric aides working with potentially violent psychiatric patients. The ability to manage violent behavior is essential for anyone working in any human service field.

The goal of crisis intervention with violent or aggressive individuals is to provide safe, non-harmful behavior management (Crisis Prevention Institute, 1999). In order to accomplish this, it is important to fit the intervention with the type of aggressive behavior presented. In other words, given that individuals may act out either verbally or physically, it is important to match the intervention to the type of aggressive behavior being displayed. For example, with someone who is acting out verbally, it is inappropriate and over-reactive to respond with physical intervention. Similarly, verbal interventions may be ineffective with someone who is acting out physically by hitting, punching, or biting.

Case Presentation: Richard, A Case Involving Threats of Murder/Suicide

Richard is a 43-year-old separated father of two. He previously sought counseling at the recommendation of a coworker who was concerned about Richard's making "threatening remarks" and depressive statements. This coworker was also worried because of Richard's increased use of alcohol and explosive temper outbursts at work. Richard explains that he recently separated from his wife, Karen after 20 years of marriage and that he doesn't know if he can go on without her. He is restless and angry as he describes how his wife "kicked him out of his home" because she wanted to "find herself." Richard suspects she is seeing a guy she works with at her part-time job. Richard states that the thought of them together "drives me crazy" and apparently, this is where his threats are focused. Richard made some vague threats about killing his wife and lover if he ever caught them together, and has also threatened to wait for him after work and "beat him up." Richard denies any domestic abuse history in his relationship with his wife. Richard is currently living alone in a rented room and has few friends other than his coworker, whom he seems to trust and confide in. Richard also confided in his coworker that he has both a handgun and a rifle in his possession.

Intervention

The crisis counselor working with Richard must therefore make an assessment of both the potential for violence/homicide as well as suicide and come up with a strategy that ensures the safety of all involved. In the following session excerpt, the crisis counselor has already established a rapport with Richard and is now trying to assess the potential of his acting out. What if Richard walked out? What would the crisis counselor do? In an instance of either homicidal or suicidal threat, the counselor needs to consider reporting these threats to the police. In keeping with the Tarasoff (1976) ruling, the counselor also needs to consider whether to report the threats to both Karen and her boyfriend. Even if Richard agrees to go into the hospital as planned, there still needs to be a consideration of whether to notify Karen and her boyfriend of the threats. It is likely, given the homicidal and suicidal threats, that if Richard tried to sign himself out of the hospital that he would be involuntarily committed; however, under the Tarasoff ruling, potential victims still need to be notified of the threats.

Case Conceptualization/Crisis Resolution

Richard's situation represents a crisis that has the potential for violent acting out, with both homicidal and suicidal outcomes. This type of crisis is one of the most frightening to work with because of its many inherent dangers; yet, one should also note that Richard does not appear to fit into any one of the diagnostic groups that are most likely to act out aggressively. Instead, the catalyst to his crisis was his recent marital separation and Richard's suspicions and fears that his wife is now involved in another relationship. His sexual jealousy fuels his anger and fear and his alcohol abuse makes the likelihood of his acting out even greater. The fact that Richard has a means of carrying out his plans for vengeance (because he owns firearms), also lends more urgency to this crisis. The research literature on murder-suicide suggests this appears to be a high-risk situation (Eliason, 2009; Marzuk, Tardiff, & Hirsch, 1992). Usually, the killer is a white, non-Hispanic man, and 76% of the victims are female (Auchter, 2010); (Violence Policy Center, 2015). The use of firearms is the primary method in nine out of ten cases (Violence Policy Center, 2015). The central theme found in most murder-suicides is that the perpetrator is overly attached to a relationship and when the relationship is threatened with dissolution, this leads to the destruction of the relationship and self (Allen, 1983; Nock & Murzuck, 1999). In fact, 72% of all murder-suicides involved intimate partners (Violence Policy Center, 2015). These relationships are often differentiated by emotional abusiveness and sexual jealousy.

In resolving this crisis, it was important to first **listen** to Richard's emotional pain over the separation from his wife that is fueling his anger and need for revenge. Richard may feel that he has no other options, therefore it is most important to validate his feelings of hurt and anger. A thorough lethality **assessment** is called for given Richard's threats. Here it is important to explore whether Richard has a concrete, organized plan for hurting his estranged wife and her lover and a means to carrying out that plan (e.g., Richard admits to owning firearms). An indicated risk of danger often mandates using a risk assessment instrument, such as the Ontario Domestic Assault Risk Assessment (ODARA) (Hilton, Harris, Rice, Lang, Cormier, & Lines, 2004) or the Danger Assessment (DA) instrument (Storey & Hart, 2014); both of which can be used in crisis situations like Richard's, where homicidal threats have been made. The ODARA is most often used with the partner who has been threatened with physical harm asking questions regarding prior domestic incidents, prior non-domestic incidents (e.g., violence perpetrated outside the home), whether the person making the threat has been incarcerated in the past 30 days, if the person making the threat has been re-incarcerated following conditional release from jail/prison, if the threatened partner has a child from a previous relationship, if there is past or current substance use, if applicable if the person making the threat has ever assaulted their partner while she was pregnant, and whether the threatened partner is isolated, or if there are barriers to his or her support networks. The Danger Assessment instrument is unique in that it was designed to be administered as a structured interview with the victim and includes items that go beyond the ODARA (see Figure 11.1).

Most importantly, given the nature of Richard's threats, the **plan** would need to involve informing the police and having Richard evaluated by a psychiatric screener at a local emergency room, and notifying Karen of the threats.

Case Presentation: Jason, A Case Involving the Threat of Violence

Jason was court ordered to the local mental health clinic for an evaluation after his landlord claimed that he threatened to kill him over a dispute involving payment of back rent. Jason is a 28-year-old, single male who is currently on parole after having served 5 years in the state penitentiary for a variety of offenses, including sexual assault, attempted rape, robbery, and aggravated assault. His parole officer provided information to the mental health clinic regarding these convictions. In addition, Jason identifies himself as a "skinhead" and a member of the Aryan nation. His landlord is from Jamaica. The threats of violence are therefore racially motivated and may constitute a bias crime. In talking with Jason, the counselor notes that he is very guarded in revealing any information about these prior convictions. Jason only states that he was "framed" and that the woman whom he was accused of assaulting had invited him into her house. The other conviction involved his assaulting an elderly man and stealing his wallet. Jason has absolutely no remorse or guilt over these incidents. Jason's history reveals that he has been in and out of institutions since he was about eight years old. There were several instances where he broke into neighbor's homes and stole valuables. He also set fire to another neighbor's garage without any cause or provocation. When

Figure 11.1   Danger Assessment (Storey & Hart, 2014)

1. Has the physical violence increased in severity or frequency over the past year?
2. Does he own a gun?
3. Have you left him after living together during the past year?
3a. (If you have ever lived with him check here _____)
4. Is he unemployed?
5. Has he ever used a weapon against you or threatened you with a lethal weapon?
5a. (If yes, was the weapon a gun? _____)
6. Does he threaten to kill you?
7. Has he avoided being arrested for domestic violence?
8. Do you have a child that's not his?
9. Has he ever forced you to have sex when you did not wish to?
10. Does he ever try to choke you?
11. Does he use illegal drugs? By drugs, I mean "uppers" or amphetamines, "meth", speed, angel dust, cocaine, "crack," street drugs or mixtures.
12. Is he an alcoholic or problem drinker?
13. Does he control most or all of your daily activities? For instance, does he tell you who you can be friends with, when you can see your family, how much money you can use, or when you can take the car? (If he tries, but you don't let him check here _____)
14. Is he violently and constantly jealous of you? (For instance, does he say, "If I can't have you, no one can")
15. Have you ever been beaten by him while you were pregnant?
16. Has he ever threatened or tried to commit suicide?
17. Does he threaten to harm your children?
18. Do you believe he is capable of killing you?
19. Does he follow or spy on you, leave threatening notes or messages on answering machines, destroy your property, or call you when you don't want him to?
20. Have you ever threatened or tried to commit suicide?

asked about these prior incidents, Jason just shrugged his shoulders and replied, "I thought it would be a fun thing to do, besides it wasn't like I was hurting anyone or anything." When he was 16-years-old, he was sent to a state reformatory for boys for allegedly beating up an elderly man and stealing his car. What was noteworthy, however, was that for each offense, Jason had an elaborate story as to why he was not responsible for the offense or how he was "framed" by someone else. When asked about the threats to his landlord, Jason merely replied that he has been "buggin' him for the rent for the past three weeks. When I get mine, he'll get his." He refuses to elaborate further on this remark.

In this case, the crisis counselor is trying to work with Jason who has come in, not so much in crisis, but more because of the court's recommendation that he submit to evaluation and possible counseling. The counselor is again faced with the dilemma of trying to assess the risk of violence, given the alleged threats that Jason has made against his landlord. Unlike Richard who had no prior psychiatric history or history of violent behavior, Jason has quite a record of both. However, because the session is court-ordered, there are certainly limits to how much truthful information the counselor will be able to obtain.

Intervention

Counselor: Jason, tell me something about the accusations and possible parole violation you are facing.

Jason: Is this being recorded? I'd rather not have what I say recorded, you know for legal purposes.

C: No, there is no audio or video recording of our meeting.

J: Doc, I swear to you, I just told the guy to get off my back, that's the way it happened.

C: Do you have any prior convictions?

J: Yeah, I got jammed up a couple of times before. Once on a rape charge, that was back in '08 and about four times on assault charges. I also did time when I was 16 in Jamesburg (a state juvenile correction facility) on an arson charge.

C: Tell me about the other assault charges.

J: What's there to tell, I was working as a construction supervisor for about six months or so, and after work some of the crew and I would go down to the bar for some drinks. One thing would lead to another and the next thing you know, somebody was calling the damn cops. I wasn't doing anything that the others weren't doing.

C: And what about the situation with your landlord, can you tell me something about that?

J: Well, Doc, there's not much to tell. I've been out of work for the past two months, so naturally, I can't make my rent and this guy won't give me a moment of peace. He is constantly on my back, so I said some things that would kind of shut him up for a while. The cops are also tryin' to pin a bias crime charge on me because the guys from Jamaica. I just know he's black and I don't get along with blacks from the time I was in Jamesburg. White kids don't do well in the system if you know what I mean?

C: What do you mean?

J: Well let's put it this way, if you didn't stand up for yourself or join the Aryans, you might as well cut your own throat.

C: So, what will you do to your landlord if he doesn't get off your back?

J: Nothing Doc, honest, I just want to get him to lighten up.

C: Do you have any weapons, guns, knives?

Jason: No, I don't because I'm on parole.

Case Conceptualization/Crisis Resolution

In this case example, Jason typifies so many of the attitudes and behaviors of those individuals with antisocial personality disorder. For example, his attitude toward the current allegation of threatening his landlord is very glib and nonchalant. He does not take responsibility for his actions. In a crisis assessment situation like that described above, it is not necessarily the counselor's role to confront Jason on his behavior or try to do the therapeutic work required in long-term therapy. Unfortunately, as indicated earlier, people with antisocial personality disorders do not often present in crisis unless they have been caught in the act, accused of something, or they are planning some criminal actions, at which point, they may be referred for assessment.

In preparation for this evaluation, the counselor and the clinic should make some plans. They should alert the office staff to be vigilant and listen for a code phrase that indicates the counselor is feeling threatened. They should occupy an office in a busy area of the building and the counselor should sit closest to the door. In the event that Jason became more agitated to the point of threatening violence (either verbally or through physical actions, e.g., slamming his fist on the table), then the crisis counselor needs to employ some **defusing** techniques. The following are some defusing strategies that might be used with a potentially violent individual:

1. *Understand the mindset of the hostile or potentially violent person:* These individuals often have a compelling need to communicate their grievance to someone, now! Even if the person is wrong, they are acting on perceptions that are real to him/her. In the overwhelming number of cases, the person just wants to be heard and to be treated fairly.

2. *Practice "Active Listening":* Stop what you are doing and give the person your full attention. Listen to what is really being said. Use silence and paraphrasing. Ask clarifying, open-ended questions.

3. *Build trust and provide help. Avoid confrontation:* Be calm, sit still, be courteous, respectful, and patient. It is important to be open and honest, but don't make promises you can't keep. Never belittle the person, embarrass them, or verbally confront a potentially violent person.

4. *Allow a total airing of the grievance without comment or judgment:* While the person is airing their grievance, make eye contact, but don't stare (that can be perceived as a challenge). Let the person have their say, while ignoring challenges or insults. Don't take venting personally; redirect their attention to the real issues.

5. *Allow the aggrieved party to suggest a solution:* A person will more readily agree to a resolution that he has helped to formulate.

6. *Move toward a "win-win" solution:* Preserve the individual's dignity. Switch focus from what you can't do, toward what you can do.

There may be times however, when you will need to call in additional resources (e.g. a supervisor, security, another counselor), or if necessary call the police if you feel you are in danger. If danger is imminent then it is not necessary to obtain consent from the client in order to call for assistance (Bohen, 2002, p. 27).

Box 11.3: Suicide Clusters

Research studies have identified instances where multiple suicides occur in quick succession, or "clusters." These clusters may occur when young people (e.g. adolescents and young adults) copy or mimic the suicidal death of a peer or a celebrity. Copycat suicides were very much a concern in the United States following the death of musician Kurt Cobain, who committed suicide by firearm on April 5, 1994. One suicide cluster that is often cited occurred in the small town of Red Deer in Alberta, Canada, when six high school males committed suicide. Several years ago, there was a similar cluster Bergenfield, New Jersey, and more recently in Manasquan, New Jersey and among students attending Palo Alto and Gunn High Schools in California. It is also noteworthy that suicide clusters have occurred among both Native Americans and Canadian First Nation Aboriginal peoples. These events have prompted much attention from the Centers of Disease Control and Prevention.

Researchers have hypothesized three types of suicide clusters: mass clusters, which involve suicides that cluster in time regardless of geographical location (e.g., there was a 12% increase in suicide deaths in the month after Marilyn Monroe's death), and point clusters, which are suicides that occur in both close time and proximity to one another. Echo clusters occur over extended periods of time from the original cluster (Olson, 2013). Although there are several factors that might contribute to suicide clusters, no true definitive cause has been identified. However, the role of news media in sensationalizing the suicide deaths of celebrities and young adults are thought to be a contributing factor, which prompted the Center for Disease Control and World Health Organization to issue guidelines to the media for reporting suicides (Olson, 2013). The impact of poverty and discrimination are hypothesized to contribute to some suicide clusters (e.g. those among poor tribal Native-American populations), while a sense of community ownership, common culture and other protective factors may serve to reduce rates of suicide (Kirmeyer, 2007). Many questions about this phenomenon remain to be answered.

Kirmeyer, et al. (2007). Suicide among Aboriginal people in Canada. Ottawa, ON: Aboriginal Healing Foundation.

Olson, R. (2013). Suicide contagion and suicide clusters. InfoExchange 10: Suicide Contagion and suicide clusters: Centre for Suicide Prevention. www.csp.Cloud8.ionhnehosting.net

SUMMARY

Threats involving suicide, violence, and other forms of lethality are among the most difficult for mental health, medical, and first responders to manage. As you can see from the cases described in this chapter, by the time intervention takes place, these crises have already begun to spiral out of control and the role of those professionals intervening is to ensure the safety of the individual making suicidal or violent threats, and to ensure the safety of those around them. These are examples of crises where responsible action must be taken and, in our experience, it is always better to err on the side of caution. These are not crises where individuals can be sent home with hopes that he or she will feel better in the morning and the crisis will have gone away. Even the most experienced professionals often seek consultation with supervisors and colleagues in these types of crisis situations. Therefore, it is even more important for less experienced mental health, medical, and other professionals to seek consultation in managing these crises.

RESOURCES FOR CHAPTER ENRICHMENT

Suggested Websites

www.suicide.org This website provides information on statistics related to suicide, warning signs, suicide myths, and correlates of suicide, such as divorce, postpartum depression, suicide among high school and college students and many other topics.

http://www.suicidology.org This is the website for the American Association of Suicidology. The association provides information and materials on suicide and suicide prevention. They sponsor an annual conference, which features top researchers and speakers on topics related to suicide and suicide prevention.

http://www.vpc.org/studies/wmmw2016.pdf This website examines instances of murder-suicide, where men murder women, as discussed earlier in this chapter.

http://www.vpc.org/studies/amroul2012.pdf This website also examines murder-suicide rates in the United States.

http://www.nij.gov/journals/266/Pages/murderfamilies.aspx This website provides statistics and other information about men who murder their families.

Recommended Films

Dead Poets Society: (1989) stars Robin Williams as a teacher at an exclusive boys' boarding school. The film depicts the suicide death of a student who feels trapped by a demanding, perfectionist father who refuses to allow his son to pursue his interests in acting. Robin Williams's character is blamed for encouraging the student to pursue his interests and is subsequently fired from his teaching position.

Girl Interrupted: (1999) based on Suzanna Kaysen's novel, this film stars Winona Ryder as a young woman who is psychiatrically hospitalized following a suicide attempt and provides an account of her 18-month stay at a psychiatric hospital in the 1960s. The film focuses on how she attempts to put her life together after her hospitalization. The film also graphically depicts the suicide death of one of the main characters.

Falling Down: (1993) stars Michael Douglas as a middle-class businessman who becomes progressively violent as the film unfolds. It is interesting to see how a chain of events and catalysts seem to push the main character toward further violent behavior. In watching this film, look for various risk factors for violent behavior like those presented in Figure 11.1 titled Danger Assessments.

Cape Fear: (1991) (stars Robert DiNiro, Jessica Lange and Nick Nolte). DiNiro provides an excellent portrayal of someone with antisocial personality disorder who uses violence and threats of violence throughout the film.

American Psycho: **(2000)** (stars Christian Bale and Edward Norton). A wealthy New York investment banking executive hides his alter-psychopathic ego from his coworkers and friends as he progresses deeper into violent behavior and fantasies.

Kurt Cobain: **(2015)** an HBO documentary that provides an intimate portrait into the life of Nirvana singer and songwriter, Kurt Cobain. The documentary delivers insights into the possible factors that resulted in Cobain's committing suicide.

Suggested Activities

1. Watch one of the films listed above (*Dead Poets Society* or *Girl Interrupted*) and determine those factors that were the prime motivators for the character taking their own life. Does the character who commits suicide fit the profile of those considered at risk for suicide? In order to determine this, you should fill out one of the Lethality Assessment—Suicide forms included in this chapter. What steps could have been taken to prevent the suicide of this character?

2. Read each of the case vignettes listed below. Rank in order which individual you feel is at highest risk to lowest risk for suicide. Discuss why you have rank ordered them as you did. In other words, justify your rank ordering.

   a. Case Vignette #1: Rebecca is a 22-year-old college student who has been dating Justin for the past two years. Approximately three days ago, Rebecca overheard two other students in one of her classes talking about seeing Justin at a party and hooking up with someone they know. At first Rebecca thought her classmates were talking about someone else, but when she asked them to describe Justin, the description they gave along with other information, confirmed for Rebecca that it was her boyfriend. Rebecca confronted Justin later that evening and although he did not deny that he was at the party, he denied that he was with another woman and became angry that Rebecca would believe these total strangers over his account of what happened. Rebecca was distraught and couldn't stop crying. That evening, when she got back to her dorm room, she took 50 aspirin and made some cuts on her wrist. Her roommate called the residence hall assistant who then called the Campus Counseling Center. Rebecca was brought to the local emergency room by campus police. The crisis screener interviewed Rebecca and found that she had been treated for depression while in high school and was given Prozac. She has not had any history of suicidal behavior, but the family history reveals that she has an uncle who committed suicide in the aftermath of being arrested for embezzling from the corporation he worked for. Rebecca indicates that she doesn't really want to kill herself, she just wanted to get back at Justin.

   b. Case Vignette #2: Sal is 62 years old and recently retired from his job working as a police captain in a small suburban town. He took an early retirement because his wife recently died of liver cancer, and because of an injury he sustained about five years ago. Sal was a shift supervisor when he received a call for backup from one of his patrolman. The patrolman was called to the scene of a domestic violence dispute where the husband was intoxicated and threatening. As Sal was about to put the husband in handcuffs, he bolted out of the door and began to run to the back of the house. Sal fell as he ran through the yard to catch him and suffered a major knee injury that required surgery. Sal experiences a lot of pain from his injured knee, even though the injury occurred five years ago. He was given Percoset for the pain, which he often takes in order to get to sleep. Sal was very proud of being a policeman and feels he is "useless" since the injury. He did feel good about taking good care of his wife during her battle with cancer, but felt lonely and empty when she died. Sal visits her grave every day and says he can't wait until he "joins" his wife. Sal still sees some of his coworkers from the police department and, every so often, they go to the pistol range for the afternoon.

   c. Case Vignette #3: Hans is 24 years old and recently moved to the United States after living in East Germany all of his life. He spent a couple of years at the University of Munich, but ran out of money, so he could not continue his studies. He planned to become an architect, but decided to put his plans on hold until he could find a job in the United States and begin to save some money. The only job Hans was able to find, however, was working as a janitor in a department store. He does not speak English very well, and finds himself feeling lonely and depressed. He says that he feels like a failure and should just give up.

   (This exercise is based on a classroom activity described by Madson and Vas (2003) in Learning risk factors for suicide: A scenario-based activity. *Teaching of Psychology, 30,* 123–126.)

3. You are in the parking lot of the local mall looking for a parking space when you see someone pulling out ahead of you. You put on your blinker as you approach the space, but see another car rounding the corner also with their blinker on. Because the car leaving the space is pulling out in the direction of the other car, it allows you to pull into the space. You turn your car off and are about to get out, when all of a sudden you're confronted by the guy from the other car who is yelling and shouting obscenities at you and threatens to drag you out of your car and "beat you to a pulp." How do you deal with this situation?

4. You are having a quiet lunch in the student center when you're confronted by another student who accuses you of "hitting on" their boyfriend/girlfriend. They start yelling and screaming and their anger is escalating. How do you manage this situation?

Recommended YouTube Viewing

https://www.youtube.com/watch? v = D1QoyTmeAYw This TED talk video provides a first person account of someone who attempted suicide.

https://www.youtube.com/watch? v = SVe4lAUyY8M This TED talk also provides an insightful first person account from someone who attempted suicide.

https://www.youtube.com/watch? v = STMp6w38k3g This TED talk delivers a first person account; however, the presenter also discusses the societal and cultural taboos regarding suicide.

https://www.youtube.com/watch? v = VCsuaVJqOh8 This brief documentary provides a chilling account of a family murder-suicide.

https://www.youtube.com/watch? v = tBcOSo6A__k This is a brief video of a crisis worker taking a call from a suicidal client.

https://www.youtube.com/watch? v = 2iBpfEEJWxk Facebook produced a video on how to support someone who may be suicidal using social media.

https://www.youtube.com/watch? v = 0XEKrRJeB5I This is a role play of a counselor helping an individual who is experiencing a suicide crisis.

https://www.youtube.com/watch? v = wH0gpp_WMkQ A behind the scenes video of a crisis call in a center for veterans. Excellent instructional tool for counselors working at hotline centers.

https://www.youtube.com/watch? v = iTdqo_7_qLE This video lecture provides useful information regarding violent behavior in adults.

https://www.youtube.com/watch? v = nnl5WF2ScNM Interesting video on the neurobiology of violent behavior.

https://www.youtube.com/watch? v = yYre7fmdFus This video provides useful information about managing violent behavior of clients and other individuals.

https://www.youtube.com/watch? v = rDrzfrtTUiU This brief video provides information on managing violent behavior.

Mental Health & Psychiatric Crises

*J*ulie is a 46-year-old housewife and mother of two sons, ages 14 and 17, who has been married to John for the past twenty years. John called his primary care physician seeking help for his wife because of his concerns about her feeling increasingly "lethargic and depressed for the past eight months." John notes, "she doesn't want to go out anyplace, not even to her women's auxiliary meetings, which she used to love going to. She won't even go out to dinner or leave the house for that matter. All she does is sit around and cry all day." John further states that although Julie has been feeling depressed, she is not suicidal because of her "religious beliefs." What prompted John to call their primary care physician was that Julie has been staying in bed for the past week and refuses to bathe or get dressed. Their doctor suggests that John bring Julie to the mental health center at their local medical center.

DISCUSSION QUESTIONS

1. There has been a great deal of debate in the media recently about mental health background checks for people purchasing guns. What are your opinions about this proposal? Does it create stigma for people suffering with mental illness or characterize all those with mental illness as potentially violent?

2. There are many who say the mental health treatment system in the United States is broken. What are some of the ways you would fix it or make improvements to treatment in your state or county?

3. In the 1990s, there was a major push to close psychiatric hospitals by discharging mentally ill people into the community, many of whom were assigned to live in substandard boarding homes. What are your opinions and what do you see as advantages and disadvantages of what was known as "deinstitutionalization?" How would you feel if a home for the mentally ill was placed in your neighborhood?

There are particular types of psychiatric conditions where people are more vulnerable to crises. What is unique to psychiatric crises is that unlike other types of crises discussed in Chapter 1 (e.g., developmental, traumatic event, existential), psychiatric crisis can come about in reaction to internal psychological emotional catalysts as well as external triggers. It is conceivable therefore, that the psychiatric condition itself can be the reason for a person experiencing the crisis (e.g., a person who experiences a manic episode) or a psychiatric condition can occur as a result of the crisis (e.g., a person who experiences PTSD symptoms following a traumatic car accident). Psychiatric crises often involve disturbances in **emotion**, **thought**, or **behavior/conduct**. The goal in effectively resolving a psychiatric crisis is to make certain that the person is not in any danger and to also make certain that an effective crisis plan is in place that addresses those issues/problems that lead up to the crisis. Therefore, it is necessary for crisis counselors to identify issues or possible triggering events in order to assist the person in developing a plan, which hopefully prevents the problem from reoccurring in the future.

It is also important to consider that with many other crises, crisis planning is done collaboratively with the client; this may not be true with psychiatric crises. Ruchlewska, Mulder, Smulders, Roosenschoon, Koopmans, and Wierdsma (2009) make distinctions between Patient Advocate Crisis Plans (PACP) and Clinician Facilitated Crisis Plans (CCP). With Patient Advocate Crisis Plans, counselors may be working with a client advocate (e.g., a case manager, a mental health counselor, a family member, or significant other) who works on behalf of the client. In some instances, the client and advocate come up with a crisis plan which is then reviewed and implemented by the crisis counselor. This type of crisis planning may occur when the client is incapable of making treatment decisions on their own behalf, as in the case when the individual is experiencing a psychotic disorder. In clinician facilitated crisis planning, the client and counselor work collaboratively to come up with a crisis plan.

SCOPE OF THE PROBLEM

According to the National Alliance on Mental Illness (2016), more than 40 million adults in the United States (i.e., nearly 20% of the adult American population) will deal with some form of mental illness this year. It is not surprising, therefore, that psychiatric crises make up such a large portion of the crises that crisis counselors encounter. Mental health crises also represent one of the most complex of the crisis issues discussed in this text. As noted in the case illustration at the beginning of this chapter, people experiencing a mental health crisis, often present with a variety of symptoms. The original *Diagnostic and Statistical Manual of Mental Disorders (DSM)*, published in 1952 by the American Psychiatric Association, contained less than 20 diagnostic categories. Today the most recent edition of the *DSM* (American Psychiatric Association, 2013) consists of over 250 diagnostic categories. Although the *DSM-5* has many advantages over its predecessors, there are still many controversies that surround psychiatric diagnoses in general. For example, the *DSM-5* includes some diagnoses that many mental health professionals feel are not true reflections of psychopathology (e.g., premenstrual dysphoric disorder or gender dysphoria) and question whether they should be included along with other mental disorders. For example, gender dysphoria is conceptualized to be a more biologically based condition where children, adolescents, and adults feel that they have been "born in the wrong body" and their identity is that of the opposite sex. Many feel that this is not truly a mental health

Box 12.1: Seattle Shooter Kills 5 in Cascade Mall, Burlington, WA

According to the *Associated Press*, Arcan Cetin, age 20 was charged in the fatal shooting of five people in the cosmetics section of Macy's on Friday September 16, 2016.

Mr. Cetin had been undergoing psychiatric treatment and was said to have been compliant with counseling, having attended a session with his therapist as recently as on September 6th. According to records obtained by the *Associated Press*, Mr. Cetin had been diagnosed with PTSD, ADHD, anxiety, and depression. There was no mention made as to why Mr. Cetin suffered from PTSD. When he threatened to harm himself, Mr. Cetin had been involuntarily committed to a psychiatric hospital approximately two months prior to the shootings. The records indicate that there had been several other prior suicide attempts. Approximately two years before, Mr. Cetin had been court-ordered into mental health treatment after allegedly attacking his mother. He had been doing well in outpatient treatment until he made unwanted sexual advances toward two 16-year-old girls in his math class, and also had punched his stepfather. At this time, there were no known reasons or motivations given for the shootings. According to Mr. Cetin's mother and stepfather, they had been helping Arcan with his rent and other living expenses and visited him frequently. Mr. Cetin's stepfather had dinner with him on Friday, just prior to the shootings.

It is important to realize that not everyone with mental illness commits violent acts, such as those of Arcan Cetin; James Holmes (the Aurora, Colorado shooter who killed 12 and injured 70 in a movie theater); or Adam Lanza (the Sandy Hook shooter who killed 20 children, and six staff members of the elementary school). However, it does raise the question whether those with serious mental illness should be able to have access to firearms. This question is posed in the Discussion Questions at the beginning of this chapter.

Source: Mele, Christopher. 2016. "5 Dead in Shooting at Mall in Washington State, Police Say." *New York Times.* https://www.nytimes.com/2016/09/24/us/mall-shooting-washington-state.html.

condition. For that reason, France took Gender Dysphoria off its list of psychiatric diagnoses several years ago.

There have been two major studies investigating how many Americans suffer from various psychiatric disorders. The two largest epidemiological surveys are referred to as the Epidemiological Catchment Area (ECA) survey (Reiger, Narrow, Rae, Manderscheid, Locke, & Goodwin, 1993; Robins & Reiger, 1991) and the National Comorbidity Study (NCS) (Kessler et al., 1994). Both came to some rather similar conclusions, even though they were conducted independently. First, these studies concluded that the three most frequently occurring psychiatric disorders are *anxiety disorders,* such as panic disorder, phobias, and generalized anxiety disorders; *mood disorders,* which would include both unipolar depression and bipolar disorders; and *substance use disorders,* which include both alcohol and drug addictions. The current prevalence estimates are that approximately 22% to 23% of the U.S. population (or about 44 million people), suffer from some type of mental health disorder within a given year. In further elucidating this data, 19% of the adult U.S. population has a mental disorder alone, while 3% have both a mental and addictive disorder, and

6% have an addictive disorder alone. It is estimated that approximately 28 to 30% of the population has either a mental health or substance use disorder. Approximately 20 to 25% of the nation's 700,000 homeless suffer from mental illness, while an estimated 50% suffer from co-occurring mental illness and a substance use disorder. A subpopulation of approximately 5.4% of U.S. adults have what is considered "severe" mental illness. The overall costs of these various mental illnesses are estimated to be at $193.2 billion in lost earnings per year (Insel, 2008). More than 80% of these costs are attributable to disabilities caused by mental illness, which results in individuals with mental illness unable to work (National Alliance on Mental Illness, 2013). Furthermore, the National Alliance on Mental Illness (2015a) estimates that approximately one in 25 American adults (4.2% or 25 million) experiences severe mental illness, which substantially interferes or limits their ability to function on a daily basis. In addition, it is estimated that one in five adolescents (ages 13 to 18), or 21.4% experience a severe mental illness (National Alliance on Mental Illness, 2015b).

DEFINING VARIOUS PSYCHIATRIC CRISES

Crises Related to Trauma and Other Stressors

Posttraumatic stress disorder or PTSD was previously grouped under anxiety disorders in the 2000 APA *DSM-IV-TR Manual*. However, in the *DSM-5* (2013), PTSD is grouped in its own category (i.e., trauma & other stressors) along with acute stress disorder, and adjustment disorders. The reason for this change was that although individuals with PTSD may experience acute anxiety in response to a traumatic event, it is also just as likely that they may experience dysphoric or depressive moods, anger and irritability, or emotional numbing. With posttraumatic stress disorder, many different types of trauma can produce PTSD. Although combat-related trauma is more often associated with PTSD, traumatic events can be as varied as witnessing the attacks on September 11th, sustaining an auto or boating accident, enduring a natural disaster (e.g., an earthquake, hurricane, tornado), being a refugee from a war zone, or being held captive in a hostage situation or concentration camp. Also, surviving an assault, such as a rape or robbery can also produce PTSD symptoms.

According to the *DSM-5* (2013), in order to be diagnosed with PTSD, there are several criteria that must be met. For example, under Criteria A the individual has to have been exposed to actual or threatened death, serious injury, or sexual violence in one of the following ways: direct exposure, witnessing a traumatic event happening to others, learning that a traumatic event has occurred to a close family member that may have occurred as the result of violence or a tragic accident, or experiencing repeated or extreme exposure to aversive details of traumatic events (i.e., firefighters, police or EMTs who are called to the scenes of horrifying events). For example, firefighters often are required to extricate dead, burned bodies out of cars or buildings. Under Criteria B, the person experiences intrusive symptoms, such as distressing memories of the traumatic event; distressing dreams or nightmares; dissociative reactions (e.g., flashbacks, where the person feels that they are reliving the event); or becoming highly distressed at exposure to internal or external cues that symbolize or resemble the traumatic event. Also, there is often intense physiological arousal to internal or external cues that resemble some aspect of the traumatic event.

Under Criteria C, there is persistent avoidance; or efforts to avoid disturbing memories, thoughts, or feelings associated with the traumatic event and avoidance of any external reminders of the traumatic event, such as any people, places, conversations, activities, objects that may be associated with the traumatic event. Under Criteria D there are negative alterations in mood or cognitions associated with the traumatic event (e.g., an inability to remember important aspects of the event); persistent and exaggerated negative beliefs about oneself, or others, or the world, such as "no one can be trusted," or "the world is a dangerous place." Persistent ongoing emotional states, such as horror, fear, anger, guilt, or shame; diminished interest in activities; feeling detached or estranged from others; and a lasting inability to experience any positive emotions, such as joy, happiness, or loving feelings. Under Criteria E there are marked alterations in emotional reactivity, such as hypervigilance, reckless or destructive behavior, irritability, exaggerated startle response, and problems with concentration, or problems falling asleep. From the aforementioned symptoms, it becomes obvious why PTSD is no longer listed under anxiety disorders given the multitude of reactions that people can experience in the aftermath of a traumatic event. Sadly, there can also be an increased incidence of suicidal ideation and suicidal behavior in the aftermath of trauma. For example, it is estimated that as many soldiers (if not more), died from suicide after returning from Vietnam as died in combat (Jordan, 2014; Lester, 2005). There also have been alarming rates of suicide in Iraq and Afghanistan veterans after returning home to the United States. Depression and suicidal ideation is also often found in physical and sexual abuse victims, especially among female victims who appear to be more prone to turning their anger and shame into abuse against themselves (Cavaiola & Schiff, 1988).

Acute stress disorder (ASD) is also included in the *DSM-5* chapter on Trauma and Stressor-Related Disorders. The main distinction between PTSD and ASD is essentially time. To receive a diagnosis of acute stress disorder, the aforementioned symptoms of PTSD are experienced within three days to one month of the trauma; if the person is experiencing these symptoms after one month of the trauma or longer, they are then diagnosed with PTSD. To receive a diagnosis of adjustment disorder rather than experiencing or witnessing a traumatic event, the individual experiences a stressful, but nontraumatic event, such as the loss of a job, or a break up in a relationship.

Crisis Intervention with PTSD and Other Trauma Disorders

Individuals suffering from posttraumatic stress disorder or acute stress disorder often have great difficulty in talking about the traumatic event as this represents tremendous apprehension about reliving the trauma. This sometimes depends on the level of guilt, shame, or fear connected to the trauma. For example, victims of sexual abuse and childhood molestation often experience difficulty in discussing their sexual traumatization, both because of the horrible memories of the trauma, and because of feelings of guilt or shame connected with the trauma. A person suffering from trauma resulting from a car accident may also have trouble discussing the events leading up to the accident, because of the anxiety-provoking memories in reliving the accident. It is not unusual to hear trauma victims state, "I should have stayed home that day," or "I knew I should have gotten more sleep before setting out" or "I should have reacted differently and this would have never happened." It appears that trauma is more difficult to deal with if the trauma is committed by another human being rather than when it is occurs as a result of a natural disaster, such as with a hurricane or earthquake. In any of these examples, however, it is not unusual for PTSD victims to experience **suppression (consciously trying to put the traumatic event out of one's mind) or repression (unconscious inability to recollect information)** of the traumatic event. Sometimes however, the person may be flooded with painful and intrusive recollections of the traumatic incident that plagues them throughout the day and disturbs his or her sleep with vivid, frightening nightmares. It is noted that many individuals who suffer from PTSD often go through stages in the aftermath of their ordeal. Initially, they may experience **denial** of the traumatic event, a feeling that this is not happening to me, which is then followed by **outcry**, at which point the person is often flooded with many painful emotions related to the trauma. In the next stage, **intrusiveness**, the person is bothered by intrusive thoughts or recollections of the traumatic incident or they may experience nightmares, all of which brings on more painful emotions. In the next stage, **working through**, the person begins the journey of coming to grips with the traumatic event by talking about what they experienced. Often it is necessary for the person to talk about the incident over and over again. The reason for this is that each time the person relives the incident, another piece of the traumatic puzzle is revealed, or often each time the person relives the trauma they are able to express more of the feelings associated with the incident. This is thought to provide some catharsis and relief. Hopefully, the person reaches a final stage of **completion** where the person can incorporate the trauma into their life experience, has learned from it and they can become a survivor of the incident rather than continuing to be a victim of the incident (Horowitz, 1985). It is common for crisis counselors to first encounter individuals with PTSD when they are experiencing **Outcry** symptoms, because this is when all of the emotions that have been suppressed during the **denial** phase come flooding in. The goal of crisis counseling in the **outcry** stage is to help the person express all that he or she is feeling, but also to help them gain some control over these emotions so that they are not overwhelmed by intrusive thoughts, recollections, or emotions that interfere with their ability to function. There are two other techniques, found to be helpful in the crisis management and ongoing treatment of PTSD and ASD. Clinical hypnosis (Kluft, 2016; Platoni, 2013; Poon, 2009) and eye movement desensitization response (EMDR) (Harford, 2010; Shapiro, 1989a, 1989b, 1995) have been used extensively to help individuals contain the impact of their traumatic symptoms. Clinical hypnosis has been employed in the treatment of various types of trauma for quite some time. Unfortunately, both clinical hypnosis and EMDR require extensive specialized training; however, most crisis counselors are versed in using techniques, such as diaphragmatic breathing, guided imagery, and progressive muscle relaxation that do not require extensive training to master. These techniques are described in more depth later in this chapter.

It is also important to note that there are several treatment modalities that can be helpful once the person experiencing trauma is stabilized. For example, some individuals with panic disorders and PTSD respond better to group therapy than to one-on-one counseling. This is especially true of individuals who may have all suffered from the same type of trauma. Such is the case with rape survivor groups or combat veteran groups. Often it is the homogeneity of the group that allows group members to identify with the thoughts and feelings of those who have been through similar experiences. One group of Vietnam

Box 12.2: College Students and Loneliness

According to a recent article that appeared in the *Washington Post*, college students often experience intense loneliness, especially when they first go off to college as undergraduates. According to the reporter Joanna Nesbit, "loneliness is part of the transition to college for just about everyone, but it's not an easy experience to weather, and many students feel uncomfortable sharing their feelings." It is common for feelings of loneliness to overlap with feelings of homesickness, anxiety, and depression. Experts agree that the best way to combat loneliness is to get involved with activities or clubs that are similar to students' interests and where they are more likely to meet other like-minded students. The worst thing is to isolate and withdraw into video games. Also, parents can help by not becoming too involved in their son or daughter's college adjustment, but rather allowing them to work on the issue themselves.

Source: Nesbit, J. (2016, Sept. 22). How to help your college student cope with loneliness. *Washington Post.*

veterans was very successful because it contained only those veterans who had experienced infantry combat. The group was very suspect of those whom they considered "RENFs" or Rear Echelon Forces. Although these soldiers may have also experienced combat trauma and death, they were considered different from those combat infantry soldiers whose lives were in peril on a daily basis. Similarly, a group of rape survivors would not be as therapeutic if they were combined with incest survivors. Crisis intervention with children who have experienced trauma is discussed in Chapter 4, which deals with crises of children and adolescents.

Crises Related to Anxiety Disorders

Anxiety disorders are a group of often complex conditions. For example, in the *DSM-5*, anxiety disorders include panic disorders, social phobias, specific phobias, agoraphobia, and generalized anxiety disorder. It is beyond the scope of this text to describe each of these disorders therefore, we focus on those disorders that are commonly linked to crisis states. It is estimated that 18.1% of American adults experience some type of anxiety disorder (National Alliance on Mental Illness, 2015c).

Anxiety is often experienced as both an emotion and as a physical state since a sufferer of anxiety often experiences intense dread, racing thoughts, perspiration, rapid breathing, and a pounding heart. Anxiety can arise in different intensities and in various settings or situations. For example, individuals with panic disorder experience intense debilitating anxiety and often fear they are having a heart attack, or that they are suffocating. Although the panic crisis is extremely intense, it usually only lasts for five to twenty minutes; although for the person suffering from panic disorder, those fifteen or twenty minutes may seem like an eternity. A person with panic disorder often reports indefinable fears. They may report a fear of losing control and doing something unspeakable, or have a fear of pending doom or death. Physical symptoms include hyperventilation, gasping for air, numbness or parasthesias, heart-pounding, dizziness, or lightheadedness; all of which are symptoms easy to mistake for a heart attack. Once medical causes have been ruled out, a crisis counselor or psychiatric screener usually evaluates these individuals. Some panic attacks may be triggered by particular situations, such as a particular place or sensory experience, while in other instances, panic attacks occur without rhyme or reason. After experiencing a first panic attack, many people begin to obsess about whether they might have another. This is why panic disorder is sometimes referred to as a "fear of fear" (Kendall & Hammen, 1998). Many individuals begin to limit their activities or places they go, which is why panic disorder can commonly coexist with agoraphobia. It is estimated that approximately 6 million Americans (age 18 and older) suffer from panic disorder (Kessler, Chiu, Demler, & Walters, 2005).

Crisis Intervention with Anxiety Disorders

As indicated above, crisis intervention with people suffering from anxiety disorders often involves helping them to manage or lessen their anxiety. Although there are many techniques that are useful in helping to reduce anxiety, it appears that unless the person in crisis has established some level of trust in the crisis counselor, no matter what technique is used, it may not be effective in alleviating anxiety. Therefore, it is important that the crisis counselor spend time with the anxiety sufferer, hearing them out, **listening** to their symptoms, apprehensions, and dreadful worries. In the process of establishing trust, it may then be possible to get some background information about this person's history of anxiety, without being intrusive or dismissive. Anxiety disorder sufferers often aptly describe, with great detail, their various physical symptoms, and apprehensions. In assessing a person with panic disorder, it is also important to find out how they have coped with their anxiety in the past and when the panic attacks began. It is of consequence to determine if he or she had received any prior treatment for anxiety, whether in an emergency room or other setting, and if it entailed medication or counseling. Also, it is beneficial to find out whether the person has experienced any periods of remission. If so, find out what may have accounted for these symptom-free periods. In order to get an idea as to how intense this person's anxiety may be, it is helpful to use a rating scale or *subjective units of distress* (SUDs), as a type of assessment rubric. SUDs or subjective units of distress or discomfort (Wolpe, 1982) are elicited by asking the patient to rate their anxiety on a scale of 0 to 10, with 0 indicating total calm and 10 indicating panic-type or extremely intense anxiety. Most individuals can come up with some estimation of their anxiety using SUD's. Once they have done that, it is now possible to have a way to measure whether the tools you provide are indeed effective.

There are several tools that crisis counselors can use to help individuals manage their immediate anxiety. Some of these tools are often used as part of ongoing therapy. One such tool or technique involves **diaphragmatic breathing**. This technique for managing anxiety is said to derive from yoga and is especially helpful for managing or preventing hyperventilation associated with panic disorder. Patients are instructed to breathe in through the nose and exhale through their mouth at their own pace, without taking deep breaths. As one inhales, they should feel their stomach inflate, when they exhale, their stomach should deflate. This technique can be used to help patients lessen their current experience of anxiety without the negative side effects of many psychotropic medications. The counselor can practice this breathing exercise with the patient for a few minutes or they may use this technique in combination with a **guided imagery exercise**. In using guided imagery, it is helpful to elicit from the patient, scenes which they find the most relaxing. It is beneficial if the safe place is unique to them and not connected with any other person (e.g., if the person has a fight or conflict with that person, their "safe place" is no longer a safe place). The patient can experience the imagery with his or her eyes open or shut, whichever is more relaxing. Another tool, which is also used to reduce anxiety, is called **progressive muscle relaxation**. In this technique, patients are prompted to tighten various muscles of their body and then to suddenly relax them. They are taught muscle relaxation exercises for the arms, legs, hands, chest, buttocks, shoulders, neck, and face. When done in sequence, the person experiences a physical sensation of relaxation, like what one would feel after a vigorous physical work out.

Case Presentation: A Case of Panic Disorder in the Aftermath of Trauma

In the following case illustration, Jeff's panic attacks brought him to the emergency room for treatment.

Jeff is a 37-year-old married father of two children, who is being seen at the local emergency room. He complains of severe chest pains, panicky feelings, and he is hyperventilating. Although he has no history of cardiac problems, he was so frightened about the chest pains that he decided he should call an ambulance. After ruling out that there are no cardiac abnormalities, the examining physician asks Jeff what was going on when he began to experience the chest pain and hyperventilation. Jeff explains that the only thing he can recall was how hot he was feeling. He goes on to tell the doctor that he has had two panic attacks since coming home from Iraq approximately four months ago. Jeff states that he is in the National Guard and his unit was deployed to an area near Kandahar, Afghanistan. He was not wounded, but he states that several of his buddies were and two were killed in action. Jeff states that he has nightmares about his friends being killed and wounded. He was reluctant to seek help through the VA because he was told that it might affect future promotions or possibly even cause a discharge from the National Guard for mental health reasons.

In Jeff's case, we note that he first seeks treatment after experiencing a panic attack that mimics a heart attack. Jeff is a good illustration of someone who is experiencing symptoms of panic disorder that is directly tied to the trauma he experienced while in combat. The counselor begins by gathering some background information.

Intervention

Counselor: Jeff, when did you first experience a panic attack?

Jeff: It was about three months ago. I remember that I was driving home from work and I began to feel really hot. I started to get this tightness in my chest, but nothing like I just had. After that first panic attack I began dreading that I was going to have another one. I remember feeling my heart began to pound, it felt like I was going to explode. I couldn't breathe and I think I began to hyperventilate, like I was suffocating. I thought I was having a heart attack or something, but it started to go away, so I didn't go to an emergency room.

C: What do you think triggered this recent panic attack?

J: Well I was driving and like I said, and I started to feel really hot. I think it reminded me of when I was in Iraq. My National Guard unit was assigned to provide escort to convoys delivering supplies to one of the main bases. I remember on one of these convoys, one of our Humvees was hit by an RPG (rocket-propelled grenade). There was nothing we could do, just sit there waiting. We didn't know if we were going to be the next to get hit or not. The worst part was when we finally were ordered to move forward we had to drive past the Humvee that was still smoldering. Some of my buddies were still in there, but they were trying to get them out. I knew they weren't alive.

C: That must have been a horrible experience for you.

J: It was one of the worst days of my life and probably one of the worst days I had over there. It's funny, most of the time we'd just be sitting around, bored and nothing would happen. Then something like this.

C: So, when you had this recent panic attack it was probably brought on by your recollections of your buddies being killed in the convoy attack? Do you experience flashbacks or nightmares very often?

J: Sometimes. I'll get them in waves. Usually it's been if I see something on TV that reminds me of being back in combat.

C: Are you receiving any treatment or counseling?

J: No, the guys from my unit keep in touch with one another, that's about it. We were told about PTSD, but most of us were reluctant to go for help because we were afraid we might get discharged. One guy did go to the outpatient VA clinic and all they did was put him on medication, which he stopped taking.

C: Jeff, on a scale from 0 to 10, with 0 representing calm and 10 representing panicky feelings, where would you say you are right now?

J: I would put myself at about a 7 right now, but if you asked me that question a half hour ago, I was definitely at a 10.

C: Jeff, would you be willing to try something right now that may help calm yourself down without having to use medication?

J: Sure, at this point, I'm willing to try anything.

C: I'd like to begin by having you focus in on your breathing, just begin to breathe in through your nose and exhale through your mouth, at your own pace, not deep breathing, okay?

J: Sure, is it okay to keep my eyes open?

C: Whatever is more comfortable for you. Now as your exhaling, Jeff, imagine that you are exhaling out all of the tension and anxiety. Now imagine the muscles of your body becoming more and more relaxed, with each breath that you take. I'd now like you to imagine a safe place. Can you think of a safe place Jeff, someplace that's totally yours, a place where you can feel total safety and in control?

J: Sure, I think the place I feel the safest is in my garage, I have a work bench there, where I like to tinker on model boats. Is that what you mean?

C: Sounds fine. Now imagine yourself in your garage working on one of your boats, feeling totally relaxed, totally calm with each breath you take. As you're doing this, you begin to feel a cool breeze across your face and feel totally relaxed.

J: I'm feeling a little better, probably about a 3 or 4 right now.

C: That's good Jeff. I'll give you some information on the techniques I've described, but I'm wondering if you'd consider some follow-up at the clinic here. This way it wouldn't be connected to the VA.

J: If it will help me to avoid another panic attack, I'll try anything you say.

Case Conceptualization/Resolution

In the illustration above, the counselor is focusing on providing Jeff with some immediate tools to manage his anxiety and hopefully in doing so, can prevent another panic attack. Some recent research suggests that panic disorder is really a "breathing disorder," because when a person is predisposed to panic attacks and begin to feel even slightly anxious, they often begin to hyperventilate. The escalation of the hyperventilation brings on more anxiety. Some counselors have their clients breathe into paper bags, which increases the carbon dioxide levels in the bloodstream, thereby decreasing the subjective experience of anxiety. In some instances, these techniques may not be offered in the initial crisis session, but may be implemented in long-term counseling, once more trust is established. If some of the various techniques do not work, and Jeff were to remain in a highly anxious state, then an antianxiety medication like Buspar might be used. Benzodiazipines (e.g., Valium, Ativan, Xanax, or Klonapin) might be prescribed on a short term interim basis, because an unfortunate disadvantage to these medications is that they can promote dependence; therefore, it is best to try some of the other techniques first. Once the initial crisis has passed, it is then advisable to convince Jeff to enter counseling on either an individual or group basis. He may benefit from clinical hypnosis or Eye Movement Desensitization Response treatments (EMDR). Individuals who suffer from posttraumatic stress disorder often have great difficulty in talking about the initial trauma. This usually depends on the intensity of the trauma they experienced or witnessed or the level of guilt, shame, or personal responsibility they feel in connection with the trauma. For example, victims of sexual abuse, or childhood molestation often experience difficulty in discussing their sexual traumatization, usually because of the experience of guilt and shame. A person suffering from trauma resulting from combat like Jeff may also have trouble discussing the traumatic events for different reasons.

PRACTICAL GUIDELINES FOR CRISIS INTERVENTION FOR SOMEONE WITH PTSD AND ANXIETY

1. When assessing individuals with an anxiety disorder, it is helpful to get background information about when they first experienced anxiety; how often they experience anxiety; how they have coped with their anxiety to date; if they experience anxiety attacks and if so, how long they last; and whether they have received any prior treatment for anxiety, for example, emergency room treatment, medication, or

psychotherapeutic efforts. Similarly, when assessing someone who presents with PTSD, it is important to find out what type of trauma that individual has experienced, how recent the trauma occurred, if the trauma was experienced first-hand or witnessed, and the individual's initial reaction to the trauma. It is also important to find out if this individual has experienced other trauma in the past.

2. Gain an understanding as to how that individual experiences the trauma: for example, numbing or intrusive symptoms, hypervigilance, or anxiety reactions, such as panic symptoms like shortness of breath, rapid heartbeat, or feelings of choking.

3. Determine whether the person has experienced any periods of remission or times when they did not experience anxiety intrusive symptoms. If so, it is helpful to find out what may have accounted for these symptom-free periods. What worked for them during this period? Also, what brings on their symptoms?

4. Ask the person to rate his or her anxiety using a SUD scale described earlier.

5. Question how the person tried to cope with the anxiety. Usually before seeking treatment, most people try to cope with anxiety on their own. Here it is important to assess what the person has done to try to cope with their anxiety or panic attacks. It is not unusual for people to self-medicate, so alcohol or drug abuse should be assessed at each session.

6. Help the person to develop some immediate strategies to alleviate their anxiety, such as a relaxation techniques, diaphragmatic breathing, or guided imagery.

Crises Related to Mood Disorders

Depression affects more than 350 million people worldwide, which is why it is one of the leading causes of disability worldwide. Also, approximately 14.8 million Americans are affected by major depressive disorder (Kessler et al., 2005; World Health Organization, 2012) and approximately 6.1 million Americans live with bipolar disorder (NAMI, 2013). The two major subtypes of mood disorders are unipolar depression and bipolar disorder. unipolar depression refers to individuals who experience depressive moods which permeate their lives. The subtypes of unipolar depression (major depression and dysthymia) really differ in terms of degree or intensity. Individuals with major depression usually have difficulty functioning in everyday life. They feel pervasive sadness; they often cannot sleep, or want to sleep all the time. The same holds true for appetite. People with major depression often lose interest in life, they lack energy and nothing really seems to give them much pleasure. They usually withdraw from all social interactions. These individuals also report having difficulty in concentrating, and this often leads to difficulty with remembering things. Naturally, all of these behaviors can impact a person's ability to perform their job or function on a daily basis. With major depression, the symptoms must be persistent for at least two months before the person meets the criteria to be diagnosed with these disorders. Crises that are common to these diagnoses include instances where a person is so depressed that they cannot function. Although suicidal behavior is common among people who are experiencing major depression and bipolar disorder, there are many instances where people who experience crises related to mood disorders do not experience suicidal thoughts or ideas. What is also noteworthy in each of these mood crises, is that the individual may not seek help on his or her own, but rather at the urging of friends or family who witness the impact of mood disorder. Such was the case with Julie (described at the beginning of this chapter) whose husband, John, reached out for help.

Crisis Interventions with Mood Disorders

In providing crisis intervention services to individuals experiencing a mood disorder, it is important to first establish rapport. Do not barrage the person with too many questions and proceed at a pace that is comfortable for the client. Many depressed individuals may talk and move slowly or may not want to talk at all. It is important for counselors to show restraint and patience and not to become frustrated or uncomfortable with silence. Let's return to the case of Julie described at the beginning of the chapter to see what happens once she is seen at the mental health clinic by the crisis counselor.

Julie is a 46-year-old homemaker and mother of two sons, ages 14 and 17. She has been married to John for the past twenty years. John called his primary care physician seeking help for his wife because of his concerns about her feeling increasingly "lethargic and depressed for the past eight months. John notes, "she doesn't want to go out anyplace, not even to her women's auxiliary meetings, which she used to love going to. She won't even go to a movie or leave the house for that matter. All she does is sit around and cry all day." After some persuading on John's part, Julie agrees to speak with someone at the clinic. The background information that Julie provides indicates that her father had gone through periods of depression in his late thirties and had been hospitalized briefly for "a nervous breakdown." Julie is unable to explain exactly when or why she began to feel depressed. In exploring possible explanations, Julie explains that when she was in high school she became pregnant by her boyfriend whom she had dated before meeting John. She gave the baby up for adoption. Julie admits that she never really forgave herself for giving the baby up and now feels that she doesn't deserve to be happy. She wonders if she really loves John or if she is staying with him for "the wrong reasons."

Julie raises several issues in this brief crisis session. From the information obtained thus far Julie appears to be experiencing a crisis related to Major Depression. If you were Julie's crisis counselor, what issues do you feel are most important to address? In helping Julie to manage this crisis, the crisis counselor first establishes rapport or connection with her and conveys that the counselor is there to help. Once trust is established, background information is explored pertaining to the onset of the depressive symptoms (usually to determine if there was a specific catalyst or not). Julie is asked how she experiences the depression, and whether there are any times when she feels better than others. The crisis counselor begins to explore the amelioration or lessening of Julie's depressive symptoms. This might involve an exploration of whether Julie is a candidate for an antidepressant medication. Once this is established, the counselor also needs to gain a commitment from Julie that she will participate in counseling beyond the crisis intervention phase. Given that Julie's depression seems to be of a long-standing nature, it is probable that her issues will not be resolved within six to eight weeks. Julie's depression may have both genetic influences (since her father was apparently depressed and needed to be hospitalized), and environmental factors (Julie's decision to give up her baby for adoption and her frustration with her marriage). The focus of this crisis intervention session however, does *not* involve uncovering these causal factors, but rather to deal with the immediate crisis—Julie is depressed and has been unable to function in everyday life. During the crisis intervention sessions, it is important that the issues Julie reveals are not minimized; rather the counselor needs to assure Julie that these issues do need further in-depth exploration as her post-crisis therapy progresses. It is imperative that the crisis counselor establish a connection with Julie by **listening** to how she experiences depressive symptoms. Next, it is helpful to explore some of the recent history pertaining to Julie's symptoms in order to **assess** her present crisis.

Case Conceptualization/Crisis Resolution

Once the counselor obtains background information regarding Julie's symptoms (e.g. how long the symptoms have lasted, how intense they are, any periods where Julie feels better, any suicidal thoughts, suicidal plan etc.), at this point the goal is to begin to take some steps to stabilize Julie's life. Provided that she indeed is not suicidal, she may be started on an antidepressant medication and begin outpatient psychotherapy to help her address the issues surrounding her depression. However, the immediate goal is to help Julie through the current crisis and to encourage her to **commit** to a **plan** involving a psychiatric evaluation for antidepressant medication and ongoing therapy.

Now let's turn to another mood disorder. With bipolar disorders, there are usually two phases: The manic phase is characterized by extremely high levels of energy, talking a mile-a-minute, sometimes grandiose ideas or plans, inflated self-esteem, racing thoughts, distractibility, and excessive activity in pleasurable often risky activities (including gambling sprees, spending sprees, or sexual promiscuity). When individuals are in the midst of a manic phase, they are usually unaware of their condition or may be so energized that they don't want the feeling to stop. This becomes a problem for people with bipolar disorder who go off of their medication (like Lithium), because they "miss" the high of the manic phase. Unfortunately, "what goes up, must come down" and when people with bipolar disorder crash into depression, they often fall hard, which is one of the reasons why individuals with bipolar disorders are considered at risk for suicide. It is also not unusual for bipolar individuals to abuse alcohol or drugs, which only exacerbates their problems and can even further increase their risk for suicidal action or other dangerous risk-taking behavior. Many people with bipolar disorder are known to abuse stimulants, such as cocaine and amphetamines in an effort to perpetuate the manic high.

In the case example of Gavin presented below, he clearly exhibits many of the signs of bipolar disorder. His presentation in the crisis interview is one of non stop talking and boundless energy. Individuals with bipolar disorder can often go days without sleep or rest. They often lack awareness or insight into how outlandish their behavior has become when they are in the throes of a manic phase, or they deny the seriousness of their symptoms. They may feel they are invincible . . . until the depressive phase sets in. When the problems do begin to sink in, or when the person becomes aware of any outrageous behavior acted out during their manic phase is when he or she may be at the greatest risk for suicide. Alcohol or drug abuse further heightens their suicidal risk. Ernest Hemingway, the Pulitzer Prize winning author, was believed to suffer from bipolar disorder. He was also known as a very heavy drinker. Unfortunately, Hemingway died by his own hand when he shot himself.

Box 12.3: L-A-P-C Completed Form for Julie

Name: _____Julie_____   Age: _____46_____

Listen   **A**ssess   **P**lan   **C**ommit

L   I   S   T   E   N

I What are they saying about the crisis? *Julie reports that she has been feeling lethargic, lacks interest, cries all the time and feels down all the time.*

S What happened? *Julie reports she doesn't know why she's depressed.*

When did it happen? *Julie has been depressed for several weeks however, her depression intensified over the past week. She reports feeling guilty about having put her baby up for adoption when she was in high school.*

T What type of crisis was it? (Traumatic event, Developmental, Psychiatric, Existential?) *Psychiatric*

E

Did they mention anything that indicates danger? *No, Julie states she would*

N *never hurt herself because of having strong religious beliefs.*

Other relevant information about the crisis: *Julie also feels guilty about not being a better wife and mother over these past eight months. She has been referred by her primary care physician, therefore it will be important to ask Julie to sign a release form allowing communication.*

A   S   S   E   S   S

S **F**eeling: Is there a predominant emotional state one of:

S   anger *No*   guilt *Yes*   sadness *Yes*   hopelessness *Yes*

E   anxiety *No*   panic *No*   numbness *No*

suicidal? If yes, complete lethality assessment/suicide. *No*

homicidal? If yes, complete lethality assessment/violence. *No*

S

Acting: Is her behavior.....

active/restless   *No*   consistent with mood *Yes*

passive/withdrawn *Yes*   good eye contact   *No*

S   lethargic *Yes*

Thinking: Is she....

logical/making sense *Yes*   coherent/expressing self well *Yes*

insightful *Yes*   focused on topic *Yes*

(Continued)

(Continued)

                evasive/changing subject *No*
                Other: Any medical problems? *No*   Physical limitations? *No*
                    Hospitalizations?   *No*   Need for hospitalization? *No*

P   **L**   **A**   **N**

L   What needs to be done now? *Julie needs to continue in ongoing counseling and should be evaluated for anti-depressant medication.*

A   What alternative plans have been discussed? *Julie is agreeable to both counseling and medication evaluation.*

N   Are these plans reasonable? *Yes*   Able to be carried out? *Yes*

C   **O**   **M**   **M**   **I**   **T**

          Which plan of action have they chosen? *Julie has agreed to ongoing*

O   *counseling and has begun to take an anti-depressant.*
          Do they have the resources/support to implement the plan? *Yes, spouse is supportive*

M   Are they motivated to implement the plan? *Yes, Julie is committed to this plan.*

          What other resources/support may be needed?

M   friend *Yes*   family member *Yes*

I   neighbor mental health provider *Yes*

             public agency (law enforcement, child protective
T   services, social services) *No*

             medical (hospitalization, medication) *Yes*

The role of the crisis counselor is to ensure the patient's safety by making certain that whatever the mood when they present, it can be managed. Fortunately, medications like Lithium and more recently Depakote, Tegretol, and Neurontin have been used to successfully treat bipolar disorder. However, it often takes time for these medications to take effect, so in many instances inpatient treatment may be necessary until the person is stabilized. One of the problems with many bipolar patients is that they often discontinue the use of their medication, either because of side effects, or because they "miss" the manic high. Consequently, the crisis counselor must impress on the patient and family the importance of taking the medication regularly, not going off of it impulsively, and to need to follow the psychiatrist's orders regarding having their Lithium blood levels checked. As is indicated in the case of Gavin, it is sometimes difficult to convince a person who is in the midst of a manic phase that they need medication and ongoing counseling; however, this is often one of the main tasks that the crisis counselor must accomplish in order to come to a successful resolution of the case.

> *Gavin is a 37-year-old attorney who is currently separated from his wife, whom he had been married to for 16 years. Gavin and his wife, Stephanie have two children, ages 10 and 8. Gavin was diagnosed with bipolar disorder when he was in college. He had periods when he would stop going to class and would become totally isolated, sleeping in his dorm room for several days. Yet, when he would cycle into periods of mania, he would become gregarious, outspoken, with boundless energy. He could go without sleep for several days, and would engage in binge drinking, gambling, and spending sprees. Gavin would become incredibly creative and productive during these manic periods and would sometimes stay up and write all night. Gavin was able to get decent grades and he did well on the LSATs, which allowed him to get into a good law school. In his second year of law school, Gavin collapsed while studying for exams and was briefly hospitalized and placed on Tegretol, a mood stabilizer.*

It is not unusual for people with bipolar disorder to do well as long as they are compliant with taking their medication. However, as is common, Gavin would go off his medication because he "missed the high" he felt when he cycled into manic phases. During one of these manic phases, Gavin became involved in an extramarital affair, which resulted in Stephanie requesting a separation.

Counselor:	Hello Gavin, my name is Matt Hooper and I'm a crisis counselor here at the medical center. I understand your brother Frank brought you to the emergency room. He was concerned that you've not been sleeping lately.
Gavin:	I didn't think Frank would actually bring me here to the ER. I'm doing okay, I guess.
C:	You don't sound sure, is something bothering you?
G:	Well, I've not been sleeping very well for the past week and I have a big case coming up and I can't concentrate. I'm too restless.
C:	Does this usually happen when you have a big court case coming up?
G:	Not usually, but I've been under a lot of stress lately. My wife and I are separated and I've not seen my kids in weeks.
C:	Sounds like the separation has been rough on you?
G:	Yes, my wife feels I need to be back on my meds. I was prescribed Lithium, but it made my hands shake, so my doctor put me on Tegretol. I don't have as many side effects, but I don't like how I feel when I'm on it.
C:	What is it that you dislike?
G:	I feel blah. Lifeless I guess. I miss the high.
C:	Like how you're feeling now?
G:	Yeah, being able to party all night, go without sleep. I love the feeling of exhilaration.
C:	Is there anything you don't like about the way you're feeling now?
G:	Well, being separated for starters. Not seeing my kids. Not being able to concentrate, not being able to focus on work. Not to mention gambling sprees,

spending sprees, and getting involved with a much younger woman who wants me to divorce my wife and marry her.

C: Sounds like you've been going through a lot of stress.

G: A lot. I guess I should be back on my meds huh?

PRACTICAL GUIDELINES FOR CRISIS INTERVENTION FOR SOMEONE WITH MOOD DISORDERS

1. Unless the client has already been diagnosed with a mood disorder, it is important to do a thorough assessment. Are the current mood disturbances or coping difficulties triggered by an external event (e.g., a breakup in a relationship, job loss, etc.), or did they come up without rhyme or reason? In the absence of a triggering event, an endogenous mood disorder may be the reason for the current mood disturbance.

2. In obtaining a history of the mood disorder, determine how often the mood disturbance occurs, and do they change over time? Determine whether the client uses any coping mechanisms when his or her mood is at its worse.

3. Do a lethality assessment. Since mood disturbances are one of the risk factors for suicide, ask the client if he or she is having any suicidal thoughts, impulses, or intentions. Do they have a suicide plan and is the plan one that he or she could carry out? (For example, one client might say, "I'm going to take a handful of pills," which may be a vague suicide threat; whereas another client may say, "I'm going to blow my brains out," and they have firearms at home. (See suicidal risk factor assessments in Chapter 10 on Suicide, Homicide, and Lethality.)

4. Listen to your client without being judgmental or critical. Hear what they have to say. Expect however, that there may be periods of silence, especially when counseling someone with major depression. The opposite is true when interviewing someone with bipolar disorder who is experiencing mania.

5. Don't jump to making suggestions or recommendations about a crisis plan until you feel that you have established a positive working rapport with your client.

Crises Related to Schizophrenia and Psychotic Disorders

It is estimated that approximately 2.4 million American adults are diagnosed with Schizophrenia (Reiger et al., 1993). According to the National Alliance on Mental Illness (2015d) approximately 1.1 % of the U.S. adult population is estimated to suffer with schizophrenia. It is calculated that schizophrenic patients occupy 25 % of all American hospital beds, and (excluding elderly patients with cognitive disorders), two-thirds of all psychiatric beds (Trotman, Mittal, Tessner, & Walker, 2013). Interestingly, rates of schizophrenia seem to be equal in other countries. It appears that African Americans and European Americans are affected by schizophrenia at equal rates. Those living in urban environments seem to have slightly higher rates when compared to those living in more rural settings, presumably because of differences in stress levels. Regarding gender differences, there are slightly higher rates of schizophrenia for men than women.

In most instances, schizophrenia begins in the late teens and early twenties. Schizophrenia is commonly known as a "thought disorder," because people with schizophrenia often experience perceptual disturbances, such as auditory, visual, tactile (touch), or olfactory (smell) hallucinations or delusional thinking (which is a false personal belief based on an incorrect inference about external reality even when evidence to the contrary is presented). Generally, auditory hallucinations are more common in individuals who experience schizophrenia. Although psychoses can occur because of a toxic reaction to certain drugs, alcohol, or medications, the majority of psychotic reactions are thought to represent a class of mental disorders known as schizophrenia. The symptoms of schizophrenia are grouped into two major categories: *positive symptoms* that include hallucinations; delusions; difficulty communicating thoughts logically; abnormal movements, such as rocking or head banging; and paranoia or anxiety, and *negative symptoms,* such as anhedonia (inability to experience pleasure in day-to-day life); lack of ability to socialize or connect with others; lack of energy; and difficulty with maintaining concentration. Usually when individuals with schizophrenia present in crisis, it is when they are experiencing active and acute *positive symptoms* (as in the case of Robert described below), as opposed to negative symptoms. Positive symptoms are often more serious and more distressing to the individual and their family. At this point, they are more likely to act out or be referred for psychiatric evaluation. Schizophrenia often makes its first appearance in the late teens or early twenties and interestingly, those individuals with acute positive symptoms are considered to have a better prognosis than individuals with chronic, long-term, negative symptoms. It should be noted that schizophrenics are also at a high risk for suicide.

In order to be able to effectively manage crises related to schizophrenia, it is important to first understand its symptomatology. As indicated above, schizophrenia is commonly referred to as a "thought disorder" because this disorder attacks logical thought processes and involves distorted perceptions of reality. Delusional thoughts are common, such as delusions of grandeur ("I am Jesus Christ"); or delusions of persecution ("The CIA is trying to steal my thoughts"). Hallucinations are also a common symptom and are reported by 75% of newly admitted schizophrenics (90% are auditory, i.e., hearing voices; 40% are visual, i.e., seeing things that are not really there) (Ludwig, 1985). Schizophrenics often are convinced that their delusions and hallucinations are real (Maxmen & Ward, 1995) and are not convinced by rational explanations to the contrary. (This was evident in the book *A Beautiful Mind* [Nasar, 1998] based on the life of Nobel Laureate, John Nash. Dr. Nash was convinced that Russian codes could be deciphered from American newspapers and magazines.) It is only once that a schizophrenic person is in remission that might admit, "I don't let those thoughts about the CIA bother me anymore."

It is important to keep in mind, that although there are some people with severe mental illness who experience violent behaviors, it is important to note that violence-prone individuals are in the minority. Those who are most likely to act out violently are often individuals who refuse treatment and/or refuse to take medication to help control their symptoms.

Crisis Intervention with Schizophrenia: The two most essential components for successfully intervening with people suffering with schizophrenia are **safety** and **stabilization**.

The safety factor comes into play both in terms of ensuring the safety of the schizophrenic and those around them. It appears that approximately 50% of those with schizophrenia are painfully aware of their symptoms and the devastating effects of this disorder on their ability to function in everyday life. The other 50% are oblivious to their symptoms or they are convinced that the distortions of thought and perception are accurate; therefore, they do not experience turmoil over these symptoms, although their family and friends do. It is not unusual then to find that about 50% of schizophrenics also experience depression. It is estimated that about 10% of schizophrenics do commit suicide and that 20% attempt it (Maxmen & Ward, 1995). Interestingly, most schizophrenics do not commit suicide in the midst of the psychosis, but rather in the aftermath or while in remission when they become more painfully aware of their illness. Those with better premorbid adjustment and higher education levels are more at risk for suicide. It seems that these individuals probably have higher expectations of themselves, so it is not unusual to find that they are hit harder by a depression in the aftermath of a psychotic episode. Therefore, safety concerns cannot be too highly emphasized.

Regarding stabilization, often antipsychotic medications are used to control delusional and hallucinatory symptoms. Phenothiazines refer to a class of antipsychotic medications that have been quite effective in ameliorating psychotic symptoms. Drugs known by their trade names, such as Thorazine, Haldol, and Stelazine were considered to be major discoveries in psychiatry when they were introduced in the 1950s. Unfortunately, as effective as the antipsychotic medications have been in controlling psychotic symptoms, they also produce major side effects, some of which mimic Parkinson's Disease (e.g., hand tremors, lip smacking, facial grimacing). These side effects are sometimes referred to as tardive dyskinesias. Some of the newer antipsychotic medications have fewer of these Parkinsonian-like side effects, such as Clozaril, Zyprexa, or Risperdal.

Case Presentation: A Crisis Involving Schizophrenia

Robert is 25 years old. He has come to the local mental health clinic today, complaining that he is "hearing voices." Robert lives in one of the group boarding homes in the area; unfortunately, it is not one of the better ones. He often goes without his medication, because no one is there to supervise that he actually takes his medication. He states that it has been about three weeks since he last took his Risperdal and he is now beginning to feel "edgy." Robert describes that he usually starts to feel restless and he then hears voices telling him that someone is trying to poison his food and steal his brain. When he felt this way once before, the examining psychiatrist had Robert admitted to a state psychiatric hospital for observation. When asked about the voices, Robert explains that the voices he hears are "from Satan" and that they also tell him to do "bad things." Fortunately, Robert has not been in trouble with the law before this and he usually knows enough that when he begins to feel this way, it is time to go back on his medication.

In the case of Robert, we see someone who most likely manifests paranoid schizophrenia. He fears that someone is trying to poison his food and steal his brain. He also alludes to hearing voices from Satan that are telling him to "do bad things;" although he does not explain what these "bad things" are. He also tells the crisis counselor that he had been in a state hospital and that he also had been taking Risperdal, all of which are indicators that Robert was most likely diagnosed with schizophrenia. When a person diagnosed with schizophrenia whose symptoms have been successfully controlled by medication begins to re-experience psychotic symptoms, we refer to them as *decompensating*. Decompensation can occur rather abruptly, or can take place over the course of several weeks.

Naturally, when making a thorough assessment, other corroborating information is needed. Here, it is helpful to talk with a reliable family member, or get permission to look at Robert's prior medical records, or talk with the psychiatrist prescribing his medication. What is difficult however, in working with individuals with paranoid schizophrenia, is that they are suspicious of any attempts to help them and may therefore be unlikely to sign a release for prior treatment records.

It is likely that Robert may not be willing to sign any releases. It does seem that he has some insight into his condition, as he states that when he begins to feel out of touch with reality, he realizes that it is time for him to go back on his medication. Stabilization then entails making certain that Robert receives the correct medication and at the proper dose. As with bipolar disorders where a person may go off of their medication against medical advice, it is common that schizophrenics discontinue their medication in order to lessen the side effects. Another complicating factor toward stabilization, is that many schizophrenics sometimes stop taking their medication because of poor supervision in their living situation (e.g., a boarding home), or because they are abusing alcohol or other drugs and do not like the effect that is produced by combining the medication with drinking or illicit drug abuse. Alcohol and drug abuse is a common factor in psychotic decompensation. Once rapport has been established, the crisis counselor interviewing Robert tries to explore factors that may have resulted in his most recent compensation in order to determine what level of treatment is necessary.

Intervention

Counselor: Robert, you mentioned earlier that the voices you hear tell you to do "bad things." Could you tell me what kind of "bad things?"

Robert: If I tell you, you're not going to lock me up in a psych ward, are you?

C: Robert, it is important that we talk about this; I don't want to lock you up, I just need to get a sense of what types of "bad things" you've been hearing.

R: (hesitates) Well, the voices tell me to hurt people. People that are bad.

C: Do the voices tell you how to hurt them or who to hurt?

R: No, just that I should hurt bad people and that I'm bad too. I think the voice is the devil's voice.

C: Robert, you don't seem to be a bad person; are there any other things that you've done or think about that make you bad?

R: No, nothing else that I can remember. I just want the voices to go away. I know I should take my medicine, but I hate how it makes me feel.

C: What do you dislike about it?

R: It makes me feel numb and spaced out. My face starts to twitch when I take it and I'm afraid people are going to know I'm crazy, and then they'll really make fun of me.

C: So, when you feel that people know you are taking the medication that is when you stop taking it?

R: Yeah . . . but that's when the thoughts about being poisoned or about the CIA trying to steal my thoughts come back really bad.

C: It sounds like you usually feel and think better when you're taking the medication, except for the twitches right?

R: Yeah, I really hate the twitches and my hands shaking all the time.

C: What other things do you do during the day?

R: Well, I wake up and then have coffee and sit in the dayroom of the boarding home where I live. Then I walk around town until it's time for lunch. Then after lunch I walk around some more until dinner time.
        Is that what you mean?

C: Yes. Were you also in a day program at one time? I thought I saw that in your chart?

R: I was in a program at Central Medical Center, but I was getting up late and the bus stopped picking me up.

C: How did you like the program?

R: It was good when I went. They gave you lunch, we had groups to work on different skills, and we got to go bowling twice a week in the winter.

C: Here's what I'd like to do. I'd like you to come into the hospital for a couple of days so we can get you started back on the medication and make sure the twitches don't come back. In the interim, I can call over to Central Medical Center and arrange for you to begin the program again.

R: What about my not getting up on time.

C: We can work on that. We can get you an alarm clock and I'll talk with the boarding home manager about making sure they wake you up. Until you get used to waking up on your own again. What do you think?

R: That sounds good. You're not going to ship me off to the state hospital, are you?

C: No, I think we can get you feeling better again.

R: Okay, just as long as you're not going to put me back in the state hospital?

C: No, I think you're going to do better in our hospital. We may look into getting you into a different boarding home. A better one than the one you're currently living. Would you be okay with that?

R: Sure, just as long as I'm not going back to the hospital.

Case Conceptualization/Crisis Resolution

In this case example, there are several noteworthy issues. First, regarding safety, when Robert refers to hearing voices that tell him to do "bad things," the counselor makes certain that Robert is not harboring plans to hurt someone else or himself. If that was the case, Robert needs to be hospitalized immediately. The goal of this crisis session is to make certain that Robert is safe, that he goes back on his medication, and that he begins to go to the day program again to avoid a future decompensation. The other issue regarding stabilization is brought out in the discussion about Robert returning to his medication. Fortunately, Robert can see more advantages than disadvantages to resuming his medication at this time. This is not always the case and it may take some persuading and convincing before some patients agree to go back on their medication. There are some medications (e.g., Artane, Benedryl, or Cogentin) that are designed to control some of the side effects that upset Robert. Often stabilization is rather difficult because a particular antipsychotic medication may work well with some patients and not with others. Also, certain doses work well, while other doses can produce stuporous or drugged states. The role of the psychiatrist is to adjust the medications to produce the greatest benefits with the least amount of side effects.

Stabilization concerns are also addressed when the counselor brings up the issue of Robert's going back to the day program. Day hospitals or day programs have been quite effective in providing schizophrenic patients with very much needed social support and social interaction, along with social and occupational skills training. Day program staff can also monitor each patient's overall physical and psychological condition. In many instances, astute counselors can head off a full-blown psychotic decompensation by recognizing the telltale symptoms of a pending break. However, what is problematic is that schizophrenic patients often drop out of these day programs due to lack of transportation, lack of motivation, they stop taking their medication, or because of alcohol and drug abuse. As a result, these patients often become the revolving door patients who police bring to emergency rooms repeatedly, or who are arrested for vagrancy, or worse.

GUIDELINES FOR CRISIS INTERVENTION FOR THOSE WITH SCHIZOPHRENIA

Murphy and Moller (1997) and Moller and Murphy (1998) offer some helpful strategies for counselors working with individuals with hallucinations and/or delusions. These recommendations include:

1. Establish a trusting interpersonal relationship. In doing so, express your feelings in an open, honest, direct manner.

2. Assess the hallucination and/or delusion, including duration, intensity, and frequency. Be patient and listen when the patient is ready to talk.

3. Focus on the symptoms and ask the person to describe what is happening. The goal is to understand the symptoms experienced or demonstrated. Pay attention to the content of the hallucination or delusion, for example, some delusions are nihilistic involving themes of nonexistence or annihilation; some are grandiose involving an exaggerated sense of self-importance; and some are persecutory involving themes of being attacked, persecuted, conspired against, or cheated.

4. Identify if drugs and alcohol have been used, including prescription drugs. Morphine and codeine often induce hallucinations in some people.

5. If asked, point out simply that you are not experiencing the same stimuli. The goal is to let the person know what is actually happening in the environment. Do not argue about what is not occurring. When a hallucination occurs, do not leave the person alone. Some auditory hallucinations called "command hallucinations" may be perceived by the client as a "command" to hurt themselves or someone else.

6. Help the person describe and compare the present and recently past hallucinations.

7. Encourage the person to observe and describe the thoughts, feelings, and actions (both present and past), as they relate to the hallucination.

8. Help the person describe needs that may be reflected in the content of the hallucination.

9. Help the person identify what triggers the hallucination.

10. Suggest and reinforce the use of interpersonal relationships as a means of helping manage their symptoms (e.g., talking with someone they trust who can give them corrective feedback).

11. Identify how symptoms of psychosis have affected the person's ability to carry out activities of daily living. It is also helpful not to push the person to disclose too quickly and to let them know that they have a right to say, "I don't want to answer that question at this time." Also, don't play "analyst" by trying to interpret the hallucination or delusion, it is better to listen and try to gain an understanding of what the person is experiencing (Bohen, 2002).

CRISIS RELATED TO PERSONALITY DISORDERS

When certain personality traits become inflexible and maladaptive, or if they cause significant impairment in everyday functioning or emotional distress, these traits may constitute a personality disorder. According to the *DSM-5* (American Psychiatric Association, 2013), there are currently ten subtypes of personality disorders. There are a few disorders however, that are most likely to experience crises. Cluster B or dramatic erratic subtypes are those most likely to present in crisis. Cluster B is composed of the following personality disorder subtypes: Narcissistic personality disorder, borderline personality disorder, histrionic personality disorder, and antisocial personality disorder. Individuals with narcissistic personality disorders are characterized by extreme self-centeredness, a grandiose sense of self-importance, preoccupations with unlimited success, power, wealth, and a drive to be admired. Individuals with borderline personality disorder (BPD) often experience tremendous difficulty in modulating or regulating emotions, especially when it comes to tolerating boredom, loneliness, or feelings of rejection or abandonment. Individuals with histrionic personality disorder are often characterized by a tremendous need to be the center of attention and often experience a great deal of drama in their everyday lives. They are often the "life of the party" and can be quite seductive and charming, but they can also be very prone to experiencing crisis. Individuals with antisocial personality disorder (APD) are known for their lack of conscience and a lack of remorse. These individuals are also known to commit criminal acts and are quite adept at manipulating or conning others. Individuals with APD also exhibit a lack of concern for the well-being of others. It is helpful to think of APD as existing on a spectrum. At one end of this spectrum are white-collar criminals, con artists, unscrupulous and corrupt politicians, while at the other end of the spectrum are rapists, murderers, and serial killers.

Out of all the aforementioned personality disorders, individuals with borderline personality disorder are considered the most likely to present in crisis and may be among the most difficult and most demanding individuals to work with, mostly because of their difficulties with emotional regulation. One of the commonalties shared by individuals with borderline personality disorder is that they appear to constantly experience crises because of the inability to self-soothe, and lack of poor coping skills. In providing crisis counseling to individuals with various types of personality disorders (e.g., especially the Cluster B personality disorders, such as narcissistic, borderline, or histrionic personality disorder), it is important to make certain that they are not harboring suicidal ideation or plans. It is possible for some individuals with these disorders to act on suicidal ideation in the face of rejection or abandonment. In that case, take the same precautions as with any suicidal patient, such as those discussed earlier in this chapter.

Individuals with narcissistic personality disorders (NPD) are characterized by their incredible self-centeredness, their grandiose sense of self-importance, preoccupations with unlimited success, power, wealth, and their drive to be admired. Individuals with NPD have difficulty in accepting rejection or criticism; therefore, when confronted with rejection or with their own imperfections (e.g., if turned down for a job or relationship), he or she may experience a crisis. These crises can take the form of either "narcissistic rage" (Ronningstam, 2005), or suicidal depression. It is as if the Narcissistic Personality individual is saying, "How could someone possibly do this to me, don't they realize how important and special I am?" One narcissistic patient, when faced with the prospect that his wife was going to divorce him, was in a continual state of crisis. He would vacillate between statements like "How can she leave me, how could she do this to me?" to "I was the best thing she ever had and once she realizes this, she'll come crawling back on her hands and knees to me." Narcissists are usually unaware of their impact on others. They are often so caught up in themselves they fail to see how their actions and behaviors impact on others. Naturally, this lends to difficulty in both work and love relationships (Cavaiola & Lavender, 2000).

In counseling someone with narcissistic personality disorder, often the impact of the initial crisis can be reduced by gaining an understanding of the narcissist's sense of wounded pride. By bolstering the client's damaged ego, by emphasizing past achievements, or by stressing his or her superiority to others, the crisis counselor may be able to help lessen the impact of the crisis. Although it may sound somewhat disingenuous to bolster the ego of someone so self-centered, remember, the goal of crisis intervention is not to provide in-depth psychotherapy. Instead, the counselor works within a short-term framework assisting the client in resolving the initial crisis. While individuals with narcissistic personality disorder are sometimes admitted for psychiatric hospitalizations during a crisis, they tend to leave early against medical advice, once the initial crisis has passed. The following is a brief case example.

Charles is a 28-year-old, single, investment broker who has just been told by his girlfriend of two years, that she is leaving him and running off with his best friend, Jerry. He has come to the local hospital-based mental health clinic because of suicidal ideation. Charles states to the crisis counselor that he had planned to take a bottle of pills when he learned that his girlfriend was leaving him. He can't understand why she would do this to him, although he then goes on to explain that the girlfriend often complained that "everything was always about Charles" and her feelings or concerns were never taken into account. Later, Charles adds that he had cheated on his girlfriend several times throughout the relationship and although he regrets having done so now, it appears that he felt entitled to his affairs.

Case Conceptualization/Crisis Resolution

Although Charles may not necessarily need to be in an inpatient unit, his having threatened suicide may make this the safest option until he is stabilized. Charles suffers from what Ronningstam (1998) refers to as narcissistic rage. This often comes about in reaction to a feeling of being wounded by others ("how dare she break up with me"). In the immediate crisis, Charles needs to feel supported by his counselor, and that he is being heard. Otherwise, Charles will direct all his rage toward the counselor. Charles is agreeable to the suggested **plan** that he admit into an inpatient unit where his needs can be better attended to and where he can get all the attention that he feels he so well deserves. While this may seem like the counselor is feeding into Charles's sense of feeling special or entitled (traits common to those with narcissistic personality disorder), it is probably best to be safe. Since Charles reports no history of violence, it is unlikely that he would harm or act out against Tara. However, it is better to further assess his risk level while Charles is in the inpatient unit.

The second type of personality disorder that is most likely to present in crisis is the borderline personality (BPD). Many mental health professionals often have difficulty treating individuals with borderline personality disorder. Patients with BPD often appear to be in a constant state of crisis because of the tremendous difficulty they have in regulating emotions. Attempts to set appropriate boundaries with someone with BPD may be interpreted as a major rejection that could send him or her into an emotional downslide or into an angry rage. People with borderline personality disorder often have difficulty tolerating boredom and have intense fears of abandonment. According to Linehan (1993), borderline personality disorder is marked by "emotional dysregulation," suggesting that people with BPD often have difficulty coping with the daily ups and downs or emotional upsets that most people experience. They seem to lack the ability to self-soothe or comfort themselves especially during times of disappointment, apprehension, or despair. Because of this emotional dysregulation, individuals with BPD are often prone to suicidal acting out and self-mutilation (e.g., cutting arms or legs with knives or razor blades) is common. These behaviors may be an attempt to regulate overwhelming emotions or sometimes to feel something because feelings of emptiness or boredom have become intolerable (Linehan, 1993). According to Maxmen and Ward (1995), "Many slash their wrists or douse lit cigarettes on their arms, not to kill or hurt themselves, but to *feel* something ('I feel so dead, cutting myself is the only way I know I'm alive') or to relieve tension." (pp. 407–408).

Borderline personality disorder is also characterized by impulsivity, unstable and intense interpersonal relationships, fears of abandonment, inappropriate and intense anger, identity confusion, problems with being alone, and chronic feelings of emptiness and boredom. Individuals with borderline personality disorder are sometimes difficult to assess especially in a crisis situation, because they often present with so many overwhelming problems. He or she may seek crisis services because of a relationship loss, sexual acting out, alcohol or drug abuse, a fight or argument, anxieties over sexual indiscretions, suicidal behavior, or some other impulsive act. Individuals with BPD also tend to be involved in very intense "all or nothing" types of relationships. Most will feel that anything less than total love and devotion is considered rejection or hate. People with BPD are very demanding of people's attention and affection; however, when others do not give this to them unconditionally, they often go into tirades and reject that person. At which point, he or she may then look for another savior and repeat the same pattern (Hooley & St. Germain, 2013). With borderline personality disorder there are very few shades of gray, as they tend to see others as either hero-saviors or as rotten bastards. He or she often includes therapists, family, and friends in these all-or-nothing perceptions.

Case Presentation: Borderline Personality Disorder

Sara is 23 years old and presently lives with her parents and her younger brother. She called the hotline stating that she had cut her arms and didn't want to "live anymore." Her parents agreed to bring her to the emergency room for an evaluation and to talk with the crisis counselor. Sara explains that when her boyfriend, Sean, had broken up with her, she felt "empty" and could not stand living without him. She states that she has a difficult time with being alone and that she cannot tolerate boredom. Sara admits that sometimes she makes superficial cuts on her arms and thighs with a razor blade when she feels "empty." She also engages in a lot of risky behaviors, such as getting drunk and racing down the highway, or going out to bars and getting picked up by strange guys.

Sara has many classic symptoms of Borderline Personality. She reports having an intense and stormy relationship with her boyfriend, Sean. She also talks about feelings of emptiness and boredom since the relationship ended. Sara reports suicidal ideation and self-mutilative behavior. One of the first rules in working with someone with BPD is to establish a contract to stop any and all acting-out behaviors. Unfortunately, individuals with BPD often relate to others by way of acting out their feelings impulsively, so to expect that someone with BPD will respond to behavioral contracting is unrealistic. In many instances, any therapeutic contract is developed with the understanding that the person has certain goals and the counselor can help them attain those goals. However, the crisis counselor would need to examine whether Sara's goals are attainable (e.g., to reunite with Sean or make him into the kind of boyfriend she wants). Obviously, these things are not going to happen. In the intervention below, the crisis counselor tries to offer encouraging support to Sara, and set boundaries while making certain that she does not interpret these remarks as abandonment.

Intervention

Counselor: Sara, from what you've told me so far, it sounds like the breakup with Sean was really tough for you, but now you're saying he was a loser. How long did you and Sean date?

Sara: Only about two months or so. We met in the Roadside Bar down on Route 7. He was really cute. We slept together the first night, although that's nothing new, I guess. I remember I was pretty drunk that night. I had just broken up with Doug . . . I found out he was married and had a kid, the rat bastard.

C: Sounds like you've been having a rough time with relationships.

S: I keep meeting up with losers. Maybe I should stop hanging out at the Roadside Bar.

C: That may help. Sara, you mentioned before about cutting yourself. Have you done that recently?

S: Last night I did, after getting off the phone with Sean. He was being such a pain in the neck. After I got off the phone with him, I was feeling really upset, like I was going to explode or something, so I cut my thighs with a razor blade, not deep though; I didn't want to kill myself. Do you want to see the cuts?

C: Maybe we can have our medical doctor check the cuts out later. Were you also drinking last night?

S: Yes, I had about three vodka and cranberry juices. Or maybe it was four, I lost count after a while.

C: Sara, I'd like to suggest something and see if you would be willing to make an agreement with me. Would you hear me out?

S: Sure.

C: Well, it sounds like there is a pattern to the types of problems you've been having. You get involved with guys who probably are not good for you, then you end up breaking up and feeling suicidal, or cutting yourself with razor blades because you feel empty or abandoned; is that right? Then when you add alcohol to the mix, things get even more out of hand. What I'd like to recommend is that we write up an agreement that you will stop these things that seem to be hurting you in the long run. What do you think?

S: What do you mean, stop hanging out at the Roadside Bar? What would I do, sit home?

C: We would have to come up with other things you could do that would be enjoyable or other ways to be social.

S: But, you mean stop having sex with strangers, stop drinking, and stuff, right?

C: Yes, exactly. Would you agree to that for now and also agree to continue with counseling? I don't want to see you getting into situations where you end up hurting yourself.

S: What if I do stop, does that mean you'll dump me or stop the counseling?

C: No, there is still a lot of work for us to do, but if you stop these dangerous behaviors, then at least that would be a beginning. Would you agree that we put some of these things on paper?

Case Conceptualization/Crisis Resolution

In this crisis session, the counselor is focused on trying to set some realistic limits to Sara's behavior; the counselor is also trying to support her emotionally while at the same time convey a sense of reassurance that Sara will not be "dumped," if she is making progress. The counselor also needs to come up with a crisis prevention plan with Sara. In other words, if she were to feel anger, rage, suicidal feelings, or become self-mutilative, then she agrees to call the crisis hotline and talk with the counselor on call. There are naturally advantages and disadvantages to this type of a plan. The advantage is that it does not promote dependency on just one counselor and allows Sara to get other points of view when she is feeling upset. The disadvantage is that individuals with borderline personality disorder often engage in other calculating behaviors, like playing one staff member off against the other, or manipulating a staff member who may not be familiar with the importance of boundary setting with BPD clients. The other disadvantage is that individuals with borderline personality disorder often are demanding of time and resources; therefore, they may call many times, and for the least little thing. For example, one BPD patient called her therapist's emergency contact phone number every Sunday morning. Weekends tend to be particularly difficult for BPD clients because they may be more prone to feeling lonely and bored. Eventually, the therapist had this patient plan her weekends during their sessions and encouraged her to call to report in how the weekend plans went. Eventually, the patient stopped calling once she realized that she was capable of adequately planning her weekend time independent of her therapist.

GUIDELINES FOR CRISIS INTERVENTION WITH BORDERLINE PERSONALITY DISORDER

Linehan's work with borderline personality disorder individuals is some of the most highly regarded work in the field. Her dialectical behavior therapy (DBT) provides counselors with effective strategies for both short-term and long-term case management of borderline personality disorder. The following guidelines are derived from some of Linehan's (1995) recommendations for use at the time of crisis and pertain to engaging the patient in ongoing treatment. The major goal is to encourage the patient to commit to ongoing therapy:

1. Encourage the patient to enter and stay in treatment for a specified period of time;

2. Encourage the patient to commit to attending all scheduled therapy sessions;

3. Work on reducing suicidal and self-injurious behavior; and

4. Engage the client in skills training that focuses on regulation of mood, and that increases problem solving.

It has been estimated that approximately 75% of individuals with borderline personality disorder are prescribed psychotropic medication to help alleviate some of the aforementioned emotional symptoms (Bradford & Holt, 2015). In some instances, psychotropic medication may be of some use in helping to stabilize the extreme mood fluctuations inherent in borderline personality disorder. According to research literature, MAO inhibitors (a subclass of antidepressant drugs and antipsychotic drugs in low doses for irritability) have proved effective in treating the transient emotional lability of some borderline individuals (Cornelius, Soloff, Perel, & Ulrich, 1993). Two studies compared the effectiveness of different medications for treating BPD. The first meta-analysis study compared the effectiveness of mood stabilizers, antidepressants, and antipsychotics in treating specific BPD symptoms, such as anger and depression (Mercer, Douglass, & Links, 2009). There were indications that some mood stabilizers were effective in reducing anger, while antidepressant medication was not very effective in treating depressive symptoms. However, antidepressants were moderately effective in treating anger. Antipsychotic medications also were moderately effective in treating anger, but were not effective in treating depression. In the second study (Haw & Stubbs, 2011), of 79 individuals with BPD who received treatment in an inpatient program, 80% were treated with medication. Most often these individuals were prescribed antipsychotics or antidepressants in hopes of alleviating certain BPD symptoms. Although overall the use of medication was found to be disappointing, the antipsychotic Clozapine was found most helpful. Unfortunately, benzodiazipines like Valium, Librium, or Tranxene can disinhibit borderline patients and may create more impulsivity and possible substance dependence. According to the research noted above, tricyclic antidepressants, such as Elavil and Triavil were not found very effective. Some anticonvulsant drugs, such as carbamazine (Tegretol) when prescribed off-label, were found to reduce self-destructive behavior in individuals with BPD. Use caution when referring individuals with borderline

Box 12.4: I Don't Believe in God, but I Believe in Lithium

On June 25, 2015, an article appeared in the *New York Times* with the above-referenced title, Jaime Lowe recounts her experiences when as a teenager she was admitted to a psychiatric institute after experiencing what appears to have been a Bipolar Manic type episode. To help manage her symptoms of boundless energy, little need for sleep, expansive mood, grandiosity, and rapid speech she was given a medication called Lithium that was approved by the U.S. Food & Drug Administration in 1970 (Lithium had been approved in France in 1967; Great Britain in 1966; Germany in 1967; and Italy in 1970). This naturally occurring salt (i.e., lithium carbonate) found in certain types of tree bark and also in vast Lithium mines in South America, was known for its curative powers long before it became an FDA approved drug. For example, at one time, the soft drink *7-Up* used to contain lithium. Also, back in the 19th century, tourists would flock to bathe in the lithium springs near Steamboat, Colorado. As reported in Lowe's article, initially lithium was tested as a possible treatment for schizophrenia, PTSD, and depression; however, in clinical trials, it proved to be most effective in treating Bipolar 1 Disorder, and in many instances brought about relief from Bipolar symptoms within 10 to 15 days.

Source: Lowe, J. (2015, June 15). "I Don't Believe in God, but I Believe in Lithium," *The New York Times.*

personality disorder for medication evaluations, as medication is often approached on a "trial and error" basis with this population (Rogers & Acton, 2012).

The aforementioned section on personality disorders raises the issue of whether there are "crisis-prone patients." According to Freeman and Fusco (2000), the crisis-prone patient is one who may become easily overwhelmed by emotions, thus have a more reactive style that lacks the ability to appropriately assess situations and use his or her strengths, supports, and resources. This lack of coping resources and coping skills often results in impulsive or dramatic gestures (e.g., suicidal gestures) in order to decrease the anxiety brought on by the crisis. The crisis-prone patient is also likely to misinterpret statements made by others in negative ways or tends to exaggerate the events he or she experiences that then only adds to the feeling of being overwhelmed. As stated by Freeman and Fusco (2000), "The high-arousal individuals are either in crisis, about to go in crisis or live their lives with crisis always on the horizon" (p. 28).

CRISES INVOLVING NEUROCOGNITIVE DISORDERS

As baby boomers are aging, crisis counselors expect to see more and more cases involving what the *DSM-5* refers to as neurocognitive disorders (ND). Two of the most prevalent disorders within this category are delirium and dementia, both of which can contribute to crisis situations. The symptoms of delirium include confusion, memory disturbance, disorientation to time, place, person, poor decision making and poor judgment, delusions, bizarre behavior, and in some instances hallucinations. At first glance, these symptoms may seem similar to schizophrenia or psychotic disorders however, there are major distinctions. For example, usually schizophrenia develops slowly over time, while delirium often develops abruptly. Schizophrenia tends to be chronic and progressive. On the other hand, if the cause can be determined, delirium can often be reversed; for example, in instances where delirium may be caused by changes in blood pressure medication, by reactions to other medications, or other metabolic changes (e.g., electrolyte imbalances).

Dementia often occurs slowly and may often be imperceptible at first as gaps in memory may be chalked up to "senior moments" or normal aging. However, usually short-term memory problems become progressive and more problematic over time. It's not usual, as an example, for people with dementia to forget to turn the stove off, or to lock the door. Some may forget their way home and drive around for hours becoming more and more confused and agitated. (Several states have instituted "Silver Alerts" for when people with dementia who wander off and become lost and disoriented while walking or driving).

CRISIS CASES INVOLVING DELIRIUM AND DEMENTIA

Bob Jones is a 35-year-old divorced father of two daughters. When Bob and his wife divorced, Bob moved back in with his 68-year-old father. Bob's father was a widower who liked playing golf with his friends at least three times a week. When Bob's father was told he needed a hip replacement, he asked Bob to take care of the house and his dog while he was recuperating in the hospital. Bob went to visit his father as soon as he was transferred from the recovery room to his own hospital room. Bob's father was agitated and was not making sense. He didn't recognize his son and instead asked him not to tell their sergeant that he forgot to clean his rifle. Bob realized that his father was not making sense and was treating him like one of his army buddies. Bob went to get the nurse to ask her what was happening.

Bob's father was most likely experiencing delirium brought on by the anesthesia he was given for his hip surgery. As mentioned above, delirium can sometimes be brought on by metabolic changes; and generally, older people have more difficulty in metabolizing anesthesia when compared to younger adults. It is fortunate that Bob's father was hospitalized as it is more difficult to manage this type of crisis were it to occur at home or in the community.

When in states of delirium, individuals can sometimes pose a danger to themselves or to others. Alice is a 62-year-old college professor who currently teaches full time at a prestigious university. Alice began to experience difficulties with her short-term memory about two years ago, when she reported her frustration over misplacing her apartment keys or her lecture notes. Her husband and daughter initially assumed that Alice was just under a lot of stress and had a lot on her mind. However, one day they received a call from the police, stating that Alice was at the police station and reported being lost and unable to find her way home. This caused concerns among Alice's family members who were uncertain how to help Alice.

Alice's story is similar to Julianne Moore's character in the film "Still Alice," which chronicles the slow, progressive nature of dementia (Alzheimer's type) in a woman who is an accomplished university professor and neurolinguistics expert.

It is not unusual for the police to become involved when individuals with dementia become lost or disoriented. In instances where these individuals live alone, with no family or friends nearby, it may be months or years before someone from the community recognizes the need for assistance.

MEDICAL CONDITIONS & MEDICATIONS
THAT CAN MIMIC PSYCHIATRIC SYMPTOMS

Earlier, it was mentioned that psychiatric crises are often complex and may involve a multitude of symptoms and problems that frequently converge to exacerbate a particular crisis. These crises can also be either created by, or intensified by, certain medical conditions. For example, there are many medical conditions that can often look like a psychiatric condition. Such is the case with hyperthyroidism (overactive thyroid hormone) that can produce symptoms, such as anxiety, irritability, grandiosity, and manic-like symptoms. Conversely, hypothyroidism often produces symptoms that are depressive in nature and include impaired cognition, social withdrawal, and sleepiness/drowsiness.

There are also particular medications that can create, exacerbate, or mimic certain psychiatric conditions. For example, there are certain medications prescribed for hypertension or high blood pressure that can cause depressive symptoms. This does not mean however, that crisis counselors recommend that an individual stop taking their high blood pressure medication. Instead, the counselor usually consults with the physician or cardiologist prescribing this medication in order to determine if they may be able to prescribe

Table 12.1 Medications that may cause depressive symptoms

Analgesics and Anti-inflammatory medicine	Antihypertensive and cardiac medications
• Ibuprofen • Indomethacin (can also create mental confusion, or acute psychosis, depression with suicide attempts)	• Alphamethyldopa • Bethanidine • Beta blockers (e.g., propranolol) • Clonadine • Digitalis • Hydralazine • Lidocaine • Procainanide • Reserpine • Rescinnamine • Veratrum
Opioids (prescription)	
• Percodan • Percoset • Darvon • Darvocet • Demerol • Methadone	
Antibacterial and antifungals	**Hypoglycemic medications**
• Ampicillin • Clycloserine • Ethnomide • Streptomycin • Sulfamethoxazole • Sulfonamides • Tetracylcine	• Oral insulin • Injectable insulin
	Prostate enlargement medications
	• Flomax

Source: Copied with permission from S. Bohen (2001) <u>Psychiatric Emergencies,</u> PESI Healthcare, Eau Claire, WI

Table 12.2   Medical conditions that may cause psychiatric symptoms

Endocrine/Metabolic Disease	Psychiatric Symptoms
Hyperadrenalism (Cushing's Syndrome) psychosis	Depression, mood lability
Adrenal cortical insufficiency (Addison's disease)	Apathy, depression
Hyperparathyroidism	Depression, anxiety, confusion, irritability, psychosis
Hypoglycemia	Anxiety, irritability, confusion
Hyperthyroidism	Anxiety, irritability, grandiosity
Hypothyroidism	Depression, sleepiness, social withdrawal
Hypernatremia (excessive sodium)	Sleepiness, drowsiness, confusion, lack of emotion, dullness
Gastrointestinal Disease	**Psychiatric Symptoms**
Wilson's disease	Personality changes, schizophrenic-like symptoms, dementia
Anemia	Decreased concentration, mood disturbance
Porphyria	Anxiety, insomnia, depression, hallucinations, paranoia, delirium
Infectious Diseases	**Psychiatric Symptoms**
AIDS	Early: decreased attention & concentration Late: dementia, personality change, apathy, agitation
Meningitis	Confusion, coma
Creutzfeldt-Jakob disease (mad cow disease)	Rapidly progressive dementia
Neurologic Symptoms	**Psychiatric Symptoms**
Intracranial tumors	Personality changes, dementia, depression, anxiety
Subdural hematoma	Irritability, confusion, extreme sleepiness
Nutritional Syndromes	**Psychiatric Symptoms**
Pernicious anemia	Anxiety, depression, mania, confusion
Wernicke-Korsakoff's (thiamine deficiency)	Amnesia, apathy, delirium, coma, confabulation, disorientation

Table derived from Assad, G. (1995). *Understanding mental disorders due to medical conditions or substance abuse: What every therapist should know.* New York, NY: Brunner/Mazel.

an antihypertensive medicine that is less deleterious to this individual's mental health. Table 12.1 above provides a partial list of some other medications that may produce depressive symptoms. It is always important when assessing any individual who is in crisis to ask questions about their medical history and what medications they are currently taking.

PSYCHIATRIC CRISIS SERVICE DELIVERY: PSYCHIATRIC CRISIS HOT LINES

Crisis hotlines have been in existence since 1906 with the inception of the National Save-a-Life League. However, crisis hotlines did not begin to really flourish until the 1970s, which coincided with the momentum generated by the community mental health movement described in Chapter 2. One can look in any newspaper or the front pages of any U.S. phone book and see listings for various hotlines. There are psychiatric hotlines, rape hotlines, alcohol and drug hotlines, child abuse, and domestic violence hotlines. These hotlines are usually available 24 hours a day, seven days a week, all year round. An assignment to answer hotline calls can be excellent training for any crisis counselor; however, it is not without its frustrations. Although there are many advantages to psychiatric hotlines, it seems that most of these advantages favor the side of the caller rather than the counselor. For example, since hotlines are readily available, the caller can determine when they call and often the length of the call; the caller has the advantage of anonymity; hotlines are free; therefore, the caller has only the expense of the phone charges. In rural areas, where services are not readily available, hotlines can serve a vast geographical area. By accessing a hotline, the caller can also get different points of view on a problem and not be restricted to the views of one counselor or therapist. Unfortunately, crisis counselors experience most of the disadvantages when it comes to hotline calls. First, it is difficult to assess someone when you are not able to read body language, facial expressions, or other observable behaviors. Also, it is almost impossible to assess someone who is extremely intoxicated or under the influence of drugs. Second, it is certainly more difficult to ensure the safety of the person who is calling when the counselor may not know their name or even where they are calling from. This is especially frightening when the caller intimates suicidal or homicidal ideation or plan. In those instances, the crisis counselor may need to have the call traced by an operator in order to have a police officer dispatched to the scene. The counselor is also at a disadvantage because they are not in control of the duration of the call. Although many callers are earnest in the need for help, there are those instances where people abuse the hotlines (James & Gilliland, 2017). Callers who are lonely, depressed, or dependent types of individuals may try to allay their fears of loneliness or boredom by continually calling crisis hotlines and keeping crisis counselors on the line for hours. Individuals with borderline personality disorders are often prone to calling hotlines because of their apprehensions surrounding abandonment, boredom, and inability to cope with loneliness. In instances like this, it is sometimes necessary for crisis counselors to set limits or boundaries. For example, a crisis counselor who has a particularly dependent caller on the line may handle the call in the following way:

Intervention

Counselor: Mark, I think we've gone over the same issues a few times now. What I'd like to suggest is that we summarize what we've talked about so far and then come up with a specific plan that you can agree to carry out today. How does that sound?

Mark: Okay, I guess. But, I don't know if I can stand being without Mary. I was so used to spending every Sunday with her. We would go to the movies or the beach, go for walks, get something to eat (etc., etc.).

C: Yes, Mark, I hear you, but what can you do today that might help you to spend the time more productively? You mentioned that you have a couple of friends from work; have you thought about calling them?

M: They have families and I'm sure they're busy.

C: Why don't you call them, the worst they can say is that they are busy, but you can always try to make plans for next week, or for one day after work. What else could you do today?

M: I guess I could go the mall. I do have to buy sneakers.

C: Good, what else?

The counselor is trying to get Mark to be more concrete in planning the day and also to discuss when would be an appropriate time to call back to check in. Sometimes, this helps to allay the person's fears that they are being left totally on their own. It is also important that the counselor get Mark to bring up ideas. If the counselor continued to bring up suggestions, Mark would merely reject those ideas, as not being good enough; therefore, it is always better to get the caller to make suggestions. In the instance of abusive callers, the counselor may need to set limits or boundaries in a different manner, as in the case example below.

F: You know, this really sucks, you're supposed to be helping me and instead all I'm getting is a lot of cliché stuff, bumper sticker therapy. I don't want to go to any damn AA meeting; but I don't want to start using again, and I'm sure as hell not going to hang out with a bunch of holy rollers.

C: Fred, I suggested AA because it helps many people with alcohol problems. Besides it is free and you could attend a meeting today if you wanted.

F: I'm not going to some damn AA meeting.

C: Well, although I feel it would be the most helpful, we can talk about other things you could do in order to avoid picking up a drink today.

F: I'm so ticked off, I'll think I'll just go and have a couple of drinks. Thanks for nothing.

C: Fred, I'm sorry you feel this way, but is it really worth picking up a drink? Instead of drinking, why don't you take an hour or so to take a walk and then we can talk again and start at the beginning.

In this instance, an abusive caller, seems to be looking to displace the responsibility or blame onto someone else. It is better that the counselor not get caught up in the "blame game" and instead explore with Fred what, if anything, has worked in the past rather than trying to offer helpful recommendations. In the example above, the recommendation the counselor made to Fred was certainly a sound, viable recommendation and Fred could have just as easily said, "No thank you, AA is not for me." However, crisis hotline callers are not always reasonable or rational. Therefore, it is better for the counselor to keep their composure, while at the same time, conveying to the person that they are concerned about them and are willing to help them work the problem through.

In handling any type of crisis call, the procedures that counselors follow from case-to-case is fairly similar to using the L-A-P-C model. The first step is to **listen** to this individual and the problem or dilemma that caused them to seek help. It is also helpful to tell the person who you are and that you are there to help them with their situation. The next step is to **assess the crisis and the individual in crisis**, or in other words, why did this person call the crisis hotline. What are they experiencing in terms of both emotional and physical symptoms. Why are they calling at this particular point in time. Most types of crises are defined as such by the patient, because they cannot cope with the situation at hand, or they have exhausted all of their own coping resources. What is unique to this person's coping style? Do they have resources they can rely on? The next step is to **explore alternatives in order to agree on a plan**; naturally, not every crisis situation has a "correct" or precise alternative that can somehow be discovered. There are many instances where hotline callers just need someone to talk to; they need to connect to another human being, and not be told what "to do." It is important that crisis counselors not get trapped into feeling that they must come up with some perfect plan or solution in every case they handle. For instance, when a parent calls in crisis, because they are having difficulty coping with a relationship breakup. Crisis calls of this type are often made simply to allow the person to express feelings of anger, hurt, or disappointment. For the counselor to jump into talking about a crisis plan or antidepressant medication could be a mistake. The next step is to obtain a **commitment to the plan.** Again, this step could represent the closure phase of the call. Here, the counselor is trying to summarize what transpired in the call. Plans could involve a follow-up call, a face-to-face appointment, or a visit to the emergency room or psychiatric clinic for an immediate assessment. Unfortunately, it is not unusual for people to neglect to make follow-up appointments. Once the initial crisis has passed, and the caller is no longer in the same emotional turmoil they were in, he or she may feel it unnecessary to follow through with further counseling. Although this is usually a mistake, the crisis counselor can only offer encouraging support to the person. The only exception to this is in the event of a suicidal or homicidal crisis that dictates that action be taken, or in a crisis situation involving child or elder abuse.

Box 12.5: Mental Health First Aid®

Mental Health First Aid provides a structured blueprint or outline for providing comfort, promoting recovery, and helping to reduced distress, trauma, or crisis for individuals suffering from mental health crises. This movement originated in Melbourne, Australia, in 2010 and has spread to the United States. Trainings in Mental Health First Aid are provided to law enforcement personnel, other first responders, medical and school personnel and to community providers. The structured blueprint for helping those with mental disorders is based on the acronym: ALGEE which represents an action plan for helping those in crisis consisting of Action A: Assessing for risk of suicide or harm; Action L: Listening nonjudgmentally; Action G: Give reassurance and information; Action E: Encourage appropriate professional help; and Action E: Encourage self-help and other support strategies. Information on Mental Health First Aid and trainings can be accessed through the National Council on Behavioral Health (2005), 1400 K Street Northwest #400, Washington, D.C., telephone (202) 684-7457, or at their website: www.TheNationalCouncil.org

PSYCHIATRIC CRISIS SERVICE DELIVERY: PSYCHIATRIC WALK-IN CRISIS CENTERS AND MOBILE CRISIS SERVICES

It is naturally more effective when assessing a person in crisis if you are sitting face-to-face with them. In these instances, crisis counselors can read facial expressions, body language, and other observable behaviors. Most psychiatric clinics and hospital emergency rooms offer some type of emergency psychiatric screening services. In some areas, there may even be particular hospitals or community mental health centers that are designated as psychiatric screening centers for adults or for adolescents and children. These centers usually provide 24 hour/7 day a week coverage for emergencies, and also have some ability to admit a person to a psychiatric inpatient unit for observation and/or treatment. These community-based psychiatric units are usually housed within major medical centers or hospitals designed to provide emergency psychiatric care to members of their immediate communities, and to take the burden off state psychiatric facilities. More recently, many

Box 12.6: Out of the Shadows: Confronting America's Mental Illness Crisis

E. Fuller Torrey is a leading authority and researcher in the study of schizophrenia. In his book *Out of the Shadows*, he describes the burden placed on communities as a result of deinstitutionalization. In the 1980s, the state governments "sold" the closing of major psychiatric hospitals to their constituents on the basis that it was inhumane to keep the mentally ill locked up in decaying mental institutions where the mentally ill were ill-treated and often abused. What state governments did not tell the public were two things: first, that the closing of state psychiatric hospitals represented a huge cost savings to the state treasuries. Second, was that surrounding counties and communities were often ill-equipped to manage the number of psychiatric patients who were now living in often substandard boarding homes within the community. These towns became "psychiatric ghettos" according to Dr. Torrey. Patients who did not take their medication quickly decompensated, which often resulted in hospitalization in community hospitals that were not equipped to handle the large influx of admissions. Even worse, however, was the increase in community violence or incarceration because of former psychiatric patients not being properly treated, and not receiving needed follow-up services. Statistics uncovered by Dr. Torrey reveal that state and county jails/prisons began incarcerating these former psychiatric patients in large numbers. Already burdened police departments and police officers often found themselves managing psychiatric crises in ever-increasing numbers, sometimes without having any proper crisis management training. Although there have been some improvements in mental health treatment delivery since this book was written (e.g., a treatment approach called "Targeted Assertive Outreach" that has been successful in preventing re-hospitalizations, and improvements in mobile psychiatric screening), deinstitutionalization was a debacle that still impacts many former patients and communities today.

Source: Torrey, E. F. (1997), *Out of the Shadows.* New York, NY: Wiley.

states and counties have been offering mobile psychiatric screening services. In these instances, trained mental health crisis counselors are dispatched (often with an accompanying police officer), to go to the client's home to provide an assessment within their home or apartment. If that individual does require psychiatric hospitalization (e.g., in instances where the person may pose a danger to self or others), then the police and mobile screener then accompany that individual to the hospital for admission.

For the crisis counselor working as a psychiatric screener in a hospital emergency room or psychiatric clinic, they are often faced with the rather daunting task of assessing the exact nature of the crisis, determining if the crisis involves alcohol, drugs, or some undiagnosed medical condition, and then making appropriate treatment recommendations. Naturally, all of this assumes that the patient is a willing participant in this process, which is not always the case. Treatment recommendations are then complicated by whether he or she has insurance and if so, what type of insurance. For example, even for a depressed, suicidal patient who needs inpatient observation/treatment and who is willing to enter the hospital as a voluntary admission, the question then becomes, "Will their health insurance cover such a stay?" One of the frustrations voiced by crisis counselors is not only encouraging the client to continue with treatment, but also convincing the health insurance company that mental health treatment is appropriate and necessary.

The procedure that most crisis counselors use to assess patients in psychiatric crisis centers is somewhat similar to the process used in psychiatric hotlines, and naturally also takes into account that in spite of some inherent similarities, each person is assessed on a case-to-case basis.

WARNING SIGNS OF A MENTAL HEALTH CRISIS

As the saying goes, "Hindsight is always 20/20." The ability to prevent or avert a mental health crisis is of paramount importance; although not all psychiatric crises can be averted, if counselors and family members are attuned to the warning signs, there are some instances where clients can be helped and hospitalization can possibly be avoided. Some of the warning signs include:

Inability to cope on a daily basis: this may be reflected by changes in daily hygiene, refusing to eat, sleeping all day, refusing to get out of bed

Rapid mood swings: may include increased energy levels, restlessness, agitation, or sudden depression, withdrawal, or calmness after depression

Increased agitation: violent, acting-out behavior, makes threats, destroys property, inappropriate language, or behavior

Abusive behavior: hurts others, self-injurious behavior (e.g., cutting, burning self, abuses alcohol or drugs)

Loses touch with reality (psychotic thinking): unable to recognize family or friends, confusion, has strange ideas, thinks they are someone they're not, hears voices, does not understand others, sees things that aren't there

Isolation from school, work, family, friends: decreased interest in social and recreational activities, changes in friendships, stops going to work or school

Unexplained physical symptoms: facial expressions change, complains of not feeling well, increase in headaches, stomachaches, etc.

Adapted from National Alliance on Mental Illness—Minnesota (2016). *Mental health crisis planning for adults.* http://www.namihelps.org/NAMI-MHCrisisPlannforAdultFeb2016.pdf

MULTICULTURAL CONSIDERATIONS

In assessing any psychiatric crisis situation, it is always important to take into consideration cultural and/or ethnic characteristics, beliefs, values, and rituals, as well as gender, religion, and age factors. All behavior, thoughts, and emotions must be viewed within their sociocultural context. For example, a person who feels comfortable with their homosexuality and lives among family or friends who support that decision (context) experiences a different view of their sexuality than a homosexual who is growing up in a strict Christian family, where there are certain religious sanctions against homosexuality. A Latina adolescent who goes against her father's wishes by dating a non-Latino male, may also suffer a greater sense of guilt or shame than an Anglo-American teenager who is dating a boy her parents might dislike. It is important that crisis counselors take these differences into account.

With ethnic groups that immigrated to the United States, primarily during the most rapid period of immigration in the early 1900s, these groups have had a longer period of time to work through issues of acculturation. Here, Polish, Irish, Italian, European Jews, Scandinavian, Slovak, and other Eastern European immigrants have had a longer time period to assimilate and meld their customs, rituals, and beliefs of their homelands with that of mainstream America. Various racial and ethnic groups that are more recent immigrants often experience major difficulties as the customs, traditions, and beliefs of their homeland clash with mainstream America. Such is the case with many immigrants from India, Japan, or Korea (McGoldrick, Giordano, & Garcia-Preto, 2005). These cultures tend to place great value on adherence to family cohesiveness and obedience to the father as the head of the home, and also place value on education and achievement. To fail academically is to fail one's family, and may be seen as a kind of disobedience. As an example, one Indian teenager was brought into a local emergency room after making a rather serious suicide attempt, which proved fortunately to be nonlethal. When the crisis counselor evaluated him, what the young man later revealed was that he had failed to gain admission to an advanced premedical program at a prestigious Ivy League school. Although he was admitted to several premedical programs at other universities, this was clearly "not good enough," and he felt he had failed to live up to the very high demands and expectations of his parents, both of whom were respected surgeons. It is imperative for the crisis counselor to be aware and culturally sensitive. To take an ethnocentric view (i.e., "American culture is all that counts" or "When in Rome, do what the Romans do") is to court disaster.

It should be noted that mental illness is also viewed differently by various cultures, and even the meaning of mental illness may be interpreted differently. For example, anthropologist Arthur Kleinman (1991) finds that most Western cultures separate the emotional and physical components of a particular disorder (e.g., depression) and give more weight to the emotional aspects. In Asian cultures, emotional experiences are thought to be inseparable from physical experiences; therefore, these cultures tend to focus on the physical aspects (e.g., lethargy, stomach distress, or sleeplessness). Whereas most Western cultures allow for a display of emotional distress, many non-Western cultures do not (Kendall & Hammen, 1998). Another assumption of Western thinking is that mental illness is caused primarily by psychological factors and therefore, the treatments are psychological in nature (i.e., psychotherapy or counseling). In non-Western cultures, greater emphasis may be placed on spiritual or religious causes (e.g., the person may feel that God is punishing them for some indiscretion, therefore they are depressed). These individuals may also seek religious or spiritual counseling. Interestingly, the prevalence and incidence of various disorders may also vary according to racial or ethnic ancestry. For example, depression is nearly nonexistent in Kenya and Rwanda, yet relatively frequent in Ghana and in Nigeria; concurrently, suicide is very rare in most African countries. Rates of depression are very low among the Amish (Maxmen & Ward, 1995); and African Americans and European-Americans have nearly the same rates of schizophrenia.

It seems that cultural beliefs and changes can also influence the prevalence of certain disorders. For example, suicidal behavior is less prevalent in Catholic and Muslim countries where there are strict religious beliefs regarding suicide as being sinful. Recently, there has been an increase in suicide among middle-age men in Ireland. Apparently, this increase has been attributed to the increased divorce rate. Apparently, as Irish couples have strayed from strict religious practices, their beliefs in sanctions against divorce have dissipated, thereby creating laxer attitudes toward divorce. Irish women no longer feel that they must stay in unfulfilling or abusive relationships, and are therefore choosing to divorce.

SUMMARY

Psychiatric emergencies represent a unique subtype of crises. In some instances, there may be a readily identifiable catalyst. Such is the case with posttraumatic stress disorder where the individual either experiences or witnesses a life-threatening traumatic event, or when an individual with schizophrenia stops taking their medication. However, in some instances there may not be a readily identifiable catalyst to the crisis. Regardless, the role of the crisis counselor is to help make certain that the person in crisis is safe and that a plan that provides stabilization of symptoms is agreed on and implemented. Individuals with particular types of psychiatric disorders are more prone to experiencing a crisis than others. Therefore, in this chapter we focused on those disorders most likely to present in crisis, such as individuals with panic disorder, PTSD, depression, bipolar depression, schizophrenia, and particularly personality disorders. Finally, we discussed crisis intervention service delivery as it pertains to hotlines and walk-in clinics, as well as the imperative of factoring in multicultural issues.

RESOURCES FOR CHAPTER ENRICHMENT

Suggested Readings

Beck, A. (1967). *Depression: Clinical, experimental, and theoretical aspects.* New York: Harper & Row.

Bellak, L., & Siegel, H. (1983). *Handbook of intensive brief and emergency psychotherapy.* Larchmont, NY: CPS.

Ellis, A. E. (1962). *Reason and emotion in psychotherapy.* New York: Lyle Stuart.

Freeman, A., & Fusco, G. (2000). Treating high-arousal patient: Differentiating between patients in crisis and crisis-prone patients. In F. M. Dattilio & A. Freeman (Eds.), *Cognitive-behavioral strategies in crisis intervention.* New York, NY: Guilford Press.

Mednick, S. A., Machon, R. A., Huttunen, M. O., & Bonett, D. (1988). Adult schizophrenia following prenatal exposure to an influenza epidemic. *Archives of General Psychiatry, 45,* 189–192.

National Alliance on Mental Illness (NAMI). (2016). *Mental health crisis planning for children.* http://www.namihelps.org/NAMI-HCrisisPlanforChildrenFeb2016.pdf

National Alliance on Mental Illness—Minnesota (NAMI). (2016). *Mental health crisis planning for adults: Learn to recognize, manage, prevent, and plan your loved one's mental health crisis.* http://www.namihelps.org/NAMI-HCrisisPlannforAdultFeb2016.pdf

Kesey, K. (1967). *One flew over the cuckoo's nest.* New York: Bantam.

Rice, D. P., & Miller, L. S. (1996). The economic burden of schizophrenia: Conceptual and methodological issues and cost estimates. In M. Moscarelli, A. Rupp, & N. Sartorious (Eds.) *Handbook of mental health economics and health policy. Vol. 1: Schizophrenia.* (pp. 321–324). New York: John Wiley and Sons

Suggested Websites

Mood Disorder Resources

Anxiety & Depression Association of America (ADAA)
This website provides information on both anxiety and depression screening as well as many other useful resources. https://adaa.org/iving-with-anxiety/ask-and-learn/screenings/screening-depression

Depression Central
This site is the Internet's central clearinghouse for information on all types of depressive disorders and on the most effective treatments for individuals suffering from major depression, manic-depression (bipolar disorder), cyclothymia, dysthymia and other mood disorders. http://www.psycom.net/depression.central.html

Depression Alliance
This website contains information about the symptoms of depression, treatments for depression, as well as Depression Alliance campaigns and local groups. http://www.depressionalliance.org/

NIMH—Depression
This website gives descriptions of major depression, dysthymia, and bipolar disorder (manic depression). It lists symptoms, gives possible causes, tells how depression is diagnosed, and discusses available treatments. The site provides help and hope for the depressed person, family, and friends. https://www.nimh.nih.gov/health/topics/depression/index.shtml

Depression Screening
This website is sponsored by the NMHA as part of its Campaign for America's Mental Health. The mission of this site is to educate people about clinical depression, offer a confidential way for people to get screened for symptoms of the illness, and guide people toward appropriate professional help if necessary. http://www.depression-screening.org/

Depression and Bipolar Support Alliance
This site provides information on mood disorders along with treatment resources and information on self-help support groups. www.dbsalliance.org

National Alliance on Mental Illness
NAMI is a nonprofit, grassroots self-help support and advocacy organization for individuals with mental disorders and their families. This site provides very useful information on resources. https://www.nami.org/Learn-More/Mental-Health-Conditions

Anxiety Disorder Resources

Anxiety Disorders Association of America
The site offers resources for clinicians, researchers, and other treatment providers in all disciplines. Resources for anxiety disorder sufferers, family members, and other interested parties are provided. The site also includes facts, statistics, and news releases. It allows you to search for treatment providers by location. http://www.adaa.org/

NIMH–Anxiety
Provides a brief overview of the symptoms and treatment of the major anxiety disorders: panic disorder, obsessive-compulsive disorder, posttraumatic stress disorder, social phobia, specific phobias, and generalized anxiety disorder. Also lists organizations to contact for further information. https://www.nimh.nih.gov/health/index.shtml

The Anxiety Panic Internet Resource (APIR)
APIR is a grass-roots website dedicated to providing information, relief, and support for those recovering from debilitating anxiety. http://www.algy.com/anxiety/

Other Mental Health Resources

Mental Health America
This site provides information on mental health, treatment resources and how to take action. www.mentalhealthamerica.net

National Council for Behavioral Health
This site also provides information on mental health and addiction treatment resources. www.TheNationalCouncil.org

National Institute on Mental Health
This site provides statistics on mental illness by age, gender, and race along with other important information and resources. http://www.nimh.nih.gov

Recommended Films

The Deer Hunter: **(1978)** (Starring Robert DeNiro, Christopher Walken). This film also provides an accurate depiction of Vietnam veterans who suffer from PTSD-related symptoms.

Born on the 4th of July: (1989) (Starring Tom Cruise, Raymond J. Barry). This film provides an accurate depiction of a disabled Vietnam veteran who suffers from PTSD-related symptoms.

Girl Interrupted: (1999) (Starring Winona Ryder, Angelina Jolie). This film is set in an exclusive Northeastern psychiatric hospital and focuses on young women who are battling major depression and borderline personality disorder. The film was based on the novel by Susanna Keyson, which provides a chilling and accurate description of women whose lives are in various states of crisis.

A Beautiful Mind: (2001) (Starring Russell Crowe, Jennifer Connolly). This film is based on the true-life story of Dr. John Nash, a mathematics professor at Princeton University and a Nobel prize winner. This film depicts Dr. Nash's struggle with schizophrenia and portrays the crises that he and his wife experienced when the disease took hold of him.

Fatal Attraction: (1987) (Starring Michael Douglas and Glenn Close). In this film, Glenn Close portrays a woman who has many characteristics of borderline personality disorder.

Alive Day Memories: (2009) This is an HBO documentary produced by James Gandolfini who interviews several soldiers who suffered near fatal wounds while serving in Iraq. This documentary also explores issues pertaining to trauma as well as recovery.

Still Alice: (2014) (Starring Julianne Moore and Alex Baldwin). This film chronicles the progression of early-onset dementia in a woman who is a neuroscience linguistics professor at Columbia University. The film also portrays the reactions of Alice's family as they come to grips with her devastating neurocognitive disorder.

First Cousin: (2013) An HBO documentary that examines the life of literary figure Edwin Honig as he struggles with Alzheimer's disease.

Suggested Activities

1. Imagine that a friend or family member is suffering from major depression and needs psychiatric hospitalization. What resources can you find in your community or within a twenty-five-mile radius that might help? Would your friend or family member need medical insurance to obtain treatment at these facilities? What about for follow-up treatment at an outpatient treatment clinic?

2. The following is a list of medications that are used to treat psychiatric problems. Find out what the medication is used for and the benefits and side effects:

   Librium

   Depakote

   Topamax

   Seroquel

   Cymbalta

   Luvox

3. The National Alliance for the Mentally Ill (NAMI) is an organization that does a lot of advocacy work for people with mental disorders. See what you can find out about NAMI and they type of work they do.

Recommended YouTube Viewing

https://www.youtube.com/watch? v = aqdQ1DJ7NZM This video explores crisis intervention with psychiatric patients in a major medical center. Very informative.

https://www.youtube.com/watch? v = uX-SP8H1lEE This video is an addendum to the above-referenced video on psychiatric emergencies in a medical setting.

https://www.youtube.com/watch? v = DUoyVVeMtpA This documentary addresses psychiatric crises in Great Britain. This is similar to problems encountered in the United States.

https://www.youtube.com/watch? v = fflQf-T155o This video provides some basic guidelines for first responders who are called on to manage a psychiatric crisis.

CHAPTER 13

Health Crisis

Tom is 72 years old, married and the father of three adult children and four grandchildren. He and his wife, Barbara were in Nashville visiting their grandchildren around the holidays when Tom suddenly began to have chest pains and it felt like his heart was beating so fast it was going to explode. He was rushed to the nearest medical center where it was determined he had a 95% blockage in one of his arteries and would need immediate surgery. Although Tom has been in good health, he has a cardiologist back home that he meets with annually to monitor his high blood pressure. Tom is uncertain what to do. He would rather have the surgery back home in Connecticut where his cardiologist is located. He is afraid of something "going wrong," and that he will not wake up from surgery. Tom is in crisis.

DISCUSSION QUESTIONS

1. Imagine you go to your family doctor for a routine medical checkup and when your lab results come back, your doctor informs you that you may have a "serious medical condition." What would your reaction be? What would you do?

2. How do you think healthcare has changed since your grandparents were your age? What changes do you expect will happen in the future; for example, will a cure for cancer be discovered in your lifetime? What about a cure for AIDS?

INTRODUCTION

Despite all of the technological advances in medicine and the increase in life expectancy, the mortality rate and incidence/prevalence rates of particular diseases are alarmingly high in the United States. Interestingly, cardiovascular diseases (like heart disease and stroke) remain among the leading causes of death, along with cancer and chronic respiratory disease (Centers for Disease Control and Prevention, 2013c). Other lifestyle-related illnesses now appear on the Leading Causes of Death list, which explains the need for crisis counselors in our emergency care system.

Table 13.1 The Leading Causes of Death in the United States in 1900 and in 2009 (rates in 100,000)

1900	Rate	2009	Rate
1. Cardiovascular disease (heart disease, stroke)	345	1. Cardiovascular disease (heart disease, stroke)	652
2. Influenza and pneumonia	202	2. Cancer	559
3. Tuberculosis	194	3. Stroke	143
4. Gastritis, duodenitis, enteritis, and colitis	143	4. Chronic pulmonary disease	130
5. Accidents	72	5. Accidents	117
6. Cancer	64	6. Diabetes	75
7. Diphtheria	40	7. Alzheimers	71
8. Typhoid fever	31	8. Influenza/Pneumonia	63
9. Measles	13	9. Homicide and legal intervention	9.9
10. Chronic liver disease and cirrhosis	*	10. Chronic liver disease and cirrhosis	9.6
* data unavailable			

Source: Figures from 1990 from *Historical Statistics of the United States: Colonial Times to 1970,* U.S. Bureau of the Census, 1975, Washington, DC: Government Printing Office. Figures for 1993 from *Statistical Abstracts of the United States* by U.S. Bureau of the Census, 1995, Washington, DC: Government Printing Office.

According to epidemiological research by Xu, Kochanek, Murphy, and Arias (2014), in 2012, the ten leading causes of death in the United States were heart disease, cancer, chronic lower respiratory diseases, stroke, unintentional injuries, Alzheimer's disease, diabetes, influenza and pneumonia, kidney disease, and suicide. In addition, there were significant declines in the number of deaths for eight of these ten leading causes. For example, mortality rates decreased 1.8% for heart disease, 1.5% for cancer, 2.4% for chronic lower respiratory diseases, 2.6% for stroke, 3.6% for Alzheimer's disease, 1.9% for diabetes, 8.3% for influenza and pneumonia, and 2.2% for kidney disease. The rate for suicide increased 2.4%. The rate for unintentional injuries remained the same.

Interestingly, the fifth leading cause of death according to this research was listed as "unintentional injuries." This term is often accidents and *iatrogenic deaths,* a term which means unintentional death due to medical or surgical procedures. Estimates of the number of unintentional deaths range from approximately 224,000 to up to 7.1 million per year depending on which criteria are used. The good news is that the average life expectancy according to Xu et al. (2014) is approximately 78.4 years for men and 81.2 years for women. This is probably attributable to advances in medical science. However, what is rather astounding is that the World Health Organization (WHO) ranks the United States as 37th out of 191 countries in the world in health care delivery (Commonwealth Fund, 2014, 2015; Hellman, 2014). Although there is a great deal of controversy over the WHO rankings, what is evident is that the United States rankings are so low because of restricted access to healthcare. Yes, our emergency department treatments are probably the best in the world; however, when it comes to access to non-emergency healthcare and palliative or end-of-life care, that's where we seem to fall short. Yet, also take

Table 13.2   Leading Causes of Death in the U.S. 2013 (Centers for Disease Control, 2013)

- Heart disease: 611,105
- Cancer: 584,881
- Chronic lower respiratory diseases: 149,205
- Accidents (unintentional injuries): 130,557
- Stroke (cerebrovascular diseases): 128,978
- Alzheimer's disease: 84,767
- Diabetes: 75,578
- Influenza and Pneumonia: 56,979
- Nephritis, nephrotic syndrome, and nephrosis: 47,112
- Intentional self-harm (suicide): 41,149

Source: http://www.cdc.gov/nchs/fastats/leading-causes-of-death.htm

Figure 13.1   Mortality in the United States: 2011 and 2012

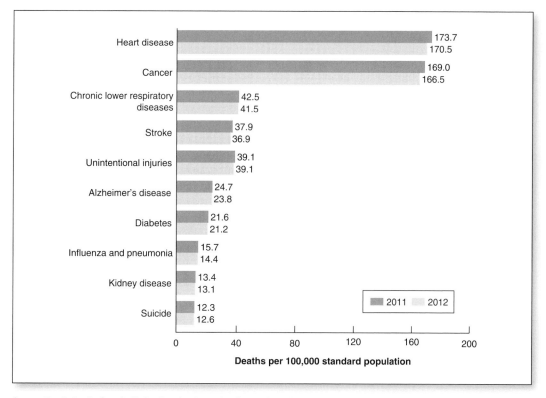

Source: Xu, J. Q., Kochanek, K. D., Murphy, S. L., & Arias, E. (2014). *Mortality in the United States, (2012)*. [NCHS data brief, no 168]. Hyattsville, MD: National Center for Health Statistics.

into consideration that the United States spends more on health care than all of the other 191 countries included in the WHO survey. Even with the rollout of the Affordable Care Act, there are still approximately 30 million Americans who have no access to routine or preventative health care due to a lack of health insurance. In a more recent comparison by Hellman (2014) of eleven Western countries (e.g., Sweden, U.K., Germany, Australia, Norway, New Zealand, the Netherlands, etc.), the United States ranked the lowest when compared to these countries on factors, such as quality of care, access to care, equity of care, cost for care, etc.). Furthermore, the United States ranked the highest when it came to administrative health care costs (Commonwealth Fund, 2014, 2015). Administrative costs encompass everything from hospital CEO salaries to nursing supervisors and those staff who do billing and insurance submissions.

So, what can we conclude from all these seemingly contradictory statistics? It appears that not only are many Americans experiencing medical crises, but the United States health care system is also in a state of crisis especially given the rising costs of healthcare in the United States and a lack of access to healthcare, despite the advances made by the Affordable Healthcare Act in reducing these numbers. For many Americans and immigrants, the fear of being denied medical treatment or being offered less than adequate medical treatment, or facing financial ruin or bankruptcy in order to access healthcare can only exacerbate any personal medical crisis.

DEFINING MEDICAL CRISES

Medical crises differ in their origin, etiology, and chronicity. For example, a medical condition that is brought on by behavioral factors (e.g., emphysema brought on by smoking, or liver inflammation brought on by excessive alcohol intake, or a cardiovascular incident brought on by poor diet and obesity), may be perceived differently than a condition where the person bears no personal responsibility, such as certain types of cancer that may be genetic in origin. Naturally, whether the condition is *acute* (e.g., influenza or ear infections) versus *chronic* (e.g., diabetes or Lupus), also has tremendous bearing on whether the individual experiences a medical crisis. Regardless of etiology or chronicity, what all medical conditions have in common is that there is a psychological or emotional response. Again, not all psychological or emotional responses to illness necessarily constitute a "medical crisis." However, the intensity of one's reaction is usually equal to the amount of disequilibrium it causes in the person's life, and the lasting effects of the disruption in functioning.

Crises often arise not only at the time of the diagnosis, but also at the time when treatment decisions need to be made. There are a variety of situations where treatment decisions could result in crises. For example, a woman diagnosed with breast cancer may be given treatment options ranging from whether a radical mastectomy should be performed, or whether a lumpectomy followed by radiation or chemotherapy treatment can best treat her cancer. Another example of treatment decision crisis can arise with a diabetic male in his late thirties who, because of extremely poor circulation, is being advised by his doctor to have his leg amputated. With an elderly woman who is living alone with advanced arthritis, a treatment decision crisis may arise when her physician recommends an assisted living facility in order to prevent injuries resulting from falling and to provide proper nutritional care. Or take for example, a 52-year-old male who is a self-employed home construction owner who is diagnosed with prostate cancer and must have his prostate surgically removed, which involves a 6- to 8-week recovery period. These treatment decision crises also involve *quality of life* issues, as individuals weigh out how their everyday life may be impacted by the recommended treatments. Will the 36-year-old diabetic be able to work after his leg is amputated? Will the construction company owner be able to do any heavy lifting after his prostate removal, and will he suffer incontinence because of the surgery? All of these factors are often the reasons why people experience crises when faced with medical illnesses.

EMOTIONAL-PSYCHOLOGICAL RESPONSE TO MEDICAL CRISES

DiTomasso, Martin, and Kovnat (2000) determined that a medical crisis is composed of the following elements: *a triggering event, cognitive factors, behavioral factors, and physical factors.* They point out that the triggering event alone (e.g., a medical illness), may not necessarily account for whether the individual is in crisis, but rather whether that event takes place in combination with other stressors, and how the person perceives the triggering event. This leads to the notion that the *triggering event* then leads to an interpretation by the person that brings into play *cognitive factors.* In other words, the person's response to the event is often influenced by "unrealistic beliefs, attitudes, and assumptions; cognitive distortions; biased recall and perception; negative view of self, world, and future; decreased self-efficacy, and lack of accurate information" (DiTomasso et al., 2000, p. 413). So, for example, a patient who unrealistically expects to make a full recovery after a surgical procedure may find himself or herself in a depressive crisis when they realize they may not have the same freedom of mobility they once had. Cognitive distortions also bring about a state of crisis when the medical condition brings about a change in self-perception and self-efficacy. Such as a young man with ulcerative colitis that results in a colostomy. He may feel that he can never date or marry, as no woman would ever want him as long as he has a colostomy bag. In biased recall and perception, DiTomasso and colleagues (2000) point out that it is more likely that people in general recall negative events when they are in a negative mood. A negative mood state brought on by medical illness is no exception. Anyone who has been immobilized by the flu, even for a week, knows how difficult it is to have a cheerful, optimistic attitude. A negative view of oneself, the world, and the future according to Beck (2011) is a recipe for a depressive response, which can lead to or exacerbate a medical crisis. The patient who feels that he or she will never fully recover, or those who are forever scarred physically and emotionally by an illness or accident naturally experience depressive emotional reactions that become an integral part of their medical crisis. Finally, a lack of accurate information also exacerbates the crisis. Misinformation or a lack of accurate information only fosters cognitive distortions and misperceptions, which only further exacerbate the crisis.

Behavioral/emotional factors also play a role in whether one experiences a crisis and the extent or severity of the crisis. For example, DiTomasso et al. (2000) indicate that a *lack of coping strategies, negative means of coping, lack of available social supports and inability to request support,* all become part of the behavioral/emotional factors that influence the course of a medical crisis. A person who has been able to handle other crises in their lives usually has a better prognosis about how well they cope with a medical crisis. For example, a man or woman who is diagnosed with bladder cancer and who has few people in their social support network may find it difficult to cope with the prospect of going through painful chemotherapy and with the prospect of needing to have the cancerous bladder

Box 13.1: The Cost of Treatment

Susan Gubar (2016) is a *New York Times* columnist and a survivor of cervical cancer. In a recent blog, she explores the issue of the cost of treating her cervical cancer and asks the question, "What does it cost to keep a cancer patient alive for a year, given the current costs of medication?" The answer she received was $50,000 dollars, on average. This figure was obtained from what medical economists refer to as a QALY (quality of adjusted life year). Basically, the QALY is a calculation of one's quality and quantity of life in order to judge "the monetary worth of medical inventions," which includes the medical worth and cost effectiveness of certain drugs used to treat cancer. However, Guber points out that "never during the four years of operations, radiological interventions and cycles of chemotherapy had I ever been informed beforehand about the cost of any consultation, procedure, equipment or drug. Nor did I understand what would be covered by insurance, what Medicare would cover (on turning 65) or what I would need to pay out-of-pocket." Katie Thomas (2016) (who is a business/health reporter for the *New York Times*) writes that some prescription cancer drugs can cost patients upwards of $100,000 dollars a year. Thomas explains that what a handful of pharmaceutical companies have done is to buy up older drugs and then jack up the prices. The most recent example was in the Fall, 2015 when Martin Shkreli, the owner and founder of Turing Pharmaceutical ignited a huge controversy when his company raised the price of a drug used to treat toxoplasmosis from $13.50 a pill to $750 dollars a pill. Cancer drug prices have skyrocketed because there is less competition and, therefore, drug companies can charge whatever they want. The same holds true for many diabetes drugs, and drugs used to treat various heart conditions. A recently developed drug used to boost the effectiveness of existing antidepressants costs $750 dollars a month. Some economists and business analysts hypothesize that pharmaceutical and health insurers are trying to grab all the profits they can now before legislative constraints or restrictions are enacted.

Sources: Gubar, S. (2016, May 5). Pricing a year of life. *New York Times.* Retrieved from http://well.blogs.nytimes.com/2016/05/05/pricing-a-year-of-life/

Thomas, K. (2016, April 27). The complex math behind spiraling prescription drug prices. *New York Times.* Retrieved from http://www.nytimes.com/2016/04/28/business/high-drug-prices-explained.html

removed surgically, if at some point the chemotherapy is ineffective. The lack of coping strategies may contribute to individuals feeling hopeless, helpless, and depressed in the face of a medical diagnosis.

Finally, the physical factors are the most obvious and most important aspects in determining a medical crisis. Here the nature and extent of the physical illness is considered. An acute physical condition, for example, an acute childhood ear infection that is easily treated with antibiotics may result in an immediate medical crisis because of the child's pain; however, if the child's hearing loss becomes permanent because of repeated ear infections, and results in several surgical procedures, then another ear infection can represent a more enduring major medical crisis. Similarly, those physical disorders which are life-threatening: cancer, leukemia, tuberculosis, coronary artery blockage can also result in a medical crisis. Similarly, illnesses or accidents that result in permanent physical or bodily change also create an intense medical crisis. Such is the case with the young teenager or college athlete who has an arm or leg disabled or amputated after a near-fatal car collision.

THE CRISIS RESPONSE OF THE FAMILY AND THE CULTURAL CONSIDERATION

Just as the person who suffers the medical crisis experiences a variety of reactions to a medical crisis, so too does the family. The family's reactions play a big role in how the crisis is experienced and how the crisis evolves over time. A warm, loving, supportive family who pull together in times of crisis, naturally have a much different impact on the person suffering the medical crisis. In general, medical crises tend to bring out the best or worst in families.

Children also react to medical crises, although their reactions and the expression of the concomitant feelings to the crisis may be quite different from that of adults. A child, for example, may develop symptoms when his or her parent or sibling is diagnosed with a medical illness. Or he or she may regress (by bedwetting or thumb sucking) or begin to act out in some way (fighting in school). Children may also adopt certain roles within the family, as a means of trying to manage the stress brought on by the illness. It is noteworthy that the roles that are often associated with growing up in an alcoholic home, for example. the hero, the scapegoat, the lost child, the mascot (Vernig, 2011; Wegscheider, 1981) were also described by Virginia Satir (1972, 1988), a pioneer in the field of family therapy who was working with families who had a parent diagnosed with cancer.

There are several factors that also come into play when considering how culture can influence how a medical crisis impacts on a family. Just as culture plays a role in determining the acceptable norms for emotional expression; so too, families of various cultures differ in how they respond to a medical crisis. For example, some cultures tend to be more stoic in response to crisis, while others are more openly expressive and do not hold back their tears or rage.

In some cultures, illnesses may be perceived as originating from "bad luck," personal behavior, evil spirits, or through the ill will of others. For example, in countries with strong Christian values, a medical illness may be viewed as resulting from sinful behavior, or it may be perceived that God has given this person the illness or injury to test his or her faith. Irish Americans find "virtue and sanctity in silent suffering," or in "offering up" their pain to God "as an imitation of Christ" (McGoldrick, 2005). In Italian culture, some believe in the notion of the "the evil eye," or *malocchio,* which suggests that others who wish harm or bad luck on a person can so do intentionally or unintentionally by casting the "evil eye" on this individual or on his or her relatives. Prior to seeking formal medical consultation, many first generation Italian Americans may seek help from a "therapeutic woman" who is usually a first-generation Italian woman consulted in cases of anxiety, depression, or stress (Ragucci, 1982). Similarly, in Puerto Rican culture, a variation of the "evil eye" exists known as *mal de ojo.* This concept is often used to explain the sudden illness of children (ranging from mild discomfort to severe pain and even death).

Culture can also influence the types of treatment (mainstream or non-mainstream) that may be sought for particular illnesses. For example, many individuals of Puerto Rican and Cuban ancestry endorse faith-healing beliefs and may be as likely to consult a spiritist as they would a medical doctor. A spiritist acts as a medium, counselor, or healer in order to exorcize the spirits that are believed to cause illness. *Santeros and espiritistas* are found throughout many Latino communities in the United States (Bernal & Shapiro, 2005). *Curanderos* are common among Mexican Americans; *bonesetters* are common treatment providers among the French Canadians; *remede-mans* are common among the Louisiana Cajuns; *singers* are found among the Navajo; and *herbalists* are common healers among the Chinese (Harwood, 1982). Many of these beliefs regarding causes of illness and non-mainstream treatments have waned somewhat among those second and third generation people of immigrant ancestry. These individuals have become more acculturated, and English is spoken as the primary language in their homes, thereby making for easier communication in accessing health care. As second and third generation sons and daughters have become more medically sophisticated and educated, there is less of a tendency to hold onto old world beliefs and customs, and this results in a greater likelihood of their accessing more traditional healthcare treatment.

In the section that follows, intervention strategies for various medical crises are discussed in great detail.

Case Presentation: A Crisis at the Time of Diagnosis

Helen is a 36-year-old divorced woman. She was referred for counseling by the Women's Health Center of her local medical center following her notification of a positive breast biopsy. Helen has been attending the Women's Health Center regularly after her sister died of breast cancer about nine years ago. Because breast cancer runs in her family, Helen initiated regular mammography exams and checkups.

Helen's medical crises began at the point when she received a phone call to return to the office. She knew the news was not good. Given the history of breast cancer in her family, she had dreaded this type of call since the time of her sister's death. After meeting with the doctor, but before making any decisions regarding what steps to take medically, Helen agreed to speak with a counselor at the Women's Health Center. The counselor introduced herself to Helen and the meeting went as follows:

Intervention

Counselor: Hello Helen, I'm Sara Smith. Your medical doctor asked that I speak with you. She told me about your biopsy results and that you were willing to come in today. Did you find the office okay?

Helen: Yes, the directions the receptionist gave me were fine. I was just so upset, because when I got the call and they said I had to come in to speak with Dr. Johnston, I knew something had to be wrong. Usually they just tell me my mammogram was negative and ask me to reschedule in a year.

C: What was your initial reaction or feeling when you received the call?

H: At first, I was in shock or disbelief, like they must have the wrong lab results or something. Then I got really upset, like afraid mostly. It's hard to describe. I kept thinking about what my sister went through and I kept flashing back to when she was diagnosed with cancer.

C: How long ago was that?

H: She was diagnosed in April of 1997, and by Christmas she was dead.

C: I'm so sorry to hear about your sister. Were you and she close?

H: I guess you can say we were. We were always competing against one another, probably because we were only a couple of years apart. So, whether it was sports, or grades in school, or boys in high school, we were always trying to see who would come out ahead. When she died, I felt like a part of me died along with her. She made me promise to get regular checkups, though. Something I always avoided. I guess you can see why?

C: So, you kept up with yearly checkups just as you promised your sister?

H: Yes, I've been coming to the Women's Health Center here for the past nine years, since she died. I've always dreaded this day though. I knew that one day I'd get a call like this. Part of me wants to know every detail of what to expect and what the treatments will be like, while the other part of me just wants to run away and never come back.

C: Did your sister go through a lot of treatments?

H: Yes, but I guess the cancer was so far advanced by then that it really didn't do her any good; I think it just made her worse. It probably would have been better to have left her alone and let her live out her last months in dignity.

C: It sounds like you've given a lot of thought to what you would do?

H: I guess I have. Since getting divorced a couple of years ago, I thought about what I'd do if I was ever diagnosed with breast cancer.

C: When will you meet with Dr. Johnston?

H: I'm scheduled to meet with her next Wednesday.

C: What steps are you willing or not willing to take?

H: If she recommends removing a lump or mass, I would do it, but I just don't know if I'd do all that radiation or chemotherapy. My sister went through all that and she was weak and throwing up all the time. Plus, it really didn't help her. And I would only do a radical mastectomy if they were certain that it hasn't spread. I don't think I'll ever get remarried anyway, so I figure it doesn't matter if I have one breast or two.

C: It does sound like you've given a lot of thought to this in terms of what you're willing and not willing to do.

H: I have. What would you do if you were in my shoes?

C: I would probably do exactly what you're doing. I'd talk with someone, get some help, get support and then I'd find out the facts and then make a decision from there. Do you have other help or support? Other friends or family you can talk to?

H: No, I mean other than a couple of friends I have at work. I have no other family living in the area, and I don't have children. I do have a brother that lives outside of Seattle, but I don't get to see him often. Plus, I don't know if I could talk with him about this kind of issue. If my sister were alive, I could talk with her.

C: What do you think your sister would recommend?

H: I think she would tell me to go out and enjoy life. She always wanted to go to Paris, but never went. I know she always regretted not having done that when she was alive and healthy.

C: Where would you want to go, or what would you want to do?

H: I've always wanted to go to Italy.

C: Tell me more about your plan? Where would you want to go in Italy?

Case Conceptualization/Crisis Resolution

One of the first tasks of intervening in a crisis situation is to try to establish a rapport with the individual, making him or her feel comfortable enough to talk. The counselor also empowers Helen by asking her what she wants to do regarding treatment rather than to impose any expectations on her. Plus, at the time of the initial crisis session, Helen has not met with her doctor yet and doesn't know what recommendations will be made regarding treatment. What Helen knows is that she doesn't want to go through the suffering her sister went through, and this also becomes a source of fear and apprehension regarding the diagnosis. By talking with the crisis counselor, Helen can gain support from someone whom she can talk to and who will help her weigh out decisions. Helen has few friends and although it would have been helpful to gain more information about her divorce and other past history, it was not relevant to the crisis at hand and therefore can be discussed at a later date.

In the vignette presented here, the counselor is intent on gathering information about the nature of the crisis; the factors that are contributing to it and maintaining it. This is all part of the **listening** stage as described in the L-A-P-C Model.

In discussing her present reactions, the counselor is trying to gain a sense as to Helen's state of mind, her feelings, and other reactions, as well as what other support systems she may have. This is all part of the **assessment** stage. In the **planning** stage, the counselor concludes this initial session by getting Helen to commit to coming back after her meeting with Dr. Johnston to discuss her reactions given any new information she receives. Helen is willing to **commit** to returning later in the day after her meeting with Dr. Johnston. The following describes some of the next session:

Counselor: I'm glad you were able to come in today Helen. How did the meeting with Dr. Johnston go?

Helen: Well, I'm not totally sure, to tell you the truth. It was very different from what I expected.

C: In what way was it different?

H: I was really expecting the worst, like I'd have to undergo radical surgery followed by months of chemo, but that's not what happened. Dr. Johnston told me that she could do a lumpectomy and that they could then do chemo for a few months. I could keep working during this time. I was really expecting that I'd have to go on disability.

C: It sounds like you're agreeable to what Dr. Johnston was proposing?

H: Yes, I think it's something I could do, something I could get through.

C: You sound much more optimistic.

H: I am, but I don't want to be overly optimistic. I feel I have to always be on guard, like I'm "hoping for the best, but preparing for the worst" as they say.

C: I see what you mean.

H: But, I'm going to take that trip to Italy. I don't want to wait until things are worse before I do some things for myself.

In Helen's medical crisis, it appears that she is trying not to be overly optimistic, and she has been cautious up to this point, especially because her sister died of breast cancer. Yet, Helen decided not to postpone things she wants to do in life. Her wanting to go to Italy is an example of this. It may be helpful for the crisis counselor to meet with Helen a few more times, especially around the time of her lumpectomy and while she is undergoing chemotherapy. Although Helen has made a good connection to the counselor, it remains to be seen whether she is willing to attend a support group for breast cancer survivors. This may be explored as a possibility in future sessions with the crisis counselor.

Case Presentation: A Treatment Decision Crisis Involving Chronic Back Pain

Antonio is a 47-year-old married father of three. After graduating high school, Antonio enlisted in the Navy where he served for six years. Upon receiving his discharge, he then went to work for his uncle in the family masonry business. He had been working successfully and had become a foreman when he was injured on one of the jobs when he was lifting a cinder block. This resulted in his herniating three lumbar discs. Antonio received physical therapy; however, it was not helpful, at which point his orthopedic surgeon recommended that metal plates be screwed into his spine in order to support the weight that the discs could no longer support. Antonio has received several other surgeries since that time, including a spinal fusion using cadaver bone, and more recently a titanium cage that is wired to his spine. All of these surgeries have provided only minor relief, and Antonio finds that he is unable to work, and unable to do much of anything in the way of physical work or exercise. Even driving a car is painful. Antonio sought crisis counseling at the advice of his pain management physician who felt that Antonio was slipping into a deep depression.

The case of Antonio represents a medical crisis involving both chronic pain brought on by a chronic back condition, and a depression resulting from a combination of factors, including the pain medication, the lack of mobility, and the loss of his occupational identity. These factors have created a synergistic effect, resulting in the current crisis. Antonio prided himself on being a hard worker and a good provider for his wife and children. Now, he finds that even driving a car is painful, and he feels that he is "useless" around the house. Antonio also once hoped that he would be able to return to work and get off medical disability; however, he is now coming to the realization that this probably won't happen. Each time he has surgery, he musters hope that this could be the one that restores him to full functioning; however, in each instance, the gains were minor and, in some instances, short-lived. Unfortunately, Antonio's quality of life has increasingly diminished with each surgery.

In this initial session with Antonio, the crisis counselor is intent on listening to the reasons why he is seeking counseling at this particular point in time. (Why now, as opposed to a month or a year ago?). The counselor is also intent on establishing some rapport with Antonio with the hope that he might avail himself of future counseling to help him cope with his present dilemma.

Intervention

Counselor: Antonio, I understand that your pain management doctor referred you here?

Antonio: Yeah, he sent me here, when I told him how depressed I was feeling lately. I didn't say that I was going to kill myself or anything, but he felt it was serious enough to suggest I come here.

C: Could you tell me how depressed you have been feeling lately?

A: Doc, I've just been miserable. I can't sleep, and when I do sleep I wake up in the middle of the night in a sweat. I don't want to eat or go out. People annoy the hell out of me; I guess I would rather be left alone.

C: How long have you been feeling this way?

A: I guess it started about four months ago. I noticed that I was feeling increasingly hopeless about my back, about all the surgeries, all the medication.

C: What was going on four months ago, that was different from before?

A: Well, for one thing, I just finished physical therapy after my most recent surgery, which was six months ago. I had the titanium cage operation. That's the one where they go in through your stomach and push all of your intestines out of the way so they can get to your spine and they then attach this cage-like thing into your spine to support the weight that the discs can't support.

C: It sounds like a really involved surgery. How long were you under anesthesia?

A: I was under for about eight hours. The recuperation was even worse though. Then once I was discharged from the hospital I couldn't get out of bed for weeks.

C: Was this recuperation different from the other surgeries you had?

A: It was in that it really took much longer for me to get to where I could even attempt to get out of bed.

C: Then you began physical therapy, right?

A: I did that religiously, but when I was done with it, I felt I was no better off than before I had the surgery. I guess that's when I went into a tailspin.

C: That must have been really tough for you, having gone through all that you did and then not feeling much better than before the surgery.

Here the counselor is providing some validation of how difficult it must have been for Antonio to have gone through such a difficult procedure and not to have derived some benefit from it.

A: Exactly. I felt like I had wasted all that time for nothing.

C: What has your orthopedic surgeon said about the operation?

A: Well, he said it was successful and that I just need to give it more time.

C: Do you feel you've given the recuperation enough time?

A: Well, I guess it may get better. I spoke with someone on line, who had this same procedure and he said it took many months before he began to feel some relief. I feel like I'm running out of time.

C: Are there options other than waiting?

A: Well, not surgery that's for sure! I can't go under the knife again. But, I did hear about some kind of morphine pump that delivers the painkiller right to the back rather than taking pills that are only going to space me out and make me even more depressed.

C: Maybe that is an option for you. Have you discussed that with your doctor or pain management specialist yet?

A: No, I just heard about it, but I think I will the next time I meet with them. I can't take this anymore. I'm either in constant pain, or I'm spaced out on the medication.

C: Antonio, are you going to be safe in the meantime?

A: I wouldn't do anything to myself. I couldn't do that to my wife and kids. Besides, I'm a devout Catholic, and I know it's a sin to kill yourself.

Case Conceptualization/Crisis Resolution

There are several things that transpired within this brief session. First, Antonio explains that he sought counseling not only at the advice of his pain management specialist, but because of how depressed he was that the surgery did not bring about the anticipated relief. It is common for patients to develop expectations about what their treatment or surgery will do for them. When these expectations are not met, or when the treatment is unsuccessful, the letdown is difficult to cope with. In Antonio's case, this letdown is exacerbated by the fact that the surgical procedure and recovery were such an ordeal. Therefore, when the expected relief is not forthcoming, it is normal for him to feel angry and depressed. It is noteworthy that in exploring alternatives there are basically two options that emerge. First, Antonio knows that more healing time may help him. It is often helpful in educating patients regarding surgical procedures to have them talk with other people who have gone through the same ordeal. Although their experiences may differ, it gives the patient some idea of what to expect. The Internet is very useful in helping to put potential surgical patients in touch with others who have had the same procedure. Secondly, Antonio also recently become aware of a device that could help him manage the pain, without the side effects of pain medication. Although Antonio has tried several other pain management techniques before (e.g., Transcutaneous electrical nerve stimulation (TENS) units which deliver electrical stimulation to the affected area to "short circuit" the pain), he is hopeful about the morphine pump because intuitively it makes sense to him. In ongoing crisis counseling with Antonio, it would be helpful to gain more information about this new pain management device and to make certain that Antonio does not let his expectations get too high.

GUIDELINES FOR COUNSELORS WORKING WITH MEDICAL CRISES

Medical crises can be very difficult to manage because of the serious implications of various medical illnesses or medical trauma. This is certainly the case with terminal conditions, such as many types of cancer, leukemia, and advanced cases of cardiopulmonary obstructive diseases (COPD). Chronic conditions also have serious implications for any individual, as is the case with diabetes; an injury that can result in permanent physical disability, an amputation, or a colostomy. Chronic conditions often result in permanent changes in the way that an individual defines him or herself. This naturally often results in a crisis. Bellak and Siegel (1983) devised guidelines for crisis counselors, psychiatrists, psychologists, medical social workers, or medical personnel working with people who are experiencing a medical crisis. These are the most relevant:

1. Explore the patient's concept of the illness or impending surgery;
2. Explore the personal meaning and role of the illness (e.g., secondary gains);
3. Educate the patient;
4. Establish contact with the treating physician or surgeon;
5. Explore the meaning of anesthesia;
6. Explore specific notions and fears of death; and
7. Explore specific types of illnesses and surgery.

Bellak and Siegel (1983) suggest that the counselor explore the specific meaning of the illness or surgery to the patient. For example, does the illness impact on this individual's self-concept as a man or woman? Does the patient associate the illness with significant others in their lives who may have had similar illnesses? It is also important to explore the personal meaning and secondary gain aspects of the illness. Is the patient gaining additional attention from being ill, or are others doing things for them that they had not done before? If so, this might represent the secondary gain aspects of the illness. There is also an exploration of the patient's anxieties and apprehensions. In other words, how is the patient responding or reacting to being ill or needing surgery? It is important that nurses, counselors, and other human service workers help to educate the patient about the illness and the potential risks and benefits. The assumption is that the more informed and educated patient is usually the more cooperative patient. It is also important that the counselor establish contact with the treating physician and/or surgeon. As Bellak and Siegel suggest, it is best not to work at cross-purposes with other medical professionals; therefore, it is highly recommended that the attending physician is kept apprised of your work with their patient. Hopefully, the physician then reciprocates and reports any changes in the patient's medical condition or changes in treatment regimen. This helps to facilitate the notion of a team approach to treatment, as opposed to having several specialists working independently, uninformed about each other's findings and treatment plans.

It is important to deal with those aspects of the illness or surgery where the patient may have other specific fears. For example, with anesthesia, many patients fear the burning and choking sensation they experience in the throat or that they may struggle for air. Others fear not being in control to keep an eye on things. Again, the more educated the patient is about both preoperative and postoperative procedures, the better. Concurrently, the fear of death arises often from the experience of not being in control—that a mistake will be made or the patient will not wake up. Bellak and Siegel talk of the importance of discussing these fears of death and dying and the patient's associations regarding death (e.g., being alone in a cold grave).

In the two cases described earlier, the counselor highlights some of the methods typically employed to establish rapport when conducting medical crisis counseling. Though certainly not complete, the crisis intervention counselor typically relies on several key features for establishing rapport, which is of key importance in providing crisis intervention services (DeWolfe, 2000). They are as follows:

Listening with genuine concern to the person in crisis as he or she talks about and often re-experiences the crisis is paramount to establishing a rapport with the client. Doing so establishes confidence in the client such that they feel their experiences are understood, respected, and not judged in any negative way. It encourages the person in crisis to unburden themselves with minimal self-consciousness. A skilled listener often adheres to the following guidelines:

Allowing for silences. Very often, the person in crisis reaches a point where there is a long silence. An experienced listener does not rush in to fill the silence with comment or further questioning right away. The crisis counselor knows that such silences often allow the person in crisis to reflect on and sometimes re-experience the intense emotional reactions to what he or she has endured. It is not uncommon for silences to be followed by a cascading of intense emotional affects that may have been suppressed, which are re-lived by the client.

Nonverbal attentiveness. The counselor can express concern and his presence in nonverbal ways. A good listener is empathetic to the client, by maintaining good eye contact, nodding in a knowing fashion at important junctures, and conveying attunement to the client's momentary state by donning caring facial expressions that are in accord with the content of what is said and the emotional state of the client. These nonverbal communications often come about quite naturally when the listener is attuned not only to the client's words, but also to the accompanying affect and the client's nonverbal body language.

Clarifying or identifying feelings. Nonverbal gestures by the client or change in tone of his/her voice serve as markers for the counselor to reflect to the client what he or she may be feeling. This is most helpful when the client is either flooded by emotion or unable to put into words what he or she is feeling. Comments like "You look terrified, or you sound angry" help the client identify and frame vague feelings of prior detachment. Identifying feelings for a client who is unable to do so on his or her own concretizes, encapsulates, and places boundary markers to feelings that are free floating and otherwise intolerable; the person in crisis usually has a sense of greater control when able to identify and label a feeling state. It may be less frightening to identify a specific fear than to try to deal with more generalized, non-focused anxiety.

Paraphrasing. The counselor can convey attunement with the client by reflecting back what the client said. Comments like "If I've understood you correctly you are saying that" confirms for the client that he is understood. It serves to validate what is being expressed by the client, and provides an opportunity for the counselor to check on the accuracy of the processed information by seeing if it is consistent with what the client acknowledges saying.

Emotional Release. Crucial to the healing work of crisis intervention is the emotional venting or release of intense feelings by the client. The crisis counselor may feel uncomfortable with the client's venting of very intense emotions, such as anger, grief, sadness, and so forth. The crisis counselor may inadvertently communicate discomfort with a client's abreaction by way of subtle facial expressions of disapproval, prematurely timed verbal reassurances, interjections that do not mirror what the client is feeling, or less subtle cues like active redirecting of the client's focus. Such cues serve to derail clients from free expression of their feelings. It stifles the flow of the client's emotional upheaval and, in doing so, may obstruct the real working through of such intense feelings that is prerequisite for the constructive problem solving that eventually follows.

SUMMARY

Health crises are often overlooked or not likely encountered by counselors who do primarily mental health or other types of crisis counseling, yet for doctors, nurses, or other medical health professionals, these types of crises are quite common. As in managing other types of crises presented in this textbook, it is important to listen to the client's fears, apprehensions, and other emotional reactions to the medical issues or problems they are dealing with as a beginning to understanding how they feel. As explained throughout this chapter, crises at the time of diagnosis and again at the time of treatment decision making are quite common.

RESOURCES FOR CHAPTER ENRICHMENT

Recommended Films

Whose Life Is It Anyway?: **(1981)** (stars Richard Dreyfuss, John Cassavetes, & Christine Lahti). Richard Dreyfuss plays a sculptor, named Ken Harrison, who is involved in a car accident which leaves him paralyzed from the neck down. The film portrays the crisis brought on by his medical condition, and his wish to be allowed to terminate his life.

The Doctor: **(1991)** (stars William Hurt & Christine Lahti). This film focuses on the medical crisis of cancer when a physician, played by William Hurt, is diagnosed with cancer. This film is unique in its portrayal of a doctor who is now in the role of being the patient and the reactions he experiences as a result.

Philadelphia: **(1993)** (stars Denzel Washington and Tom Hanks). Hanks is a gay attorney who is dying from AIDS-related complications. In this Oscar-winning performance, the issues of the psychological-emotional crises surrounding AIDS is well-portrayed, as well as the bias and discrimination issues that individuals with AIDS often face.

The Savages: **(2007)** (stars Philip Seymour Hoffman and Laura Linney). This is the story of a brother and sister who are faced with the crisis of needing to put their estranged, elderly father in a nursing home. This film accurately depicts the devastating impact of dementia (Alzheimer's) on both the elderly parent and his adult children.

Alive Day Memories: **(2009)** this is an HBO documentary produced by James Gandolfini who interviews several soldiers who suffered near-fatal wounds while serving in Iraq. This documentary also explores issues pertaining to trauma as well as recovery.

Sicko: **(2007)** this documentary by filmmaker Michael Moore provides a highly critical examination of the greed fueling America's private enterprise healthcare system.

Suggested Activities

1. Find someone who has gone through a major illness or accident who will agree to talk with you. Ask them how they reacted at the time of the illness or accident. How are they coping with that illness or accident now? How did the accident or injury change their life? What helped them to cope with the illness or accident. What didn't help?

2. In July 2007, Michael Moore released his documentary "Sicko" that deals with the state of health care in America. After watching the film, discuss your reactions. What stood out most about the film? What would you do to change our current health care system?

3. Interview someone who deals with people who are experiencing health care crises, for example nurses, doctors, EMT workers, police, or first aid squad volunteers. What does this first responder find is the most difficult aspect of his or her job? What is the most gratifying part of his or her work?

Recommended YouTube Viewing

https://www.youtube.com/watch? v = XPcYIZO6FZo This brief video provides an example of a hospital social worker helping a medical patient who is noncompliant with dialysis treatment.

https://www.youtube.com/watch? v = o-FDfp8DC1Y This video presents information on managing depression in the face of chronic illness.

CHAPTER 14

Crises in the Workplace

*S*andra works for a major airline in the maintenance department. Her job is to help guide planes to their gates, and she is also responsible for setting up refueling and baggage unloading. Her boss, Jim Groper, often makes remarks about how slow Sandra is in getting her work done, and he often makes inappropriate sexual remarks about her appearance. Sandra finds herself the brunt of other jokes made by male employees. When Sandra tried to talk with Mr. Groper about how his remarks were making her uncomfortable, he became angry and defensive and said she was being "too sensitive." He commented that "the airline industry was no place for women anyway." Sandra is a single parent and cannot lose this job or health benefits. She feels angry, frustrated, and trapped.

DISCUSSION QUESTIONS

1. Workplace crises often come about as a result of sexual harassment, as in Sandra's case. Do you think that sexual harassment is more prevalent in certain types of jobs or industries? What would you recommend that Sandra should do?

2. Workplace violence is a particularly dangerous and frightening type of workplace crisis. How would you manage a coworker who threatens to harm a boss or supervisor?

INTRODUCTION

The crisis situation presented above is just one of the many crises that are common in today's workplace. For many, work settings can be stress-filled environments. Given that most Americans devote at least a third or more of their waking life to work, and given the many pressures that most employees find themselves under, it is not unusual to find that these stressful environments are a breeding ground for various types of crises. Naturally, work stress and work crises are much worse during times of economic recessions; however, even during times of a booming economy, the United States continues to witness the stresses and strains of downsizing, corporate takeovers, increased work demands, and longer work hours. For example, in 2016 although the economic reports were favorable as evidenced by lower unemployment rates and overall growth in production (GDP—gross domestic product), there are still concerns about corporations laying off many employees because of American companies building factories overseas. Many families find that in order to provide their children with basic necessities, better opportunities, or health insurance, both parents must work outside the home. Also, consider that for many years, it was common for an employee to put in twenty-five or thirty years at the same job and then retire. However, these types of secure "cradle-to-grave" jobs are unfortunately a thing of the past. Some workers feel that holding a job for five years is the maximum that can be expected in today's economy and job market. Just as employees feel that their employers hold no sense of loyalty toward them, so too in many cases, employees feel a lack of loyalty toward their employers. The downfall of corporate giants, like Enron and WorldCom, because of mismanagement and greed only served to strengthen these attitudes. Yet, there are also many corporations and other work organizations (e.g., nonprofits, medical centers, universities, and government) that pride themselves on treating employees with respect and civility.

In response to the various crises that are common to the workplace, many companies provide employee assistance counseling services to help employees cope with some of the crises that we discuss in this chapter. These employee assistance counselors or EAPs (employee assistance professionals) are available to help employees with any type of stressors they may encounter, whether within the workplace or from outside. Some larger corporations provide excellent in-house EAP programs to their employees. These programs can range from having one EAP counselor who provides assessment and referral for employees in crisis, to having several counselors on staff, who not only can provide assessments, but who can also provide on-going counseling services beyond the initial crisis assessment. Smaller companies or organizations that cannot justify having an employee assistance professional on staff often contract with managed care insurance providers or mental health clinicians to provide employee assistance services via hotline access. These employee assistance counselors usually provide immediate crisis intervention, and act as gatekeepers in providing employees with information and referrals.

The cases and scenarios presented in this chapter address three common types of workplace crises, including crises pertaining to violence, crises pertaining to downsizing/job termination, and crises pertaining to supervisor-employee and coworker conflict.

According to recent statistics, from 1992 to 2012 there were approximately 14,770 incidents for workplace homicides, which averages to about 700 workplace homicides per year (Centers for Disease Control & Prevention, 2014). Of course, when considering the fact that more than 120 million people in the United States are employed, the total number of deaths per year may seem like a rather small percentage, yet the number of workplace assaults is more commonplace. It is also important to note, however, that most workplace deaths occur during the course of robberies (e.g., convenience stores or cab drivers), while only 9% to 10% are attributed to business disputes, and of that percentage, only 4% to 6% were committed by employees or former employees. According to OSHA (Occupational Health & Safety Administration, 2002), it appears that workplace violence resulting from disputes with coworkers make up the minority of the instances of workplace violence. The Centers for Disease Control—National Institute of Occupational Safety & Health (2014) estimates that from 2003 to 2012, over 50% of workplace homicides occurred within three occupational classifications: Sales and related occupations (28%) protective services (17%) and transportation (13%). This suggests that the rates of violence and homicide are highest for law enforcement officers, corrections officers, taxi drivers, private security guards, bartenders, mental health professionals, gas station attendants, and convenience or liquor store clerks. Therefore, the potential for violence is much greater for those dealing with the general public than for those dealing with coworkers or supervisors. The following is a quote from one of OSHA's Workplace Violence Fact Sheets:

> Some 2 million American workers are victims of workplace violence each year. Workplace violence can strike anywhere, and no one is immune. Some workers, however, are at increased risk. Among them are workers who exchange money with the public; deliver passengers, goods, or services; work alone or in small groups during late night or early morning hours; work in high-crime areas; or work in community settings and homes where they have extensive contact with the public. This group includes health-care and social service workers, such as visiting nurses, psychiatric evaluators, and probation officers; community workers, such as gas and water utility employees, phone and cable TV installers, and letter carriers; retail workers; and taxi drivers. (Occupational Health & Safety Administration Fact Sheet, 2002)

In instances where workplace violence occurs as a result of disputes or conflicts between workers or between supervisors and employees, Lewis and Zare (1999) have identified several factors that may predict or exacerbate workplace violence. One of these is what is often referred to as a "toxic" work environment. Toxic work environments are defined as jobs that lack upward mobility and job security; offer limited benefits; low wages; heavy workload; long hours with weekends required; unexpected shift changes; expected or mandatory overtime; no autonomy; no input in decisions; and managers who are inconsistent, inflexible, untrained, and who show favoritism. According to Lewis and Zare (1999), any organization or company that manifests these toxic workplace characteristics may be placing themselves at greater risk for workplace violence.

Obviously, not all individuals who work in toxic work environments commit acts of workplace violence. Therefore, it is important to determine what distinguishes the potentially violent employee from those who are able to cope with a toxic workplace. Although there are no foolproof ways to predict who will become a potentially violent worker, there are some signs that need to be considered. In terms of work-related employee behaviors, Lewis and Zare (1999) suggest that absenteeism, tardiness, ignoring work assignments, frequent absences from one's workstation, leaving work early, or arriving late for work are significant factors. Coworkers or managers may notice faulty judgments, poor decision making, inconsistencies in work quality and productivity, and failure to remember instructions. From an attitudinal and emotional perspective, if an employee's mood swings are frequent; negative attitudes persistent; frequent complaints received from customers, vendors, or coworkers are common; and the employee overreacts to any criticism, then these characteristics evidence as red flags. The aforementioned mood swings may be characterized by irritability, high anxiety, depression with crying jags, and hostility. Potentially violent individuals often feel that they have been wronged or betrayed by their boss or supervisor (as in Ted's case, described below). As their behavior escalates, they may display temper outbursts, frequent arguments with coworkers or supervisors, and they may display violence by throwing things, smashing things, or they may abuse alcohol or drugs flagrantly. Alcohol and certain drugs (e.g., cocaine, amphetamines, and steroids) tend to exacerbate the potential for violent acting out. As these behaviors escalate over time, the potentially violent individual may or may not verbalize threats. If, and when this happens, responsible individuals in the work setting, whether human resources staff, employee assistance professionals, or supervisors/managers, must be prepared to take action.

CRISES PERTAINING TO WORKPLACE VIOLENCE

Case Presentation: When Violence Threatens

Ted has been employed by a large telecommunications company for the past five years. During that time, he has been assigned to a work unit where Sandra Brown is his direct supervisor. Ted has been increasingly agitated by Sandra's treatment of him over the past few months. He feels that she has been unreasonable when assigning him extra work assignments with impossible deadlines. Ted was also promised a faster computer in order to do his work more efficiently; however, after several months, he still has not received the computer. As Ted has become increasingly upset, he reports that he has been unable to sleep. He has been drinking more frequently and neglecting his personal hygiene. One day after being reprimanded by Ms. Jones for missing a deadline, Ted stated in front of several coworkers, "If Ms. Brown dumps one more job on me, I'm going on a rampage that will make Columbine look like a day in the park." Background information reveals that Ted had been fired from a previous job for having a physical altercation with his supervisor although he claims that he didn't make a direct threat and that his comments about wanting to hurt the supervisor were "misunderstood." Because Ted's company doesn't have an on-site employee assistance counselor, he was referred to an EAP counselor by one of the staff in the Human Resources Department who usually handles conflicts between employees and supervisors.

Case Conceptualization/Crisis Resolution

Ted feels that he has been wronged by his supervisor, Ms. Jones, and that he has been treated unfairly. His frustrations and complaints have resulted in his making a threat to commit acts of violence. All threats of this nature must be taken seriously and not ignored or minimized in such a way to conclude that "Ted is just blowing off steam." In fact, Ted had voiced his frustrations to another supervisor and to his coworkers and feels that he has "gotten nowhere" and that no one is listening to his complaints. In this type of situation, the role of an employee assistance counselor or crisis counselor is to hear out Ted's complaints and to convey to Ted that he is willing to help and intervene on his behalf. Also, given the seriousness of Ted's complaints and threats, he can't merely send him back to work. Therefore, the EAP counselor makes an agreement with Ted that he will intervene on his behalf provided that Ted goes for a psychiatric evaluation. The EAP counselor is careful not to use the term "psychiatric evaluation" immediately because he doesn't want Ted to become more agitated or respond with something like, "you think I'm crazy?" It would be essential in a situation like this to ascertain whether Ted has a past history of violence, a concrete plan, and access to weapons to carry out his plan. In order to ensure safety of all those involved, it would be best to have Ted escorted from the building and to the emergency room or clinic where he will be psychiatrically evaluated. The last thing the Employee Assistance counselor wants is for Ted to leave agitated and hostile, go out to his car to get a weapon, and return to the building (this is what happened at a workplace shooting at a meatpacking plant in the Midwest).

There are two important questions to consider. What if Ted refuses the Employee Assistance counselor's recommendation that he must have an evaluation? In an instance like this, Ted would most likely be suspended from his position pending an investigation; however, the police would need to be called, and a restraining order would be requested from the courts given his direct threat to harm Ms. Brown. The restraining order would specify that Ted could not come near any company building, nor could he contact (by phone, e-mail, text, or through another employee) or come near Ms. Brown. The other question pertains to the psychiatric evaluation. What if the psychiatrist assesses Ted as having a high potential for committing violence? In this instance, inpatient psychiatric treatment may need to be court-ordered until such time that it is determined by his doctor and the judge that he is no longer a threat to others. There is a possibility that inpatient treatment may be the safest option, given that Ted is not sleeping, he has increased his use of alcohol, and he has admitted to having a history of violence in the past.

In an attempt to predict, and hopefully prevent workplace violence, it is also helpful to view workplace violence as arising from a combination of personality factors, AND workplace factors, AND instigating situations, because instances of violence rarely occur because of one isolated incident that pushes a person over the edge.

Even with what is known about profiles of individuals who may be prone to workplace violence, there are still exceptions to the rule. Therefore, individual coworkers, bosses, or supervisors must sometimes learn to trust their instincts or reactions when faced with coworkers who engender unease. In order to prevent workplace violence, steps should be taken when some of the aforementioned behaviors are first noted. Sometimes, a non-threatening meeting with a managing supervisor early on in the process can help to "clear the air" and in doing so, come up with some strategies for making this person's work situation more tolerable. What is difficult is that once the potentially violent worker feels "wronged," then there is often very little that can be done to diffuse this person's anger at their supervisor, coworkers, or at the organization. This is especially true if the person has some other mental disorder. Individuals who manifest any kind of psychotic thinking, especially paranoid thinking, or who may be an estranged or loner type of individual may be prone to becoming increasingly more violent, or they may perceive violence as a means of achieving their goals. It is always best to intervene with these individuals as early as possible, for example, when peculiarities in their behavior or attitudes first begin to become evident. When a potentially violent employee is referred for psychiatric evaluation, one of the first things that is done is a *lethality assessment*.

In assessing someone for potential violence, one of the best predictors of future violence is **a past history of such behavior**. It is important to keep in mind however, that the violence-prone individual may not always be forthcoming about such information. In some instances, the person may sign a release so that the counselor may speak with a trusted family member or a mental health counselor who may have previously treated this individual. In examining past violent behavior (which includes both verbal and physical assaults), it is important to determine what might have provoked these incidents and whether the individual has any insight into whether his or her behavior was inappropriate.

Figure 14.1 LAPC Form: Ted

Name: _____ Ted _____   Age: __32__

<u>L</u>isten   <u>A</u>ssess   <u>P</u>lan   <u>C</u>ommit

L   I   S   T   E   N

I   What are they saying about the crisis? *Ted claims that his supervisor, Mrs. Brown, has been treating him unfairly and has been harassing him.*

S   What happened? *Frank made a verbal threat to harm Mrs. Brown.* When did it happen? *Earlier today*

T   What type of crisis was it? (traumatic event, developmental, psychiatric, existential) *Traumatic event*

E   Did they mention anything that indicates danger? *Yes, Ted's comments suggest physical harm/homicidal intent.*

N   Other relevant information about the crisis: *Yes, Ted has a prior history of physical violence.*

A   S   S   E   S   S

S   <u>F</u>eeling: Is their predominant emotional state one of:
S
E

anger *Yes*	sadness	hopelessness
anxiety	panic	numbness

suicidal? If yes, complete lethality assessment/suicide.   *No*
homicidal? If yes, complete lethality assessment/violence.   *Yes*

S   <u>A</u>cting: Is their behavior

active/restless *Yes*	consistent with mood *Yes*
passive/withdrawn *No*	good eye contact *No*

S   <u>T</u>hinking: Are they

logical/making sense *No*	coherent/expressing self well *Yes*
insightful *No*	focused on topic *Yes*
evasive/changing subject *No*	

Other: Any medical problems?   *No*   Physical limitations?   *No*
Hospitalizations?   *No* Need for hospitalization?   *Yes*

P   L   A   N

L   What needs to be done now? *Psychiatric evaluation for possible admission to inpatient hospital for observation.*

A   What alternative plans have been discussed? *None given seriousness of threat*

N   Are these plans reasonable? *Yes*   Able to be carried out? *Depends on whether Ted is willing to go for an evaluation.*

C   O   M   M   I   T

O   Which plan of action have they chosen? *Ted has agreed to evaluation.*

M   Do they have the resources/support to implement the plan? *Yes, the Psychiatric Evaluation will be paid for by the company.*

M   Are they motivated to implement the plan? *Yes, it is a condition of his continued employment.*

I   What other resources/support may be needed?

T   friend   family member
           neighbor   mental health provider   *Yes*
           public agency (law enforcement, child protective
           services, social services)
           medical (hospitalization, medication)   *Yes*

Lethality Assessment Form - Homicide/Violent Threat

Client: Ted   Age: 32

1) *Is there a past history of any of the following:*
   - **violent behavior**   *yes, prior assault charge involving fight in bar*
   - **property destruction**   *yes, destroyed girlfriend's property*
   - **attempted homicide**   *no*

(Continued)

Figure 14.1   (Continued)

- other criminal behaviors — *unknown*
- intimate partner violence — *yes*
- other family violence — *unknown*
- bullying of others — *yes*
- child abuse (client) — *unknown*
- incarceration — *yes*
- job loss due to threats — *yes, in prior job*
- school expulsion — *unknown*
- animal cruelty — *unknown*
- psychiatric treatment — *denied*
- alcohol/drug abuse — *yes*

  If yes, specify substances abused   *alcohol*

2) Present threats of violence? — *yes, threats directed to supervisor*
3) Violent or homicidal plan? — *denies specific plan*
4) Recent homicidal plan or behavior? — *no*
5) Violent ideation or obsessions? — *yes, feels "wronged" and unfairly treated*
6) Means or methods to carry out plan? — *denies specific plan, minimizes his threats*
7) Recent disruptions in interpersonal
   relationships (e.g. separation) — *yes, separation due to alcohol abuse and subsequent abusive behavior*

GUIDELINES FOR CRISIS INTERVENTION WITH A POTENTIALLY VIOLENT EMPLOYEE

Lewis and Zare (1999) recommend that companies and other work organizations develop "Crisis Response Teams" that can be activated in instances of extreme violent behavior in the workplace like a shooting. A Crisis Response Team may be composed of employee assistance counselors, representatives from management and labor, occupational health, legal, safety, and security personnel, and an outside liaison to community resources like mental health professionals. Each member of the team is designated a specific role. For example, one member of the team is designated as the media liaison, another provides information to employees, another sets up debriefing sessions. The U.S. Department of Labor Occupational Safety and Health Administration also provides valuable information on workplace violence that can be accessed on their website (www.osha.gov). Certainly, the old adage, "an ounce of prevention is worth a pound of cure" applies to workplace violence. In a majority of cases, early intervention can prevent potentially volatile workers from acting out and harming others.

Table 14.1   Factors Predictive of Workplace Violence

Personality Factors   Prior history of violent behavior   Antisocial personality disorder   Explosive personality   Schizoid personality disorder   Paranoid personality disorder   Borderline personality disorder
Toxic Workplace Factors   Autocratic management   Lack of control over workload   No upward mobility   Lack of job security   Lack of input into job   Mandatory overtime
Instigating Factors   Divorce or separation   Job termination or lay off   Verbal altercation with boss or coworker   Feeling "wronged" or cheated by company   Major job change or stressor   Corporate merger with job uncertainty

Table 14.2   Factors Associated with Increased Risk of Violence

Think of the acronym "ARM PAIN"
     Altered state of consciousness like delirium
     Repeated assaults or history of violence
     Male gender- males are more prone to violent acts then females
 	
     Paranoia (as in schizophrenia, mania, or delusional disorder)
     Age – younger individuals are more likely to become violent
     Incapacity – brain injury or psychosis
     Neurological disease

Or think of the acronym: MADS and BADS
     Mania (high energy level and poor judgment)
     Alcohol (intoxication or withdrawal)
     Dementia
     Schizophrenia (especially paranoid subtype)
 	
     Borderline personality disorder (intense anger)
     Antisocial personality disorder (disregard for safety of self/others)
     Delirium (with hallucinations or delusions)
     Substance abuse (especially PCP, cocaine, methamphetamines)

Reprinted with permission from S. Bohen, (2001). *Psychiatric Emergencies* (p.24). Eau Claire, WI: PESI Healthcare.

Box 14.1: A Different Kind of Mass Shooting: Kansas rampage doesn't fit the usual pattern

On Thursday, February 18, 2016, Cedric Larry Ford went to his place of employment, Excel Industries, a lawn mower factory and began shooting fellow employees, killing three coworkers, and injuring many others. Ford was armed with a semiautomatic pistol and an assault-style rifle. What was unusual about this workplace shooting was that, unlike most perpetrators, Mr. Ford is African American; the other factor that makes this shooting unusual is that Mr. Ford had a history of felony criminal convictions that should have precluded him from obtaining weapons under Kansas gun laws (the shootings took place in Hesston, Kansas). Another unusual factor was that when Mr. Ford entered the factory, he appeared to be shooting random employees. Usually, shooters have specific coworkers or supervisors they target, but this was not the case with Ford. The Hesston, Kansas, shootings came just five days after another shooting rampage where a gunman killed six people.

Earlier in February, Ford was accused by his girlfriend of assault, when she alleged that he put her in a "chokehold" from behind. Mr. Ford's girlfriend filed for an order of protection on February 5, 2016, and it so happened that the order was served to Mr. Ford on Thursday February 18th, the day of the shootings at the Excel factory. Mr. Ford's girlfriend stated, "He is an alcoholic, violent, and depressed. It's my belief he is in desperate need of medical and psychological help."

Source: Haxel, Christopher, Mark Bermna, and Jerry Markon. (2016, Feb. 26). "Kansas Shooting Rampage Deviated from Pattern of Recent Tragedies." *The Washington Post.*

CRISES PERTAINING TO DOWNSIZING AND JOB TERMINATION

Downsizing has become one of the most pervasive yet understudied phenomena in the American workplace. In April 2009, unemployment in the United States hit a new all-time high of 8.6%. Job loss and downsizing is common during times of economic recession (Andrews, 2008) and it's common that corporations differ in the ways they reduce their workforce. Although there have been recent decreases in unemployment (United States Bureau of Labor Statistics, 2017) there are some who claim these estimates are lowered because of the number of workers who have stopped looking for work. Hickok (2000) refers to the notion of "corporate culture" as a reflection of the ways in which companies downsize. According to Hickok, ". . . culture is to an organization what personality is to an individual." Therefore, it is not unusual to find many ways that corporations use to downsize their workforce (Cameron, 1993, 1994). Some companies conscientiously plan a layoff and allow employees time and assistance (such as executive coaching) to make the transition smoother. These companies often initiate voluntary reductions as a first step measure (e.g., job buyouts, job sharing, early retirement). Some companies provide explicit criteria for who is laid off versus who stays on (Hickok, 2000). This type of downsizing is far different from the company that reacts impulsively to declining profits by arbitrarily laying off employees, giving them a cardboard box to clean out their desk, and having a security guard escort them to the parking lot. "Survivors" of corporate downsizing often experience high stress (Leana & Feldman, 1992; New York Times, 1996); lower morale (Armstrong-Stassen, 1993), and a "syndrome" characterized by anger, envy, and guilt (Noer, 1993). Work relationships also suffer during periods of downsizing, which can take the form of backstabbing, blaming, and failure to cooperate by remaining employees (Mohrman & Mohrman, 1983).

The stages that employees experience when they lose their jobs are somewhat like those experienced with other types of losses, in that employees go through a grieving process. The outcome of this process is that the person either becomes apathetic, depressed, and angry or they accept the loss and begin to move on with their lives. What is important for crisis counselors working with individuals who have experienced job loss it to determine what will help this individual move on. Leana and Feldman (1992) mention in their

Box 14.2: Congratulations . . . You're Fired

In an April 9, 2016, article in the *New York Times*, reporter Dan Lyons talks about a recent trend at many tech companies, start-ups, and established Fortune 500 industries, where employees are terminated or fired after a year or two without due cause, rhyme, or reason. For example, at HubSpot, a software company, when employees are fired, it is called a "graduation." Employees get these "cheery emails" from their boss saying, "Team, just letting you know that X has graduated and we're all excited to see how she uses her superpowers in her next big adventure." Lyons, who was an employee of HubSpot states, "One day this happened to a friend of mine. She was 35, had been with the company for four years, and was told without explanation by her 28-year-old manager that she had two weeks to get out. On her last day, that manager organized a farewell party for her. It was surreal, and cruel, but everyone at HubSpot acted as if this were perfectly normal. We were told we were 'rock stars' who were 'inspiring people' and 'changing the world,' but in truth, we were disposable."

Unfortunately, many start-up IT companies are "proud of this kind of culture," according to Lyons. Citing Amazon as an example, CEO Jeff Bezos states that employees who don't like the company's grueling environment are free to work elsewhere. He has stated, "We never claim that our approach is the right one—just that it's ours and over the last two decades, we've assembled a group of like-minded people." Some viewed the statement as a sign that Mr. Bezos at least seems to recognize that it's not normal for employees to cry at their desks. But, it was also a defiant message that he had no intention of letting up.

Lyons goes on to state, "Treating workers as if they are widgets to be used up and discarded is a central part of the revised relationship between employers and employees that techies proclaim is an innovation as important as chips and software. The model originated in Silicon Valley, but it's spreading."

Source: Lyons, D. (2016, April 9). Congratulations...You're Fired. *New York Times,* pp. 25–26.

research with workers who had experienced job loss that "many had used metaphors of death and dying in their descriptions of the experience" (p. 50). One worker stated, "Besides the death of a loved one, losing my job was one of the greatest hurts I have had in my life" (p. 51). Eisenberg and Lazarsfeld (1938) were among the first to recognize that workers go through various stages in response to job loss. They were studying individuals who lost their jobs during the Depression of the 1930s. The stages that they discovered all workers went through included shock, then followed by an active job hunt, at which point the person is usually optimistic and hopeful. When these efforts fail, however, the person experiences pessimism, anxiety, and active distress. This stage is followed by a fatalistic period where job attainment is viewed as hopeless or unattainable. Kaufman (1982) describes a four-stage model of response to unemployment. This first stage is characterized by *shock, relief, and relaxation*. In the second stage, the person begins to *search for a new job;* however, if these attempts prove futile, the person then moves into a third stage in which they may feel *self-doubt, anger, and vacillation*. In the fourth stage, the unemployed person experiences *resignation and withdrawal*. Kaufman suggests that this process may occur over a five- to seven-month period. Leana and Feldman's (1992) research attempts to determine what factors account for whether people succumb to a state of apathy following their job loss or whether they respond by viewing the job loss and re-employment as a challenge. Generally, they found that individuals with higher self-esteem (prior to the job layoff) and Type A personality were predictive of those individuals who take a more problem-focused coping approach. Type A personality is characterized by traits, such as competitiveness, ambitiousness, and aggressiveness. These individuals are often driven and exhibit a great deal of goal-directed behavior with a high energy level. In contrast, the Type B personality is more laid back and less likely to become stressed. They tend to be more cooperative than competitive. Problem focused coping behaviors include making an active job search, retraining for another type of work, increasing employability skills, or relocating to another town or city where jobs are more plentiful. Regarding the job search process, it is recommended that an active job searcher treat the search process as if it is a full-time job.

It is difficult sometimes for crisis counselor to work with individuals who have recently been laid off, especially if the person is floundering in a mass of emotions that keep them immobilized, such as blame, self-doubt, or pessimism. As with individuals who are going through a bereavement crisis, the role of the crisis counselor is to help facilitate the grieving process; that is to help the person experience the myriad of emotions that people naturally feel after going through such a loss while continuing to take active steps in their job search.

Case Presentation: "I've Been Downsized"

Kathleen has been working for a financial investment firm for the past eighteen years. Over the years, she rose up the ranks and within the past few months, she was promoted to senior vice president. Unfortunately, about three months after her promotion, her company announced that they were going to lay off several staff members; this action was a direct result of a lawsuit brought against the company that ended in a large payoff to the complainant. Subsequently, Kathleen and three other senior vice presidents were laid off. Kathleen was emotionally traumatized when she was told by her boss that she was one of the senior vice presidents eliminated. Making matters worse was that Kathleen was within five years of retirement, and she has two children who are attending expensive private universities. Since Kathleen was given notice of the layoff six weeks ago, she just sits and stares out of the window all day. She feels immobilized, angry, and betrayed.

Kathleen can probably best be described as in the stage of shock or depression. She is immobilized by the news of the layoff, as evidenced by her sitting and staring out the window all day. Kathleen is also experiencing regret for taking the promotion. However, the saying, "hindsight is always 20/20," applies here. She also knows that she would have regretted not taking a promotion that resulted in higher pay, more prestige, and better benefits. But, she also fears that no other company will hire her at her age, particularly given that she is close to retirement. The most important question is: How can the counselor assist Kathleen in mobilizing her internal resources and her external network so that she can begin the road to healing from this loss? Kathleen has sought counseling through her health insurance plan, which she was allowed to keep as part of her severance package. The following is a possible scenario of this type of session.

Intervention

Counselor: Kathleen, I understand that you were laid off from your job because of downsizing at your company. When did you learn that you were being laid off?

Kathleen: It was about six weeks ago. I keep losing track of time. I feel like I'm in limbo right now, and I can't seem to get moving. I had just been promoted to senior vice president too! I finally got to a point where all the hard work I put in, all the overtime I put in, had finally paid off and bang, they give me my pink slip.

C: Sounds like you felt blindsided?

K: Really!!! I heard about a lawsuit that had been settled against the company, but I didn't think they were going to lay people off, especially not senior vice presidents. I have another few months, which allows me to train my replacement. Do you believe that? And then I'll get a year's severance pay with full benefits. I'm thinking of moving to Tahiti for a year. Just kidding, of course. I have two kids in college, so I'm not going anywhere, least of all Tahiti!

C: Have you given any thought to what you'll do during this upcoming year?

K: Well, that's why I agreed to see you. I admit I was resentful at first when my ex-husband suggested I come and speak with you, but then I thought to myself, why not take advantage of my health insurance why I still have it?

C: You mention you have two kids in college? How are they coping with the news of your layoff?

K: They were pretty upset, but like most college kids, they're more focused on their own lives and how this will eventually impact on them. My one son was pretty supportive. He works all summer to save money to pay for his expenses during the school year. My daughter is less motivated to work. She still thinks we have a money tree growing in the backyard. She's not as realistic when it comes to the harsh realities of life.

C: And your ex-husband, does he help with college expenses?

K: He does help a little, but he was laid off from his job as a computer programmer about a year ago. His company had downsized and outsourced their computer work to a company in Bangalore. He was never great when it came to helping out with the kids.

C: Had you ever been through a layoff before or anything like this?

K: Well, not exactly like this. What it feels like is when I went through my divorce about ten years ago. That was pretty bad also. We had to sell our condo, I had no money, no place to live. I felt like a lost soul, I guess.

C: Tell me Kathleen, what helped you to get through that crisis? They say that going through a divorce is like grieving a death. How did you get through it?

Here, the counselor is not as interested in the details of the divorce, as they are in talking about how Kathleen was able to get through the emotional pain of the divorce. This might provide some clues for how Kathleen coped with the loss and what might help her through the present crisis. It is not unusual for those who react the most intensely to a job loss crisis have already experienced some other major loss.

K: Well, after I sulked and moped around for about two months, I finally found myself feeling angry at my ex. You know, it was similar.
Here I was thinking I was a good wife. I worked hard and then one day, he says "I don't think I love you anymore, I need time to figure this out."
About a month later he's living with a woman he worked with. I guess he "figured things out."

C: What helped you get through all this?

K: Well, I have a great group of friends, some I've been friends with since grammar and high school, and I was able to talk with them a lot. I spent time with my kids. I got into a support group at my church. I just got out of the pity pot and began doing things, like dating again.

C: Do you think you'll get to that point with this crisis?

K: Probably . . . you're right. I got through that crisis, I can get through this one. I hope you're right. I don't know though; this one is pretty bad. Besides, who is going to hire me at 59 years old? I don't see things turning around, at least not in the near future anyway.

C: So maybe you weren't kidding about throwing in the towel and moving to Tahiti?

K: I don't see many options here. The job market sucks. I don't even know how to begin a job search or even where to start. The last time I applied for a job, I sent in a paper CV. Now most jobs you apply for online, right?

C: There are a number of things we can work on. For example, I know of a headhunter that specializes in your industry, and he can coach you on how to redraft your CV. That is, providing that you see yourself working in the same industry?

K: Yes, I don't want to make a total career change, I know this industry inside and out. Plus, I got to be pretty good at what I do, and I liked the work.

C: Okay, so I will give you the headhunters email and cell number so you can set up a meeting with her. What about networking? What I mean is that over the years, you have met many people in this industry. What about putting out feelers, making some calls?

K: Funny you mention that, I've kept every business card of everyone I've met in this business since I started out. I just feel lousy about calling them. Like I've failed, like I'm some sort of failure or charity case or something.

C: That's the first thing we need to work on. You know that the workplace has changed. Very few people have lifelong jobs anymore, so what makes you different? What's wrong with your asking if these contacts know of any job openings? What if one of the people whose card you have, called you looking to see what you know about possible openings?

K: I would try to help the person, unless they were a total loser or something.

C: So, you're not a "total loser," don't you think some of your friends or colleagues would be willing to help you?

Case Conceptualization/Crisis Resolution

In the case illustration above, there are both emotional as well as practical goals. As with any grief counseling, the counselor tries to facilitate the grief process. By facilitation, we mean that the counselor tries to get the person to express the feelings associated with the particular stage that they are experiencing. If they are angry, then the counselor tries to facilitate the expression of this anger. If they are depressed, then the counselor tries to facilitate the expression of these depressive feelings. In the latter part of the session, the counselor uses a cognitive behavioral strategy. Kathleen indirectly expresses one of Ellis's Irrational Beliefs (Ellis, 1952), "I must be thoroughly adequate, competent, and achieving in everything I do," therefore Kathleen feels that losing her job is a sign that she is basically incompetent and flawed. The counselor is trying to get Kathleen to refute this irrational perception.

GUIDELINES FOR CRISIS COUNSELING WITH A DOWNSIZED EMPLOYEE

1. *Listen to the person's story and understand his or her reactions.* It is important to hear the events leading up to the downsizing and listen for various emotional reactions (e.g., feelings of betrayal, of sadness and loss, of anger). This is key to understanding how and why the person is reacting to the downsizing.

2. *Assess whether there is depression, anxiety, or anger that has become immobilizing.* There are many instances where individuals can become totally immobilized by a job loss. If so the crisis counselor needs to assess strategies according to the primary reaction evinced. For example, would this person benefit from an antidepressant medication to help get them mobilized?

3. *Facilitate the feelings of loss.* As with bereavement counseling, the role of the counselor is not to "push" the person, but rather to help facilitate their expression of grief.

4. *Refer for additional resources as appropriate.* In Kathleen's case, the counselor saw that she had fought her way through other crises (e.g., her divorce) and was open

to using support systems. Therefore, Kathleen may have been open to job-finding self-help groups, or in this instance a referral to a headhunter.

5. *Watch for signs of apathy.* As indicated earlier, there are many instances where job hunters become apathetic and stop searching or become isolated. It is important to keep watch to make sure the person stays active in their job search.

6. *Assist the person to become open to other options.* In some instances, the job outlook for certain careers may not be as promising as others. If that's the case, it may be more helpful to encourage the person to be open to other possibilities.

CRISES PERTAINING TO SUPERVISOR—COWORKER CONFLICT

Additional aspects of workplace crises are those brought about by interactions between managers and employees, and interactions among coworkers. Because this area involves power, we have found that the abuse of power can often lead to crises in the workplace. There are different types of power that each individual in the workplace possesses. It is obvious that certain administrative or managerial positions give one the authority to make decisions involving others. Naturally, there are some bosses or managers who flagrantly abuse this power. It is also not uncommon for supervisors or administrators to demand more work from their employees for less pay. Sexual harassment is probably at the top of the list of such abuses of power. However, abuses of power may take several forms. When employees attempt to rectify such situations, he or she may be confronted with responses like "you should consider yourself lucky you have a job." When someone's job responsibilities are not clearly defined, this can result in potential abuses, as in the case of an employee faced with more job responsibilities and receives little or no additional compensation. When workers are subjected to demeaning comments, are excluded from decisions that directly affect their ability to do their jobs, or their expertise is diminished in some way, then this is a form of abuse (Einarsen, Hoel, Zapf, & Cooper, 2011). When an administrator makes decisions arbitrarily, promotes arbitrarily, or raises and bonuses are doled out arbitrarily, then this too may feel abusive to those who are passed over. In some instances, promotions can merely be an insignificant title, which translates to more work, more responsibility, and the same pay. We have also witnessed several instances where companies have merged and many managers were given increased responsibilities within the newly merged company, with no pay, no recognition, and no promotion.

Keep in mind, however, the abuse of power can run both ways. For example, the employee who refuses to complete a needed work assignment on time may use passive-aggressiveness to wield power. An employee who is continually negative about every idea for change even if it may be positive, uses that negativity to wield power. People's attitudes toward others can be very abusive. The employee who goes after an administrator by criticizing him at every opportunity, or who goes behind his back to other administrators is being abusive in the way they are wielding their power. It may appear on the surface that the supervisor or manager has all the power, but this is not always true. Workplace

Box 14.3: Sexual Harassment and Sexual Abuse at Nation's Service Academies

In 1975, then President Gerald Ford signed legislation that permitted women to apply for admission to the nation's service academies (i.e., West Point, Annapolis, Air Force Academy). For centuries, these esteemed institutions have been considered to be among the finest military leadership training programs in the world, and they were exclusively for male candidates. Men and women who are fortunate enough to gain admission to these revered institutions are deemed to be of the highest moral, intellectual, and physical character. So, when allegations of rape and sexual harassment began to surface in the media, there were many taxpayers who were dumbfounded that this type of behavior could occur in our nation's esteemed service academies.

The sexual abuse scandal at the Air Force Academy began in 2003 when an anonymous email was sent to the Secretary of the Air Force, the Chief of Staff of the Air Force, and several senators and congressmen alleging that there was a significant sexual assault problem at the Air Force Academy, and that the problem was being ignored by Academy leadership. The Secretary of the Air Force ordered an immediate investigation of the allegations. A 2003 survey of female cadet graduates revealed that 12% reported having been raped or victims of attempted rape, while 70% of the 579 female cadets reported having been victims of sexual harassment, and 22% had been pressured for sexual favors. NPR (National Public Radio) reported (Halloran, 2013) instances of sexual harassment at West Point involving videotaping of females in a woman's locker room. In 2012, a female midshipman at the U.S. Naval Academy alleged having been raped by three male midshipman who were on the football team (Clark, 2013). The aforementioned allegations prompted New York Senator Kirsten Gillibrand, and Missouri Senator Claire McCaskill, both members of the Senate's Armed Services Committee, to propose legislation that would mandate the military to create a separate legal process to deal with sexual assault claims. The Gillibrand Amendment was later voted down in the U.S. Senate.

Sources: Halloran, L. (2013) Stunned by military sex scandals, advocates demand change. Retrieved from http://www.npr.org/2013/05/23/186335999/stunned-by-military-sex-scandals-advocates-demand-changes

Wikipedia (2003). 2003 United States Air Force Academy sex scandal. Retrieved from https://en.wikipedia.org/wiki/2003_United_States_Air_Force_Academy_sexual_assault_scandal

Clark, M. (2013, Sept. 4). Naval Academy sexual assault hearing underscores flaws in system. Retrieved from http://www.msnbc.com/melissa-harris-perry/naval-academy-sexual-assault-hearing-0

bullying is a topic that has received a lot of attention in both the popular and scholarly literature (e.g., Einarsen et al., 2011; Rayner, 2000).

Sexual harassment and sexual abuse often involve yet another form of abuse of power. All too often, people in positions of power use that power to take sexual advantage of a subordinate. Two forms of sexual harassment are described in the literature: "quid pro quo" and "hostile working environment" (Sexual Harassment—Fact v. Myth, 1994). In the quid pro quo type, the harassment message is straightforward: "Sleep with me or you're fired." In other words, employment (hiring, promotions, raises, or retaining one's job) is contingent on the victim's providing sexual favors. In defining a hostile workplace environment, the job becomes permeated with discriminatory intimidation, ridicule, and insult that is sufficiently severe or pervasive to alter the conditions of the victim's employment and create abusive working conditions. In determining whether a work environment is hostile or abusive, the U.S. Supreme Court also handed down some guidelines by which all circumstances could be taken into account: a) the frequency of the discriminatory conduct; b) its severity; c) whether it is physically threatening or a mere offensive utterance; and d) whether it unreasonably interferes with an employee's work performance.

In United States labor law, a **hostile work environment** exists when one's behavior within a workplace creates an environment that is difficult or uncomfortable for another person to work in. Common complaints in sexual harassment lawsuits include fondling, suggestive remarks, sexually suggestive photos displayed in the workplace, use of sexual language, or off-color jokes. Small issues, annoyances, and isolated incidents typically are not considered illegal. To be unlawful, the conduct must create a work environment that would be intimidating, hostile, or offensive to a reasonable person. An employer can be held liable for failing to prevent these workplace conditions, unless it can prove that it attempted to prevent the harassment and that the employee failed to take advantage of existing harassment counter-measures or tools provided by the employer. According to the U.S. Equal Employment Opportunity Commission (EEOC) (2017), it is unlawful to harass a person (an applicant or employee) because of that person's sex. Harassment can include "sexual harassment" or unwelcome sexual advances, requests for sexual favors, and other verbal or physical harassment of a sexual nature. Harassment does not have to be of a sexual nature, however, and can include offensive remarks about a person's sex. For example, it is illegal to harass a woman by making offensive comments about women in general. Both victim and the harasser can be either a woman or a man, and the victim and harasser can be the same sex. Although the law doesn't prohibit simple teasing, offhand comments, or isolated incidents that are not very serious, harassment is illegal when it is so frequent or severe that it creates a hostile or offensive work environment or when it results in an adverse employment decision (such as if the victim is fired or demoted). The harasser can be the victim's supervisor, a supervisor in another area, a coworker, or someone who is not an employee of the employer, such as a client or customer.

Unfortunately, when sexual harassment does occur in the workplace, many companies often deny that the event occurred, admit no wrongdoing, and then turn against the victim. It is common for the harasser to deny the allegations. To make matters worse, coworkers sometimes place blame on the victim, by alleging that it was somehow his or her fault. Some coworkers even become angry with the victim for coming forward with the complaint and quickly run to the defense of the harasser, instead of offering their assistance and understanding to the victim; the victim is then left standing alone. However, the other case scenario is when one victim of sexual harassment comes forward which is then followed by other employees who come forward also alleging harassment by the same individual (e.g., See Box 14.4: Covert, 2016; Stewart, 2016). Unfortunately, many cases of sexual harassment go unreported. As with other forms of sexual assault, such as rape or intimate partner violence, there is fear that reporting the incident will result in retaliation or reprisal. Victims of workplace harassment fear that they will lose their jobs. They fear that others will not believe them, and that they will be attacked for having come forward.

It appears that sexual harassment is more common in professions considered male-dominated (e.g., the military, law enforcement, transportation, law, medicine, media, and academia). As more women assimilated into the workforce, one of the unfortunate by-products is an increase in sexual harassment allegations. Such is the case in the military with the increase of both sexual assault and sexual harassment cases. In 2014 alone there were 160,500 military service members who claimed to face severe and persistent sexual harassment or gender discrimination (1 in 4 women, and 1 in 14 men). Approximately 20,300 service members were sexually assaulted in 2014 (10,600 men and 9,600 women). Junior enlisted men and women experienced the highest rates of sexual assault (1.4% of men, 7.3% of women), and 90% of these assaults were alleged to have taken place in military settings, and most often perpetrated by higher-ranking service members who knew the victim. Sixty-two percent of women who said they reported the sexual assault also indicated that they faced retaliation from superiors and commanders (Department of Defense, 2014; Rand Corporation, 2014). Allegations of sexual harassment unfortunately have gone beyond the military ranks to the military service academies (See Box 14.3).

Case Presentation: A Case of Sexual Harassment

Let's return to the case described at the beginning of this chapter. Sandra reports feeling uncomfortable by sexual remarks made by her boss. She also finds herself the brunt of sexual jokes made by her coworker, which her boss finds amusing and not the least bit inappropriate. In Sandra's case, she is faced with the dilemma of whether or not to report the abuse. She decides that she will speak to the employee assistance counselor because she heard that whatever is said in the session is confidential. The role of the employee assistance counselor is to first validate Sandra's feelings. Sandra reports that she feels trapped and powerless, but more so, she feels humiliated whenever she is at work and also feels that her coworkers have either joined Jim Groper in his abusive remarks, or they have totally turned their back on her. It is important that the employee assistance counselor validate these feelings; in other words, to make certain that Sandra's feelings are heard and understood. The counselor's role is not to play judge and jury, or to determine whether the abuse has occurred, or whether the remarks constitute a violation of the law; rather the counselor's role is to help Sandra to define the problem and provide her with support. It is also important that the counselor not force Sandra to make any decisions as to what course of action to take, rather to provide her with information to use so that she can then make a more informed decision. The following session illustrates how the counselor might help Sandra through this crisis.

Intervention

Counselor: Sandra, when you called earlier today to meet with me, you sounded really upset. Were you able to finish out your shift today?

Sandra:	Yeah, it was really tough going though; I've not been sleeping very well since all this is happening.
C:	What type of problems have you been having?
S:	First of all, before I get into anything, this is confidential, right? I mean you can't tell my boss about what we talk about, or make me go to Human Resources, right?
C:	Yes, it is confidential. The only time the law mandates me to break confidentiality is in instances of threats of homicide, suicide, or child abuse. Anything else remains between us and the only time I'm allowed to reveal anything is with your signed release. Okay?
S:	Okay, well what's been happening is that my boss, Mr. Groper, started (begins crying), this is really tough.
C:	Yes, I can see it is, why don't you take a minute to catch your breath. Do you want some water or some tissues?
S:	No, I'll be all right. Well, about six months ago, Mr. Groper, my immediate boss began making remarks, sexual type remarks. When I was unloading baggage from the trucks, he would say some really horrible things and make comments about my breasts. At first, I wouldn't say anything and just go about my business, then about a month ago, he started groping me, grabbing my butt as I walked by. You know, things like that. Some of the other guys on the crew also began making remarks. I warned them that I would talk with Mr. Smith, the VP in charge of maintenance, but they'd laugh and would keep doing it. I was going to see Mr. Smith, but then I thought I would end up losing my job.
C:	What made you think that you would lose your job?
S:	Well, a friend of mine had the same thing happen at her job. She doesn't work here, she works at a retail chain store and her boss said that if she didn't do "favors" for him, he was going to fire her, the next time she came in late. She refused and he fired her. She tried to report him, but the company denied that it happened, and so did her coworkers. It was her word against his.
C:	Sandra, this must have been very tough for you to come here and talk about this. It sounds from what you've said, this has been happening for several months. Have you told anyone else besides me?
S:	No, I felt like I couldn't tell anyone. I was afraid that if I told my brother or anyone in my family, they would put out a contract on Groper's life or something. My ex-husband split, not that he would care. I can't lose my job, he doesn't pay any child support and I bring in the only paycheck. If I lose this job, I'll lose my kids. My ex-husband's parents have already threatened to have them taken from me.
C:	Why have they threatened to do that?
S:	Because they want more time with the kids. I'm pretty good about making sure the kids spend time with their grandparents, but the more time I give, the more they seem to want.
C:	I can see the bind you're in. What have you done so far?
S:	I did try to talk with Mr. Groper; I told him I was uncomfortable with the things he was saying and his grabbing me, but he laughed it off and said I was being too sensitive. He said since women have been working the flight line, everything has to be "nicey nice." I feel bad that I didn't try talking

	with him when this first started or with his boss, but I'm afraid they would just fire me.
C:	You did the right thing by trying to talk with him first. Sandra, you are a victim of sexual harassment. There are laws which prevent any employee from harassment in the workplace and protects them from being fired in retaliation.
S:	The laws didn't help my friend though.
C:	Maybe her situation was different. Do you know if she filed an EEOC complaint?
S:	What is an EEOC?
C:	The EEOC is the Equal Employment Opportunity Commission. They are responsible for making certain that companies are in compliance with EEOC regulations. This covers subjects like making sure that companies do not discriminate against people because of gender, race, ethnicity, disability, and so forth, and also enforces laws pertaining to sexual harassment and hostile work environments. You could file a complaint through the EEOC office here at the airline or through one of the regional offices.
S:	And then I suppose I would get my pink slip in my next paycheck, no way!
C:	No Sandra, once you file a complaint, your job is protected. Mr. Pritchard cannot fire you unless there was some major infringement of company policy. Basically, you are protected.
S:	What happens once I file a complaint?
C:	Usually, the EEOC staff conduct an investigation to determine if the allegations are valid. If they are, then the airline needs to take steps to rectify the situation. Sometimes, this might also involve sitting down with a mediator.
S:	But, once this is all over, can Groper turn around and fire me?
C:	Not if you're doing your job.
S:	I do my job, don't worry about that. I'm never late, I never take a day off, my performance reviews are all "Outstanding."
C:	That's in your favor. Sandra, what do you suppose will be the reaction of your coworkers, if you file a complaint?
S:	Well, I know the guys I work with will be ticked off. I don't care. There is one other woman that works part time, though, and she has put up with some of the same stuff. I don't think as much as I have; so, I don't know how she will react. Why?
C:	What is unfortunate in instances like this, is that it is not uncommon for coworkers to turn against the person who files the complaint; therefore, they often feel as if they are out there alone once they file.
S:	So, what are you saying, don't file?
C:	No, I just want to give you as much information as possible in the event that you do file. Let's take the other case scenario, what if you don't file?
S:	Well, I guess Groper will keep pawing me and making nasty remarks. I don't know if I can put up with that.
C:	Sandra, there is nothing to say that you have to file a complaint today. Why don't you think about it for a little bit? Find out if your friend has filed an EEOC complaint. You don't have to do anything right now. Also, you can continue to come for counseling here, or I can refer you to a counselor close

by where you live. Sometimes, it's helpful to get another opinion on some-thing like this anyway. Your insurance plan covers you seeing an outside counselor.

S: Can I think this over a bit, and can we meet in a few days, maybe?

C: That is fine. Sandra, how are you feeling right now? Are you going to be okay?

S: Believe it or not, I do feel a little better. I feel as if at least I have some options now. I don't feel as trapped.

C: Sounds good. Let's meet again on Thursday.

Case Conceptualization/Crisis Resolution

In the case illustration above, the counselor is careful to validate Sandra's feelings that she is being mistreated by her supervisor. Often victims of sexual harassment doubt their own perceptions and feelings, and believe that it is something they are doing that is caus-ing the harassment. They may also question whether they should report the harassment. For example, in Sandra's trying to deal directly with Mr. Groper, he downplays the harass-ment and accuses Sandra of being "too sensitive." This is unfortunately very common.

The counselor is also careful to provide Sandra with information about options, while at the same time, not forcing her to make a decision. According to EEOC guidelines, a complaint must be filed within 180 days of the alleged act; however, in some jurisdictions, a complaint may be filed up to 300 days after the alleged act. Since Sandra's harassment has been ongoing, it is likely that her case falls within these guidelines. It is also important that Sandra is given all the facts in order to weigh the merits of whether to file a complaint. This is why the EAP Counselor suggested that she may want to speak with a neutral coun-selor outside of the company.

Before concluding this section, it is important to point out that sexual harassment and hostile work environments (although primarily a male-to-female phenomena), can also include instances where men are subjected to sexual harassment by female supervisors or by fellow male coworkers. Such was the case with a male employee working for a construction crew who was continually subjected to ridicule and harassment by other male employees who taunted him by calling him "a pansy," "a fairy," and "a homo." This person was subjected to this ridicule because he was not as brash or vulgar as his cowork-ers. Because this employee was quiet and nonthreatening, he was an easy mark for bul-lying and sexually demeaning remarks. Eventually, this person quit the job, but only after filing an EEOC complaint alleging that his foreman condoned the "hostile work environ-ment" created by his coworkers. Male-to-male sexual harassment has become more commonplace, and according to recent legal rulings, does constitute a form of "hostile work environment," which is often cited in sexual harassment suits (Talbot, 2002).

There are many other instances other than sexual harassment of coworker and supervi-sor created conflicts; for example, incidents of workplace discrimination and workplace aggression. In addition, there's a growing body of research on covert aggression and rela-tional aggression in work settings, which also creates a great deal of stress for employees (e.g., Björkqvist, Osterman, & Lagerspetz, 1994; Crothers, Lipinski & Minutolo, 2009; Kaukiainenet al., 2001).

In prior research, it appears that much of the stress created in the workplace by admin-istrators, coworkers, or subordinates may be produced by individuals with personality disorders (Cavaiola & Lavender, 1999; American Psychiatric Association, 2013). Because individuals with personality disorders often lack insight into their behavior, this naturally leads to problems in interpersonal relationships. Since most workplaces involve social interaction, individuals with personality disorders often generate a great deal of stress for those with whom they work. For example, the narcissistic administrator (Levinson, 1994), is a classic example of how an individual with narcissistic personality disorder or narcissistic traits can create stress in the workplace. An illustration of this is the story of a 28-year-old administrative assistant to an up-and-coming vice president of an investment banking firm who became pregnant, but unfortunately lost the baby after three months. When she called her boss to let him know that she needed to take a few days off to recover both physically and emotionally from the miscarriage, he screamed at her, stating, "This is unacceptable, you know we have the month-end report due by next week. If you're not in here by tomorrow, don't bother coming in at all." Narcissistic managers or bosses are known for their lack of empathy and compassion. Instead, they see things only from the vantage point of how it impacts on them or their careers.

It is also possible to have narcissists working for you as an employee or as a subordinate. Characteristically, when trying to manage this type of employee, they feel that they are "special" and therefore, should be treated in a special way. They may also feel that the rules that apply to others do not apply to them. The more pathological or problematic narcissist thinks nothing of going after their boss' job, or going behind their back to upper management (Cavaiola & Lavender, 2000). These are just a couple of examples where individuals with personality disorders, by the very nature of their personality, lack of social skills, or lack of ethics and fair play, can create stress and crises in the workplace.

Box 14.4: Sexual Harassment Complaints at Fox News

Fox News recently had two high profile lawsuits filed against former Fox News Chairman, Roger Ailes. The first lawsuit filed by popular Fox News host, Gretchen Carlson, alleged that Ailes made comments to her like "I think you and I should have had a sexual relationship a long time ago." On September 6, 2016, the *New York Times* reported that Fox News settled the suit for $20 million. In the second suit, Fox News host Andrea Tartaro alleges that Ailes asked her to "turn around to get a look at her." According to Bryce Covert of the *New York Times*, Fox News had evolved into a corporate culture where "sexual harassers roamed free," as there had been many such complaints of sexual harassment filed over the years, including one suit brought against Fox News anchor, Bill O'Reilly by a female intern. It was further alleged that Fox News had paid out millions in sexual harassment suits over the years, prior to the Roger Ailes accusations.

Sources: Covert, Bryce (2016, August 27). Sexual harassment training with Roger Ailes. *New York Times,* Sunday Review.

Stewart, James B. (2016, August 18). Secrecy of settlements at Fox News hid bad behavior. *New York Times.*

CRISES PERTAINING TO THE CONVERGENCE OF WORK STRESSORS AND OUTSIDE-OF-WORK STRESSORS

In this section, we address other types of work crises. Some stressors may relate to work stress itself. These can include low pay, increased workload, long commute, change in job responsibilities, mergers, and transfers. The common denominator to most of these sources of work crises is that the employee usually has very little say or control over the work stressors. Such is the case with a transfer. One supermarket chain was notorious for transferring department managers with incredible frequency. A produce or dairy manager might be working fifteen minutes from their home one day, and then on the next day have to commute for hours to get to the new job assignment. Naturally, burnout and turnover rates were quite high. At one point, when IBM was experiencing a declining market share in personal computers because of "IBM clone" computers, it was not unusual for IBM to regularly transfer their middle managers. In the computer industry, it was said that the acronym "IBM" stood for "I've Been Moved." So, stress can come from a variety of sources and each source of stress has the potential of sending an employee and their family members into crisis. One colleague called frantically one day, stating that her husband's company had just transferred him to the Hong Kong office and that the move was to take place within weeks. Imagine having to sell or rent your house, sell your car, enroll your children in new schools, and learn a new language? That is enough to send any family into a state of crisis.

Given the growing number of dual career families, this also has placed tremendous strain on the nuclear family. Crises often develop because of *family/work spillover*. This refers to when home problems are taken to work or "spillover" into the workplace. Burley (1991) notes that there is less tolerance of family/work spillover for men than for women. Women are often more likely and/or willing to take time off from work for child-oriented problems, problems with elderly parents, or other family obligations (Young & Long, 1998). However, this often creates an incredible amount of stress for women who are trying to juggle the demands of both work and family responsibilities as is illustrated in the following case example.

Case Example

Janet has been working for a large telecommunications company for the past fourteen years. She started out as an administrative assistant to one of the section project chiefs, and she now has risen to the level of being a project chief; a job that she really had to fight hard to attain. Janet feels good about her work and feels that she is well respected by the people she supervises. Although things are going well in her career, the same cannot be said of things at home. Janet is married to Tom who is an active alcoholic who has been out of work for the past ten months. In addition, their 12-year-old son, Tommy Jr. has attention deficit hyperactivity disorder, and Janet is constantly getting calls from the school that Tommy has been acting out in class and is on the verge of being suspended. Janet cannot afford to take any more time off, as she is presently working on a deadline. Yet, she cannot count on her husband to effectively deal with their son's problems at school. She feels that she is losing control of herself and fears she will have a nervous breakdown.

Intervention

Janet is experiencing stress from both within and outside the workplace. Her within-work stress is generated by her having "moved up the ladder" in her company. While this has its benefits, it also has many disadvantages because coworkers who may have been passed over for the same position may hold resentments and would not be very interested in seeing Janet succeed. In addition, she has a son with attention deficit hyperactivity disorder, and a husband who is an active alcoholic. Dealing with either disorder requires tremendous patience and understanding. Dealing with both disorders concurrently can tax the patience and endurance of a saint. Janet is like "an accident waiting to happen," as she tries to get through each day the best she can; however, her ability to manage the stress is limited, which is why she feels she is on the verge of having "a nervous breakdown." If you were Janet's crisis counselor, what interventions might be helpful in preventing this "nervous breakdown" or some other crisis from occurring? How can a crisis counselor be of help to Janet?

If Janet accessed the services of the employee assistance counselor where she works, she takes a positive first step. In many instances, managers or employees like Janet become so overwhelmed by their stress that they feel they have no one to turn to, or no one that can help them. They often feel that they must manage everything themselves and do it perfectly. Up to now, this certainly has been Janet's frame of reference for how things are going at home. She feels she cannot count on her husband for support or to help with their son. So, Janet has every right to feel "if you want something done right, do it yourself."

One of the first things that an employee assistance counselor or crisis counselor needs to do is to let Janet vent her feelings about all that she is going through. Here it is important that the counselor is an active listener, by asking Janet for points of clarification (e.g., "How long has your husband been drinking?" or "When did Tommy begin to have problems in school?"), or by validating her feelings (e.g., "I can see why you would feel overwhelmed" or "It must be very tough for you just to get through the day."). In doing this, the counselor is conveying to Janet that he or she is willing to hear her out and help her come up with some solutions. This first step is similar to what we refer to in the L-A-P-C model as the "listening" step.

Knowing that it was difficult for Janet to reach out for help, it is important for the counselor to support Janet's decision to seek help (e.g., "You know Janet, with all that you have going on in your life, it was really courageous of you to seek help"). The next step is to help Janet explore some solutions to her current crisis. In doing so, it appears that there are three main areas, which are factors in her crisis: 1) her job stress and fear of losing her job, 2) her son's ADHD, and 3) her husband's alcoholism and lack of participation as a functional family member. It is therefore helpful to assist Janet in prioritizing these areas; in other words, which does she consider to be the most important in her life right now?

Counselor: Janet, of all the areas we've talked about, which one is troubling you the most right now?

Janet: I am most worried about my son, Tommy. He really seems to be having a rough time, both with school work and, also with his Dad's being out of work for so long.

C: I know you mentioned having been to the school several times. Is there anything else you could do to help Tommy right now?

J: Well, apart from quitting my job, I just can't think of anything. The guidance counselor wants me to have Tommy evaluated by a pediatric neurologist to see if he might benefit from medication. They think he might respond to Ritalin. I'm just afraid of putting him on something that he might not need. Also, I wonder how much of his hyperactivity is related to the problems at home right now.

C: I see what you mean. So, it's like one problem area impacts on the other. They all tie in somehow.

J: Exactly. If I'm worried about Tommy or taking calls from his teacher every day, then I'm not doing my job here at work. Or, if my husband had a bad night drinking, then Tommy is more hyper in school the next day. You're right, it all ties in.

C: You mentioned you have a best friend, Susan, that you keep in touch with. I was wondering what she suggested.

Sometimes family or friends have a different perspective on a situation because they know the person in crisis and some of the factors involved. Susan may also be an influential person in Janet's life.

J: Susan feels I should kick Tom out and tell him to go into a rehab. We have medical insurance to cover his being in treatment and he's not doing anything to help my situation anyway. Susan also feels I should be going to Al-Anon, but, I just don't have the time to go. I would like to go if I had the time or someone to watch Tommy.

C: I do know of an Al-Anon meeting in Stockton that has babysitting. Getting back to Susan's advice though, what's your reaction, when she suggests this?

J: I agree with her, I just don't think that Tom would go for treatment. He'd get angry, move out for a few days, and then come begging to come back. I usually give in.

C: How do you feel Tommy would react to his father's being out of the house, say, if he were to go for help?

J: He would be relieved. He worries about his father all the time. Even when we've been separated for the few days, Tommy seems to calm down a lot.

C: I see what you're saying. Tommy may still have ADHD, but he is able to focus a lot more when he's not worried about his father.

J: I think Susan is right. I can't control Tom's drinking, I at least know that, but I can control what kind of life we have at home. Maybe that is the place to start.

C: Whether Tom goes for treatment or not, it would still be helpful for you to go to Al-Anon.

J: Yes, I will go, could you give me the address of the meeting in Stockton?

C: Janet what about your job? You're still on the firing line there quite a bit, what can we do to help you with that? Would it help to take a few days off?

J: It might if and when Tom goes to rehab. In the meantime, I just need to get into work every day on time and try to stay focused on work while I'm here. I really like my job and would be doing a lot better if I didn't have all this other stuff to contend with.

Case Conceptualization/Crisis Resolution

At this point in the session, the counselor and Janet begin to explore some of the things that Janet can do at work to make things less stressful for her. The counselor is also willing to become Janet's advocate while she is going through these crises and is taking steps to resolve them. You can imagine that the worst-case scenario is if Janet refused to see the employee assistance counselor and/or decided to deal with these problems totally on her own. This does not mean that the goal is to make Janet dependent on the counselor. If anything, especially with crisis counseling, the goal is to provide brief counseling and to assist the person in mobilizing his or her own strengths and resources to deal with the crisis at hand. If necessary, a referral can then be made to appropriate treatment providers for ongoing counseling.

SUMMARY

Today's workplace can often be the source of many stressors and potential crises; the most obvious and dangerous of these crises involve workplace violence and workplace shootings. Many of the crises described in this chapter have come to light in recent years as corporations, organizations, and nonprofits have become more sensitive to issues of workplace bullying and sexual harassment. Issues of downsizing and unexpected job terminations are often experienced during times of economic recession; however, the American job market is rapidly shifting even during times of economic growth as corporations shift manufacturing overseas in order to take advantage of cheaper labor costs. Finally, many individuals find themselves experiencing high degrees of stress juggling the responsibilities of having to handle both work demands as well as the demands of managing a household, children, or elderly parents. These problems are often compounded when there are the added hardships or having to care for a special needs child, or an elderly parent with medical problems or cognitive disorders like Alzheimer's. Employee assistance counselors and crisis counselors play a vital role in helping individuals manage these crises.

RESOURCES FOR CHAPTER ENRICHMENT

Suggested Readings

Baumol, W. J., Blinder, A., & Wolff, E. N. (2003). *Downsizing in America: Reality, causes and consequences*. New York: Russell Sage Foundation.

Cavaiola, A. A., & Lavender, N. J. (2000). *Toxic co-workers: How to deal with dysfunctional people in the workplace*. Oakland, CA: New Harbinger.

Einarsen, S., Hoel, H., Zapf, D., & Cooper, C. L. (2011). *Bullying and harassment in the workplace*. Boca Raton, FL: CRC Press/Taylor & Francis.

Joyce, S. P. (2016). Surviving a job layoff. Retrieved from http://www.job-hunt.org/layoffs/surviving-a-layoff.shtml

Levinson, H. (1994). Why the behemoths fell: Psychological roots of corporate failure. *American Psychologist, 49*, 428–436.

Lewis, G. W., & Zare, N. C. (1999). *Workplace hostility: Myth and reality.* Philadelphia, PA: Taylor & Francis.

Noer, D. (1993). *Healing the wounds: Overcoming the trauma of layoffs and revitalizing downsized organizations.* San Francisco, CA: Jossey-Bass.

Nowrouzi, B., & Huynh, V. (2016). Citation analysis of workplace violence: A review of the top 50 annual and lifetime cited articles. *Aggression and Violent Behavior, 28,* 21–28.

U. S. Equal Opportunity Commission. (2016). Sexual harassment. Retrieved from https://www.eeoc.gov/laws/types/sexual_harassment.cfm

Woodward, H., & Buchholz, S. (1987). *Aftershock: Helping people through corporate change.* New York, NY: Wiley.

Suggested Websites

Job Loss Resources

Job Loss
How to cope if you are fired. Help dealing with emotional issues and practical topics like severance pay and unemployment benefits. http://careerplanning.about.com/cs/jobless

Surviving Job Loss
Site offers strategies, techniques, and tools to help survive losing a job. Includes information on personal finance, job searching, and places to get help. http://www.helpguide.org/articles/stress/job-loss-and-unemployment-stress.htm http://www.forbes.com/sites/womensmedia/2012/06/12/bouncing-back-from-job-loss-the-7-habits-of-highly-effective-job-hunters/#52201a635b15

Job Loss Grief Stages
Detailed information on the stages of job loss grief, symptoms of, how to help, and suggestions for managing your own job loss grief. http://members.tripod.com/ ~ jobnet/joblossc.htm

Downsizing
Provides helpful suggestions and recommendations for people who have lost their jobs through downsizing. The article also explains why corporate downsizing often doesn't work to improve a company's bottom line. http://www.hrma.ca/wp-content/uploads/2012/07/rb-forcedlayoffs.pdf

Workplace Violence Resources

Preventing and Protecting Yourself from Workplace Violence and Harassment
This site explores some of the sources and origins of violence at the workplace, what can be done to prevent it, and what to do when it happens. http://www.uslawbooks.com/books/violence.htm

Guidelines for Preventing Workplace Violence for Health Care and Social Service Workers
U.S. Department of Labor Occupational Safety and Health Administration (OSHA) material contained in this publication: violence prevention program elements, work-site analysis, hazard prevention and control, training, and education. https://www.nami.org/Learn-More/Mental-Health-Conditions

Workplace Violence
These websites provide valuable information on identifying and preventing workplace violence incidents. https://www.cdc.gov/niosh/topics/violence/default.html; https://www.fbi.gov/file-repository/stats-services-publications

Sexual Harassment

Sexual Harassment Worksite

These websites provide useful information on sexual harassment in the workplace. They also contain links to many other resources and vital information on EEOC regulations.

http://www.aauw.org/what-we-do/legal-resources/know-your-rights-at-work/workplace-sexual-harassment/

http://employment.findlaw.com/employment-discrimination/sexual-harassment-at-work.html

http://money.usnews.com/money/careers/articles/2015/02/12/6-things-to-know-about-workplace-sexual-harassment

Recommended Films

Nine to Five: (1980) (stars Jane Fonda, Lily Tomlin, Dolly Parton, and Dabney Coleman). This film depicts the story of three women working for an egotistical, narcissistic, harassing boss played by Dabney Coleman. The movie is loosely based on a true story, and although it is basically a comedy (due to the revenge that these women exact from their tormentor), it does give a good depiction of workplace harassment and the inappropriate boundary violations that can and do occur.

Office Space: (1999) (stars Ron Livingston and Jennifer Aniston). This film depicts office workers who are tormented by a narcissistic, exploitative boss. This film provides an excellent illustration of a narcissistic boss and the employees who are forced to put up with his bad behavior. *Office Space* has a cult following and is still quite popular because it deals with workplace problems and crises that are still timely.

Fun with Dick and Jane: (2005) (stars Jim Carrey, Tea Leonie, and Alec Baldwin). This movie depicts a couple who are on top of the world financially and occupationally until they are downsized from their jobs. The film is a comedy, but portrays an accurate depiction of the financial panic and fear of ruination that can beset individuals with this type of crisis. It is based on the 1977 film of the same name which starred George Segeal and Jane Fonda.

Confirmation: (2016) (stars Kerry Washington and Wendell Pierce). This docudrama depicts the 1991 confirmation hearings of Supreme Court Justice Clarence Thomas in which Anita Hill, a law professor, came forward to disclose allegations of sexual harassment by Judge Thomas during the time she was a law clerk under his supervision. This film is a gripping portrayal of the impact of sexual harassment and a portrayal of the courage of Anita Hill in coming forward at the U.S. Senate confirmation hearings of Supreme Court Justice Thomas.

Suggested Activities

1. What services are available in your area for someone who has been laid off from their job and their unemployment benefits are running out?

2. Check out the EEOC website listed above. If you had a friend that wanted information on how to file an EEOC complaint, what could you tell them about the website to help them file?

3. What types of prevention programs are available to employers or corporations who wish to prevent workplace violence and/or sexual harassment? Do an Internet search.

Recommended YouTube Viewing

Job Loss

https://www.youtube.com/watch? v = uWf-gn0guhY This brief video provides some good suggestions for building self-esteem after job loss.

https://www.youtube.com/watch? v = 988hezLBwGs Dr. Frank Doberman discusses how to cope with job loss.

https://www.youtube.com/watch? v = _9A_d-vxtIU From a human resources professional, ten things to do if you've suffered a job loss. Good practical advice.

https://www.youtube.com/watch? v = vBM_VegvLBM A news interview on how to cope with job loss.

https://www.youtube.com/watch? v = YpgvoXv3o-w This video provides an illustration of a role play in the aftermath of a job loss using cognitive-behavioral strategies. The sound quality is poor, but the video does provide useful strategies.

https://www.youtube.com/watch? v = PfmdGFZ6wFk First person account of a couple who managed a job loss and the impact it had on them.

Sexual Harassment

https://www.youtube.com/watch? v = NGc7KfQ3uWs Informative video on sexual harassment in the workplace.

https://www.youtube.com/watch? v = _TcRyqdnSGE Video consists of PowerPoint slides with voice presentation of what constitutes sexual harassment and what to do and what not to do; along with how corporations/companies can prevent sexual harassment in the workplace.

https://www.youtube.com/watch? v = ovIsy-NVHh4 This video provides a preview of the PBS program on an underreported phenomena, teen sexual harassment at work. Interesting and informative video.

https://www.youtube.com/watch? v = vzN3CKaZZKk New reporter interview regarding sexual harassment in the workplace. Describes how sexual harassment impacts on those victimized.

Workplace Violence

https://www.youtube.com/watch? v = W6tjFNDN-EI This video describes the early warning signs of workplace violence.

https://www.youtube.com/watch? v = oiuWLkdUZ5o This video presents information on workplace violence and workplace violence prevention. Good stats on workplace violence.

https://www.youtube.com/watch? v = WtmpuTZ3MKs Produced by a human resources consulting firm, this video focuses on how to prevent workplace violence. Good information.

https://www.youtube.com/watch? v = cpHdC_-eAiQ This is a preview of a training program offered by a management consulting firm and provides useful information on preventing workplace violence and workplace bullying.

CHAPTER 15

Disaster Response

DISCUSSION QUESTIONS

Take a tour of your own community. Do you see potential sources of crises? Consider all types of possible crises, such as those posed by one's location to industrial areas, power plants, sources of natural weather-related events, potential terrorist targets, and so forth.

What do you think should be the public's responsibility in responding to a crisis event that has a significant impact on the community?

Have you ever been involved in a volunteer effort in the aftermath of a crisis to assist someone in need? Has anyone assisted you after a personal crisis without your requesting the assistance?

INTRODUCTION

In true crisis/disaster events which devastate whole communities, the federal government is able to step in with financial and physical supports to assist the community to return to some semblance of normalcy. Once a governor declares a state of emergency, then the state can request federal assistance from the Department of Homeland Security's Federal Emergency Management Agency (FEMA). The Robert T. Stafford Disaster Relief and Emergency Assistance Act (Federal Emergency Management Agency, 1988) created a system by which the president can issue emergency or disaster declarations that trigger both financial and physical assistance and gives FEMA the responsibility of coordinating any relief efforts.

The Act distinguishes between emergency and disaster declarations. The former declaration is made to protect property and the public's health and safety and to lessen or avert the threat of a major disaster or catastrophe. Emergency declarations can be made when a potential crisis is recognized, even before it occurs; for example, an emergency declaration was made for New Orleans by President George W. Bush in 2005 in advance of Hurricane Katrina hitting landfall. One of the deadliest hurricanes in United States history, it devastated the city and killed over 1,000 people. Most emergency declarations are for hurricanes, followed by snow-related events, droughts, and severe storms.

In contrast, a major disaster declaration is made as the result of a catastrophic event and constitutes a broader authority that helps states, local communities, families, and individuals recover from the damage caused by the event. Most disaster declarations are for severe storms, flooding, hurricanes, and tornadoes and represent tragic and devastating incidents. However, it must be noted that the differences between these two declarations remain an area of study for the federal government as it attempts to parse out what event qualifies for what type of declaration (Liu, 2014).

FEMA responds to 27 different disaster types, both natural and man-made, from chemical/biological catastrophes to terrorism to winter storms. The amount of assistance provided through presidential disaster declarations so far has exceeded $140 billion. Various forms of assistance are provided: financial aid to families and individuals for uninsured needs, and assistance to state and local governments and certain nonprofit groups for rebuilding or replacing damaged infrastructure.

The federal government also has long promoted the cause of community volunteering among its citizenry, so the purpose of this chapter is to illustrate, in one particular community's story, how people respond to others in crisis.

Who helps in times of crisis?

Many people do, according to *A Survey of Charitable Giving After September 11, 2001* (Independent Sector, 2001). This survey reported that seven in ten Americans donated money, blood, or time in response to the terrorist attacks of 9/11, whereas 30% of those surveyed claimed that they participated in one or more community, spiritual, or local neighborhood events or activities commemorating the 9/11 event. Candlelight vigils, religious services, prayer vigils, and town meetings were only some of the participating activities in a spontaneous display of support.

Researchers have long distinguished between helping (spontaneous helping) and volunteerism (planned helping) (Clary et al., 1998). The helper is one who experiences an unexpected need for help from someone and who makes an immediate decision to act; the volunteer, however, is someone who actively seeks out the opportunity to help others. The helper's act involves one relatively brief instance of helping, whereas the volunteer may commit to an ongoing relationship with a person, a cause, or an organization.

This sustained nature of volunteering is what distinguishes it from the more spontaneous act of helping, otherwise known as bystander intervention, the object of considerable earlier research efforts in investigating the reasons behind prosocial actions (Finkelstein, 2007). Later research (Clary et al., 1998) into volunteering, however, identified six potential motives of the volunteer:

- Values—expressing altruistic and humanitarian values

- Understanding—acquiring learning experiences and/or exercising unused skills

- Social—strengthening social relationships

- Career—gaining career-related benefits

- Protective—reducing negative feelings about oneself or addressing personal problems

- Enhancement—growing psychologically

Nevertheless, regardless of the motives which drive the helper and the volunteer to provide assistance to those in need, it is clear that volunteers represent an integral part of this country's workforce (Finkelstein, 2007). According to the Bureau of Labor Statistics's *Volunteering in the United States, 2015* report, approximately 24.9% of the population, or about 62.6 million people volunteered through or for an organization at least once in the previous year. Almost half of these volunteers (43%) became involved with their primary volunteer organization after being asked to do so by a member of the organization, and a slightly smaller proportion of volunteers (40%) initiated contact with the organization on their own initiative.

A greater proportion of women than men (27.8% versus 21.8%) volunteer. People between the ages of 35 and 54 and 45 to 54 are the most likely age groups to volunteer (28.9% and 28%), whereas the least likely age group to volunteer were people in their early 20s (18.4%). The main organizations where volunteers worked the most hours were most frequently religious (33.1% of all volunteers), educational and youth service-related (25.2%), and social or community service organizations (14.6%).

This large number of helper and volunteer hours must surely be considered a minimal estimate of the total number of hours given in the volunteer effort. Individuals who are not necessarily connected to an organization when they contribute time, effort, or money constitute another whole cadre of volunteers, the numbers of whom elude even rough approximations. People who organize their own bake sales, garage sales, or other fund-raising activities to provide donations to victims of a natural or man-made disaster are not counted among this number, nor are individuals who provide comfort, shelter, or any form of support to rescue workers or crisis survivors. Donations of all kinds done in anonymity ensure that the true numbers of helpers and volunteers and their donated hours will never be known.

Large numbers of volunteers, however, are not always without their share of problems. In the aftermath of 9/11, for example, the city of New York had to turn down offers of blood donations after it reached its capacity to test and store the blood properly. It even had to refuse all but the most skilled and essential volunteers who offered their services, considering the vast numbers of individuals who appeared on the scene (Cavaiola & Colford, 2006). The National Voluntary Organizations Active in Disaster (NVOAD), a group created in 1970 to coordinate the efforts of volunteer groups in responding to disasters, reported on the serious challenges presented by the large numbers of volunteers after a disaster, particularly those events of a significant magnitude like 9/11. In fact, just several months after 9/11, NVOAD sponsored the first National Leadership Forum on Disaster Volunteerism to discuss ways to provide guidance to the public on the management of volunteers in disasters.

The focus of this chapter is on one particular community's response to the events of 9/11. It documents the coordinated efforts of the municipal government and of two volunteer groups that spontaneously developed from the needs of a community devastated by the attacks on that day. Although there have been more recent crises with profound consequences on different communities, such as the natural disasters of hurricanes Katrina, Rita, and Ike; the California wildfires; and the severe flooding in the Midwest; one of the current authors of this text is a resident of the community highlighted below. He thought it fitting that he relates this story.

In the early morning hours of September 11, 2001, American Airlines Flight 11 and United Airlines Flight 175 left Boston, MA, for different destinations. Within hours, a group of terrorists crashed Flight 11 into the north tower of New York City's 110-story World Trade Center. Flight 175 hit the south tower 18 minutes later. It will never be known how many people died at impact or in the minutes immediately after in the incinerating heat of the jet fuel fireballs. As hundreds of firefighters, police, and other emergency workers struggled to help thousands of office personnel get out of the buildings, both of the towers collapsed in an avalanche of concrete and steel. The death toll reached almost 3,000 people.

MIDDLETOWN, NEW JERSEY: A COMMUNITY IN CRISIS

Townships known as Middletown number approximately 35 and stretch across the United States, with 19 states claiming to have one or more of them listed among their rosters of municipalities. Urban and rural, large and small, the name connotes a settlement somewhere between two larger and more established ones, making the name appear as a mere footnote to more substantial, more important settlements. Middletown, New Jersey, a 42-square mile town and home to almost 70,000 residents was once just another Middletown, named for its strategic geographic position midway between New York City and Philadelphia. Located approximately 43 miles south of the Manhattan site where the World Trade Center Twin Towers once stood, this Middletown was the perfect commuter town, sending many members of its 23,000 households into Manhattan each day by car, train, bus, or ferry. And so it was on September 11, 2001.

Thirty-seven of these same commuters were barely at their desks somewhere in the Towers that morning when the first attack came; 37 died that day, the largest concentration of victims from any town in America. Suddenly, this Middletown became the international representative for human tragedy; no longer would this Middletown be confused with any of its 34 namesakes.

Pictures of unclaimed cars in Middletown's bus and train station commuter parking lots, many of them belonging to those who would never again return to claim them, made the local newspapers the next day. One of the police department's first duties that week was to visit these lots and record license plate numbers in order to track their owners, all potential victims of the attack. Missing persons' reports filed by local residents as well as requests for prayers from the local clergy suggested early what later was confirmed: many Middletown residents lost their lives that day.

Among the dead were youth baseball and basketball coaches, volunteer firefighters, the PTA president of a local parochial school, and 26 parishioners of the local Catholic parish. One of these coaches, Paul Nimbley, had been sworn in as the new Middletown Youth Athletic Association basketball commissioner just the night before; he was proud to be able to oversee a 500-player program, although his special interest was in enlarging the girls' league in town. He left behind a wife, two daughters, a six-month old son, and a household packed in boxes in anticipation of a move to a new neighborhood just days later.

News of the large number of Middletown dead soon spread around the globe. A front-page story of the town's loss in *The Washington Post* garnered international attention. Reporters and film crews descended on the town over the next few weeks, many of them looking for friends and family members of Nimbley who was featured prominently in *The Washington Post* story.

During one of the girls' basketball games at one of the town's middle schools where Nimbley would have been coaching, a reporter from *The Baltimore Sun-Times* sat in the bleachers interviewing some of his acquaintances, while a film crew from the British Broadcasting Company set up shop in one corner of the gym and conducted a series of interviews with those who knew him. In yet another corner of the gym that night was a film crew from the Japanese Broadcasting System show described as the Japanese counterpart to America's own news magazine show, *60 Minutes*; Dai Koyama, the host, conducted these on-camera interviews.

Reporters from other countries, including Belgium, Italy, France, and Australia also arrived in Middletown within days of the attacks. Best-selling author, Gail Sheehy spent much of the next two years in the township interviewing victims' family members as well as a host of others involved in the recovery effort for her book, *Middletown, America: One Town's Passage from Trauma to Hope.* This suburban setting would never be the same again.

MIDDLETOWN'S RESPONSE TO 9/11

The modest basement office was unassuming. Besides the requisite office furniture consisting of a half-moon desk separating a swivel chair from three side chairs, there was little more to distinguish this simple office arrangement from any other in the bustling police department headquarters in Middletown, New Jersey.

Little more, save for the constant reminders of that day, September 11, 2001, which shared much prominence in this small, intimate room and kept it frozen in time. Were it not for the desk calendar, one might think that the day of this interview (November 28, 2007) was just shortly after the terrorist attacks on the Twin Towers of New York City over six years earlier.

All three of the framed pictures hanging on the office walls were of the Towers and of the 9/11 nightmare: a night photograph of the New York skyline with the twin beams of light commemorating the Towers not long after the attack, a *Remember the Heroes, September 11, 2001* framed poster picturing the Towers adorned with the colors of the American flag, and a framed artist's rendition of a police officer and a firefighter arm-in-arm inside a cloud of smoke above the Towers, entitled *Always Honored, Never Forgotten, New Jersey State PBA* (**Policemen's Benevolent Association**).

Propped up in the small window ledge was an article from the local newspaper, the *Asbury Park Press*, laminated onto a wood frame with the title, *Cop Calls on 9/11 Families and Helps.* And resting atop the office desk was a glass and chrome clock given by FAVOR, a local volunteer group in the aftermath of 9/11 (see below), with an inscription commemorating this same person for his *Leadership and Initiative That Lead to Our Success.* Still somewhere else in this office was a Middletown *Employee of the Year* plaque honoring its occupant for his work in the year after 9/11.

The recipient of these honors and the keeper of all these memories was Joe Capriotti, at the time a Detective Sergeant. It was immediately after 9/11 when Detective Sergeant Capriotti became the liaison between the police department and the Middletown families of all victims of the attacks. Detective Capriotti's job was to contact each of these families with offers of assistance. A more gruesome series of tasks he assumed, however, included personal visits to notify families of victims whenever body parts had been identified. He performed 12 of these visits over a seemingly never ending three-year period; his last such visit was just days before the third anniversary of 9/11. After that, notifications then became the responsibility of the New York City Medical Examiner's office. Remains of only 16 of the 37 Middletown victims had been identified by that time.

The Attorney General's Office called for a specific protocol for death notifications; at least two police officers had to knock on the door of the family of the deceased, one of whom had to be in uniform, to inform them of the death. Plain-clothed Detective Capriotti typically took with him for these visits a uniformed officer, a neighbor/friend or family member, and a member of the clergy. "Whenever I knocked, most people knew why I was there," Detective Capriotti claimed. Reactions varied among those who allowed him entry into their homes. "Some people could deal with it and didn't want me there, whereas others needed additional comfort and assistance, such as calling a funeral director or the New York City medical examiner for further assistance."

The reactions of others, however, were varied. Some respondents wanted to grieve privately, while others preferred the hours long solace of Capriotti and his entourage before they were able to let him go. Another diminutive woman threw objects around her living room, while Capriotti and the parish priest attempted to calm her rage over the news of her loss.

At the time of the attacks, Detective Capriotti was a 44-year-old detective in his 19th year on the Middletown police force and in his 34th year as a township resident. A former little league coach himself and a frequent visitor to the local scholastic sporting events, he was quite familiar with the town's children and families. His identity around town, however, changed with the events of 9/11. Suddenly, he was no longer the coach or the team supporter, becoming instead the bearer of tragic news. "It's tough being remembered for the most traumatic event in your life," he claimed, sensing that those he knew before 9/11 looked at him differently now.

Capriotti undertook his responsibilities to the Middletown victims' families seriously, as documented by the accolades described above. Calling it "my proudest accomplishment in my 25 years as a police officer," he began this task in earnest. He became a partner with a grassroots group of "helpers" (see below) who banded together after the Towers fell to take care of the town's families.

MIDDLETOWN'S FAVOR ANSWERS THE CALL

It was the unforeseen response to the Boys Scouts's car wash, scheduled for the Saturday after the attacks, that got at least one Middletown resident to thinking about what else she could do to help. A scout leader in the local troop thought that the car wash might be a fitting way for the Scouts to respond to the events of 9/11 by raising some money to donate to the American Red Cross. What she didn't anticipate, however, were the spontaneous donations which the customers made to the Scouts that Saturday morning for the wash; contributions in the amounts of $10 and $20 rather than the more typical $5 were common. The Scouts also collected four donations of $100 that day.

Just under a mile away from the car wash site, the Boy Scout leader also commissioned other Scouts to man the entrance to the local donut shop to go "canning," the practice of soliciting donations, for the Red Cross effort. "People were just throwing money at us," she claimed; "Women would stop and kiss the kids and thank them for their work." The Scouts collected over $4,000 in just a few hours that day. It was as if their generosity was the direct response to the attacks. An observer mused about the reason for such largesse, "Everybody felt so helpless, so they needed to do something. Giving was their way of doing something." With people in such a giving mood, she thought, it might be easy to raise money right here in Middletown for the victims' families. And so it began.

Soon after the car wash, two other Scout leaders came up with an idea to help the families of the 9/11 victims by capitalizing on this spirit of giving. One of the organizer's business acumen from her years as a Certified Public Accountant and management consultant helped with the organizational aspect of what was to follow. Before long, Middletown's FAVOR was born, Friends Assisting Victims Of terroR. Others soon joined the group as well as the chief of police, a state senator, and the superintendent of the Middletown schools. All decided that perhaps FAVOR could do more than just raise money for the families, believing that the amount collected might not be substantial enough to make a difference, anyway. Rather, the group chose to provide goods, services, and money to those families according to need. "We wanted to restore those little things that make a difference, like pizza on Fridays; we wanted to keep normalcy as much as possible," they said. FAVOR's mission statement was clear. It stated, in part:

Middletown's Friends Assisting Victims Of terroR is a not-for-profit organization created to help those residents of Middletown who have lost an immediate family member as a result of the horrific attack on the World Trade Center on September 11, 2001. It is our mission to provide our beneficiaries with services, goods, and monetary assistance donated by local businesses, Middletown residents, and other friends. We cannot bring back their loved ones. However, we hope to assist them so that they may continue in their normal lifestyle.

So off to local businesses and to other families and individuals the FAVOR founders went, asking for donations. Pizzerias donated gift certificates for pizzas; hardware stores provided tools and equipment for typical household repairs; clothing stores gave clothing; and local markets donated gift certificates and food supplies of all kinds. Families also received free counseling, financial and accounting services, memberships to a local health club, art classes, dry cleaning, and even an hour of massage therapy. Even the state Realtors Association offered to pay for three months rent or three months mortgage for the families.

Local community folks gave time and labor: they mowed the families' lawns, raked their fallen leaves, fixed their leaky roofs, shoveled snow from their porches and driveways, and ran all kinds of errands for them. Others gave according to their own specialty areas of interest: the captain of the nearby charter fishing boat took the surviving children of the victims to sea and taught them how to fish, the family with a house at the shore offered it to families for vacation time, the contractor refinished both bathrooms in the home of a 9/11 widow, and the local train enthusiast known for his elaborate model train display opened his home for a special showing and party for the families just before Christmas. The volunteers numbered 150 in all.

As word of FAVOR's existence spread, "FAVOR became the funnel of all donations from around the world and the country," a founder explained. "We couldn't envision what happened." Holidays brought yet more giving: turkeys and turkey dinners, more money, and toys galore. She recalled one family who drove four hours from their home in Pennsylvania to drop off teddy bears they had made for the families, only to turn around and return home without availing themselves of FAVOR's offer of hospitality after their ride. There also was the quilting club in Florida that made quilts for all the children in town who lost their parents.

The mayor, the police chief, and the chief financial officer from the town of Middletown, Virginia arrived in town with a check for $10,100 for FAVOR; almost half the amount came from their community's yard sale, with the rest coming from a matching donor and assorted other contributors. In all, FAVOR collected between $200,000 and $300,000, according to its founder, the value of the goods and services donated reached approximately $500,000.

When asked why people were so generous, the founders mused, "Giving makes people feel good. When you have no control, at least you can do something." FAVOR's efforts did not go unnoticed. The group was a recipient of one of New Jersey's Ramapo College's annual *Russ Berrie Award for Making a Difference,* a financial award "to recognize unsung heroes from New Jersey who made a significant difference to the well-being of their community." FAVOR used the $2,500 award to fund a social gathering of the 150 volunteers and the surviving members of the 9/11 victims' families, the first time that both groups had ever been together as one.

MIDDLETOWN AND FAVOR WORKING TOGETHER

The process by which FAVOR offered these various donations to the town's families was an organized one. The founders selected an Executive Director, and the other four FAVOR members (chief of police, a state senator, and the superintendent of the Middletown schools) each took primary responsibility for an equal number of the families to be served by the organization. "We each became advocates for our families," the director said. She continued, "This way we got to know the families, and the families depended on us; there was a big connection." These core members each made from six to eight visits to their assigned families, sometimes to deliver a package of donated goods, sometimes just to respond to a phone call to visit and talk.

The group then created an introductory letter explaining FAVOR's mission and purpose along with an application form for any family wishing to be recipients of FAVOR's largesse. The application itself included questions pertaining to the names and ages of the surviving children as well as a checklist of the types of goods and services useful to each family. One of the FAVOR women, in the company of both Capriotti and the Chief of Police, visited the homes of the families and presented the paperwork to them.

All but one family completed the application to begin its participation in the program. Once received, the FAVOR members set about the task of matching those donated services, monies, and materials to the indicated areas of need on the application forms. The director's basement, filled to the brim with boxes and packages of all kinds, became the base of operations for the distribution effort. She and her friends each created packages for the seven or eight families assigned to their care, lobbying each other for certain items which best fit their families' needs.

There was typically more than just one delivery per family; Thanksgiving and the Christmas seasons brought more donations to FAVOR for these families and yet more deliveries. Despite the clause in its mission statement that "FAVOR will exist for a very limited duration, up to six months," the group was unable to abide by this timeline. Well after this six-month period, donations continued to arrive, some Easter-related gifts, beach-related paraphernalia for the upcoming summer season, and still more money. Each anniversary of the event also brought in donations. "You can't walk away from this now," someone said to the FAVOR members who made the last donations to the families a full five years later.

Some of the last checks given to the families remained uncashed. One recipient didn't take it, but used it to send her son's friend to college instead. Capriotti's connection to FAVOR remained strong. As he prepared to make his own visits to families to notify them that their members' body parts had been identified, he always called FAVOR first. "Is there anything I should know about the family?" he asked.

The community's response to the attacks now are literally written in stone; the memorial garden dedicated to the victims contains 37 granite stones, one per victim, emblazoned with their names and images along with a brief description provided by the surviving spouses or other family members. The experience, however, lingers. The founders recall the days of FAVOR tearfully, while Capriotti still sits in his office among various reminders of that day. From time to time he thinks that it's time to remove them and move on. "I looked at them the other day and said to myself, 'Maybe it's time to take them down,' but then I said, 'Nah!'"

A PARISH RISES UP TO HELP

Eileen Theall, both a volunteer and a helper was at a loss to explain how she became involved in the recovery effort in Middletown. A registered nurse with a career of service to others, Theall served as the head of the Parish of St. Mary's Nursing Ministry for a few years before the attacks of 9/11. The parish was a busy one, the largest in the diocese, serving over 4,000 families. It was just such a position that placed her in the forefront of the parish response to the tragedy; a parish which lost 26 members that day.

The Parish of St. Mary had opened a 24-hour-a day, seven-days-a week Adoration Chapel just four years prior to 9/11; two parish volunteers were present in the chapel in one-hour increments all throughout the daytime and evening. The 100-seat chapel was open to anyone, parishioner or not, who wanted some time in silence to reflect or to pray. In the wee hours of a typical early morning, only a small handful of individuals were usually present. And then came 9/11.

Immediately after the news of the attacks, attendance changed dramatically; the number of people at the chapel increased to a "standing room only" crowd all throughout the day and night. Some sat or stood in silence and prayed, some sobbed uncontrollably, and others stoically tried to hold back tears. The overwhelming turnout was a surprise to Theall and to the parish clergy. Stunned by this unanticipated mass outpouring of grief, Theall and others thought that they should be doing something else to assist with the emotional recovery of the community. Although she remains unclear to this day who first proposed the idea, she and others made the decision to open up a crisis center.

The chapel itself was adjacent to the former parish convent, a building which once housed as many as forty Catholic nuns. With declining numbers of the religious sisters over the years, however, the building had lain vacant and unused for some time. It consisted of a large, open community room with a kitchen area, and a long, narrow corridor that provided access to many small, dormitory-like rooms that once served as homes for the nuns. This setting, Theall and others thought, would serve quite well as the site for the 24-hour-a-day, seven-day-a-week crisis center they envisioned.

"We all got together and said, 'We have to have some place for people to go, some place for people to talk,'" Theall recalled. And so this vacant space became the busiest crisis center in town for the next month. Theall put calls out to community members with professional training: psychologists, counselors, nurses, art therapists, and social workers. For the next thirty days, there was never a moment when there was not one or more of these helpers available to the center visitors whenever they stopped by, regardless of the hour. The community room served as the site of informal group counseling and support, while the smaller rooms accommodated those wishing for a more private setting for their expressions of grief. Approximately fifty people visited the center each day, Theall claimed, "and sometimes more." This number was Theall's best guess at the turnout, since, as she said, "We kept no records; it was so unplanned, we just did it."

There were those friends and family members of the deceased who came, and there also were those who "just wanted to be around familiar people, they wanted reassurance," added Theall. In they came, sitting in groups with others or in one-to-one encounters with one of the counselors. They offered support to others and gained support themselves. Many were repeat visitors; others were one-timers only. The center itself had a nonstop flow of visitors in the days immediately following the tragedy.

Just as the staff was discussing chipping in some money of their own to buy pizza for the visitors and for the staff members themselves that first night, food arrived. Unsolicited and unexpected, individuals from the community dropped off trays of hot and cold food. These food donations went on throughout the life of the crisis center; one woman made a delivery of breakfast at 5:00 a.m. each day, and others made similar daily donations at lunchtime and dinnertime. Most of the food was dropped off by anonymous donors. "At no point did we put out one penny," Theall recalled.

As word of the center spread, more people came. The volunteer staff also kept a watchful eye on the visitors to the Adoration Chapel, ushering those more visibly bereaved individuals into the crisis center. Soon community members began referring friends and neighbors to the center as well. As time passed and as the community returned to some sense of normalcy, the crisis center closed its doors. What continued for several years, however, was an ongoing support group for the spouses and other family members of those lost in the attacks, staffed by some of the volunteer counselors from the crisis center. The number eventually dwindled from the initial group of fourteen members as some moved away and others "got their lives back," Theall said.

When asked to reflect on the experience, Theall had no explanation as to how it all started. "It's hard to explain," she said, "We were in awe. We never knew that this would happen. We all just did what had to be done at the time." She was equally unsure about why people help out in times of crisis; she posed, "It's just what people have to do; people are kind and care for other people. They want to help, it's as simple as that."

As simple as that.

SUMMARY

Federal and state governmental agencies and grassroots organizations composed of simple folks from the neighborhood, such as lay people and professionals, the trained and the untrained, the blood donor and the counselor, all contribute to a community's response to tragedy. The word *system* refers to a complex of interacting and interdependent parts that comprise a united whole; changes to even one of the individual parts most certainly affect the other parts of the system. A tragedy in even one component reverberates through the other components.

The serious illness of a young child, for example, generates waves of concern, not just among family members, but also among classmates, neighbors, and other community members who may have been only remotely acquainted with the child. Similarly, the death of a high-profile celebrity from the entertainment industry sparks strong reactions of grief throughout the country. Repeated televised images of terrorist-sponsored bombings, mass shootings, or devastating natural disasters seem to call people to action to help.

Perhaps poet John Donne said it most eloquently when he wrote in "Meditation XVII":

No man is an island, entire of itself; every man is a piece of the continent, a part of the main . . . any man's death diminishes me, because I am involved in mankind, and therefore never send to know for whom the bell tolls; it tolls for thee. (p. 441)

This chapter concludes with this poet's words.

RESOURCES FOR CHAPTER ENRICHMENT

Recommended Films

9/11: Hosted by actor Robert De Niro, this documentary film chronicles the attack on the Twin Towers in New York's World Trade Center. The reactions of the firefighters who were first responders are showcased as much in this film as were the actual minute-by-minute events of the day.

World Trade Center: The film is the true story of two Port Authority policemen, John McLoughlin and William Jimeno, two of the last survivors extracted from the rubble of Ground Zero and of the rescuers who saved them. The themes of courage, persistence, and personal resilience mark this film.

Triumph Over Disaster: The Hurricane Andrew Story: In August of 1992, Hurricane Andrew, the most destructive U.S. hurricane on record, pummeled southern Florida with winds of 164 miles an hour. Twenty-nine people died, and property damage in three states reached almost $27 billion. This film examines the lives of several people affected by the storm and their attempts at recovery.

Suggested Activities

1. Log onto the Federal Emergency Management Agency website (www. fema.org) and find the listing of all FEMA emergencies to which it has responded. What kinds of crises prompted its involvement?

2. Hurricane Katrina devastated the better part of New Orleans. Even though there are parts of the city which are uninhabitable to this day, investigate those agencies which contributed goods and services to its recovery.

3. Make a list of local community groups, agencies, or organizations on a county-wide level in your area that provide volunteer opportunities for its citizens. Categorize them according to the services they provide and the volunteer opportunities offered for people like you.

References

Acierno R., Hernandez, M. A., Amstadter, A. B., Resnick, H. S., Steve, K., Muzzy W., & Kilpatrick, D. G. (2010). Prevalence and correlates of emotional, physical, sexual, and financial abuse and potential neglect in the United States: The national elder mistreatment study. *American Journal of Public, 100*(2), 292–297.

Aguilera, D. C. (1998). *Crisis intervention: Theory and methodology*. St. Louis, MO: Mosby-Year Book.

Aguirre-Molina, M., & Molina, C. (1994). Latino populations: Who are they? In C. W. Molina & M. Aguirre-Molina (Eds.), *Latino health in the U.S.: A growing challenge* (pp. 3–22). Washington, DC: American Public Health Association.

Albuquerque, S., Pereira, M., & Narciso, I. (2016). Couple's relationship after the death of a child: A systematic review. *Journal of Child and Family Studies, 25*(1), 30–53.

Allen, K., Byrne, S., Oddy, W., Schmidt, U., & Crosby, R. (2014). Risk factors for binge eating disorders: Differences based on age of onset. *International Journal of Eating Disorders, 47*(7), 802–814.

Allen, N. H. (1983). Homicide followed by suicide: Los Angeles, 1970–1979. *Suicide & Life-Threatening Behavior, 13*, 155–165.

American Foundation for Suicide Prevention. (2016). *Annual report*. New York, NY: Author.

American Medical Association. (1991). *Report of the Council of Scientific Affairs: Violence Against Women* [Proceedings of the House of Delegates]. Chicago, IL: Author.

American Psychiatric Association. (2013). *The diagnostic & statistical manual of mental disorders* (5th ed.). Washington, DC: Author.

American Psychological Association. (2008). Are zero tolerance policies effective in the schools? An evidentiary review and recommendations. Zero Tolerance Task Force. *American Psychologist, 63*(9), 852–862.

Andrews, E. (2008, March 8). Sharp drop in jobs adds to grim economic picture. *New York Times*.

Andrews, J. A., & Lewinsohn, P. M. (1992). Suicidal attempts among older adolescents: Prevalence and co-occurrence with psychiatric disorders. *Journal of the American Academy of Child & Adolescent Psychiatry, 31*, 655–662.

Anestis, M. D., Khazem, L. R., Keyne, C. L., Houtsma, C., LeTard, R., Moberg, F., & Martin, R. (2015). The association between state laws regulating handgun ownership and statewide suicide rates. *American Journal of Public Health, 105*(10), 2059–2067.

Anorexia and Related Eating Disorders (ANRED). (2004). *Statistics: How many people have eating disorders?* Retrieved from www.anred.com/stats.html

Anthony, J. C., & Petronis, K. R. (1991). Suspected risk factors for depression among adults 18–44 years old. *Epidemiology, 2*, 123–132.

Armstrong-Stassen, M. (1993). "Survivors" reactions to a workforce reduction: A comparison of blue-collar workers and their supervisors. *Canadian Journal of Administrative Sciences, 10*, 334–343.

Asaad, G. (1995). *Understanding mental disorders due to medical conditions or substance use: What every therapist should know*. New York, NY: Brunner/Mazel.

Athey, J., & Moody-Williams, J. (2003). *Developing cultural competence in disaster mental health problems: Guiding principles and recommendations*. Washington, DC: U.S. Department of Health and Human Services.

Auchter, B. (2010). Men who murder their families: What the research tells us. *National Institute of Justice Journal, 266*. Retrieved from http://www.nij.gov/journals/266/Pages/murderfamilies.asp

Bachman, J. G., O'Malley, P. M., Johnston, L. D., Schulenberg, J. E., & Wallace, J. M. (2011). Racial/ethnic differences in the relationship between parental education and substance use among U. S. 8th, 10th, and 12th-grade students: Findings from the Monitoring the Future Project. *Journal of Studies on Alcohol and Drugs, 72*, 279–285.

Badenes-Ribera, L., Bonilla-Campos, A., Frias-Navarro, D., & Pons-Salvador, G. (2016). Intimate partner violence in self-identified lesbians: A systematic review of its prevalence and correlates. *Trauma, Violence & Abuse, 17*(3), 284–297.

Barlé, N., Wortman, C. B., & Latack, J. A. (2015, August 3). Traumatic bereavement: Basic research, and clinical implications. *Journal of Psychotherapy Integration,* 1–12.

Basile, K. C., Arias, I., Desai, S., & Thompson, M. P. (2004). The differential association of intimate partner physical, sexual, psychological, and stalking violence and posttraumatic stress symptoms in a nationally representative sample of women. *Journal of Traumatic Stress, 17*, 413–421.

Bates, E. A. (2016). Current controversies within intimate partner violence: Overlooking bidirectional violence. *Journal of Family Violence, 31*(8), 937–940.

Battered Women's Shelters. (2015). *Battered women's shelters: What are they? How to find one*. Retrieved from http://www.healthyplace.com/abuse/domestic-violence/battered-women-shelters-what-are-they-how-to-find-one/

Beck, A. T., Kovacs, M., & Weissman, A. (1979). Assessment of suicidal intention: The Scale for Suicidal Ideation. *Journal of Consulting & Clinical Psychology, 47*(2), 343–352.

Beck, A. T., Wright, F. D., Newman, C. F., & Liese, B. S. (1993). *Cognitive therapy of substance abuse*. New York, NY: Guilford Press.

Beck, J. S. (2011). *Cognitive behavior therapy: Basics and beyond* (2nd ed.). New York, NY: Guilford Press.

Beebe, D. K., & Walley, E. (1991). Substance abuse: The designer drugs. *American Family Physician, 43*, 1689–1698.

Bellak, L., & Siegel, H. (1983). *Handbook of intensive brief and emergency psychotherapy*. Larchmont, NY: C.P.S. Berglas, S. (1985). Why did this happen to me? *Psychology Today,* 44–48.

Berman, A., Jobes, D., & Silverman, R. (2006). *Adolescent suicide: Assessment and intervention* (2nd ed.). Washington, DC: American Psychological Association.

Bernal, G., & Shapiro, E. (2005). Cuban families. In M. McGoldrick, J. K. Pearce, & J. Giordano (Eds.), *Ethnicity and family therapy* (3rd ed.). New York, NY: Guilford Press.

Birnbaum, H. G., White, A. G., Schiller, M., Waldman, T., Cleveland, J. M., & Roland, C. L. (2011). Societal costs of prescription opioid abuse, dependence, and misuse in the United States. *Pain Medicine, 12*(4), 657–667.

Björkqvist, K., Österman, K., & Lagerspetz, K. M. J. (1994). Sex differences in covert aggression among adults. *Aggressive Behavior, 20*, 27–33.

Black, M. C., Basile, K. C., Breiding, M. J., Smith, S. G., Walters, M. L., Merrick, M. T., & Stevens, M. R. (2011). *The National Intimate Partner and Sexual Violence Survey (NISVS): 2010 summary report*. Atlanta, GA: National Center for Injury Prevention and Control. Centers for Disease Control and Prevention.

Blair, J. P., & Schweit, K. W. (2014). *A study of active shooter incidents, 2000-2013*. Washington, DC: Texas State University and Federal Bureau of Investigation.

Blumenreich, P. E., & Lewis, S. J. (1993). *Managing the violent patient: A clinician's guide*. Philadelphia, PA: Brunner/Mazel.

Bohen, S. (2002, June). *Psychiatric emergencies*. Eau Claire, WI: PESI Healthcare.

Bohner, G. (1998). *Rape myths.* Landau, Germany: Verlag Empirische Padagogik.

Boira, S., del Castillo, M. F., Carbajosa, P., & Marcella, C. (2013). Context of treatment and therapeutic alliance: Critical factors in court-mandated batterer interventions programs. *The Spanish Journal of Psychology, 16*(1), 14–23.

Bonanno, G. A. (2004). Loss, trauma, and human resilience. *American Psychologist, 59,* 20–28.

Bowlby, J. (1969). *Attachment and loss: Attachment* (Vol. I.). New York, NY: Basic Books.

Bowlby, J. (1973). *Attachment and loss: Separation* (Vol. II.), New York, NY: Basic Books.

Bowlby, J. (1980). *Attachment and loss: Loss, sadness, and depression.* (Vol. III.). New York, NY: Basic Books.

Bowman, S., & Randall, K. (2004). *See my pain! Creative strategies for helping young people who self-injure.* Chapin, SC: Youthlight.

Bradford, J. M. W., Greenberg, D. M., & Motayne, G. G. (1992). Substance abuse and criminal behavior. *Psychiatric Clinics of North America, 15,* 605–622.

Bradford, R., & Holt, C. (2015). The use of psychotropic drug therapy in borderline personality disorder: A case report. *Psychiatria Danubina, 27*(1), S371–S374.

Brammer, L. M. (1985). *The helping relationship: Process and skills* (3rd ed.). Englewood Cliffs, NJ: Prentice-Hall.

Brecher, M., Wang, B. W., Wong, H., & Morgan, J. P. (1988). Phencyclidine and violence: Clinical and legal issues. *Journal of Clinical Psychopharmacology, 8,* 397–401.

Brieding, M. J., Basile, K. C., Smith, S. G., Black, M. C., & Mahendra, R. (2015). *Intimate partner violence surveillance: Uniform definitions and recommended data elements* (version 2.0). Atlanta, GA: National Center for Injury Prevention and Control, Centers for Disease Control and Prevention.

Briggs, J. T., & Tabarrok, A. (2014). Firearms and suicide in U.S. States. *International Review of Law and Economics, 37,* 180–188.

Briody, L., Albright, D., & Denman, K. (2016). Deterring future incidents of intimate partner violence: Does type of formal intervention matter? *Violence Against Women, 22*(9), 1113–1133.

Brock, S. E. (1998). Helping classrooms cope with traumatic events. *Professional School Counseling, 2,* 110–116.

Brock, S. E. (2002). Crisis theory: A foundation for the comprehensive crisis prevention and intervention team. In S. Brock, P. Lazarus, & S. Jimerson (Eds.), *Best practices in school crisis prevention and intervention* (pp. 5–17). Bethesda, MD: National Association of School Psychologists.

Brock, S. E. (2003). School Suicide Postvention. In S. E. Brock, P. J. Lazurus, & S. R. Jimerson (Eds.), *Best practices in school crisis prevention and intervention: The PREPaRE model.* Bethesda, MD: National Association of School Psychologists.

Brock, S. E. (2006). *Crisis intervention and recovery: The roles of school-based mental health professionals.* Bethesda, MD: National Association of School Psychologists.

Brock, S. E. (2015). President's message: Homicide in school: What are the odds? *Communique, 43*(7), 1–3.

Brock, S. E., Nickerson, A. B., Reeves, M. A., Jimerson, S. R., Lieberman, R. A., & Feinberg, T. A. (2009). *School crisis prevention and intervention: The PREPaRE model.* Bethesda, MD: National Association of School Psychologists.

Brock, S. E., Sandoval, J., & Hart, S. (2006). Suicidal ideation and behaviors. In G. G. Bear & K. M. Minke (Eds.), *Children's needs III: Development, prevention, and intervention.* Bethesda, MD: National Association of School Psychologists.

Brock, S., Sandoval, J., & Lewis, S. (2001). *Preparing for crises in schools: A manual for building school crisis response teams.* New York, NY: John Wiley.

Bronfenbrenner, U. (1979). *Ecology of human development.* Cambridge, MA: Harvard University Press.

Brooks, K., Schiraldi, V., & Ziedenberg, J. (2000). *School house hype: Two years later.* Washington, DC: Justice Policy Institute/Children's Law Center.

Bryan, C. J., & Rudd, M. D. (2016). The importance of temporal dynamics in the transition from suicidal thought to behavior. *Clinical Psychology: Science and Practice, 23*(1), 22–25.

Bureau of Justice. (2009). *Female victims of violence.* Washington, DC: U.S. Department of Justice, Office of Justice Programs. Retrieved from http://www.bjs.gov/content/pub/pdf/fvv.pdf

Bureau of Justice. (2012). *Intimate partner violence, 1993–2010.* Washington, DC: U.S. Department of Justice, Office of Justice Programs. Retrieved from http://www.bjs.gov/content/pub/pdf/ipv9310.pdf

Bureau of Justice. (2013). *Intimate partner violence: Attributes of victimization, 1993–2011.* Washington, DC: U.S. Department of Justice, Office of Justice Programs. Retrieved from http://www.bjs.gov/content/pub/pdf/ipvav9311.pdf

Bureau of Justice. (2014). *Non-fatal domestic violence 2003–2012.* Washington, DC: U.S. Department of Justice, Bureau of Justice Statistics.

Bureau of Labor Statistics. (2015). *Volunteering in the United States, 2015.* Washington, DC: Author.

Burley, K. A. (1991). Family-work spillover in dual-career families: A comparison of two time perspectives. *Psychological Reports, 68,* 471–480.

Butcher, J. N. (1980). The role of crisis intervention in an airport disaster plan. *Aviation, Space, and Environmental Medicine, 51,* 1260–1262.

Cafferky, B. M., Mendez, M., Anderson, J. R., & Stith, S. M. (2016). Substance use and intimate partner violence: A meta-analytic review. *Psychology of Violence, 31,* 116–126.

Cameron, K. S. (1994, Summer). Guest Editor's note: Investigating organizational downsizing: Fundamental issues. *Human Resources Management, 33,* 183–194.

Cameron, K. S., Freeman, S. J., & Mishra, A. K. (1993). Best practices in white-collar downsizing: Managing contradictions. *Academy of Management Executive, 5,* 57–72.

Cantor, C. H., & Slater, P. J. (1995). Marital breakdown, parenthood, and suicide. *Journal of Family Studies, 1,* 91–104.

Caplan, G. (1961). *An approach to community mental health.* New York, NY: Grune & Stratton.

Caplan, G. (1964). *Principles of preventative psychiatry.* New York, NY: Basic Books.

Carkhuff, R. (1969). *Helping and human relations: A primer for lay and professional helpers.* New York, NY: Holt, Rinehart, & Winston.

Carkhuff, R. R., & Berenson, B. G. (1977). *Counseling and psychotherapy: Theories and interventions.* Englewood Cliffs, NJ: Prentice-Hall.

Carnegie Foundation. (1995). *Great transitions: Preparing adolescents for a new century.* New York, NY: Author.

Case, A., & Deaton, A. (2015, June). *Suicide, age, and well-being: An empirical investigation* [Working Paper series]. Cambridge, MA: National Bureau of Economic Research.

Castro, F. G., Proescholdbell, R. J., Abeita, L., & Rodriguez, D. (1999). Ethnic and cultural minority groups. In B. S. McCrady & E. E. Epstein (Eds.), *Addiction: A comprehensive guidebook.* Oxford, England: Oxford University Press.

Cavaiola, A., & Colford, J. (2006). *A practical guide to crisis intervention.* Boston, MA: Houghton Mifflin.

Cavaiola, A., & Colford, J. (2011). *Crisis intervention case book.* Belmont, CA: Brooks/Cole.

Cavaiola, A. A., & Dolan, D. (2016). Some considerations in the civil commitment of individuals with substance use disorders. *Substance Abuse, 18,* 22–26.

Cavaiola, A. A., & Lavender, N. J. (1999, March). *Personality disorders in the workplace: Are we driving each other crazy?* Paper presented at the APA-NIOSH Conference on Work, Stress and Health, Baltimore, Maryland.

Cavaiola, A. & Lavender (2000a) Working with Difficult People. Workshop series provided for New Jersey Natural Resources Human Resources sponsored by Monmouth University, West Long Branch, NJ

Cavaiola, A. A., & Lavender, N. J. (2000b). *Toxic co-workers: How to deal with dysfunctional people in the workplace.* Oakland, CA: New Harbinger.

Cavaiola, A. A., & Schiff, M. (1988). Behavioral sequalae of sexual and /or physical abuse in chemically dependent adolescents. *Child Abuse & Neglect, 12,* 181–188.

Center for Behavioral Health Statistics and Quality. (2015). *Behavioral health trends in the United States: Results from the 2014 National Survey on Drug Use and Health* (HHS Publication No. SMA 15-4927, NSDUH Series H-50). Retrieved from http://www.samhsa.gov/data/

Centers for Disease Control and Prevention. (CDC). (2005). *Youth risk behavior surveillance survey.* Washington, DC: Government Printing Office.

Centers for Disease Control and Prevention. (2010). *Homicides—United States, 2007–2009. Morbidity & Mortality Weekly Report.* Washington, DC: Government Printing Office. Retrieved from http://www.cdc.gov/mmwr/preview/mmwrhtml/su6203a28.htm

Centers for Disease Control and Prevention. (2013a). *Alcohol Related Disease Impact (ARDI) application, 2013.* Retrieved from http://nccd.cdc.gov/DPH_ARDI/Default.aspx. http://www.cdc.gov/alcohol/data-stats.htm

Centers for Disease Control and Prevention. (2013b). *Data, trends, and maps.* Retrieved from http://www.cdc.gov/alcohol/data-stats.html

Centers for Disease Control and Prevention. (2013c). *Leading causes of death in the United States, 2013.* Retrieved from http://www.cdc.gov/nchs/fastats/leading-causes-of-death.htm

Centers for Disease Control & Prevention. (2014a, July 7). *National Institute of Occupational Safety & Health—Workplace Violence Statistics.* Retrieved from http://www.cdc.gov/niosh/topics/violence

Center for Disease Control & Prevention. (2014b). *Marriage and divorce rates in the United States, 2014.* Retrieved from http://www.cdc.gov/nchs/fastats/marriage-divorce.htm

Centers for Disease Control. (2014c, January 9). *Suicide Prevention.* Retrieved from http://www.cdc.gov/violenceprevention/pub/youth_suicide.html

Centers for Disease Control and Prevention. (2015a). National Center for Health Statistics, National Vital Statistics System, Mortality File. *Number and age-adjusted rates of drug poisoning deaths involving Opioid analgesics and heroin: United States 2000-2014.* Atlanta, GA: Author. Retrieved from http://www.cdc.gov/nchs/data/health_policy/AADR_drug_poisoning_involving_OA_Heroin_US_2000–2014.pdf

Centers for Disease Control and Prevention. (2015b). *Suicide facts at a glance, 2015.* Retrieved from http://www.cdc.gov/violenceprevention/pdf/suicide-datasheet-a.pdf

Centers for Disease Control and Prevention (CDC). (2016a). *Web-based injury statistics query and reporting system.* National Center for Injury Prevention and Control. Atlanta, GA: Author.

Centers for Disease Control and Prevention (CDC). (2016b). *Increase in the suicides in the United States, 1999–2014.* Atlanta, GA: Author.

Child Welfare Information Gateway. (2014). *Child maltreatment 2014: Summary of key findings.* Washington, DC: Department of Health and Human Services, Children's Bureau.

Chu, J. A. (1999). Trauma and suicide. In D. G. Jacobs (Ed.), *The Harvard Medical School guide to suicide assessment and intervention.* San Francisco, CA: Jossey Bass.

Chu, J. A., Floyd, R., Diep, H., Pardo, S., Goldblum, P., & Bongar, B. (2013). A tool for the culturally competent assessment of suicide: The Cultural Assessment of Risk for Suicide (CARS) measure. *Psychological Assessment, 25*(2), 424–434.

Clary, E., Snyder, M., Ridge, R., Copeland, J., Stukas, A., Haugen, J., & Miene, P. (1998). Understanding and assessing the motives of volunteers: A functional approach. *Journal of Personality and Social Psychology, 74,* 1516–1530.

Clayton, P. J., Desmarais, L., & Winokur, G. (1968). A study of normal bereavement. *American Journal of Psychiatry, 125,* 64–74.

Collins, B. G., & Collins, T. (2005). *Crisis and trauma.* Belmont, CA: Cengage.

Commonwealth Fund. (2014a). *Mirror, mirror on the wall, a 2014 update: How the U.S. health care system compares internationally.* Retrieved from http://www.commonwealthfund.org/publications/fund-reports/2014/jun/mirror-mirror

Commonwealth Fund. (2014b, September 8). A comparison of hospital administrative costs in eight nations: U.S. costs exceed all others by far. Retrieved from http://www.commonwealthfund.org/publications/in-the-literature/2014/sep/hospital-administrative-costs

Commonwealth Fund (2015, October 8). *U.S. healthcare from a global perspective.* Retrieved from http://www.commonwealthfund.org/publications/issue-briefs/2015/oct/us-health-care-from-a-global-perspective.

Congressional Research Service. (2015). *Stafford Act Declarations 1953-2014: Trends, analyses, and implications for congress.* Washington, DC: Government Printing Office.

Copeland, A. R. (1985). Dyadic death revisited. *Journal of the Forensic Science Society, 25,* 181–188.

Cornelius, J. R., Soloff, P. H., Perel, J. M., & Ulrich, R. F. (1993). Continuation pharmacotherapy of borderline personality disorder with haloperidol and phenelzine. *American Journal of Psychiatry, 150,* 1843–1848.

Covert, B. (2016, August 27). Sexual harassment training with Roger Ailes. *New York Times,* Sunday Review.

Crisis Prevention Institute. (1999). Nonviolent crisis intervention: A practical approach for managing violent behavior. *Violence Prevention Resource Center.* Milwaukee, WI: Author. Retrieved from http://www.crisisprevention.com

Cross, T. L., Bazron, B. J., Dennis, K. W., & Isaacs, M. R. (1989). *Toward a culturally competent system of care.* Washington, DC: Georgetown University Child Development Center.

Crothers, L. M., Lipinski, J., & Minutolo, M. C. (2009). Cliques, rumors, and gossip by the water cooler: Female bullying in the workplace. *The Psychologist-Manager Journal, 12,* 97–110.

Cuevas, D. A., & Bui, N. H. (2016). Social factors affecting the completion of a batterer intervention program. *Journal of Family Violence, 31*(1), 95–107.

Dana, R. H. (1993). *Multicultural assessment perspectives for professional psychology.* Boston, MA: Allyn & Bacon.

Dardis, C. M., Amoroso, T., & Iverson, K. M. (2016, July 14). Intimate partner stalking: Contributions to PTSD Symptomatology among a national sample of women veterans. *Psychological Trauma: Theory, Research, Practice, and Policy.*

Davidson, M. W., Wagner, W. G., & Range, L. M. (1995). Clinician's attitudes toward non-suicide agreements. *Suicide & Life-Threatening Behavior, 25,* 410–414.

Decker, K. P., & Ries, R. K. (1993). Differential diagnosis and psychopharmacology of dual disorders. *Psychiatric Clinics of North America, 16,* 703–718.

Delva, J., Wallace, J. M. Jr., O'Malley, P. M., Bachman, J. G., Johnston, L. D., & Schulenberg, J. E. (2005). The epidemiology of alcohol, marijuana, and cocaine use among Mexican-American, Puerto Rican, Cuban American, and other Latin American eighth-grade students in the United States: 1991–2002. *American Journal of Public Health, 95,* 696–702.

Department of Defense. (2014). *Sexual Abuse Prevention Report* (SAPR). Washington, DC: Author. Retrieved from www.sapr.mil/public/docs/reports/FY14_annual_dod_FY14_annual_reports_on_sexual_assault

Dershimer, R. A. (1990). *Counseling the bereaved.* New York, NY: Pergamon Press.

DeVoe, J. F., Peter, K., Noonan, M., Snyder, T. D., & Baum, K. (2005). *Indicators of school crime and safety: 2005.* U.S. Departments of Education and Justice. Washington, DC: Government Printing Office.

DeWolfe, D. J. (2000). *Field manual for mental health and human service workers in major disasters* [DHHS Publication No. (ADM) 90-537]. Washington, DC: Government Printing Office.

Dinwiddie, S. W. (1994). Abuse of inhalants: A review. *Addiction, 89,* 925–929.

DiTomasso, R. A., Martin, D. M., & Kovnat, K. D. (2000). Medical patients in crisis. In F. M. Dattilio & A. Freeman (Eds.), *Cognitive-behavioral strategies in crisis intervention.* New York, NY: Guilford Press.

Dobie, K. (2016, January 5). To catch a rapist. *New York Times.*

Dolan-Delvecchio, K., & Saxton-Lopez, N. (2013). *The pet loss companion: Healing advice from family therapists who have led pet loss groups*. North Charleston, SC: Create Space.

Donne, J. (1624). Meditation XVII. In H. Alford (Ed.), *Devotions upon emergent occasions*. London, UK: John W. Parker.

Doweiko, H. E. (2014). *Concepts of chemical dependency* (9th ed.). Stamford, CT: Cengage Learning.

Drapeau, C. W., & McIntosh, J. L. (2015, April 24). *U.S.A. suicide 2013: Official final data*. Washington, DC: American Association of Suicidology. Retrieved from http://www.suicidology.org

Dutton, D. G. (1995). *The batterer: A psychological profile*. New York, NY: Basic Books.

Dutton, D. G. (1996). *The domestic assault of women*. Vancouver, British Columbia: UBC Press.

Dutton, D. (1998). *The abusive personality*. New York, NY: Guilford Press.

Eckhardt, C., Barbour, K., & Davison, G. (1998). Articulated thoughts of martially violent and nonviolent men during anger arousal. *Journal of Consulting and Clinical Psychology, 66,* 229–269.

Edelson, J. L., & Tolman, R. M. (1992). *Interventions for men who batter: An ecological approach*. Newbury Park, CA: SAGE.

Egan, M. P. (1997). Contracting for safety: A concept analysis. *Crisis, 18,* 17–23.

Eigsti, I., & Cicchetti, D. (2004). The impact of child maltreatment on expressive syntax at 60 months. *Developmental Science, 7,* 88–102.

Einarsen, S., Hoel, H., Zapf, D., & Cooper, C. L. (2011). *Bullying and harassment in the workplace: Developments in theory, research, and practice* (2nd ed.). Boca Raton, FL: CRC Press.

Eisenberg, P., & Lazarsfeld, P. E. (1938). The psychological effects of unemployment. *Psychological Bulletin, 39,* 358–390.

Eliason S. (2009). Murder-suicide: A review of the recent literature. *Journal of American Academy of Psychiatry Law, 37,* 371–376.

Elkind, D. (1967). Egocentrism in adolescence. *Child Development, 38,* 1025–1034.

Ellis, A. (1952). *Reason and emotion in psychotherapy*. New York, NY: Citadel.

Erikson, E. (1963). *Childhood and society* (2nd ed.). New York, NY: Norton Press.

Erikson, E. (1968). *Identity, youth, and crisis*. New York, NY: W.W. Norton.

Evans, P. (2010). *The verbally abusive relationship* (3rd ed.). Avon, MA: Adams Media.

Everly, G. S., Jr., & Mitchell, J. T. (1999). *Critical Incident Stress Management (CISM): A new era and standard of care in crisis intervention* (2nd ed.). Ellicott City, MD: Chevron.

Fang, X., Brown, D., Florence, C., & Mercy, J. (2012). The economic burden of child maltreatment in the United States and implications for prevention. *Child Abuse and Neglect, 36,* 156–165.

Featherstone, S. (2015, July 8). Spike nation: Cheap, unpredictable, and hard to regulate, synthetic marijuana has emergency responders scrambling to save lives. *New York Times*.

Federal Bureau of Investigation (FBI). (2015). *Uniform Crime Report: Crime in the United States 2015, Table 16*. Washington, DC: Author. Retrieved from https://ucr.fbi.gov/crime-in-the-u.s/2015/crime-in-the-u.s.-2015/tables/table-16

Federal Emergency Management Agency (FEMA). (1988, November 23). *The Robert T. Stafford Disaster Relief and Emergency Assistance Act* (Public Law 100-707). Amended the Disaster Relief Act of 1974 (Public Law 93-288). Washington, DC: Government Printing Office.

Felitti, V. J., & Anda, R. (2009). The relationship of adverse childhood experiences to adult medical disease, psychiatric disorders, and sexual behavior: Implications for healthcare. In R. Lanius, E. Vermetten, & C. Pain (Eds.), *The hidden epidemic: The impact of early life trauma on health and disease*. Cambridge, England: Cambridge University Press.

Fernandez-Montalvo, J., Echauti, J. A., Martinez, M., Azcarte, J. M., & Lopez-Goni, J. J. (2015). Impact of a court-referred psychological treatment program for intimate partner batterer men with suspended sentences. *Violence & Victims, 30*(1), 3–15.

Finkelstein, M. (2007). Correlates in satisfaction in older volunteers: A motivational perspective. *The International Journal of Volunteer administration, 24,* 6–12.

Fitch, F. J., & Papantonio, A. (1983). Men who batter: Some personality characteristics. *Journal of Nervous and Mental Disease, 17*(1), 190–192.

Flannery, J. B., Jr. (1998). *The assaulted staff action program: Coping with the psychological aftermath of violence.* Ellicott City, MD: Chevron.

Flannery, R. B., Jr., & Everly, G. S., Jr. (2000). Crisis intervention: A review. *International Journal of Emergency Mental Health, 2*(2), 119–125.

Foran, H. M., & O'Leary, K. D. (2008). Alcohol and intimate partner violence: A meta-analytic review. *Clinical Psychology Review, 28*, 1222–1234.

Fox, S. (2009). *Divorce rate among the bereaved.* Retrieved from http://www.opentohope.com/divorce-rate-among-bereaved/

Frazier, P. A. (1990). Victim attribution and post-rape trauma. *Journal of Personality and Social Psychology, 59*(2), 298–304.

Freeman, A., & Fusco, G. (2000). Treating high-arousal patients: Differentiating between patients in crisis and crisis-prone patients. In F. M. Dattilio & A. Freeman (Eds.), *Cognitive-behavioral strategies in crisis intervention.* New York, NY: Guilford Press.

Frierson, R. L., Melikian, M., & Wadman, P. C. (2002). Principles of suicide risk assessment. *Postgraduate Medicine, 112*(3). Retrieved from www.postgradmed.com/issues/2002/09_02/frierson4.htm

Froeschle, J., & Moyer, M. (2004). Just cut it out: Legal and ethical challenges in counseling students who self-mutilate. *Professional School Counseling, 7*, 231–236.

Furman, E. (1974). *A child's parent dies: Studies in childhood bereavement.* New Haven, CT: Yale University Press.

Galea, S., Nandi, A., & Vlahov, D. (2004). The social epidemiology of substance use. *Epidemiological Reviews, 26*, 36–52.

Gallo, J. J., Royall, D. R., & Anthony, J. C. (1993). Risk factors for the onset of depression in middle age and later life. *Social Psychiatry & Psychiatric Epidemiology, 28*, 101–108.

Ganim, S. (2011, November 17). Exclusive: Jerry Sandusky interview prompts long-ago victims to contact lawyer. *The Patriot News.*

Gannon, T., Collie, R., Ward, T., & Thakker, J. (2008). Rape: Psychopathology, theory, and treatment. *Clinical Psychology Review, 28*, 982–1008.

Garrison, C. Z., McKeown, R. E., & Valois, R. F. (1993). Aggression, substance use and suicidal behaviors in high school students. *American Journal of Public Health, 83*, 179–184.

Geffner, R., Mantooth, C., & Franks, D. (1989). A psychoeducational, conjoint therapy approach to reducing family violence. In P. L. Caesar & L. K. Hamberger (Eds.), *Treating men who batter: Theory, practice, and programs.* New York, NY: Springer.

Geffner, R., & Pagelow, M. D. (1990). Mediation and custody issues in abusive relationships. *Behavioral Science & the Law, 8*, 151–159.

Gilliland, B. E., & James, R. K. (1997). *Crisis intervention strategies* (3rd ed.). Pacific Grove, CA: Brooks/Cole.

Gladding, S. (1999). *Counseling: A comprehensive profession* (4th ed.). New York, NY: Prentice-Hall.

Gold, J., Wolan Sullivan, M., & Lewis, M. (2011). The relation between abuse and violent delinquency: The conversion of shame to blame in juvenile offenders. *Child Abuse and Neglect, 35*(7), 459–467.

Goode, E. (2001, September 16). After the attacks: Counseling; Some therapists fear services could backfire. *New York Times.*

Granvold, D. K. (2000). The crisis of divorce: Cognitive-behavioral and constructivist assessment and treatment. In A. R. Roberts (Ed.), *Crisis intervention handbook: Assessment, treatment, and research.* New York, NY: Oxford University Press.

Greenstone, J., & Leviton, S. (1993). *Elements of crisis intervention.* Belmont, CA: Brooks/Cole.

Greenstone, J. L., & Leviton S. C. (2002. *Elements of crisis intervention: Crises and how to respond to them*. Pacific Grove, CA: Brooks/Cole.

Group for the Advancement of Psychiatry. (1989). *Suicide and ethnicity in the United States* (GAP Report 128). Formulated by the Committee on Cultural Psychiatry. Dallas, TX: Author.

Grych, J. H., Jouriles, E. N., Swank, P. R., McDonald, R., & Norwood, W. D. (2000). Patterns of adjustment among women of battered children. *Journal of Consulting and Clinical Psychology, 68*, 84–94.

Gubar, S. (2016, May 5). Pricing a year of life. *New York Times*. Retrieved from http://well.blogs.nytimes.com/2016/05/05/pricing-a-year-of-life/

Halpern, C. T., Oslak, S. G., & Young, M. L. (2001). Partner violence among adolescents in opposite-sex romantic relationships: Findings from the National Longitudinal Study of Adolescent Health. *American Journal of Public Health, 91*, 1679–1685.

Hamberger, L. K., & Hastings, J. (1986). Personality correlates of men who abuse their partners: A cross validation study. *Journal of Family Violence, 1*, 323–341.

Hare, R. D. (1993). *Without conscience: The disturbing work of psychopaths among us*. New York: NY: Guilford Press.

Harford, P. M. (2010). The integrative use of EMDR and clinical hypnosis in the treatment of adults abused as children. *Journal of EMDR Practice and Research, 4*(2), 60–75.

Harkavy Friedman, J. M., & Asnis, G. M. (1989). Assessment of suicidal behavior: A new instrument. *Psychiatric Annals, 19*(7), 382–387.

Harrell, A., & Smith, B. E. (1996). Effects of restraining orders on domestic violence victims. In E. S. Buzawa & C. G. Buzawa (Eds.), *Do arrests and restraining orders work?* Thousand Oaks, CA: SAGE.

Harwood, A. (1982). Mainland Puerto Ricans. In A. Harwood (Ed.), *Ethnicity and medical care*. Cambridge, MA: Harvard University Press.

Haw, C., & Stubbs, J. (2011). Medication for borderline personality disorder: A survey at a secure hospital. *International Journal of Psychiatry in Clinical Practice, 15*, 280–285.

Heisel, M. J., & Flett, G. L. (2006). The development and initial validation of the Geriatric Suicide Ideation Scale. *The American Journal of Geriatric Psychiatry, 14*, 742–751.

Heisel, M. J., & Flett, G. L. (2016). Investigating the psychometric properties of the Geriatric Suicide Ideation Scale (GSIS) among community-residing older adults. *Aging & Mental Health, 20*(2), 208–221.

Hellman, M. (2014, June 17). U.S. health care ranked worst in the developed world. *Time Magazine*, 24–27.

Hendin, H., & Hass, A. P. (1991). Suicide and guilt as manifestations of PTSD in Vietnam combat veterans. *American Journal of Psychiatry, 148*, 586–591.

Hendricks, J. E., & McKean, J. B. (1995). *Crisis intervention: Contemporary issues of on-site interveners*. Springfield, IL: Charles C. Thomas.

Herman, J. (1997). *Trauma and recovery: The aftermath of violence—From domestic abuse to political terror*. New York, NY: Basic Books.

Hickok, T. A. (2000, Nov.). *Downsizing and organizational culture*. Retrieved from http://www.pamij.com/hickok.html

Hilton, N., Harris, G. T., & Rice, M. E. (2007). The effect of arrest on wife assault recidivism: Controlling for pre-arrest risk. *Criminal Justice & Behavior, 34*, 1334–1344.

Hilton, N. Z., Harris, G. T., Rice, M. E., Lang, C., Cormier, C. A., & Lines, K. J. (2004). A brief actuarial assessment for the prediction of wife assault recidivism: The Ontario Domestic Assault Risk Assessment. *Psychological Assessment, 16*(3), 267–275.

Hooley, J. M., & St. Germain, S. A. (2013). Borderline personality disorder. In W. E. Craighead, D. J. Miklowitz, & L.W. Craighead (Eds.), *Psychopathology: History, diagnosis, and empirical foundations* (pp. 511–549). Hoboken, NJ: Wiley.

Horowitz, M. J. (1985). Disasters and psychological responses to stress. *Psychiatric Annals, 15*(3), 161–167.

Hotaling, G. T., & Sugarman, D. B. (1986). An analysis of risk markers in husband to wife violence: The current state of knowledge. *Violence & Victims, 1,* 101–124.

Hudenko, W., Homaifar, B., & Wortzel, H. (2016). *The relationship between PTSD and suicide.* Washington, DC: U. S. Department of Veterans Affairs, National Center for PTSD. Retrieved from http://www.ptsd.va.gov/professional/co-occurring/ptsd-suicide.asp

Independent Sector. (2001). *A survey of charitable giving after September 11, 2001.* Washington, DC: Author.

Insel, T. R. (2008). Assessing the economic costs of serious mental illness. *American Journal of Psychiatry, 165*(6), 663–665.

Jacobson, G. F., Strickler, M., & Morley, W. E. (1968). Generic and individual approaches to crisis intervention. *American Journal of Public Health: Nations Health, 58*(2), 338–343.

Jacobson, N., & Gottman, J. (2007). *When men batter: New insights into ending abusive relationships.* New York, NY: Simon and Schuster.

James, R. K., & Gilliland, B. E. (2002). *Crisis intervention strategies* (4th ed.). Pacific Grove, CA: Brooks/Cole.

James, R. K., & Gilliland, B. E. (2017). *Crisis intervention strategies* (8th ed.). Boston, MA: Cengage Learning.

Jimerson, S. R., & Huff, L. C. (2002). Responding to a sudden, unexpected death at school: Chance favors the prepared professional. In S. E. Brock, P. J. Lazarus, & S. R. Jimerson (Eds.), *Best practices in school crisis prevention and intervention* (pp. 449–487). Bethesda, MD: National Association of School Psychologists.

Johnson, V. E. (1991). *I'll quit tomorrow: A practical guide to alcoholism treatment* (2nd ed.). San Francisco, CA: Harper Collins.

Jordan, B. (2014). *Older vets committing suicide at alarming rates.* Retrieved from http://www.military.com/daily-news/2014/08/31/older-vets-committing-suicide-at-alarming-rate.html

Kaiser Family Foundation. (2014). *National survey of adolescents and young adults: Sexual health knowledge, attitudes, and experiences.* Menlo Park, CA: Author.

Kaiser Family Foundation. (2015, November). Most Americans report a personal connection to prescription painkiller abuse. *Kaiser Health News.* Retrieved from http://www.khn.org/news/policy

Kanel, K. (1999). *A guide to crisis intervention.* Pacific Grove, CA: Brooks/Cole.

Kanel, K. (2003). *A guide to crisis intervention* (2nd ed.). Pacific Grove, CA: Brooks/Cole.

Kassinove, H. (Ed.). (1995). *Anger disorders.* Washington, DC: Taylor Francis.

Kastello, J. C., Jacobsen, K. H., Gaffney, K. F., Kodadek, M. P., Sharps, P. W., & Bullock, L. C. (2016). Predictors of depression symptoms among low-income women exposed to perinatal intimate partner violence (IPV). *Community Mental Health Journal, 52*(6), 683–690.

Kaufman, H. G. (1982). *Professionals in search of work.* New York, NY: Wiley.

Kaukiainen, A., Salmivalli, C., Björkqvist, K., Österman, K., Lahtinen, A., Kostamo, A., & Lagerspetz, K. (2001). Overt and covert aggression in work settings in relation to the subjective well-being of employees. *Aggressive Behavior, 27,* 360–371.

Kendall, P., & Hammen, C. (1998). *Abnormal psychology: Understanding human problems.* Boston, MA: Houghton Mifflin.

Kessler, R. C., Chiu, W. T., Demler, O., & Walters, E. E. (2005). Prevalence, severity, and comorbidity of 12-month DSM IV disorders in the National Comorbidity Survey Replication. *Archives of General Psychiatry, 62*(6), 617–627.

Kessler, R. C., McGonagle, K. A., Ahzo, S., Nelson, C. H., Hughes, M., Eshleman, S., Wittchen, H., & Kendler, K. S. (1994). Lifetime and 12-month prevalence of DSM-III-R psychiatric disorders in the United States, from the National Comorbidity Survey. *Archives of General Psychiatry, 51*, 8–19.

Kilgus, M. D., Maxmen, J. S., & Ward, N. G. (2016). *Essential psychopathology and its treatment* (4th ed.). New York, NY: W. W. Norton.

Kim, S., McLeod, J. H., & Shantzis, C. (1992). Cultural competence for evaluators working with Asian American communities: Some practical considerations. In M. A. Orlandi, R. Weston, & L. G. Epstein (Eds.), *Cultural competence for evaluators* (pp. 203–260). Washington, DC: Office of Substance Abuse Prevention.

Klassen, D., & O'Connor, W. A. (1988). A prospective study of predictors of violence in adult male mental health admissions. *Law & Human Behavior, 12*, 143–158.

Klein, A. (1996). Re-abuse in a population of court-restrained male batterers: Why restraining orders don't work. In E. S. Buzawa & C. G. Buzawa (Eds.), *Do arrests and restraining orders work?* Thousand Oaks, CA: SAGE.

Kleinman, A. (1991, April). *Culture and DSM-IV: Recommendations for the introduction and overall structure*. Paper presented at the National Institute of Mental Health-sponsored Conference on Culture and Diagnosis. Pittsburgh, PA.

Klingbeil, K. S., & Boyd, V. D. (1984). Emergency room intervention: Detection, assessment and treatment. In A. R. Roberts (Ed.), *Battered women and their families: Intervention strategies and treatment programs* (pp. 7–32). New York, NY: Springer.

Klingspon, K. L., Holland, J. M., Neimeyer, R. A., & Lichtenthal, W. G. (2015). Unfinished business in bereavement. *Death Studies, 39*(7), 387–398.

Kluft, R. P. (2016). The wounded self in trauma treatment. *American Journal of Clinical Hypnosis, 59*(1), 69–87.

Kochanek, K. D., Murphy, S. L., Anderson, R. N., & Scott, C. (2004). Deaths: Final data for 2002. *National Vital Statistics Report, 53*(5), 1–115.

Kolko, D. J. (2002). Child physical abuse. In J. B. Myers, L. Berliner, J. Briere, C. T. Hendrix, C. Jenny, & T. A. Reid (Eds.), *The APSAC handbook on child maltreatment*. Thousand Oaks, CA: SAGE.

Korchmaros, J. D., Ybarra, M. L., Langhinrichsen-Rohling, J., Boyd, D., & Lenhart, A. (2013). Perpetration of teen dating violence in a networked society. *Cyberpsychology, Behavior and Social Networking, 16*(8), 561–567.

Kowalski, G. (2012). *Goodbye, friend: Healing wisdom for anyone who has ever lost a pet*. Novato, CA: New World Library.

Kraanen, F. L., Vedel, E., Scholing, A., & Emmelkamp, P. M. (2014). Prediction of intimate partner violence by type of substance use disorder. *Journal of Substance Abuse Treatment, 46*, 532–539.

Krase, K., & DeLong-Hamilton, T. (2015). Comparing reports of suspected child maltreatment in states with and without universal mandated reporting, *Children and Youth Services Review, 50*, 96–100.

Kress, V., Gibson, D., & Reynolds, C. (2004). Adolescents who self-injure: Implications and strategies for school counselors. *Professional School Counseling, 7*, 195–202.

Kristiansen, M. (2016). Experiencing loss: A Muslim widow's bereavement narrative. *Journal of Religion and Health, 55*(1), 226–240.

Kristiansen, P., Weisaeth, L., Hussain, A., & Heir, T. (2015). Prevalence of psychiatric disorders and functional impairment after loss of a family member: A longitudinal study after the 2004 tsunami. *Depression and Anxiety, 32*, 49–56.

Kroger, J. (2000). *Identity development: Adolescence through adulthood*. Thousand Oaks, CA: SAGE.

Kubler-Ross, E. (1969). *On death and dying*. New York, NY: Macmillan.

Lachkar, J. (1998). *The many faces of abuse: Treating the emotional abuse of high functioning women*. New York, NY: Jason Aronson.

Lanceley, F. (1999). *On scene guide for crisis negotiators*. Boca Raton, FL: CRC Press.

Langenderfer, L. (2013). Alcohol use among partner violent adults: Reviewing recent literature to inform intervention. *Aggression and Violent Behavior, 18,* 152–158.

Langhinrichsen-Rohling, J., Misra, T. A., Selwyn, C., & Rohling, M. L. (2012). Rates of bidirectional versus unidirectional intimate partner violence across samples, sexual orientation, and race/ ethnicities: A comprehensive review. *Partner Abuse, 3*(2), 199–230.

Leana, C., & Feldman, D. C. (1992). Coping with job loss: How individuals, organizations and communities respond to layoffs. New York, NY: Lexington Books.

Legrand, L. N., Iacono, W. G., & McGue, M. (2005, March-April). Predicting addiction. *American Scientist,* 140–147.

Lehman, L. B., Pilich, A., & Andrews, N. (1994). Neurological disorders resulting from alcoholism. Alcohol Health & Research World, 17, 305–309.

Lehman, D. R., Wortman, C. B., & Williams, A. F. (1987). Long-term effects of losing a spouse or child in a motor vehicle crash. *Journal of Personality & Social Psychology, 52,* 218–231.

Lester, D. (2005). Suicide in Vietnam veterans: The suicide wall. *Archives of Suicide Research, 9*(4), 385–387.

Levenkron, S. (1998). *Understanding and overcoming self-mutilation.* New York, NY: W.W. Norton.

Levin, D. (2016, April 21). Vancouver finds success in treating drug addicts: Prescription program gains new attention. *The New York Times,* pp. A4, A9.

Levinson, D. J. (1978). *The seasons of a man's life.* New York, NY: Knopf.

Levinson, H. (1994). Why the behemoths fell: Psychological roots of corporate failure. *American Psychologist, 49,* 428–436.

Lewis, G. W., & Zare, N. C. (1999). *Workplace hostility: Myth and reality.* Philadelphia, PA: Taylor & Francis.

Liddell, H. G., & Scott, R. (1968). *The Greek-English Lexicon.* Oxford, England: Clarendon Press.

Lieberman, R. (2004). Understanding and responding to students who self-mutilate. *National Association of Secondary School Principals: Principal Leadership, 4(7),* 10–13.

Lieberman, R., Poland, S., & Cassel, R. (2008). Best practices in suicide intervention. In A. Thomas & J. Grimes (Eds.), *Best practices in school psychology V.* Bethesda, MD: The National Association of School Psychologists.

Lifeline. (2016). *Survivors of suicide booklet.* Retrieved from https://www.lifeline.org.au/static/uploads/ files/survivors-of-suicide-booklet1-

Lifespan of Greater Rochester, Inc., Weill Cornell Medical Center of Cornell University. & New York City Department for the Aging. (2011). *Under the radar: New York State Elder Abuse Prevalence Study.* New York, NY: Author.

Lindemann, E. (1944). Symptomotology and management of acute grief. *American Journal of Psychiatry, 101,* 141–148.

Lindenmeyer, J. P., Czobar, P., Alphas, L., Nathan, A. M., Anand, R. Islam, Z, & Chou, J. C., & The InterSePT Study Group. (2003). The InterSePT scale for suicidal thinking: Reliability and validity. *Schizophrenia Research, 63,* 161–170.

Linehan, M. M. (1993). *Cognitive-behavioral treatment of borderline personality disorder.* New York, NY: Guilford Press.

Linehan, M. M. (1995). *Treating borderline personality disorder: The dialectical approach* (Program Manual). New York, NY: Guilford Press.

Linehan, M. M. (1999). Standard protocol for assessing and treating suicidal behavior for patients in treatment. In D. G. Jacobs (Ed.), *The Harvard Medical School guide to suicide assessment and intervention.* San Francisco, CA: Jossey-Bass.

Litwack, T., Kirschner, S., & Wack, R. (1993). The assessment of dangerousness and prediction of violence: Recent research and future prospects. *Psychiatric Quarterly, 64,* 245–273.

Liu, E. C. (2008). *Would an influenza epidemic qualify as a major disaster under the Stafford Act?* [Congressional Research Service Report RL34724]. Prepared for Members and Committees of Congress. Washington, DC: Government Printing Office.

Lowe, J. (2015, June 25). I don't believe in God, but I do believe in lithium. *New York Times,* Sunday magazine section.

Ludwig, A. M. (1985). Cognitive processes associated with "spontaneous" recovery from alcoholism. *Journal of Studies on Alcohol, 46,* 53–58.

Madson, L., & Vas, C. (2003). Learning risk factors for suicide: A scenario-based activity. *Teaching of Psychology, 30,* 123–126.

Malamuth, N. M., & Check, J. (1983). Sexual arousal to rape depictions: Individual differences. *Journal of Abnormal Psychology, 92,* 55–67.

Malley, P. B., Kush, F., & Bogo, R. J. (1994). School-based adolescent suicide prevention and intervention programs: A survey. *The School Counselor, 42,* 130–136.

Mallory, A. B., Dharnidharka, P., Deitz, S. L., Barros-Gomes, P., Cafferky, B., Stith, S. M., & Van, K. (2016). A meta-analysis of cross-cultural risk markers for intimate partner violence. *Aggression and Violent Behavior, 30,* 114–126.

Maltsberger, J. T. (1992). The psychodynamic formulation: An aid in assessing suicidal risk. In R. W. Maris, A. L. Berman, J. T. Maltsberger, & R. T. Yufit (Eds.) *Assessment and prediction of suicide* (pp. 362–380), New York, NY: Guilford Press.

Marcia, J. (1994). The empirical study of ego identity. In H. Bosma, T. Graasfma, H. Grotebanc, & D. DeLivita (Eds.), *The identity and development.* Newbury Park, CA: SAGE.

Marin, G., & Marin, B. V. (1991). *Research with Hispanic populations.* Newbury Park, CA: SAGE.

Maris, R. W. (1992). The relationship of nonfatal suicide attempts to completed suicides. In R. W. Maris, A. L. Berman, J. T. Maltsberger, & R. T. Yufit (Eds.), *Assessment and prediction of suicide* (pp. 362–380). New York, NY: Guilford Press.

Marzuk, P. M., Tardiff, K., & Hirsch, C. S. (1992). The epidemiology of murder-suicide. *Journal of the American Medical Association, 267,* 3179–3183.

Mash, E. J., & Dosois, D. J. A. (2003). Child psychopathology: A developmental-systems perspective. In E. J. Mash & R. A. Barkley (Eds.), *Child psychopathology* (pp. 3–71). New York, NY: Guilford Press.

Maslow, A. H. (1958). A dynamic theory of human motivation. In S. L. Chalmers, M. DeMartino (Eds.), *Understanding human motivation.* Cleveland, OH: Howard Allen.

Maxmen, J. S., & Ward, N. G. (1995). *Essential psychopathology and its treatment* (2nd ed.). New York, NY: W. W. Norton.

May, A. M., & Klonsky, E. D. (2016). What distinguishes suicide attempters from suicide ideators: A meta-analysis of potential factors. *Clinical Psychology: Science and Practice, 23,* 5–20.

Mayer, N. (1978). *The male mid-life crisis: Fresh starts after 40.* Oxford, UK: Doubleday.

McConaughy, S. (2005). *Clinical interviews for children and adolescents: Assessment to intervention.* New York, NY: The Guilford Press.

McGhee, T., & Munio, N. (2016, Feb. 23). Marijuana sends more Colorado tourists to ER than locals. *Denver Times.*

McGirr, A., Tousignant, M., Routhier, D., Pouliot, L., Chawky, N., Margolese, H. C., & Turecki, G. (2006). Risk factors for completed suicide in schizophrenia and other chronic psychotic disorders. *Schizophrenia Research, 84*(1), 132–143.

McGoldrick, M., Giordano, J., & Garcia-Preto, N. (2005). *Ethnicity and family therapy* (3rd ed.). New York, NY: Guilford Press.

McKinney, C. M., Caetano, R., Rodriguez, L. A., & Okoro, N. (2010). Does alcohol involvement increase the severity of intimate partner violence? *Alcoholism: Clinical and Experimental Research, 34,* 655–658.

McNeil, D., & Binder, R. (1991). Clinical assessment of risk of violence among psychiatric inpatients. *American Journal of Psychiatry, 148*, 1317–1321.

McNeil, D., & Binder, R. (1994). The relationship between acute psychiatric symptoms and diagnosis and short-term risk of violence. *Hospital & Community Psychiatry, 45*(2), 133–137.

McVey-Noble, M. E., Khemlani-Patel, S., & Neziroglu, F. (2006). *When your child is cutting: A parent's guide to helping children overcome self-injury*. Oakland, CA: New Harbinger.

Mee-Lee, D. (Ed.). (2013). *The ASAM Criteria: Treatment criteria for addiction, substance-related and co-occurring conditions*. Washington DC: American Society of Addiction Medicine.

Meloy, J. (1987). The prediction of violence in outpatient psychotherapy. *The American Journal of Psychotherapy, 41*, 38–45.

Men against Sexual Assault (1998). *Test your knowledge*. University of Rochester: Author. Retrieved January 3, 2008 from http://sa.rochester.edu/masa/truefalse.php

Mercer, D., Douglass, A. B., & Links, P. S. (2009). Meta-analysis of mood stabilizers, antidepressants, and antipsychotics in the treatment of borderline personality disorder: Effectiveness for depression and anger symptoms. *Journal of Personality Disorders, 23*(2), 156–174.

Messman-Moore, T., Walsh, K., & DiLillo, D. (2010). Emotion dysregulation and risky sexual behavior in revictimization. *Child Abuse and Neglect, 34*(12), 967–976.

Miller, D. (1994). *Women who hurt themselves*. New York, NY: Basic Books.

Miller, L. (2014). Rape: Sex crime, act of violence, or naturalistic adaptation? *Aggression and Violent Behavior, 19*, 67–81.

Miller, M. C. (1999). Suicide-prevention contracts: Advantages, disadvantages and an alternative approach. In D. G. Jacobs (Ed.), *The Harvard Medical School guide to suicide assessment and intervention* (pp. 463–481). San Francisco, CA: Jossey-Bass.

Milliman, D. P., & Soderstrom, C. A. (1994). Substance use disorders in trauma patients. *Critical Care Clinics, 10*, 595–612.

Mohrman, S. A., & Mohrman, A. M. Jr. (1983). Employee involvement in declining organizations. *Human Resources Management, 22*, 445–465.

Moller, M. D., & Murphy, M. F. (1998). *Recovery from psychosis: A wellness approach*. Spokane, WA: P.R.N.

Monahan, J. (1995). *The clinical prediction of violent behavior*. Northvale, NJ: Jason Aronson.

Morley, W. E., Messick, J. M., & Aguilera, D. C. (1967). Crisis: paradigms of Intervention. *Journal of Psychiatric Nursing, 5*, 537.

Moscicki, E. K. (1995). Epidemiology of suicidal behavior. *Suicide and Life-Threatening Behavior, 25*, 22–35.

Motto, J. A. (1999). Critical points in the assessment and management of suicidal risk. In D. G. Jacobs (Ed.), *The Harvard Medical School Guide to suicide assessment and intervention* (pp. 224–238). San Francisco, CA: Jossey-Bass.

Moulton, H. G. (2014). *Report to the Attorney General on the investigation of Gerald A. Sandusky*. Commonwealth of Pennsylvania, Office of Attorney General, May 30, 2014.

Muehlenkamp, J., Claes, L., Havertape, L., & Plener, P. (2012). International prevalence of adolescent non-suicidal self-injury and deliberate self-harm. *Child and Adolescent Psychiatry and Mental Health, 6*(10), 1–9.

Mulvey, E., & Lidz, C. (1995). Conditional prediction: A model for research on dangerousness to others in a new era. *International Journal of Law & Psychiatry, 18*, 129–143.

Murphy, S. A., Johnson, C., & Cain, K. C. (1998). Broad spectrum group treatment for parents bereaved by the violent deaths of their 12–28-year-old children: A randomized controlled trial. *Death Studies, 22*, 209–235.

Murphy, M. D., & Moller, M. F. (1997). The three R's rehabilitation program: A prevention program for the management of relapse symptoms associated with psychiatric diagnoses. *Psychiatric Rehabilitation Journal, 20*(3), 42–49.

Myer, R. A. (2001). *Assessment for crisis intervention: A triage assessment model.* Belmont, CA: Wadsworth/Thomson Learning.

Myer, R. A., Williams, R. C., Ottens, A. J., & Schmidt, A. E. (1991). Crisis assessment: A three-dimensional model for triage. *Journal of Mental Health Counseling, 14,* 137–148.

Nasar, S. (1998). *A beautiful mind: The life of mathematical genius and Nobel Laureate John Nash.* New York, NY: Touchstone-Simon & Schuster.

National Center for Health Statistics. (2016). *Vital statistics in the United States* (Vol. 75, No. 9). Washington, DC: Government Printing Office.

National Coalition Against Domestic Violence (NCADV). (2015). *Domestic violence national statistics.* Retrieved from http://ncadv.org/images/Domestic%20Violence.pdf

National Alliance on Mental Illness (NAMI). (2013). *Mental health facts in America.* Retrieved from http://www.nami.org

National Alliance on Mental Illness (NAMI). (2015a). *Serious mental illness (SMI) among adults.* Retrieved from http://www.nimh.nih.gov/health/statistics/prevalence/serious-mental-illness-smi-among-us-adults.shtml

National Alliance on Mental Illness (NAMI). (2015b). *Any disorder among children.* Retrieved from http://www.nimh.nih.gov/health/statistics/prevalence/any-disorder-among-children.shtml

National Alliance on Mental Illness (NAMI). (2015c). *Any anxiety disorder among adults.* Retrieved from http://www.nimh.nih.gov/health/statistics/prevalence/any-anxiety-disorder-among-adults.shtml

National Alliance on Mental Illness (NAMI). (2015d). *Schizophrenia.* Retrieved from http://www.nimh.nih.gov/health/statistics/prevalence/schizophrenia.shtml

National Alliance on Mental Illness (NAMI). (2016). *Mental health crisis planning for adults: Learn to recognize, manage, prevent, and plan your loved one's mental health crisis.* St. Paul, MN: Author. Retrieved from http://www.namihelps.org/publications.html

National Association of School Psychologists & National Association of School Resource Officers (NASP & NASRO). (2014). *Best practice considerations for schools in active shooter and other armed assailant drills.* Bethesda, MD: National Association of School Psychologists.

National Association of School Psychologists. (2017). *Helping children cope with terrorism—Tips for families and educators.* Bethesda, MD: National Association of School Psychologists.

National Center for Health Statistics. (1998). *Vital statistics in the United States* (Vol. 47, No. 9). Washington, DC: Government Printing Office.

National Center for Health Statistics. (2001, Oct. 11). *Suicide as a leading cause of death* by age, race, and sex: 1999. National Vital Statistics Report, 49 (11). Retrieved from http://www.cdc.gov/nchs/fastats/suicide.htm

National Center for Victims of Crimes. (2007). *Sexual assault.* Washington, DC: Author. Retrieved from http://www.victimsofcrime.org

National Center on Shaken Baby Syndrome. (2009). *All about shaken baby syndrome (SBS) and abusive head trauma (AHT).* Farmington, UT: Author. Retrieved from http://www.dontshake.org/sbs.php

National Highway Traffic Safety Administration. (NHTSA). (2012). *Driving related fatalities in 2012.* Retrieved from http://www.nhtsa.gov/About+NHTSA/Press+Releases/NHTSA+Data+Confirms+Traffic+Fatalities+Increased+In+2012

National Research Council; Committee on National Statistics. (2013). *Report brief: Estimating the incidence of rape and sexual assault.* Washington, DC: Author.

National Volunteer Organizations Active in Disaster. (2002). *Preventing a disaster within the disaster: The effective use and management of unaffiliated volunteers.* Arlington, VA: Author.

Neill, C., & Leigh, A. (2009). Do gun buy-backs save lives? Review of evidence from time series variation. *Current Issues in Criminal Justice, 20*(2), 145–162.

Nekvasil, K. S., Cornell, D. G, & Huang, F. L. (2015). Prevalence and offense characteristics of multiple causality homicides: Are schools at higher risk than other locations? *Psychology of Violence, 5*(3), 236–245.

New York Times. (1996). *The downsizing of America.* New York, NY: Time Books.

No Child Left Behind Act (NCLB). (2001). Pub. L. No. 107-110.

Nock, M. K., & Marzuk, P. M. (1999). Murder-suicide: Phenomenology and clinical implications. In D. G. Jacobs (Ed.), *The Harvard Medical School guide to suicide assessment and intervention.* San Francisco, CA: Jossey Bass.

Noer, D. (1993). *Healing the wounds: Overcoming the trauma of layoffs and revitalizing downsized organizations.* San Francisco, CA: Jossey-Bass.

Occupational Health & Safety Administration. (2002). *Workplace Violence Fact Sheet.* Retrieved from http://www.osha.gov/OshDoc/data_General_Facts/factsheet-workplace-violence.pdf

Odem, M. E., & Clay-Warner, J. (1998). *Confronting rape and sexual assault.* Wilmington, DE: Scholarly Resources.

Ohlheiser, A. (2015, February 23). A dozen hospitalized after apparently overdosing on Molly at Wesleyan University. *The Washington Post.*

Osman, A., Bagge, C. L., Gutierrez, P. M., Konick, L. C., Kooper, B. A., & Barrios, F. X. (2001). The Suicidal Behaviors Questionnaire-Revised (SBQ-R): Validation with clinical and nonclinical samples. *Assessment, 8,* 443–454. Retrieved from http://www.integration.samhsa.gov/images/res/SBQ.pdf

Pagliocca, P. M., Nickerson, A. B., & Williams, S. (2002). Research and evaluation directions in crisis intervention. In S. E. Brock, P. J. Lazarus, & S. R. Jimerson (Eds.), *Best practices in school crisis prevention and intervention* (pp.771–791). Bethesda, MD: National Association of School Psychologists.

Paine, C. (1998, November). Tragedy response and healing: Springfield unites. *NASP Communique, 27*(3), 16–17.

Papp, L. J., Liss, M., Erchull, M. J., Godfrey, H., & Waaland-Kreutzer, L. (2016, August 11). The dark side of heterosexual romance: Endorsement of romantic beliefs relates to intimate partner violence. *Sex Roles, 76*(1–2), 99–109.

Parad, H. J. (1965). *Crisis Intervention: Selected readings.* New York, NY: Family Service Association of America.

Parad, H. J., & Caplan, G. (1965). A framework for studying families in crisis. In H. Parad (Ed.), *Crisis intervention: Selected readings.* New York, NY: Family Service Association of America.

Parad, H. J., & Parad, L. G. (1990). Crisis intervention: An introductory overview. In H. J. Parad & L. G. Parad (Eds.), *Crisis intervention: Book 2: The practitioner's sourcebook for brief therapy.* Milwaukee, WI: Family Service America.

Peled, E., & Krigel, K. (2016). The path to economic independence among survivors of intimate partner violence: A critical review of the literature and course for action. *Aggression and Violent Behavior, 31,* 127–135.

Platoni, K. T. (2013). Hypnotherapy in the wartime theater: OIF, OEF, and beyond. In R. M. Scurfield & K. T. Platoni (Eds.), *Healing wartime trauma: A handbook of creative approaches* (pp. 159–171). New York, NY: Routledge/Taylor & Francis,

Poland, S., & Gorin, S. (2002). Preface. In S. Brock, P. Lazarus, & S. Jimerson (Eds.), *Best practices in school crisis prevention and intervention* (pp. xv–xviii). Bethesda, MD: National Association of School Psychologists.

Poland, S., & McCormick, J. (1999). *Coping with crisis: Lessons learned.* Longmont, CO: Sopris West.

Polivy, J., & Herman, C. P. (2002). Causes of eating disorders. *Annual Review of Psychology, 53,* 187–213.

Poon, M. W. (2009). Hypnosis for complex trauma survivors: Four case studies. *American Journal of Clinical Hypnosis, 51*(3), 263–271.

Pope, H. G., & Katz, D. L. (1990). Homicide and near-homicide by anabolic steroid users. *Journal of Clinical Psychiatry, 51,* 28–31.

Pope, H. G., & Katz, D. L. (1994). Psychiatric and medical effects of anabolic-androgenic steroid use: A controlled study of 160 athletes. *Archives of General Psychiatry, 51,* 375–382.

Popenoe, D., & Whitehead, B. (2005). *The state of our unions: The social health of marriage in America.* New Brunswick, NJ: National Marriage Project.

Posner, K., Brown, G. K., Stanley, B., Brent, D. A., Yershova, K. V., Oquendo, M. A., Currier, G. W., Melvin, G. A., Greenhill, L., Shen, S., & Mann, J. J. (2011). The Columbia-Suicide Severity Rating Scale: Initial validity and internal consistency findings from three multisite studies with adolescents and adults. *American Journal of Psychiatry, 168*(12), 1266–1277.

Prevent Child Abuse America. (2006). *Annual report: Winds of change.* Chicago, IL: Author.

Ragucci, A. T. (1982). Italian Americans. In A. Harwood (Ed.), *Ethnicity and medical care.* Cambridge, MA: Harvard University Press.

Rand Corporation. (2014). *RAND military workplace study.* Santa Monica, CA: Author. Retrieved from www.rand.org/nsrd/projects/rmws/publications.html

Rando, T. (1984). *Grief, dying and death: Clinical interventions for caregivers.* Champaign, IL: Research Press.

Rape, Abuse, and Incest National Network. (2016). *Statistics.* Washington, DC: Author. Retrieved from https://rainn.org/statistics

Raphael, B. (1986). *When disaster strikes.* New York, NY: Basic Books.

Rayner, C. (2000). Bullying research: Global Allies Bullying at Work, Survey Report—UNISON (UK union), Campaign Against Workplace Bullying, P.O. Box 1886, Benicia, CA 94510.

Reddy, M., Boram, R., Berglund J., Vossekuil, B., Fein R., & Modzeleski, W. (2001). Evaluating risk for targeted violence in schools: Comparing risk assessment, threat assessment, and other approaches. *Psychology in the Schools, 38,* 157–172.

Reed, B. F., & May, P. A. (1984). Inhalant abuse and juvenile delinquency: A control study in Albuquerque, New Mexico. *International Journal of Addictions, 19*(7), 789–803.

Reiger, D. A., Narrow, W. E., Rae, D. S., Manderscheid, R. W., Locke, B. Z., & Goodwin, F. K. (1993). The de facto U. S. mental and addictive disorder delivery system. Epidemiologic Catchment Area prospective 1 year prevalence rates of disorders and services. *Archives of General Psychiatry, 50,* 85–94.

Rice, F. P., & Dolgin, K. G. (2008). *The adolescent: Development, relationships, and culture* (12th ed.). New York, NY: Allyn & Bacon.

Rizo, C. F. (2016). Intimate partner violence related stress and the coping experiences of survivors: "There's only so much a person can handle." *Journal of Family Violence, 31*(5), 581–593.

Roberts, A. R. (1981). *Sheltering battered women.* New York, NY: Springer.

Roberts, A. R. (1990). Contemporary perspectives on crisis intervention. Englewood Cliffs, NJ: Prentice-Hall.

Roberts, A. R. (Ed.). (1996). Crisis management & brief treatment: Theory, technique, and applications. Chicago, IL: Nelson Hall.

Roberts, A. R. (1998). Crisis intervention: A practical guide to immediate help for victim's families. In A. Horton & J. Williamson (Eds.), *Abuse and religion* (p. 606). Lexington, MA: D. C. Heath.

Roberts, A. R. (Ed.). (2000a). *Crisis intervention handbook: Assessment, treatment, and research.* Oxford, UK: Oxford University Press.

Roberts, A. R. (2000b). An overview of crisis theory and crisis intervention. In A. R. Roberts (Ed.), *Crisis intervention handbook: Assessment, treatment, and research.* New York, NY: Oxford University Press.

Roberts, A. R. (2002). *Crisis intervention handbook: Assessment, treatment, and research* (2nd ed.). New York, NY: Oxford University Press.

Roberts, A. R., Knox, K. S., & Tesh, M. (2013). School-based adolescent suicidality: Lethality assessments and crisis intervention protocols. In C. Franklin, M. B. Harris, & P. Allen-Meares (Eds.), *The school services sourcebook: A guide for school-based professionals.* Oxford, UK: Oxford University Press.

Robins, L. E., & Reiger, D. A. (Eds.). (1991). *Psychiatric disorders in America: The Epidemiological Catchment Area Study* (pp. 343–350). New York, NY: Free Press.

Robinson, R. C., & Mitchell, J. T. (1995). Getting some balance back into the debriefing debate. *Bulletin of the Australian Psychological Society, 17,* 5–10.

Robinson, R., Perry, V., & Carey, B. (1995). *African Americans. In U.S. DHHS, PHS,* SAMHSA, & CSAT, Implementing cultural competence in the treatment of racial/ethnic substance abusers (pp. 1–21). Rockville, MD: Technical Resources.

Rock, R. C., Sellbom, M., Ben-Porath, Y. S., & Salekin, R. J. (2013). Concurrent and predictive validity of psychopathy in a batterers' intervention sample. *Law & Human Behavior, 37*(3), 145–154.

Rogers, B., & Acton, T. (2012). "I think we're all guinea pigs really": A qualitative study of medication and borderline personality disorder. *Journal of Psychiatric and Mental Health Nursing, 19,* 341–347.

Rogers, C. (1951). Client-centered therapy: Its current practice, implications, and theory. Boston, MA: Houghton-Mifflin.

Ronningstam, E. F. (Ed.). (1998). *Disorders of narcissism: Diagnostic, clinical and empirical implications.* Washington, DC: American Psychiatric Press.

Ronningstam, E. F. (2005). *Identifying and understanding the narcissistic personality.* New York, NY: Oxford University Press.

Rosewater, L. B. (1982). *An MMPI profile for battered women.* [Doctoral Dissertation], Union Graduate School, Ann Arbor, Michigan.

Rosewater, L. B. (1985a). Schizophrenic or battered? In L. B. Rosewater & L. E. A. Walker (Eds.), *Handbook on feminist therapy: Psychotherapy with women.* New York, NY: Springer.

Rosewater, L. B. (1985b). Feminist interpretations of traditional testing. In L. B.

Rosewater, L. B., & L. E. A. Walker (Eds.), *Handbook on feminist therapy: Psychotherapy with women.* New York, NY: Springer.

Rosner, R. (2015). Prolonged grief: Setting the research agenda. *European Journal of Psychotraumatology, 6.*

Ross, H., & Heath, N. (2002). A study of the frequency of self-mutilation in a community sample of adolescents. *Journal of Youth and Adolescence, 31,* 209–217.

Rouse, B. A. (1995). *Substance abuse and mental health statistics sourcebook.* U. S. Department of Health & Human Services [Publication No. (SMA) 95-3064]. Washington, DC: Government Printing Office.

Ruchlewska, A., Mulder, C. L., Smulders, R., Roosenschoon, B. J., Koopmans, G., & Wierdsma, A. (2009). The effect of crisis plans for patients with psychotic and bipolar disorders: A randomized controlled trial. *BMC Psychiatry, 9*(41), 1–8.

Rudd, M. D. (2006). Fluid vulnerability theory: A cognitive approach to understanding the process of acute and chronic risk. In E. T. Ellis (Ed.), *Cognition and suicide: Theory, research, and therapy* (pp. 355–368). Washington, DC: American Psychological Association.

Runyan, D., Wattam, C., Ikeda, R., Hassan, F., & Ramiro, L. (2002). Child abuse and neglect by parents and other caregivers. In E. Krug, L. Dahlberg, J. A. Mercy, A. B. Zwi, & R. Lozano (Eds.), *World report on violence and health.* Geneva, Switzerland: World Health Organization. Retrieved from http://www.who.int/violence_injury_prevention/violence/global_campaign/en/chap3.pdf.

Rynearson, E. K. (1987). Psychotherapy of pathological grief. *Psychiatric Clinics of North America, 10,* 487–499.

Sandler, I., Wolchik, S., & Ayers, T. (2008). Resilience rather than recovery: A contextual framework on adaptation following bereavement. *Death Studies, 32,* 59–73.

Sandoval, J. (1985). Crisis counseling: Conceptualizations and general principles. *School Psychology Review, 14,* 257–265.

Sandoval, J., & Lewis, S. (2002). Cultural considerations in crisis intervention. In S. Brock, P. Lazarus, & S. Jimerson (Eds.), *Best practices in school crisis prevention and intervention* (pp. 5–17). Bethesda, MD: National Association of School Psychologists.

Satir, V. (1972). *Peoplemaking.* Palo Alto, CA: Science & Behavior Books.

Satir, V. (1988). *The new peoplemaking.* Palo Alto, CA: Science & Behavior Books.

Schaal, S. (2015). Is prolonged grief distinct from depression? *Journal of Loss and Trauma, 20*(1), 46–55.

Schmookler, E. (1996). *Trauma treatment manual.* Albany, CA: Author. Retrieved from http://trauma-pages.com

Schneider, J. (1984). *Stress, loss, and grief* (pp. 262–263). New York, NY: Aspen Publishers.

Schneidman, E. (1999). Perturbation and lethality: A psychological approach to assessment and intervention. In D. G. Jacobs (Ed.), *The Harvard Medical School guide to suicide assessment and intervention.* San Francisco, CA: Jossey Bass.

Schuckit, M. A. (1995). Alcohol related disorders. In H. I. Kaplan & B. J. Sadock (Eds.), *Comprehensive textbook of psychiatry* (6th ed., pp. 120–138). Baltimore, MD: Williams & Wilkins.

Schuerger, J. M., & Reigle, N. (1988). Personality and biographic data that characterize men who abuse their wives. *Journal of Clinical Psychology, 44,* 75–81.

Scully, D. (1990). Understanding sexual violence: A study of convicted rapists. Boston, MA: Unwin Hyman.

Seligman, M. (1990, 1998). *Learned optimism.* New York, NY: Pocket Books.

Shaffer, A. (2012). *Child maltreatment: Risk and resilience in ages birth to 5.* Retrieved from https://www.cehd.umn.edu/ssw/cascw/attributes/PDF/publications/CW360-CEED_Winter2012.pdf

Shaffer, D. A., Gould, M. S., & Hicks, R. C. (1994). Worsening suicide rates in black teenagers. *American Journal of Psychiatry, 151,* 1810–1812.

Shapiro, F. (1989a). Efficacy of the eye movement desensitization procedure in the treatment of traumatic memories. *Journal of Traumatic Stress, 2,* 199–223.

Shapiro, F. (1989b). Eye movement desensitization: A new treatment for post-traumatic stress disorder. *Journal of Behavior Therapy & Experimental Psychiatry, 20,* 211–217.

Shapiro, F. (1995). Eye movement desensitization and reprocessing (EMDR): Basic principles, protocols, and procedures. New York, NY: Guilford Press.

Sharfstein, S. S. (2000). Whatever happened to community mental health? *Psychiatric Services, 51,* 616–620.

Sheehan, D. V., Giddens, J. M., & Sheehan, I. S. (2014). Status update on the Sheehan-Suicidality Tracking Scales (S-STS). *Innovations in Clinical Neuroscience, 11*(9–10), 93–101.

Sheehy, G. (2005). *Middletown, America: One town's passage from trauma to hope.* New York, NY: Random House.

Shepard, B. (2001). *A war of nerves: Soldiers and psychiatrists in the twentieth century.* Cambridge, MA: Harvard University Press.

Showalter, K. (2016). Women's employment and domestic violence: A review of the literature. *Aggression and Violent Behavior, 29.*

Simpson, J. A., & Rholes, W. S. (1998). *Attachment theory and close relationships.* New York, NY: Guilford Press.

Siris, S. G. (2006). Suicide and schizophrenia. *Journal of Psychopharmacology, 15*(2), 127–135.

Slaikeu, K. A. (1984). *Crisis intervention: A handbook for practice and research.* Newton, MA: Allyn & Bacon.

Slaikeu, K. A. (1990). *Crisis intervention: A handbook for practice and research* (2nd ed.). Boston, MA: Allyn & Bacon.

Slovic, P., & Monahan, J. (1995). Probability, danger, and coercion: A study of risk perception and decision making in mental health law. *Professional Psychology: Research & Practice, 26,* 499–506.

Smith, J., & Williams, J. (1992). From abusive household to dating violence. *Journal of Family Violence, 7*, 153–165.

Smith, G. D., & Munafo, M. (2015). Why is there a link between smoking and suicide? *Psychiatric Services, 66*(3), 331.

Smolak, L. (2005). Eating disorders in girls. In D. J. Bell, S. L. Foster, & E. J. Mash (Eds.), *Handbook of behavioral and emotional problems in girls* (pp. 463–487). New York, NY: Kluwer Academic.

Sontag, D. (2002, April 28). A suicide at M.I.T.: *In loco parentis* is dead. Is that why Elizabeth Shin is, too? *New York Times,* Section 6, 57–61.

Sonkin, D. J., & Durphy, M. (1997). *Learning to live without violence* (4th ed.). San Francisco, CA: Volcano Press.

Stark, E. (1996). Mandatory arrests of batterers: A reply to critics. In E. S. Buzawa & C. G. Buzawa (Eds.), *Do arrests and restraining orders work?* Thousand Oaks, CA: SAGE.

Steinberg, L. (2005). *Adolescence* (7th ed.). New York, NY: McGraw Hill.

Steinglass, P., Bennet, L. A., Wolin, S. J., & Reiss, D. (1996). *The alcoholic family* (2nd ed.). New York, NY: Basic Books.

Steinhardt, S. J., Moore, T. R., & Casella, S. D. (2014). Have you seen Molly? A review of Molly in primary literature. *Mental Health Clinician, 4*, 231–235.

Stewart, J. B. (2016, August 18). Secrecy of settlements at Fox News hid bad behavior. *New York Times.*

Stordeur, R. A., & Stille, R. (1989). *Ending men's violence against their partners: One road to peace.* Thousand Oaks, CA: SAGE.

Storey, J. E., & Hart, S. D. (2014, March). An examination of the Danger Assessment as a victim-based risk assessment instrument for lethal intimate partner violence. *Journal of Threat Assessment and Management, 1*(1), 56–66.

Stosney, S. (1995). *Treating attachment abuse: A compassionate approach.* New York, NY: Springer.

Strauss, M. A., Gelles, R. J., & Steinmetz, S. K. (2006). *Behind closed doors: Violence in the American family* [Reissued from 1980 with new Forward by R. J. Gelles & M. A. Strauss). New Brunswick, NJ: Transaction.

Substance Abuse and Mental Health Services Administration (SAMSHA). (2011). *Drug abuse warning network: National estimates of drug-related emergency department visits* [HHS Publication No. (SMA) 13-4760, DAWN Series D-39]. Rockville, MD: Author. Retrieved from http://archive.samhsa.gov/data/2k13/DAWN2k11ED/DAWN2k11ED.html

Substance Abuse and Mental Health Services Administration (SAMSHA). (2014, June 10). *A day in the life of young adults: Substance use facts.* Rockville, MD: Center for Behavioral Health Statistics & Quality. Retrieved from http://www.samhsa.gov/data/sites/default/files/CBHSQ-SR168-TypicalDay-2014/CBHSQ-SR168-TypicalDay-2014.pdf

Substance Abuse and Mental Health Services Administration (SAMHSA). (2015, Aug. 14). *Trauma-informed approach and trauma-informed care.* Retrieved from http://www.samhsa.gov/nctic/trauma-interventions

Suyemoto, K., & Kountz, X. (2000). Self-mutilation. *The Prevention Researcher, 7*, 4.

Swannell, S. V., Martin, G. E., Page, A., Hasking, P., & St John, M. J. (2014). Prevalence of nonsuicidal self-injury in nonclinical samples: Systematic review, meta-analysis, and meta-regression. *Suicide Life Threat Behavior, 44*, 273–303.

Symoens, S., Colman, E., & Bracke, P. (2014). Divorce, conflict, and mental health: How the quality of intimate relationships is linked to post-divorce well-being. *Journal of Applied Social Psychology, 44*, 220–233.

Symoens, S., VandeVelde, S., Colman, E., & Bracke, P. (2014). Divorce and the multidimensionality of men and women's mental health: The role of social-relational and socio-economic conditions. *Applied Research in Quality of Life, 9*(2), 197–214.

Talbot, M. (2002, Oct. 13). Men behaving badly. *New York Times*.

Tarasoff v. Board of Regents of the University of California, 551 P2d 334 (1976).

Tarullo, A. (2012). *Effects of child maltreatment on the developing brain*. Retrieved from http://www.cehd.umn.edu/ssw/cascw/attributes/PDF/publications/CW360-CEED_Winter2012.pdf

Thomas, K. (2016, April 27). The complex math behind spiraling prescription drug prices. *New York Times*. Retrieved from http://www.nytimes.com/2016/04/28/business/high-drug-prices-explained.html

Thomas, M. D., Bennett, L. W., & Stoops, C. (2012). The treatment needs of substance abusing batterers: A comparison of men who batter their female partners. *Journal of Family Violence, 28*, 121–129.

Tolman, R. M. (1989). The development of a measure of psychological maltreatment of women by their male partners. *Violence & Victims, 4*, 159–177.

Torrey, E. F. (1997). *Out of the Shadows*. New York, NY: Wiley.

Tozzi, F., Thornton, L., Klump, K., Fichter, M., Halmi, K., & Kaplan, A. (2005). Symptom fluctuation in eating disorders: Correlates of diagnostic crossover. *American Journal of Psychiatry, 162*, 732–740.

Trotman, H. D., Mittal, V. A., Tessner, K. D., & Walker, E. F. (2013). Schizophrenia and the psychosis spectrum. In W. E. Craighead, D. J. Miklowitz, & L. W. Craighead (Eds.), *Psychopathology: History, diagnosis, and empirical foundations* (pp. 403–444). Hoboken, NJ: Wiley.

Trovato, F. (1986). The relationship between marital dissolution and suicide: The Canadian case. *Journal of Marriage and the Family, 48*, 341–348.

Truman, J., Langton, L., & Bureau of Justice Statistics. (2014). *Criminal victimization*. Washington, DC: Bureau of Justice.

Truscott, D., Evens, J., & Mansell, S. (1995). Outpatient psychotherapy with dangerous clients: A model for decision making. *Professional Psychology: Research & Practice, 26*, 484–490.

United Nations Secretariat. (1996). *Demographics yearbook*. New York, NY: Department for Economic and Social Information and Policy Analysis, Statistical Division, United Nations.

United States Equal Employment Opportunity Commission (2017). *Sexual Harassment*. Retrieved from https://www.eeoc.gov/laws/types/sexual_harassment.cfm

U.S. Department of Education, Office of Elementary and Secondary Education, Office of Safe and Healthy Students. (2013). *Guide for developing high quality school emergency operations plans (K-12)*. Washington, DC: Author.

U.S. Department of Health and Human Services, Administration for Children and Families. (1974). *The child abuse prevention and treatment act*. Washington, DC: Government Printing Office.

U. S. Department of Health and Human Services, National Institute of Mental Health (NIMH). (2001), p. 27. Washington, DC: Government Printing Office.

U.S. Department of Health and Human Services. (DHHS). (2006). *Monitoring the future: National results on adolescent drug use*. [Investigators: Institute for Social Research: University of Michigan]. Washington, DC: Government Printing Office.

U.S. Department of Health and Human Services (DHHS), Administration for Children and Families (ACF). (2013a). *National survey of children and adolescent well-being, 2013*. Washington, DC: Government Printing Office.

U.S. Department of Health & Human Services. (2013b). *Administration on Aging*. Washington, DC: Government Printing Office. Retrieved from http://www.aoa.gov/AoA_programs/elder_rights/EA_prevention/whatisEA.aspx

U.S. Department of Health and Human Services (DHHS). (2015). National Center on Child Abuse and Neglect. *Child maltreatment 2014*. Washington, DC: Government Printing Office.

U.S. Department of Homeland Security (DHS). (2004, March). *National incident management system*. Washington, DC: Author.

U.S. Department of Justice. (1998). *Violence by intimates: Analysis of data on crime by current or former spouses, boyfriends, and girlfriends*. Washington, DC: Bureau of Justice Statistics.

U.S. Department of Justice. (2000). *Violence by intimates: Analysis of data on crime by current or former spouses, boyfriends, and girlfriends*. Washington, DC: Bureau of Justice Statistics.

U.S. Department of Justice. (2004). *A national protocol for sexual assault medical forensic examinations*. Washington, DC: Author.

U.S. Department of Justice. (2005). *National crime victimization survey*. Washington, DC: Author.

U.S. Department of Justice. (2011). *National violence against women survey*. Washington, DC: Author.

U.S. Department of Justice. (2012). *Attorney general Eric Holder announces revisions to the uniform crime report's definition of rape*. Retrieved from http://www.fbi.gov/news/pressrel/press-releases/attorney-general-eric-holder-announces-revisions-to-the-uniform-crime-reports-definition-of-rape.

U.S. Department of Justice. (2015). *Uniform crime report: Crime in the United States*. Washington, DC: Government printing Office.

U.S. Department of Justice. (2016). *Office on violence against women*. Washington, DC: Author.

U.S. Bureau of Labor Statistics. (2017). *Labor force statistics from the current population survey*. Washington, DC: Author.

U.S. Secret Service and the U.S. Department of Education. (2002). *The final report and findings of the Safe School Initiative: Implications for the prevention of school attacks in the United States*. Washington, DC: Author.

van der Kolk, B., McFarlane, A., & Weisaeth, L. (Eds.). (1996). *Traumatic stress: The effects of overwhelming experience on mind, body, and society*. New York, NY: Guilford Press.

Vernig, P. (2011). Family roles in homes with alcohol-dependent parents: An evidence-based review. *Substance Use and Misuse, 46*(4), 535–542.

Violence Policy Center. (2015). *American roulette: Murder-suicide in the United States*. Retrieved from http://www.vpc.org/studies/amroul2012.pdf

Walker, L. (1980). *The battered woman*. New York, NY: Harper & Row.

Walker, L. (1989). Terrifying love: Why battered women kill and how society responds. New York, NY: Harper & Row.

Walker, L. (1994). *The abused woman: A survivor therapy approach* [Manual & Video]. New York, NY: Newbridge.

Walker, L. (2000). *Abused women and survivor therapy*. Washington, DC: American Psychological Association.

Walker (2009). *The battered woman syndrome* (3rd ed.). New York, NY: Springer.

Waller, B. (2016). Broken fixes: A systemic analysis of the effectiveness of modern and postmodern interventions utilized to decrease IPV perpetration among Black males remanded to treatment. *Aggression and Violent Behavior, 27*, 42–49.

Walsh, F. (1998). *Strengthening family resilience*. New York, NY: Guilford.

Wang, L., Seelig, A., Wadsworth, S. M., McMaster, H., & Crum-Cianflone, N. F. (2015). Associations of military divorce with mental, behavioral, and physical outcomes. *BMC Psychiatry, 15*, 28–35.

Washton, A. M., & Zweben, J. E. (2006). *Treating alcohol and drug problems in psychotherapy practice*. New York, NY: Guilford.

Wegscheider, S. (1981). *Another chance: Hope and health for the alcoholic family*. Palo Alto: CA: Science & Behavior Books.

Weis, R. (2008). *Abnormal child and adolescent psychology*. Thousand Oaks, CA: SAGE.

Weiss, R. D., & Hufford, M. R. (1999). Substance abuse and suicide. In D. G. Jacob (Ed.), *The Harvard Medical School guide to suicide assessment and intervention*. San Francisco, CA: Jossey Bass.

Weissman, M. M., Bruce, M., Leaf, P., Florio, L., & Holzer, C. (1991). Affective disorders. In L. Robins & E. Reiger (Eds.), *Psychiatric disorders in America* (pp. 53–80). New York, NY: Free Press.

Weitzman, J. (1985). Engaging the severely dysfunctional family in treatment: Basic considerations. *Family Process, 24*, 473–485.

Wekerle, C., & Wolfe, D. A. (2003). Child maltreatment. In E. J. Mash and R. A. Barkley (Eds.), *Child psychopathology*. New York, NY: Guilford.

Whiteside, L. K., Bonar, E. E., Blow, F., Ehrlich, P., & Walton, M. A. (2015). Nonmedical prescription stimulant use among youth in the emergency department: Prevalence, severity, and correlates. *Journal of Substance Abuse Treatment, 48*(1), 21–27.

Widom, C., Czaja, S., Bentley, T., & Johnson, M. (2012*).* A prospective investigation of physical health outcomes in abused and neglected children: New findings from a 30-year follow-up. *American Journal of Public Health, 102*(6), 1135–1144.

Wikipedia. (2017). *Hostile workplace.* Retrieved from https://en.wikipedia.org/wiki/Hostile_work_ environment

Wilhelm, R. (1967). *The book of changes or the I Ching.* Princeton, NJ: Princeton University Press.

Winkler, K. (2003). *Cutting and self-mutilation: When teens injure themselves.* Berkeley Heights, NJ: Enslow.

Winstok, Z. (2016). A new definition of partner violence. *Aggression and Violent Behavior, 28,* 95–102.

Wollman, D. (1993). Critical incident stress debriefing and crisis groups: A review of the literature. *Group, 17,* 70–83.

Wolpe, J. (1982). *The practice of behavior therapy.* New York, NY: Pergamon Press.

Woolfolk, A. (2007). *Educational psychology* (10th ed.). Boston, MA: Allyn & Bacon.

Worden, J. W. (2008). Grief counseling and grief therapy: A handbook for the mental health practitioner (4th ed.). New York, NY: Springer.

World Health Organization. (2010). Mental and behavioural disorders due to psychoactive substance use (pp. F10–F19). In D. A. Yost (Ed.). (1996). *The International Statistical Classification of Diseases and Related Health Problems* (10th Revision (ICD-10). Geneva, Switzerland: Author.

World Health Organization. (2012). *Depression Fact Sheet.* Retrieved from http://www.who.int/mediacentre/factsheets/fs369/en/

World Health Organization's Ranking of the World's Health Systems. (n.d.). Retrieved August 30, 2017, from http://thepatientfactor.com/canadian-health-care-information/world-health-organizations-ranking-of-the-worlds-health-systems/

Xiangming, F., Brown, D., Florence, C., & Mercy, J. (2012). Child maltreatment, youth violence, and intimate partner violence: Developmental relationships. *American Journal of Preventative Medicine, 33*(4).

Xu, J. Q., Kochanek, K. D., Murphy, S. L., & Arias, E. (2014). *Mortality in the United States, 2012.* [NCHS data brief, no 168]. Hyattsville, MD: National Center for Health Statistics.

Yang, B., & Lester, D. (2009). Is there a natural suicide rate? *Applied Economic Letters, 16*(2), 137–140.

Ybarra, M. L., Espelage, D. L., Langhinrichsen-Rohling, J., & Korchmaros, J. D. (2016). Lifetime prevalence rates and overlap of physical, psychological, and sexual dating abuse perpetration and victimization in a national sample of youth. *Archives of Sexual Behavior, 45*(5), 1083–1099.

Yost, D. A. (1996). Alcohol withdrawal syndrome. *American Family Physician, 54,* 657–664.

Young, M. (2001). *Victim assistance: Frontiers and fundamentals.* Washington, DC: National Organization for Victim Assistance.

Young, M. (2002). The community crisis response team: The national organization for victim assistance protocol. In S. Brock, P. Lazarus, & S. Jimerson (Eds.), *Best practices in school crisis prevention and intervention* (pp. 5–17). Bethesda, MD: National Association of School Psychologists.

Young, M. E., & Long, L. L. (1998). *Counseling and therapy for couples.* Pacific Grove, CA: Brooks/Cole.

Zetterqvist, M. (2015). The DSM-5 diagnosis of nonsuicidal self-injury disorder: A review of the empirical literature. *Child & Adolescent Psychiatry and Mental Health, 9*(31), 1–13.

Zetumer, S., Young, I., Shear, M. K., Skritskaya, N., Lebowitz, B., Simon, N., Reynolds, C., Mauro, C., & Zisook, S. (2015). The impact of losing a child on the clinical presentation of complicated grief. *Journal of Affective Disorders, 170,* 15–21.

Zila, L., & Kiselica, M. (2001). Understanding and counseling self-mutilation in female adolescents and young adults. *Journal of Counseling and Development, 29,* 46–52.

Zisook, S., Schuchter, S. R., & Lyons, L. E. (1987). Predictors of psychological reactions during the early stage of widowhood. *Psychiatric Clinics of North America, 10,* 355–368.

Index

Pages followed by b, f, or t indicate boxes, figures, or tables, respectively.